POLITICS OF CAIN

POLITICS OF CAIN

One Hundred Years of Crises in Somali Politics and Society

Hussein A. Bulhan

TAYOSAN INTERNATIONAL PUBLISHING
Publisher and Distributor of African Books,
Magazines, and Audio-visual Products
P.O.Box 30602
Bethesda, Maryland, 20824

First Printing
Tayosan International Publishing
P.O. Box 30602
Bethesda, Maryland, 20824

Book Design: HAB
Cover Design: HAB
Cover Photo: Patrick Wiggers

ISBN-13: 978-0-9814745-0-2 (Paperback)
ISBN-10: 0-9814745-0-0 (Paperback)

Library of Congress Cataloging-in-Publication Data

Bulhan, H. A.
Politics of Cain: One Hundred Years of Somali Politics/ H.A. Bulhan
p. cm
Includes bibliographic reference and index

I dedicated this book to my mother.

After she fled tyranny and violence of Cain in two countries—first Ethiopia, then Somalia—she died in Canada, far from her ancestral land she never wanted to leave.

ACKNOWLEDGMENTS

I would not complete this work without the assistance of many persons to whom I am very grateful. Unfortunately, I can mention only a few of them here.

I most grateful to my sister, Sahra, for her constant love and support. I am also thankful to my wife, Nuura, who steadfastly and with love stood by me in both good and bad times; to Mohamed Ábdirahmaan Áli and Ábduláziz Jaamá Badawi for helping, each in their different but essential ways. I am also grateful to Marty Hawkins who edited the bulk of this work in its early draft, to my friend, Oumie Jouf, for typing the corrections and serving as my point of contact in the United States, and to the many friends, acquaintances, and fellow researchers (some of them mentioned in footnotes) who, through personal communication or their writing, shared valuable information.

Of the persons who shared valuable information, I want to specially thank Aves O. Hagi and Ábdiwahid O. Hagi whose detailed listing of the names, clans, and sub-clans of key Somali officials from 1960-1990 offered important data for my analysis on Somali politics in post-independence.

Lastly but not least, I want to thank all my children whose very sight and sound cheered me while writing about the depressing history and plight of Somalis. No doubt, they and other African children deserve a better world than my generation has found and lives through. If this work somehow contributes to improving this troubled and tormented world, then the labor in writing this work is worthwhile.

INSERT
MAP OF SOMALIA AND SOMALILAND

TABLE OF CONTENTS

"Those who cannot remember the past are condemned to repeat it."
Santayana

PREFACE

Milil dushi lama dhayo.
Never dress a bad wound superficially.
—Somali Proverb

The Somali state was not the first to collapse in Africa. Congo experienced the same as early as 1960-1961, Uganda in 1979-1981, Chad in 1980-1982. Other African states like Rwanda, Liberia, Sierra Leone, and Ivory Coast followed suit—the last appearing in the nineteen-eighties as one of the most stable and prosperous countries in the continent.

More recently in 2008, Kenya and Zimbabwe were on the brink of chaos and state collapse when the ruling party annulled presidential elections it had lost, demonstrating clearly that democracy has yet to take root in Africa. Following international pressure, the ruling elite in Kenya finagled a compromise but costly solution. President Mugabe, on the other hand, insists on continuing his long reign by use of brutal violence while the economy is in total shambles, turning one of Africa's breadbaskets into a basket case of horrendous suffering for citizens, all because a dictator wants to rule for life.

In 1993, Nellier estimated that about half of the African states were in serious danger of collapse.[1] Nellier's is an underestimate since many seemingly stable African states are on the verge of, or headed toward, crisis and chaos unless fundamental changes in their system of governance, justice, and economy take place.

Several important questions therefore arise: Why has the modern state—a politically organized body of people, occupying a definite territory and conferred with sovereignty—failed to work well for Africans? How can we explain the succession of state collapse in Africa? Is the state that Africans inherited from European colonizers fundamentally flawed—so deeply flawed that Somali reactions manifest reflexive rejection of it, as the body rejects alien organ transplant? On the other hand, are Africans culturally or psychologically unprepared to use effectively the political institutions that have worked well for other peoples? And how do generations of people who lived through state hegemony to its collapse view their collective predicament?

The Somali experience provides answers to these questions and serves as an example of what ails Africa. With its tumult and torment, the Somali experience places in sharp relief problems that make Africa a junkyard of unworkable systems, a continent of death and destruction, a dumping ground for international charity, and a convenient receptacle for racial stereotypes.

Further, the Somali example shows that homogeneity (in ethnicity, language, culture, and religion) shields no society from conflict of identities, chaos, or cruelty in a flawed system of governance, particularly so when the leaders are tyrannical, incompetent, and corrupt. Is this a case of mismanaged diversity or mismanaged homogeneity?

The world has come to know of the Somali disaster from sketchy newspaper accounts and quickly flashed TV reports. These horrid reports and images, though largely true, do not tell the whole story. Indeed, the selected tidbits and innuendoes of reports covertly suggest that Somalis and generally Africans cannot rule themselves—at least that they cannot do without the guidance and charity of those who once colonized them.

Thus, in addition to killing themselves, Somalis unwittingly confirm old myths attributing to the African natural incompetence and need for external rule. In reality, these images of violence and death are symptoms of deeper malaise and crises in making for decades. Those who wish to understand the causes and contributors to this explosion of rage and violence must examine the history of Somalis from the late nineteenth century to the end of the twentieth century—a history of grim tales that begs critical analysis if Somalis and those who want to help them are to learn lessons from past mistakes.

This work examines why Somalis experienced a succession of disasters before and after the collapse of the state in 1991, followed by years of anarchy and chaos during which Somalis hurled explosives and hate at one another. I wrote the *Politics of Cain* so that Somalis, seventeen years after the collapse of the state, can learn lessons from their past and social scientists can find in the Somali experience an example of a failed state, failed leadership, and failed quick fixes.

Other Africans too can benefit from the Somali experience described in this work, learning at least *what not to do* to avoid the ruinous consequences that precede and follow the kind of state collapse Somalis have known. As will be evident later, I argue that the Somali state, being deeply flawed and impervious to demand for reform, deserved to collapse, but how state collapse came about and its consequences were mismanaged by the so-called Somali elite and their external supporters. Although I explain that this group does not deserve to be called elite in the best sense of the name, I refer to them as such for want of a better a term.

My approach in analyzing these problems of the Somali state and the ruling elite is not to marshal a litany of "facts," for facts themselves are casualties of oppression and armed conflict, but to interpret key events and trends in Somali politics and history in order to help Somalis draw lessons from their past. If I succeed in identifying some of these lessons and offer new approach of analyzing Somali problems, it is then up to the reader to choose what to do with these lessons and formulations.

Perhaps some members of the Somali elite will find in these lessons new excuses to join the violent fray, vigorously fanning the fires of clan wars. Others may find new justification to continue burying their heads in the sand, seeing or hearing no evil. Still others may discover in this work a few ideas that extend critical analysis or promote the change Somalis and other Africans desperately need.

Of course, no author who publishes his work retains control of how his ideas are used. My case is not an exception, although I know that this work can be a manual on how to destroy a country, or how to discover the causes of a society's ruin in order to rebuild it on sound foundation and human values. I had in mind the latter goal in writing this work, but I leave it to the reader to make his or her choice on the two options and assume responsibility for that choice.

Consciously or by default, we all make choices. Albert Camus said that even a man forced to the gallows chooses on *how* he faces certain death. Saddam Hussein, however profoundly repugnant were his political record as President of Iraq, had shown his choice of meeting certain death at the gallows: refusing to wear a hood, holding the Qur'an in hand, and confronting death with singular calm, while his hooded executioners shouted barrage of insult and taunts at him. None who witnessed the courage and dignity with which he faced his televised hanging would disagree with Camus.

Collectively and individually, the Somali elite too must make a choice in *how they die* if not *how they live*. Political and social conditions in their land are so violent and messy that it is never easy to make choices under these conditions. Many Somalis, including the best and the mediocre, sought refuge abroad or in madness. Others chose to remain in their country to serve their people.

Sometimes, the choice the Somali elite make on the fundamental issues of life and death takes most peculiar form. A case in point is the choice of a Somali who lives in the United States. In a public gathering abroad, the man declared that he is so content with his life in the United States, so satisfied with his achievements, so desirous of distancing himself from Somalis that he already bought a plot in the United States for his burial when he dies. By that decision *and* public declaration, this Somali expressed his antipathy for his people.

The irony is that this man earns living by teaching Americans about Somalis, the very people upon whom he heaps contempt. I suppose that even a zoologist has more sympathy for the fauna he studies than does this man for Somalis. Further, his obsession with a burial place, his flaunting of personal success, and his contempt for his own people suggest profound disturbance of identity.[2]

Still, we should give credit to this man for making a *conscious choice*, regardless of how we disagree with his choice, since the timid souls who fail to choose except by default are worse. We readily become tools and minions of others when we do not consciously make life choices, then fail to take responsibility for how we live. At minimum, this work defines the choices available to the so-called Somali elite.

After all, this group belongs to the most fortunate minority among the wretched population in the Horn of Africa. They owe their privileged status to relatives and compatriots who, despite abject poverty, spent the family assets and national resources to educate them.

Hence, their people expect from them tangible contribution to improve living with dignity, not private and macabre obsession on where the egotistic wish to be buried when they physically die.

Death actually comes in different forms—fools know only its physical form. As we shall see in this work, there are also *social* and *psychological* forms of death under conditions of prolonged oppression. Those who benefit the most from collectively owned resources bear the greatest obligation to prevent premature death in all its forms. *For to whom much is given, much is expected.* The Somali experience proves the reverse.

1

INTRODUCTION

Fooli timyaaba gudo qarsimo hadhan.
In child delivery, hiding private parts is absurd.
—Somali proverb

The start of a new millennium, like the beginning of a new year, stirs a surge of hope for better life. It also offers an opportunity to look back on the past, to evaluate major achievements as well as failures in order to learn lessons and to set new goals. Eight years into the twenty-first century, it may be useful to look back to the Somali past to draw lessons and to chart a new course away from oppression and war, economic misery and social despair, preventable disease and death, mass trauma and tragedy.

This work examines Somali history over the past one hundred years—a tumultuous period which began with colonial rule, followed by independence and a false start, replaced by military dictatorship that promised revolution but unleashed a reign of terror. When armed political groups ousted the military dictator, the state collapsed, anarchy and chaos followed in Somalia, giving way to a succession of warlords and wars, mass famine and trauma, ineffective foreign peacekeeping forces and several failed attempts to reinvent the flawed state for Somalis. (Somaliland broke away and restored fragile peace and democracy, but so far won no political recognition from any country and is sliding into the flawed state of the past.[1])

After the failure of fourteen reconciliation conferences sponsored by the international community to rebuild the state for Somalia, the Union of Islamic Courts filled the power vacuum in the summer of 2006 and rapidly took control of large territories in Somalia. The UIC was defeated six months later by Ethiopian military invasion, with United States assistance, repeating in the twenty-first century the religious wars, unholy alliances, and bitter defeats of the sixteenth century and the turn of the twentieth century.[2]

This chapter describes the task I set for myself in this work and how I approach that task.

Primary Questions

It is of course one thing to be at the center of the complex drama Somali leaders found themselves in the heady and difficult years of post-independence, quite another to sit alone in front of a computer nearly a half-century later, pointing out the mistakes of political actors in the early years of post-independence. The discussion presented in this work would be frivolous if Somalis today were at peace, blessed with leaders who knew their responsibility, or fashioned a state that served the basic needs of its citizens. None of this conditions being the case, we must therefore inquire into what went wrong using the benefit of hindsight.

In fact, all historical critiques rest on analysis of events that had taken place in the past and on the benefit of hindsight. In this work, I seek answers for the following general questions: How does the state—supposedly the most organized body of people for harnessing human and material resources for the common good—repeatedly turn into a violent and ruinous system, an endless curse for Somalis? What role do the Somali elite play in creating and perpetuating this tragedy? How did colonial rulers and later the local elite distort the clan system to manipulate and oppress the majority of Somalis?

Related to the above questions are the following: Why do Somalis remain caught in ceaseless political disaster, much of it fabricated and therefore preventable? Why have they become wretched recipients of charity from the international community when in the past they were self-reliant, proud, and resourceful people? Why do majority of them acquiesce to oppression and go against their self-interest?

The tragic predicament of Somalis, their amnesia on the past, and their grim prospects in the future prompt these questions. One thing is for sure: Somalis cannot solve their predicament or expect better future unless they analyze the past and tease out the conditions and factors that gave rise to colonial rule, then to the auto-colonial state, followed by the military dictatorship—the ultimate outcome of the flawed state.

According to Sören Kierkegaard, the Danish philosopher, we understood life only backwards; but it must be lived forward. The past—its torment and tribulation—overwhelms Somalis and quickly recede to collective amnesia as psychological defense. In addition, living forwards has become impossible for them because conflict and violence abound; trauma and tragedy multiply; despair and doom permeate life. Merely surviving the day dominates the thoughts and activities of Somalis. One counts his blessing if not killed, wounded, or persecuted by his fellowman; if frequent droughts and raging disease (including AIDS) do not snuff out life; if the state, where it exists, permits private space without intrusion and intimidation.

In the midst of war and tragedy, all good in life and people turn malign and malevolent. Hence, this preoccupation with imminent danger and death leaves little opportunity to plan the future or to enjoy momentary laughter with friends and loved ones. In the midst of violence and trauma, even laughter and love also lose some of their natural spontaneity and joy. What indeed is laughter when it so frequently bursts out as masked hostility at others, jeering at their misfortune or inadequacies? And how is love to be a gift of life when always accompanied by constant worry and anxiety that a loved one becomes the next victim of a stray or intended bullet, perhaps indiscriminate artillery or aerial bombardment hurled by your government or a foreign power?

Even when Somalis live abroad and enjoy geographic distance from this collective obsession with destruction, relatives mired in utter despair and desperation in the motherland call for help at odd hours of the night, in shrilled and distressed voices, emotionally pulling back Somalis living in distant lands into their experience of death and disaster that had forced them to seek refuge abroad. In response to the call for help, they send steady and large remittance spent mostly on *qat* (an amphetamine-like stimulant) providing fleeting euphoria and self-medication against trauma and depression.

In short, something deep and disturbing has gone wrong in society and life, requiring Somalis to think and rethink in order to nudge events in the twenty-first century in a direction that offers them a better life, at least less disgraceful ways of dying than they experience today. Victims of oppression can in fact turn the tide of history in their favor if they first understand the causes of their suffering and act collectively to take control of their destiny. Externalizing causes of their problems or blaming others for them is in the final analysis a convenient crutch, a self-defeating rationalization, an escape from responsibility. Through critical analysis and concerted action, people can solve their problems. Understanding life backward, they solve problems and live forward.

Thus by analyzing the Somali past, I want to answer the above questions, identify fundamental causes of political crises in Somali society, and show that neither constructive change nor sustained development can come unless Somalis, particularly the so-called elite, abandon their self-deception and clan delusion. I also want to demonstrate the heavy price society pays for the flawed systems, the inept leaders, and the distorted clan system.

Central Argument

In essence, I argue that the state Somalis have known before and since independence was fundamentally flawed, founded on flawed laws, institutions, policies, and practices. Two factors—the clan system and the local elite—have combined with the flawed state to produce the auto-colonial state which by its nature is in perpetual conflict and crisis.

Diagram 1 below summarizes my argument.

Diagram 1

Causes and Consequences of the Flawed State

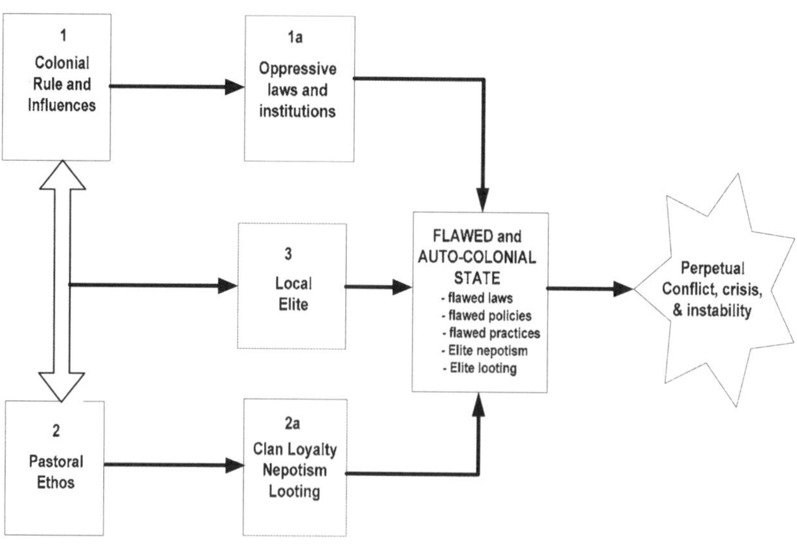

In brief, the auto-colonial state is a product of three joint influences. The first is colonial rule (# 1) and its oppressive laws and institution (# 1a). The second is the traditional Pastoral Ethos (# 2) misapplied to contemporary Somali politics as clan loyalty, nepotism, and looting (#2a). The third is the malfeasance and ineptitude of local elite (# 3) who in childhood internalized the Pastoral Ethos (# 2) and as colonial protégés assimilated colonial influences (# 1). The resulting auto-colonial state is inherently and inexorably prone to instability, conflict, and crisis.

A brief discussion below clarifies my argument that subsequent chapters elaborate with supporting evidence.

The colonial state imposed on Somalis from the late nineteenth to the first half of the twentieth centuries was from the start flawed because of its violence, exploitation, and racism. Following colonial occupation, the flawed state came up against the Pastoral Ethos and the clan system that governed the hitherto stateless Somalis. At first, the colonial state (with its oppressive laws and institutions) collided with traditional society's values and practices. The collision of the two systems and cultures in time brought an integration of components from both, resulting in the auto-colonial state that rests on uneven and confused mix of incompatible worldviews, values, and practices.

At the same time, the local elite emerged during this collision of systems and cultures. They internalized the pastoral ethos in childhood and assimilated alien values in colonial schools. Their upbringing in traditional society and the identity they share with the population gave them personal knowledge of their suffering, defense, and aspirations. In addition, their western education provided them access to the state and the material resources it controlled. It also provided them the opportunity to bring about systemic change ameliorating the abject poverty and oppression of their people.

After independence, the elite exploited their access to state power and material resources but had forsaken their responsibility to effect change for the common good. Instead of changing the flawed state and therefore society, they reinstated the worst aspects of the colonial state, turning it into a most oppressive and killing machine. In the few instance when they attempted reforms, as they did in the early years of military rule, they quickly reverted to the auto-colonial state in the name of "socialist revolution."

To sustain injustice and exploitation, the auto-colonial system often winnows out the competent, honest, and socially committed members of the local elite, selecting the technically inept and the financially unscrupulous to assume leadership for critical posts in government. Thus, contrary to elite theories like Vilfredo Pareto and Gaetano Mosca, the most competent in society do not necessarily lead or govern. I provide evidence in subsequent chapters that the so-called elite actually mislead and misgovern, at least so in Somali society.

This work, *Politics of Cain,* covers key political and social events that transpired from 1890 when Europeans imposed an alien state on Somalis to 1991 when the state collapsed from internal decay. It examines Somali politics in the past one hundred years, identifying the flaws of the colonial state from the beginning and how it degenerated into auto-colonial system, a modern replica of colonialism with black face. It should be clear from the above that the closer the historical period discussed to our time, the more I present detailed exposition on it.

Why Invoke the Metaphor of Cain?

Most analyses of oppression begin with dichotomous opposition—for instance the slave and the master, the serf and the lord, the bourgeoisie and the working class, the power elite and the masses, in general the oppressor and the oppressed. These dichotomous oppositions are paradigmatic tools used by different disciplines and ideologies.

Yet these dichotomous oppositions are never pure, exclusive, or exhaustive. Each of them therefore contains overlaps, middle range groups, and exceptions. For this reason, they do not reflect reality, but are conceptual tools that provide points of reference for shedding light on certain problems of society. I use here the dichotomies of *Cain* and *Abel* for purpose of initial analysis of Somali political problems while acknowledging the same limitations found in other dichotomous concepts.

According to Christian and Islamic scriptures, Cain is the eldest son of Adam who murdered his brother Abel. Genesis IV, 1-10 in the Bible and Sura V, 27-30 in the Qur'an explain the circumstances in which Cain (Qaabiil) murdered Abel (Haabiil). These scriptures affirm that Cain was the elder of the two brothers—for this reason, he felt entitled to have more rights than his younger brother. Harboring jealousy and resentment, Cain eventually murdered Abel, his innocent and devout brother. As a result, Cain took upon himself a double burden: his own sin of murder, and the sins of his brother whom he had murdered. In contrast, Abel was absolved of all his sins. On these basic features of the story, Christianity and Islam agree by condemning arrogance, jealousy, and murder.

In Islam and Christianity, Cain (Qaabiil) symbolizes the perpetrator of injustice, and Abel (Haabiil) the victim. Two aspects of the legend in particular interest us here. The first is the gist of the story—that the two brothers shared much to unite them in filial bond, yet one murdered the other, bringing upon him a lasting curse. The second aspect concerns how Cain and Abel are metaphors of the oppressor and the oppressed.

I chose the title *Politics of Cain* for two reasons—first because Somalis share close kinship, second because they inflict recurrent violence upon one another. Regarding kinship, Somalis are a homogeneous people who share the same ethnic origin, the same religion, the same culture, the same language, and ultimately the same destiny, even when their current political differences create superficial lacuna and separate governments.[3]

Each clan-family links to another through *abtirsiimo* or *abtirsinyo*—reckoning of male ancestors—and secondarily through maternal kinship and marital relations. As I detail in *Kinship and Conflict,* the clan system had originated from the nuclear family that in time took on clan organization and character. To this day, the clan system simulates the nuclear family and draws inspiration from it, although it became unlike the nuclear family in practice as it grew in size.

Thus, if one can invoke the term "family" to discuss the relations of a people anywhere, Somalis can rightly summon the same metaphor because they belong to the same *family writ large.* Yet, paradoxically, violent conflicts bedevil this homogeneous people belonging to the same *tribe*, speak the same language, share the same culture, and profess the same religion.[4] The metaphor of Cain came to mind when I reflected on these acts of violence among so homogenous group as Somalis. In invoking the metaphor of Cain, I refer not to the occasional incidence of individual violence but to the patterned, systemic, and massive violence Somalis inflict on one another.

Thus, despite clan and even filial relationship binding Somalis, we find two broad groupings—one group compulsively exploits and oppresses, the other repeatedly suffers exploitation, mystification, trauma, and death. As in the scriptural story of Cain and Abel, Somali politics turned fratricidal—politics of violence and exploitation among brothers and sisters motivated for greed, arrogance, and selfishness.

The metaphors of Cain and Abel are apt for another reason. The violence Somalis inflict on one another exceeds the usual frequency and intensity of groups fighting over ideology, power, or material gain. For when conflict erupts among Somalis, the violence each group unleashes upon the other is as destructive as if each wanted to eliminate the other from the face of the earth; each group acts as if members of the other group are deadly and eternal enemies. Each group casts reason and compassion to the wind. This is so not because Somalis are by nature more violent and cruel than other nationalities or ethnic groups, but because the core cultural beliefs they assimilate in childhood and the political system under which they live contain fundamental flaws that set brother against brother. Thus, the political system aggravates problems in the clan system and the associated pastoral ethos, bringing out the worst in people. It is therefore a breeding ground and host for Cain—and where Cain exists, Abel suffers and dies.

More generally, I employ the metaphors of Cain and Abel to underscore two universal human tendencies—the tendency toward violence and evil, and the tendency toward suffering and victimization. Sigmund Freud, the founder of psychoanalysis, discussed these proclivities in terms of instincts of aggression and love, or generally death and life. Other students of human and animal behavior propose similar theories. Therefore, the Cain I describe in Somali society and behavior is not peculiar or unique to Somalis. Because of flawed systems, however, Somalis show the extremes of the same proclivities and behaviors found in other peoples of the world.

In reality, each person contains elements of Cain and Abel. It is therefore a question of which tendency dominates his or her personality and social behavior at a given time and in a particular situation. The same person appears Cain or Abel, depending on the social context and power relations in which he or she is involved.

How often do we observe in Somali society a gentle and Abel-like person appointed to a position of authority in government suddenly transform into Cain—a monster committing the same abuse of power about which he complained when he was not in government? The reverse too occurs with equal frequency. Kicked out of power, the same man turns angelic, acting like Abel suffering the abuse of Cain. Such observations emphasize how Cain and Abel readily surface, given opportunity and congenial circumstance.

This work presents evidence for the hypocrisy and duplicity of the Somali elite who, by history and habit, are today's Cain in Somali society but also know how to disguise as Abel to exploit others.

Clan and Klan

One class of Cain whom this work analyzes is the *Klan* who by history, organization, and mission is distinctly different from the *clan*—a social and political organization which I briefly outline below because the clan system plays a pivotal role in Somali politics and society.

The Somali clan system rests on a chain of paternal ancestors reaching back to a mythical founding ancestor whose name all members of the clan take for collective identity. The system is patrilineal and, by acknowledging only male ancestors, favors male dominance. Agnatic relations, reinforced by explicit social contract (*xeer*) define all social and political relations. A new child born enlarges not only the size of the nuclear family but also augments the number and strength of the sub-clan and clan. No social relation exists without invoking or engaging the clan. Birth, marriage, divorce, and death too invariably involve the blessing, consent, or participation of the kinfolk.

The clan is the crucible of identity, social defense, and social security. Providing social insurance and social control, it supports members in time of need and defends the individual from external attack. It also serves as social control to regulate the behavior of members and avoid collective reprisal for injury or murder committed by a member. Unless the perpetrator's clan pays blood-compensation, the aggrieved clan or sub-clan retaliates by injuring or killing any other member of that clan, even if he were in no way personally involved in the crime.

The clan is to this day a continuing and pervasive system, permeating all social relations in Somali society. As in the past, the clan and sub-clan comes to the assistance of the members in time of financial and social problems. In birth and death, marriage and divorce, employment and joblessness, war and peace, the clan pervades and influences social relations. When a person dies, the clan and sub-clan buries him/or her. The members arrange the burial, pay the expenses, and carry out the pertinent religious rituals. In short, clan identity is a source of cleavage, the cause of division and conflict, but also the source of affiliation, unity, and mutual assistance.

I adopted the term *Klan* from the Ku Klux Klan, an organization of white supremacists known for its anti-Black and sometimes anti-Semitic diatribe. Ex-confederate whites established the secret society in Pulaski, Tennessee, in December 1865 and its leader, General Nathan B. Forrest, took the title of "Grand Wizard." By intimidation and violence, The KKK denies civil and human rights to black people in the United States. In the past, they used lynching and cross-burning to force submission before the state took responsibility to protect African-Americans, showing how a small group can masquerades as the legitimate representatives of a larger collective to carry out its ideology and programs. The KKK acted in the name of the white race, although the overwhelming majority of Caucasians reject their racist ideology.

In choosing the term *Klan,* I mean to emphasize that the Somali elite are in many respects similar to the infamous KKK. The members of the Somali elite, like the members of the KKK, belong to an exclusive club, viewing with contempt those in whose name they act. The Somali elite are different in one respect: the KKK uses race for its hatred and oppression; the Somali the elite exploit both the western education they acquired and the clan system to which they remain identified. They exploit western education to justify their claim that they deserve the best in society, including the right to rule others and to accumulate wealth. They also exploit the clan system to rally members for their clan in pursuit of personal power and wealth.

Theodore Roosevelt said this: "To educate a man in mind but not in morale is to educate a menace to society." Auto-colonial education in Somali society educates neither intellectually nor morally—hence, it produces far greater menace to society than Roosevelt had probably imagined. Worse, the victims are confusedly stuck in primordial clan loyalty and identify; in consequence, they willy-nilly die in wars instigated by their kinsmen in the *Klan*—the new Cain of Somali society.

The *Klan* acquire from western education a diploma, a degree, or often minimally literacy which gives them sense of entitlement that society owes something, not the understanding that they owe their people service and self-sacrifice to pay back for society's investment into their education. They also take from the clan system its divisive and distorted aspects that satisfy their greed for power and wealth in the midst of poverty and misery. This work shows the menace of the *Klan* to Somali society.

We will see that this group, the *Klan*, demonstrates the psychopathic syndrome Robert W. Rieber (1997) calls the *Mephisto Syndrome* identified by four salient characteristics: thrill-seeking, pathological glibness, antisocial pursuit of power, and absence of guilt. They seek thrill by rushing into dangerous undertakings that others prudently avoid. Because ordinary life is too predictable and boring for them, they engage in activities or situations of threat and danger (involving lying and cheating) that makes them excited, energized, and truly alive.

Their pathological glibness is shown by their ability to speak well, dramatically, and persuasively about themselves and their causes which invariably promote self-interest. They speak volubly and persuasively because there is no limit to the deceit and lies they use to manipulate communication with others. Extremely sensitive to power relations, they continually seek to obtain maximum power over others and use this power mainly for self-serving ends. They also ceaselessly carry on exploitative behavior that at least inconvenience or often hurting others because they do not feel guilt for the suffering they cause people.

These four characteristics of the *Mephisto Syndrome* are found to a substantial degree in the politics of the Somali elite, the *Klan*, because Somali politics by its very nature is rooted in oppression and exploitation, whether colonial or auto-colonial. In addition, the Somali elite who engage in this type of politics are socialized into two drastically different cultures—traditional and colonial—both of which they had internalized but only partially and selectively use aspects of each to serve their interest. Lacking therefore coherent values and consistent moral structure, they egoistically behave as they wish, avoiding punishment or obtaining rewards by whatever means available to them, regardless of the consequences of their behavior for others.

The dialectics and key actors of Somali politics we discuss in this work show the relevance of Rieber's *Mephisto Syndrome* and the price Somalis collectively pay for the ruling elite's thrill-seeking behavior, their intense passion for power, their manipulation of communication for exploitation, and their lack of guilt on the suffering of their people.

Kinsmen and Camels

In addition to western education, two traditions in particular facilitate *Klan* exploitation of society. The first is the tradition of rallying clans by crying *"tollaayey!"*—have I no kinsmen to defend me! The second is the tradition of camel looting which in contemporary society the *Klan* transfer to looting the public treasury and anything that catches their fancy. Since these two traditions resurface in different forms in our historical narrative, we must clarify both in anticipation.

The tradition of crying *"tollaayey*!" goes back to the time when Somalis lived exclusively under the clan system without a central state or law enforcement to protect individuals from attack by others. It was accepted and expected that individuals fell back on the collective defense of the clan. Thus, individuals cried this code word when forces arrayed against them exceeded their capacity to avert danger to their person or property. To rally the clan for self-defense, one therefore cried *"tollaayey*!"

Using the spirit and message of *"tollaayey!"* but not necessarily uttering the code word, members of the *Klan* similarly rally their kinsmen in time of competition and conflict over power with other members of the *Klan* who likewise rally theirs. Thus, the competition and conflict within the elite quickly generalize to clan competition and conflict. Clan members jump into the contest and conflagration of the *Klan* because, as we shall see later, they internalized the Pastoral Ethos and obtain vicarious subjective gains. Members of the *Klan* know the emotional and social pull of *"tollaayey!"* and exploit the code word by covert means, producing the same effect as loud declaration of it.

The tradition of camel looting emerged when camels and the practice of herding them occupied central position in the life of traditional Somalis. Camels not only provided milk and meat for the pastoralists but also served as beast of burden enduring long treks in the semi-desert. They were also the currency of exchange and the symbols of prestige. A specified number of camels covered blood compensation for murder or bodily injury. Young men who wanted to marry also paid dowry in camels, although cattle, guns, and cash could take their place or supplement them.

Because camels were prized possession and symbol of prestige, camel looting developed into a quick means of obtaining wealth and prestige. In addition, camel looting offered adventure and sport, a test of bravery and clan superiority, an activity of camaraderie and bonding for young men belonging to the same clan. Frequently, the camel looting sortie began in clan revenge for camels the other clan had looted in the past; it also gave vent to old grievances (like unpaid blood-compensation for injury or murder) the other clan failed to redress. Sometimes too, it was driven by impulse for adventure or desire material gain.

The practice of camel looting had its rules and rituals. Typically, a gang of armed men belonging to the same clan ventured to the settlement or grazing areas of another clan to loot their camels. Before the gang divided the camels looted, they recruited a religious man to sanctify or purify *(xalaaleeyo)* the camels from sin of looting prohibited it is prohibited in Islam. This ritual by which the religious man sanctified the looted camels was called *booli-reeb* (purifying the loot)—suggesting that both camel looting and *booli-reeb* developed before Somalis converted to Islam, though today the ritual of purification has been abandoned my most clans.

After the religious man read conveniently selected quotations from the Qur'an, the gang divided the looted camels following an established tradition. First, the gang gave the religious man a few of the camels. Then the leader of the camel-looting gang received the choice camels. Thereafter, other members received a share commensurate to their power or influence in the group. If the looted camels were in excess, other clan members who did not participate in the raid might get some of the looted camels as expression of kinship and to implicate them in future defense of the loot. From there on, each beneficiary of the loot branded his newly acquired camels with his clan and sub-clan insignia.

Old traditions die hard—particularly so when the socialization of children, the economic relations, and belief systems do not change. The ritual of sanctifying looted camels is no longer practiced by most clans, but the practice of camel looting persists to this day. We will see in subsequent chapters that the ruling Somali elite, the *Klan*, transferred the traditional looting of camels to looting the resources of the state, in particular the public treasury. Moreover, the Somali public who consciously want equality and inclusion in the political order actually feel little or no outrage on the *Klan's* blatant looting of the state because they too internalized what I call the Pastoral Ethos and Delusion of Clan Superiority detailed in Chapter 13. On the contrary, they experience vicarious pride and satisfaction that members of their clan boldly loot commonly owned resources.

The preceding should therefore forewarn the conclusion of this work that change in Somali politics and society requires fundamental change in three critical domains—the flawed political system, the pathologic behavior of the elite, and the distorted aspects of the traditional clan system. Change in the three domains need not take place simultaneously since change in one has repercussion on the other two. However, transforming one or all three domains is possible only after we comprehend the historical evolution of Cain and Abel in Somali society—an evolution this work traces during the past one hundred years.

Perils of the Somali Past

Pierre Nora stated that history is a reconstruction of what no longer exists except in the memory of living people. Therefore, it is always an incomplete representation of the past.[5] Reconstruction based on memory, history permanently evolves, successively changed by the dialectics of remembering, forgetting, and retold by different individuals, from different perspectives, with different interests.

If this is true of the history of peoples who for centuries recorded their past in writing, it is more so of Somali history for which we have scanty or no written record.[6] In addition, colonial distortion and the biases of local elite who grew under colonialist tutelage contaminated the limited record that exists on Somali history. Somali history is therefore subject not only to the dialectics of remembering, forgetting, and retelling but also to self-serving interpretation and biases of those in power.

Being myself a member of the so-called Somali elite, I am aware that the perils of clan and class distortion lurk on the path of my inquiry, as they do for every Somali who grew up in the eco-pathological conditions of the past several decades. Still, I offer no apology for my critique of the elite whom I consider the bane of Somali society and key contributors to Somali suffering. On the other hand, I regret if I appear to vilify any clan when I analyze the vicious competition for power among elites of different clans. The distinction between a clan and its elite is clear to me, but I am not sure most Somalis make such distinction for subjective reasons I explain later.

That is why my analysis shifts from the real to the mythic clan and from the objective to the subjective, invoking Clan X or Clan Y, sometimes referring to an actual group (like Daarood, Hawiye, and Isaaq), at other times their fictional representation by the elite who pursue their interests using the mantle of the clan. Yet we should not confuse the actual group with its fictional representation by the elite, nor should we generalize the malfeasance of the elite to culpability of the clan with whom they share lineage. Guilt by association is a common error among Somalis. It is part of the pastoral legacy to hold a whole clan responsible for the crimes of one person.

Inquiry into Somali politics and history, full of peril and pain, is in some respects akin to an onion. As you peel each layer, you shed tears. That indeed has been my experience in writing *Politics of Cain.* As I wrote about the disaster of decades, I could not help but grieve the loss of life that Somalis could prevent if they intelligently analyzed their predicament and garnered the will to change their self-destructive behavior. At the same time, I found stimulating the experience of piecing together scattered information into a coherent narrative on the Somali political predicament. Thus, despite many jarring and painful experiences, I feel fortunate that my return home almost ten years ago dispelled illusions bred by decades of life abroad, and that I had the opportunity to observe firsthand how political oppression distorts the social relations and behavior of the Somali people.

An obvious limitation in my analysis of Somali history is the omission on the role and plight of the minority clans, women, and agrarian communities in Somali history. These groups are in fact the prime victims of Cain in Somali politics and society. The omission of these groups is not my preference but rather a proof that pastoralists who are intensely chauvinists dominate Somali politics.

My use of the masculine pronouns is an inherent limitation of language where shifting pronouns for the two genders can confuse rather than clarify or show fairness when, in the male dominated Somali society, *history* in effect is *'his-story'*. Nonetheless, my use of masculine pronouns should not be taken literally but generically to include men and women. My hope is that future studies will uncover their unacknowledged but substantial contributions of women and others to Somali history and society.

My reference to the name 'Somali' also deserves clarification. Somalis straddle various political borders including those of Kenya, Ethiopia, the Republic of Djibouti, and the former Somali Republic formed in 1960 and later called the Somali Democratic Republic. The former British Protectorate, now called Somaliland, withdrew on May 18, 1991 from the union after the collapse of the regime on January 26 1991. The Republic of Djibouti became independent in 1977 while Somalis in Ethiopia and Kenya remain parts of their respective countries.

Although the political history of the now defunct Somali Republic is the focus of this work, much of what I present here concerns and implicates Somalis in Kenya, Ethiopia, and the Republic of Djibouti. This is because Somalis in the region, despite the colonial borders segregating them, are interdependent; their life and destiny are also inextricably bound. No doubt, the specific political events and contexts vary from region to region, but Somalis everywhere share the same political and historical crises I discuss in this work. Besides, Somalis across the border have been active participants in the politics and wars of the Somali Republic to which they fled in pursuit of freedom and opportunity. In fact, no territory is safe or insulated from the numerous wars, the massive import of lethal arms, and the constant flow of refugees taking place in the region.

In reality then, the problems Somalis experience today, turning them into their own worst enemies and keeping them in abject poverty and oppression, know no borders. Although the population in the former Somali Democratic Republic experiences successive disasters, similar but less cataclysmic problems also plague Somalis in Kenya, Ethiopia, and Djibouti. If not, the same fate as that of the former Somali Republic awaits them. Hence, they too can learn from this work.

Approach and Orthography

To reiterate, I focus on the state, the elite, and the clan because the trio deserves in-depth analysis. The fundamental function of the state is to protect the physical security of its citizens, even if it fails to provide social and economic security. The Somali state did not meet this minimum requirement, the original *raison d'etre* of the state. On the contrary, it became the cause of oppression, hence its collapse. The elite also deserve critical analysis because they have been at the center of degeneration since independence. The clan system too distorted that it hardly serves its original function as it bolsters the flawed state and interests of the malfeasant elite.

To meet the challenge I set for myself, I freely use every discipline and data at my disposal. To the extent possible, I draw not only on written records but also on popular poems and songs that serve as remarkable repositories of Somali history. Somali poems and songs reveal public sentiment, mood, and frame of mind. Giving voice to Abel, they affirm the hopes and suffering of the oppressed. The Somali proverbs and sayings quoted at the beginning of each chapter and throughout the work also express Somali values.

Translation of poems, songs, and proverbs from one language to another is highly risky, especially when the metaphors and nuances of words in one language differ drastically from another. I admit my translations do not capture the full meaning and flow of the original Somali poems, songs, and proverbs. However, I offer these translations so that the non-Somali speakers can understand the mood and thought prevailing at the time. Somali-speaking readers will find the selection of poems and songs in their original Somali form in the notes I present at the end of work, giving them opportunity to interpret these poems and songs as they wish.

One point on orthography is worth noting here. Writing names of people and places in adopted Latin script presents difficulty for outsiders who do not know how Somalis use the letters of *'x'* and *'c'*. Yet the correct pronunciation of names is lost when written in English version. For compromise, I use mostly the Somali version of names with the exception of two letters: I replace the Somali *'x'* sound with *'h'* (like Mohamed instead of Maxamed) and the *'c'* sound with *'á'* (as in Ábdi instead of Cabdi). I hope this way of writing names helps Somali- as well as non-Somali speakers.

In short, Somali history during the past one hundred years has been a cycle of promises made and betrayed, a seesaw of hope and disillusionment, a fluctuation between short-lived euphoria and chronic despair. While analyzing the trio of the flawed state, the distorted clan system, and the malfeasant elite, this work traces this cycle and seesaw in Somali history, illustrating the promises made and the trust betrayed, the fluctuation between euphoria and disillusionment, the swing between hope and despair. The poems and songs illustrate the mood prevailing in Somali society in different periods in the late nineteenth century to the collapse of the regime.

Obviously, the history of one hundred years is a long time to which one cannot do it justice in one volume. Yet I did not set out to detail here all the critical events but only to present the broad outlines of the Somali predicament during the past century in the hope of distilling some basic lessons that can be useful for Somalis in the twenty-first century. This work does not therefore catalogue facts but interprets key examples of them for their heuristic and practical value.

I also hope that the narrative presented here gives voice to the suffering of Abel in Somali society.

2
COLONIAL PARTITION AND RULE

Addoonsi cabsi bu ka abuurmaa.
Slavery (oppression) begins in fear.
—*Somali Proverb*

The days when Africans blamed colonial rulers for all the ills of their country have long passed. Not only has passage of time made colonialism a stale topic but also much that does not compliment African leaders has transpired in the politics and history of Africans since they gained independence over forty years ago. Who could have anticipated four decades ago that Africans would experience as much misrule by their own leaders as they had known under colonialism? The Somali experience I discuss in this work is a case in point.

Yet, stating so does not exonerate colonial dehumanization nor recommend external rule as a solution to Somali problems. Far from it! We must search solution within the formerly colonized societies that obtained symbols of independence but not genuine freedom. But to find solution, we must first critically examine the colonial past and comprehend how and why things had gone wrong in Somali life.

After all, the flawed state and the malfeasant the Somali elite are products of colonial rule. Only when we understand the colonial conditions that gave birth to the flawed state and it servile elite can we grasp the root causes of contemporary problems and move forward, avoiding errors of the past. Only then can we also make sense of what Somalis do to themselves and why they engage in their self-destruction. Understanding the ways Somalis experienced colonial rule clarifies how little has changed in the vertical state violence during the past one hundred years.

To begin with, how did colonial rule and partition of Somalis take place, and how did ordinary Somalis understand and experience this rule and partition? What is the role of leaders and arms in protecting Abyssinia from colonial rule while making Somalis victims of it? Were there social, cultural, or political vulnerabilities of Somalis to colonial rule? If so, what were they?

Prelude to Colonial Rule

The land Somalis inhabit was a battleground for different forces within and without the region before Europeans arrived on Somali shores. Many writers on Somali recent Somali history, including this author, benefited from the contributions of I.M. Lewis. I will sketch key aspects of that history, interpreting and drawing lessons from them.

The ancestors of Somalis had intimate commerce and cultural exchange with Pharaonic Egypt over three thousand years ago. There are also indications that the territory had commerce with distant lands like India, China, and Indonesia. Contact and commerce with the Arab world also existed long before Islam reached the Somali coast about the eighth century. European attempts to colonize followed, the first of which was in 1487 when the Portuguese forces under Pero De Cavilhan invaded ports on the Somali coast.

The Portuguese in the sixteenth century had two goals: pursuit of material gain and proselytizing Christianity. In that era, religion provided the justification for colonization. The Portuguese first sought to colonize Somalis, then to assist political expansion of fellow Christians in Abyssinia. The Portuguese tried to blockade Somalis from the Muslim world and deny them access to arms. Similar attacks followed in subsequent decades – most notably by Vasco Da Gama and later by his son, Christopher Da Gama who was killed in a battle against the Muslim forces of Imam Ahmed Garaad Ibraahim, the charismatic leader whom Somalis know as *Ahmed Guray*—*'Ahmed the Left-handed.*[1]

Imam Ahmed's military forces comprised Somalis, Oromos, Afars, and other Muslims in the region. They overran much of Abyssinia by carrying out *jihad* – a holy war not only to defend Islam but also to proselytize it in non-Muslim communities. The Imam and his followers received arms from Muslim countries (notably Turkey) while the Portuguese armed Christians in Abyssinia.

Confident after resounding victories, the Imam sent away his Turkish advisors. This proved too hasty: with support of the Portuguese, the Abyssinians defeated his forces and killed him near Lake Tana. As we shall see later, different players have since fought similar proxy wars, but this war had lasting repercussions in the region. To this day, one finds emotional and social residues of those wars in the fears haunting Christian Highlanders and Muslim Lowlanders.[2]

In addition, as I show in *Archeology of Forgotten Experience,* the Crusades that began over ten centuries ago still rages on in different guises repeatedly benefiting Highland Christians while making Somalis victims of causes they neither comprehended nor controlled. This work does not concern itself with the history and consequences of the Crusades. However, it presents below an outline of the external forces that shaped Somali history since the nineteenth century, setting the stage for the primary focus of its inquiry—the evolution of auto-colonialism and dynamics of self-victimization in Somali society.

Scramble for Somali Colonies

Following the Imam's death in early 1543 and the subsequent defeat of his forces, Somalis once again fell back into their traditionally nomadic life. They scattered in the large expanse of semi-desert land, without a unifying leader or organization. A scramble to colonize Somalis began in earnest in the late nineteenth century by three European powers—Britain, France, and Italy. Abyssinia joined the fray, using religion and benefiting from astute leaders, to obtain a share of the land grab.

As the colonial occupation and partition of Somalis began, the Ottoman Empire revived its claim of the Red Sea coast, transferring in 1866 control of the Somali coast to Kediev Ismaíil of Egypt. In 1887, the Governor of Kediev Ismaíil residing in Sudan visited Tajura, Zeylá, and Berbera. Subsequently, Mohamed Jamal Bey representing the Kediev hoisted the Egyptian flag in Bulahaar and Berbera. Egyptian forces moved inland and established a garrison in Harar.

Meanwhile, the other four powers (Britain, France, Italy, and Abyssinia) kept a close eye on developments on the Somali coast with their own claims and interests. Britain was determined to avoid control of the coast by its rival, France; hence, it encouraged Egyptian occupation of the Somali coast. During their presence on the Somali coast, the Egyptian colonizers developed the ports of Berbera and Zeylá, constructed a piped water system for Berbera from the springs of Dubaar, built many mosques, and established a basic administrative structure. Most probably, Somalis moderated their reaction to Egyptian rule for two reasons. First, Egyptian colonial rule was couched in the name of Islam. Second, Somalis considered Turkish and Egyptian forces their protectors from the ever-present threat of encroachment by Christian Abyssinia.

As early as the 1820's, British ships frequently came to the Somali coast, provoking Somali suspicion and resentment. In 1825, for instance, the inhabitants of Berbera plundered a British ship. In retaliation, the British navy imposed a blockade of the coast until 1833 when the local Somali inhabitants paid £6,000 in compensation. Initially, British interest in the Somali coast was to secure a free flow of trade from the interior that supplied fresh meat to its garrison in Aden, the strategic port located in the Arabian Peninsula, which served as a coaling station for ships traveling to India. When the Egyptian forces withdrew from the Somali coast in 1884 to focus resources on the Mahdist rebellion in Sudan, the British who, like the French and Italians, were poised to establish a colony on the Somali coast signed agreements of "protection" with Somali elders.

With the opening of the Suez Canal in 1869, passage through the Red Sea offered a faster and cheaper route to the Persian Gulf, India, and the Far East than travel around the southern tip of Africa. The Red Sea and Somali coast therefore gained greater strategic value, intensifying competition for control ("sphere of influence") between Britain and France, two major of that era. As we shall see later, the United States and the former Soviet Union also competed during the Cold War for geopolitical advantage in the Horn of Africa.

In 1854, Richard F. Burton embarked on an expedition to explore the Somali interior inhabited by "a most dangerous race." A year earlier, he disguised himself as a Muslim and successfully carried out pilgrimage to Mecca and Medina, making him the first European to visit these two holy sites forbidden to non-Muslims. Disguising himself this time as an Arab merchant and a learned Muslim, Burton landed on the ancient port of Zeylá and undertook an arduous trek into the hinterland. He recorded his observations in *First Footsteps in East Africa*.

Burton's opinion of Somalis reflected the European racism of the time. Comparing Somalis with "Red Indians" of America and the "Kaffir" of South Africa, he declared:

> "They [the Somali] have all the levity and instability of the Negro character; light-minded as the Abyssinians... soft, merry and affectionate souls, they pass without any apparent transition into a state of fury, when they are capable of terrible atrocities." [3]

Following his brief visit (which lasted for four months), Burton wrote about Somali genealogy, history, culture, and even sexual behavior. Though the breadth and depth of his observations are impressive, considering his brief visit, Burton wrote with the same arrogance with which Europeans approached discussions on "natives." For instance, writing like someone who conducted a comprehensive survey of private sexual behaviors of Somalis, Burton affirmed: "Curious to say, throughout the Somali territory, kissing is entirely unknown." Nevertheless, he also made an ominous prediction sadly realized after independence over a century later:

> "At the present, a man armed with a revolver would be a terror to the country; the day, however, will come when the matchlock will supersede the assegai [spear], and then the harmless spearman in his strong mountain will become... a formidable foe." [4]

Somalis did indeed acquire lethal weapons after independence and they have become a formidable foe—but in the end foe to whom except to themselves? After independence, armed with imported and lethal arms, they killed one another for causes this work examines and identifies so that Somalis find solution for their auto-destructive behavior.

Burton concluded his book by appealing for complete occupation of Somaliland and positioning the British as the "sole judges of all disputes" for the sake of British interest and raising "fellow man in the scale of civilization." One hundred and fifty years later, were Somalis raised in the "in the scale of civilization?" What is civilization anyway?

In the same year, Burton, Herne, Speke, and Stroyen carried out another expedition. During their second expedition, about 300 Somalis attacked the four men and the forty-two armed men they brought with them to the coast. They killed Stroyen; inflicted eleven wounds on Speke; they hurled a spear at both cheeks of Burton who lost four teeth; Herne escaped without injury. The survivors (including Burton) reached Aden never to return to the Somali coast.

In retaliation, the British authorities in Aden sent two vessels to blockade the Somali coast until Somalis handed over the murderers of Stroyen to British authorities for reprisal. Somali elders assured the British authorities that they would execute Stroyen's murderers. In addition, they offered $15,000. However, the British were not satisfied with these offers. They forced Somalis to sign a treaty acceding to British needs for commerce and the appointment of a British Resident in Berbera. This paved the way for British colonization of the Somali. The attack of the explorers and the compensation imposed on Somalis only hastened the colonial occupation the British wanted in the first place.

The French and Italians too had their own "pioneers" like Burton and Speke who "explored" the land Somalis inhabit. France was one of the early powers to send its explorers and weapons dealers into the region. From the start, France focused attention on the section of the Somali coast closest to the gateway of the Red Sea. French engineers and financiers were instrumental in digging the Suez Canal, the control of which promised greater competitive advantage over their rival, the British Empire.

When France lost control of the Suez Canal because the British purchased a majority share, the French sought to acquire a port on the Somali coast near the gateway to the Red Sea and close to Aden, an important coaling station, to which they had limited access. In 1862, the French "purchased" concession from the local inhabitants to hoist their flag in Obokh in 1862.

By 1881, France used this "possession" as a strategic foothold to extend its control of *Cote des Somali* from which it launched its Franco-Ethiopian trading company. In 1884, Leonce Lagarde became the governor of Obokh. He not only began colonizing the inhabitants but he also enlarged French influences deep into Ethiopia.

Similarly, Italy armed with lethal weapons and ready-made treaties, entered into the land grab. Italy's entry into the colonial adventure started with equivocation but it soon turned into consuming obsession. For instance, the Italian Foreign Minister, Mancini, declared in 1884 that "any effort to acquire political colonies by annexation or conquest [must be] repugnant to the true interests of the Italian nation."[5]

After less than a year, Mancini reversed the anti-colonial argument with equal conviction. Defending his government's colonial adventure, Mancini declared, "It would not in any case have been possible for Italy to watch, idle and indifferent, the peaceful crusade undertaken by all the great powers in order to civilize the population of Africa, without seeing Italy's good name disgraced in Europe."[6]

Indeed, the crusades in all its disguises had neither peaceful goals nor enlightening civilizing consequences. On the contrary, invoking the crusades against non-Christians justified war on faith, dislocation of indigenous cultures, or occupation of lands. By invoking the crusades, the Prime Minister appealed to the emotions and rationalizations that would resonate with his European constituency. And it worked.

In 1889, Vincenzo Filonardi, the Italian Consul in Zanzibar, signed treaties with Sultans of the Mijeerteen who had accepted "protection" of Italy in return for 1,800 tallers per year. In 1891, Robecchi-Brichetti trekked into the Somali hinterland, starting from Mogadishu, crossing the Ogaadeen and leaving from Berbera. In the same year, Baudi di Vesme and Candeo reached the Ogaadeen; they managed to find among the Ogaadeen signatories for their ready-made treaty of protection.

In 1893, Prince Ruspoli trekked from Berbera and signed a similar treaty with inhabitants of Baardeera and Juba. In the same year, Filonardi and his colleagues drafted a treaty of protection with the elders of Merka. However, as they were boarding their warship, the inhabitants attacked, mortally wounding one of them. In reprisal, twelve Somali elders were taken hostage and the town was heavily bombed.

Filonardi quit his diplomatic job, formed his own commercial venture called V. Filonardi e Co., and obtained a contract to manage the Benaadir coast on behalf of Italy. Filonard's company failed three years later. In 1896, Somalis attacked Cecchi who was the Italian Consul in Zanzibar and his companions at Lafoole, near Mogadishu, killing fifteen of the seventeen Italians. A year later, Giorgio Sorrentino, a commander of a warship, arrived with arms and soldiers (including "native troops") to restore order in the area and punish those who attacked Cecchi and his companions. He did. Several years later, Italy used the treaties of "protection" and "lease" to establish a Somali colony and extend its area of control.

Fraudulent Treaties

Bombarding inhabitants to sign a treaty of "protection" was common practice. First, the future colonizers sought local inhabitants willing to sign gratis or with small monetary inducements. The signatories could be chiefs, elders, or persons with little claim to legitimacy. Often, the colonizers did not inform or consult the inhabitants. If they did, they invented stories of impending threats or exaggerated existing conflicts, sometimes mobilizing and arming their opponents to confirm the propaganda. Thus frightened by fabricated or exaggerated accounts of threats, the inhabitants signed treaties of 'protection.'

In reality, threats to Somali freedom and life grew in the very incursion of Europeans into the region. If one colonizer did not attack, another was poised to do the same, reproducing the classic case of the fox protecting the chicken coop. Nevertheless, the offer of "protection" was not an offer at all. The population had no choice of either accepting or refusing the so-called offer. It was an ultimatum covered up with legal jargon the signatories did not understand. Resistance of the 'offer' invariably brought brutal reprisal. One way or another, the inhabitants were forced or induced to sign the so-called treaty of protection. And once signed, the treaty provided a convenient legal pretext to occupy the land and colonize the people.

Moreover, these treaties were explained as a *favor* for which the colonized were to be grateful. For instance, the agreements the British wrote with Somali elders started with the following preamble: "The British Government, in compliance with the wish of the undersigned Elders … hereby undertakes to extend to them and to the territories under their authority and jurisprudence, the gracious *favor* and *protection* of Her Majesty the Queen-Empress." The favor and protection turned out to be outright colonialism and partition without the consent of Somalis.

Such agreements did not only pave the way for colonial occupation and rule; they also became the bitter and enduring heritage of generations who to this day live with malfeasance and machination of leaders. For one thing, inducing the weak, defenseless, or misinformed populations to sign 'treaties' sustaining and justify oppression continued after the colonialists had ostensibly left. In post-independence, the Somali elite replaced the colonial treaties with high-sounding terms like 'constitutions', 'legislative decisions', and 'democratic elections' declared to protect the rights of the ruled. In reality, these declarations of rights, parliaments, and rituals of elections contradict the obvious abuse of power and pillage of public resources which the ruling elite carry on in practice, demonstrating that the declaration written on paper and announced in the media are fraudulent 'contracts' or 'covenants' which the ruling elite enter with the ruled but conceal their abuse of power and corruption.

For another, Somalis continue to be victims of the 'protection' treaties European colonialists had induced unsuspecting elders or unqualified persons to sign more than a century ago. These treaties were to serve specific and time-limited interests of colonial powers, but they have permanent legal fixtures hemming Somalis in artificial "colonial boundaries" that today are considered sacrosanct and fixed under international law. The Somali signatories of those treaties did not know that their signature would provide legal pretext for colonialism and victimize their descendants centuries later, pitting them against their neighbors.

What is remarkable here is not only the cunning and cupidity of the colonizers but also the ignorance and naivety of the Somali signatories. Worse, the inhabitants of the region, stuck with old fashioned notions of nation and nationalism, continue to hurl at one another expensive explosives imported from abroad, giving vent to reciprocal hate and acrimony that leaves them economically poorer and morally bankrupt each time they fight for causes that no longer make sense in a world where even Europeans who fought world wars have broken down boundaries to pool material and human resources.

Outcome of the Scramble

The Anglo-French Treaty of 1887 fixed the boundary between the British Protectorate of Somaliland and the French Somaliland, later called the French Territories of Afars and Íise. From 1889 to 1925, a series of Anglo-Italian treaties divided and re-divided colonial spoils, leading to the formation of Italian Somaliland. In the Anglo-Ethiopian Treaty of 1897, Britain ceded on paper, without the knowledge or consent of Somalis, a significant portion of Somaliland to Ethiopia. They neither published the secret treaty, nor marked the boundary until the early nineteen-thirties. Without Somali knowledge, Britain and Ethiopia signed a military convention in 1942 while Haile Selassie was an exile in Britain. The military convention gave Britain temporary administrative rights. Somalis learned of the original 1897 Treaty in 1954 when Britain transferred the "Haud" to Ethiopian authorities.

The Anglo-Ethiopian Treaty of 1897 was not the only instance of agreement in which European colonizers ceded the land of the Somalis to Ethiopia without their knowledge or consent. The Franco-Ethiopian Treaty of 1897 also ceded a considerable part of French Somaliland. The Italo-Ethiopian Agreements of 1897 attempted to define the boundary between Ethiopia and Italian Somaliland. A second agreement in 1908 attempted to define a precise boundary, but it did not succeed. After decades of colonial intrigues and bartering, colonizers partitioned the land without the knowledge or consent of Somalis.

Though driven by the same mission to colonize for material gain and self-aggrandizement, European colonial powers nonetheless had different objectives for colonizing Somalis. France occupied the northern portion of Somali territories in order to acquire a coaling station for its ships bound for Southeast Asia. Using its foothold in Djibouti, it also wanted to link the Red Sea with its colonies in Equatorial Africa. Britain occupied Somaliland in order to obtain a steady supply of meat for its garrison in Aden and to deny competing colonial powers (particularly France) access to the source of the Nile and to the Suez Cannel.

Italy, a late starter in the colonial scramble since it unified into an independent nation in 1860, was determined to hold on to Eritrea and Somalia partly for the prestige of possessing colonies. It also sought the rewards of colonization: to gain a strategic foothold, to exploit resources and perhaps to create settler communities in agriculturally rich areas. In addition, all three European powers considered their colonial footholds on the coast as strategic gateways to Ethiopia.

Viewing Ethiopia a formidable threat to their colonial possessions, they all wanted to forge an alliance with Menelik II— an alliance they thought would give them access to the riches of the Oromo hinterland that he was rapidly usurping into his empire. Italy in particular wanted nothing less than colonizing Abyssinia to avenge its devastating loss in the Battle of Adowa in 1896—the first instance in which black Africans had indisputably defeated white Europeans. At least, it wanted to even the score in order to restore the prestige it had lost.

In the end, the land of the Somalis was effectively partitioned into five colonies: British Somaliland, French Somaliland (with a substantial Afar population), Italian Somaliland, the Northern Frontier District (now part of Kenya), and the Somali territory under Ethiopian rule (now called the Somali Region of Ethiopia). The fraudulent treaties leading to the partition, developed without Somali knowledge or consent, continue to have a lasting effect on Somalis, as if they were cast on stone and Somali destiny was fixed in the late nineteenth century.

The Abyssinian Advantage

While Europeans were partitioning Somalis and their land, the burgeoning Abyssinian Empire joined the colonial melee under the leadership of the astute Menelik II who understood that European cannons, firearms, and advisors were critical in gaining power and a share of the land occupied without consent of its inhabitants. In an 1872 letter to European powers, Menelik wrote, "Be so kind as to send me a doctor, an engineer, a mechanic, and good men specializing in woodwork and ironwork. I will respect them and treat them well and reward them properly."[7]

If Machiavelli was an astute political strategist in theory, Menelik was its consummate practitioner. In the period when Abyssinian kings were fighting for ascendancy, he allied himself with King Yohannes, the most powerful king in the region, conceding to him "King of Kings" with the agreement that Menelik would assume that coveted rank after Yohannes' death. Yohannes agreed. To ensure the agreement endures, he arranged marriage of his daughter to Yohannes' son. In the meantime, Menelik enlarged his forces and defeated other kings who vied for the same title. When Yohannes died, Menelik became the Emperor—the King of Kings—and the region's most formidable king with whom each Europeans power wanted to forge alliance in order to realize its colonial ambition.

One historical coincidence—shared religion with Europeans—favored Menelik, Yohannes, and other Abyssinian kings in developing good relations with Europeans. The powers that hailed from Europe and grew into global victors since the sixteenth century were Christian. The passion for the Crusades still possessed them and they had a soft place for a Christian nation in need of aid, so long as assistance to it did not contradict their economic and political interests.

Thus in an era when religion offered convenient cover and metaphor for political and economic interest, Abyssinian kings exploited maximally their religious affinity with Europeans and couched their economic and political interest in terms of religious wars. So did the Muslims in the region when Turkey was a global power. In fact, the victories of Ahmed Guray in the sixteenth century would not continue without a steady supply of arms from the Ottoman Empire, the same way the defeat of his forces would not take place without decisive Portuguese support for his Christian opponents.

This was one of the earliest proxy wars in the Horn of Africa. The Portuguese and the Turks who at that time were the primary competitors for hegemony in the world had respectively allied themselves with Highland Christians and Lowland Muslims in the region. The two local parties had their conflict but it became subsumed under a larger conflict involving the Portuguese and the Turks. Hence they engaged in a war within a larger war—a pattern of conflicts that was to recur until to this day.

Conditions in the nineteenth century had their specific configuration and context. Although Highland Christians enjoyed better prospect than Muslim Somalis and Oromos to win and exploit alliance with Europeans, more was actually involved in the repeated success of Abyssinia than shared faith with Europeans. For one thing, Abyssinian leaders cultivated knowledge of Europe and developed social capital that would be bulwark to foreign occupation of their land. Not so with Somalis who for centuries continued their parochial and isolated existence.

Menelik was not alone in learning much about Europeans and their interests. For instance, Tewodros (born in 1818 and whose original name was Kasa) was an educated man for his time. He studied in a convent and rose from poverty to becoming a powerful king. He studied ancient and modern European history; he was even familiar with Shakespeare.[8] Other Abyssinian kings (like Yohannes and Menelik II) were at least able to read, understand maps, and craft treaties with Europeans, ensuring that their interest are not thwarted.

Most of all, they understood the importance of strategic weapons—particularly the cannon—and they knew how to acquire them for defense of their kingdoms and for expansion to other territories. Tewodros had demonstrated his political acumen when he chose the cannon of the Europeans over the education and religious proselytizing they offered. The Ethiopian kings who succeeded him, like Menelik and Haile Selassie, adopted Tewodros' preference for guns and cannon but they also embraced Western advisors and education.

In the days of Tewodros and Menelik II, Somalis confined themselves to their own world, unaware of the coming European onslaught. If some of them had inkling of the impending occupation, as did Faarax Nuur, they lacked the social capital—the national consciousness, the institutions, the inter-clan solidarity, and the military organization—with which to protect their land and freedom. Competing for scarce resources, they engaged in incessant clan conflicts that collectively weakened them and sapped their human resources. Their trade and strategic links with the defeated Arab world neither inspired them to do better nor helped them to defend themselves against the European onslaught. Moreover, their tools of offensive and defensive war remained primarily the spear, the shield, and the dagger—no match to the guns and cannons arrayed at them.

During the scramble for colonies, Menelik invoked Christianity while vilifying his neighbors as heathens—people who have little or no religion and therefore deserved to be ruled if not decimated. Like Abyssinian leaders before and after him, Menelik described Abyssinia as "an island of Christians in a sea of pagans" to win European sympathy and support for a besieged and isolated kingdom. Menelik understood and used the metaphor and tactics that worked in his time and other before him. As I have shown in *Archeology of Forgotten Experience*, this was the language of the Crusades that raged on since the twelve century and has been resurfacing in differ forms to the present.

Somalis and other Muslims in the region lacked this skill for subterfuge and awareness of political trends in the world. When the fire and fury of Crusades reached their region centuries ago, they did not understand why they became target of European aggression. Unaware of the economic and political motives of Europeans, they interpreted Abyssinian and European assault in purely religious terms, as if European bias for Abyssinia was inevitable or irreversible. To this day, they do not understand the ascendancy of material and geopolitical interest in the European mind over spiritual loyality and the dictates of the church, that therefore societies survive and prosper if they develop proper strategy and policies while holding on to their faith.

Somalis often underestimate two critical factors in particular. The first factor is that Menelik had a political system akin to the state that Europeans elaborated in their societies. He possessed the institutions, the written script, and the human organization to sustain this political system. This factor was product of historical trajectory Christian Highlanders took long ago in developing kingdoms that approximated European experience, in contrast to the Muslim Lowlanders (including Somalis, Oromos, and Afars) who at best developed weak and insular city-states like Ifat based in Harar or Adal based in Zeylá, although the majority ived in pastoral disarray.

The second factor had to do with Menelik the person and the leader. Menelik aligned his ambition for conquest and annexation with Europeans passion for colonies. Having demonstrated by skill and organization that he was a force with whom they must reckon, he offered Europeans alliance to not only proselytize or defend Christianity but also exploit rich Oromo resources—two offers no European power could refuse. In return, Menelik wanted and received profusion of arms denied to Somalis and other Muslims in the region. Indeed few African leaders in his time could boast of Menelik's prescience and success.

The Vital Role of Arms

Of the many advantages Abyssinia had—including shared faith with Europeans, burgeoning national consciousness, state-like structure, and astute leaders—the most decisive factor that brought victory to Menelik's expanding empire and sealed the fate of Somalis to oppression was the study flow of arms to Abyssinia, at the same time as Somalis were systematically denied access to arms.

As the scramble for colonies escalated to a feverish pitch, each colonial power pursued its own interests and plans in the region. The British, as mentioned earlier, were concerned first with the free flow of food supplies to its garrison in Aden that served as a coaling station en route to India. Later, the British used the Somali colony they acquired (euphemistically called the "British Protectorate")as a bargaining chip to prevent the burgeoning Abyssinian Empire from involvement against the British in the Mahdist war in the Sudan.

The French wanted to develop the port of Djibouti to compete with Aden and to extend its influence into Ethiopia. The Italians had their eye on Eritrea and Somaliland. Beyond the regional interests, each European country had its own long-term plans on the African continent. The British had plans to build a trans-African railway from Cape Town to Cairo. The French schemed to connect by rail their colonies in West Africa to the Red Sea.

Abyssinia thus became a prized acquisition for whichever power had succeeded in pulling her into its sphere of influence due to its strategic location on the Nile and easy access to the rich Oromo interior, contiguous to it. Each European power sought to sign treaties with its rival kings. The British first supported King John (Yohannes) of Tigre until his death, while the French, the Italians, and the Russians supported King Menelik of Shoa who later became the acknowledged "King of Kings." Playing one European power against another, Menelik not only succeeded in preserving sovereignty of his people (where his contemporaries in the region had failed) but also obtained continued flow of arms from the French, the Italians, and the Russians.

In aligning his interests with those of Europeans, Menelik became a junior partner to European powers he knew were determined to occupy and partition the region. In return, he saved his empire and obtained a share of the land grab. At the same time, Menelik also used one power against another. He even misled Italians to think he had an "agreement of protection" with them, obtaining as a result massive arms supply, advice, and diplomatic support from them, only to defeat them with their arms and tactics.

When Menelik obtained enough arms and developed relations with other European powers, he revoked the "agreement of protection" he had signed with Italians by arguing that the Amharic version did not contain the same terms as the Italian version. The dispute led to a war between Menelik's forces and Italian colonialists, resulting in a resounding defeat of Italians—the most decisive victory of European colonialist in African history. This victory also became a symbol that lifted the aspirations and pride of oppressed Blacks, particularly in the Caribbean, North America, and South Africa. On the other hand, Somalis, the Oromos, and the other Muslim nationalities bore the brunt of the Abyssinian expansion. They were more cognizant of their growing loss of land and liberty than symbolic gains for the black race. On the contrary, they found Menelik's victory as another indication that their oppression would grow and deepen.

The 1890 Brussels General Act that prohibited access of firearms to Africans exempted Abyssinia, making it the only African territory enjoying the legal right to import arms and to deal directly with European arms suppliers without restriction. Therefore, by 16 September 1890, the steady stream of firepower flowing to Menelik became a deluge; arms of all types and sizes poured in from various European sources. Italy sponsored the Abyssinian exemption from the prohibition of the 1890 Brussels General Act. The other European powers also endorsed the proposal.

Using this steady and unhindered flow of arms, Menelik conquered the Oromo and their neighbors, annexing their territories and plundering their resources. Encouraged by his success and European support, Menelik's self-aggrandizement grew beyond bounds, as his circular letter of 1891 declared:

> While tracing today the actual boundaries of my empire, I shall endeavor ... to reestablish the ancient frontiers of Ethiopia up to Khartoum, and as far as Lake Nyaza of the Gallas. Ethiopia has been for fifteen centuries a Christian Island in a Sea of Pagans. If powers at a distance come forward to partition Africa between them, *I do not intend to be an indifferent spectator.*

Menelik wrote this letter at the instigation and advice of Italy. On 18 July 1890, Italian Prime Minister Crispi instructed his ambassador in Addis Ababa to forewarn Menelik that Europeans planned to divide the region into spheres of influence and, before they executed plan, Menelik should make his claims known.

On 20 August 1890, Count Antoneli wrote the following advice to Menelik: "The countries that your Majesty should put in the list are specifically all the tribes of the Adal and Somalis, those of Ogaden, the countries beyond Kaffa and always insist on Gidessa, Harar and Lake Assal."

Actually, the Brussels General Act only legitimized the ongoing flow of arms to Abyssinia. Several decades before signing the Brussels General Act, European governments and weapon traders poured firearms into Abyssinia. In 1882, M. C. Hunter wrote, "As soon as the port of Assab was opened, the Italians began to pour arms through it in a steady stream into Shoa [Menelik's Kingdom]; the French did the same through their protectorate first at Abokh and next at Tajoura."

Ironically, the Italians who sponsored Abyssinians to acquire these rights for being Christians were later to suffer military defeat by Menelik's forces using imported arms.

The importation of arms continued in subsequent years. For instance in 1885, a French arms dealer, Savoure, sold to Menelik 30,000 cartridges, 600,000 repercussion caps, 3,000 muskets and 24 cannons. In the same year, Russia brought for Menelik 50,000 rifles, 50,000 carbines, 5,000 revolvers, 40 cannons, 5,000 swords, and extensive ammunition.

A year later, a French trader sold to Menelik's empire 2,590 rifles, 198,200 cartridges and 80,000 repercussion caps. Because of the 1887 Treaty of Alliance with Italy, Menelik's forces received 50,000 Remingtons and 10,000,000 cartridges. Two years later, King Hubert of Italy sent to Menelik a gift of 28 cannons and 38,000 rifles.

Harrington, a British Consul, observed this deluge of arms and wrote in 1900, "It is impossible to travel between Harar and Addis Ababa without repeatedly meeting caravans of rifles and cartridges. I should think there are more rifles, Gras and Remington, in the country than there are men to carry them."[8] Visiting the Somali hinterland nearly two decades earlier, Swayne reported that the chief complaint he heard was the constant raiding by better-armed Abyssinians. Swayne's biographer wrote:

> At many points on the route he was the first European who had been seen by the [Somali] natives, and when he told them he was English, he heard many complaints of raiding by the Abyssinians ... beseeching him to ask the Great Queen to arm their country and stop the Abyssinian raids! [9]

Little wonder Somalis, fearing occupation by well-armed forces of Menelik, had readily accepted European offers of "protection." The European powers on their part exploited Somali fears and wrote ambiguous agreements that did not prevent them from making deals with the shrewd Menelik of Abyssinia. If the agreements Europeans reached with Somalis conflicted with their aims, they simply reneged or changed them at will.

As a result, the world as Somalis knew it collapsed or distorted. Isolated in small communities and cut off from the world of politics, they bore the brunt of the colonial scramble in the eastern Horn of

Africa, suffering colonial occupation and division into colonial enclaves—historical and lasting assaults for which Somalis were least prepared. The world as Somalis knew it therefore collapsed or it irretrievably distorted. That world was never the same since.

Obviously, none can recreate that bygone world, any more than adults recover childhood. Whether we recall the past with nostalgia or dread, we can some lessons from it. One thing is certain: the social capital—the worldview, the values, the institutions, the social relations, and the means of war—Somalis inherited did not prepare them to anticipate the coming colonial onslaught or to defend themselves from it. As we shall see in subsequent chapters, their social capital contradicted the development of a nation and state, keeping Somalis stuck in clan-based consciousness and politics, producing after independence clan-based form of auto-colonialism.

Nonetheless, the transition from a pre-colonial society, to colonized society, subsequently to auto-colonialism involved significant transformation in the world and life Somalis had known before the colonial rule and partition. How then did Somalis react to colonial rule and partition?

3
FROM RESISTANCE TO BETRAYAL

Ninku mas qaniinay baa mulac ka baqa
A man bit by snake fears small lizards
—*Somali Proverb*

The struggle for freedom is a never-ending process. It is the human nature to strive for freedom whose appetite intensifies with more freedom. Each struggle for freedom brings disappointments and those who risked their lives wonder if what they attained was worth the sacrifice. Worse than this disappointment is the self-blame and self-denigration following defeat and prolonged oppression.

Somalis have gone through the whole cycle. They fought against colonial rule, for independence, and against the oppression of the ruling elite on whom they entrusted power. Each victory whetted the appetite for more freedom only to result in disappointment and each defeat brought erosion or distortion of the self, at least that part of it Somalis embraced with pride and confidence.

Somalis in the nineteen-forties and nineteen-fifties did not fight for independence in violent ways that the Somali Dervishes did. Their armed struggle against colonialism reached its peak under the leadership of Mohamed Ábdulle Hassan and his dervish movement. Similar struggles for freedom followed in subsequent decades, particularly against Ethiopian and French rule, but the thirst for independence bore fruit in the former Italian colony and the former British Protectorate. Still, the fruits of freedom and development—the motive goal of all political struggles—eluded Somalis. Why?

First, I present a highlight of the armed resistance to colonial rule, followed by the quest for independence, then the causes and agents of betrayal.

Resistance to Occupation

When Somalis realized they were powerless by lacking arms and organization, they quickly signed agreements with a colonial power or lamented the colonial encroachment into their life. The capitulation to colonial rule quickly turned into active collaboration to gain advantage over the next clan or to find protection from Abyssinian expansion.

Poetry of lament was indeed a form of resistance. Most memorable among the laments on colonial rule is that of Faarah Nuur, the great poet and warrior who in a poem concluded that the end of the world was imminent.

The British, the Ethiopians, and the Italians are squabbling
Whosoever is stronger divides and snatches the country,
Without our knowledge the country is sold piece by piece,
And for me, all this is the teeth of the last days of the world.[1]

The world did not literally end, but it changed drastically as colonial powers took "possession" of Somalis. From that point on, Somalis became "possessed" in two meanings of the word. Firstly, colonial powers "owned" their land and they too became owned. Secondly, the colonizers who took "possession" of them crept into in their psyche, turning into inner controls.[2] The former type of "possession" was obvious and it was thought be reversible only when political independence was granted in 1960; the latter type of "possession" remains barely understood and continues growing with intensity.

Qamaan Bulhan too lamented the colonial problems in one of his poems. Like Faarah Nuur, he knew that Abyssinia and powerful European powers carried out simultaneous assault on the Somali. He stated:

The Amhara raging from the west is an enemy
Those marauding on the seas are French soldiers
The English will come in large force from Aden
Armed to the teeth, are the Italians not ready to occupy? [3]

The first organized movement of colonial "possession" dates from early 1900 when Mohamed Ábdulle Hassan and the Dervish Movement kept the British at bay for over twenty years. Mohamed Ábdulle Hassan was born in 1856 in Balli Sac Madeeqa, a village seven miles north of Buuhoodle, now in the Republic of Somaliland.[4]

After travels in the Arab peninsula and studies in Mecca under Sheekh Mohamed Saalah, the founder of the Salihiyya Order, Mohamed returned to Somali society. On his way from Saudi Arabia, he passed through Sudan and encountered the Mahdist Movement that left lasting impression on him. When he arrived in Berbera, a British officer demanded that the Mohamed pay custom duties. He answered: "You're an Englishman. Who collected custom duties from you when you entered the land?" An intense argument ensued, the British officer explaining the law and Mohamed continuing his anti-colonial tirade.

Mohamed's defiant attitude and fiery words took the British officer by surprise. Calling him "Mad Mullah", he let him go without paying the required duty. The derisive nickname stuck to Mohamed in colonial literature. While in Berbera, Mohamed's outrage intensified when he saw churches built in Berbera and Somali children wearing the cross around their neck. The British administration ignored his repeated complaints. Mohamed was outraged when early one morning he witnessed the *Mu'addun* calling Muslims to prayer shot down by a British officer. When asked why he did so, the officer explained: "He had disturbed my sleep!"

By then, Mohamed was determined to wage *Jihad* against the infidels who had imposed colonial rule converted them to Christianity. The rest is history – one that I cannot detail here. The key points are essentially five. First, colonizers did not impose their rule without resistance after Somalis understood their true designs. Second, the Somali struggle to preserve liberty was undermined by a misunderstanding of the world and of the motivation of European powers. Third, limited access to arms reduced Somali capacity to defend freedom. Fourth, Somalis vigorously defended their faith – Islam – but they gave in to colonial occupation and partition of their land. What they did not know was that occupation and partition of land leads to occupation and partition of psyches. Five, clan politics deeply infected the Dervish leader even while he claimed to wage a *Jihad* whose goals transcend clan politics. This attests the truth of the proverb, *"Fiqi tolki kama jano tago"*—even the most learned man of religion forsakes paradise if his clan is excluded from it."

To carry out *Jihad* against the infidels, Mohamed relied mostly on his maternal clan. He had a character flaw common to Somali leaders. His was profoundly clannish even when he claimed to fight for a lofty religious cause. He also interpreted opponents to his cause as expression to his clan identity. Caught in clan identity and loyalty, he was incapable of wooing to his cause others outside his paternal and maternal clan. His actions were often vindictive, his condemnations categorical, and he relied on violence to recruit others to his cause. Mohamed Siyaad Barre suffered from similar character flaws, even though he was far less gallant (though more crafty) than Mohamed Ábdulle Hassan.

As we shall see in the wars of Mohamed Ábdulle Hassan at the turn of the twentieth century, Somalis fought to defend their land and freedom against colonial rule. But that resistance, with all its spectacular bravery, did not achieve its aims because it was woefully uninformed about global developments and trends, it lacked conscious political goals, preferring redemption in the hereafter to success in this world. It was also corroded by the same blunder—clan myopia—that always compromises Somali aspiration toward freedom.

If Mohamed Ábdulle Hassan had not alienated other clans and had not known how to counteract the colonial tactic of divide-and-rule, his political movement might have endured longer. It might possibly have preserved Somali liberty. Nevertheless, protecting political liberty and building a modern nation was not his primary goal. Instead, he wanted to save Islam and to cease Christian proselytizing. In that, he clearly succeeded. The British ceased building churches and they prohibited missionaries from proselytizing.

I. M. Lewis affirms that the memory and image of Mohamed Ábdulle Hassan haunted British colonial administrators in the Protectorate for decades. According to him, it tempered their colonial rule and made them weary of policies that might offend "the prickly Muslim Somalis."[5]

The history of colonial rule would have been different if Mohamed Ábdulle Hassan had possessed the diplomatic skills like those of Menelik II and Haile Selassie. The political and social balance of power in the region would shifted drastically if the alliance between Mohamed Ábdulle Hassan and Lij Iyasu had not been nipped in the bud.[6] However, history does not progress in hindsight, nor can the quality of leaders be justly assessed on a universal standard. Nor indeed do all societies pursue the same goals, under the same the conditions.

Mohamed Ábdulle Hassan lived in a society committed to social, religious, and historical precepts different from that of Europeans and Abyssinians. His was a defensive reaction to an external assault to his land, people, and religion. Since action taken controls the *reaction* that follows it, the timing and tactics of the oppressed are often stuck in anger and rejection, not by proactive thought on end and means. Mohamed tried to end the external assault but he did not succeed in turning his reflexive *reaction* to successive *responses.* He could not overcome the strong clan contradictions in Somali society and its vulnerabilities to colonial occupation and partition. Therefore, it is not surprising that he drew support from the Daarood (mainly the Dhulbahante sub-clan, his maternal kin) and alienated other Somalis that would have made his struggle successful.

Still, Mohamed's determined struggle should not be underestimated. His remarkable genius for organizing people for guerrilla war is obvious from his ability to fight and befuddle the British for twenty years. The fact that the British resorted to aerial bombardment, the first of its kind in Africa, proves that he was a formidable opponent. In fact, his poetic description of the aerial bombardment is so moving that it transports one to the era of the colonialism, evoking images of "birds" raining bombs of destruction. Mohamed Ábdulle Hassan died on November 23, 1921 from natural causes.

In one of his poems—*Dardaaran*— meaning 'last words of counsel or will'—Mohamed Ábdulle Hassan began with words depicting the death and destruction caused by the British aerial bombardment. He ends his poem with words that underscore his intense hatred of the European colonizer and his worries of what was to come if Somalis acquiesced to colonial rule:

No benefit comes from cooperating with the white man
The infidel to whom you're lenient always deceives you
He throws you money to poison you to death
First he disarms you like women
Then he makes you accept his authority
Later he tells you to sell your land
Then he heaps loads on you, like donkeys…[7]

Following the death of Mohamed Ábdulle Hassan, the British extended their rule in the territory they euphemistically called *the Protectorate.* One of the measures colonial forces took to bring Somalis into submission was to send convoys of armed soldiers to capture camels and other livestock, to burn villages, to imprison leaders, and to kill anyone considered a threat to their rule. These soldiers included recruits from India, Kenya, other foreigners, and local Somalis. Led by British officers with sophisticated weapons, they imposed draconian measures to "pacify" Somalis who, since the Brussels General Act of 1890, could not obtain arms for self-defense. The period from 1922 to 1940, was especially grueling for Somalis whom the British, the Italians, the French, and the Ethiopians considered as the backbone of Somali resistance to colonial rule.

To contain resistance, the colonial forces focused on strategic watering points to which Somalis inevitably flocked. Contemporary Somalis have forgotten the suffering and destitution of Somalis in that era. It is not simply forgetting the past for lack memory. It is primarily due to a desire not to recall and relive the painful past. In addition, the unusual has become the usual and the abnormal, normal. Oppression and injustice became acceptable. With the demise of tradition, a new breed of compromised and confused men came to be "the elite." Instead of being the cream, they turned into the dregs and trash of society.

Contemporary Somalis have taken for granted European domination, corrupt government, and the habit of local elite, created and pampered by colonial masters, and the greed of the elite. In fact, they think oppression and exploitation the norm. Therefore, they try to live their lives the best they can in an oppressive and pathogenic environment. Mohamed Ábdulle Hassan was a visionary who saw that the external colonizing forces wanted to change Somalis according to their beliefs and values. He seems to have understood that the change they wanted to impose derailed Somalis from the path of development inherent in their history. Nonetheless, he did not know, as did Menelik II, how to bring his vision, his belief, and Somali values to survive the onslaught.

The armed resistance and poems of Mohamed Ábdulle Hassan are widely known but so well are the resistance poems of ordinary Somalis of that time. A close examination of the Somali past and poetic heritage shows many ordinary people who resisted the imposition of colonial occupation and partition. Of the poets today rediscovered after years of social amnesia is Mohamed Ábdulle Áli (known generally as Gamuute) who was born in village close to Buró in about 1882. Gamuute became a respected poet a decade after the death of Mohamed Ábdulle Hassan. Like Mohamed Ábdulle Hassan, he was a strident opponent of colonial rule and he rallied people against occupation. However, unlike Mohamed Ábdulle Hassan, he did not organize or lead an armed resistance.

Gamuute's poems reveal that he had traveled widely. He had intimate knowledge of Somalis clans and of their tragic lives. Like Mohamed Ábdulle Hassan, Faarah Nuur, and others, Gamuute was pained pain by the imposition of colonial rule. He too lamented the partition of land and concluded that colonial rule and partition brought Armageddon, the final battle between the forces of good and evil (with Somalis depicted as losers to evil). The swift colonial occupation of the land, using technology like airplanes also baffled Gamuute.

By the gateways to water reservoirs, armies are posted ...
It is a world sold and bought without our consent
A monster soars in the skies, rending it apart
Moving without wheels, leaving no tracks behind
It is a world showing signs of doomsday...[8]

The poems of Faarah Nuur and Gamuute share the same lament over the colonial occupation and partition. The two men also used the same vowel of alliteration. They also used literally the same words in one line—*Waa duni la kala iibsaday aan nala ogaysiin ee*—the country is bought and sold without our consent. Which of the two preceded the other is not clear. Speculation of who first composed that famous statement is of little consequence. More importantly, the two men, living in different parts of the country, lamented their land bought and sold without their consent. Both expressed a sentiment widely shared by their contemporaries.

In the poem *Garwaaqsi* (translating to understanding, recollection, or empathy), Gamuute tells his brother about the strenuous efforts that he (Gamuute) made to save the family herd of camels when the colonial forces captured the land of the Somalis. The poem is remarkable in depicting the danger and suffering Gamuute experienced and the indiscriminate colonial plunder. In another poem, he recalled a favorite cow he lost and the suffering colonial forces inflicted on livestock and people alike.

Showing his knowledge of developments in different communities, Gamuute described the scorched-earth tactics and plundering of livestock carried out by colonial forces on different clans. In moving poetic language, as if he carried out a grand and fresh tour of land, near and distant, Gamuute concludes his poem in a way that recalls the doom and gloom Mohamed Ábdulle Hassan and Faarah Nuur had predicted.

So long the up country and rural areas are feared...
Coastal cities destroyed, even shunned by the rustic
They trampled on the religion and justice that redeem...
Society remains unprotected, lost forever
And the one who would heal it, undermines it
I swear by Allah, durable peace shall never prevail...[9]

Contemporary Somalis have no memories of those harsh decades, but Gamuute and Faarah Nuur remind us that people who were content with their lives in the past had been pushed by colonial rule to such extremes as to yearn for death. The decades that followed ushered more colonial repression and taxation without representation. Nevertheless, British attempts to impose taxes brought the same violent reaction from Somalis, as did the harsh tactics of "pacification."

One such attempt occurred in 1922 in Buró. The colonial officers in Buró demanded that nomads coming to the town for water pay tax in heads of livestock. Somalis refused. A violent confrontation ensued, resulting in murder of one British officer named Mr. Gibbons (known by Somalis as Giib). The administration apprehended a Somali in the mob and accused him for the murder of Giib.

A traditional judge, Sheekh Muhumed Warsame Guuleed (known as Sheekh Muhumad Yare), was asked to adjudicate. He declared that the perpetrator to pay thirteen heads of camel and a fraction of one *(saddex iyo toban halaad iyo hal daloolkeed)*. The verdict infuriated the since they understood the Somali custom of blood-compensation that set payment of 100 camels for a man killed. They fired the judge and imposed a penalty of 30,000 heads of camel on the clan of the accused. What a contrast in the value each society had on the life of a British officer! Equally remarkable, this judge who came up with this bold verdict was employee of the colonial administration. Like dinosaurs, these men disappeared long ago. Today, whoever pays money owns the judge—money dictates the verdict.

Once colonizers divided the land of Somalis into colonies before the turn of the twentieth century, each colonial power subjugated the inhabitants according to its own requirements. For instance, Italian administrators enforced in their colony color segregation in all public places. British racism in the Protectorate was more subtle but no less pernicious than Italian and French racism. There was segregation in neighborhoods and government. Above of all, British racism existed in the attitude and stereotypes of administrators. Their system of indirect rule spared Somalis the daily humiliations fascist Italian administrators practiced in Somalia. To implement it, the British fanned clan conflicts and conducted expeditionary raids in the country. With money and nominal positions of authority, they also bribed the elders and religious leader, thus undermining the old trust and respect for traditional leaders.

Langton P. Walsh who started colonial rule in Somaliland illustrates the manipulation and subterfuges with which British colonial rule started and continued in subsequent decades. With a handful of Arab and Somali supporters recruited from Aden, Walsh occupied Berbera and installed himself as the governor, the police commissioner, the judge, and the tax collector. He prohibited rural Somalis from entering the city unless they brought two boulders needed for building colonial offices and mansions. He required them to leave their arms in a police station. If he caught men fighting, he confiscated their arms and ordered them to dig a grave. After they complied with the order of digging to his satisfaction, Walsh returned their arms and urged them men to resume their fight with the explanation that the victor would bury his adversary. A hired town crier then walked in the city to publicize the time and place of the contest![10]

Walsh also meted out cruel punishment for whatever he deemed criminal. He recounts an instance when a representative of the new colonial system dealt with a case of tampering with the pipes supplying water to Berbera. To punish the "mischievous rascals," an agent procured two donkeys and loaded them with dates, rice, sugar, tobacco, and "other delicacies specially appreciated by the Somalis." Included in the load was "soda-water bottle containing dynamite, arranged to explode if the contents of the panniers were interfered with." A native boy then drove the loaded donkeys to the outskirts of the town and told to leave the donkeys and hide in a bush as soon as he saw Somalis approaching. He did as ordered. The unwary Somalis captured the donkeys. But the moment they started to unload the enticing contents, dynamite exploded, blowing up the three Somalis and the donkey.[11]

In short, colonial punishment from start to end was harsh even for minor offences. It spared none—not even an innocent boy inducted to administer official crime and training him and his peers to colonial cruelty. Based on pitting brother against brother, it created a population of Cain and Abel. The policy had the goal of weakening the colonized and undermining their collective power. Having set up this system, it did not take long for colonizers to reverse the guilt and accuse 'the natives' of unspeakable cruelty. Still, as we shall see later, Italian colonialists armed with Mussolini's fascism were more violent and racist than the British.

Struggle for Independence

Colonialism in place in Somali society at the turn of the twentieth century, it took until the nineteen-forties for the Somali elite to rekindle the quest for freedom and Pan-Somali-Unity. World War II had a pivotal influence on anti-colonial struggle. Somali soldiers who risked their lives to free Britain or France came back with a new passion for freedom. Participation in wars abroad also hardened them. The soldiers saw at a close range that the colonizer is not superhuman but a mortal like the colonized; he can be frightened, wounded, even killed.

Life abroad also broadened the horizon of the soldiers as they gained a broader perspective to life's opportunities. Their return to home raised conscience of the public who until then lived insulated in their clan settlements clan and partitioned colonial boundaries. The soldiers brought tales of adventure and violence, of personal hardship and valor, of sacrifices for freedom and honor. Those who listened to their accounts were emboldened to think beyond their immediate clan conflicts. From there, it was only a short step for Africans to demand the same rights as their colonizers. They demanded the freedom to occupy the same office, to live in the same neighborhood, to eat at the same table, to sleep in the same bed—perhaps with the same woman.

The Somali too benefited from these consequences while they served colonial aggrandizement at home and abroad. There were specific local experiences that fuelled the Somali quest for freedom, such as the rise of Benito Mussolini and his Fascist Party in October 1922. The Fascists intensified colonial abuses in Somalia and later instigated war in the region. Cessere De Vecchi, one of four leading members of the Fascist Party, arrived to govern Somalis. He believed in brutal force to subjugate resistors and developed a program of disarming Somalis by use of violence and imprisonment.

By early December 1934, Italian and Ethiopian forces engaged in armed confrontation at Walwaal. Italy demanded compensation and an apology from Ethiopia for the loss it incurred due to the Walwal Incident. Efforts at mediation by Britain and France failed. By January 1935, Italy started preparation for war on Ethiopia. In October 1935, Italian forces made a frontal attack on Ethiopia from two directions – from Eritrea in the North and Somalia in the East. Included in the invading forces were 53,226 Eritreans and 29,511 Somalis and Libyans. By January 1, 1935, Italian forces took control of Addis Ababa and soon after much of Ethiopia.

Some of the Somali soldiers—including Mohamed Siyaad Barre—were members of the armed forces who invaded Ethiopia in 1935.[12] The experience of these soldiers organized by Italian fascists and ordered by Benito Mussolini was to have enormous impact on the politics in the Italian colony and later in Somali society in general. They cut their teeth on fascism in Ethiopia during the occupation and most certainly in Somalia in the decades of Italian rule. After the fascists took over Ethiopia, they brought Somalis ruled by Ethiopian under the same administration as other Somalis already under Italy's control. Ironically, although fascism has been fundamentally inimical to freedom or unity, the participation in the war revitalized the Somali desire for freedom.

Following the defeat of Italian forces by Britain, Italy abandoned all Somali territories under its control on 14 March 1941. These territories came under British rule as the "Occupied Enemy Territories Administration" which in 1943 was renamed "British Military Administration". In the first three years, the BMA encouraged a resurgence of political consciousness and a desire for Somali unity because previously partitioned Somali territories came under one administration. At the same time, it established institutions of social control, including the Somali Gendarmerie started on August1, 1941. Consisting of Somalis personnel and their foreign officers, the Gendarmerie consisted of comprised two main units—the Police Wing charged with enforcing peace in the cities, and the Field Force Wing whose responsibility was to secure peace in nomadic and rural communities. Significantly, as we shall see later, Mohamed Siyaad Barre was among a member of the Police Wing.[13]

Emergence of Political Parties

The British Military Administration (1941-49) was sympathetic to Somali wishes to remove the artificial borders imposed on them. In 1946, Ernest Bevin, the British Foreign Secretary, went further. He advocated unification of all Somali territories under one colonial administration and said:

> ... In all innocence, therefore, we propose that British Somaliland, Italian Somaliland, and the adjacent part of Ethiopia, if Ethiopia agreed, should be lumped together as a trust territory, so that the nomads should lead their frugal existence with the least possible hindrance and there might be a chance of a decent economic life, as understood in that territory.

Ethiopia, the United States, the USSR, and France rejected the plea inspired more by British ambition for a larger colony in the region rather than the declared sympathy for Somalis. Faced with insurmountable objections, Bevin explained: "All I wanted to do is to give those poor nomads a chance to live ... It is to nobody's interest to stop the poor people and cattle from getting a decent living." The plea unheeded, Britain made deals with Ethiopia and other colonial powers on re-partitioning the land of Somalis.

The colonial powers again sealed the fate of Somalis by dint of superior arms after re-partitioning. In fact, from the late twentieth century to 1954, the history of British policy and behavior toward Somalis contradict Bevin's proposal. Cases in point are the 1897 Anglo-Ethiopian Treaty, the eventual disposal of the Haud and Reserved Area in 1954 without the consent of Somalis, and the disregard by the British to development concerns in the British Protectorate of Somaliland.

It was also during the British Military Administration that nascent political movements emerged. The Somali National Society (SNS) was formed in the British Protectorate in 1938, at first a social club of the Somali elite in the Protectorate. Its political aims, if articulated by its members, were unclear at the time. The nascent Somali intelligentsia who were educated by and worked for the colonial administration did not begin their organization with clear political mission. As a social club, they were primarily concerned with their needs of association, education, and entertainment.

Faarah Omaar who was most educated and political informed was an exception. He had obtained higher education abroad and familiar with independence movements taking place in other colonies. He was one of the founders of the Somali National Society (SNS) the predecessor of the Somali National League (SNL), later the leading political party advocating independence of the Protectorate. He also used the tactics of Gandhi to oppose British colonialism. The SNS formed in the 1938, five years before the Somali Youth Club, later called Somali Youth League, was established.

The son of Michael Mariano, the late Rooble Michael Mariano, reported that Omaar was a 1933 graduate of London University, probably the first Somali graduate of a university. He also said that Omaar was brought up a Christian, perhaps one of the orphans whose conversion to Christianity had enraged Mohamed "Ábdulle Hassan and intensified his resolve to mount a Jihad. Omaar reconverted to Islam upon his return to the Protectorate, subsequently making a pilgrimage to Mecca.[14]

Other individuals who knew the personal past of Omaar question Rooble's claim that Omaar was once Christianity. They also state that he studied in India where he met or learned about Mahatama Gandhi. In any case, there is little dispute that Faarah Omaar was an early pro-independence leader who studied in higher institutions of learning abroad. Often, political movements under oppression start with innocuous social clubs and social causes because the oppressive system denies them freedom of speech and association. These early efforts organize people and gradually test the system. In some instances, the organizers themselves are not aware of the political outocme of organizing themselves. Only after they coalesce into a group do new ideas on their political aspirations become articulated, followed gradually by agitation for independence.

The purpose of the SNS was to educate the people, to promote the struggle for freedom, and to realize political unity of Somalis. Ironically, the British Military Administration was more tolerant of political organization in the former Italian colony than in the Protectorate, indeed BMD officials hoped to keep the Italians at bay, leaving British control of most Somali territories.[15]

The treatment meted out for Faarah Omaar in the Protectorate illustrates the point. Omaar regularly wrote letters to the British Parliament to advocate for Somaliland independence and to complain about the abuses of British officers in the Protectorate. His letter-writing campaign offended the colonial officials and they decided to silence him. They exiled him to an isolated island in the Red Sea called Sáad El Diin. When he succumbed to tuberculosis, Omaar sought treatment in Jigjiga. In 1948, Omaar died in the hospital where Somalis believe he was poisoned.

Another example is that of Haaji Yuusuf who was a leading member of the Dervishes led by Mohamed Ábdulle Hassan. His son, Bashiir, was nine years old when the Dervishes were defeated. In subsequent years, Bashiir became a highly learned and respected man of religion known for his striding opposition to colonial rule. At the end of World War II, Sheekh Bashiir organized a rebellion in Buró against British colonial rule. A preemptive attack by British colonial forces killed Sheekh Bashiir and that of eight of his followers in April 1948.

Reacting to the mistreatment of Bashiir's remains by the British colonial administration, Haaji Aadan Afqaloó recited one of the poems lamenting the fallen hero and the absence of public outrage:

Bashiir was attacked the other day near you
With bullets they tore up his back and chest
They added to it gloating, insults, and kicks
When his sanctified remains was taken outside
You were there and saw his burial prohibited
Instead of feeling pain, you rejoice [his death]
Noble if you were, never would you simply walk away
Weakness is your distinction other people never accept.[16]

Another ostensibly non-political association formed in the former Italian colony. On 15 March 1943, thirteen members of the Somali young elite in Mogadishu formed the Somali Youth Club (SYC). The members of this new organization were young and middle-aged clerks and business who wanted to form a social club with little over political overtones. Since the British Military Administration was more liberal than the fascist regime it replaced, the founders of this new organization articulated political goals the fascists prohibited.

As we shall see later, the British were "liberal" only in comparison to the fascists and because they sought to woo Somalis to opt for British colonial rule. In reality, however, their colonial rule was as inherently forced occupation and oppressive.

Table 1 presents the list of the thirteen founders of the Somali Youth Club, later called the Somali Youth League.[17]

Table 1

Founders and Members of the SYL
1943

NAME	CLAN	SUB-CLAN
Yaasin Haaji Ósmaan	Daarood	Mijeerteen
Mohamed Hirsi Nuur	Daarood	Mijeerteen
Áli Hassan Verdure	Daarood	Mijeerteen
Daahir Haaji Ósmaan	Daarood	Mijeerteen
Mohamed Sheekh Ósmaan	Digil	Tunni
Ábdilqaadir Sheekh Sakhawadin	Digil	Tunni
Ósmaan Geedi Raage	Hawiye	Abgaal
Mohamed Faarax Hilowle	Hawiye	Habar Gidir
Khaliif Huurdo Maálin	Hawiye	Sheekhaal
Mohamed Abdalla Hassan	Isaaq	Habar Awal
Dheere Haaji Dheere	Reer Hamar	Bandhaw
Haaji Mohamed Hussein	Reer Hamar	Dhabarwein
Mohamed Áli Nuur	Reer Hamar	Reer Hamar

Chart 1 shows the clan distribution of the founders.

Chart 1

Clan Distribution of SYL Members

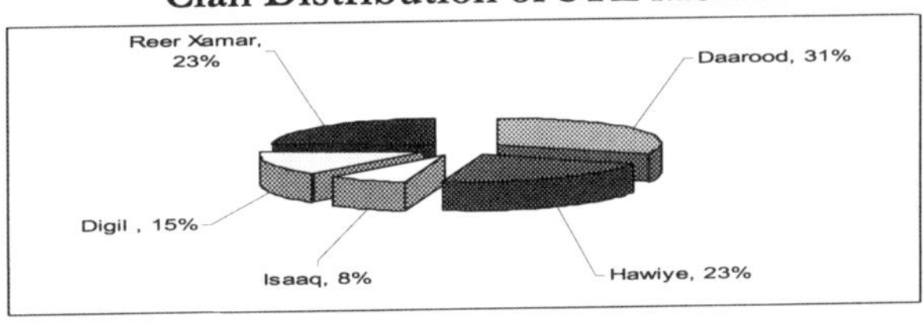

The chart shows that the Daarood had the highest representation (31%), the Hawiye and the Reer Hamar were next (23% each), and the Digil was third (15%). Unfortunately, the Reer Hamar, who had contributed significantly in the development of the SYL, did not receive the recognition they deserve. This illustrates the tyranny of numbers that readily translate to unequal representation in Somali politics. The representative from the Isaaq is surprising because his clan-base was in the British Protectorate, and he was a longtime resident of Mogadishu.

Clan distribution of SYL founders was a precursor of things to come in subsequent decades of Somali politics. It suggests that Somalis are members of clans first even when they pursue nationalist or pan-Somali goals. In fact, clan and nation are two complementary yet contradictory aspects of Somalis. One first learns to identify with the clan at a young age and that identity remains integral throughout one's life. In addition, socialization in later years and the demands of adult life —such as for instance paying blood-compensation (*mag*) and mutual assistance (*qaadhaan*)—to keep the old identity, loyalty, and commitments alive.

Nationalism, in terms of unity and equality of all Somalis, builds on the old loyalties of the clan, even as the so-called nationalists consciously condemn the clan system. Thus, the nation that Somalis seek to build turns out to be an enlarged concept of the clan, subsuming all traditional clans under a new national identity, as the clan comprises a group of nuclear families. Yet the clan and nation cannot coexist without contradictions and conflicts. The question facing the SYL founders in the nineteen-forties was which of the two (clan and nation) dominates Somali identity and becomes the defining element. Repeatedly, clan identity and loyalty took precedence over national identity and loyalty.

Because the prevailing colonial climate did not permit the SYL to articulate these aims, its initially state mission was exchange of ideas and knowledge among its members. However, SYL later transformed into a political organization; it advocated for Somali freedom and unity. When it hoisted a red flag as its emblem, it appeared as if it were a communist organization. For this reason, the British Military Administration banned the organization, but soon lifted the ban after the founders explained their intent to the colonial administration. Despite control by BMA, Somalia continued to follow the segregationist laws of the Italian Fascist administration. The BMA was more tolerant of the political campaigns the new organization had undertaken.

By 1947, the Somali Youth Club (SYC) changed its name to Somali Youth League (SYL). Its agenda was more explicitly political. It had focused on four main goals: to unite all Somalis by removing colonial oppression and the clan system, to augment the knowledge of youth by developing modern educational institutions, by legal means to remove all impediments to Somali well-being, and to use the Ósmaania writing script as national script.[18]

The primary membership of the SYL consisted of the Hawiye and the Daarood, and it spread to different parts of the Somali territories. A notable exception was its strong foothold in Jigjiga uprooted after Ethiopian forces attacked it during the late nineteen-forties, leading to an uprising and scores of Somalis killed. However, the SYL never found a substantial membership or presence in the former British Protectorate. Instead, the elite and public of the Protectorate joined the Somali National League (SNL), the dominant political organization in Somaliland.

The role of Michael Mariano in the advocacy campaigns of the SYL to the United Nations and to the international community is not widely known. He acquired catholic education in Aden and, fluent in English, was well versed in international politics. While he was running his own business in Dire Dawa, Mariano learned that the SYL sought his assistance in publicizing its cause by means of writing and word of mouth. Faarah Omaar recommended Michael Mariano to the SYL and Mariano in turn recruited Clement Salool (known generally as Ina Salool) who lived in Addis Ababa at the time. Also well educated, Clement Salool was of mixed blood—his mother was English, his father an Isaaq. Mariano and Salool moved to the Mogadishu and worked closely with the SYL leaders and, with their help, the SYL presented its case to the United Nations.

When SYL representatives requested the assistance of the two men, they enthusiastically responded as Somali patriots. Subsequent developments in Somalia and later in Somaliland would force Michael Mariano into his clan identity and constituency—a proof that even most diehard nationalists in Somali society cannot escape the mark and burden of his clan! If Michael Mariano, a man of impeccable nationalist credentials, had no choice but enter the nasty pit of clan politics, who could stay clear from the same? Clement Salool returned to Aden where he became a judge.

An interesting story is that Mariano and Salool arrived in Mogadishu while the apartheid established by Italians was still in force in European facilities. Somalis could not enter employment except to provide menial service. Racial segregation of hotels was enforced. Before arriving there, Michael Mariano and Clement Salool obtained reservations at *Croce del Sud*—at that time the largest hotel and reserved exclusively for Europeans. When they arrived, the owners of the hotel were dumbfounded since they had assumed the two guests with Christian names were white and European. Argument ensued when the owners cancelled their reservation but, after intervention of the British authorities, the Italian owners relented. Thus, Mariano and Salool were the first Somalis—indeed the first black persons—who stayed at *Croce del Sud*, breaching the segregation laws of the period.

Soon after, the two men immersed themselves into the work of the SYL. Among their contributions was the detailed program of development the SYL leaders presented to the Four Power Commission who arrived in Mogadishu on January 6, 1948 to assess Somali grievances and aspirations. The Italian politicians and residents in Mogadishu who resented the work of these two men organized a plan to assassinate them. The last attempt to get rid of the two men involved a secret plan in which armed men were to storm their residence. When the British Military Administration responsible for security in Mogadishu learned of the plan, they took the men to Hargeysa where they were safe from Italians. But Mariano continued his advocacy for independence in the Protectorate by forming the National United Front in 1954. Three years later, the NUF became one of the two leading political parties in Somaliland. For years, the British Administration considered Mariano a communist and kept file on him in the Special Branch.[19]

It is also interesting to note that young Somalis—like Faarah Omaar, Michael Mariano, Clement Salool, and Alex Qolqolle—had come of age only to take up the struggle for freedom from colonial rule.[20] These men were members a minority community whose conversion to Christianity Mohamed Ábdulle Hassan and his Dervishes inspired them to wage a Jihad against infidels. The missionaries took members of this community to Djibouti or Aden where the population was more tolerant.

Did Mohamed Ábdulle Hassan misjudge in assuming that conversion to Christianity made these men less Somali than those who professed Islam? He did. After Mohamed Ábdulle Hassan's death, the struggle changed from a Jihad—focused on defending Islam, for rewards in the hereafter—to a nationalist struggle with a goal of anticolonialism and recovering political rights. Despite their childhood conversion, some of them (like Faarah Omaar) had reconverted to Islam and proved, beyond doubt, that they were patriots ahead of their time.

These patriots were better educated than most of the Somali elite, they spoke European languages better than all Somalis, and they were experts who understood the laws and thoughts of the colonizer, and all these attributes had served well Somali struggle for freedom. Yet, in the conservative mind of the predominantly Muslim Somali, their childhood conversion to Christianity had remained a blot on their record. After independence, as we shall see later, Michael Mariano's Christian faith impeded his political career in a highly conservative Muslim society.

By 1954, Michael Mariano and his colleagues formed the National United Front (NUF), and the establishment of the United Somali Party (USP) followed. In fact, 1954 was a year of shock and outrage throughout the Protectorate because Britain withdrew from the Haud and the Reserved Areas, a large expanse of pastureland (65,000 sq. km), and it handed over legal control to Ethiopia. This loss of this territory outraged Somalis, as did the dishonesty of the British whose promises of protection from Ethiopian domination had softened their opposition to European colonialism.

Somalis believed that Britain violated the joint agreements entered it entered with the inhabitants before the turn of the twentieth century. However, they soon realized that those agreements were meaningless. The consequences of this breach of faith are with us today. Little wonder Somalis give no credence to or enforce agreements governments enter with the people!

The Giddy Decade

The passion for independence swept everywhere Somalis inhabited during the nineteen-fifties. The former Italian colony was placed under United Nations Trusteeship to be granted independence in 1960. Somalis in other territories anticipated that they too would enjoy the freedom denied them previously. Enormous excitement took place in the emotional life of Somalis everywhere. By the late nineteen-fifties, Somalis, regardless of their place of residence, huddled around shortwave radios to listen to news of independence, patriotic poems and songs aired by stations in Hargeysa and Mogadishu.

The passion for unity is expressed voice in the popular song composed by the late Yuusuf Haaji Aadan:

Wake up, Somalis
Wake up and lean on one another
Whoever among you is weak (needy)
Support him forever.[21]

The song by Ábdilaahi Qarshi in 1947 called for resistance against the arrival in Somaliland of Gerald Reese who governed the Northern Frontier District in Kenya and allegedly committed mass killings to quell resistance to British rule:

Arise! Arise
It's time for battle, rise
Jokes have ended, rise
Kooraleey is burned down, rise...[22]

Similarly, Ábdilaahi Qarshi's other song applauds the national sentiment of the youth under colonial rule:

The youth of the land we are
Male and female, we decide
To either die or be (re) born
Between the two we've no other choice![23]

Another poet who expressed Somali sentiment during the nineteen-fifties was Mohamed Ismaíil Baasará (know as Barkhadás). Friends invited him to an event welcoming the Duke of Gloucester who visited Somaliland in 1958. Burkhadás rejected the invitation and he took offense in the visit of a representative of the colonial power that oppressed Somalis. His poem began thus:

The man who blinded my grandfather
The man who enslaved my father
The man who sold me
I hate this man to no limit
Powerlessness placed me in this predicament
So long as I cannot avenge myself
So long as I cannot kill him
I hate the sight of that man
Close the doors so I may weep alone.[24]

From the beginning, Britain was determined to mollify Abyssinian rulers and it readily breached agreements with Somalis whenever it suited its interest.[25] Ceding the Haud and Reserved Area was in the 1897 Anglo-Ethiopian Treaty signed between Britain and Abyssinia without the knowledge of Somalis. They became aware of it only in 1934 when a joint commission, representing Britain and Ethiopia, started to demarcate the boundary stipulated in the 1897 treaty. Handing over sovereignty of this territory to Ethiopia in 1954 was the only logical conclusion to an agreement signed with Ethiopia 57 years earlier.

Perhaps Britain would have made changes in the 1897 treaty with Ethiopia if its plan to bring Somalis under British rule (alluded to in the Bevin proposal) had materialized. But Britain ended assertions on justice and sympathy to Somalis and chose instead to make alliance with Ethiopia. The same betrayal took place in the Northern Frontier District in early 1963, forcing the new Somali Republic to end diplomatic relations with Britain.[26]

During the nineteen-fifties, coordination continued between the SYL and political parties in the Protectorate since they shared the basic goals of Somali freedom and unity. The fledgling parties shared several key characteristics. First, members of the westernized, urban-based elite led them. Second, they emulated colonial masters and assimilated Western values while they looked down on rural people and traditional society. Third, they exploited the biases and advantages extended to westernized Somalis in the colonial system. Fourth, they marginalized traditional leaders, their competitors to influence and power in a free society.

Nevertheless, when they needed the traditional leaders to win votes, they rewarded and bought them. As a result, they weeded out traditional leaders with integrity and principle. That is why it is as difficult today to find traditional leaders of integrity as it is to see pink elephants—indeed any type of elephant—in the land Somalis inhabit. Despite clan composition and inevitable clan bias, all the pre-independence parties (except the NUF) invoked "Somali" in their name in the same way as do contemporary movements like the Somali Salvation Democratic Front (SSDF), Somali National Movement (SNM), United Somali Congress (USC), Somali People's Movement (SPM). It is a pattern of hypocrisy recurring in Somali politics, although the SYL, SNL, and NUF are relatively innocuous in comparison to the narrow mission and violent tactics of recent political movements.

One of the unfortunate developments in the history of party politics is the treatment Michael Mariano received. Despite his record of patriotism, he suffered discrimination because of his faith. For instance, the public maligned him and the party he founded, the NUF, in nasty party politics; they shouted both down with "*Allahu Akbar!*"—Allah Is Great! Some who were active in politics then report that the Chairman of the NUF, Ahmed Hassan Ibraahim, himself a devout Muslim, took offense in this declaration! When asked why Ahmed took offence, he responded: "Any word, even if pious, turns offensive if hurled at you by a crowd." I wonder what Michael Mariano felt on hearing disparaging remarks about his faith declared by the very people for whose freedom he had valiantly struggled for years?

Still, with courage and determination, Michael Mariano stood up for his political convictions in an intolerant Muslim society. He remained undeterred even when his faith became a campaigns issue, as shown by the song:

Michael is a Christian
But Ahmed is Muslin
Support them Patriots...[27]

The Ahmed cited is Ahmed Hassan Ibraahim, Chairman of the NUF. Michael was then the Secretary General. On the one hand, the song defended the NUF; on the other, it described that the Muslim faith of its Chairman outweighed Michael's liability as a Christian. In fact, Mariano's faith remained a sore point for both the NUF and

Mariano's political career. The opposing political party, the SNL, often exploited Mariano's religious affiliation. Another lyric expressing this is:

Listen, clueless lady
Watch out for Michael
For the snake behind him
And for Michael watch out
He carries with him a knife
Watch out for Michael
To avert his betrayal
Watch out for Michael.[28]

In spite of these vicious attacks, Michael remained steadfast. His son, the late Rooble Michael Mariano, recounted an incident during which opponents derisively and publicly shouted down Michael as a Christian. His colleagues and supporters angrily defended him, with evident risk that the confrontation could get out of hand.

Michael turned to his defenders and calmed them by declaring: "It seems that you're more Christian than me!" This demonstrates the substance and determination of the man. A lesser man would have abandoned his patriotic zeal, finding a more comfortable life in Europe, harboring a loathing for anything Somali. Compare Michael's reaction to the Muslim member of the NUF who could not tolerate the public shouting of "*Allahu Akbar.*"

In the end, Somalia gained its independence on July 1, 1960 after ten years of UN trusteeship. Preparing the Protectorate for independence did not started until 1959. The British granted independence with the usual disregard of Somali needs even though they had administered the colony since taking control of it before the turn of the twentieth century. When granted independence on 26 June 1960, Somalis in the former Protectorate threw themselves into unity with their brothers in Somalia.

Unity without condition turned out to be unity on unequal terms. They conceded the Presidency, the Prime Minister, the key members of the cabinet, unequal representation in the parliament, and location of the capital city. It was as if Somalis in the Protectorate were in pan-Somali trance. They threw themselves headlong into unity at all cost, dispensing insults to anyone advising prudent negotiation for unity with equity.

Thus, the hope of Somalis everywhere focused on developments in Somalia and Somaliland during the nineteen-fifties and nineteen-sixties. Once the two territories gained independence and spontaneously united, the new republic became the fulfillment of Somali dreams. Somalis in Ethiopia, Kenya, and Djibouti flocked to the new republic in large numbers in search of opportunity and freedom, convinced that the Somali unity of these two territories would bring about freedom for them.

It was not to be. The elite who inherited the colonial state had a different goal and, although they looked like the ruled in every respect, they differed from the majority of Somalis who entrusted them with power and their future. The early disillusionment with their leadership in the new republic is important because it provides a window to the bitter experience that was to be the fate of Somalis in years to come

Early Signs of Disappointment

Within the first year of unity, the euphoria for nationalism waned. Several years later, it turned into despair. A 1964 poem by Ahmed Ismaíil Diiriye (Qaasim) illustrates the public disillusionment and cynicism following the independence and unity that only a few years earlier symbolized new dawn for freedom and Somali brotherhood. (Carroll represented the Queen in the transfer of power to Somalis.)

Augmented population and prosperity in vain I anticipated
That goal too frustrated, did I lick the [bitter] juice of aloe vera?
To the footpaths I walked the day before, did I [confusedly] return?
As one totally disoriented, did I lose my way again?
Nothing changed with the white man I ejected, and with those who replaced him
In surface appearance, Somalis, black in color they look
But they bring misery to the heart, being the offspring of Carroll.[29]

Qaasim's poem underscored that people of the former British protectorate gave up their sovereignty for unity with the hope that other Somalis in Ethiopia, Kenya, and Djibouti would join them. This was not to be. In fact, the unity of two territories out of the possible union of five proved unattainable. Worse, the colonial system remained unchanged except that black leaders replaced white colonialists on June 26, 1960. The song also underscores the public confusion and disorientation produced in the aimless march along the beaten track of indignation.

Another popular song by Áli Sugulle, *Hiddiyo Hiddii*, sung with sadness by the talented singer, the late Shimbir, also reaffirmed the same disillusionment and despair:

Surge [of hope] appeared which lured me
I saw lightning and I woke up startled
Yet I lost it all and I felt despair....[30]

Camels, as we have seen earlier, were critical in the economic and social life of traditional Somali society. They also played a central role as a political metaphor prior to and after independence. The most famous of this symbolic use of camels in politics is the she-camel called *Maandeeq*—a literally meaning that which satisfies or heals the soul. Historically, *Maandeeq* evoked dreams of political and economic independence in the former British Protectorate. To this day, the name is popular in Somaliland. *Maandeeq* is a symbol of freedom and hope. In the early sixties, poets and singers evoked the she-camel to underscore the depth of discontent with the politics of the elite:

A she-camel was my only possession
A predator took away the she-camel
I [now] carry an empty milking bowl.[31]

In short, the long-awaited independence and unity turned into a bitter and toxic pill. The nine-years of civilian rule brought profound disappointment; the unity of the two Somali states also led to despair. The ruling elite had no interest in heeding the changed public mood. They went about their petty squabbles over power, get-rich-quick schemes, and lavish public ceremonies, even their binges of Johnny Walker and Black Label in plush private quarters. Then the armed forces took power on October 21, 1969.

By the early and mid nineteen-seventies, the repression of the state turned into a nightmare and pan-Somali nationalism became a dirty word. Meanwhile, the clan system reasserted itself in Somali communities as the primary means of political organization and social cohesion. Worse, *Klannism*—the habitat of Cain in politics—took root in Somali society in the name of freedom and progress. What is *Klannism*?

Emergence of Klannism

As explained earlier, I adopted the term 'Klan' from the racist organization called the KKK. In some respects, the Somali elite are similar to the KKK. The members of the Somali elite, like the members of the KKK, belong to an exclusive club, viewing others in society with contempt. The Somali elite are different however in one respect: the KKK uses race for hatred and oppression; the Somali the elite exploit the western education they acquired and the clan system to which they remain identified. They exploit western education to justify their claim that they deserve the best in society, including the right to rule others and to accumulate wealth. They exploit the clan system to rally members for their personal power and wealth. I refer to this group the *Klan,* their exploitative politics to *Klannism.*

Klannism evolved gradually. During the nineteen-fifties and nineteen-sixties, the public believed the elite's condemnation of what they called "tribalism," the use of clan identity to favor some members or discriminate against others. They took these condemnations seriously because they wanted merit, not favoritism or discrimination to sour their dream of Somali unity. They trusted leadership to the elite whom they called *indheer-garad*, those who foresee long-term trends, who therefore have intelligence to guide them. The public complied as best they could with the elite's prescriptions for injunctions against "tribalism" which was condemned in the media. Therefore, the public felt that the anti-clan poet, Ábdilaahi Suldaan, Timaádde, spoke for them when he said:

Until we end our self-inflicted wounds
Until we shun clannism and the qaat addiction
Until we share mission and trust one another
You Somalis, immature are your passions today.[32]

In fact, when we examine the progress of clannism since independence, we discover that it fell out of favor during the nineteen-sixties, and came back with vengeance thereafter. Clannism alone did not return. The elite's distortion of the clan system and their addition of *Klannism* into Somali politics had a devastating effect on society. We can cite numerous illustrations showing that the clan system lost its grip on the Somalis during the nineteen-sixties.

Two significant examples are the election of Mohamed Bihi

(known as Shuuriye) in 1960 and Úmar Mohamed Ábdirahmaan (known as Úmar Dheere) for parliamentary seats in 1964. The two men won election in Hargeysa, the second largest city in the newly independent republic. The predominant Isaaq inhabitants chose two men who belonged to two minorities—the first born to the culturally despised Tuumaal, the second to the Ogaadeen who did not inhabit the territory. The opposition was of the Isaaq clan, yet the two candidates were elected without regard to their clan.[33] The election of Shuuriye and Úmar represents a momentous shift in clan outlook of the time, a shift that was seen neither before nor after in Somali society. Their election affirms that, in rare moments and under special conditions, Somalis can choose a candidate on qualification and conviction, not on the grounds of clan affiliation.

The passion for Somali unity which every clan and region shared during the nineteen-sixties is another example of how Somalis set aside their traditional allegiance to the clan system. No political leader, including the dictator, could ignore the pro-unity passion that bound Somalis during the first two decades of independence. From 1960 to 1978, Somalis poured immense resources into liberating their "brothers" and "sisters" from Ethiopian, Kenyan, and French rule across the border. Everywhere, they postponed their dreams for economic advancement as they channeled their meager resources to feeding, clothing, and arming the Somali military. They also accepted the unacceptable – poverty, persecution, and tyranny – in the hope that liberty of all Somalis would compensate for their sacrifice.

The public commitment to Somali nationalism during the late nineteen-fifties and early nineteen-sixties went hand in hand with their passionate attachment to the new republic's flag that was blue with a five-pointed white star in the middle. The blue color did not signify sadness (like the blues of Afro-Americans) but hope and freedom. It signified the open sky without clouds. The five points of the star symbolized unity of the five Somali colonies. In fact, the love of this symbol was such that blue was a national color for Somalis everywhere. Many people wore blue clothes; they painted their houses blue; they even furnished their homes in blue.

The refrain of the most popular song of the day, composed by Hussein Aw Faarah and sang by Ábdilaahi Qarshi's, the late master guitarist, composer, and singer was:

The color of each nation is different
Ours is like the sky
Clear, without clouds, and let's love it.[34]

The song was popular in every territory Somalis lived like a sacred mantra. In the Somali region in Ethiopia where I lived then as a young boy, the color blue represented a form of resistance against oppression. It also symbolized a silent vote of confidence in the new Somali republic. During the early and mid nineteen-sixties, I remember that the color blue dominated the bustling marketplace of Jigjiga. Women and men wore blue, covered the stalls with blue shades, and painted their houses blue. I do not know if the Ethiopian authorities understood the veiled resistance to their rule contained in the color blue that dominated the landscape and, right under their nose. At the time, color blue that signified freedom and hope and resistance for Somalis made clan system appear obsolete.

In addition, many other songs and poems expressed the public euphoria for independence and Pan-Somali-Unity. One of the most memorable of these poems is that of Ábdilaahi Suldaan, known generally as Timaádde. The poet recited it in Hargeysa on the eve of independence, June 25, 1960, the night Douglas Hall, the British representative transferred power to Somalis. The famous poem was called, "*Kaa na sib, kan na saar!*"—pull that one down, raise this one up!—celebrating the historic moment when he British flag came down as the Somali flag replaced it.

The poem is intensely emotional, reflecting gratitude and pride in hoisting the Somali flag. The following excerpt suggests the feelings of the poet and the prevailing public euphoria on the departure of the colonialists:

Somalis raising flag
This morning we're the first
If you feel as I do
Or differently I don't know
Three weeks and days
If food I don't eat
I shall feel no hunger
Nothing shall I miss.
The sorcerer left in disgrace
The Lofty and the Perfect

Let me see how it looks
Pull that one down, raise this one up. [35]

In fact, those who lived through the euphoria of independence thought that "tribalism" was on its deathbed, that allegiance to it would die and replaced by nationalism, that all Somalis, with one culture and faith, would one day come under one flag, one state. Others believed that the clan system would vanish of its own accord as western education spread among the populace and a cosmopolitan culture emerged in the urban centers. Meanwhile, every educated Somali strained to avoid reference to his clan. When one found it necessary to invoke the clan, he declared, "my *ex* is such and such", or he asked, "what's your *ex*?" The "ex" implied disassociation from the clan in the same way one refers to a divorced spouse as "my *ex*." It implied rejection of the clan system.

In those years, the traditional clan mind-set I discussed in *Kinship and Conflict* had shifted to a de-clannized nation mind-set. The opposition of 'us' and 'them'—as in the delusion of clan superiority detailed in Chapter 13—was also repressed. However, the elite that so condemned "tribalism" could not (and did not) abandon it in practice. The public soon realized that the elite's condemnation of clannism and glorification of nationalism were insincere. They said one thing but did the opposite. Their hypocrisy soon became a cause for disillusionment. The public was confused and disillusioned.

It turned out that while the public tried to shed clan identity and embrace nationalism, the *Klan* with whom it entrusted leadership was busy securing its position while the majority continued to suffer poverty and exploitation. Even when disillusionment with the *Klan's* leadership emerged, the elite persisted in its self-serving politics and strengthening the flawed state. After independence, the *Klan's* power and exploitation enlarged. It took thirty years before the state over which the *Klan* presided would explode.

The Klan Comes of Age

A close examination of the history of Somali politics would shows two basic facts. First, most nationalists including poets like Timaádde condemned the exploitation of the clan system by the Somali elite. But they did not clearly differentiate the clan system from the

Klan system—a distinction that would have separated Cain from Abel in Somali society.

Second, the examination would reveal the Somali elite's hypocrisy—they never mean what they say and they do not say what they mean. Behind every politician's clan identity, there lies *Klan* affiliation. The former is a mask he wears in public; the latter is his chosen nexus and destiny. Clan identity binds him to his lineage, rooted in the culture, Klan affiliation links him to his social class of urban predators tutored in reading and speaking a foreign language.

Often the two identities complement each other. Clan identity remains dormant until members of the elite belonging to different clans threaten his personal or political fortunes. It is then that he rallies his traditional clan with calls of *"tollaayey!"*—'help kinsmen!' His kinsmen come to his aid because, grounded in traditional clan identity and loyalty, they assist him in the same way they assisted one another in time of war. Yet every member of the elite acts and considers himself an individual, free from traditional clan system and its obligations, so long he enjoys a state of peace and privilege. He disassociates himself from the clan system when he does not need its support. He condemns it as regressive and primitive. Only when he faces competition for power and privilege does he invoke the clan as his sole identity, his essential armor, his last line of defense.

Not distinguishing *clan* and *Klan* has misled many commentators on Somali politics. Clan is a genealogically based kinship that can be invoked for social, political, and economic reasons. *Klan* is economic and political organization of the elite bound by shared clas interests and educational experience. Only when we distinguish the two concepts do we understand how on the one hand nationalism and Pan-Somali-Unity degenerated into a *clan* feud over power and privilege, on the other hand the *Klan* worked in collaboration (as a class) against their majority. *Klan* collaboration affords the elite the power and privilege in society, but clan identity provides them grass roots support for their ambition in time of competition and conflict over power. Exploiting this Janus-faced character of social affliation, elite politics incorporated clan and *Klan* dynamics from the beginning in order to confuse the majority. The *Klan* sustains itself by exploiting the distortion of the clan system.

For instance, the Somali Youth League made Somali unity a

linchpin of its ideology. However, the Hawiye and the Mijeerteen members of the elite dominated the SYL and two groups competed for power. It remained dominated by the two clans until its demise in 1969. Despite the SYL's loud anti-clan ideology, disputes on clan leadership and control of the party simmered throughout its history.

On occasions, the dispute came out in the open, as on the eve of independence, when two leading members of the Mijeerteen (Ábdirashiid Áli Sharmaarke and Ábdirazaaq Haaji Hussein) broke away from the SYL. They were unhappy with the policies of Ábdulaahi Íise Mohamuud, the Prime Minister from the Hawiye clan, and they formed their own caucus known as the *"Croce del Sud Group"*, named after the popular Italian restaurant where they frequently met.[36] Mohamed Abshir Muuse, the powerful Commissioner of the Police, himself a Mijeerteen, joined the influential duo to make it a formidable trio. The three leading members of the Mijeerteen had opposed the policies of Ábdulaahi Íise Mohamuud and his staunch supporters like Sheekh Áli Jumáalle, an influential member of the General Assembly and prominent leader of the Hawaadle clan.

In 1956, the Italian Trusteeship Administration—*Administratione Fiduciariea Italiana della Somali*, often known by its acronym AFIS—passed a law granting Somalis the right to form an interim administration. The Italian administration named Ábdulaahi Íise Mohamuud (Hawiye, Habar Gidir and leader of the SYL) the Prime Minister along with a cabinet consisting of five Ministers. The ensuing conflict over personal power smacks of clan politics which presages conflict of the so-called elite over power in subsequent decades.

Table 2 below lists the clans and sub-clans of the six members of the first Somali government formed by the Italian administration.

Table 2

The First Somali Government Under Italian Administration 1956

Name	**Post**	**Clan**	**Sub-Clan**
Ábdulaahi Íise Mohamuud	Prime Minister	Hawiye	Habar Gidir
Haaji Muuse Boqor	Minister of Internal Affairs	Daarood	Mijeerteen
Sheekh Áli Jumáalle	Minister of Social Affairs	Hawiye	Hawaadle
Haaji Faarax Áli Úmar	Minister of Economic Affairs	Hawiye	Habar Gidir
Salaad Ábdi Mohamed	Minister of Finance	Daarood	Mijeerteen
Mohamed Ábdi Noor "Juje"	Minister of General Affairs	Dir	Gaadsan

Chart 2 presents the clan distribution of cabinet members.[37]

Chart 2

Clan Distribution the First Government, 1956

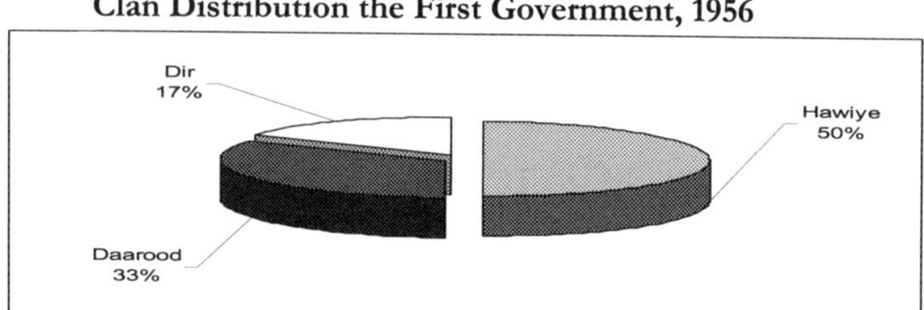

The proportion of the Hawiye and Daarood composition was respectively 50% Hawiye to 33% Daarood. Clearly, the Hawiye had dominated the new government and the Habar Gidir sub-clan received a lion's share of power. The Mijeerteen constituted sole representative of the Daarood. The Rahanwein were not included at all in the cabinet. In addition to appointing the Prime Minister and the five-member cabinet, the Italian administration had formed a Legislative Assembly. The deputies elected Aden Ábdulle Ósmaan (Hawiye, Ujejen) as the President of the Assembly.

As we see in this example as in subsequent decades of Somali politics, there is the illusion of clan distribution of power and the men vested with power looked as if they represent clans when in fact they did not. Yet the illusion and myth of clans sharing power persists even today. In fact, the clan illusion has kept the *Klan* in power. Thus, one must realize that behind every clan identity in contemporary politics lie the ruling elite who exploit clan identity and loyalty in their quest for personal power and wealth.

The so-called elite actually have two group identities—one with their clan, the other with the Klan. They used the first for personal advantage, but the live and wholeheartedly identify with the later. This should dissuade us from condemning a whole group for the actions of a politician who superficially identities with that clan. Still, even though the Somali elite use clan when it serves their purpose, I note in this work the name of politicians and their clan details in the analyses that follow.

The illusion of clan power struggle was a game played out subjectively with little objective gains for the clan. The Prime Minister and the cabinet had little legal authority to make decisions. The Prime Minister and the cabinet were accountable not to the Assembly but to the Italian administration that had the power to appoint and dismiss the cabinet ministers, including the Prime Minister. The competition for clan supremacy had begun and continued to have adversely consequences for Somali politics. The *Klan's* power tactic, involving personal contest for power camouflaged as clan conflict was in place.

This rush for power generated personal animosity that made Somali politics acrimonious prior to and after independence. The elite's condemnation of clannism on the one hand and their compulsive use of clan politics on the other gave the Somali politician duplicity that made Somali politics confusing and destructive. It reminds one of the "split-mind" that Emil Kraepelin associated with the schizophrenic caught in ambivalence and torn with conflicts. The intense competition and duplicity continued before and after independence.

The Italian Administration formed the second government in 1959. Again, Ábdulaahi Íise Mohamuud became the Prime Minister. Appointed were also nine other Ministers. The expanded Cabinet had five Ministers, including the Prime Minister, some of whom were from the previous administration. However, there was a significant change—Haaji Muuse Boqor (Daarood, Mijeerteen) dropped from the new list. In addition, the two new Cabinet members, one from the Ogaadeen, the other the Rahanwein, emerged for the first time.

Table 3 identifies the cabinet Ábdulaahi Íise appointed.

Table 3

The 2nd Government under Italian Administration (1959)

Name	Post	Clan	Sub-Clan
Ábdulaahi Moh. Íise	Prime Minister	Hawiye	Habar Gidir
Mohamuud M. Faarax	Min. of Justice & Grace	Daarood	Ogaadeen
Sheekh Áli Jumáalle	Min. of Health and Labor	Hawiye	Hawaadle
Haaji Faarax Áli Úmar	Min. of Comm. and Indus.	Hawiye	Habar Gidir
Mohamuud Ábdi Noor	Min. of Works & Comm.	Dir	Gaadsan
Mohamuud Y. Aadan	Minister of Education	Daarood	Mijeerteen
Ósmaan A. Roobleh	Minister of Finance	Hawiye	Abgaal
Salaad Ábdi Mohamuud	Min.of Ag. & Animal Hus.	Daarood	Mijeerteen
Ali Úmar Sheego	Min. of Liaison & Gov't	Digil	Tunni
Ábdi Nuur Mohamed	Min. of General Affairs	Rahanwein	Gedofade

Chart 3 also presents the clan distribution of the 1959 Cabinet.

Chart 3

Clan Distribution of the 2nd Government (1959)

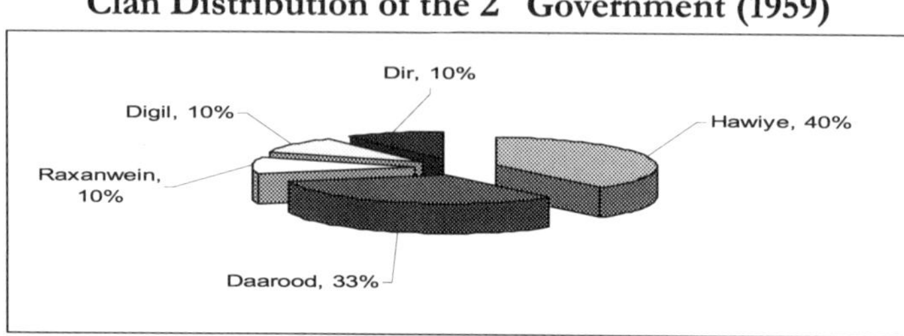

The inclusion of an Ogaadeen member shifted the Hawiye-Mijeerteen balance; therefore, the Hawiye and Daarood proportions fulfilled the implicit rule of clan balance. The Mijeerteen received smaller share of cabinet members than in the previous administration.

That Ábdulaahi Íise dropped Haaji Muuse Boqor from the list angered the Mijeerteen. In addition, the way Ábdulaahi maneuvered out Muuse Boqor also added insult to injury. Haaji Muuse Boqor was declared unfit due to old age (some even alleged that he suffered mental disorder). They also felt that the new Daarood members were too weak to balance the weight of influence exerted by men like Sheekh Áli Jumáalle. These changes angered the Mijeerteen politicians, in particular Ábdirazaaq Haaji Hussein and Mohamed Abshir Muuse who with Sharmaarke belonged to the *"Croce del Sud Group"*.[38]

Mijeerteen members resorted to walkouts and boycotts of the National Assembly. Increasing the clan imbalance, Mohamed Sheekh Gabiou (Hawiye, Abgaal) emerged as Minister for the Constitution and International Affairs. The Hawiye-Daarood competition, particularly the competition between the Habar Gidir and the Mijeerteen continued for years until General Mohamed Siyaad Barre installed his dictatorship and replaced it with Mareehaan-Mijeerteen conflict. Sheekh Áli Jumáalle himself was later dismissed by using tactics similar to those the Hawiye employed against Haaji Muuse Boqor. Note again that persons listed in the table collectively belong to the *Klan* but they distinguish themselves by clan identity when in competition for power.

Following acrimony over Ábdulaahi Íise Mohamuud's last cabinet, the contestants for power in the former Italian colony reached an understanding that moderate clan balance must be maintained power between the Daarood and the Hawiye. Most Hawiye thought that Ábdulaahi Íise would become the Prime Minister of independent Somalia and that he would form the first independent government. Whether

Ábdulaahi would become the Prime Minister depended on who won the Presidency.

The Daarood politicians rallied to oust Ábdulaahi Íise by finding a more acceptable Hawiye President. They campaigned for Aadan Ábdulle Ósmaan, a Hawiye and the President of the Legislative Assembly during the last years of the Trusteeship. The latter won 107 out of 114 votes in the Assembly to become the Provisional President of the Somali Republic.

There was no other contestant for this post. Ábdulaahi Íise could not stand for the post because of a procedural article that lowered the age of presidential candidates. The appointment of the provisional President was for one year until a referendum on the constitution. Aadan Ábdulle Ósmaan was in temperament a conciliatory man, moderate in political behavior, and married to a Mijeerteen, the aunt of Mohamed Abshir Muuse. Thus, Aadan had the confidence and trust of the Mijeerteen. His qualifications—paternal Hawiye), affine Mijeerteen—combined with his personal attributes to make him the first President of the Somali Republic. He continued in that position until 1967.[39]

In his *A Modern History of Somalia*, I.M. Lewis credits (p.158) the expulsion of Haaji Mohamed Hussein from the SYL to Aadan Ábdulle Ósmaan. Haaji Mohamed became President of the party in July 1957. However, Haaji Mohamed, a militant advocate of Pan-Somali-Unity and pro-Arab relations, criticized the party and the President of the Assembly, Aadan Ábdulle Ósmaan, for their lukewarm views and policies toward the freedom and unity of all Somali territories. Following his dismissal from the party, Haaji Mohamed formed his own party called the Greater Somali League. Though popular with the public, the SYL and the Italian dominated administration suppressed his party in the municipal elections of 1958, later closing its headquarters. Haaji Mohamed and his G.S.L. continued to be a thorn in the SYL that eventually succeeded to undermine him and his party.

In addition, Aadan Ábdulle Ósmaan was a darling of the Italian Administration that exerted great influence on politics even during the UN Trusteeship. He grew in an orphanage managed by Italian missionaries. Therefore he was knowledgeable about Italian culture.[40] His Italian connection served him well in politics but also all of his children—four of them medical doctors—who, it is said, had special educational dispensation in Italian universities. Yet those of them I have known are so competent and deserving that they would rise in their chosen professions without the power or influence of their father. Aadan Ábdulle Ósmaan's dual loyalty to Italy and Somalia later created lasting animosity between himself and his Prime Minister, Ábdirashiid Áli Sharmaarke, when he succeeded to gain parliamentary endorsement for a military treaty with the former Soviet Union while the President was away on a visit to Italy. If true, this incident illustrates the distrust and backstabbing that existed in *Klan* politics.

Competition for clan influence was similar in the British Protectorate. Here too, the distribution of power within the *Klan* had the illusion of clan distribution of power. Each minister in the government pursued his own personal ambition for power while he identifying himself as a member of a clan. The competition and conflict over personal power was as intense as before, often escalating into competition and conflict of clans. Yet as in the former Italian colony, the first government of the former British Protectorate had limited power.

The first general election in the former British Protectorate took place on 8 March 1959. The Governor served as the President of the Legislative Council. There were 15 official British members and 14 Somalis members considered unofficial members of the Legislative Council.

The first Somali government in the Protectorate formed in 1959. It consisted of four members who together formed the Executive Council.

Table 4 identifies the leaders of this government.

Table 4

The First Somali Government

1959

Name	**Post**	**Clan**	**Sub-Clan**
Mohamed Ibraahim Égaal	Prime Minister	Isaaq	Habar Awal
Ahmed Haaji Duáale	Min. of Natural Resources	Isaaq	Habar Jélo
Áli Garaad Jaamá	Min. of Communication	Daarood	Dhulbahante
Haaji Ibraahim Ósmaan	Minister of Social Service	Isaaq	Habar Yoonis
Yuusuf Ismaíil Samatar	Assistant Minister	Isaaq	Habar Awal

*He was also Minister of Local Government

Chart 4 shows the clan distribution of the first Somaliland Government under British rule.

Chart 4

Clan Distribution of the First Somaliland Government, 1959

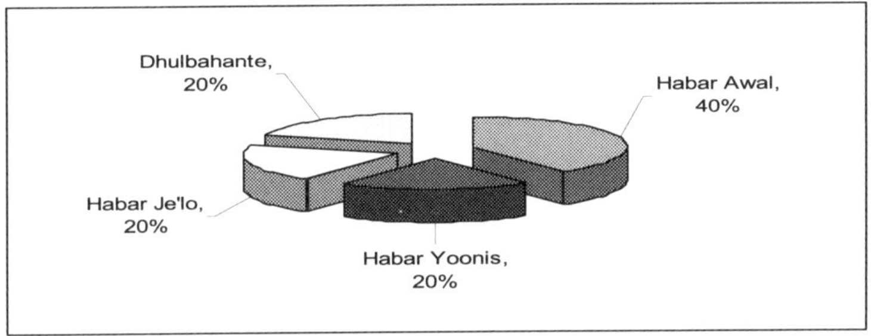

An overwhelming percent of members (80%) in the first Somaliland government were Isaaq and only 20% Daarood. There was no representation of Gadabuursi, Warsangali, Íidagale, Arab, Íise, or others in the Executive Council. The chart below summarizes the distribution percentage of members in sub-clans. Each of these four members had departmental responsibilities.

In this first Somali government, Égaal was not only the Prime Minister; he was also Minister of Local Government that provided him experience in dealing with traditional leaders and local administrators. That experience proved valuable experience to him later in his political career of manipulating both urban and rural politics with skill and finesse but now with admirable goals of advancing the economic and political development of his people.

In fact, Mohamed Ibraahim Égaal had a mercurial and unpredictable personality, showing remarkable charm at the times and sudden shift of mood for causes unknown until, when the occasion arose, he frankly shared rumors of one's supposed opposition fabricated by those who sought monetary gifts from him.

The chart illustrates the pattern of politics of the *Klan* in subsequent decades. Western education and service to the colonial system qualified members to assume power and privilege. Though a few, the elite comes from different clans. Birth to a father who was a chief—a *boqor*, *suldaan*, *ugaas*, or *garaad*—augmented or replaced the requirements of western education. The necessary level of education was minimal – many got by with basic literacy in a European language.

Members of the *Klan* rallied the clan their clan when involved in competition or conflict with others; they were aloof from when not so involved.

Distribution of power among the elite always gives the illusion of clan representation. In fact, the earliest cabinets before independence confirm unequally representation of clans. In Somalia, representation in the cabinet of the late nineteen-fifties showed that the Hawiye and the Daarood locked in competition, with Hawiye holding an edge. In Somaliland too, there was unequal clan representation in the pre-independence government of the late nineteen-fifties. This inequity continued after independence between clans as well as between Somalia and Somaliland.

The competition for power within the *Klan* in Somalia and Somaliland simmered for years. As we shall see later, unity of the two former colonies provided a diversion and delay from a clan crisis and conflict within each territory until January 26, 1991 when the state collapsed. The brutal repression of Barre regime that increasingly identified itself as Daarood hegemony brought reprisal against the Daarood in Mogadishu after the collapse of the regime. Somaliland declared independence on May 18, 1991, but inter-clan armed conflicts broke out among the Isaaq in 1994-96. Examining these conflicts closely shows that the *Klan* instigated the armed clashes and that competition for power among the *Klan* masquerading as clan conflict often produces disastrous consequences.

Today as in the past, clan distribution of power among the elite does not reflect the actual size of clan constituency. There is no census of clans or of the population as a whole. The *Klan* uses the social fiction of clan representation to give the public the illusion of power and participation in government. It is a ruse to confuse the public about clan power. Even after the state collapse in 1991, the *Klan* resurface and Somalis continue to entertain the illusion of clan power. We will discuss the underlying psychology of this enchanting illusion in Chapter 13.

Since Somalis repeatedly reenact the tactics of the *Klan* and the associated illusion, we must examine both closely and historically to understand the essence of Somalis politics. Thirty years of Somali experience (from 1960-1991)—the longest Somalis enjoyed independence in recent years—offers lessons worth uncovering and learning. How then did the tactics of the *Klan* and the illusion unfold and develop after independence?

4

CAIN IN CIVILIAN GARB

Run sheeg waa ceeb sheeg.
Telling truth exposes the unseemly
—Somali Proverb

Before colonial rule, Somalis lived in their traditionally pastoral world cut off from international politics and commerce with the exception of the coastal areas where ancient emporia existed. Clans interacted, intermarried, and fought contiguous clans, but they had little contact with distant clans, although they shared the same language, religion, and culture. As explained in Chapter 2, colonial rulers partitioned the land of Somalis into colonial enclaves administered by different colonial powers. But the colonial occupation and partition provoked not only resentment of Somalis to artificial borders but also a shared passion for independence and Pan-Somali-Unity.

The independence granted in 1960 to the former Italian colony of Somalia and the former British Protectorate of Somaliland brought jubilation and high expectation to Somalis in these territories. It also raised the hopes of other Somalis in the Northern Frontier District in Kenya, the Somali Region in Ethiopia, and the former French colony, today the Republic of Djibouti. Somalis in all five territories took for granted that independence of Somalia and Somaliland would usher a new era of freedom and unity for all Somalis under one state, one flag.

After independence, however, these dreams of freedom and unity dissipated and turned into bitter disillusionment and despair. Independence did not bring freedom, but derailed and distorted it. The aspiration of Pan-Somali-Unity also diminished and later died. Why?

The answer lies primarily in the direction to which the civilian ruling elite, the *Klan*, took the newly independent and united territories of Somalia and Somaliland in the first nine years, from 1960-1969.As we shall see in this chapter and the next, the rule of the civilian elite was marred by internal feud, corruption, and nepotism that set the stage for clan hegemony, then oligarchy and dictatorship. A review of the first nine years therefore provides an essential backdrop for decades of tragedy that followed.

Bogus Beginning

Before independence, Somali politicians applauded freedom and Somali unity, leaving no doubt that they identified with *the people* and with their quest for *liberty*. Wearing pinstriped suits and colorful ties, they presented themselves in colonial offices and international venues as the chosen representatives of their people. Yet they kept social distance from the ordinary person except in moments of self-serving political campaigns. Most of the time, they retreated to their private homes, cordoned off by high walls and armed guards. Behind these high walls, they indulged in fine food and western pleasures while their people endured abject poverty and misery.

Though these politicians projected desire for independence, they did not critically analyze the type of state they wanted to build and how the clan system would integrate into the fledgling state. Instead, they mimicked forms of nationalism fashioned in European context and founded on European history. Impersonating their colonial mentors, they condemned the clan system as sign of ignorance while glorifying the nation and nationalism as proof of enlightenment. Echoing the Eurocentric views of their colonial mentors, they also declared that nation and clan were totally incompatible. However, they never spelled out their presumed contradictions, let alone solve problems arising from their muddled mix. Neither did they figure out how they would change the state to accommodate the clan system on which Somalis depended for centuries, or by which magical means they would root out the clan system they demonized as "tribalism."[1]

Independence and unity of Somalia and Somaliland put to test these beliefs and outlook of the politicians who inherited the colonial state. As we shall see in this and the subsequent chapters, Somali politicians failed to deliver the freedom they promised their people because they did not develop the proper state and the appropriate institutions to govern justly or usher economic development. Naïve or misinformed, they thought hoisting a flag, singing an anthem, and having Somali leaders were sufficient condition to establish a nation and enjoy freedom. They did not realize that freedom and nation-building require the development of legitimate institutions; that these institutions must have a consistent policy based on realistic means and ends; that public service is not the royal road to wealth; that government cannot provide solutions to all problems; that freedom is not a free lunch—that therefore every right has its responsibility.

The failure to develop legitimate and functional institutions was one of the most serious barriers to state development. Government institutions mediate between the individual and the state; the state inspires confidence only when its institutions are accountable to the ruled and responsive to their needs. Calls for nation-building are therefore insincere when the mediating institutions are corrupt. After independence, the existing institutions (for instance, the legislature, police, courts, schools, and hospitals) were those inherited from colonial rulers. Somali leaders did not critically examine what services those institutions provided and for whom. They assumed that change from white to black managers necessarily changed the function of these institutions, not recognizing that social systems determine behavior and outcome, that therefore oppressive systems remain oppressive regardless of the color or nationality of those who manage them.

In addition, government became the sole employer—indeed the only 'industry'—to which the elite and the public looked for satisfaction of all their needs. Instead of turning to commerce and the market for material reward, they flocked to government, making it the sole arena for competition over power and wealth rather than the best means for public security and service when government is properly started and maintained. The leaders also invested little on livestock development (the backbone of the economy) and agricultural expansion that would employ and meet the needs of the majority. On the contrary, government became top-heavy—burdened by large number of officials, administrators, auxiliaries, and parasitic appendages—while it rested on weak economic and social foundation. At the same time it overtaxed the private sector while the elite pillaged state resources like the modern day equivalent of gangs looting camels.

Unable to support the state on local resources, the politicians turned to foreign aid as if such assistance was inexhaustible, their natural right, and available at their request. The Somali saying *maba dhalan eh dhawrtaysan ogaa*—'Not yet born, it excelled in begging'—had gained new meaning. In time, the elite and the government became too dependent on foreign aid. Initiative and hard work gave way to lethargy and dependence on the state which in turn became addicted to foreign aid that seldom produced the results supposedly intended by donors.

Little wonder then that, by the early nineteen-sixties, the Somali Republic was known as "the graveyard of foreign aid."

Further, the ruling politicians did not promote merit in hiring, pride in producing, honor in public service, or commitment to the common good. They understood freedom not as recognition of necessity but as absence of restraint on pursuit of self-interest, the right to obtain whatever one wished, by any means. That is why every Somali reached out for the breast of the proverbial she-camel *Maandeeq* which was extolled by popular poems and songs as symbol of the state, the supposed guarantor of freedom and prosperity for all. After independence, however, *Maandeeq* became the exclusive property of whoever wrested it like the traditionally looted camel. And who else but the politicians controlling the state were best placed to wrest *Maandeeq*?

Yet, as in the tradition of camel looting, wresting *Maandeeq* directly or indirectly implicated the clan of the looters. Further the elite used the clan system in their contest over power and privilege. Inevitably, then, the specter of clan politics which prior to independence was condemned as divisive and sign of ignorance had reared its head right after independence, dominating Somali political life from the birth of the new republic in 1960 to the collapse of the state in 1991.

Thus as the years progressed, it became clear that independence did not bring the material and social progress expected. Corruption and nepotism were rife, as were official abuses of power. The state failed to replace the social functions the clan system provides. It did not offer an alternative social support, nor did it extend protection for the person and property of citizens the way the clan system did. It also failed to build institutions that ensure justice and equality.

On the contrary, the state collected taxes but returned little return in health and social services. It gave license for the few to enrich themselves by illegal means, to loot *Maandeeq* and pursue get-rich-quick schemes. As a result, loyalty to the state, feigned and fleeting at first, lost ground to clan identity and commitment. But the clan identity and clan loyalty of post-independence were not those of traditional society which emphasized reciprocal assistance and survival of the group. They were distorted by colonial rule and urban life extolling survival of the craftiest and greediest by exploiting the unwary and poorly defended, including kinsmen.

The elite bred under colonial rule and in urban centers knew best how to exploit clan identity and loyalty for their own ends. They ran the government not as tool to serve the people but as instrument with which predators at the top looted the treasury and foreign aid while a swarm of scavengers, wearing the uniforms and insignia of the state, preyed on the weak and defenseless. Their hypocrisy on clannism—on the one hand their overt public denouncement of the clan system, on the other covert use of it to dispense jobs and privileges—reinforced not only public confusion and despair but also the cynical belief that only one's clan is the most reliable recourse for security and support.

The elite caught in competition for power also generalized their private struggles into contest of clans, inducing their kinsmen into believing that other clans are out there to do harm to them. Their class wishes and fears translated into clan paranoia; in reaction, the ordinary people of necessity threw themselves to the fold of the clan, taking shelter in the herd and huddling in psychological bunkers of the clan. Thus the clan system that for centuries kept Somalis to collectively survive the harsh elements of the semi-desert turned into a fetish, an object of irrational reverence and obsessive devotion, while to the same degree the state lost relevance and loyalty.[2]

By early nineteen-sixties, poets and ordinary citizens gave voice to their disillusionment and despair at the bankruptcy, injustice, and material greed of the ruling elite. Jaamá Ahmed Jaamá *(Gámadheere)* was one of the poets who expressed the frustrations of people and described the elite's greed and corruption in post-independence.

In one of his poems, he explored the relation between the ruling civilian elite and their people:

I get promotion, living in a tall building, but never ever touch it
I gorge myself, eating nourishing foods, but never ever feel resentment
Pay the debt you owe me, though I annulled what I owe you.
This indeed is state of dictatorship people will not tolerate
Only the fool accepts this, but we reject it all.[3]

The following pages show how this bogus beginning with an unproductive and top-heavy government became the vortex of the *Klan's* competition and conflict using clan politics while they claimed to manage the state for the common good. We focus on politics at the top echelons of the power because conflict at this level best demonstrates the tension and contradictions permeating the political system in Somali society. The conflict at the level of Presidents, Prime Ministers, ministers, and parliamentarians in the early years of independence also set the stage for the crisis-ridden auto-colonial system pitting one group against another until the state collapsed thirty years later.

Equally important, the list of cabinet members each leader appointed offers us a glimpse to the political (clan) problems he wanted to solve and the type of persons he trusted to take responsibility for key state functions. How he dealt with people and problems during his tenure also reveals his personality and style of leadership.

Sharmaarke's False Start

Many problems of today began when the Somali Youth League (SYL) and the Somali National League (SNL) formed after World War II. Both organizations drew membership from different clans, though certain clans or sub-clans dominated each organization and its leadership. These political parties that would have served as leverage of change were themselves as flawed as were the state and its institutions. Even during the nineteen-fifties when nationalism reached its zenith, this clan configuration eroded nascent political consciousness and continued to corrode unity of Somalis in subsequent decades. Yet for a while the elasticity of clan identity gave the illusion of broad-based participation and sharing of power. Lack of distinction between *clan* and the *Klan* also allowed the elite to carry out elite mischief.

The politics of the SYL, the dominant party, shows how its leaders exploited the illusion of broad-based participation while they engaged in personal and clan competition for power. In the former Italian colony where the SYL held absolute dominance, the Hawiye and the Daarood—in particular the Habar Gidir and the Mijeerteen—were locked in fierce clan competition and, until 1967, the Hawiye enjoyed political dominance over the Daarood. They held the leading posts in government headed by Prime Minister Ábdulaahi Íise Mohamuud before independence and the Presidency by Aadan Ábdulle Ósmaan until 1967. They also had greater representation in the cabinet until that year. From 1967 onwards, including the 21 years of military rule, the Daarood took dominant share of power, symbolically and in reality.

Instigated and maintained by their respective members of the elite, the Hawiye-Daarood competition for power was a critical factor in post-independence politics and the chief contributor to the instability and eventual collapse of the state. It also has been the primary barrier to rebuilding the state for Somalia during the past eighteen years, despite numerous reconciliation conferences and massive funds spent by major powers on the elusive search for peace and order.

Similar clan competition and conflicts no doubt existed at other levels of Somali politics, involving other clans and their elite, but the Hawiye-Daarood conflict is both paradigmatic and pivotal. It exemplifies elite conflict enlarged to clan conflicts in Somali society; it is also at the core of problems turning Somalia into a hornet's nest thwarting solution to this day. Tracing this conflict shows not only how Somali politics often degenerates into petty personal feuds but also how the public are duped to serve as fodders and foot soldiers of wars instigated by the elite.

The competition between the Hawiye and Daarood came out to the open in 1959 when Prime Minister Ábdulaahi Íise Mohamuud dropped Haaji Muuse Boqor (a leader of the Mijeerteen) from the second government he had formed. Anger at the Prime Minister's treatment of Haaji Muuse Boqor brought an alliance of Mijeerteen politicians who later plotted to end the leadership of Ábdulaahi Íise as Prime Minister. Thus on the eve of independence, clan competition threatened the prospect of peaceful transition from colonial rule to independence until a compromise leader, Aadan Ábdulle Ósmaan, emerged. Though a Hawiye by clan, he was a moderate person by temperament and married to a Mijeerteen of an influential family. For these personal attributes, the Daarood accepted President Ósmaan. After his election, politicians and the people waited anxiously whom the President would nominate as the Prime Minister.

The two competitors were Ábdulaahi Íise Mohamuud, a Hawiye, and Ábdirashiid Áli Sharmaarke, a Daarood. If Ábdulaahi Íise became the Prime Minister, the clan balance would tilt to the Hawiye as in the past. President Ósmaan therefore appointed Ábdirashiid Áli Sharmaarke to become the first Prime Minister of the new republic, declaring him the "most qualified" man for the post. His qualification for being the best qualified was not stated; neither was it questioned since people in the former Italian colony understood the importance of keeping clan balance in the persistent Hawiye-Daarood competition. Sharmaarke thus formed the first cabinet of the independent republic.

The Hawiye and the Daarood accepted the first government formed by Sharmaarke because it gave them equal representation in the cabinet. In addition, both clans were content with the arrangement because they shared the two most important posts of President and Prime Minister. The Isaaq and other clans were pushed to ancillary status with regard to the two top offices; they also obtained smaller representation in the cabinet and parliament. The neglect of other clans distressed mostly the Somaliland politicians who enthusiastically had pushed for union without condition.

Viewing Somalia as a category and Somaliland as another, they expected that President Ósmaan would nominate one of them, most probably Mohamed Ibraahim Égaal who had led the largest political party in Somaliland. Instead, the President from Somalia appointed another politician from Somalia. As we shall see later, Égaal never forgot this devaluation of him, forcing him into unholy alliance with politicians from Somalia who had little regard for the aspiration and interests of the people he had led to independence.

Table 1 shows the composition of Sharmaarke's first government.

Table 1

Composition of the First Government Appointed 22 July 1960

Name	**Post**	**Clan**	**Sub-Clan**
Aadan Ábdulle Ósmaan	President	Hawiye	Ujejeen
Ábdirashiid Áli Sharmaarke	Prime Minister	Daarood	Mijeerteen
Ábdi Hassan Buuni	Dep.Prime Minister	Gadabursi	Samaroon
Ahmed Haaji Duáale	Min. of Agriculture	Isaaq	Habar Jélo
Mohamed Ibraahim Égaal	Min. of Defense	Isaaq	Habar Awal
Ali Garaad Jaamá	Min. of Education	Daarood	Dhulbahante
Ábdilqaadir M. Aadan "Zoppe"	Min. of Finance	Rahawein	Disow
Ábdulaahi Íise Mahamuud	Min. of Foreign Affairs	Hawiye	Habar Gedir
Sheekh Áli Jumáalle	Min. of Health & Labor	Hawiye	Hawaadle
Sheekh Ábdulle M. Mohamed	Min. of Industry & Com.	Daarood	Mareehaan
Ali Mohamed Hiraabe	Min. of Information	Hawiye	Abgaal
Ábdirazaaq Haaji Hussein	Mini. of Interior	Daarood	Mijeerteen
Mahamuud Ahmed M. Aadan	Min. of Justice	Hawiye	Abgaal
Ábdi Nuur Mohamed Hussein	Min. of Pub.W. & Com.	Rahawein	Geedowfade
Ósmaan Mohamed Ibraahim	Min. of Somali Affairs	Daarood	Ogaadeen

Chart 1 presents the clan distribution of the new government.

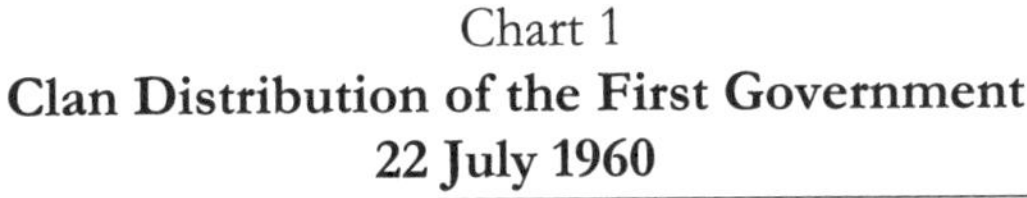

Chart 1
Clan Distribution of the First Government
22 July 1960

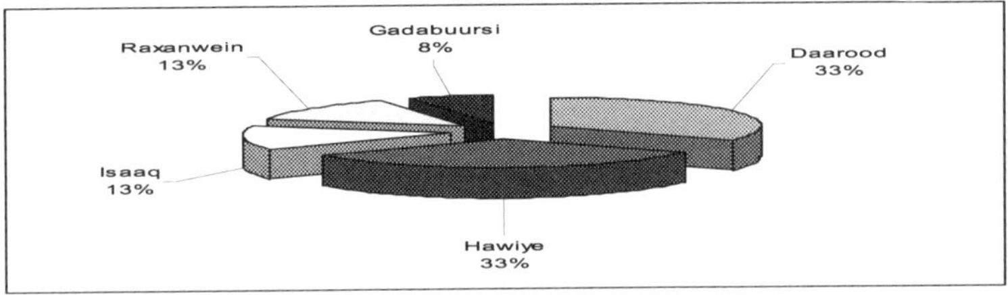

When the President and the Prime Minister were included, the Daarood and Hawiye obtained equal representation (33%) to keep parity of two intensely competing clans. In this first post-independence government, other major clans like the Isaaq and Rahanwein obtained limited share in government as if they were minorities. Égaal who expected to become the Prime Minister had little choice but to accept Minister of Defense.

The year during which Aadan Ábdulle Ósmaan was to serve as the Provisional President ended after a referendum on the Constitution on 20 June 1961. An overwhelming majority (97%) in the South (Somalia) and a minority (less than 50%) in the North (Somaliland) voted in favor of the Constitution. This regional disparity should have prompted the political leaders of Somalia to question why the people of Somaliland were dissatisfied, but these issues were of little interest to them. The approaching contest for the Presidency claimed their attention.

The two candidates for the Presidency, Aadan Ábdulle Ósmaan and Sheekh Áli Jumáalle, were both Hawiye and from Hiiraan Region. It was a close contest. Aadan Ábdulle Ósmaan allied himself with the Daarood, particularly with the Mijeerteen, while Sheekh Áli Jumáalle lobbied the other clans, including the Isaaq. The two candidates received an equal number of votes in the first round. Sheekh Áli Jumáalle won by one vote in the second round, and Aadan Ábdulle Ósmaan eventually won by two votes (62 to 59) in the third round of voting.

The majority of Daarood members in the Assembly voted for Aadan Ábdulle Ósmaan not only for the reasons mentioned above but also they dreaded the prospect of handing the Presidency to Sheekh Áli Jumáalle, a strident advocate of Hawiye dominance in politics. For this reason, the Daarood politicians disliked Sheekh Áli Jumáalle for years, particularly so when he was in Ábdulaahi Íise's cabinet. They believed that he was behind the dismissal of Muuse Boqor on grounds of advanced age or even mental disorder. Several years later, the opponents of Sheekh Áli Jumáalle dismissed him from the Assembly using the same pretext that he had used against Muuse Boqor.[4]

President Aadan Ábdulle Ósmaan again nominated Ábdirashiid Áli Sharmaarke on July 11, 1961 and the Assembly approved the nomination. On 27 July 1961, Sharmaarke presented the list of his 14 cabinet members, most of them from his previous cabinet with the exception of the Deputy Prime Minister, Ábdi Hassan Buuni, whom he had replaced. He also replaced Ahmed Haaji Duáalle (Isaaq, Habar Jélo) with Sheekh Áli Ismaíil (Isaaq, Habar Yoonis) who became Minister of Defense. Égaal moved to the post of Education Minister.

The Assembly rejected Sharmaarke's government on grounds that the 14 ministers he proposed exceeded the limit of 12 ministers required by the law they had passed on August 14, 1961. Angered by this rejection of his government, Sharmaarke offered his resignation to the President who refused his resignation and urged him to follow the law. When Sharmaarke reduced the cabinet to 12 ministers, the Assembly approved the list.

Again, the clan distribution of ministerial appointment stayed within the unwritten rule of balance between the Daarood (31%) and Hawiye (39%), giving advantage to the latter by a small margin which the Daarood accepted. The Isaaq and the Rahanwein obtained 15% each, which was far less than they had expected. After Sharmaarke announced the list of his cabinet members, dissatisfaction of Somalilanders with the Somalia-dominated government hardened into bitter resentment that further augmented to the other crises already weakening Ábdirashiid's government.

The revolt of military officers of Somalialnd in December 1961 followed by the revolt on taxation and salary cuts in Somaliland in May 1962 (explained in Chapter 5) was aggravated by another when Mohamed Ibraahim Égaal, the Minister of Education, and Sheek Áli Ismaíil, the Minister of Defense, resigned from the Sharmaarke government on October 13, 1962. The resignation of Égaal and Ismaíil, both leaders of the Somali National League, ended the coalition of the Somali National League (SNL with the Somali Youth League (SYL).

The resignation and the withdrawal from the SYL coalition also gave Égaal free hand to engage in political campaigns opposed to Ábdirashiid and his government. Forming alliance with Sheekh Áli Jumáalle, he found a new rhetoric and leverage that would raise his stake and disturb the Prime Minister in carrying on business as usual.

Earlier, in June 1961, the Prime Minister dismissed Sheekh Áli Jumáalle from the cabinet, but Sheekh Áli Jumáalle was not a push-over. A highly influential advocate of Hawiye political dominance, he ran for the Presidency in June 1961 and, as we have seen, barely lost to Aadan Ábdulle Ósmaan. Sharmaarke and Sheekh Áli were at political loggerheads for years on clan superiority but they had managed to keep their differences under control while they were in the Council of Minister whose members Sharmaarke had appointed.

However, the conflict erupted again between the two men and Sharmaarke dismissed Sheekh Áli Jumáalle. The latter refused to resign. When the conflict turned ugly, President Aadan Ábdulle Ósmaan intervened and forced the resignation of Sheekh Áli Jumáalle by a Presidential Decree he issued on 4 December 1961. Sheekh Áli Jumáalle, like Égaal, sought a means of reprisal against the Prime Minister and what he viewed as Daarood hegemony. Sheekh Áli and Égaal therefore formed a clan coalition based on *Iririsrn*—referring to *Irir*, the earliest ancestor which the Isaaq and the Hawiye share in common. This coalition put the Sharmaarke government under pressure until the election of March 1964.

Sharmaarke was popular for his commitment to pan-Somali nationalism, many remembering him with admiration for his remark—Somalis would vote with one hand, while defending their country with the other— when Ethiopian forces attacked the new republic during the 1964 parliamentary elections. However, Ábdirashiid was not an effective manager of people, nor a good administrator, nor an effective crisis manager. Somewhat distant and reclusive, he tended to leave management of people and programs to his cronies, intervening with inflexible decisions when conflicts escalated to crises.

Very religious and self-righteous, Sharmaarke also tended to see things in black and white when he encountered problems that could be resolved through dialogue and compromise. Augmenting his problems, Sharmaarke did not appoint others to the posts Égaal and his allies vacated. This shows that Sharmaarke seldom delegated power and, when he did, his management style was lackadaisical and distant, with little follow-up and demand of accountability.[5]

How Sharmaarke managed the resignations of Égaal and the dismissal of Sheek Áli Jumáalle was a case in point. By not resolving conflict with them, he was on a collision course with two highly influential politicians who would (and did!) stir trouble for him. By failing to appoint others to their vacated posts, he also lost the support of more allies who could have helped him face the challenges of these two vociferous men now poised in opposition to him. That he assumed the responsibilities of the ministerial posts Égaal and Sheekh Áli Ismaíil had vacated, as if the Prime Minister did not have enough to keep him busy, also shows Ábdirashiid's muddled priorities and the lackadaisical way he dealt with conflict.

Little wonder then that dissatisfaction with his government grew and more resignations followed less than a month later. Thus on 6 November 1962, Sheekh Ábdulle Mohamuud Mohamed, Minister of Industry and Commerce, a Daarood of the Mareehaan sub-clan, and Ábdi Nuur Mohamed Hussein, the Minister of Public Works and Communication, a Rahanwien of the Geedowfade sub-clan, resigned from their posts. Sharmaarke again avoided the problem and announced a cabinet shuffle on 19 November 1962. He moved Ábdirazaaq Haaji Hussein from the Ministry of Interior to become the Minister of Public Works and Communication. He appointed Hilowle Moálin, a Daarood of the Ogaadeen sub-clan, to become the Minister of Defense, and Mohamuud Ábdi Nuur "Juje," a Dir of Gaadsan sub-clan, to become Minister of the Interior.

The Prime Minister continued to hold on to the ministerial post of Education and Industry until 2 February 1963 when he appointed as Minister of Education Yuusuf Áli Samatar, an Isaaq of the Habar Awal sub-clan. On the same date, he also appointed Haaji Ibraahim Ósmaan Fod "Basbaas", an Isaaq of the Habar Yoonis sub-clan, to become Minister of Industry. By these and earlier changes, Sharmaarke started the practice of replacing a minister with another appointee from his clan. Subsequent leaders used the practice for political reasons, compromising integrity and merit in government. The practice also created enmity between members of the same clan. Otherwise, Sharmaarke's cabinet reshuffle Sharmaarke retained almost the same clan distribution as his previous government: 38% Hawiye, 32 % Daarood, 15% Isaaq, and 8% each Rahanwein and Dir.

The shift of Ábdirazaaq from the powerful post of Interior Minister to that of Public works and Communication may have been provoked by a simmering conflict between Ábdirashiid and Ábdirazaaq, two former allies and power brokers of the Mijeerteen before independence and soon after it. As mentioned in Chapter 3, the two men in collaboration with Mohamed Abshir Muuse formed the *"Croce del Sud Group"* who led the Mijeerteen opposition to the Hawiye political dominance prior to independence. Many understood that Ábdirazaaq and his two clan allies attacked Prime Minister Ábdulaahi Íise Mohamuud in quest of Daarood equity if not hegemony.

Ábdirazaaq and Mohamed Abshir had a fall out with Sharmaarke after independence for reasons not fully known but could be inferred from developments after 1962. Some state that the Prime Minister was dissatisfied with how Ábdirazaaq had managed the growing conflict in Somaliland over taxes and salary cuts that provoked mass protest to which the government responded with siege of cities. Actually, the conflict between the two men goes deeper, although the crises in Somaliland and the shift of Ábdirazaaq from one ministry to another had intensified it. No doubt involved was conflict of personal ambition for power, as subsequent developments attest.

The conflict of the two former allies was almost coterminous with and certainly not independent from the conflict between Sharmaarke and Mohamed Abshir Muuse, the powerful Commander of the Police, who was himself a member of the *"Croce del Sud Group"* and related to President Aadan Ábdulle Ósmaan by marriage. Sharmaarke's conflict with these two highly influential members of his clan would haunt him until his assassination seven years later. Though the two men have been rumored to be involved in the assassination, no evidence exists to prove their guilt.

Not unrelated to the above conflict between former allies, the relationship between President Aadan Ábdulle Ósmaan and Ábdirashiid Áli Sharmaarke also strained after Sharmaarke entered into an agreement with the former Soviet Union to provide military and technical assistance to the new republic. The West offered a total of $6 million while the former USSR offered $11 million. Sharmaarke took the latter offer for pragmatic reasons since no evidence exists that he was an avid or even closet socialist. Further, Sharmaarke knew that the West would not offer Somalis greater financial and military assistance that it already extended to Ethiopia and later Kenya—two countries with which the new republic had border dispute.

On the other hand, Aadan Ábdulle Ósmaan was known to be a close and loyal friend of Italy and Mohamed Abshir Muuse was a darling of West Germany which provided training and arms to the police force he commanded. Still, ideology was not as critical in provoking conflict between these men and Sharmaarke as was personal differences and conflict of loyalties. President Ósmaan objected to the USSR offer of aid and took offense in how his Prime Minister maneuvered the Assembly to endorse the agreement without the President's knowledge and during his absence in Italy. Ábdirazaaq and Mohamed Abshir sided with the President against the Prime Minister

Still, the conflict between these men in high places with their opposing camps, without significant ideological differences, stumbled into to the Cold War by force of circumstance. As a result, their conflict over personal ambition diverted into a whirlwind of superpower geopolitical conflict, throwing the Somali state into a trajectory neither of the competing camps understood or anticipated. As a result, their mindless feuds left a violent and confusing legacy for generations to come. The heavy guns and the all-pervasive AK-47 that to this day cause mayhem and destruction for Somalis and for the region are in part consequences of hasty decisions the ruling civilian elite took in the first few years after independence.

As we shall see in the next chapter, the dream of Pan-Somali Unity had pushed the civilian regimes deeper into the whirlwind of the Cold War for which Somalis had little preparation or power to survive its freezing chill and dizzying turns. The military regime that overthrew the civilian government also pushed to extreme limits the policy of opportunism and personal squabble started by the civilian elite and enlarged into clan conflicts.

Ábdirazaaq's Failed Reforms

The conflict between Aadan Ábdulle Ósmaan and Ábdirashiid Áli Sharmaarke simmered until individuals formed into two strident camps. Sharmaarke held firm on his decision to woo the Soviet Union while President Ósmaan never forgave him for failing to consult him.

Thus after the election of 1964, President Ósmaan dropped Ábdirashiid Áli Sharmaarke and instead nominated Ábdirazaaq Haaji Hussein for Prime Minister. By nominating Ábdirazaaq, the President solved two problems: getting rid of someone whom he did not trust and pacifying the Mijeerteen with whom he had strong alliance.

However, Ábdirazaaq's first cabinet appointment quickly ran into problems. First, Ábdirazaaq broke the unwritten rule of clan balance between the Hawiye and the Daarood. His appointments favored the Daarood, reversing Sharmaarke's conciliatory approach to the Hawiye. Second, his *Posto Rosa* program, so called because dismissal of civil servants came in red envelop, was supposed to clean the bureaucracy, dismissing technically inept or financially corrupt employees. But this reform program failed as soon as it started in part because the new Prime Minister's government faced staunch opposition from the start. Third, Ábdirazaaq appointed mostly new ministers and rejected all former ministers except Ábdilqaadir Mohamed Aadan "Zoppe." In addition, he again ignored the state's chronic problems with Somaliland.

His decision to ignore the implicit rule of clan balance between the Hawiye and the Daarood suggested that he was a staunch supporter of Daarood political superiority, recalling his opposition to Ábdulaahi Íise Mohamuud before independence. His *Posto Rosa* program created fear and resentment in the civil service and in particular those from clans different from his own. This led to charges that the aim of *Posto Rosa* was not reform, as declared, but a tool with which the Prime Minister punished those whom he disliked for clan or other reasons, replacing them with his cronies. In Somali politics, cynicism is always keener and sharper to reformers than to guardians of the status quo.

His appointment of new persons to the cabinet also alienated former ministers, including former ministers who were Mijeerteen. Not surprisingly, then, the former Mijeerteen ministers joined in the opposition to Ábdirazaaq. His strict economic policies also alienated deputies in the National Assembly who routinely exploited their status for personal gain. Frustration of personal and clan interest therefore mobilized broad opposition against his government As a result, Ábdirazaaq's government lost vote of confidence one month after he had formed it, confirming a persistent pattern in Somali politics—personal interest *before* clan loyalty and clan loyalty *before* national interest.

Once again, President Aadan Ábdulle Ósmaan intervened to help resolve the problems between Ábdirazaaq and his opponents in the Assembly. Ábdirazaaq Haaji Hussein subsequently formed a new government. He announced the list on 14 August 1964; the Assembly approved it on 2nd September of the same year. The Daarood obtained 5 ministers (31% of the cabinet) while the Hawiye obtained 4 minister (25%), and the Isaaq 3 minister (19%). In addition, he included 1 minister (6%) each for the Rahanwein, the Digile, and the Gadabuursi.

This distribution of Ábdirazaaq's cabinet suggests that he was uncompromising on Daarood hegemony. However, he sought this time to moderate Isaaq but not Hawiye discontent with his government. But the gesture to the Isaaq was simply too little, too late. Their resentment to his government persisted, although Ábdirazaaq as Prime Minister had appointed a greater number of Isaaq in his second cabinet than Sharmaarke did as Prime Minister; he also recruited more Somalilanders the civil servants than Sharmaarke ever did as Prime Minister.

Yet the Isaaq did not dislike Ábdirazaaq more than Sharmaarke. The difference was partly one of history, partly of personality. Ábdirazaaq had serious problems with Somalilanders generally and the Isaaq particularly when he was Minister of Interior. As Minister of Interior, he harshly dealt with them when they revolted against tax increase simultaneous with salary cuts of movement employees. The harsh measures, including siege of Hargeysa, only intensified the crisis. To show Ábdirazaaq's insensitivity to public grievance and his abusive language, Somalilanders cite one incident in which Hargeysa residents turned their back to him during his visit and he retorted that the image of those who turned their back to him looks better seeing them from behind than meeting them face-to-face. Ábdirazaaq's reaction was understood not only as sign of dictatorial streak in the man but also an insult with sexual connotations that deeply offended people.

The two men also had contrasting personalities. Ábdirazaaq is a frank man who expresses his views without mincing words. Some consider his style highly abrasive and opinionated, forgetting the virtues of the lion that roars in contrast to the one that waits quietly for the kill. Ábdirashiid was indirect and reclusive, giving the impression of being more congenial and sincere. The two men were also different in how they managed people. Ábdirazaaq was a hands-on manager who appeared highly controlling while Sharmaarke was remote and appeared easygoing.

Somalilanders resented the arrogant and dismissive way that Ábdirazaaq treated them when they presented their grievances to him as Interior Minister and Prime Minister. In contrast, Sharmaarke had reputation of being the most ardent pan-Somali nationalist than all the Prime Ministers who succeeded him. Themselves intoxicated with pan-Somali nationalism, Somalilanders were therefore willing to ignore Ábdirashiid's meager appointments of their own in the cabinet and key government posts. After all, these people had sacrificed their independence for Somali unity without condition and they would also forsake any regional or clan gain for the sake of Somali unity.

To reduce growing opposition to his government, Prime Minister Ábdirazaaq announced a cabinet change in March 21, 1966. Table 2 below presents the list of ministers he had appointed.

Table 2

The Government Appointed by Ábdirazaaq Haaji Hussein 21 March 1966

Name	Post	Clan	Sub-Clan
Aadan Ábdulle Ósmaan	President	Hawiye	Ujejen
Ábdirazaaq Haaji Hussein	Prime Minister	Daarood	Mijeerteen
Mohamuud Ábdi Nuur "Juje"	Minister of Agriculture	Dir	Gaadsan
Ábdirahmaan Haaji Mumin	Minister of Defense	Hawiye	Galjeél
Kenadiid Ahmed Yuusuf	Minister of Education	Hawiye	Ajuuran
Áli Úmar Sheego	Minister of Finance	Digile	Tunni
Ahmed Yuusuf Duáale	Minister of Foreign Affairs	Isaaq	Habar Awal
Haaji Bashkir Ismaíil	Minister of Health & Labor	Daarood	Mijeerteen
Ábdulaahi Íise Mohamuud	Min. of Industry & Commerce	Hawiye	Habar Gidir
Yuusuf Ahmed Bookah	Minister of Information	Daarood	Dhulbahante
Ábdilqaadir Mohamud Aadan	Minister of Interior	Rahawein	Disow
Hassan Ábdulaahi Faarah	Min. of Justice & Religious Affairs	Isaaq	Habar Yonis
Mohamud Mohamed Faarah	Minister of Somali Affairs	Daarood	Ogaadeen
Ósmaan Ahmed Roble	Minister of State	Hawiye	Abgaal
Aadan Isaaq Ahmed	Minister of Transport & Com.	Gadabursi	Makahiil

Chart 2 shows clan distribution of the third cabinet Ábdirazaaq had appointed.

Chart 2

Clan Distribution of Government, 21 March 1966

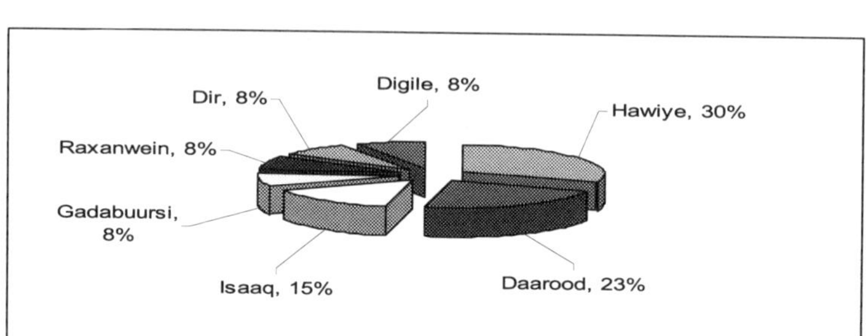

By this change of cabinet members, Ábdirazaaq wanted to solve the Hawiye dissatisfaction which inflame Hawiye-Daarood conflict over dominance. Thus for the first time in his role as Prime Minister, Ábdirazaaq gave greater representation in his cabinet to the Hawiye (30%) than the Daarood (23%). This time, however, he reduced the Isaaq representation in the cabinet to 2 ministers (15%) while in 1964 he appointed 3 (19%) ministers from this clan. The Rahanwein, the Digile, the Dir, and the Gadabuursi each had one minister (8%) each.

To accommodate these changes, Ábdirazaaq added four new cabinet posts, enlarging the size of the cabinet. He also replaced some ministers with new persons from the same clan. For instance, he replaced Ósmaan Mohamuud Ádde (Daarood, Mijeerteen), the Minister of Industry and Commerce, with Haaji Bashiir Ismaíil (Daarood, Mijeerteen). He also replaced Ismaíil Duáale Warsame (Isaaq, Habar Jélo), the Minister of Agriculture, with Sheekh Hassan Ábdilaahi Faarah (Isaaq, Habar Yoonis). Áwil Haaji Ábdilaahi (Isaaq, Habar Yoonis) resigned from his post, but no member of the Isaaq replaced him.

Thus Ábdirazaaq institutionalized Sharmaarke's practice of substituting one person with another of his same clan. This practice which gave priority to clan identity over merit also became the *modus operandi* in other levels of government. As we shall see, the Égaal administration from 1967-1969 and the military regime that ruled for twenty-one years followed the same practice.

Even today, nearly forty-two years after Ábdirazaaq premiership, the practice not only continues in Somalia and Somaliland but the ministries and major offices of government have turned into clan turfs where kinsmen of the minister expect of him to doll out the greatest services and perks as their exclusive right. They also hang around his office and its environs like their clan settlement and act in the manner of camel herders on the outlook for looters on the attack.

If Ábdirazaaq had avoided conflict with the Hawiye by giving them greater representation in his second cabinet, he could not avoid a formidable challenge from another quarter, this time from his former ally and clansman, Ábdirashiid Áli Sharmaarke, who established a coalition with Mohamed Haaji Ibraahim Égaal. The two former enemies have found a common target for their ire in the camp of President Aadan Ábdulle Ósmaan and Ábdirazaaq Haaji Hussein. They wanted to inflict on these men the political humiliation and isolation they had experienced while out of office.

But the revenge of Sharmaarke and Égaal took three years to unfold. After 1964, Sharmaarke moved out of the limelight and in late afternoons rode his old car to public cinemas with no visible sign of the Prime Minister that once attracted public attention and admiration. Égaal on his part retired to private life in his home, watching western movies, reading western novels, drowning his frustration with expensive and imported liquor. In desperate moments, especially when broke and isolated, he turned to the Qur'an for consolation and strength.

Yet the public image of political inactivity and withdrawal of the two men was deceptive. Behind the scene, they plotted, garnered support, and coordinated action. They focused their energy on the National Assembly which had the power to withdraw vote of confidence from the government and even replace the President. In time, the alliance of Sharmaarke and Égaal brought decisive inroad into the Assembly's loyalty to President Ósmaan and his camp.

The outcome of the Sharmaarke-Égaal alliance became obvious in the summer of 1966 when the government of Ábdirazaaq faced a stiff challenge in the National Assembly and among the SYL members on whose support its survival depended. Thus on June 26, 1966, the new cabinet Ábdirazaaq had appointed only three months earlier unanimously resigned in protest to laws passed by the Assembly. These were innocuous laws designed to enrage Ábdirazaaq and his cabinet. They had the intended effect when the cabinet resigned. President Aadan Ábdulle Ósmaan overruled the resignations. With the intervention of the President, the Assembly eventually reaffirmed the vote of confidence on the government. However, the conflict between the two camps resurfaced when the SYL leadership expelled 13 members of the SYL from the party.[6]

This expulsion solved one problem for the leaders of the SYL (i.e. the President and the Prime Minister) but created another. It removed the "troublemakers" from the party but it also reduced the margin (from 91 to 78 deputies) with which the leaders of the SYL dominated the Assembly. Worse, the 13 dismissed joined the camp of Ábdirashiid Áli Sharmaarke and his allies. Thus the conflict within the SYL and reorganization of its members swept from power not only Ábdirazaaq but also President Aadan Ábdulle Ósmaan himself.

The showdown came in the presidential elections of June 10, 1967 when Sharmaarke won in all three rounds of voting by members of the parliament, but failed to win a two-thirds majority of the 123 deputies in the first and second ballot. He won 63 and 67 votes respectively in the first and second round, in comparison to Ósmaan's 57 and 55 votes in the same two rounds. Sharmaarke won the contest when he secured 73 votes to Ósmaan's 50 votes in the third round.

In consequence, Ábdirashiid Áli Sharmaarke emerged victorious over his former boss, Aadan Ábdulle Ósmaan, and over his former ally, Ábdirazaaq Haaji Hussein who, like the President, was stripped of power and consigned to civilian status, reversing roles of victor and vanquished.

Égaal's Dance with Danger

Ábdirashiid Áli Sharmaarke carried out his swearing-in ceremony as President on 6 July 1967. Soon after becoming President, Sharmaarke named Mohamed Ibraahim Égaal the Prime Minister. But unknown to Sharmaarke and his colleagues, a plot to assassinate him on that day was in place. The plot failed because of unexpected glitch in the plans of the plotters. Unknown to him and to his colleagues, his rise to power also set in motion a highly secretive plot for military coup.

As we shall see in the next chapter, it is not only the plot on the day of his swearing-in ceremony that failed. Other assassination plots followed and also failed. Unfortunately, however, one plot to assassinate the President and the planned military coup succeeded two years and four months after Ábdirashiid Áli Sharmaarke ceremonially swore to serve as the President of a nation whose elite conflict escalated while public misery and insecurity intensified. Whether the men plotting the assassination and the military coup were separate men working independently or members the same team remains unclear. Still, we shall return to this tragic aspect of Somali history in subsequent chapters to suggest hypotheses of who was behind it and its long-term consequences for Somalis.

Of course, the new President and his allies had no prescience to know these concealed plots to snuff life and usurp power. Thus in the two and four months they wielded power, they behaved with the pomp and self-confidence of victors whose scheming behind the scene and luck had vindicated them. They also worked strenuously to ensure that power did not slip out of their grasp again, forcing them to the isolation and obscurity they had known in the past and to which they now consigned their foes. Returning to the limelight, they therefore set out not only to even the score with their enemies but also retain power by any means.

It was not only President Sharmaarke who was in peril. Without realizing, Égaal too danced with danger throughout his tenure as Prime Minister. The danger came from chiefly three sources. The first source was within the very camp with which Égaal was allied. Driven by personal ambition, he had thrown himself in the intense personal and clan conflicts of Somalia without garnering and mobilizing the support of his Somaliland constituency.

Not that his constituency would necessarily take up arms for his defense but, in the smoke-and-mirror dynamics of Somali politics, a man who appears cut off from his clan is most vulnerable while another surrounded by his kinsmen appears well-defended. Égaal did not only enter the den of his opponents who earlier had consigned him to political irrelevance and obscurity; he also took sides in their bitter feuds that in time led to assassination of the President and to the military coup—two sordid chapters in Somali history. Insiders in the deadly politics of Somalia would have taken more caution than this Somalilander who alone floated in perilous waters by his own steam and speed.

This was vintage Égaal who dumped his constituency when in power but came back to its fold when out of power. While the Prime

Minister, Égaal distanced himself from his Somaliland constituency and particularly the Isaaq to whom he belonged by clan affiliation and social perception. No doubt this talented politician and adept Machiavellian was capable of blazing a new trail on his own, exploiting his new coalition for his ends, the same way the other parties exploited him. Yet in this arrangement of power and allies, Égaal was alone and therefore like a sea turtle swimming with sharks without a protective shell or shield. For reasons we shall note later, the desire to win alone and deny the limelight to his kinsmen were some of Égaal's character flaws. On the occasion he warmed up to his kinsmen or generally his constituency, Égaal pursued self-interest by exploiting clan identity, like mobilizing votes for a political campaign or attacking political opponents.

The second source of danger was his abrupt abandonment of the Hawiye-Isaaq alliance he had formed with Sheek Áli Jumáale and his betrayal of the *Iririst* ideology the two men spearheaded to oppose Daarood hegemony. The anger of the Isaaq and the Hawiye who found hope in this new alliance and ideology but whom he betrayed might have peacefully ended his political career in the long-term, but more formidable opponents to him had carried out swifter and deadlier plans which unveiled in 1969 and thereafter.

The third source of danger was less obvious but most perilous. As we shall see later, Égaal quickly jumped into the superpower conflict on geopolitical dominance. Reversing the policy of confrontation and possibly armed conflict with Ethiopia, Kenya, and French-controlled Djibouti on territorial claims, Égaal started a policy of détente which relaxed strained relation with these countries. He also actively wooed the West, particularly the United States, while quietly distancing himself from the USSR to which his country had become a client state under the leadership of Sharmaarke when he was Prime Minister.

Not only did he dismiss General Mohamed Abshir Muuse, the influential Commander of the police, but also rumor circulated that Égaal entertained plans to dismiss General Mohamed Siyaad Barre, the Commander of the armed forces which the USSR trained and armed. For this and sundry other grudges, his boss Sharmaarke paid the ultimate price six days before the military coup while Égaal suffered twelve years of solitary confinement after the coup. The resulting trauma stayed with him for those years, forcing him to alternate between the consolation of the Great Book and the amnesia of Black Label until his death in 2002.

These three dangers which Égaal activated as Prime Minister did not emerge quickly or simultaneously. They evolved gradually to allow Égaal and Sharmaarke to wield their power as they saw fit, taking revenge on their foes and rewarding their allies. Aadan Ábdulle Ósmaan graciously left the Presidency and retired to private life without the anger or rancor characteristic of Somali politicians. But his allies, Ábdirazaaq Haaji Hussein and General Mohamed Abshir, remained active opponents of Sharmaarke and Égaal, each according to their career and style.

Ábdirazaaq formed his own opposition party and continued political life as the most vocal and strident opponent of the two men. General Mohamed Abshir lost his luster and power after his two foes dismissed him from his powerful post as Commander of the Police. Of course, that was not the end of Mohamed Abshir or the political drama that was to unfold in subsequent years. The conflict and behind-the-scene plots continued while the politics of appointing ministers and dismissing others followed the usual path and pathos of Somali politics.

The victors acted with arrogance and feeling of invincibility; the vanquished nursed wounded pride and plotted for revenge; the public too anxiously awaited the next moves of their leaders and the dark cloud hovering over the nation. Although none knew in advance how events would unfold, most people had a vague premonition of something drastic and tragic was on the offing. Even the plotters did not know whether their plans would succeed, yet there was an air of uncertainty and anxiety as the drama was building to a climax after Sharmaarke and Égaal rose to power. But how did the two men behave at the peak of their power while the assassination and coup plots proceeded?

Though Sharmaarke retreated to the office and chores of the Presidency, Égaal took the political limelight of the executive Prime Minister, assuming leadership of the government with the pomp and ostentatious display characteristic of him when in power. His exercised his power for the first time as Prime Minister when he selected a list of cabinet members and presented the list to the President and the National Assembly. An active lobbyist for his causes, his list was soon approved by the President and National Assembly, no doubt after extending the usual consultation and monetary inducement such rituals involve and Égaal knew too well.

Égaal lobbied to increase the size of the cabinet from 15 to 17 ministers. The President and the National Assembly granted his wish.

Table 3 shows the list of cabinet ministers Égaal cabinet.

Table 3

The Government Appointed by Égaal
July 21, 1967

Name	**Post**	**Clan**	**Sub-Clan**
Áli Álio Mohamed	Minister of Agriculture	Rahawein	Elai
Haaji Yuusuf Imaan Guuleed	Minister of Defense	Isaaq	Habar Yoonis
Aadan Isaaq Ahmed	Minister of Education	Gadabuursi	Makaahiil
Haaji Faarax Áli Úmar	Minister of Finance	Hawiye	Habar Gidir
Áli Mohamed Ósooble	Minister of Health & Labor	Hawiye	Murasade
Mohamed Áli Daár	Minister of Industry & Commerce	Daarood	Mijeerteen
Hassan Haaji Úmar Amel	Minister of Information	Daarood	Dhulbahante
Yaasiin Nuur Hassan	Minister of Interior	Daarood	Mijeerteen
Aadan Shire Jaamá	Minister of Justice & Religious Aff.	Daarood	Mareehaan
Ábdulaahi Mohamed Qablan	Minister of National Planning	Daarood	Warsangeli
Mahamuud Ábdi Nuur "Juje"	Minister of Public Works	Dir	Gaadsan
Ismaíil Duáalle Warsame	Min. State/Mineral Res. & Fishing	Isaaq	Habar Jélo
Ábdulaahi Giire Duáalle	Min.of State/Rural Development	Isaaq	Habar Awal
Mohamed Sh. Yuusuf "Derbi"	Minister of State/Somali Affairs	Daarood	Ogaadeen
Áli Mohamed Hirave	Min. of State/Coun. of Presidency	Hawiye	Abgaal
Áli Úmar Sheego	Min. of State/Foreign Affairs	Digile	Tunni
Hareed Faarax Nuur	Min. of State/Transport & Com.	Hawiye	Jajeele

Chart 5 presents the clan distribution of the cabinet.

Chart 3

Clan Distribution of Ministers under Égaal, July 21, 1967

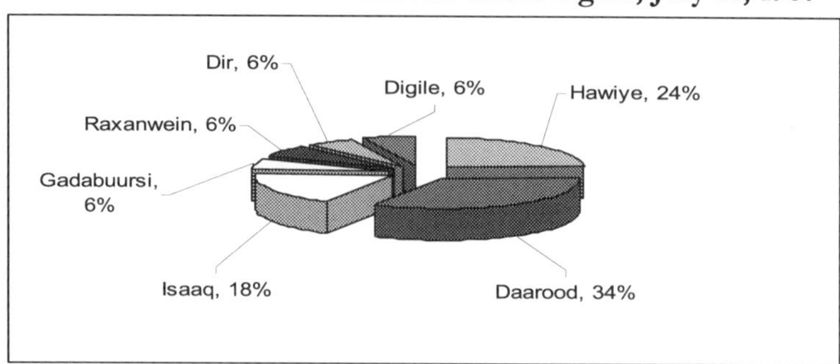

Like the leaders preceding and following him, Égaal's first cabinet permits us to glean into his political tactics and personal attributes.

The Daarood and the Hawiye, who in Ábdirazaaq's last cabinet had obtained 23% and 30% respectively, received 6 (34%) and 4 (24%) ministers in Égaal's first cabinet. Égaal thus reaffirmed Daarood dominance in the cabinet which Ábdirazaaq had reversed under pressure in his third ministerial appointments. This time, however, a member of the Daarood also occupied the Presidency, giving the Daarood decisive advantage at all levels. Breaching the implicit rule to keep clan balance between the Hawiye and Daarood was therefore most prominent under Égaal's government.

In this first cabinet he had formed, Égaal increased the number of Isaaq ministers from 2 (15%) to 3 (18%) ministers, but the increase was minimal and symbolic, repeating Ábdirazaaq's second ministerial appointment. It showed that Égaal was not as committed to his constituency as were his peers from Somalia. Neither did he change the proportion that Ábdirazaaq gave to other clans: He gave the he Rahanwein, the Gadabuursi, the Dir, and the Digile one (6%) ministers each.

Though he increased the representation of the Daarood, Égaal in fact had no personal preference for them. A Machiavellian politician, his friends were those who advance his interests and his foes were those who frustrated them. Giving the Daarood dominance in the cabinet demonstrated Égaal's desire to appease his two Daarood colleagues, President Ábdirashiid Áli Sharmaarke and Yaasiin Nuur Hassan, the powerful Minister of Interior and a key bulwark to Ábdirazaaq whom they shared clan affinity at the level of sub-clan and therefore split Ábdirazaaq's potential supporters.

To accommodate egoistic needs and clan demands, Égaal appointed five ministers of state, all of them enlarging the prestige and power of the Prime Minister. In addition, Égaal did not appoint anyone as Minister of Foreign Affairs but kept that role for himself saying, "I thought it best to keep this responsibility for myself. I will have the assistance of my colleague Áli Úmar Sheego as Minister of State of Foreign Affairs."[7]

Though his explanation was unclear, Égaal revealed for the first time his passion to hold on to the post of Foreign Minister. Even as President of Somalialnd from 1993-2002, Égaal continued to enlarge his cabinet and keep the Ministry of Foreign Affairs to himself. On the occasion he appointed someone to this post, the Minister of Foreign

Affairs was from a minority clan who presumably presented no threat to his power. Égaal seldom trusted his appointee to foreign affairs. He believed that an independent person with a large clan constituency could use the ministry and his foreign contacts against him. Besides, Égaal believed that he knew international affairs better than any Somali on earth. His over-confidence in this regard nearly pushed him to madness when, as President of Somaliland in the early nineteen-nineties, the international community ignored his letter-writing campaigns to win recognition for the breakaway republic.

As a person, Égaal could be a very charming and generous person. However, he distributed his charm and money always with a political scheme in mind. The only child of a wealthy family, he grew up highly pampered and protected, always with enough money in his pocket to purchase friends and punish foes. Unlike most Somali politicians who hoard ill-gotten money for its sake, Égaal used money almost exclusively for political ends. By his own admission, he spent much of his inheritance to promote his political ambition and dallying of youth.[8]

No only did Égaal lavish charm and money to whoever advanced his interests, he also was vindictive to those who offended him—not an infrequent event in politics anywhere and most treacherously so in Somali politics where competition for power is often vicious and desperate because the elite believe that there is no other arena of life where one can achieve success and contentment except by controlling people and the public purse. Most members of the elite also did not acquire a profession (as in accounting, engineering, health services, and the like) that would provide them alternative to politics. In fact, many had set their mind at a tender age on politics because they observed that power is the royal road to wealth and prestige. Only in adulthood do they discover its pathos and perils.

Égaal was also a highly intelligent and articulate man. He spoke glibly in private and public, recruiting to his cause many who otherwise would oppose or sneer at it if they did not persuade them. He also had the biting words with which he disparaged and derided his opponents. Yet despite his intelligence, he judged people by sheer intuition and unverified rumor. Once he concluded that an individual was his opponent, he retaliated without the restraint of conscience or the prudence of verifying rumor. The only saving grace in his impulsive conclusion and action was his frankness in telling the victim what perception or whose tattletale drove him to act in the cruel way he did. Often, however, this admission and clarification, presented with grin of self-satisfaction, came too late for the puzzled but stung victim.

It did not matter for Égaal whether or not the victim deserved the punishment; what mattered was how the person handled the abuse thereafter. Égaal was warm and generous if the person submitted to the show of power, but cold and vindictive if the victim seemed to hold grudge. Even without suspicion or rumor provoking his attack, Égaal used this tactic as part of his honed stratagem to test the independence and malleability of persons he considered for official appointment. If the person rolled with the punches, showing no resistance of holding no grudge, he extended confidence and trust in him. If on the other hand the person responded in kind or showed resentment, he found a rebellious streak in him and therefore kept him at a distance, but followed his whereabouts and activities.

In short, like other Somali leaders, Égaal valued loyalty to him more than the person's capability or public honesty. Often, he appointed cronies with ill-repute because they knew that they would not attain the position and power he bestowed upon and therefore they did his bidding and remained loyal to him. Dictatorship, in both its civilian and military form, not corrupts the dictator but he in turn corrupts those around him. They make sure that those with integrity have their hands and character tained because the need the protection of the leader against legal action, they are alienated from the people, and they make "the old man" look good.

Power by its nature changes people, giving the holder the illusion of being invincible and his place at the top assured in the future. Égaal was by no means an exception. But the change of character and style he revealed was all his own. In power, he acted like a king who at last found the throne that he was his natural and social right so long as he used his power and money effectively. And while hoisted on the throne, he distanced himself from relatives, including his children. With power, he exuded authority and arrogance. He was impetuous and impatient. Without power, he was humble and patient, seeking and accepting the help of kinsmen and acquaintances alike.

His greatest dread, it seems, was the prospect of another kid in "the family" or clan constituency emerging to challenge him for the national pedestal (and as a child maternal lap) that was his natural place and exclusive right. In particular, he disliked clan members who showed political promise and anyone with good access to foreigners, unless such individuals came under his control and corrupting influence. By direct and indirect means, he made sure that younger and potential leader in his clan were either politically eliminated or emasculated. Égaal had a knack for orchestrating *af-miinshaars* (men whose words cut like saw) he hired for character assassination of his opponents.

On May 21, 1969 Égaal reorganized his second cabinet. He added two new ministerial positions raising his 1969 cabinet to 19 ministers, the largest cabinet since independence. At the time, this number of ministerial appointments was considered too many while in subsequent decades the number steadily increased. Ministries and their deputies today exceed sixty. Their inflation is in inverse relation to the growth of the economy and political stability.

Table 4 presents the composition of Égaal's cabinet of 1969.

Table 4

The Government Appointed by Égaal
21 May 1969

Name	**Post**	**Clan**	**Sub-Clan**
Ábdulaahi Mohamed Hired	Min. of Agriculture	Isaaq	Habar Yoonis
Áli Alio Mohamed	Min. of Communication	Rahawein	Elai
Hilowle Moálin Mohamed	Min. of Defense	Daarood	Ogaadeen
Aadan Isaaq Ahmed	Min. of Education	Gadabursi	Makaahiil
Sufi Úmar Mohamed	Min. of Finance	Digile	Geledi
Mohamed Sh. Mohamed Daahir	Min. of Health & Labor	Rahawein	Yantar
Ábdulaahi Íise Mohamuud	Min. of Industry & Commerce	Hawiye	Habar Gidir
Ismaíil Jumáalle Óssoble	Min. of Information	Hawiye	Abgaal
Yaasiin Nuur Hassan	Min. of Interior	Daarood	Mijeerteen
Aadan Shire Jaamá	Min. of Justice	Daarood	Mijeerteen
Hirsi Bulhan Faarax	Min. of Livestock	Daarood	Mijeerteen
Haaji Muuse Samatar	Min. of Mining	Daarood	Mijeerteen
Michael Mariano	Min. of National Planning	Isaaq	Habar Jélo
Jaamá Gaanni Ahmed	Min. of Public Works	Daarood	Dhulbahante
Ábdulaahi Giire Duáale	Min. of Rural Dev. & Self-Help	Isaaq	Habar Awal
Élmi Ahmed Duáale	Min. of State for Foreign Affairs	Hawiye	Hawaadle
Haaji Ábdulaahi Sh. Ibraahim	Min. of Religious Affairs	Isaaq	Tol Jélle
Hareed Faarax Nuur	Min. of State for Somali Affairs	Hawiye	Jajeele
Ósmaan Ahmed Rooble	Min. of State/Council of Presidency	Hawiye	Abgaal

Chart 4 presents the clan distribution of the cabinet.

Chart 4
Clan Distribution of Ministers under Égaal
21 May 1969

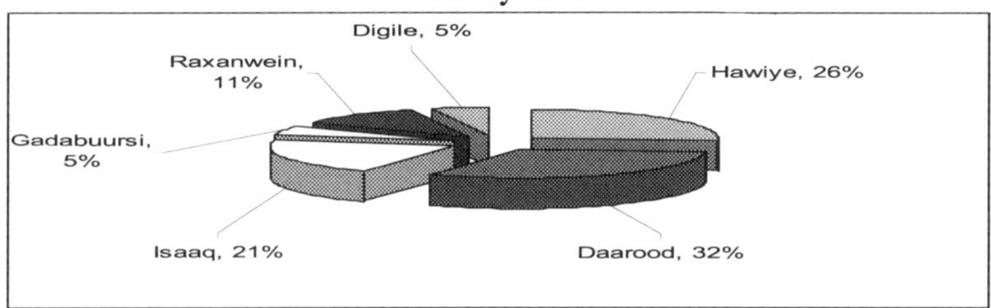

As shown in Chart 4, Égaal again gave 6 Ministers (32%) to the Daarood while he appointed 5 Hawiye Ministers (26%), 4 Isaaq Ministers (21%), 2 Rahanwein Ministers (11%), one Digil Minister (5%), and one Gadabuursi Minister (5%).

Égaal's abiding desire to monopolize foreign relations or appoint least threatening cronies for foreign relations was not peculiar to him. All Somali leaders consider the ministerial posts of finance and foreign relations as the most important posts to which they assign loyal cronies who also set aside for them a lion's share of the loot from the public treasury and foreign aid. The Governor of the Bank and the Managers of the Ports are also important for the same reason. Whom they appoint to Ministries of Interior and Defense are also significant because these posts keep the population and competitors in check.

As we shall see later, President Mohamed Siyaad Barre revealed the same inclination when he appointed his unqualified and inept half-brother to become the longest reigning Foreign Minister in Somali history since independence. The same man also served as the Minister of Finance for several years when Somali politics moved from clan hegemony to oligarchy and the 'rule of the family.' Ministries like those of health, education, agriculture, and industry that would provide public service and stimulate the economy are often pushed to low priority in the political agenda. Ministries like those of religion and culture that would rehabilitate the society's moral confusion and identity crisis are always lowest in the totem pole.

If previous Prime Ministers were marred by disappointments, Égaal tenure as Prime Minister pushed their flaws to extremes. Disappointment with his government was most intense for another reason—people expected better from the Sharmaarke-Égaal coalition.

Because this coalition was the first in the short history of the republic that brought into alliance two men—one from Somalia, the other from Somaliland—people expected economic and political reforms, including solution to the drifting apart of the two former colonies since the *de facto* union of 1960. The country desperately needed reforms to the growing official malfeasance, mass misery, and dependence on foreign aid. It also needed freedom from the suffocating clutch of the *Klan*, whose corrosive feuds, corruption, and nepotism preoccupied the leaders and the led alike.

However, reform was in not in the political agenda of Sharmaarke and Égaal; hence, they attempted no reforms, as did Ábdirazaaq Haaji Hussein. Neither did they try to solve the chronic problems simmering in the relation between Somalia and Somaliland. On the contrary, the economic and political conditions of the country worsened as the two men gave priority to fighting their foes and ensuring perpetuation of their reign by use of money and if necessary intimidation. Somaliland and Somalia also continued to drift apart.

Ábdilaahi Suldaan (Timaádde) recited a long poem of the Geeraar genre that expressed the hope for reform in government and warned Égaal about the perils of continued corruption. The following is an excerpt:

These people consigned to rags...
Enduring rain without shelter
From the meager livestock they herd...
Paying taxes from black-headed lamb
The one shilling they gain [in profit]
The [official] looted and wasted
Erecting for himself high-rise building.
And so long as he is not apprehended
No verdicts issued quickly [against him]
Égaal, [the land} will never be stable.[9]

Neither Sharmaarke nor Égaal heeded the warnings that, if they took to heart, would have saved them and their regime. However, they ignored these warnings and failed to bring about the needed reforms. Most of all, Égaal's policies brought the greatest let down for the people of Somaliland whose independence he had negotiated away as leader of the delegation sent to Mogadishu to consummate union with

Somalia. As a result, relations between the Somalia ("the South) and Somaliland (the "North") further degenerated in Égaal's watch

It was not Somaliland alone that suffered under the reign of Sharmaarke and Égaal. The rest of the country did not fair better. Égaal's *laissez-faire* policies gave free reign to corruption and nepotism as well as to vote-rigging and get-rich-quick schemes through government contracts. The appointment of Yaasiin Nuur Hassan to the key post of Interior Minister ensnared him to become a tool of the Mijeerteen against other clans, particularly the Hawiye. Yaasiin Nuur Hassan was an influential Mijeerteen, and a skillful schemer who was among the first beneficiaries of government largesse. Using his power, he enlarged his thriving business concerns in the republic and extended it to East and Southern Africa. In addition, people believed that Yaasiin was the covert Prime Minister while Égaal held the post symbolically.

One thing is however certain: Yaasiin who was personally close to President Sharmaarke made clan the primary criterion for reward and punishment in the conduct of government, particularly regarding monetary policies and disbursement. For this reason, all types of opportunists, including the Commander of the Armed Forces, General Mohamed Siyaad Barre, visited Yaasiin's office and home, convinced that the Interior Minister was the primary arbiter of power in the nation. Often where the crafty and the crowds flock is the seat of power and the place where money is disbursed in the form of cash, contracts, checks, and personal letters to the Bank.

Another thing is also certain: Every smart fox finds another that outsmarts it, the same way every sucker finds a less wary and less skilled sucker to exploit. The crafty Mohamed Siyaad Barre used to visit Yaasiin's at home and on occasions swing Yaasiin on a hammock while they talked. It is not clear if Mohamed Siyaad Barre also sang him lullaby as if Yaasiin were his infant son. But, as we shall see later, the Commander of the Armed Forces had something else in mind while he carried out this fatherly chore. The Minister of Interior later landed in one of the Commanders jails; released from prison, he talked on his death bed about the confounding tricks the General had used to ensnare him with Byzantine-like subterfuge and flattery.

Fake Democratic Elections

Sharmaarke and Égaal assured their victory in the parliamentary elections of 1969. To discourage splintering of parties and to keep the dominance of the SYL, Mohamed Ibraahim Égaal, the Prime Minister, and Yaasiin Nuur Hassan, the Interior Minister, introduced an amendment for proportional representation. Because their supporters dominated the Assembly, the amendment passed.

The amendment established an "electoral quotient." It was a convenient formula dividing the number of votes cast in a district by the number of seats allocated to that district. Any candidate whose votes were below the quotient did not obtain a seat in parliament. By this arrangement, Sharmaarke and Égaal assured their victory, but fate too had its own concealed plans.

As it turned out, the SYL won 74 seats and the SNC won 11 seats. Together, the two parties won an overwhelming majority of 85 seats. To this day, many bitterly remember the system of "quotients" which denied them their place in the parliament. Even more disturbing was the way votes tallied using questionable tactics.[10]

That the promises of independence had failed were clear from the first nine years and fully evident after the 1969 election. Democracy in Somali society was troubled from the beginning. The economy was in shambles and public misery rampant. Personal ambition for power among the elite superseded national interest. Rule of the *Klan* took precedence over public participation in politics. While they sang the virtues of "anti-tribalism", the ruling elite exploited clan and clannism to rally support when this served their interest. Often, they simultaneously pontificated on nationalism while rallying kinsmen to promote personal and class (i.e., *Klan*) interests.

This hypocrisy of the ruling elite, stated before independence, had become the norm in Somali politics which rested on Polly tricks. The public who put their trust on the elite did not know what to believe. Talk of nationalism fired their passion and imagination beyond the humdrum of poverty and drudgery of everyday life. Talk of clan conflict instigated by conflict within the *Klan* played on their traditional fears, identity, and loyalty. Kinship with others and paranoia about them co-existed. The constant move back and forth between the high emotions of nationalism to the cold freeze of clan feuds made hypocrisy adaptive, neurosis inescapable. In time, the hypocrisy of the *Klan* grew into a sub-culture; their neurosis also enlarged into a social neurosis that later grew to national psychosis.

Sharmaarke and Égaal raised the politics of subterfuge, corruption, and vote rigging to a level Niccoló Machiavelli would probably consider a welcome development in a far off African country that knew independence and state management for only nine years. However, he might have urged these African princes of doom that they better take caution in playing the deadly a game at which they are novice but had led to the demise of more seasoned monarchs with long family histories of usurping and defending their power.

Karl Marx too would also lament the deepening suffering of the masses easily duped and dismayed by a new breed of robber barons. Bastards of two systems—one colonial, the other clan—they took the worst of each and turned them into the politics of despair. Convinced that pre-capitalist societies are not ready for revolution, he might have advised that the bastards of two systems and their victims should not take themselves seriously, or view their fate optimistically, as long as *work* and *production* are neither their vocation nor avocation.

Of course, ordinary Somalis did not wait for Machiavelli or Marx to make sense of their plight. They were the experts of their experience even when their leaders denied them the right of being its primary authors. Knowledge of contributions to political thought by Machiavelli and Marx would no doubt help, but ordinary Somalis were not at a lost to articulate their suffering under the misrule of their leaders.

For instance, the following poem captures the public frustration during the civilian rule, particularly with regard to ministers who campaigned by mobilizing the clan but did little for its members.

As before, in roasting Makale
and under the sun I idly waste away
As before, morsels cooked in pots
and trivial amounts I eat
As before, education I lack
and centers of religious teaching...
It's him who pursues his interest
as he manages nothing [for the public]
What else, tell me, has he done for me
the minister I had elected? [11]

Sharmaarke, Égaal, and the ruling civilian elite before them ignored these cries of pain. They continued their feuds and their shift of alliance in pursuit of personal power and wealth. But the time of harvesting the seeds they sowed was near; the monsters they bred were also ready to flex their muscles and test their teeth.

Brash and overconfident, they did not realize that their illusion of invincibility and permanence had an expiry date. Had they heeded the warnings of darker days to come, they might have avoided assassination in the case Sharmaarke and enduring trauma with regard to Égaal.

What then were harbingers of the darker days ahead?

5

DARKER DAYS AHEAD

Dhubuq-dhubuqda hore dhabano-hays dambay leedahay.
Overconfidence at the beginning brings befuddlement at the end.
—Somali Proverb

The foremost challenge that faced the elite who inherited the colonial state was to substantiate the freedom that formal independence implied. The second was to consolidate the unity of Somalia and Somaliland that came about spontaneously as the first step toward Pan-Somali Unity. The third was to improve the economic and social life of citizens whose poverty, morbidity, and mortality were and continue be among the highest in the world.

Independence and the dream of Somali unity were embraced by all Somalis with joy and fanfare. Yet both entailed awesome responsibilities for the Somali elite who, by an accident of history, were the only credible leaders available at the time and whom their people as well as the colonialists anointed to take over power. The traditional leaders were long ago overshadowed presumably because the new elite acquired the requisite education to govern and dispense justice for the population that trusted them. However, the ruling elite failed to rise to these challenges because they understood neither the primary goal of *de-colonization* nor the responsibilities thrust upon them.

As the preceding chapter argued, the ruling elite failed to establish a viable state because they could not find common vision and cooperation with one another. Caught in incessant competition among themselves, they put material self-interest and personal power above the common good. They also ignored hints of darker days to come, in the end setting the stage for the division, destruction, and death constituting the wretched existence of Somalis today.

What then were the harbingers of darker days ahead? The first is the erosion of the union of Somaliland and Somalia that was lynchpin for the Pan-Somali dream; the second was the rise of *Klannism* and clan hegemony; the third was the elite's resort to violence in competition for power. This chapter outlines how these problems began while subsequent chapters elaborate their evolution and consequences.

Death of the Dream

Independence of Somaliland and Somalia in 1960 was one of the most momentous events in Somali history. Achieving spontaneous unity between Somalia and Somaliland was another. This unity of the two former colonies provided concrete proof that all Somalis can and must unite, despite different colonial experience, legacies, and administrative systems. For the dream to be fully realized, it was believed, the remaining three colonies had to be incorporated into the new Somali Republic so that all Somalis would equally share the same state, the same flag, and the same destiny. Thus the independence of the two formers colonies and their spontaneous union intensified Somali commitment substantiate the dream, thereby reversing domination and partition by foreign powers, near and distant.

Somaliland became independent on June 26, 1960. Five days later, on July 1, 1960, Somalia also became independent and unity of the two former colonies took place on the same day. Because these two historic events—independence and unity—took place spontaneously on about the same dates, they were for years fused in the Somali mind as twin victories, each inseparable from the other, each giving meaning to the other. While Somaliland's day of independence was annually commemorated on June 26, Somalia's independence and the day of unity were jointly celebrated on July 1. The fusion of independence and union was therefore most obvious on July 1.

However, the meaning of these events changed in the last three decades. Today, the people of Somaliland commemorate only June 26, but not July 1. Following their unilateral declaration of independence in 1991, they no longer officially commemorate July 1. This demonstrates not only the dissolution of the union but also erosion of shared belief in common destiny. On the other hand, the people of Somalia continue to celebrate July 1 as the day of independence and unity, even though no viable state exists and the unity of the two territories had ended in 1991, following Somaliland's UDI.

The commemoration of one date and not the other in Somaliland is not a small matter considering Somali aspirations in the past because it shows a sea change in the thought and emotion of Somalilanders who used to pride themselves as pioneers of Somali unity—the ones who first became independent and pressed for unity without condition. These same people today believe that July 1 is a date of no concern or consequence to them. If at all, they remember it as the day of error when they abandoned their independence in pursuit of an illusion that took years of violent struggle to retrieve and reclaim the independence they gave up for unity. What caused this drastic reversal of thought and emotion leading to the unilateral declaration of independence? Who is responsible for it? And what are its consequences?

When we examine the Somali past, we discover that there was indeed more to the union of Somaliland and Somalia than the merging of two former colonies. Firstly, the union of these two former colonies represented the first step toward the greater dream of enlarging freedom and unity by incorporating the Somali territories in Ethiopia, Kenya, and Djibouti into the new Somali Republic. Secondly, the dream of Pan-Somali unity served essential psychological and social functions for Somalis everywhere. The dream gave Somalis something bigger and better than the daily and grinding travails they had known, living in poverty in urban anonymity and rural desolation.[1]

For at least the two decades between1960-1980, the dream of unity infused Somalis with hope and pride in a pan-Somali nation nested in the mind but never objectively existent prior to or after independence. This irredentist nation in the mind was symbolized by a light blue flag at the center of which was a white five-pointed star, each point of the star representing the five Somali territories the colonial rulers had partitioned. The flag represented not only freedom and fraternity of all Somalis but also symbolized share identity and destiny.

Even when the promises of independence had failed to materialize, the dream of Pan-Somali Unity continued to hold together people who in the past had no political creed or conviction outside the clan. It rallied them for goals more animating and larger than the barren and parochial pursuits they had known for centuries. It also enabled them to endure stubborn if not deepening poverty and oppression, imbuing them with confidence that emancipation and prosperity would come when all Somalis are free and united.

In addition, Somalis who by culture and habit are not given to delay of gratification and sacrifice for the intangible, except faith, found in the dream of Pan-Somali Unity a welling reservoir of hope, the commitment to sacrifice for an idea, and bullheaded persistence against the odds to unite. Hence Somali people who previously would die for nothing except for defense of the family or the clan have after independence rallied for the Pan-Somali Unity in both war and peace. The 1977-78 war with Ethiopia to which we shall return in subsequent chapters presents the best example of this mass mobilization and sacrifice.

Thus the survival and sustaining value of dreams should not be underestimated. Dreams are essential to living. In their nocturnal form, they protect sleep that refreshes the mind and body; they also help us solve problems eluding comprehension and resolution in normal consciousness. In their political and social form, they give us something we can enthusiastically look forward to, fight for with the energizing camaraderie of others, and endure daily misery that with dreams can torment us. In short, dreams are antidote to despair. When they die, living too turns dreary, dull, and depressing, thereby inviting death that assails us in its physical, social, or psychological forms.

That is why the crash of Pan-Somali Unity combined with the crushing disappointments of independence brought a chain of successive collapses in Somali society and psyche of its members. For nearly two decades, Somalis were trying to pick up the pieces driven not by an alternative dream but sheer instinct of survival. That is also why today many Somalis turn to the assuring certitude of faith or the clarion call of the clan for escape and refuge, allowing other ambitious actors to exploit broken and exhausted souls for political ends.

As we shall in this chapter, the drifting apart of Somaliland and Somaliland began soon after union and this gradual drift was the first harbinger of the coming death of the Pan-Somali dream. That the ruling civilian elite could not govern justly the two spontaneously united territories should have brought doubts on how they would firstly free three Somalis territories from formidable powers and, in the event they freed them, how they would govern justly a far larger territory and population than the two former colonies they already misgoverned.

However, these doubts did not emerge among the ruling elite who are not given to analysis or reflection. Nor did the public enchanted with the unity of all Somalis want to part with a dream that gave them a hallucinated ray of hope in the dark caves of their existence, convinced that impediments to the dream would somehow clear away in due course when the right leaders emerge or Somalis garner their might. Dreams of this type that have mythic quality have enduring power even when objective facts contradict them. So long as they serve psychosocial function in the life of individuals and the groups, they continue to live until suffering exceeds intolerable threshold.

Thus the union of Somaliland and Somalia continued for at least three decades, although the drift between the two former colonies had begun soon after independence. The repeated failure of the ruling elite to heed warnings or their failure to heal the growing rift was characteristic of the elite's inattention to the common good and obsession with personal ambition promoting clan hegemony. The eventual consequence of this inattention and obsession for personal power is the collapse of the state on January 26, 1991 and the unilateral declaration of independence of Somaliland four months later.

Underlying the collapse of the state and end of the union was the collapse of a dream that bound people together and encouraged them to look forward to a future of fraternity and freedom. Efforts to restore peace and recreate the state in Somalia did not succeed during the past eighteen years precisely because there is no substitute dream to hold it together and the old elite is replaced by another more hungry for personal power and committed to clan hegemony.

Start of the Drift

The passion for Somali unity found new stimulus between 1941-49 when four of the partitioned Somali territories (excluding only the French colony) came under British Military Administration, following defeat of Italy and its withdrawal from Somalia and Somaliland.[1] This period of unification under one colonial power had encouraged the growth of Pan-Somali-Unity. It also found new momentum when in 1946 Ernest Bevin, the British Foreign Secretary, appealed to the three allied powers (USA, USSR, and France) to keep Somalis under one colonial rule in order to allow them free mobility they need for their nomadic existence.

The three powers rejected the proposal because it implied British trusteeship that would enlarge Britain's sphere of influence in the Horn of Africa. When colonial rulers again repartitioned Somalis, the Somali Youth League in particular continued advocacy for Pan-Somali-Unity. For this reason, the SYL with headquarters in Mogadishu opened branches outside the Italian colony in order reached out to Somalis in other territories. Its popular motto was *Soomaaliiya hanoolaato!—Long Live Somalia!* For them, unity meant the expansion of *Somalia* by incorporating into it other Somali territories.

Somalia historically referred to the territory ruled by Italy. Somalis inhabiting outside the Italian colony mistakenly interpreted the motto as *Soomaali hanoolaato! – Long live Somalis!*—without implying what the name of the united entity would. They assumed that it could be called Somalia, Somaliland, or any other name negotiated by the parties forming union under one state and flag. The difference in semantics and assumption was an important hint of problems that would subsequently arise, though the leaders of Somalia and Somaliland had considered the difference a minor if not irrelevant problem.

The leaders of the former Italian colony also took for granted that the SYL, the largest party in that territory, would continue to spearhead unity and maintain dominant position in a *united Somalia.* After the union, the territories where formally called the Somali Republic, not Republic of Somalia, suggesting a consequence of behind-the-scene negotiation that had taken place between representatives of Somalia and Somaliland before July 1, 1960. Nonetheless, the *Somalia* in the mind of the ruling elite of the former Italian colony and their anticipated dominance of the SYL became reality after on July 1, 1960 when the two territories united. Still, these early hints of problems did not evoke suspicion in Somaliland because disagreement on what seemed merely semantics was out of favor among its elite and public. And if anyone was troubled by these early hints, none expressed his worries in public or on record.

The monopolistic tendencies of Somalia's elite came to the fore as soon as the two territories united. It is then that Pan-Somali-Unity translated into G*reater Unity of Somalia* or simply *Greater Somalia.* Later, the Somali territory under Ethiopian rule came to be called *Western Somalia*, although the movement established to remove Ethiopian rule of this region was formally called the Western Somali Liberation Front (WSLF). To this day, the most enlightened persons from Somalia equate *Somaliness* with *Somalia* and interpret rejection of that label as renunciation of Somali identity, as if the name *Somalia* has intrinsic and unquestionable value over Somaliland, Puntland, or Republic of Djibouti. In reality, what is in a name when the people whom it is supposed to identiy have no meeting of minds and hearts on politics?

The association of Somali sovereignty with Somalia alone also concealed another ominously constricted meaning—that Somali unity referred mostly to the unity of one or two clans dispersed in different colonial territories, not a unity of all Somalis. It took more than a decade before this constricted and distortion meaning of Somali unity became obvious. It is not only the clan policies of the Somali state that unveiled the constricted and distorted meaning of Somali unity. A surfeit of so-called liberation movements that defended the tyrannically regime as expression of clan loyalty also turned their guns on other Somalis, indiscriminately harassing and looting them.

Somaliland's elite too had contributed to the false start. Unprepared and divided, they entered into the union hastily, negotiated poorly, and gambled on the future of their people. The National United Front (NUF) led by Michael Mariano advocated for delay of unity for at least six months until independent Somaliland achieved internal development and attained strong negotiating position ensuring equality with Somalia. As we have seen in Chapter 3, Michael Mariano was not adversely disposed to Somalia since he was one of the early advocates for its independence. His party's concern was to avoid a blind rush to a union in which Somaliland was ill-prepared, considering that Somalia had undergone ten years (1950-1960) of UN Trusteeship which prepared it for independence. He wanted Somaliland to develop its institutions and manpower before it entered into union with Somalia.

The Somali National League (SNL) led by Mohamed Ibraahim Égaal at first agreed to the postponement of unity advocated by the NUF. It is not only the NUF and the leaders of the SNL that advocated for postponement of union with Somalia. According to Úmar Árte Qaalib, the leaders SYL too had suggested postponement of union for their own reasons. When these leaders of Somalia saw that nothing would dissuade Somalianders from a blind rush to union, they also suggested that they at lease present their conditions for union. These early thoughts on delay of the union and at least setting clear conditions for it fell by the way side when the majority of SNL members and the United Somali Party (USP), the latter formed of non-Isaaq members, pushed for union without condition.

The Somaliland public insisted on unity without condition because they were convinced that pan-Somali would was boon for Somalis everywhere and a solution to the specific problem of the Haud and Reserved Areas transferred by Britain to Ethiopia in 1954. The NUF and SNL leaders buckled in to the public pressure and rushed into the union against their better judgment. None of the elite wanted the label of anti-Somali nationalist—a most damaging label at the time. Hence all advocated for union without condition. Michael Mariano who had the additional burden of being the only Christian leader in a conservative Muslim society and Égaal who did not want lose the support of his party also joined the herd, thereby giving up what they believed to be the best interest of their people.

Their first disappointment came when President Aadan Ábdulle Ósmaan nominated Ábdirashiid Áli Sharmaarke for Prime Minister. They expected that Somalilanders would obtain the post to ensure fair share of power. But the leaders of Somalia saw it differently. Engrossed with the Hawiye-Daarood competition and with their personal power, they focused attention on finding clan balance between these two clans and apportioning key posts among themselves. For them, the union of Somaliland with Somalia was a complicating and even inconvenient factor which they sought to manage by incorporating it into the Hawiye-Daarood competition for power instead of considering it a separate problem deserving equal consideration or weight.

The Somaliland politicians thought differently. After conceding to Somalia the presidency, the commanders of the armed forces and the police, greater representation in parliament, and the capital city, they expected to obtain the post of Prime Minister, with Mohamed Ibraahim Égaal as its primary candidate. That President Ósmaan appointed Ábdirashiid disappointed them and angered Égaal—a man who until then played a critical role in the politics of Somaliland and led the largest political party, the Somali National League, in the British Protectorate of Somaliland. As we saw earlier, the residual anger of being denied the appointment of Prime Minister remained with him for years and forced him to enter unholy alliance with Sharmaarke from whose cabinet he earlier resigned.

In reality, the leaders of Somalia and specifically of the SYL had no intention of equally sharing power or even acknowledging the leaders of Somaliland as equal partners in the newly united republic. Instead, they viewed them and their people as unwanted intruders disturbing their newly acquired state, clan balance, and anticipated prosperity.

Since they could not get rid of them, however, they succeeded in dividing them. Hence the Harti members joined the Daarood confederacy in Somalia while the other Somaliland representatives made their own separate deals in pursuit of individual self-interest.

The way Somalia's ruling elite approached Somaliland is illustrated by an account Égaal offered three decades when he was President of Somaliland. He explained that the National Assembly tabled discussion on the union on a holiday without informing the Somaliland representatives. He reported that he and other Somaliland members of the Assembly planned to enjoy an outing in Afgooye, in the outskirts of Mogadishu, when they learned of a parliamentary session scheduled on that holiday without their knowledge. Changing their plans, they rushed to the parliament to present their views on a matter that specifically concerned their constituency.

When the Somaliland representatives entered the parliament, they found neither apology nor explanation. On the contrary, Somalia's ruling elite changed tactics to keep them in the dark—they used Italian to continue their discussion, a language the Somaliland representatives did not speak. This parliamentary discussion scheduled on a holiday, the failure to inform the Somaliland representatives, and the use of Italian to excluded them from participation underscore for the Somaliland representatives that their presence in the National Assembly was unwanted and irrelevant not only on that day but also on all other days.

Nonetheless, Égaal and other Somaliland leaders could not wind the clock back and reclaim the independence they hastily gave up for dreams of Pan-Somali-Unity. Caught in the euphoria for independence and unity, neither they nor the people they represented knew then that this first denial of equality and reciprocity was a harbinger of worse things to come. Yet, for the sake of preserving Somali unity, they ignored this incident in at the parliament the same way other blatant show of disregard to them.

What they did not realize is that anything is negotiable except freedom and equal rights which if not demanded and defended are never given or granted even by 'brothers' with whom one joins in unity for emotional or pragmatic reasons. To compromise on freedom and equality is to forget that there is no greater or higher principle than freedom and equality in human relations and that the cost of compromise in this regard is heavy, tortuous, and lasting. The price is paid in successive installments: first, the party allowed superior advantage take the other for granted and make decisions as they wish; later they sideline the compromising and compromised party, considering them weak, dependent, foolish, even crazy; in the end, he is made victim of oppression and exploitation.

Remember the scriptural story of Cain and Able whom we invoked here as metaphors of the oppressor and the oppressed? After all, they were brothers but power and greed broke their filial bond and led to the murder of one by the other. The story is relevant not only to the relations of Somaliland and Somalia but also to the Daarood-Hawiye conflict that escalated to the most violent assaults and reprisals that rage on to this day, leaving countless civilians, including women and children, to suffer death and trauma in the struggle to prove the delusion of clan or personal superiority. As I argue in the work, the relevance of the Cain and Abel metaphors is also demonstrated by how the ruling elite treat their people.

The elite based in Mogadishu gave priority to enlarging their personal and clan interest over of Pan-Somali Unity. Using winner-takes-all philosophy of Somali politics, they ignored fair representation in the National Assembly of the united Republic of Somalia. They imposed their own constitution and flag, and secured major leadership positions. They took the posts of President, Prime Minister, key cabinet portfolio, and the commanders of the police and armed forces. They insisted naming Mogadishu as the capital city and the headquarters of all government institutions.

In effect, then, SYL became the dictator of all political parties, Somalia's elite the dictator of all the Somali elite, and Mogadishu the dictator of all cities. Somalilanders who sought a cabinet post had to abandon their party and become a member of the SYL. Somalia's civil servants also took key posts in government. In addition, any Somalilander who wanted to appeal an unfair court verdict, sought a job or a passport, advanced education or better health services had to go to Mogadishu where, lost in Italian language and culture, Somalilanders were called *Qaldaan*—'the Strange or Crazy People.'

During a visit by Prime Minister Ábdirashiid Áli Sharmaarke to Somaliland in August 1960, Timaádde, the foremost pan-Somali nationalist poet, expressed dismay at how the southern leadership ignored the disparity of power between Somaliland and Somalia. He cited a poem which complained about the government's disregard of Somaliland (symbolized by its main port Berbera) while Somalia (represented by *Hamar*, i.e. Mogadishu) enjoyed the seat of government, including a thriving port.

After explaining the struggle it took to achieve liberty, Timaádde complained about the elite's pursuit of private interest, ending his poem with the following stanza:

The parliamentary establishment
The Port too Hamar owns
Let Berbera drown in disastrous flood
No dhows (boats) anchor to its port
You, honorable delegates,
End the [unequal] two-track policy
Never overlook this matter.[2]

Timaádde's poem hinted at the building up and frustration in Somaliland at the two-track policy. but the politicians ignored these warnings. Although poets like Timaádde saw hints of the elite's betrayal after independence, the majority of the public nursed their disillusionment in the hopes that their dreams for more inclusive unity and a better future would come true. It did not.

Meanwhile, the elite continued jockeying for power and the politics of clan deception intensified. Inequity was built in the National Assembly from the beginning. This distribution of seats was not based on population ratio or any other rational criteria. Seats were allocated according to the original number of the two Constituent Assemblies formed before independence and the merger of the two territories. Of the 123 members of the National Assembly, Somaliland had 33 members and Somalia had 60 representatives.

The unequal representation in the parliament further weakened Somaliland representatives in the National Assembly. Being a minority in the General Assembly, they could not initiate or produce legislation on behalf of Somaliland nor reverse decisions their southern counterparts reached on behalf of Somalia. Even the three political parties of Somaliland—the SNL, the NUF, and the USP—were reduced to insignificance and later disintegrated by the SYL, the political juggernaut that required everyone seeking cabinet post to abandon his party and join the SYL. Most did.

Inequity in the civil service also started on July 1, 1960, the very first day of unity. On that day, all officers and government personnel in Somalia obtained a promotion as independence bonus. On the other hand, only senior officers in Somaliland obtained promotion on the day of independence on June 26, 1960 while the majority of civil servants did were not promoted. Moreover, the police officers and the new military recruits of Somalia obtained higher rank on that day while their counterparts in the Somaliland police and the army officers did not. The government dominated by *Southerners* (people of Somalia) did not adjust this inequity in promotion and salary; hence resentment built up in Somaliland.[3]

Disparity in taxes and salaries also existed between Somaliland and Somalia before the union. Before independence and union, civil servants in Somaliland earned higher salaries than did civil servants in Somalia. Somalilanders also paid lower taxes. To coordinate salaries and taxes, the Sharmaarke government reduced salaries and raised taxes on Somaliland in 1962. As Somalilanders saw it, this was a policy of double whammy against them. The changes in taxes and civil service salaries imposed double burden on them while giving advantage to residents of Somalia who had obtained higher salaries but no increase in taxes.

The double whammy of higher taxes and reduced salaries deepened the feeling of inequality felt in other aspects of the union. A mass revolt against the raised taxes followed. Neither the southern President nor the Prime Minister took the time to understand the source of anger of Somalilanders. Instead of finding reasonable solutions, the Sharmaarke government aggravated the conflict. On 2 May 1962, it adopted a decree of siege on Hargeysa in order to put down the mass revolt. That only added fuel to the fire. The Isaaq elders insisted that Somaliland would secede unless the government withdrew the unjust tax measures. The threats of the elders fell on deaf ears.

The rebellion by Somaliland military officers led by Hassan Ábdulle Walanwal (known as Hassan Kayd) in December 1961 was also a reaction to unequal promotion and pay in the armed forces. Some call the rebellion a coup when it was simply a rebellion for which the officers paid a heavy price. Because they rebelled against the inequity imposed on them and their people, they lost their career and almost their lives. Misunderstood by their politicians and people, they marched ahead of history—a perilous adventure like that of Girmame and Mengistu Neway undertook in about the same period to overthrow Haile Selassie.

Hassan Kayd and his fellow officers did not meet the same fate as the two Ethiopian brothers—death by suicide in Girmame's case and execution in Mengistu's. According to the unpublished biography of Dubbe Áli Yare, Somalia's leading politicians, including Ábdirashiid Áli Sharmaarke, wanted to try in the officers in a military court and summarily execute them, but later relented to pressure the more transparent procedure of public trial in which the government prosecutor demanded execution of the officers for treason.

Fortunately, the presiding British judge dismissed the charge against the officers. He argued that, n the absence of an act of union between Somalia and Somaliland, the treason for which they were accused had taken place outside the court's jurisdiction. Although released, the Somaliland officers were dismissed from the armed forces and the cause for their rebellion was lost and forgotten in return for their release. The military career for which they trained and considered their life vocation therefore ended.

The two Ethiopian brothers and Hassan Kayd's colleagues faced the same dilemma of all those who want to change an unjust system. If they wait for conditions to improve on their own, nothing may happen in their lifetime. The same conditions of injustice may continue undiminished, if not further aggravated. But if they act according to their conscience, they may jump ahead of history and act before their people are ready for change. For this, they pay a heavy price.

The Sandhurst-trained officers and the two Ethiopian brothers took the bold step of nudging history in the direction they thought proper and just. But they failed either because conditions were not ripe for their intervention, their people were not ready for change, or their tactics betrayed them. Yet their failure would haunt society years later. It took about a decade after the death of Girmame and Mengistu Neway for the rebellion against Haile Selassie to mushroom into anarchic violence removing the monarchy. These two brothers sowed the seed of rebellion the monarchy nurtured it with its continued oppression and exploitation. Hassan Kayd and his colleagues also sowed the seeds of Somaliland rebellion against inequality.

Many mistakenly think that the break up of the union dates to 18 May 1991, not realizing that the process of drifting away and regrets had started soon after the union in 1960. On the contrary, Somaliland's reclamation of independence on May 18, 1991 was the culmination of a process of drift and rift started soon after independence. May 18, 1991 was also the last nail hammered on the coffin on the grand dream that was gradually dying since 1960. The death throes of the state also began soon after independence when the ruling civilian elite turned their competition for personal power into competition for clan hegemony. As we shall see in subsequent chapters, the military regime only aggravated the process of degeneration that started under successive civilian governments, pushing the simmering crisis into cataclysmic explosion and implosion.

If the ruling civilian elite had paid attention to the early harbingers of Somaliland's drift away from the union—for instance the simmering frustration of the Somaliland politicians, the rebellion of military officers, and the mass revolt against high taxes simultaneous with salary cuts—they might have saved the union and perhaps the Pan-Somali dream.

Birth of Clan Hegemony

It is not only the gradual dissolution of the union that was precursor of darker days to come. There was also the emergence of clan hegemony which would have alerted the ruling civilian elite to the growing rot of the political system over which they presided. However, as they ignored the simmering frustration in Somaliland, they also disregarded the plight of people in Somalia. Using *clannism* and *Klannism*, they focused attention and energy on securing clan hegemony to cover up and defend their personal power and wealth.

Clannism, a bias *for* one group and *against* others becomes most perilous when combined with *Klannism,* the prejudice and deception of a power-hungry elite viciously competing for personal ascendancy and wealth within its ranks. Using *Klannism*, the elite kept the powers and privileges of the state to itself. It also used *clannism* to exploit the majority who remained steeped in clan bias. Each time conflict within the elite erupted, the cry of "*toolaayey*!" rallied the clan and its animus. The elite who sought new positions of power and privilege used the same tactic since independence.

Because all members of the elite had no equal talent or inclination for manipulation and deception, some remained at the periphery of the *Klan*, attaining minimal power and wealth while others remained at its core and rotated political power, not by consensus and cooperation but deceit and betrayal. I suggested in Chapter 1 that a high degree of psychopathy—for instance the predisposition to cheat, lie, abuse, and feel no guilt—is necessary if one is to survive and succeed in Somali politics. In particular, Rieber's *Mephisto Syndrome*—consisting of thrill-seeking, passion for power, glibness, and absence of guilt—is most apt to Somali politicians who successfully attain high office. They also need the same characteristics to retain power.

The *Mephisto Syndrome* is most salient in the *Klan*—the class of Somalis who often assume power because they acquired western education and they were socialized in the indigenous society. Western education gives them the qualification to rule and their socialization provides them access to the hearts and minds of the population. The western education they acquired is often minimal but it qualifies them to high office in the midst of illiterate population in whom colonial rule had fostered belief of personal and cultural inferiority, therefore respect for all things western.

Living in a gray zone where the alien and local cultures meet, the ruling elite are host to a muddled mix of values, beliefs, and morality. They are of the two cultures, but belong to neither fully. Their western education instilled in them not the value of ideas for solving problems or as a force of history, nor the virtue of work in creating the world or recreating the self. On the contrary, they use it as license for entitlement and comfortable life, a right to govern and enrich themselves. But since the high places of power and opportunities for wealth are limited, competition between the elite is rife and intense. More so as proliferating schools produce a new crop of the entitled and the cost of imported trinkets soar.

Invariably, the organization of *Klan* in power has clan configuration, with some clans being overrepresented in it. Clan affiliation and mobilization intensify when the competing members of the elite belong to different clans. When in competition with a member of the same clan, one exploits the clan system by moving down one notch down into the next level of genealogy, rallying support from closer kinsmen. That one can always move up or down over twenty ancestors allows the *Klan* to exploit these dynamic relationships interminably.

The same pattern of conflict or alliance took place with regard to Aadan Ábdulle Ósmaan and Sheekh Áli Jumáalle, both Hawiye, the former of Ujejen sub-clan, the former of the Hawaadle sub-clan. In the competition between Ábdirashiid Áli Sharmaarke and Ábdirazaaq Haaji Hussein, the former two allies later became intense enemies when their personal ambitions for power brought them into conflict. Each also found support from his sub-clans within the Mijeerteen.

The same politics of clan manipulation and illusion continues to the present. It is a treacherous game we will analyze in detail in this work in order to gain insight into Somali politics and tactics of the *Klan.* I provide below an overview on how the ruling elite divided ministerial posts by clan and sub-clan during the nine years of civilian rule. From this overview, a clear pattern emerges to show how the ruling civilian elite used clannism and clan hegemony to attain and retain power. We shall return to the same theme in subsequent chapters discussing power relations during the twenty-one years of military rule.

Table 1 below presents the distribution of ministers in the civilian administrations from 1960 to 1969.

Table 1

Clan and Sub-Clan Distribution of Ministerial Posts 1960-1969

	Sub-Clan																									
Clan	Majerteen	Abgaal	Habar Awal	Dhulbahante	Habar Gidir	Habar Je'lo	Ogaadeen	Disow	Habar Yoonis	Mareexaan	Ujejeen	Gaadsan	Xawaadle	Makaahiil	Tunni	Ajuraan	Eelaay	GaalJe'el	Geedowfade	Jajeele	Geledi	Murasade	Samaroon	Warsangeli	Yantar	**Grand Total**
Daarood	17			7			6			5														1		**36**
Hawiye		10			7						5		4			2		2		2		1				**33**
Isaaq			9			6			5																	**20**
Raxanwein								5									2		2						1	**10**
Gadabursi														4									1			**5**
Digile															3						1					**4**
Dir												4														**4**
Grand Total	**17**	**10**	**9**	**7**	**7**	**6**	**6**	**5**	**5**	**5**	**5**	**4**	**4**	**4**	**3**	**2**	**2**	**2**	**2**	**2**	**1**	**1**	**1**	**1**	**1**	**112**

Chart 1 summarizes the same information graphically.

Chart 1

Clan Distribution of Ministerial Posts 1960-1969

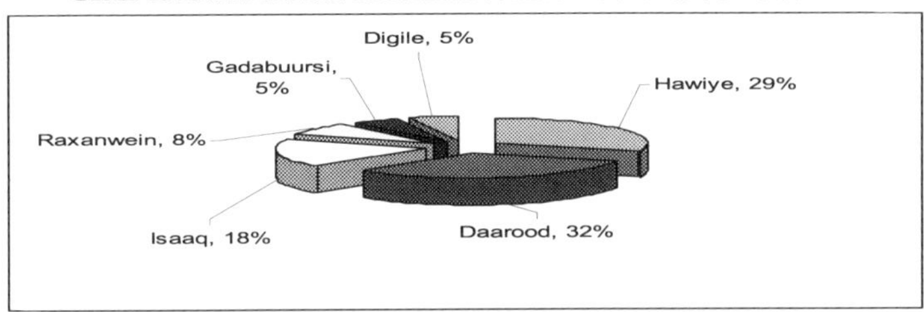

Note that throughout this period the Daarood had 32% (36 ministers) out of 112 ministerial posts appointed from 1960-1969. The Mijeerteen had 11% (17 ministers) of the 112 appointed for all clans and 47%, one out of the 36 ministers appointed to the Daarood. Similarly, the Hawiye had 29% (33 ministers) of the 112 appointed. When we combine the numbers of Abgaal (10) and Habar Gidir (9) ministers, the two sub-clans obtained 57% of the ministerial posts allocated to the Hawiye.

The Isaaq, always the distant third in the clan competition for power, had 20 ministers (18%) of the total number of ministers appointed for the nine years period of civilian rule. Within the Isaaq, the Habar Awal sub-clan obtained 8% of the 112 ministers, and 45% of the 20 ministers were allocated to the Isaaq. The Rahanwein and the Gadabuursi respectively had 8% (nine ministers) and 5% (six ministers). The Daarood and Hawiye together had 69 (61%) of all appointed ministers. We will see later that the inequity in power distribution grows larger under the military regime, with Daarood gaining even larger share than under the civilian administrations, the Hawiye getting less, and the Isaaq fairing the worst.

Inequity was not confined to unequal distribution of ministers. Similar inequity existed throughout the system. For instance, the same inequity was found in the appointment of depute ministers, although these posts were used to compensate some clans for low number of ministers appointed to them.

Table 2 presents the clan distribution of the deputy ministers from 1960 to 1969.

Table 2
Deputy Ministers Appointed by the Civilian Governments 1960-1969

	Ábdirashiid Áli Sharmaarke 1960-1964		Ábdirazaaq Haaji Hussein 1964-1967		Mohamed Ibraahim Égaal 1967-1969	
Clans	**Number**	**Percent**	**Number**	**Percent**	**Number**	**Percent**
Daarood	4	26	2	22	7	38
Hawiye	6	40	3	33	8	41
Isaaq	1	7	2	22	1	5
Rahawein	3	20	1	11	2	11
Digile	0	0	1	11	0	0
Dir	1	7	0	0	1	5
Gadabursi	0	0	0	0	0	0
Others	0	0	0	0	0	0
Grand Total	15		9		19	

Chart 2 summarizes the clan distribution of deputy ministers from 1960-1969.

Chart 2
Clan Distribution of Deputy Ministers 1960-1969

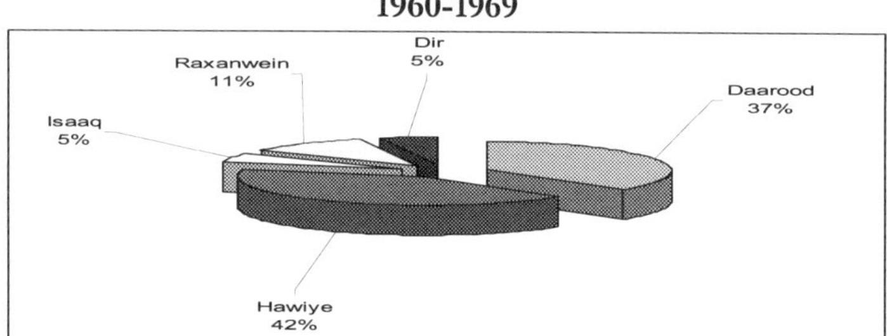

Note that under Prime Minister Ábdirashiid Áli Sharmaarke (1960-1964), the Hawiye obtained 40% of the Deputy Ministers, the Daarood 27%, and the Rahanwein 20%, and the Isaaq only 7%. Under Prime Minister Ábdirazaaq Haaji Hussein, there was a reduction in the number of Deputy Ministers for the Hawiye (33%) and the Daarood (22%), and the Rahanwein (11%); the Isaaq and the Digil gained (22% and 11% respectively.)

Under Mohamed Ibraahim Égaal, the Daarood gained substantially (37%) and the Hawiye (42%) at the expense of the Isaaq (5%) and the Digile (5%). The other clans experienced neglect by all administrations in this regard, particularly the Gadabuursi. None of the three administrations appointed a Gadabuursi Deputy Minister.

For the entire nine years, the Isaaq had four Deputy Ministers (5% of total deputy ministers) and the Gadabuursi had none at all. Again, the table and chart show the inequity among clans and of the union. The Égaal Government gave dominance to the Daarood in the ministerial posts and in its appointments on the level of Deputy Ministers. Other institutions such as the police and civil service followed the same pattern as that of the ministers.

Taken together, the tables and charts presented above show that the civilian governments from 1960 to 1969 had the clan identity as their primary criterion for the distribution of key government posts and power. They also affirm that not all clans are created equal, or have equal share of power. Thus clannism was consistently practiced in Somali politics, although the Somali politicians who led Somaliland and Somalia to independence passionately declared that "tribalism" is evil.

Yet the clannism that permeated Somali politics seldom benefited the clans in whose name the elite distributed power. The names of clans were used and their members were rallied by cries of "*tollaayey!*" but benefits obtained served the *Klan* and its members. It is therefore important not to confuse actual clans existing in reality, sharing misery and underdevelopment of their society, with symbolic clans the elite invent and manipulate to advance their class and personal interests. The confusion on the real and symbolic clans had made Somali politics an incomprehensible and insoluble quagmire.

In short, clan and clannism in urban politics got worse after independence. The elite transformed the traditional clan system into the urban *Klan*—a political and social means through which the elite obtains personal power and wealth. On the one hand, *Klannism* enabled the elite to monopolize power and exploit the majority. On the other hand, *Klannism* encouraged vicious infighting among the elite and permitted the victors to rotate through the cabinet and other centers of power.

The above data suggests a hierarchy based on which clan had the largest share of power. The Daarood and the Mijeerteen sub-clans with it had the largest share of posts and power. The Hawiye were next in power, with the Isaaq a distant third. All other clans, like the Rahanwein, the Digle, the Dir, and the Gadabuursi were deemed insignificant and worth only symbolic gestures of an occasional ministerial post. Excluded were others, like the Reer Hamar whose members were among the founding fathers of the SYL back in the nineteen-forties. Also left out were women who constitute the majority of the population. Not one single woman rose to the higher echelons of power. If a woman gained a position, it was informal and based on her husband's political status. This was often the case with the wives of Somali presidents since independence; Mohamed Siyaad Barre's wife exploited her status to the maximum, as did the wives of Presidents that came to power in Somalia, Somaliland, and Puntland within it after 1991.

Again, we should not confuse clans with the *Klan* that wields power in Somali society since those who share clan identity with members of the ruling *Klan* do not benefit greatly from the victory of their so-called kinsmen. They are generally as poor and powerless as the majority of the population. What they gain at most is subjective identification with victors of power. A few of them may gain some advantage in jobs and promotion, but most members of the clan remain as poor and powerless as the rest of the population. As we shall see later, they often pay a heavy price for the subjective gain they obtain and for defending their kinsmen in power. They become guilty by association and target of reprisals for crimes their kinsmen in the Klan commit in their name.

Because clan representation in the *Klan* had its evolution, unequal representation in this cabal began early after colonial occupation. Perhaps proximity of clan settlement to colonial garrisons and administrative headquarters gave special advantages to some clans. Others had ancestors who were seafarers (the so-called "seamen") who traveled abroad extensively and had some fluency in foreign languages. Still others took advantage of colonial schools close to their clan settlement. For whatever reason, the emerging *Klan* distorted the clan system to meet the new requirements in the policy of divide-and-rule. This new cabal appearing like the elite was the chief advocate for independence and nationalism to attain personal power and wealth. It was also the primary cause for the failure of genuine independence and nationalism.

Years later, 'Ábdi Muhumad Amiin summarized in a poem what had happened:

Since the call for mobilization

The stinking oppressor
Against whom people rallied
Except for a few misfits
Seeking only crumbs
Passions (for freedom) was total
Wresting independence as a result
But no steps were taken forward
Let alone achieving anything
Value of government and
Nationalism discarded
Clannism embraced.[4]

Clan Hegemony in the Police

Early signs of clan politics were not confined to the high echelons of power as in the distribution of cabinet members. They were also manifest at all levels of government, including the police which is the institution closest to the public and on whom they count for their security and render justice.

A report published by an Arabic newspaper called *Al-Youm* (the Somali version was *Maanta*) on 7 September 1967, three months after Ábdirazaaq's government fell and about a month after Égaal announced his first cabinet, confirmed Ábdirazaaq's inattention or outright bias for the clan inequity in police appointments.

The list is indeed instructive, as shown by Table 3 below.

Table 3
List of Police Chiefs and their Clan
1967

Name	Post	Clan	Sub-Clan
Major Ábdi Sugulle	Chief in Mogadishu Region	Daarood	Mijeerteen
Major Aadan Hirsi	Chief in Benaadir Region	Daarood	Mijeerteen
Major Mohamuud Mire	Chief in Kismaayo Region	Daarood	Ogaadeen*
Major Ismaíil Áli	Chief in Baydhabo Region	Daarood	Mijeerteen
Major Úmar M. Nimáale	Chief in Galkáyo Region	Isaaq	Habar Yoonis
Major Husseen Faarah	Chief in Bosasso Region	Daarood	Mijeerteen
Major Hirsi Úsmaan	Chief in Baladweyn Region	Daarood	Mijeerteen
Major Khaliif Faarah	Chief in Ádala Region	Daarood	Dhulbahante*
Major Mohamed Jaamá	Chief in Buró Region	Isaaq	'Iidagale*

Information with asterisk excluded from the original article.

Chart 3 shows the clan distribution of the police chiefs.

Chart 7

Clan Distribution of Police Chiefs, 1967

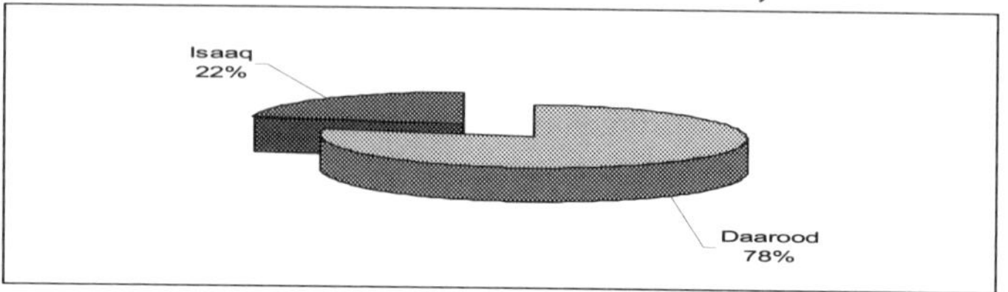

The article (supposedly written by Mohamuud Jaamá Urdooh) listed the clan distribution of the heads of police at different levels. The article exposed clan nepotism in the police force under General Mohamed Abshir Muuse and Ábdirazaaq Haaji Hussein. It was a wake-up call for all Somalis (particularly the Isaaq and Hawiye).

Table 4 lists the identities of sector chiefs.

Table 4

List of Police Sector Chiefs and their Clan 1967

Name	Post	Clan	Sub-Clan
Major Faarax Sugulle	Chief of CID, Mogadishu	Daarood	Mijeerteen
Major Ábdalla Mohamuud	Chief of Intelligence	Daarood	Mijeerteen
Major Ábdilqaadir Hassan	Chief of Immigration	Daarood	Mijeerteen
Major Aadan Ábdi	Chief of Special Forces	Daarood	Mijeerteen
Major Úmar M. Nimcaale	Chief of Police in Galkáyo Region	Isaaq	Habar Yoonis
Major Muuse Dudee	Chief of Logistics	Daarood	Mijeerteen
Colonel Ábdulaahi Faarah	Chief of Police Training Center	Daarood	Mijeerteen
Colonel Mohamuud Áagane	Chief of Daraawish (Field Force)	Daarood	Mijeerteen
Captain Mohamed Faarah	Head of Communication	Daarood	Mijeerteen
Captain Abshir Áli Guureh	Chief of Medicine and Stores	Daarood	Mijeerteen
Major Mohamed Áli	Chief of Finance and Housing	Arab	Yemeni
Lt. Colonel Mohamed Jaamá	Chief of Operations and Guidance	Hawiye	?

Chart 4 shows clan distribution of sector chiefs.

Chart 4

Clan Distribution of Sector Police Chiefs 1967

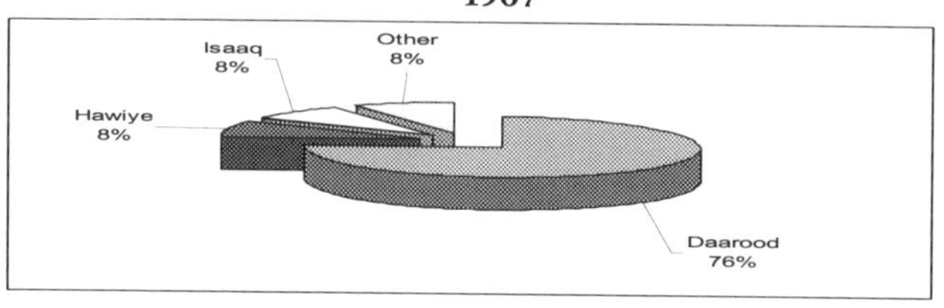

Most remarkable is that the Hawiye, the Rahanwein, the Dir, and other clans had no representation in chiefs of police throughout the country. Further, as Chart 3 below shows, 78% of police chiefs were Daarood and 22% Isaaq.

The Mijeerteen alone constituted 56% of the total number of chiefs of police. One may think the above to be a fluke, not a proof of clan pattern in the police force. However, the same results obtain when one considers chiefs of key police functions and headquarters. While 76% of police chiefs were Daarood (all Mijeerteen), there was only one Hawiye and one Arab.

When we consider the police stations throughout the country, we discover the same clan inequity—over-representation of Daarood, and Mijeerteen dominance. Of the 51 stations, including the CID and Immigration in Hargeysa, 35 of the heads were Daarood, Hawiye, 2 Isaaq, 2 Dir, 1 Íise, 1 "My-My", and 1 Arab. Of the 51 total, 20 were Mijeerteen.

Also of interest is that the Mijeerteen and the Daarood obtained the choice and most strategic stations in the country. For instance, the Daarood headed two of five stations in Mogadishu (Anzioletti and Villa Nord Police Stations) in addition to the police stations in Hargeysa (Mijeerteen), Berbera (Mijeerteen), Éerigaabo (Mijeerteen, also the Intelligence Unit in Hargeysa (Mijeerteen) and the CID Unit in Hargeysa (sub-clan unspecified). Of the two members of the Isaaq, one headed the Gabiley Police Station and the other headed the Immigration Office in Hargeysa.

Chart 5 below presents the clan distribution of police station heads.

Chart 5

Clan Distribution of Police Station Heads

1967

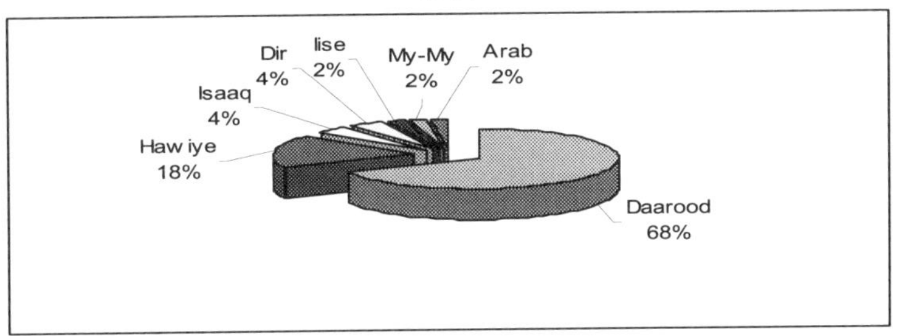

Not included in the above lists are the Daarood (particular Harti sub-clan) who occupied top posts in the police: Major General Mohamed Abshir Muuse (Mijeerteen), Major General Jaamá Áli Qorsheel (Warsangeli), Major General Ábdi Mohamed Áli (Dhibo, Dhulbahante), Major General Jaamá Badwi (Mijeerteen), Colonel Faarah Mohamed Ádde (Warsangeli), Major Jaamá Faarah (Kosofaare, Dhulbahante), and Brigadier Mohamed Jibriil (Mijeerteen). The posts and the rank these men held in the police far outweighed the combined power and influence of the posts held by any other clan in the police force.

As pointed out earlier, the report on clan distribution of police was published three months after the government of Ábdirazaaq fell and a month after Égaal announced his first cabinet. It is ironic that this state of clan inequity in the police and other aspects of government existed during the premiership of Ábdirazaaq who, Sharmaarke who preceded him and Égaal who succeeded him, is considered to have undertaken serious reforms in government. He is credited to dismiss inept and redundant civil servants, introduce merit system of qualification and competition for jobs, demand government employees to follow strict rules of work, and dismissed ministers for corruption.

Yet this man of reform did little to change the predominance of the Daarood and in particular of his sub-clan, the Mijeerteen, in the police force—a key institution that is in close and daily contact with the population. Perhaps the clan inequity was so deeply entrenched that he could not do much to change the system in the relatively short period he served as Prime Minister. But there is another explanation: despite the rhetoric of the elite, even leaders tooted as reformist are not significantly different from other Somali politicians on the fundamental question of clan bias and nepotism. For Ábdirazaaq, as for his peers, clan loyalty and bias were the *sine qua non* of politics—the essential and indispensable conditions no politician can disregard except at his peril.

It is this type of clan inequity in government and clan hegemony that eventually begot the violence that forced collapse of the state, massive death, and extensive destruction of property, including cities. The ruling elite could have anticipated that such clan inequity in government would only enlarge in time and bring about violent convulsions. However, they ignored these early indicators of darker days to come as they did others.

Some argue that the ruling civil elite carried on their mischief through peaceful means and that use of violence began with the military regime of General Mohamed Siyaad Barre. On the contrary, there were also concealed plots to commit mayhem during the civilian rule serving as harbingers of darker days to come. One such plot had transpired in 1967.

Plot to Blow up the Parliament

A military general, now a refugee in the United States, told me about a plot following the 1967 election of President Ábdirashiid Áli Sharmaarke who then appointed Prime Minister Mohamed Haaji Ibraahim Égaal.[5]

The losing candidates were former President Aadan Ábdulle Ósmaan and former Prime Minister Ábdirazaaq Haaji Hussein. Like General Mohamed Abshir Muuse, this military general and others sought victory for Aadan "Ábdulle Ósmaan and Ábdirazaaq Haaji Hussein. Soon after the election, the military general and his colleagues attempted to end the victory of their opponents by plotting to kill Sharmaarke, Égaal, and their supporters.

On the day before Sharmaarke carried out the swearing-in ceremony in the parliament, the military general and his colleagues planted scores of mines around the building. They placed the fuse in a small business establishment across the parliament. The general and his colleagues were determined to blow up their archenemies and everyone else who had come to attend the swearing-in ceremony at the parliament.

This plot remains a secret to this day; nonetheless, the general shared this secret to affirm that it was not a rumor but a plot to which he confessed as an active accomplice. The general was not out of his mind or drunk while he shared this secret with me. We were drinking coffee in a Starbuck's Restaurant in Silver Spring, Maryland. One may dismiss the general's story as fabricated but one should also wonder why a man of his caliber would share this violent, self-incriminating plot based on political differences with adversaries.

Fortunately, an unsuspecting person inadvertently disconnected the fuse a few minutes before it blow up the parliament building. The general and his colleagues could not reconnect the fuse and the secret plot therefore failed. The general and his accomplices cleared the buried mines the next night. As he spoke about the plot, the general had not shown a troubled conscience or any sign of regret. On the contrary, he seemed disappointed that the plot failed—a disappointment that, more than thirty years later, seemed alive within him.

When I questioned the general why he and his colleagues resorted to this reckless and heinous plan, he justified it as an act of national salvation. This is an example of how Somalis generally and competitors over power particularly justify a murderous action with false idealism. I give credit to the general for being so candid about this plot, but how many other plotters and plots exist and not known? Perhaps, it is better they remain hidden because it is sometimes better we do not know all evil plans in the hearts and minds of people. Yet whatever one makes of the general's admission, many people concur that the assassination of President Sharmaarke on October 15, 1969 involved more than a lone assassin and that it was the result of a secret conspiracy.

Ábdirashiid escaped another assassination attempt when a grenade exploded near his car while being driven from the airport. The general told me that a Mijeerteen colonel friend of his, Saadiq Mohamed Aw Mohamuud, who specialized in landmine operations, told him of his plans to blow up the President on the road to Afgooye. He said the same colonel was behind the assassination attempt when the President's entourage drove him from the airport in 1968. However, he explained that the colonel later died when a grenade blew him up while he was training opponents of President Ábdirashiid Áli Sharmaarke.

Another highly informed person reported that Saadiq was not only married to Ábdirazaaq Haaji Hussein's niece but was also was training his younger brother when the mine killed Saadiq.[6] Another highly knowledgeable person reported that, following the death of Saadiq, General Mohamed Siyaad Barre provided continued financial support to the wife of Saadiq, even though Mohamed Siyaad Barre had no personal relations with the wife of Saadiq.[7]

All these might have been mere chance coincidences, but questions arise who really was involved in the assassination of President Sharmaarke.[8]

In any case, as fate would have it, or as his enemies planned all along, President Ábdirashiid Áli Sharmaarke was assassinated on 15

October 1969, following a highly contested and controversial election in which over 1,000 candidates competed for 123 seats in parliament. A policeman shot him at close range in broad daylight. Although most Somalis were dismayed at the policies of the Sharmaarke and Égaal Government, few were prepared when they heard of the President's assassination. The burgeoning nation had never experienced such a brutal murder. However, the incident brought home two facts to Somalis everywhere—first, that politics is a deadly game; second, that one bullet can bring a faltering and unpopular government to its end.

The questions foremost in people's minds then were the following: Who was behind the assassination? Who would succeed the fallen President? Would the change bring better or worse conditions? The question behind the President's assassination never settled, other hypotheses had subsequently come up. One of them is that President Sharmaarke was victim of the Cold War and superpower geopolitical competition that were rife and intense in that era.[9]

There is an intriguing suggestion that the KGB was somehow involved in the assassination plot if not the planning and execution of it using Somali pawns. This line of thought seems ironic because it was Sharmaarke who in the first place negotiated collaboration with the former Soviet Union when he was the Prime Minister—a decision he took without the knowledge of President Aadan Ábdulle Ósmaan and therefore was a primary cause for their enduring conflict.

The suggestion sounds plausible when considered that Sharmaarke had changed allegiance to the West under the influence of Prime Minister Mohamed Ibraahim Égaal whose close relations to the United States was widely known even if charges of his being a CIA agent is discounted. Égaal became a darling of the West when he started a policy of détente with neighboring countries and diffused the growing armed conflict burgeoning with Ethiopia, Kenya, and French colonial administration in Djibouti under earlier Somali regimes.

Giving credence to this suggestion is that during his last trip abroad as Prime Minister, Égaal enjoyed the warmer reception and promises of support from President De Gaul and President Johnson than any Somali leader had known before him or thereafter. The conclusion is therefore that the leaders of the former USSR found in the Sharmaarke-Égaal attempts to woo the West imminent threat to their geopolitical interest in Somalia and that the Somali armed forces they trained and armed had advice, support, and blessing of a superpower. Aggravating the problems was the rumor that Sharmaarke and Égaal had secret plan to replace General Mohamed Siyaad Barre, the Commander of the Somali armed forces using, devious means in which he excelled..

In the absence of clear answer to the assassination plot and the urgency for filling the leadership vacuum, the question of succession gained special prominence. Before the President was buried, the jockeying for power began. Égaal was in the United States when the President was assassinated. He was on a diplomatic tour as well a vacation with his friend, William Holden, an American actor who had interest in game reserves in Kenya. Égaal also collected for his American friend a rare species of Somali wild animal, a Gumburi, found only in the Nugaal area.

The politicians sought a successor among themselves, never anticipating that the armed forces were poised to take power by force. As we shall see later, Haaji Muuse Boqor was being groomed to replace President Sharmaarke. But that was not to be. While the politicians bargained, exchanging bribes and promises of privilege, the military forces were ready to implement their plot which they had systematically planned for at least two years. The time for action came and they executed their plot methodically and suddenly.

Rumor had circulated that a coup of some type involving military officers would be attempted. But the ruling civilian elite did not know when and by whom. The public on their part hoped that the army would step in to end the corruption of the civilian administration and the chaos that seemed imminent. And they did.

Thus the military usurped power on October 21, 1969, six days after the assassination while the parliamentarians fought over power. From that time on, Somalis entered a new drama that once again began with euphoria and optimism but once again ended in tragedy. This time, the tragedy took years to unfold and, when it did, it was not only one leader killed and others traumatized in prison. The whole population paid a heavy price in blood before and after the state collapsed.

In the previously cited poem, Ábdi Muhumad Amiin anticipated the trouble and torment in the offing,

Smoke rose high above
The rain gathered in fury
Bringing drops of hail
The true bandits had come
Servants of colonialism
Whom nothing ever satisfies.[10]

6

RISE OF CAIN IN UNIFORM

Harag sagaaro "iiga kac" mooyee, "iga durug "ma leh.
A dik-dik hide permits only "get off it", not "let's share it".
—Somali proverb

The history of a group and the biography of its leaders interlace and enrich our comprehension of why events take a certain course and which forces nudged them toward a particular path. We saw earlier how colonialism set a course for Somalis that defined their history through occupation and partition of their land. If effects of colonial occupation diminished overtime, the partition of Somalis into different colonies left lasting borders and division among Somalis.

After independence, the civilian elite in the former British Protectorate and former Italian colony embraced the state as their own, without an attempt to heal injustices endured by Somalis. They exploited the people and betrayed their trust. Using the failure of civilian rulers for justification, the armed forces wrested power in a military coup. The man behind the military coup was General Mohamed Siyaad Barre.

Every generation has individuals who stand out among their contemporaries by using their power to heal past injuries and improve living conditions. There are also those who misuse their power and inflict massive damage that ruins lives and society. Such a man in Somali society is General Mohamed Siyaad Barre. Somali history from independence in 1960 to the collapse of the state in 1991 would be incomplete and inaccurate if we exclude his role as an individual and leader.

Since the subsequent chapters frequently invoke his name, who was Mohamed Siyaad Barre? How did he come to power? What aspects of Somali history and society shaped his character? What political and social forces influenced him to become the ruthless dictator of people whom Richard Burton referred to 150 years ago as "a race of republicans"?

Biographical Sketch

Little has been made public about the life of Mohamed Siyaad Barre partly because Somalis do not inclined to write memoirs and partly because written record would uncover embarrassing details on his long service under colonial rule. Nonetheless, some information exists of his past. He was born around 1910 in Shiilaabo, now in the Somali Region of Ethiopia. His mother was of the Ogaadeen clan, his father of the Mareehaan—both of the Daarood clan-family. His father was murdered when Mohamed Siyaad Barre was young, a loss that probably left him with a grudge against society and those he thought responsible for his father's death. The nickname of *Af-weyne*—'the big mouth'—was given to him in childhood and it stayed with him throughout his life.

At about the of age twenty years (in approximately 1930), Mohamed Siyaad Barre joined the Corpo Zaptie, *Polizia Africana Italiana*, enforcing Italian rule, subjugating Somalis, and protecting Italian residents (some of them settlers) in the colony. Prior to the establishment of the Corpo Zaptie, the Italian colonialists established a coastal police and a rural constabulary (*goggle*) which, by the nineteen-thirties, numbered about 300 men. The rural constabulary (*goggle*) was equivalent to the armed rural constabulary (*illaalo*), the Somali branch of the Somaliland Police Force. The roles of the *goggle* and *illaalo* was to quell resistance to colonial rule, patrol urban and rural areas, enforce law and order, and intervene in clan conflicts.[1]

The Corpo Zaptie, established soon after the fascists took power in Italy, was trained and commanded by the Italian carabinieri. It grew to 800 men, increasing to 6,000 when Italy invaded Ethiopia in 1935. Following the defeat of Italy in 1941, the Somali territory ruled by Italy came under the British Military Administration (BMA) which dissolved the Corpo Zaptie and replaced it with the Somalia Gendarmerie; the latter grew to more than 3,000 men in 1943. Five years later (1948), the Gendarmerie was renamed the Somali Police Force. After the Italian trust territory was established in 1950, the force became the Police Corps of Somalia (Corpo di Polizia della Somalia). It included Italian officers of the carabinieri and their Somali subordinates

During the British Military Administration, Mohamed Siyaad Barre continued to serve in the police as an ambitious law enforcement agent enforcing laws opposed to nationalist aspirations of his people.

He was regularly promoted, attesting to the vigor of the man and his commitment to pro-colonial policies. Service to a violently anti-nationalist system and betraying one's people can adversely affect one's morality, character, and behavior, but Mohamed Siyaad Barre's ambition had inoculated him from such adverse effects. As a member of the Corpo Zaptie, Siyaad Barre also participated in the invasion of Ethiopia in the nineteen-thirties.[2]

From the nineteen-thirties to independence in 1960, Mohamed Siyaad Barre was the most experienced member of the police force in Somalia. His experience ranged from years of service in the Corpo Zaptie to his rise as Commander of Police in the Benaadir region in 1957, the year an Egyptian diplomat, Kamel Eldin Salah, was assassinated. The Egyptian diplomat, a member of the Internal Control Commission monitoring the U.N. Trusteeship of Somalia, criticized the mismanagement of the Italian Administration. Many believed that Mohamed Siyaad Barre was involved in that assassination.

It is also said that his father was killed when Mohamed was young. The circumstances of the murder remain uncertain, but there are three theories. One is that Mohamed's father was killed by the Habar Gidir, a sub-clan of the Hawiye, who live in an area contiguous to that of the Mareehaan, a sub-clan of the Daarood. The second is that Mohamed's father was killed while he was defending his livestock against looters who harbored no political or clan grudge. The third suggests that a Mareehaan murdered him for unknown reasons.

Some have gone so far as to allege that Mohamed was an illicit child since, as rumor has it, his father was known to be sterile. However, we discount this claim because scurrilous rumors of false ancestry are common tactic of character assassination in Somali society. In fact, such rumors are tools of retaliation against a powerful leader and all types of scandals are often invented to undermine their character. Those who knew Mohamed Siyaad Barre and his family or origin contradict his rumor.[3]

Whatever the family history or childhood tragedies of Mohamed Siyaad Barre, the political environment in which Mohamed Siyaad Barre cut his teeth is also important because it suffused him and his peers with a view of the state that significantly influenced their perception and practice once they came to power. In particular, Benito Mussolini and his fascist representatives had a formidable influence on

Mohamed Siyaad Barre at a formative stage in his development from 1930-1940 when he served as a young and highly ambitious law enforcement agent of the Italian colony.

The fascist ideology is best articulated by Benito Mussolini, its founder and leader. For Mussolini, the state represented the absolute arbiter of justice. He felt that individuals and groups have no value or rights independent of the state. He also viewed the liberal state as being incapable of guiding the development of people. Mussolini wrote (allegedly with the help of Giovanni Gentile) the following in the 1932 *Enciclopedia Italiana* to explain the fascist state:

> The foundation of fascism is the conception of the State, its character, its duty, and its aims. Fascism conceives of the state as an absolute, in comparison with which all individuals or groups are relative, only to be conceived of in their relation to the State... the Fascist State is itself conscious and has itself a will and a personality – thus it my be called the "ethic" State.[4]

According to him, individuals should not enjoy all "useless and possibly harmful freedom." This view of the state as supreme and the individual subservient to it was to have a profound and lasting influence on politics of the Italian colony.

In the same document, Mussolini who once advocated a proletarian revolution and the rights of the disenfranchised majority denounced majority rights and the electoral process.

> Fascism denies that the majority, by the simple fact that it is a majority, can direct human society; it denies that members alone can govern by means of a periodical consultation, and it affirms the immutable, beneficial, and fruitful inequality of mankind, which can be permanently leveled through the mere operation of a mechanical process such as universal suffrage...

If Mussolini repudiated democracy and the rights of the majority in Italy, his agents in the Somali colony were convinced that Somalis, like other Africans, were less human than Europeans and therefore they had no rights whatsoever. But they practiced racism in excess of the racism known in other African colonies, except apartheid South Africa, the Belgium Congo, and Portuguese colonies. As we shall see later, the Italian fascists practiced outright slavery and they brought punished any sign of resistance. In addition to affirming the inequality of mankind, Il Duce became a rabid warmonger. He adopted an extreme form of nationalism and sought to make the Mediterranean "mare nostrum" ("our sea").

Taking George Sorel as one of his intellectual mentors, Mussolini embraced his exaltation of violence and argued:

> [Fascism] repudiates the doctrine of Pacifism, born of a renunciation of the struggle and an act of cowardice in the face of sacrifice. War alone brings the highest tension in all human energy and puts the stamp of nobility upon the peoples who have courage to meet it.

Sorelian adulation of violence gave Italian colonialists further ideological motives for absolute tyranny in their Somali colony—a form of tyranny far more cruel and blatant than those Somalis had experienced under the British and the French, although comparison of colonial abuse turns absurd when considered from the perspectives of the victims.

Still, the Italians who ruled Somalia did not need Mussolini and his fascism to embolden them on racism and the practice of colonial cruelty. Long after antislavery laws were enforced by other colonial powers, the Italian government legalized slavery in Somalia. Moreover, Italian colonialists indiscriminately bombarded resisting Somalis with artillery; they also commandeered labor to build roads, to erect forts, and work in plantations.

Pankhurst who wrote on Italian colonialism presents gruesome accounts of cruelties inflicted on Somalis. He also includes images of decapitated heads displayed to the public and Somali political prisoners with hands tied behind their back and bound to a truck driven until the body was broken up. Pankhurst explains that the latter practice was a punishment the fascists used with political prisoners in Italy and exported it to the colonies. They also enforced apartheid-like policies in public facilities.[5]

Mohamed Siyaad Barre and his contemporaries in the Italian colony assimilated fascist ideology and practice more by osmosis and emulation than by reading Mussolini and his intellectual mentors like George Sorrel. Colonialism everywhere is a negation of freedom and human rights, but the fascism practiced in Somalia did not concede the humanity of Somalis—at best, it consigned them to the lower rungs of human evolution. The fascist leaders who steadfastly held to belief in Italy that state was supreme also viewed and treated colonial subjects as fodder to the whims and pleasures of colonial administrators and white settlers planted in Somalia.

As we shall see later, the effects of those influences emerged after Mohamed Siyaad Barre came to power. The way he dealt with his own people recall the fascist cruelty he had observed and learned as a law enforcement officer. We know for sure that Mohamed Siyaad Barre admired and modeled himself after other dictators like Gamal Abdul Nassir of Egypt, Kim Il Sung of North Korea, Sekou Toure of Guinea, and Nicolae Ceausescu of Romania.[6] Yet Mohamed Siyaad Barre took these leaders as models at a late age and at the height of his power while Benito Mussolini and his fascist representatives in Somalia had formative and lasting influence on Mohamed Siyaad Barre at a young age. His admiration for dictators suggests inclination for despotism that he had formed early in his life.

In short, then, Mohamed Siyaad Barre started life in modest circumstance and with family tragedy that might have left him with wish for revenge either because his father was killed or he was an illicit child.[7] More importantly, he grew in a political zeitgeist that shaped his perspective to the state and influenced his character development. In addition, his service as law enforcement agent under fascist rule involved him in shady activities that kept him constantly vigilant against reprisal for crimes he alone knew but were closed book for the generation he ruled.

Whatever the impact of his personal past and service under fascism, it is certain that Mohamed Siyaad Barre was a highly ambitious man who possessed a gift for gaff and survival, a knack for endearing and mollifying his superiors, and a genius for setting traps that his opponents seldom suspected. It is by using these personal abilities, not personal wealth or clan might, that brought him power and to rule Somalis for twenty-one years.

Garnering Animus

The brief biography of Mohamed Siyaad Barre above suggests that since childhood he nursed a grudge against society. We know that he had a difficult childhood but his troubles did not end there. As he rose in the ranks of the police, he also found himself discriminated against as a member of the Mareehaan, outnumbered and dominated by other clans. Even after independence, the Mareehaan continued to be a powerless minority in politics, business, and law enforcement.

Ambition for power is not always a product of adverse life experience; it can also be a product of the individual's natural predisposition. Neither is it always maladaptive unless used in antisocial and pathological ways to exploit others or compensate for personal inadequacies. If Mohamed Siyaad Barre's ambition for power or lifelong need for revenge did not crystallized after his father was murdered, both may have developed when he moved to Mogadishu where he experienced isolation and discrimination for belonging. to a minority subclan of the Daarood.

Those who knew Mohamed Siyaad Barre since his childhood say that he suffered from inferiority complex for which he compensated with hard work, cunning, and shady activities. If true, the course of events after independence in the area of law enforcement and politics—for instance the highest rank in the police, then of the armed forces, subsequently becoming President—did not heal him of this inferiority complex. On the contrary, megalomania combined with the inferiority complex and, instead of healing society, reproduced his psychopathy in society with the consequence that a generation of orphans and victims of state violence were infected with impulse for revenge he had known in his past.

The discrimination Mohamed Siyaad Barre experienced is illustrated by how he lost the position of Commander of the police or the armed forces soon after independence. In August 1952, Mohamed Siyaad Barre was one of eight noncommissioned police corps sent to Italy to train as a commissioned officer of Somalia.[8] As a sergeant (saddex xarigle), he held the highest rank among the noncommissioned policemen. The newly commissioned officers returned to Somalia after completing their studies to become the leaders of the police, and some of them became the leaders of the newly formed Somali Army. Mohamed Siyaad Barre expected to become either the Commander of the Police or the Commander of the Armed Forces since he was the most senior member of the force. However, he was granted neither post.

The SYL political leaders selected Mohamed Abshir Muuse (a Mijeerteen) as the Commander of the Police and Daauud Ábdulle Hirsi (a Hawiye) as the Commander of the Armed Forces. Some argue that, although Mohamed Siyaad Barre was more qualified than either appointee, the politicians chose these two men to strike balance between the two most influential clans. If so, the SYL that publicly condemned clannism as a social evil made this political decision based on clannism. This decision also intensified Mohamed Siyaad Barre's antipathy and grudge against society. He continued to complain of discrimination, claiming that the two highly coveted posts were given to his juniors for clan reasons while his seniority was ignored because he belonged to the minority clan of Mareehaan.

Others say that Mohamed Muuse Abshir and Daauud Ábdulle Hirsi won the two posts because they had the best examination scores during their training in Italy. Ábdilaahi Íise was the Prime Minister when the appointment was made and therefore had access to the information. While serving as Ambassador in Sweden a few years later, Ábdulaahi Íise told General Jaamá Mohamed Ghalib, a police professional and once Minister of Interior, that Mohamed Siyaad Barre came third after Mohamed Abshir (first) and Daauud Ábdulle (second).[9]

After the usual lobbying and maneuvering of politicians, Daauud Ábdulle Hirsi offered Mohamed Siyaad Barre an appointment as the Deputy Commander of the Armed Forces. Although resentful that he was deputy to one of his juniors, Mohamed Siyaad Barre preferred to work under Daauud than Mohamed Abshir. Mohamed Abshir Muuse and Mohamed Siyaad Barre were never amicable; so, there was no question of Barre ever working for the Muuse. Mohamed Abshir, the handsome playboy, who viewed Mohamed Siyaad Barre as a backward and dishonest man, one who in addition inspired only distrust and contempt. According to General Mohamed Hussein Hiirane, Mohamed Abshir Muuse believed that Mohamed Siyaad Barre ws of illegitimate birth and attributed his proclivity for evil to this illigitimacy.[10]

On the other hand, Mohamed Siyaad Barre considered Mohamed Abshir cocky and arrogant, successful only because of his clan identity and the support of Aadan Ábdulle Ósmaan, his relative by marriage and the Chairman of the SYL. Personal preferences and enmity aside, the appointment of Mohamed Siyaad Barre as a deputy to Daauud actually fulfilled clan strategy—the Daarood kept the Hawiye in check so long as Mohamed Siyaad Barre (himself a Daarood) was the second-in-command of the armed forces. By campaigning for him to become the Deputy Commander, the Daarood found a highly crafty and experienced detective whose presence in the armed forces prevented the Hawiye from usurping power.

In fact, the delicate clan balance the politicians sought to keep broke down by the appointment of Mohamed Siyaad Barre as Deputy of the armed forces. The Daarood had the edge over the Hawiye in the power struggle. The police and the army were divided into clan turfs. The police were allied with the Mijeerteen, with Mohamed Abshir Muuse as its Commander. The army was the turf of the Hawiye, with Daauud Ábdulle Hirsi, as its Commander. The split along clan lines was so intense that the Mijeerteen in the army had more loyalty to Mohamed Abshir Muuse than to Daauud Ábdulle Hirsi. The Hawiye in the police had also greater loyalty to the latter than to the former.[11]

Thus placing Barre to become second-in-command gave advantage to the Daarood. Nonetheless, Mohamed Siyaad Barre viewed his appointment as deputy to Daauud humiliating, though it would have felt far more humiliating if he were he appointed as deputy to Mohamed Abshir Muuse—a person with whom he shared mutual antipathy. Mohamed Siyaad Barre was hurt and angry over the decision denying him the rank of Commander, but, he bore it with calm acceptance of one who must patiently bid his time until the right opportunity avails itself. I did.

Using his underdog status and acting like the spook who sat by the door, Mohamed Siyaad Barre developed alliance with other military officers who felt discriminated against for their clan identity. With their help and patient planning, he grabbed power and took his revenge, firstly on those who in the past discriminated against him and later on society at large. Mohamed Siyaad Barre used these alliances to grab power.

Plotting the Coup

We know that Mohamed Siyaad Barre was planning a military coup years before 1969 when the coup actually took place. In 1967, Mohamed Ibraahim Égaal told Jaamá Mohamed Ghalib that in 1964 Mohamed Siyaad Barre had threatened a coup if Égaal and his parliamentarian colleagues continued opposing the government of Ábdirazaaq Haaji Hussein. If this account is true, Mohamed Siyaad Barre knew for five years that carrying out a coup was an option even though he was only a Deputy Commander of the Armed Forces.[12]

Mohamed Siyaad Barre was not bluffing. According to General Ismaíil Áli Abokor, a close ally of Mohamed Siyaad Barre, plans for a coup dated back to at least 1967.[13] General Abokor was one of the Sandhurst graduates from Somaliland and a trusted colleague of the Commander. A strident believer in the revolution promised by the coup plotters, General Abokor broke with the dictator after 1976 when the military regime had become so rife with nepotism and corruption that he could not remain indifferent or silent. His criticism of the regime came to the open and his relationship with the dictator strained.

Colonel Ábdulaahi Yuusuf Ahmed, currently the President of the transitional government formed in October 2004 in Mbagathi, Kenya, reported that Mohamed Siyaad Barre had tried to enlist him into a plot for a coup nearly ten months before it actually took place. Barre had confidence in the colonel because he was a well-trained officer who assisted the commander in key jobs. The colonel reports that, one afternoon in late January 1969, Barre came to the colonel's house asking to have a confidential talk with him. The colonel had no idea why the Commander of the Armed forces had come to him, but Barre drove the colonel to an isolated area in the outskirts of Mogadishu where a tank battalion was garrisoned. [14]

On the way back, Mohamed Siyaad Barre told the colonel that a coup was necessary to prevent having Somali territories administered by Kenya and Ethiopia, which was Égaal's intention. The colonel responded that the Somali armed forces were established to defend the country against external aggression and, therefore, energies should be focused on this goal and the politicians should sort out their own problems. Mohamed Siyaad Barre fell silent before replying with reference to clan, "I am convinced that no other group but yours can properly run our country."

The colonel was shocked, but he answered, "I did not speak to you as a clan member; I spoke to you as a Somali. What group are you including me in?"

The Commander said, "I mean you, the Mohamuud Saleeban [a sub-clan of the Mijeerteen]."

When the colonel held firm to his views, the Commander left him at his house and drove away. The colonel adds that their conflict began that day. Barre approached other military officers (including Mohamed Faarah Áydiid, Mohamed Nuur Baarqab, Ábdilqaadir Dheel, and Hassan Gaamuur) with the same intent and all of them refused to join him in the plot. The exception, the colonel reports, was Colonel Salaad Gabeere Kediye and young officers from the "North" who were not familiar with the Commander's character.

Ábdulaahi Yuusuf claims that he tried to dissuade his friend, Salaad Gabeere, from participating in Mohamed Siyaad Barre's coup, but Salaad, ignored the advice. Gabeere was the son-in-law of Aadan Ábdulle Ósmaan who lost the presidential election to Ábdirashiid Áli Sharmaarke, therefore, Gabeere wanted to topple the government of Sharmaarke and Égaal. Sadly, Ábdulaahi's prediction came true—Salaad was one of the first officer's Mohamed Siyaad Barre and his colleagues executed on charges of plotting a coup on July 23, 1972. Ironically, Ábdulaahi who had refused to participate in Mohamed Siyaad Barre's plot had concocted a plan of his own in 1978 that aborted and forced his flight from Somalia.

Ábdulaahi was the primary architect of 1978 foiled coup.[15] However, it is doubtful that Ábdulaahi rejected Barre's plot for a coup for patriotic reasons. It is more likely that he was in the thick of his own plot, perhaps in collaboration with others including perhaps Mohamed Faarah Áydiid. Mohamed Siyaad Barre could have suspected Ábdulaahi's plot and may have hoped to get Ábdulaahi to admit to it when in he approached him to join Barre's plot. If Ábdulaahi shared with the Commander his own plans for a coup, Barre would then set him up for treason. Ábdulaahi knew of the Commander's ploy and took cover in claims of opposing all military coups.

There is in any case little doubt that plans for a coup was explored over a period of a year, and that these two men were not only involved in it, but were the instigators. Distrust developed between them and both men informed the authorities of their opponent's plans. Ábdulaahi's secret plot surfaced in the early nineteen-nineties under unusual circumstances. After release from prison in Ethiopia, Ábdulaahi returned to the territory now called Puntland where most Mijeerteen retreated after the collapse of the regime. The debate occurring among Mijeerteen politicians was who would become the Chairman of the Somali Salvation Democratic Front (SSDF).

The candidates for the position were General Mohamed Abshir Muuse and Colonel Ábdulaahi Yuusuf Ahmed. The conflict tore apart the Mijeerteen community and weakened their movement at an inopportune time. Elders and politicians of the Ósmaan Mohamuud tried to mediate between Mohamed 'Abshir (of the Íise Mohamuud) and Ábdulaahi Yuusuf (of the Úmar Mohamuud)—the Ósmaan Mohamuud, the Íise Mohamuud, and Úmar Mohamuud being sub-clans of the Mijeerteen. The Ósmaan Mohamuud believed that Mohamed Abshir was involved in the coup plot of 1969 and even in the assassination of President Ábdirashiid Áli Sharmaarke. The primary concern of the mediators was not to dig up the past but to mend the rift between the two men and therefore to forge unity among the Mijeerteen.

When the two men were brought to the mediation session, Mohamed Abshir gave Ábdulaahi Yuusuf the right of presenting his grievance first. He used a clan ploy admitting that Ábdulaahi's ancestor was the senior sibling and that therefore the latter had the right to speak first. Ábdulaahi began by accusing Mohamed Abshir of negligence regarding the Mijeerteen clan at a critical time. He explained that Mohamed refused to participate in the coup that Ábdulaahi proposed to him in 1969. Ábdulaahi was accusing Mohamed of blocking an opportunity that he (Ábdulaahi) and the Mijeerteen had of wresting power before Mohamed Siyaad Barre executed his coup.[16]

Mohamed Abshir responded that he had refused to participate in Ábdulaahi's coup because, although politically opposed to Ábdirashiid, he never believed in the violent overthrow of a government. Ábdulaahi, who intended to depict himself as a promoter of Mijeerteen interest while portraying Mohamed as an adversary to it, had forgotten that Ábdirashiid was himself a Mijeerteen and that he was of the Ósmaan Mohamuud. He also exonerated Mohamed 'Abshir from rumors that suggested he participated in the assassination of Ábdirashiid.

Upon hearing this shocking exchange, the mediators adjourned the meeting and left, disturbed with what they learned. Their anger focused on Ábdulaahi Yuusuf Ahmed and the Úmar Mohamuud (including another key member of this sub-clan—Ábdirazaaq Haaji Hussein, the former Prime Minister and strident opponent of the assassinated President). The conflict between the Ósmaan Mohamuud and the government of Ábdulaahi Yuusuf in 2000 was due primarily to the illegal extension of Ábdulaahi's term, denying succession by Jaamá Áli Jaamá, another Ósmaan Mohamuud.

History has its mysteries. Those driven by passion for power may also become victims of traps they set for others. Now the President of the Transitional Federal Government created in Kenya in 2004, Ábdulaahi still pursues raw power, although his health is compromised by a liver transplant for which he needs regular care. He evaded fate many times and baffled his enemies by his unswerving determination to hold on to power and life.

The colonel, no doubt a tough survivor of many odds, does not care the history he leaves behind and how many suffer for his ambition for power. When elected President of the Transitional Federal Government, he said that the best qualification for leading Somalis is *habaar qabe*—'the cursed one'—and that he was therefore eminently qualified for the post he possesses those qualities. He was not bluffing. Three years after his election, he proved to be not only the cursed one but Cain incarnate when, in pursuit of power, he brought Ethiopian forces to indiscriminately bombarded Mogadishu and its civilian population. Instead of changing the politics of anarchy and greed, he augmented it with outright violence that will remain as one of the darkest chapters of Somali history.

Gathering Allies for a Coup

Colonel Ábdulaahi Yuusuf characterized Mohamed Siyaad Barre as a man who would push the country and its people into a catastrophe if his plans for a coup succeeded. Decades later, the colonel himself found the opportunity to push Somalis into the precipice of disaster when he became the President of the Transitional Federal Government formed in October 2004 in Kenya. But, how did Mohamed Siyaad induce the officers from Somaliland to join him in his plot but also to become his most loyal supporters?

When he was Deputy Commander of the Armed Forces, Mohamed Siyaad Barre cultivated a firm relationship with the young, frustrated officers from the former British Protectorate. The encounter of two former military officers from Somaliland with Mohamed Siyaad Barre in 1961 suggests how warmly Mohamed Siyaad Barre treated them when they came to Mogadishu to present their grievances to General Daauud Ábdulle Hirsi, then the Commander of the Armed Forces. The two officers were Hussein Áli Duáalle (known generally as Áwil) and Ábdilaahi Aadan Rayiid (know commonly as Ábdilaahi Congo).[17]

When the two men who belonged to the officer corps from the former British Protectorate approached the office of the Commandant, they heard him and his staff communicating in Italian. Neither of the two visitors understood Italian because they grew up in Somaliland where the language of instruction and administration was English.[18] When the two officers walked into the Commandant's crowded office, they greeted General Daauud who asked them who they were and why they had come to him. The two officers presented their complaint of inequity and clan discrimination among the officers in the Somali Army.

Before they completed their account, the defensive general dismissed their complaints as unfounded. Disappointed with the general's verdict and with his attitude, the visitors left and walked into Mohamed Siyaad Barre's office next door. In contrast to Daauud, the Deputy Commander welcomed them. They noticed the office of the Deputy deserted, his desk was clear with only a cup of coffee and an ashtray on it. Behind the desk sat the Deputy Commandant, calm and alone. When he learned that the visitors were Sandhurst trained officers from the former British Protectorate, his interest peaked and he listened to their complaints with rapt attention.

After presenting their complaints, Mohamed Siyaad Barre explained that he himself was unjustly treated for his clan identity for many years. He explained that the politicians chose younger and less experienced men like Daauud Ábdulle Hirsi and Mohamed Abshir Muuse over him when in fact he was more qualified than by seniority and experience. He advised the two Somaliland military officers not to give up and told them that the true measure of courage is not to strike back out of anger but to wait patiently until the opportune moment comes to effect change. In stark contrast to Daauud, Mohamed Siyaad Barre spoke with impeccable Somali and he used not one word of Italian as he spoke to them. This presented a stark and impressive contrast to General Daauud.

The two officers left the officer of Mohamed Siyaad Barre heartened by his warm reception and wise words. By his statements and demeanor, Mohamed Siyaad Barre also revealed not only the grudge that he harbored for losing the post of Commander, but also the strategy he adopted toward his adversaries. This welcome reception of the two visitors foretold the close working relations Mohamed Siyaad Barre subsequently cultivated with disgruntled officers, like General Ismaíil Áli Abokor, enabling him to carry out his military coup eight years later. According to General Ismaíil, the coup had been planned for at least two years (from 1967 to 1969) when it was successfully carried out.[19]

The plight of the officers from the former British Protectorate had exemplified the inequity with which the union of the two former colonies began and continued thereafter. From their perspective, the Somali Army's upper echelon, like General Daauud Ábdulle Hirsi and General Mohamed Siyaad Barre, were only police officers in military uniform while the Somaliland officers were trained as army officers. Thus, the Somaliland officers believed that they alone were professional with the requisite training and credentials in the Somali Armed Forces. Yet, they were unappreciated and discriminated against while the Hawiye and Daarood men were quickly promoted.[20] Similar inequities existed in the integrated civil service of the new nation.

The civil servants from the former British Protectorate believed that they were more disciplined and skilled than the civil servants of the South who copied the behavior and values of their Italian mentors. The former, taken from their home turf to serve in the South, felt exploited and rarely rewarded. Attempts to standardize taxes and salaries in the new republic also had the effect of imposing higher taxes and reducing salaries in the North, giving the advantage to the South.

Thus, disillusionment with the union was felt by the officers in the North and their counterparts in the civil service and in the business sector. Impatient with the pace of change, the Somaliland military officers participated in a poorly organized revolt in 1961.[21] The organizers of the revolt were soon apprehended and released, some of them assigned to diplomatic posts abroad, in effect, honorably exiled.[22]

General Daauud Ábdulle Hirsi died in 1965 and a debate followed on who would succeed him. The Hawiye wanted one of their own to replace him; the Mijeerteen wanted the post for one of their own as well, but not Mohamed Siyaad Barre. Mohamed Siyaad Barre was a compromise candidate, following a vigorous campaign on his behalf by Ábdirazaaq Haaji Hussein, the Prime Minister. Neither camp thought he would become the enduring dictator he turned out to be. Most acquiesced to his appointment as Commander of the Armed Forces because they believed that he was an old man, tired and ineffective. Some thought that he would serve as a temporary fill-in of a critical post until a more appropriate Commander was chosen. Others felt that his competence would become quickly apparent and show the need for an alternative Commander.

Both groups were wrong. Mohamed Siyaad Barre lasted longer than his detractors expected, and he rose to heights of power they could never imagine. Part of his success as Commander came from his genius to appoint politically or professionally frustrated officers to balance his Mijeerteen and Hawiye adversaries. Included among these officers were the Somaliland officers in the army who, since independence, felt discriminated against. He needed them to wrest power, and they needed a friend in power.

With Mohamed Siyaad Barre in power, they believed there was a chance for the recognition they deserved. The officers worked for him with zeal and, in return, Barre rewarded them, and relied on them. Barre waited for the opportunity for him to wrest power. Time was running out for the civilian leaders as public outrage against them built up. Soon, a major military action would change the power balance. The President was assassinated on 15 October 1969 and the military assumed power on 21 October 1969, bringing with them a "revolution" of expectation but not of substance.

Examples of the allies that Barre cultivated included key military officers like Ismaáil Áli Abokor and Ahmed Suleymaan Ábdulle who were in the inner circle of the coup plotters and implementers. The two young colonels were from Somaliland and belonged to the group of military officers trained in Britain's Royal Military Academy of Sandhurst. Ismaáil and Ahmed were outside of Somaliland when their colleagues attempted a poorly planned and hastily executed revolt in Hargeysa on 4 December 1961. Both therefore remained in the armed forces to become the protégés and confidants of Mohamed Siyaad Barre. Ahmed was in addition the son-in-law of Mohamed Siyaad

Barre. Salaad Gabeere Kediye was another key contributor to the execution of the coup.

We shall return to the story of these key officers since how Mohamed Siyaad Barre brought each of these men into his circle of trusted allies is as interesting as the fate he eventually meted out for them. To anticipate, however, suffice it to mention that, once Gabeere helped him to attain power, Mohamed Siyaad Barre executed him. After Ismaíil assisted him in the coup and consolidating his dictatorship, Mohamed Siyaad Barre reduced Ismaíil to the status of outcast, subsequently detaining him incommunicado for six years in a high security prison. Ahmed Suleymaan Ábdulle remained in the inner circle of the dictator's cronies and confidants until the collapse of the regeme, as did Mohamed Áli Samatar who later joined the inner circle of cronies and confidants.

The "revolution" that the military officers began after the coup had changed society but not in the direction that the military leaders promised. The promise of socialist revolution raised hopes of a poor population desperate for change, and it provided a convenient cover for the *Klan* to manipulate and exploit them. Somalis expressed their dreams of change in songs and poetry. Soon, the dream turned into nightmare and the lyrics of jubilation changed to wails of grief.

Prelude to the Coup

The controversial election of 1969 is memorable for ballot rigging and politics of greed. For instance, over 88 parties fought for 123 parliamentary seats. Believing that politics is the road to wealth, each clan jumped into the political fray and spent huge sums of money to win representation in the assembly. In fact, this election was dubbed *Cod Khasaaray*—Wasted Votes—because the results contradicted the actual number of votes cast, huge sums of money were wasted on buying votes, and many people died competing for seats in the assembly.

The disillusionment and anger with the civilian administration deepened and spread throughout the country. Before the election of 1969, many of the opposition politicians called for an end of the civilian administration led by Prime Minister Mohamed 'Ibraahim Égaal and President Ábdirashiid Áli Sharmaarke. In speeches and in the press, they appealed to the armed forces to intervene and save the country. Ordinary citizens were frustrated and looked for someone to come along and save the country from a government gone from bad to worse. This hope paved the way for Mohamed Siyaad Barre who waited for this opportunity.

According to Colonel Ábdulaahi Yuusuf, a plot for a coup was almost carried out on the night of 26 March 1969, nearly seven months before it was actually successfully executed.[23] On that night, key government leaders including the Prime Minister and the Minister of the Interior planned a meeting on the election results. Mohamed Siyaad Barre persuaded them to hold it in the military headquarters as he planned to capture them and then announce that the armed forces had successfully carried out a military coup.

This time, Mohamed Siyaad Barre's plans fell through. The Prime Minister and his colleagues were secretly informed that Mohamed Siyaad Barre and his colleagues had set a trap for them in the military headquarters. With this advance warning, the civilian leaders held the event instead in the Police Headquarters where they felt secure from attack by the Armed Forces. The West, particularly by West Germany and Italy was trained and armed by the police force, while the armed forces obtained support by the Eastern bloc, particularly the former Soviet Union. The two institutions reenacted the Cold War by pulling Somalis in opposing directions.

Colonel Ábdulaahi Yuusuf insists that he was not the informant of the impending coup, yet his insistent denial and his known ambition for power invite speculation. Mohamed Siyaad Barre arrived at the same conclusion, and two days later, Barre summoned Colonel Ábdulaahi and imposed house arrest on him. The next day after completing 40 days of detention, Ábdulaahi received a letter from the Commander informing him that he was transferred to Hargeysa. No reasons for the detention and exile from Mogadishu were publicly given, but the two men knew why.

Probably both men had their own plans for a coup but Mohamed Siyaad Barre had greater success. In October when President Sharmaarke visited Hargeysa, the colonel learned that the government had abandoned plans to send the Commander to Russia and force his retirement. Before boarding the plane to Laas Áanood, the President urged Ábdulaahi to work with the Commander. Feeling defeated, Ábdulaahi asked that he be sent abroad for training, a request the President turned down.

The President's trip to Hargeysa was a public relations tour to neutralize the unpopularity of his government. Before coming to Hargeysa, the President visited Bossaaso, Állula, Éerigaabo, and Buró, prompting concerns about his safety. Many of his friends and supporters advised against the trip but he insisted on it, despite rumors of plans to assassinate him. Accompanying the President on this tour were Sheekh Mukhtaar Mohamed Hussein, the Speaker of the Parliament, and General Jaamá Áli Qorsheell, the Commander of the Police.

When they reached Allula, the elders of the Siwaakhroon (a subclan of the Mijeerteen) presented a litany of complaints including charges of neglect and mistreatment by his administration. Instead of assuring them that he would take corrective action, he told them that he would pass their complaints to the Minister of the Interior whom they distrusted. They were offended by this response.

One of the elders, Hassan Mohamed Áwad, stood up and recited the following poem:

Rashid, you're not the one appointed by Allah
You divided Somalis and caused their dispersal
Misery descended upon the world with your leadership
So long as you're not accepted as Prime Minister Jaamál
[We pray] that terror overwhelms you and disease disables you
That you find no treatment in Russia, Rome, or Kenya
That your power is shaken and the army pushes you out.[24]

The tour began with concern but developed into anxiety after Alula's visit. A disagreement with the Warsangali before the group reached Éerigaabo only added to the worries. Col. Mohamed Saqadhi Dubad, the police officer in charge of security, reports that he wanted to rush through the visit to Éerigaabo and take the President to secure environment before the sun set but the President's speech in Éerigaabo took more time than planned. After the speech, the entourage toured the Daallo Mountains which was not scheduled, heightening the anxiety of Mohamed Saqadhi Dubad. A vehicle with unfamiliar occupants followed them, but, when the police tried to check who was in it, the vehicle sped away, veered into a thickly wooded area, and its occupants disappeared as quickly as they appeared out of nowhere.[25]

The President and his entourage reached Buró, then Hargeysa, without incident, and supporters again told the President to cancel his trip to Laas Áanood but he refused. Two days before President Ábdirashiid Áli Sharmaarke reached Laas Áanood, an advance team of soldiers was sent to ensure his security. When he arrived in Laas Áanood on 15 October, he was escorted by security to the guesthouse prepared for him. At 11 o'clock in the morning, with the Speaker of the Parliament by his side, a 22 year-old policeman named Saíid Yuusuf Ismaíil shot him at close range.

The assassin was a policeman but he was not a member of the security detail. The police officer in charge, Mohamed Saqadhi Dubad, did not know who had posted him by the entrance of the guesthouse where he fired at the President. The Speaker and other officials near the President were unscathed, confirming that the plot to kill the President was planned and executed well, with no collateral damage.

Questions arise from this sad event. Was there a conspiracy or simply an isolated act of murder by a disgruntled policeman? Was the poet of the Siwaakhroon aware of the conspiracy when he recited the poem, or was he an example of the uncanny prescience and clairvoyance that Somalis credit to poets? Why was the President assassinated in broad daylight and in the presence of others including the Speaker of the Assembly and the Commander of the Police? If the assassination was indeed a conspiracy, who else was behind it? Who included the assassin in the security detail and posted him in a place where he could shoot the President at close range?

These questions remain a mystery. Some speculate that there was no conspiracy, that the assassin was driven by a family or clan vendetta and that he acted on his own. They add that the Speaker and others escaped injury or death because they had no part in the family or clan feud that motivated the assassin to kill the President. Others suggest that the assassin, though alone in committing the murder, was part of a wider conspiracy involving key players in national politics, in the armed forces, and in the police. Still others add that the assassination was hoped to solve a shared Daarood anger at the President's politics. These are mere speculations. The fact remains that assassination has never been solved. Circumstantial evidence suggests that Mohamed Siyaad Barre was somehow involved in the conspiracy, but who else was involved is still shrouded in mystery.

Whatever the motive for the assassination, it is certain that the nation took an unprecedented turn. Five days after the assassination, on 21 October 1969, General Mohamed Siyaad Barre and his military associates came to power by means of what they called a bloodless coup, although in fact the coup and its aftermath were anything but bloodless. In fact, the coup gained strength by spilling blood and ended with torrents of blood. With regard to the assassination, Mohamed Siyaad Barre and his unknown coconspirators obstructed full investigation of the crime and quickly executed the assassin to silence him.

The public mood gave them a convenient cover. The assassination of President Sharmaarke though shocking, did not evoke in Somalis the grief of a fallen hero. Those who knew the Sharmaarke described him as a modest man without the arrogance often associated with the powerful in Somali society. His modesty was paired with a lack of charisma and, although his personal integrity remains in dispute, it is agreed that his administration was thoroughly corrupt. Sharmaarke believed that cronyism and embezzlement were inevitable and that therefore all efforts to root them out of society were hopeless. He is remembered as a dedicated leader to Pan-Somali-Unity, but also, unlike Ábdirazaaq Haaji Hussein, Sharmaarke was a poor administrator who gave his subordinates free rein to pursue their mission of power grab and economic greed.

Sharmaarke was a victim of contradictions in Somali culture. It is generally accepted that any official who do not raid the public treasury is *dogon*, a fool. This attitude is summarized by the proverb: *Nin daaád ah doqooniimo ka ma madhna*—'an honest man has an element of foolishness in him.' In contrast, another proverb states: *Daaádi ma hungowdo*, 'honesty does not bring disappointment (failure).' The latter proverb has little application in Somali politics. The ethics of looting has greater appeal than that of honesty. The nomadic culture of the past placed a premium on cleverness and courage in looting the camels of other clans. Urban politics under the flawed state and led by the Klan have made acceptable the practice of looting the state. Thus he who enriches himself at the expense of other is *"nin rag ah"* (a man with balls or manhood), or he is *"fariid"* (a clever person). In contrast, he who fails to do so is *"doqoon"* (a fool).

So long as looting camels in traditional society is readily transferred to looting the public treasury in contemporary society, ending corruption in Somali society will be quite a challenge. A story recalls the poem of Faarah Laanjeer who recited a poem in which he glorified the looting of camels. Illustrating the same point, another man was caught after he looted camels and was taken to court. The judge asked him: *"Geela miyaad xadday*—did you steal the camels?" The man answered: "*Maya, maan xadin, waan dhacay!*—No, I did not steal them, I looted them!"[26]

In defending himself this way, the man was distinguishing stealing——in his view, an act committed only by cowards and dishonorable people——from looting which implies manly courage and proof of dominance. In so defending himself, the man was actually boasting instead of showing guilt or shame. Even when he knew that he could be sent to prison, he wanted to make sure that the judge had understood the distinction between stealing and looting because his sense of honor depended on it.

Ironically, President Sharmaarke might have been a victim of his own fiduciary integrity. Had Sharmaarke enriched himself while in power, he might have been called *"nin rag ah"* or *"fariid."* It is interesting that his Interior Minister, Yaasiin Nuur Hassan, and his Prime Minister, Mohamed Ibraahim Égaal, were never accused of foolish acts. Both were seasoned in the politics of cronyism as well as the art of corruption, and they pushed society and malfeasance well beyond the limits of tolerance. In particular, Yaasiin Nuur Hassan siphoned off enough of the public treasury to become a wealthy man owning, among other assets, a major cross-border transport company shuttling goods in East Africa. Unlike Sharmaarke who was reclusive and traditional, these two men were inclined toward western pleasures including parties, lavish dinners, frequent libations, and periodic pilgrimages to Western capitals.

More generally, the President was a victim of a population that wanted to rid themselves of the corrupt and inept government Sharmaarke and Égaal headed. The majority of Somalis were fed up with misrule by the civilian administration and they wanted the army to intervene, to clean up the mess, and to chart a new course for a nation in despair. Rigged ballots and unjust elections offering no solution, the desire to get rid of the government meant getting rid of these leaders. Some individuals exploited this shared desire by translating it literally. They physically eliminated the President, thereby forcing the end of a regime. This was the opportunity for that General Mohamed Siyaad Barre had waited for years. When the opportunity came, he acted swiftly, deftly, and callously.

Cover Up of the Assassination

The assassination of President Ábdirashiid Áli Sharmaarke on 15 October 1969 was the most tragic event that the young Somali Republic had experienced since independence. The violent death of the President was significant to Somali politics and the world. The tragedy involved not a murder of just one person but also of a President who represented the hopes and aspiration of millions, a symbol of unity and shared destiny. It was not murder by a lone policeman but a political assassination planned and coordinated by powerful men whose ambition required killing the President by a policeman supposedly protecting his life.

Mohamed Siyaad Barre had a motive to get rid of the President. He planned the coup for months and carried it out soon after the assassination of the President. He and his colleagues took unusual measures to cover up evidence and eliminated the assassin without due process of law. The assassin was kept in a secured cell that denied him access to anyone but men Mohamed Siyaad Barre trusted and his execution was hastened in order to protect his accomplices' identity.

There is little doubt that Mohamed Siyaad Barre was involved in the crime and its cover up. The assassination has the imprint of unmistakable style, as it had been so in the assassination of Kamel Eldin Salah in 1956 and Bishop Colombo in 1989. In all three assassinations, Mohamed Siyaad Barre obstructed the investigation of the assassination by an independent commission; and when the assassin was captured, he blocked public trial of the perpetrator to hide his role in the assassination.

Mohamed Siyaad Barre's shady past was known to the key politicians like President Aadan Ábdulle Ósmaan and Prime Minister Ábdirazaaq Haaji Hussein. Mohamed Ibraahim Égaal recalled the threat of a coup that Mohamed Siyaad Barre made in 1964 but Égaal did little to stop him. These politicians who had the power to avert violence failed. After the coup, all three men were among the politicians Barre sent to prison for three and a half years. Mohamed Ibraahim Égaal fared the worst—altogether, he spent 12 years in prison.

The public ignored Mohamed Siyaad Barre's shady past and violent manner of governing. His colleagues who helped him carry out the coup also underestimated the man. They saw the writing on the wall, but they ignored it. In particular, the arrest and subsequent execution in May 1971 of General Mohamed Áynaanshe, Colonel Salaad

Gabeere, and Major 'Ábdilqaadir Dheel Ábdulle, emboldened Mohamed Siyaad Barre to continue eliminating those he found to be a threat to his power.

Ever so misinformed about the political and social consequences of injustice committed in their name, the public watched the execution and accepted as fact the guilt of the three men, although these men were not given a fair trial. These executions were carried out with this chilling song of death:

Repudiator of good will
Awaiting you is a trap
By which you will be executed
You, opportunist, your fate
Is death by hanging.[27]

Subsequently, the song became the signal alerting the public to forthcoming executions. It was heard from the radio and mobile speakers on the eve of the executions.

The execution of the three military officers was significant. It served as a test of the three major clans since the General was Isaaq, the Colonel was a Hawiye, and the Major was Mijeerteen. Lack of reaction from these three clans and the absence of public outrage encouraged Mohamed Siyaad Barre to get rid of whomever he wished. Silence to the executions sent a message of submission throughout the land, proving that only violence pays. The executions kept other members of the SRC in line, making them compliant and subservient.

It is understandable that Somalis did not investigate the President's assassination. They feared the military regime that forced them into submission had a hand in the assassination. Over the last four decades, the majority of Somalis have been busy grieving the death of a loved one; few possessed the emotional energy to focus attention on the assassination of President Sharmaarke. To this day, the significance of that assassination in Somalia history remains neglected. However, the cost for neglecting this assassination has been heavy.

The assassination of President Ábdirashiid opened a new and bloody chapter in Somali history. It gave license for political murder when everyone carried on business as usual after the assassination. It represented the most blatant abortion of justice. And, it emboldened the military regime to use violence. Had the public demanded full inquiry into the assassination, whoever came into power next would have understood that committing murder has penalty. Perhaps, the death and disaster that has plagued Somalis during the last forty years could have been averted.

After the assassination of the President, Somali politics took a violent turn. Introducing change became synonymous with the use of violence. Socialism was misinterpreted not as a political means toward equality and prosperity but a systematic tool to run roughshod on people—using detention without trial, torture, and summary execution to force submission. It changed from a system for humanizing to one that dehumanizes. Socialism of the former USSR with its Stalinist legacy, imported blindly as other alien systems, further reinforced this distorted meaning of socialism and humanity.

But once the regime of Mohamed Siyaad Barre took root, he dictator and his cronies wanted to keep intact the status quo of oppression. Talk of change was considered subversive oppression. But, in spite of the regime's oppressive measures, change took place by use of counter-violence to the violence of the state. The result was anarchy and chaos.

In short, the assassination that began with Sharmaarke was reenacted in geometric proportion. Assassination of individuals enlarged to mass murder, fighting clans to bombardment of cities, and auto-colonialism to auto-destruction. These tragedies were followed by more violence after the collapse of the regime.

How did this sad turn of history come about?

7
BIRTH OF THE CAINETIC SYSTEM

Addoonsi cabsi buu ka abuurmaa
Enslavement begins in fear
—Somali proverb

Power abhors vacuum. If not filled quickly, anarchy follows. When a leader dies suddenly in the absence of a plan of succession, ambitious men throw themselves into competition for power. Sometimes, the least likely candidates for succession emerge, wresting power by force or accepted by others as temporary leaders until disagreement on who best qualifies is settled.

Somali society was not prepared for the assassination of the President on 15 October 1969. When the President was assassinated, Mohamed Ibraahim Égaal was in the United States arguing in the General Assembly of the United Nations for the rights of Palestinians and the inclusion of China in the UN. He met with the Johnson administration and vacationed in California with his friend, William Holden, the American actor who had business interests in Kenya.

Égaal ignored the crisis his country faced while he argued for Palestine and China, or he vacationed with William Holden. Égaal hurried home after he learned that Sharmaarke was assassinated. After his return, the parliamentarians approached the problem of succession the same way they approached all legislative agendas—they argued, they broke into cliques, and were ready to sell votes to whichever candidate offered the best deal. Finally, they decided to support Muuse Boqor to succeed Ábdirashiid Áli Sharmaarke. This was not to be. Unknown to them, the armed forces were planning for a takeover. They took power before Muuse Boqor was installed, herding into prison anyone they deemed a threat—including parliamentarians, the Prime Minister, and the Interior Minister.

What did the military coup leaders do after they took power? Did the power they usurped change the state permeated by corruption and nepotism? Did they deliver on their promises of justice and development? Did they heal the wounds of decades or inflict more of the same?

Cost of Indecision

It is not only power that abhors vacuum. People also abhor anarchy. Faced with anarchy, they embrace any leader who promises order and peace. The need for security often takes precedence over the yearning for justice. Thus, to avoid anarchy, people accept any system as long as it promises peace and security. When they feel threatened by anarchy, public anxiety rises and everyone waits for a savior to take the reigns of power and bring peace. In a state of shock after the President's assassination, Somalis desperately wanted a leader who can save them from anarchy. If that leader promised peace and justice, they were ready to adore and glorify him.

Six days after the President's assassination, the armed forces did exactly that—they wrested power and assured the public that they were in charge. After the mass arrest of the politicians, the coup leaders promised a revolution that would change their lives for good. Public excitement soared due to their need for someone to save and to lead them. Two years later, reality set in and Somalis returned to the despair they had known since colonial times.

Following the assassination, the political atmosphere was volatile. Grief and insecurity gripped the nation. The question of succession arose, generating more intrigue. The National Assembly was embroiled in debate on succession. On 20 October 1969, the Assembly adjourned a special session with agreement that the members would resume early the next morning. Meanwhile, the armed forces were ready to act on orders from the Commander. By 3:00 A.M. on the night that the Assembly adjourned, the armed forces took control of strategic locations in Mogadishu. When people woke up that morning, they heard the news: the armed forces toppled the civilian government and took full control of the nation in a "bloodless coup."

Somali society changed drastically at that point, and the majority of Somalis received news of the coup with jubilation. Outraged by the politics of corruption and nepotism, they wanted change, even if it occurred by violent means. Except for a few who knew Mohamed Siyaad Barre personally, the public mood was mostly one of joy. How did the coup take place?

The military coup of 21 October 1969 did not take place without long and careful preparation. General Ismaíil Áli Abokor, a key organizer and executor of the coup, affirms that the military coup had been planned for two years—that is as soon as Sharmaarke and Égaal assumed power.[1] Only a small circle of the organizers knew about this preparation, although the civilian politicians and the public heard conflicting rumors of plans for a coup in the months before October 1969.

No one expected the President would be assassinated and that the military would exploit the grief and confusion. In retrospect, one sees that the coup and the assassination were closely linked, and that powerful opponents of the civilian administration had an active role in the assassination.

The coup took place on the sixth day after the assassination of President Sharmaarke. The night before, the armed forces invaded the homes of parliamentarians and key politicians. They pulled them out of their homes, and herded them into prison, like common criminals. The parliamentarians and politicians would have received public sympathy if their policies and actions had been respected. On the contrary, they were bankrupt and corrupt, and the majority of citizens agreed that they deserved to be treated like criminals. Anger toward the politicians was so intense that the public did not care if some of them were executed.

In the days after the assassination, Barre's plans for a military coup intensified as the politicians searched for a successor and jockeyed for power. Barre took as little risk as possible while his subordinates carried out the coup. Colonel Ismaíil Áli Abokor, an Isaaq, and Colonel Salaad Gabeere Kediye, a Hawiye, were in charge of operations for the coup. The former was a member of the Sandhurst graduates with whom Barre cultivated close personal relations since he had become the Commander.

Colonel Salaad Gabeere Kediye was the son-in-law of former President Aadan Ábdulle Ósmaan whom President Ábdirashiid and Égaal outmaneuvered in the political campaigns of 1967. Colonel Gabeere thus harbored a family grudge against President Ábdirashiid and Prime Minister Égaal. For this reason, he was a convenient and committed ally. Though inducted at the last stage into the coup plotted for two years, Salaad had other qualifications in addition to his intense hatred for the civilian government. He was an effective officer and member of the Hawiye sub-clan (Abgaal) who were the predominant residents of Mogadishu.

Barre's subordinates in the armed forces were busy preparing the coup, while the Commander-in-Chief remained in the company of Yaasiin Nuur Hassan, the powerful Interior Minister and a key player in the civilian administration. Ábdirashiid Áli Sharmaarke was considered a weak leader, and he left Yaasiin Nuur Hassan to govern as he wished. His presidential powers thus were symbolic only. Égaal was not a man of either detail or consistency either. His choice as Prime Minister came about as a tactical maneuver in the conflict with Ábdirazaaq Haaji Hussein. Égaal was thus a convenient partner whom the Mijeerteen powerbrokers in Sharmaarke's camp chose to win the election.

Mohamed Siyaad Barre was masterful at scheming. Having understood that Yaasiin held the power in the civilian administration, remaining glued to him late at night offered Barre four advantages. First, he ensured that the Interior Minister was securely at home and out of touch with his political colleagues. Second, it offered him deniability if the coup failed. Third, it lulled the civilian government in complacency. Four, it provided him an opportunity to monitor the news of which the civilian leaders talked, to whom, as well as their whereabouts every hour of the day.

Years later, in the nineteen-eighties, General Mohamed Abshir Muuse recounted a story while still in prison.[2] The General said that, after he learned that a contingent of armed forces led by Mohamed Siyaad Barre was ready to wrest power, he called Muuse Boqor who was preparing to be voted in as President that night. Alarmed, Muuse Boqor called the Interior Minister, Yaasiin Nuur Hassan, who assured him that Mohamed Siyaad Barre was wrongly accused, that the story was patently false because Mohamed Siyaad Barre himself was with him at that moment. Muuse Boqor was assured by this and continued to prepare for the moment of victory that never came.

Evidently, Mohamed Siyaad Barre left nothing to chance in carrying out his plot. He knew that winning the confidence of the powerful Interior Minister would be advantageous, but still, he did not spare the Interior Minister from being imprisoned. He unceremoniously escorted him to prison, like the other politicians. The Interior Minister regretted that he underestimated Mohamed Siyaad Barre, and even at his death, he still talked about the deception of the man he mistakenly trusted. Yaasiin was not alone in dying with regret and grief. Many others who trusted Mohamed Siyaad Barre met fate in the same way.

Plans for the coup proceeded in secrecy, yet, despite the army's capacity for secrecy, rumors about an impending military coup spread. It was unclear then who leaked the news, although it became clear that the invisible hand of Mohamed Siyaad Barre was somehow involved. A veteran officer in the criminal investigation of the police, he knew how to ferret information and confuse others with disinformation. Even if he did not plant the rumor, one thing is certain: Somali society is porous and nothing remains a secret for long. In particular, secrets concerning interpersonal conflicts, sexual or financial scandals, attract and entice Somalis. The keeper of a secret often has a strong compulsion to share it with others. A secret also tempts every Somali to listen with rapt attention and to retell it with relish.

The pastoral culture relishes news of conflict and war because both are rampant. Confidential news is reserved for kinsmen but, since Somalis are linked in a wide network of relations, no news remains confidential for long. A secret binds the teller and listener in complicity, and evokes trust between them. It affords membership in the same camp, however fleetingly. Indeed a Somali who has no secret to tell or is unable to relish one is a bore if not an idiot. Therefore, if a Somali has no secret to tell, he must invent one or give a new twist to an old one for he knows that Somalis savor and embellish and disseminate a scandal, true or fabricated. Unemployment, pervasive misery, and lack of other forms entertainment also give rumor an important role in social and psychological life of Somalis.[3]

There were rumors of at least two other groups of coup plotters, one led by Ábdulaahi Yuusuf Ahmed and Mohamed Faarah Áydiid, the other led by General Mohamed Ibraahim Mohamed (Liiq-Liiqato). Actually, the latter group did not exist but it provided a cover for Mohamed Siyaad Barre's plot. Mohamed Siyaad Barre leaked "news" of these plots for a coup to confuse the civilian administration. This 'leaking' allowed him to appear loyal to the civilian administration while providing him cover to his ongoing plot. It also enabled him to eliminate opponents of his plot (like Ábdulaahi Yuusuf Ahmed and Mohamed Faarah Áydiid). This ruse worked.

The political climate in the capital city and the countryside was quite tenuous. Local elections were to take place in August 1968 and the national presidential election was scheduled in 1969. Rumors of a coup had everyone on edge. Mohamed Ibraahim Égaal, worried about the rumors had considered sending Mohamed Siyaad Barre abroad, honorably exiling him from the country until a new Commander was selected and the threats of coup d'etat had abated. However, Égaal did not act on this plan, thereby giving Barre time to consummate the coup.

The political climate throughout Africa during the nineteen-sixties was one of declared revolution that often brought the armed forces to the forefront. Somalis too looked to the armed forces for change when the civilian government failed them. Mohamed Siyaad Barre's rise to power provides testimony to how an adroit leader can control people who are fearful and desperately want change. Somalis found Mohamed Siyaad Barre to be a charismatic leader with a good sense of timing. He addressed their fears and dreams and gave them reason to trust him.

As Ábdi Muhumad Aamin—initially a supporter of the regime, later a disillusioned opponent—explained in a poem, the armed forces found justification for use of guns after the civilian regimes failed to deliver on the promises of independence:

In the African Continent
We share the general laws
And methods of topsy-turvy
Where possessors of guns
And power-grabbers prevailed
But opportunities exist to enable them
Because they find justification
By declaring nothing has been achieved.[4]

Two weeks before the coup, Mohamed Siyaad Barre received a letter announcing Égaal's decision to send the Commander for study abroad.[5] Sending the Commander far away, the Prime Minister would have forced Barre's retirement while abroad and appointed a new Commander in his absence. Before ensuring that the decision announced in the letter was carried out, Égaal left for the United States on diplomatic matters after he sent the letter. The civilian government he headed and society paid a heavy price for indecision and procrastination.

Égaal wanted to replace Mohamed Siyaad Barre as early as 1967 when he became Prime Minister. Jaamá Mohamed Ghalib reflects on a conversation he had with Égaal in 1966 when Égaal explained that in 1964 Mohamed Siyaad Barre, then the Deputy Commander of the Armed Forces, threatened both him and parliament with a coup if they withdrew their votes regarding Ábdirazaaq's government. Barre said, "If you do not stop (such votes) we will do our duty."[6] Égaal warned, if Barre was not stopped in time, he would fulfill his threat, and he did.

Égaal and Ábdirashiid had agreed to send Mohamed Siyaad Barre to the Soviet Union for further military training, thereby getting him out of the country. Yaasiin Nuur Hassan objected to the plan. Jaamá Mohamed Qaalib reported that, after the coup, President Mohamed Siyaad Barre told him that he used Daahir Haaji Ósmaan, a cousin of Yaasiin, whose mother was Mareehaan, and the influential director-general of the Interior Ministry, to intercede on his behalf and convince Yaasiin not to send the General abroad.[7]

There is still another version of why Égaal did not get rid of Mohamed Siyaad Barre.[8] According to this version, Égaal decided to dismiss Mohamed Siyaad Barre; however, Ábdirashiid Áli Sharmaarke, the President, Yaasiin Nuur Hassan, the Interior Minister, and Aadan Faarah Shirwaá (Aadan Law), the Minister of Justice, rallied in support of Mohamed Siyaad Barre. In a meeting at Afgooye in May 1969, they argued that removing Mohamed Siyaad Barre would be ill-advised because another Daarood, General Mohamed Abshir, had been removed from office and a large clan (meaning theirs) would be alienated. They also stated that Mohamed Siyaad Barre was not the danger that the Prime Minister assumed him to be. They saw little threat in a provincial man burdened by a large family, a man considered lightweight, without ambition and content with his position.

It is said that Yaasiin wondered how someone could find danger in a man who, in spite of being the Commander, comes to Yaasiin's home and finds joy in helping him relax in his hammock, gently rocking him like a child in a crib. Adan Faarah Shirwaá, himself a Mareehaan and married to the sister of Mohamed Siyaad Barre's oldest wife, remarked that he (Aadan) and Mohamed Siyaad Barre were among the very few Mareehaan members who held significant posts in the government and therefore, that sacking the Commander would be tantamount to dishonoring an entire clan. Persuaded or outvoted, Égaal decided against getting rid of Mohamed Siyaad Barre.

Regardless of which version is true, Mohamed Siyaad Barre remained in his post. There are three interesting side stories related to this matter. First, Ábdirazaaq Haaji Hussein was an advocate for General Mohamed Siyaad Barre to succeed as Commander of the Armed Forces when General Daauud Ábdulle Hirsi died in 1965, confirming the long association between the civilian leader and the military general. Ábdirazaaq may have lobbied for Mohamed Siyaad Barre's promotion in order to forestall another Hawiye to replace Daauud. Despite Ábdirazaaq's reputation for promoting people based on merit, he may have chosen in this case to affirm loyalty to another Daarood. Somalis are seldom free from clan bias and Ábdirazaaq is no exception, as we have seen in Chapter 4 with regard to his cabinet appointments and his membership in the *"Croce del Sud Group"* affirms.[9]

However, there is more involved here than clan bias. The two men found a common enemy in Ábdirashiid Áli Sharmaarke. They both belonged to an influential group that worked for the end of Sharmaarke's government. In addition, there is circumstantial evidence that some key officials were involved in the assassination of President Sharmaarke. In particular, Mohamed Siyaad Barre and Salaad Gabeere Kediye had a motive for getting rid of the President—the first knew that victory of Sharmaarke threatened his job; the second was the son-in-law of the former President. Both men also nursed intense political ambition, as subsequent developments confirmed. Unfortunately, the authorities did not carry out proper investigation of the assassination and they executed quietly and quickly—all of which provides further credence to the alleged complicity.

The policeman who assassinated the President in Laas Áanood resided in an orphanage when the would-be assassin was a child and General Mohamed Abshir later enrolled him in the police force. The assassin felt a personal obligation to avenge his benefactor who had been unjustly dismissed from his job by the government led by Sharmaarke, or he had powerful accomplices who enabled the assassin to shadow the President.

The police officer in charge of the President's security detail, Mohamed Saqadhi Dubad, reports that he others had gotten wind of a plot to assassinate the President.[10] He says that while they were in

Éerigaabo, before arriving in Laas Áanood, an unidentified Land Rover followed them in the thick woods of the Daallo Mountains. The officer in charge of the security detail reports that the assassin had the help of powerful allies who gave him cover as he stalked the President in Éerigaabo, Buró, and Laas Áanood.

No evidence exists to implicate Mohamed Abshir or Ábdirazaaq Haaji Hussein in the assassination, although rumors of their involvement circulated because of the intense and expressed hatred the two men harbored toward Sharmaarke. Unlike Mohamed Siyaad Barre's with a known and shady past, the two men had no record of complicity in such cruel and devious action. Still, the absence of proper investigation gave rise to wild rumors on who was behind the assassination, leaving in the dark a sordid chapter of Somali history.

Promises of Revolution

On 23 October, two days after the coup, Mohamed Siyaad Barre made a public speech that, for the first time, revealed his talent for oratory. He explained in the long speech why the military coup was necessary. He explained that the coup was necessary, legal and patriotic duty of the armed forces when the nation was in imminent peril. The Commander said that neither he nor his "friends" in the armed forces could tolerate the increasing nepotism, corruption, and the lack of discipline. Though denouncing the assassination of the President, Mohamed Siyaad Barre compared it to a payback for crimes Sharmaarke had committed against the people. With the armed forces fully in control, he assured the public there was to fear nothing.

Until then, few had heard Barre speak in public. With remarkable skill, he emotionally condemned colonialism, old and new, renewed the commitment to strengthen Islam, pledged to abolish clannism, and to restore equality for all Somalis. Emphasizing the need for discipline, he added: "Indeed, even for the family, it is impossible to advance its economy, education, self-defense, and human rights when the family fails to maintain discipline, when it fails to abide by the law, and when it fails to behave according to custom." He concluded his speech with appeal for unity for the "revolution." *Long live Somalia! Long live the Somali masses! Long live the revolution!*

So ended his speech, and so began a new chapter of Somali history in which a Cain in uniform ruled for twenty-two years. Following his speech, new decrees and institutions of social control were announced. On 30 October, the coup leaders announced a 13 point-program called *Axdigi Kaánka 21ka Okboober 1969kii*—'the Pledge of the 21st October 1969 Revolution.' Seven points addressed "internal politics" and six points focused on "external politics."

A. Internal Policy

1. To constitute a society based on the right to work and on principles of social justice considering the environment and social life of the Somali people;
2. To prepare and orientate the development of economic, social and cultural programs in a timely manner;
3. To eliminate illiteracy and develop an enlightened patrimonial and cultural heritage of the Somali people;
4. To constitute with appropriate and adequate measures the basic development of the writing of the Somali language;
5. To eliminate all corruption, all forms of anarchy, the malicious system of tribalism in every form and every other example of destructive customs in State activities;
6. To abolish all political parties;
7. To conduct at the appropriate time a free and impartial election.

B. External Policy

1. To support international solidarity and national liberation movements;
2. To oppose and fight against all forms of colonialism and neo-colonialisms;
3. To struggle to maintain the Somali National Unity;
4. To recognize the principle of peaceful coexistence between all peoples;
5. To continue and preserve the policy of positive neutrality;
6. To respect all legally signed international commitments of the Somali Republic.

Nothing in the program seemed out of tune with public sentiment or with the zeitgeist of the nineteen-sixties when military coups began with revolutionary rhetoric. On 2 November 1969, twelve days after the coup, the coup leaders announced the formation of the Supreme Revolutionary Council (SRC) consisting of 24 officers. This body was the new supreme *Klan* that was to run the country with iron fist. The dominant question was who would be the new leader of the Klan. Not used to collective leadership, the people wanted a single leader to emerge and take control.

A year later, on 21 October 1970, the Supreme Revolutionary Council announced it had adopted "scientific revolution". The SRC set a course that would look for models of leadership in other socialist countries where western democracy was abhorred. Marx and Lenin became the ideological idols; Mao and Kim Il-Sung became models for revolutionary practice.

The Somali public, outraged and frustrated by the policies of the civilian governments, had found hope and inspiration in this political program. While the public was enamored with the rhetoric of revolution, the coup leaders set up the political framework ensuring the supremacy of their rule. Among the first to give voice to the feeling relief were the poets and composers. The following song composed by Áli Sugulle captures the public support and appreciation for the coup:

If last night by nine[11]
Our obligation succeeded
And today the army is in control
Praise be to Allah
Our name (honor) is liberated
Our name (honor) is liberated
Celebrate in clear conscience.
With clannism the regime
And with misdeed all gone
Since it has all been liberated
And today the army is in control
Our name (honor) is liberated
Our name (honor) is liberated.
Celebrate with clear conscience.[12]

Composers and singers rallied in support of the "revolution," and they encouraged the public, to trust and submit to the coup leaders. The coup leaders were winning the hearts and mind of the population but also were recruiting the most talented poets and composers to their cause. When the new regime did not recruit poets and composers the poets wrote of their pleasure in the takeover by the armed forces. Ábdilaahi Suldaan (Timaádde) welcomed the military regime with a long poem of the *Geeraar* genre which included:

If truth be told
Fearing our Creator
You men in charge of the army
For you to take over [power]
We wanted [for a long time]
We've been eager [for it]
Only you dragged your feet.[13]

For a while, the coup leaders did not need to rely on arms. Those who had command of the spoken word—the poets and composers supported the coup leaders and, as a result, they had better tools than military arms. Moreover, the poets and composers who rallied behind the coup gave voice to the public sentiment expecting that the military takeover would save society.

The people idealized the coup leaders as the guarantors of their hopes and the "revolution" as the royal road to their redemption. The coup leaders, however, were not reassured even by this adoration and welling support. They knew that power taken by force invites retaliation, and that, other men of ambition, following their example, would seek power. They did not let down their guard, and they did not leave matters to chance. They remained suspicious and vigilant. In case the spoken word failed to mollify the public, leaders of the coup had lethal weapons; they placed soldiers in strategic locations, and they were ready to act swiftly against any opponent.

Achievements of the Regime

The first five years of the "revolution" introduced a series of bold policies. In fact, the coup leaders seemed genuinely committed to change in the first three years. They wanted to solve endemic and stubborn problems of corruption, poverty, and illiteracy. No other regime in Somali society has been as innovative in introducing significant change as the military regime from 1969-1975.

That is why in the midst of anarchy and chaos after the collapse of the military regime in 1991, some members of the public remember with nostalgia how the military regime kept the law and order with iron fist. This is not surprising because the need for peace and security has prior claim to the demand for justice and freedom for a public unaware that in the long-term peace and security are untenable without justice and freedom. Still, the achievements of the early years of military rule should neither be ignored nor minimized.

These achievements included:

- Injecting hope and optimism in a society experiencing despair;
- Introduction of discipline and national pride for people who accepted unruliness and shame as a way of life;

- Setting up hard work and integrity as new standards for a society rife with idleness and dishonestly;
- Building of schools and institutions of higher learning for different disciplines (including the first colleges of medicine, agriculture, and animal husbandry);
- Mobilization of communities for self-help schemes including neighborhood clean ups and reclamation of land from encroaching sand-dunes;
- Writing Somali script; the literacy campaigns for rural communities; and
- Resettling drought victims in agricultural and fishing communities.

These and other achievements (mentioned below) were indeed remarkable and no regime that came after the military regime can boast of similar record.

The first five years of the "revolution" unleashed a reservoir of creativity, vigor, and hope. New poets and poetry emerged, new singers and songs appeared, new composers and themes could be heard; old ones came back with renewed life and meaning. The spoken word, the most valued of all for Somalis when put into poetry, was unleashed with new vigor and meaning. It was as if a dam, hidden and suppressed for generations, had broken and swept society into a collective trance of creativity. Later, the poetry and songs changed to that of resistance to the regime. Who can forget the series of poetry—like the *Siinlay*, *Miimleey*, and *Deellay*—that unleashed passion and ideas throughout the country.

These were momentous developments in a society that only knew a state that constantly took but gave little back, a society whose ruling political elite mercilessly exploited its citizens. Civilian governments avoid any project involving controversy, but not so with the military regime on matters necessary to the public interest.

Take, for instance, the regime's decision on writing Somali in Latin script. The civilian administrations preceding the military regime did not solve the controversy of which script to adopt. Many religiously inclined people argued that Arabic should be used because the Qur'an is written in Arabic and Somalis are universally Muslim. Others (like Osmaan Yuusuf Kenadiid and Hussein Sheekh Kadare) invented their own script. Still others (like Muuse Galaal, Shire Jaamá, and Ábdulaahi Insaaniye) argued that adopting Latin script suited Somalis because existing typewriters and computers could be used without purchasing new ones and expending resources needed for other social services.[14]

Eight attempts to write Somali were proposed, the earliest dating back to Sheekh Yuusuf al-Kawnayn who in the fifteenth century taught Somalis how to read the Qur'an and Arabic by devising a readily comprehensible system to Somalis. Seven even other attempts followed in the twentieth century but none were accepted until the military regime set up a committee of 21 members to study the options and eventually accepted the recommendation for using Latin script.

The religious argument for writing Somali had an emotional impact for the public. Deciding whether Arabic, Latin, or an invented script was most useful for Somalis was something the civilian administrations avoided. Mohamed Siyaad Barre made a bold decision, when he adopted the Latin-based script in 1972. Thanks to this bold decision, Somali is today a Latin-based, written language, and used by all. He announced the decision to write Somali in Latin script on 21 October 1972 and explained that Somalis cannot advance in development or their quest for freedom, unless the high rate of illiteracy is reduced. Barre said that the best means of advancing knowledge is to write Somali and to adopt the Latin script. His explanations were accepted.

The military regime endorsed the adoption of Somali script proposed by the 21-member committee and it ensured that people used the new script. It ordered all officials to learn and become proficient in it, to use it in their work, or forfeit their jobs. As a result, officials who otherwise would have procrastinated enrolled in training programs. The public took advantage of literacy programs in schools and at "orientation centers," and many illiterate adults who never thought they would learn the magic of the written word turned literate.

Government officials were ordered to be functionally literate in the new script by a stated deadline. Fearing to lose their jobs, the officials complied. With amazing speed, all civil servants, law enforcement agents, and teachers adopted written Somali as the official medium of communication and instruction. Suddenly, official and written language was de-colonized. In addition, the so-called "Orientation Centers" located in every neighborhood taught the public the new magic of reading and writing in Somali. Students were sent to the country to teach nomadic and farming communities how to read and write. Consequently, the population's literacy rate soared so quickly and widely that the success of the regime attracted the attention and admiration of the United Nations and others organizations concerned with literacy.

Even more remarkable, the regime started a Rural Development Campaign in July 1974 that sent 30,000 students and teachers to farming communities all over the country. Dispatched in trucks, provided with folding blackboards and basic health kits, the students and teachers taught literacy, hygiene, animal husbandry, and civic education. Eight students were in a group led by a teacher. However, there were instances where one student, often a young female, lived in the rural communities, taught reading and writing to adults who had never held a pencil or a book.

The decision to carry out this campaign was momentous, illustrating that Somalis can accomplish remarkable achievements if led creatively and boldly. Not only did the students teach their less fortunate compatriots how to read and write they also saw first hand how life was in rural communities, as compared to life in the comfortable homes of the elite in urban centers.

In 1974, a devastating drought struck in parts of the country while the Rural Development Campaign was underway. Again, the regime carried out the most ambitious resettlement program ever conceived in Somali history. Unlike the Mengistu Regime of Ethiopia that concealed from the international community the devastating drought decimating its citizens in 1972, the Somali military regime appealed for help and did what it could on its own to save its people. Using trucks and Russian provided planes, the government moved thousands of the drought victims into farming and fishing communities hundreds of miles away from the drought affected areas. This "crash program" was another momentous achievement, although like the literacy campaign, it stumbled due to lack of forethought and follow-up.

Ordinarily, Somalis live in managed chaos. Discipline is often lax, authority not revered, spontaneity dominates ordinary life, and delay of gratification is encouraged by neither the pastoral culture nor the fatalism of Islam. The regime of Mohamed Siyaad Barre is the only regime that herded civil servants, diplomats, teachers, and students into training camps, forcing them to wear uniforms, to endure a Spartan life-style and to obey second-rate soldiers. The wardens of these training camps bluntly ordered them to "leave their testicles at the gate." While there, they left behind their testicles and their pride, under the iron fist of new rulers.

At first, the poets and the people extended blind support to the regime. They were intoxicated with the rhetoric of revolution and hoped for tangible achievements the people could experience. They found tangible achievements in when the SRC ended the debates on the appropriate script for writing Somali and they adopted the Latin script in 1972. They appreciated SRC reforms when it imposed strict discipline on both government employees and all citizens and when it canalized people's energy in self-help schemes including cleaning-up the neighborhoods and reclaiming arable land from encroaching sand dunes. They found pride in the regime's response to the severe drought of 1974, using the very bold and creative "experiment" of resettling thousands of victims from nomadic communities to farming and fishing communities. They also found encouragement in the regime's attempt to teach nomads how to farm and fish, two activities they culturally despise, affirming belief in the human capacity to change and the commitment to transformative action.

Taken together, these "crash programs" were an experiment in self-help in solving Somali problems using the human and material resources at hand. Mohamed Siyaad Barre and his regime must be given credit for organizing and mobilizing Somalis to realize these historic achievements. Innovations like writing Somali, reclaiming arable land and resettling nomads were no mean achievements in a society previously in disarray. These programs demonstrated that, given proper guidance, Somalis change their behavior.

Unfortunately, most of the changes introduced by the military regime did not last because they relied on flawed principles and used autocratic practice. Psychologists who study human behavior indicate that changes in behavior brought about by punishment or fear may be successful but the change does not endure when force and fear are no longer stimulus for change. In addition, revolution ordered from the top, using force and fear, intoxicates the leaders with power they usurped to the same degree that their people become subservient and fearful of taking initiative.

Dictatorship diminishes creativity and commitment to the common good. Based on fear, it fosters temporary obedience. At the same time, resentment builds up and simmers, waiting for an opportunity to explode when the lid held by an iron fist lifts. This is precisely what eventually happened in Somali society. But in 1975, neither the SRC nor the public had the prescience to know the explosion and the state collapse that was to take place sixteen years later. The best one suspected then was that the military regime derailed from the "revolution" it promised and from the initial programs of change it introduced.

As Mohamed Siyaad Barre gained absolute power, his cult grew rapidly until it turned into a new religion with a dictator as its demigod. How did Mohamed Siyaad Barre emerge as a dictator?

Slide to Dictatorship

At first, it appeared that the coup leaders had adopted a system of collective leadership with representation from the major clans. Because Mohamed Siyaad Barre was perceived to be an old man surrounded by ambitious young officers, his leadership of the SRC did not diminish the illusion of collective leadership and clan representation. He himself played to the illusion by couching SRC decisions in collective terms like "my friends and I."

In the first few days after the coup, it was not clear who really was the leader of the SRC's inner circle of leaders or of the country. During this period, the coup leaders decided who to include and who to exclude from their inner circle. The process of culling members took days until the Supreme Revolutionary Council was announced. Some (like Mohamed Siyaad Barre and Ismaíil Áli Abokor) belonged to the core planners and executors of the coup, and others (like Hussein Kulmiye, Mohamed Áynaanshe Guuleed, and Jaamá Áli Qorsheel) joined the SRC only after the coup succeeded.

According to General Ismaíil Áli Abokor, a member of the core group and the most knowledgeable living person on the topic, the coup was in planning since 1967—two years before it took place. Most probably, Mohamed Siyaad Barre had planned the coup long before, perhaps since 1964 when he became the Commander of the

Armed Forces, following the death of General Daauud. While planning the coup, Mohamed Siyaad Barre sent the lead group he did not trust to training abroad or remote assignments. These included Ábdulaahi Yuusuf Ahmed, Mohamed Faarah Áydiid, and Saleebaan Gabeere Kediye. Most arrived after the coup or when plans could not be reversed. Table 1 presents the identities of the first SRC members.

Table 1

Members of the Supreme Revolutionary Council
21 October 1969

Name	Rank	Clan	Sub-Clan
Major General Mohamed Siyaad Barre	President	Daarood	Mareehaan
General Mohamed Áynaanshe	Vice President	Isaaq	Habar Yoonis
General Jaamá Áli Korsheel	Vice President	Daarood	Warsangali
Brigadier Hussein Kulmiye Afrah	Member	Hawiye	Abgaal
Major Ismaíil Áli Abokor	Member	Isaaq	Habar Jélo
Lt. Colonel Salaad Gabeere Kedi	Member	Hawiye	Abgaal
Lt. Colonel Mohamed Áli Samatar	Member	Tumaal	Íise-'Aade
Lt. Colonel Abdalla Mohamed Faadil	Member	'Arab	Yemeni
Lt. Colonel Mohamed Mire Musa	Member	Daarood	Ogaadeen
Lt. Colonel Mohamed Sheekh Ósmaan	Member	Hawiye	Murasade
Lt. Colonel Áli Mataan Haashi	Member	Daarood	Mareehaan
Major Ahmed Sulieman Abdalla	Member	Daarood	Dhulbahante
Major Muuse Rabiileh Good	Member	Gadabursi	Mahad-Case
Major Faarax Waáys Dulleh	Member	Íise	Wadool
Major Mohamed Yuusuf Élmi	Member	Hawiye	Habar Gidir
Major Mohamed Áli Shire	Member	Daarood	Dhulbanate
Major Ahmed Mohamed Faarax	Member	Isaaq	Habar Awal
Major Mohamuud Geelle Yuusuf	Member	Daarood	Mijeerteen
Captain Ábdirazaaq Mahamuud Abubakar	Member	Daarood	Mijeerteen
Captain Ábdilqaadir Haaji Mohamed	Member	Daarood	Mareehaan
Captain Mohamed Úmar Gees	Member	Daarood	Ogaadeen
Captain Ábdi Warsame Isaaq	Member	Dir	Gaadsan
Captain Ahmed Mahamuud Ádde	Member	Hawiye	Abgaal
Captain Ósmaan Mohamed Jeelle	Member	Hawiye	Hawaaadle
Captain Ahmed Hassan Muuse	Member	Isaaq	Habar Jélo

Chart 1 presents the clan distribution of SRC members. Of the twenty-five SRC members, Daarood had 11 members (40%). Since Mohamed Siyaad Barre was himself a member of the Daarood clan, people assumed that the Daarood would have the greatest share. The Hawiye had six members (24%) and the Isaaq four members (18%). Thus, the composition of the SRC maintained the old distribution of power that had favored the Daarood since independence, with the Hawiye second, and the Isaaq third.

Chart 1
Clan Distribution of SRC Members
21 October 1969

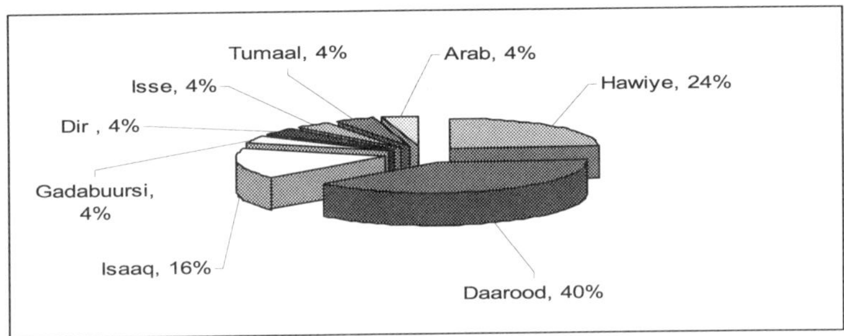

In the era of revolutionary zeal, few Somalis critically examined the clan composition of the cabinet when the SRC announced the members. Besides, the citizen had no choice but to accept the dictates of the Supreme Revolutionary Council.

Note that members of the three power usurping clans—the Daarood, the Hawiye, and the Isaaq—have occupied the top offices, with the Daarood having a decisive advantage. This sample provides a hint of how power was organized and what was to come later.

Note also that the SRC included clans (like the Gabooye and Tumaal) that, in the past, were excluded from power; but this was symbolic representation. Mohamed Siyaad Barre had a plan for including some members like General Mohamed Áli Samatar in the SRC because he knew that Samatar would be loyal having been elevated to a position of power to with which others had never entrust him.

Soon after the armed forces carried out the coup, they assembled 50 of the best civil servants and intellectuals to devise a plan of administering the country and of carrying out the "revolution." Among those assembled was Ahmed Mohamed Mohamuud (Silaanyo), then the Director General of the Ministry of Planning and later the Minister of Planning. Ahmed explained that, soon after the coup, even the assembled did not know who belonged to the core leaders or who was in charge. While the coup leaders sorted out internal problems, the assembled civil servants worked on proposals on how to govern the country.

According to Ahmed, the assembled intellectuals and civil servants proposed strategic ideas that the armed forces implemented initially but abandoned soon after. Some of the ideas proposed included that the coup leaders avoid responsibility for managing the government since they lacked training and experience, that they relinquish this responsibility to civil managers, that they form a central committee to monitor the work of these civilian managers, and that the civilian managers and military committee at all times function independently.[15]

At first, only a few of the military leaders joined the government. Most members of the Council of Ministers were therefore civilian whose members were impressive compared to the civilian government it replaced.

Table 2 presents the list and clan of the members.

Table 2

Composition of the Government
21 October 1969

Name	**Rank**	**Clan**	**Sub-Clan**
Mohamed Siyaad Barre	President	Daarood	Mareehaan
Abdalla Aw Faarax Hirsi	Minister of Agriculture	Daarood	Mijeerteen
Jaamá Áli Korsheel	Minister of Interior	Daarood	Warsangali
Úmar 'Arte Qaalib	Minister of Foreign Affairs	Isaaq	Habar Awal
Hassan Áli Mire	Minister of Education	Daarood	Mijeerteen
Mohamed Aadan Sheekh	Minister of Health	Daarood	Mareehaan
Mohamed Ábdi Árraale	Minister of Finance	Isaaq	Habar Yonis
Mahamuud Gelle Élmi "Dhurwa"	Minister of Industry & Commerce	Hawiye	Habar Gidir
Mahamuud Jaamá Ahmed "Juje"	Min. of Information & Nat. Guidance	Daarood	Mareehaan
Ósmaan Nuur Áli	Minister of Justice, Religion, & Labor	Daarood	Mijeerteen
Mohamed Buraaleh Ismaíil	Minister of Mining	Daarood	Dhulbahante
Mahamuud Mohamed Ósmaan	Min. of Livestock & Animal Husbandry	Hawiye	Hawaadle
Ahmed Mohamed Mohamuud	Minister of Planning	Isaaq	Habar Jélo
Ábdilqaadir Aadan Ábdulle	Minister of Public Works	Hawiye	Ujejen
Mohamed Ánshuur	Min. of Transport & Communication	Hawiye	Habar Gidir

As the list above shows, the selected civil servants included some of the most qualified Somalis in the country—for instance, Dr. Mohamed Áli Mire, Ahmed Mohamed Mohamuud (Siilaanyo), Dr. Mohamed Aadan Sheekh, and Ábdilqaadir Aadan Ábdulle. The last appointment was especially interesting because Ábdilqaadir was the son of former President Aadan Ábdulle Ósmaan. The composition of the government also shows the coup leaders' attempt to first mollify the "large" clans. All members were exclusive from the Daarood, Hawiye, and Isaaq. No member had been appointed from the "smaller" clans.

Chart 2 presents the clan distribution of the 1st Council of Ministers.

Chart 2
Clan Distribution of Ministers under SRC
October 1969

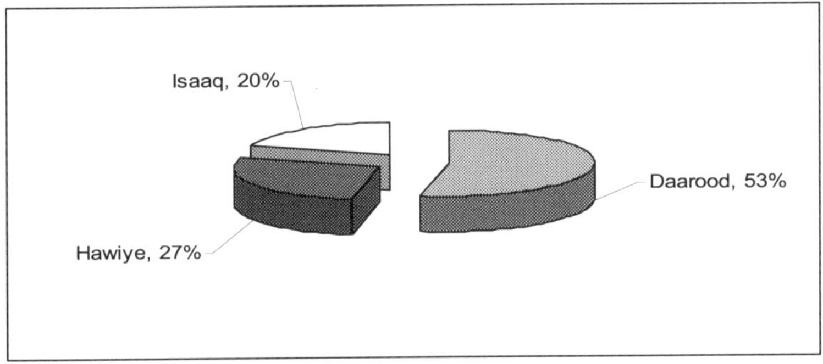

The Daarood had eight (53%) of the 15 members in the Council of Ministers and therefore the largest percentage since independence. The Hawiye had four (27%) members and the Isaaq three (20%) members. This core group constituted the ruling supreme Klan composed of different clan members. Still entranced by the rhetoric of revolution, people paid little attention to the overwhelming advantage given to the Daarood.

Even the non-Daarood members of the SRC seem to have been oblivious to the clan hegemony resurging, despite the rhetoric of revolution. If they were aware of this and Mohamed Siyaad Barre's gradually self-promotion to dictator, they might have been victims of the Somali flaw in which all overlook problems and take a rosy picture of the world if one and his clan is included in the cabal and conspiracy. Even the opponents of the coup joined with alacrity once given a role in the 'revolutionary' march to dictatorship.

The public ignored the clan composition of the SRC because they wanted change above all. They did not want to scrutinize key posts of the government; hence, they ignore which clan had the greatest representation in the government. However, the dominance by the Daarood in the SRC and the Council of Ministers was so blatant that it is difficult to conclude that Somalis who are given to clan suspicion and scrutiny were oblivious to it. Perhaps the public were assured by the presence of kinsmen in the SRC, whatever their number or proportion. Perhaps too, their desperation for change took priority over clan loyalty.

In fact, the manufacturing of a dictator began soon after the coup as did the clan oligarchy and the "rule of the family" that was to emerge a decade later. Not only did the SRC members permit Mohamed Siyaad Barre to usurp power while they underestimated him as the "Old Man" but also they conceded that he include in the SRC his relatives by clan or marriage. For instance, included in the SRC were two in-laws (Major Ahmed Suleymaan Ábdulle and Lt. Colonel Áli Mattaan Haashi, the latter also Mareehaan). The Council of Ministers had two Mareehaan—Dr. Mohamed Aadan Sheekh, then a primary confidant and advisor of Mohamed Siyaad Barre, and Mohamuud Jaamá Ahmed "Juje", Minister of Information and National Guidance.

Despite these early harbingers of troubles to come, the hand-picked team of civil servants did a superb job in raising the level of competence and credibility of the regime initially. Without their help, the military coup leaders would have quickly failed to manage and administer the affairs of the state they took over by force.

Ahmed Mohamed Mohamuud (Siilaanyo) was among this hand-picked civilian elite and recalls that, before the coup, Mogadishu became the meeting place for elders, campaign managers and *af-miinshaars* (spinners of rumor). The came to the capital city from different regions, expecting rewards for their support in the election. The city teemed with crowds of people waiting to be rewarded for the way they voted but soon after the coup, most of them returned to their village empty handed. Mogadishu was suddenly empty and quiet. Something had to be done to bring it back to normal.

The Ministry of Planning which Siilaanyo headed came up with creative and bold initiatives called "crash programs" intended to solve urgent problems ignored by the civilian regime and to channel human energy into constructive social programs. These were self-help schemes, neighborhood cleanup schemes, reclamation schemes, and literacy campaigns. These programs were the pride of the regime and a tangible example of its "revolution."

However, when the armed forces infiltrated the Council of Ministers, rigidity and inexperience set in which gradually eroded the creativity of these programs. Stern orders from the top and threats of punishment, acts inconsistent with creativity but typical of the armed forces, nipped these programs in the bud. By then, the dictatorship had gained momentum that could not be stopped.

Immediately after the coup, Mohamed Siyaad Barre adopted collective leadership for the SRC. Other members of this organization deferred to him as "the Old Man" because he was the oldest in the group.[16] At first, he used this geriatric privilege to his advantage, exploiting the deference it afforded him. He quietly pushed his ideas and power while he positioned himself as the leader of the pack, waiting for the opportunity to assert dominance in both the SRC and the country. He carried out behind-the-scene tactics of splitting the SRC members into camps, pitting one group against another and sowing suspicion among them. These behind-the-scene tactics soon enabled him to usurp power for himself.

General Ismaíil Áli Abokor, the closest ally of Mohamed Siyaad Barre in plotting and carrying out the coup, recalls that he and other SRC members lost power to Mohamed Siyaad Barre in gradual and small steps.[17] He recalls one incident in which the Mohamed Siyaad Barre appointed someone to a key post in government on his own, breaching SRC agreement that such appointments must be made jointly. Ismaíil states that he and the other SRC members confronted him by asking why he this appointment without consulting them. Mohamed Siyaad Barre, feigning shock and timidity, answered that he exercised authority due to being the oldest in the group. The other members let him get away with this breach although it paved the way for worse infractions, allowing him to increase his power and diminish theirs. The next morning, Mohamed Siyaad Barre said to them tongue in cheek: "I realized last night that the revolution has its vigilant owners and protectors." Ismaíil says that is when he and his colleagues lost out to the wit and will of the "Old Man."[18]

Mohamed Siyaad Barre outdid the rest of his colleagues in the SRC from the start when they acceded to him the leadership of the SRC and accepted less powerful ministerial posts themselves. If they had rotated leadership of the SRC, history might have been different. However, their indecisiveness cost them dearly: two of the SRC members lost their lives, the others their power; hopes for a better future for Somalis also vanished.

By the time Mohamed Siyaad Barre's colleagues woke up to his machination and to their mistakes, it all too late. The seasoned spy and skilled master of subterfuge divided them into groups, set them against one another, identified who was malleable to his influence, who a potential competitor. Among the skills that served the would-be-dictator was his unusual capacity to listen, all the while gather information he needed. Often too, he used the speaker's words and admissions to incriminate, intimidate or humiliate him in front of others. He also created adversarial camps competing for his alliance, giving ambiguous signals of support that induced one to let his guard, biding his time until he was ready to act decisively.

Seven months after the coup, in May 1971, General Mohamed Áynaanshe Guuleed and Colonel Salaad Gabeere Kediye were arrested on charges of antirevolutionary activities. Áynaanshe was one of the two Vice Presidents; Gabeere was Minister of Defense. The other Vice President, General Jaamá Áli Qorsheel, was arrested in April 1970, for the same charges of counterrevolutionary activity. However, Qorsheel was released after a period of confinement; Áynaanshe and Gabeere were executed in July 1971. As we shall see later, the execution of these men and others did not only get rid of men whom Mohamed Siyaad Barre wanted to get out of his path to dictatorship but also it had terrorizing impact on the public, particular members of three clans—the Isaaq, the Hawiye, and the Mijeerteen. No doubt, the execution had its intimidating effect on his colleagues in the SRC.

By then, Mohamed Siyaad Barre was supreme. His dictatorship consolidated and grew. In time, only the most loyal and subservient of the lot stayed with him to the end. These were the type Mohamed Siyaad Barre knew how to cultivate and keep around him. The others who questioned him or gave hint of their resentment suffered his castigation one way or another. For instance, he imprisoned in solitary confinement for almost six yeas and tried him for capital crime of sedition General Ismaíil Áli Abokor, a key architect of the coup and a sincere believer in the "revolution."

Perhaps that is what saved the General in the end, despite his public criticism of the "revolution" at a time the slightest remark threw most to the growing pack of torturers and executions waiting to unleash their sadistic impulse on victims. Reliable information has it that Mohamed Siyaad Barre did whatever he could—including offer of immense fortune—to dissuade his colleague from becoming an 'anti-revolutionary' which in essence meant opposition to the dictator. However, Ismaíil held on to his strident views, regardless.

It was not only the dictatorial behavior of Mohamed Siyaad Barre that alienated Ismaíil Áli Abokor. It was also the active campaign of his colleagues for clan hegemony that shocked and disappointed him. That he miscalculated on his expectations of "the revolution" and belief in human integrity was driven home by a visit he made to the office of his long-term friend and colleague, General Ahmed Suleymaan Ábdulle. Though Ahmed was Daarood and Ismaíil Isaaq, the two men were school mates in Somaliland and Britain. Ahmed was in a meeting when Ismaíil and another colleague arrived at his office. Without Ahmed's knowledge, they waited for him in next room where they could hear him urging a group of Mareehaan officials to realize "that every country in the region is ruled by a clan or tribe" and that therefore they must consolidate and protect Daarood power in Somalia.

That such strident fanning of clan antagonism and partisanship came from his friend of manay decades whose mother was in addition Isaaq had dissipated any last mists of illusion Ismaíil entertained about the so-called revolution. Thus, his doubts in the early seventies grew to alienation after 1976 until it emerged as open and vitriolic criticism of the regime by the end of the decade. Alienated from the regime and Mohamed Siyaad Barre, General Abokor withdrew to his home and religious life, although indirectly he was involved in the rise of Isaaq opposition to the regime. Behind the scene he urged and helped Isaaq officer in the armed forces to join the Somali National Movement. In the early 1982, Ismaíil was jailed in a high security prison and held in solitary confinement for nearly six years.

General Ismaíil recounted an incident that shows vintage Mohamed Siyaad Barre. A year or two before their estrangement had become clear both and to the public in 1980, the two traveled to Saudi Arabia. One night, the two men found opportunity to talk in Taif in breezy and pleasant night outside a secure compound, starting in the evening and ending their talk until sunrise.

As General Ismaíil tells it, Mohamed Siyaad Barre let Ismaíil to talk all night about how the revolution had derailed and what they must do to put back on tract while Mohamed Siyaad Barre calmly and intently listened. It was in fact a monologue but nothing in Mohamed

Siyaad Barre's non-verbal communication betrayed discomfort or disagreement. On the contrary, he seemed to agree with Ismaíil's analysis and recommendations. After sunrise, Mohamed Siyaad Barre promised to follow up on those issues when they returned home.

In the first meeting they had with their colleagues, Mohamed Siyaad Barre reported that he and Ismaíil had a long and intense discussion about the revolution while abroad. Ismaíil expected that Mohamed Siyaad Barre would present on the wisdom of what they talked about and how the needed correction would be made. Instead, Mohamed Siyaad Barre criticized Ismaíil's views and concluded that Ismaíil, a key member of the revolution, was greatly misinformed.

Until then, Ismaíil who knew the man well did not get the slightest hint of Mohamed Siyaad Barre's disagreement on what he had said that night in Taif, Saudi Arabia. This was one of ways in which Mohamed Siyaad Barre picked the brain and hearts of others, only to entrap them and castigate them in public. In so criticizing Ismaíil in front of his colleagues, Mohamed Siyaad Barre communicated that Ismaíil fell from grace and issued an implicit threat to others that criticism of the revolution would not be condoned.

From there on, the relationship of the two men deteriorated. By 1980, Ismaíil took public criticism of the regime that many thought was openly suicidal. None was therefore surprised when he was imprisoned and held in solitary confinement for at least six years. By 1980, Ismaíil exceeded public criticism and tread on a most dangerous path: he encouraged Isaaq officers to desert government service and to form an armed movement of their own outside the country. They did so to give birth to the Somali National Movement—a fact not acknowledged by those who today claim to be the founders or leaders of this movement. Such a campaign was indeed a highly risky undertaking for someone known for his growing opposition and under continual surveillance. However, Ismaíil was not a man who acted on his belief without fear of consequences.

Of course, Mohamed Siyaad Barre did not limit himself to subduing or punishing his colleagues. From the beginning, he and his colleagues had set up a system with which to terrorize and force submission of the public. They wrested power and exploited public frustration against the misrule of civilian governments. A few years into their so-called revolution, they realized that speeches and propaganda were not enough to control and govern. Hence, they issued a series of decrees that gave them freedom to investigate, interrogate, and persecute the opponents of the regime. These decrees at first seemed innocuous, but they become a chilling threat to society.

Laws for Terror

In 1970, the SRC weeded out all those whom it deemed a threat to the regime and its "revolution." On 10 November 1970, it issued another decree on *Difaaca Bulshada*, 'Protection of Public Order'. Among other things, the decree abolished traditional titles like *Boqor, garaad, Suldaan,* and *Ugaas*, and replaced them with a new name: *Nabaddoon*, 'Peacemaker'. It also abolished many traditional laws and social contracts.

Mohamed Siyaad Barre made a speech on 8 November 1969 in which he urged the armed forces to serve the people who actually pay their salary. On 26 November, a circular followed that announced the formation of a new office, the Public Relations Office, which was later changed to the Political Office of the Presidency and the Supreme Revolutionary Council. The SRC offered amnesty to all convicts except officials of the previous government and issued a new law imposing punishment (including death) to anyone compromising the sovereignty of the nation. Soon, the regime launched a vigorous campaign against the *Kaándiid* (the "anti-revolutionaries") and accused many government employees of mismanaging public resources. Early targets of the campaign were former officials of the civilian government and religious leaders.

In December 1970, the regime declared its desire to abolish the clan system. It began with a public murder and burial of an effigy that represented the clan system. It burned books and records on clans were burned, as if these public rituals alone could erase the clan system and clannism. On 10 January 1970, less than four months after the coup, the SRC issued a decree giving it full authority to imprison anyone suspected of subversive acts. This law gave the regional and district councils the right to detain anyone suspected to be a threat to the objectives and spirit of the "revolution." The law was so ambiguous that anyone could be detained without evidence.

On 26 January 1970, the SRC also issued Law No. 8 that amended the Code of Criminal Procedures and authorized evidence gathering by any means on any crime related to national security. As result of this law, torture became a common method of interrogation.[19] On 2 February 1970, the SRC established the National Security Services (NSS) to gather intelligence on internal and external threats against the regime, and to monitor the actions of suspected "anti-revolutionaries."

On 10 February 1970, the SRC established a special court called the National Security Court (NSC) to punish by death or long-term imprisonment those accused of being a threat to the regime. Mohamed Siyaad Barre who appointed judges for this court was closely monitored and directed in all major trials from the time the NSC was established to the collapse of the regime. The President also appointed the Special Prosecutor and his deputies who were selected from the armed forces.[20] The NSC had its extension in smaller courts in every district and region; members of the armed forces controlled and managed the lower courts.

The NSC frequently ordered executions based on minimal evidence; therefore, it came to be known as *Kawaanka Dadweynaha*, 'the Slaughterhouse of the people'. On 15 February 1970, the SRC issued Law No. 14 authorizing the NSS to search the person, property, or home of anyone suspected of being "anti-revolutionary." It also gave authority to confiscate personal possessions and property if found guilty. Soon, merely a charge of endangering "national security" became grounds for long-term imprisonment or even death.

On 26 February 1970, the constitution that had governed the nation since independence was abolished. Four days later, existing political parties were abolished and new parties were not allowed to form. A few days later, Mohamed Siyaad Barre announced that public servants would be offered a salary adequate to cover their needs and there would be a merit evaluation. The pool of talented composers and singers rallying behind the "revolution" took this promise at face value, as shown by the following song composed by 'Áli Sugulle in which the failed system based on nepotism ("who you know?") is contrasted with the new order based on merit ("what you know?).

You stumbled
You fell down, fell down
Who do you know?
You can not walk
You fell down, fell down
Who do you know?

You lost guidance and you got lost
Who do you know
And so what do you know?[21]

On 26 March 1970, Mohamed Siyaad Barre declared: "Any official who does not follow the mission of the revolution has the responsibility of quitting his job."[22] Since few would quit on their own, the draconian laws of the military regime pushed them out of jobs and out of the country. On 10 September 1970, the SRC issued Law No. 54 listing 26 articles, 20 of which carried a mandatory sentence. Referred to as a law safeguarding "national security," this law constituted a legal document by which a suspected *kacaadiid* (anti-revolutionary) could be executed or punished with long-term incarceration. The law allowed confiscation of the condemned person's property, thereby doubly the penance by punishing his family. In fact, Law No. 54 was a legal noose the SRC used to hang its opponents. The primary advocate of Law No. 54 was said to be Salaad Gabeere Kediye who ironically turned out to be among the first the regime executed using this law to justify its cruel action..

In August 1970, the SRC authorized government officials to receive and store farm produce. This decree gave the regime a monopoly on agricultural produce in the country. Anyone hiding or misdirecting produce from his farm was severely punished. The decree eliminated market and questioned the ownership of farms, leading to a decline in agricultural production.

Between 1970 and 1972, the SRC issued a series of decrees nationalizing industries, wholesale companies, banks, and insurance companies. To expand its power and to control key sectors of the economy, the SRC invoked socialist jargon justifying the nationalization of program by the need to regain "ownership of the means of production." These actions were validated by the historic role of the "working class" even though the intent of these decrees concentrated power only in the SRC. The difference between the productive working class and the parasitic armed forces seems to have conveniently escaped them.

On 17 September 1970, the Supreme Revolutionary Council ordered all government employees to appear for military training at a camp called *Bootiko* and later known as *Halane*. On 10 October 1970, the SRC abolished habeas corpus. Known as Law No. 64, the decree removed legal protection against arbitrary arrest. Like the other decrees preceding it, the law justified the SRC and its agents to detain any person, any time, without evidence. It also gave authorities freedom to punish opponents by using the death sentence. In addition, Law No. 17 issued on 7 April 1970 limited a detainee's access to legal council while authorities investigated the matter. In the rare cases where access to counsel was permitted, the accused was not granted right to private consultation with his defense attorney.

In January 1971, the SRC issued a decree prohibiting writers, journalists, and composers from disseminating their work without screening by the *Guddiga Faaf Reebka,* the Censorship Board that decided if a work was offensive to the "revolution." This decree enforced the culture of silence that is the hallmark of the dictatorship. On 4 March 1971, the SRC issued a law enabling the National Security Court to sentence to death by firing squad anyone destroying or misusing public property or who accepting bribes from the public. The decree includes anyone engaged in propaganda or working with foreigners in ways the authorities perceived a threat to 'the integrity of the government.'

On 6 March 1971, the regime entered into a comprehensive political, economic, and military agreement with the former Soviet Union. By January 1972, socialism was promoted and the number of NSS agents increased. In April 1972, the SRC issued Law No. 38 that declared Mohamed Siyaad Barre the supreme authority to revise the National Security Court, to hear appeals, and to give clemency. On 11 January 1975, the Family Law was issued. Many religious leaders opposed this law because they considered it in conflict with Somali culture and Islam.

In a speech on 13 January 1975, Mohamed Siyaad Barre explained that the Family Law was compatible with Islam but he added two views that outraged the religious community. First, he declared, "If the Prophet was alive today, he would have kept pace with modern society and its requirements." In other words, the Prophet would have endorsed the Family Law and the socialism that Mohamed Siyaad Barre imposed. Second, Mohamed Siyaad Barre said, "The statements or articles contained in *Al-Nisa Sura* concerning inequality of women and men have been rendered irrelevant."[23]

The soldier who knew little about Islam had presented himself as an authority of Islam and a preacher of its precepts. This man also presented himself as a staunch socialist with his picture displayed in public places along with those Marx and Lenin. Mohamed Siyaad Barre's arrogant statements and the Family Law itself led to demonstrations, and to the execution of ten religious leaders chosen as sacrificial lambs. Further violent confrontations significantly weakened the regime.

The arrogant statements and ignorance of Mohamed Siyaad Barre, leading to the execution of the religious men, breached the traditional separation of the *waranleh* (armed man) and the *wadaad* (religious man). Each category had its own function in society—the *waranleh* protecting the community from external attack, the *wadaad* teaching Islam, administering the spiritual needs of the community, and mediating social conflict. In times when a leader usurped the two roles, as did Mohamed Ábdulle Hassan at the turn of the twentieth century, society was in utter confusion and armed conflict.[24]

By the end of 1971, the legal justification for repression was fully in place. Yet the public, entranced by poetry and songs, was in no mood to imagine the peril ahead. Among the songs that lulled the public to complacency and intensified the arrogance of Mohamed Siyaad Barre was one composed and sung by Ábdi Muhumed Amiin. Its refrain was:

The clear path you set your feet upon
Tread [on it] all the way
Live forever
Live, live
Keep holding the reign
Hold, hold
Hold it forever…
Correct the way of thought
Healthy in essence
You guided us to it
Live forever
Live, live
Keep holding the reign
Hold, hold…[25]

As fate would have it, the progressive singer and composer of this song came to regret the propaganda that lulled his people to complacency and submission.

Internationally too, Cain was ready to flex his muscle and join in the struggle for liberty. As soon as the Cain in uniform came to power, Somalia leaped into the forefront of African nations supporting liberation movements like FRELIMO of Mozambique, the EPLF and ELF of Eritrea, the OLF of Ethiopia, and the ANC of South Africa. It even allowed North Vietnam to use the Somali flag on ships to evade the embargo during its war with the United States.

Not so widely known is that Somalia became a hotbed of terrorists and hijackers (like the infamous "Carlos" who spent some time in Mogadishu). Terrorists were secretly trained on Somali soil so that, in the name of "revolution" and for the benefit of "socialism," they could strike terror in western countries. In addition, the military regime sent some its finest military officers to train guerrilla fighters elsewhere in Africa.[26]

In short, the coup leaders presented themselves locally and globally as bona fide revolutionaries and the public readily believed them. Although bankrupt in all respects, the supreme ruling *Klan* was ready to unleash terror on its people in the name of revolution.

Propaganda and Fear

Systems of oppression need a hierarchical structure with a leader at the top. This is why collective leadership in the Supreme Revolutionary Council did not last long. The members of the SRC competed among themselves, and Mohamed Siyaad Barre demonstrated skills developed during his service under colonial rule. He sowed conflict among the SRC members, dividing them into camps. To ensure personal survival, each member of the SRC worked hard to please and mollify the "Old Man" in the hope of belonging to the camp Mohamed Siyaad Barre most favored and trusted. Thus, the cult of personality began within the SRC before it permeated public consciousness through propaganda in the government-controlled press and the neighborhood "orientation centers."

As Mohamed Siyaad Barre outwitted the other members of the SRC, his name and image became larger than life. The song writers, singers, and poets praised him and he became the supreme hero—

Guulwade Siyaad, 'the beacon of victory,' *Aabihi Ummadda*, 'the father of the nation,' even *Aabihi Garashada*, 'the father of the knowledge'—as shown by the following song that for years could be heard in schools, workplaces, and public events.

Siyaad, the victory pioneer
The Father of Knowledge
Of our land
Socialism is the system
Leading us to prosperity
This surging light
This glowing brilliance
The echoes of voices
Is that of the youth and workers
All of whom are united
Standing by their revolution
The ideas emanating from it
That had promised
Ha... Ha...
To defend socialism.[27]

Students, soldiers, civil servants, all chanted the song in unison. Mohamed Ósmaan Úmar, a Somali diplomat, reports that all embassy personnel in London and elsewhere were required to sing this song every day. This was tantamount to daily declaration of loyalty to Mohamed Siyaad Barre and to his "revolution."

Mohamed Siyaad Barre took his revolutionary and paternal credentials seriously as the population continued to sing his praises and pander to his larger-than-life image. The lyrics of the song are telling: they enlarged Siyaad Barre's megalomania while they demeaned and infantilized the rest of society. To the degree the leader is glorified, to the same the degree are the led degraded.

A political office headed by Ábdilqaadir Haaji Mohamed, a relative of Mohamed Siyaad Barre, coordinated the ideological propaganda. Some members of the intelligentsia exaggerated the facts and burdened their conscience by cataloguing the revolutionary and patriotic credentials of Siyaad Barre. Mohamed Ósmaan Omar, a Somali diplomat, reports that all embassy personnel in London and elsewhere were required to sing this song every day. This was tantamount to daily declaration of loyalty to Siyaad Barre and to his "revolution." [28] A daily newspaper and a mouthpiece of the regime called *The October Star*, on its front page, had Siyaad Barre's picture and a caption of his *Tusaalooy-inka Madax Weynaha*—'Guiding words of the President.[29]

Radio programs also carried his "revolutionary speeches," aired evocative songs that praised Siyaad Barre, and threatened opponents with harsh retribution. Neighborhood associations were organized for the "self-help" schemes the President witnessed in the Democratic Republic of Korea. The goals of these schemes were to advance the common good (e.g. to clean the neighborhoods or to reclaim land lost to the encroaching dunes). However, the primary intent was to cultivate the public obedience and loyalty to the regime.

In 1972, Siyaad Barre visited the People's Republic of China and the Democratic Republic of Korea. He was particularly impressed by how the Chinese revered Chairman Mao and the Koreans worshipped Kim Il Sung, their "Great Leader." These visits were significant in defining how Mohamed Siyaad Barre made Somali society the setting for his megalomaniac ambition. He returned fired up with determination to become the "Great Leader" of Somalia and, like Kim Il Sung of the Democratic Republic of Korea, to insinuate himself in the hearts and minds of people in the Democratic Republic of Somalia.

Soon after his return, the posters portraying him as a revolutionary leader had grown bigger and more pervasive. Billboards in the streets presented profiles of him standing with Marx, Engles and Lenin. Siyaad Barre, a barely literate man, became the "revolutionary leader" of Somalia. Even though unable to read a book on socialism, he was hailed as a leading authority on socialism. His profile in the streets showed him rubbing shoulders with Lenin, Marx, and Engles, the founders of socialism. At the same time, Mohamed Siyaad Barre shaved his moustache in a style reminiscent of Adolf Hitler. The contradictory mixture of influences and boundless ambitions of the man were indeed astounding.

One member of the civilian intelligentsia reports that Mohamed Siyaad Barre ordered him to draft written texts for his speeches, although the dictator set aside the written speeches as soon as he faced his audience.[30] In these impromptu speeches lasting for two to three hours, Mohamed Siyaad Barre often detracted from the written speech and plunged into tirades of threats and contradictory statements. Sweating profusely, he heaped invectives on the audience and castigated some of his henchmen for incompetence or corruption. By these skillful stratagems, the dictator implied that his integrity and sincerity were impeccable.

Still, what amazed this well-informed source is the conviction with which Siyaad Barre delivered these speeches. His razor-sharp castigation and his knowledge of Somali oratory were impressive and frightening. One favorite theme of his public speeches was to threaten merchants, teachers, and civil servants for their corruption. He accused traders of overpricing; he berated teachers for the colonial content of their education; and he rebuked civil servants for self-serving "anti-revolutionary" practices.

Barre identified and exploited the vulnerabilities and fears of his audience. In his speeches, he adeptly delineated the good from the evil, and patriotism from national betrayal. Having clearly juxtaposed these attributes, he cast himself in the camp of the good and others in that of evil. At least he implied that his personal integrity was above reproach while that of his listeners was in doubt. Once he aroused suspicion, he threatened retribution, sometimes citing the punishment meted out to specific persons or groups as examples of what might await opponents.

Siyaad Barre knew well how to exploit the psychology of people whose public and private lives were racked by doubt, frustration, and conflict. He knew well how to develop in the public a mind-set that he alone was concerned about the common good and was concerned about their well-being. Yet the standard by which he judged people was based on loyalty to him, not on competence or personal integrity. The internal competition and mutual spying he nurtured among his subordinates ensured that none of them could emerge untarnished or with a clear conscience.

Propaganda was not enough for people to internalize Mohamed Siyaad Barre's image and to force submission to the regime. The military regime developed institutions of social control of which the neighborhood orientation centers were among the most pervasive institutions. Established in 1970, the Orientation Centers were designed to infiltrate the neighborhoods and family life. The *Gulwadayaal* (Victory Pioneers), established in the same year, administered the neighborhoods and orientation centers through surveillance and terror.

The Orientation Centers were established in every urban center of the country. Mogadishu alone had 14 Centers, one located in each of the 14 administrative neighborhoods into which the city was divided.[31] Each center had its administrators and staff, a large hall for neighborhood meetings, an open space to accommodate mass rallies, stores offering basic supplies, courts for trying domestic quarrels and persecution of minor "anti-revolutionaries" (*Kaán-diid*), and its own temporary detention center.

There were two types of Victory Pioneers. The first type consisted of a force called "militia," headed by General Ábdirahmaan Ábdi Hussein, one of the President's sons-in-law. It was the fourth strongest force in the country. The second strongest consisted mostly of social misfits, mostly unemployed young men with no idea from where their next meal would come. They were either unpaid or minimally paid for their service. This group hung around the orientation centers, harassing the citizenry, and living mostly on bribes exacted from the public. They wore a green uniform and cap, and were known as "green dogs" because they moved together in packs like hounds following a trail of blood. Their insignia was a 'Big Eye' implying obvious scrutiny in public places. They meddled in domestic affairs, often spying on and harassing husbands while pretending to protect and defend their wives. Like gangs, they had their own turf, and their control over families.

The *Guulwadayaal* represented a key institution of social control in the regime of Mohamed Siyaad Barre. In its divide-and-rule tactic, the Barre regime recruited into this institution social misfits and persons with a grudge against society. By selecting what Marxists called the "lumpen proletariat," the misfit, the petty thieves and social rejects, the Barre regime lumpen-proletarianized society, making all forms of immorality and evil a staple of everyday living. Ten years after the fall of the regime, Somali society had not yet recovered its values. In politics, as in business and in public service, one finds gangsters and greed reigning supreme.

The Orientation Centers came under the administrative guidance of the Public Relations Office (PRO) headed by Colonel Ábdilqaadir Haaji Masale, a member of the 25 officers who staged the coup and continued to serve in the Supreme Revolutionary Council (SRC). Like his boss Mohamed Siyaad Barre, Colonel Masale was a believer in guiding the thought and behavior of the masses by a bait-and-hook policy. The bait (employment, promotion, security) was for supporters of the revolution, and the hook (unemployment, demotion, harassment, detention, and even execution) was for its opponents.

The Orientation Centers focused on breaking down family relations, in particular on creating a wedge between the husband and wife. Their tactic was to recruit women, to keep them preoccupied with the orientation centers, thereby disrupting traditional family routines, and to indoctrinate them as supporters and protectors of the state. Husbands coming home after a grueling day of harassment in the workplace found their wives away, their children abandoned, family chores neglected. Some of them harbored the suspicion that the claim of being at the orientation center was a cover for extramarital activities. If they questioned their wives, the victory pioneers bounced on them and came to the rescue of wives. The husband was labeled as *Kaán-diid* (anti-revolutionary). He was interrogated, persecuted, and humiliated. The traditional family roles were thus shaken to the roots and, the oppressive state manifested itself in family life. Not only did Cain occupy the land, the state, and the political power but also he occupied the private life of the citizen.

In fact, taking a looking closer look as to how General Mohamed Siyaad Barre talked, dressed, and spoke to others, one might detect an admiration for Benito Mussolini whose armed forces ruled Somalia and had once occupied Ethiopia. Remarkable indeed is how the past repeats itself. Mussolini did not scheme to have a protégé in Somalia who, decades later, would carry out the fascist mission of evil and cruelty,

My first encounter with the Victory Pioneers was during a short visit Mogadishu in 1976. I came from the United States and I had no knowledge of how harshly the Victory Pioneers mistreated citizens. Two of us were accosted standing by a car and we were charged with the crime of "Sitting on the President." My friend who was the son of former President Adan Ábdulle Ósmaan knew that the Victory Pioneers could use any pretext to detain a person for any length of time without due process of law.

Not understanding the charge leveled at us and shocked at the absurdities to which the regime's harassment reached, I responded: "Who can possibly sit on the President?" My friend was shocked by my unwise remark. Coming from abroad, I was naïve about the vindictiveness of the regime that the slightest remark could put one in jail without due process of law. My words and attitude gave them further reason to harass us. Only after a brief exchange did we realized that my friend had unintentionally sat on *Xiddigta Okoober* (October Star), the government daily newspaper on which the picture of the President was printed in the top right-hand corner of the front page. Before arresting us, their boss recognized my friend and ordered them to leave us alone. They did.

Like a pack of hungry wolves, they left us in the same frenetic pace in which they had descended upon us. As they disappeared in the busy marketplace, I got a bitter taste of how crude were these organized thugs known derisively called *Ayda Ágaaran* (Green Dogs) for their green uniforms and cruelty. Others accused of similarly absurd "crimes" were not so lucky. They were detained, tortured, and left to rot in prison. When and if released, the Victory Pioneers and their BIG EYE insignia left the victims with lasting dread. As the population of victims increased, a culture of dread developed in Somali society. The collapse of the regime and succession of wars left a population intensely traumatized.

While the omnipresent Gulwadayaal made certain that the neighborhood association kept citizens under constant fear and control, the educated class was herded into Halane Camp in the outskirts of the capital city for political "orientation." All civil servants were required to enlist for three months of ideological indoctrination and military exercises with the threat of dismissal from work or imprisonment for "anti-revolutionary" behavior. The Halane Camp too had a song, with its own lyrics of indoctrination and refrain stating: *Qalbiguu xalaa, Halane; Maskaxdu xala, Halane....* 'It cleans the soul, Halane; it cleans the mind, Halane...'

In reality, the camp experience was designed to break the will of the intelligentsia and force their total surrender to Siyaad Barre's dictatorship. The soldier reigned supreme in this camp, demanding and receiving obedience to their orders. Initiation of each newcomer (including ambassadors and teachers) began with orders to collect trash or learn how properly to address military supervisors. For the duration of their stay in camp, the "trainees" woke up at 4:30 AM and ended their strenuous drills at 6:00 P.M. Their khaki uniforms were checked to determine if they properly ironed, if their shoes were polished, and if they obediently accepted orders.

The obedience required through these grueling and humiliating exercises was transferred to the military establishment and ultimately to Siyaad Barre. No doubt, many of them left "training" physically fit but psychologically broken. Most were happy to return to their families and jobs. Why bother with other social interests (e.g. human rights and the common good) as long as one escaped personal hardship?

This is the narrow and self-centered logic that Siyaad Barre sought and received. Some of those sent to Halane voiced their private but shared feeling of humiliation in the rigors of military training and resentment toward the regime. A teacher sent the following sad lyrics to his girlfriend whom he did not see for months:

Do you know that I wander about the Indian Ocean
Do you know that I take orders from an ignorant soldier
Do you know that I eat food without nourishment
Do you know my real tormentor is the Old Man? [32]

Students as young as eleven years old were sent to a summer camp called *Ceel Jaalle* (The Comrade's Well) between Shalaanbood and Marka, two towns close to the capital city.[33] The Comrade's Well was presumably the repository of the President's wisdom, because each group of students spent two weeks receiving ideological indoctrination and military training. The stay in the camp was short but fast-paced and intense which permitted authorities to indoctrinate students, one group after another.. By the end of the vacation, the camp had hosted and processed a multitude of students from different schools. Pressure by the authorities and the parent's fear of persecution was the incentive to force students to register and enroll in this program.

In addition to these controlling institutions, there were others founded on propaganda. They included *Ubaha Kaáanka Oktober* (the Flowers of the October Revolution) that had offices in all regions of the country. The members consisted of children who were taught to sing the praises of "Jaale Siyaad" (Comrade Siyaad) and other nationalistic songs. They wore special uniforms and they welcomed Mohamed Siyaad Barre with flowers when he visited their communities. Associations for youth, women, workers, and members of cooperatives were also included in the list of institutions that advanced the image and cause of the regime.

Although *Waaberi* (Dawn) was the biggest of the musical bands, they included the following song and theater groups with names beginning with '*kooxda*' (the group):

1. *Kooxda Danan* (Dynamic) representing the Youth Association
2. *Kooxda Halgan* (Struggle)representing the Victory Pioneers
3. *Kooxda Heegan* (Vigilant) representing the Police

4. *Kooxda Hilaac* (Lightening) representing the Association of Cooperatives
5. *Kooxda Horseed* (Vibrant) representing the Armed Forces
6. *Kooxda Iftiin* (Light) representing the Ministry of Education
7. *Kooxda Onkod* (Thunder) representing the Custodian Corps
8. *Kooxda Xusuus* (Reminiscence) representing the Workers' Association.[34]

Mohamed Siyaad Barre was not content with songs praising him, billboards showing his picture along with those Marx, Engels, and Lenin, or military parades honoring him. He also became a marriage counselor to his cronies, as he had pathological interest in rumors of marital discord and sexual scandals. With extensive information on the private affairs of his subjects, he would call an official or his wife for a private discussion on whether what he had heard was true and what he could do to help.

Taken aback by this bizarre offer by the President, some divulged their private agonies and complaints to him. He would then call for further discussion with the others involved and gather more juicy and unflattering information that he would use to control and humiliate when it suited him. Worse than his pathological interest in rumors were his frequent sexual escapades with the wives of his subordinates. Like the rumors, he used sex to control and humiliate subordinates.

In short, the dictator's abuses of power coincided with other forms of personal and sexual abuse, showing that absolute power corrupts absolutely. Yet, in spite of his widely known abuses, officials and civilians continued to sing:

Siyaad, the victory pioneer
The Father of Knowledge
Of our land
Socialism is the system
Leading us to prosperity...[35]

The song illustrates how social and political paranoia becomes pervasive in the auto-colonial situation. In time, the song turned into moans of pain in prisons, on the battlefield and in homes. Somalis entered an era when politics came to mean *Polly tricks* in which abuse and dehumanization went hand in hand with unfulfilled promises of change and revolution. The double-talk and dishonesty turned out as corrosive as physical depravation and abuse. However, this was only the beginning—worse was yet to come.

A Somali proverb says *hal booli ahi nirig, xalaal ah ma dhaso*, 'a plundered she-camel does not give birth to legitimate offspring. The armed forces took power illegally, producing unjust rule and tragic consequences, thereby giving the proverb ring of truth, as we shall see in subsequent chapters.

8

CAINETIC SYSTEM AT WORK

Ninki xoog laa xaq leh.
A man with right has every right.
—Somali proverb

The regime of Mohamed Siyaad Barre adopted from the beginning a revolutionary posture. It claimed that it used power not for its own sake, rather to save Somalis from the civilian administration steeped in corruption, nepotism, and mismanagement. The military regime disseminated propaganda declaring that the awaited revolution had come and that the new regime would improve their lives.

While the regime heightened public expectations, it issued a series of draconian laws limiting basic freedoms to ensure that opponents real and imagined were unable to undermine its authority. The majority of Somalis accepted the rhetoric of revolution on face value, and hoped that their dreams for a better life would finally materialize. At the same time, they feared that they could meet the fate of the opponents of the regime who had been branded *Kaán-diid* (antirevolutionary).

Extensive psychological studies exist contrasting the benefits by reward and the damaging effects of punishment in human learning and social relations. To teach or lead by reward presupposes firstly a teacher or a leader who is comfortable with who he is and therefore able to tolerate human difference, secondly one who focuses on outcome that improves knowledge and practice of better living. Solutions learned from this way often stays longer even in the absence of reward.

The "revolution" that was supposed to improve living in Somali society in fact rested on punishment and revealed the psychopathic tendencies of the leader and his cronies. It was a violent system—one that left Somalis worse than they have ever known in the past.

How did Cain's system of violence—what I call *Cainetic System* or *Auto-colonialism*—work under the leadership of Mohamed Siyaad Barre? Was the violence sporadic and discriminate or was it systemic? Does a systemic perspective provide insight into Mohamed Siyaad

Barre and his regime? Did the prisons *incarcerating citizens* and the laws propaganda *incarcerating the mind* succeed in producing the intended submission of the ruled?

Rude Awakening

Mohamed Siyaad Barre was a shrewd and charismatic leader .Those who knew him acknowledge his intelligence, patience, and perseverance. Some say he ruled the country by patiently listening to others, using experience as a seasoned criminal investigator, and exploiting his insight into human nature. He was a quick learner who adopted as his own the ideas he learned from others. He spoke intelligently in public speeches about "scientific socialism" or Marxism, although he never read a book on the subject. As long as this ideology advanced his authoritarian rule, earning him in addition military and financial aid from the former USSR, Mohamed Siyaad Barre talked about socialism like a fervent believer and tireless promoter of it.

He was an effective manager of people, starting his "revolution" with innovative projects. Writing in Somali script, initiating self-help schemes, building schools and higher institutions of learning, implementing desert conservation programs, mobilizing national resources to help drought victims, and advancing the rights of women would have made Mohamed Siyaad Barre the most revered and celebrated leader in Somali history. However, this was not to be because power corrupts, corrupting absolutely in a society where political institutions are weak and the citizens know little about their rights and responsibilities.

Moreover, Mohamed Siyaad Barre could not overcome his past, his inferiority complex, or his vindictive streak. The more his personal power grew, the more his control manias and delusion of grandeur grew to destructive proportions. He assembled "yes-men" around him who were as mean and niggardly as himself but lacking his capacity for leadership. Responding to his penchant for rumor and enemies, they cultivated in him the most base and cruel features of Cain.

During the first three years of the coup, the majority of Somalis were entranced with the language of revolution that the "progressive" wing of the intelligentsia, including poets and song composers, propagated. Mohamed Siyaad Barre too, used the magical power of the spoken word by cajoling and threatening the public to embrace his leadership. By 1974, the revolutionary rhetoric of the regime lost steam, and the propaganda and institutions of social control—like the "orientation centers"—were weakening.

People began to see through the empty rhetoric of the so-called "revolution," and they discovered that Mohamed Siyaad Barre was a power-hungry and brutal dictator whose promises of liberty and better life were contradicted by his oppressive laws and cruel actions. His true nature became obvious only when it was too late to stop him. The regime was now strong due to institutions of social control and because fear was an insurmountable barrier to overcome. The dictator, internalized and lodged in the psyche, could not be easily ejected anymore that his regime, bolstered by stern laws and institutions of social control, could be openly challenged.

Mohamed Siyaad Barre knew the honeymoon would end sooner than later, that people would no longer be pacified by false promises of change and revolution. Hence, his language of reform and salvation changed to one of intimidation and violence. In a speech during the late nineteen-seventies, Mohamed Siyaad Barre admitted that he and his "friends" (as he liked to call his supporters) usurped power by violence and that they intended to keep it by violence. He said, *"Waxaan ku qabsanay qori, qori baan ku illaalinayna*—we took power by the gun, we shall protect it by using the gun.'

The truth of that statement was obvious to people years before Mohamed Siyaad Barre publicly admitted. By the time he made the statement, he found the need for blunt language—no more cajoling or false promises. Skepticism set in among the public and among those in the inner circle of power like the SRC and the Council of Ministers. Of course, those who usurp and keep power by the gun also lose power by the gun. Mohamed Siyaad Barre and his "friends" were not an exception. However, neither the regime nor society at this time reached the point where the violence of the state would meet counter-violence of the people. The system of oppression was still intact.

A system is a combination of parts forming a complex unitary whole; systems vary in origin, complexity, and scope. For instance, systems of nature like the solar system are complex and eternal. Man-made mechanical systems like the clock are simpler and relatively short-lived. In addition, people consciously create social systems (like a political organization, a social club, a government), or they evolve naturally on their own (the family or the clan system). A social system has a *name* and a *function*. It exists in a physical *territory* and possesses a psychological *boundary*. It also has a *structure* by which members are organized in relation to each other and to the whole. It has *rules* that members are expected to follow. In time, these rules become group *norms*, *values*, *beliefs*, and *rituals*. Not least, there is a *history* and perhaps elaborated *myths*.

A political system has the above characteristics; it has a name and function, a territory and boundary, a structure and rules, norms, values, beliefs, and rituals. A political system designed to meet human needs can derail from the purpose for which it was intended; it can become oppressive when it was supposed to be liberating. A political system exerts greater influence over the individuals of which it is constituted than the influence each of them can exert over it. In fact, the very individuals who invented and developed the political system may find that their power of directing or controlling it diminished to such an extent that the *subjects* of the system became its *objects*.

Even the dictator who seems to be in control of a political system may be controlled by the very political system he created. A political system can have a life of its own, independent of the intention and wishes of the individuals who brought it into existence. A political system endures for a long time because not only leaders promote and enforce it by means of propaganda or brute force but also those whom the political system exploits and oppresses internalize the system. By internalizing it, they make it part of the self, even when the system is abusive and unjust toward them. A political system is also resists change because the interests vested in it shun change.

That is why a changing political system often includes a fundamental social and psychological rupture or violent "revolutions." Yet what goes under the label of "revolution" is often the old order revived, repackaged, or amplified. Despite what self-styled revolutionary promise, we never start from a clean slate. The past reasserts itself through the institutions of the old order, the childhood socialization we experienced, and the culture we internalized.

False revolutions of the type Mohamed Siyaad Barre and his colleagues imposed on Somalis only brought out with vengeance the worst features of the past. The tradition of looting camels turned into looting the state treasury and clannism intensified as the dictator trusted only his kinsmen. The regime identified "anti-revolutionaries" in clans it deemed threat to the dictator and made law enforcement tool of oppression.

Inevitably, a political system has longevity than individuals. It outlives its original designers, beneficiaries, and victims, continuing to exert inordinate influence on subsequent generations. In short, the force, scope and perils of the political system are far greater than the influence of those who invent the system, benefit from it, or suffer under it at the beginning. In time, the system gains a life of its own; it develops its own logic, it changes along its own direction and in its own pace.

The dictator himself is a critical player and a creator of the system just as he is created by it. The point becomes clear when realize that a dictator at first assumes the mantle of reform and speak as if he were the long awaited 'man of the people.' He could not have come to power unless his colleagues and the people did not invest hope and trust in him. Once in power, they also praise him and make him larger than life that in time he comes to believe as veritable truth. From there on, he does not tolerate differences, let alone opposition. He believes that there exist only two options: either force total submission, or totally annihilate opponents. The Somali dictator too saw only these two options after he hoisted himself in the pinnacle of power.

Mohamed Siyaad Barre was a glib man, highly talented in the spoken word. Unlike Benito Mussolini who made his ideological commitment known in writing, Mohamed Siyaad Barre had the habit of saying one thing and doing another. He was characterized by the same hypocrisy and double-talk which are central flaws in the character of the Somali elite and which historically have undermined its politics and social practice. Yet, unlike the majority of the elite, his hypocrisy and double-talk worked miracles for twenty-two years. Somalis applauded and praised him "as the father of knowledge, the father of the nation…"

In reality, the success of his rule derived from not only effective propaganda and the terror it unleashed but also the vulnerability of ordinary Somalis equally infected with the hypocrisy and double-talk popularized by the Somali elite. In other words, there was a fit in the characteristics of the leader with those of the people he led. The violence and oppression flourishing in Somali society were products of their complicity. If this fit had not existed, a dictatorship of the type seen in Somali society would not have emerged. At least, it would not have lasted for twenty-two years. It is because a form of synergy existed in people, institutions, and historical forces that enabled oppression and violence to become durable.

To understand this, we must examine the promise with which the coup began, why people were inclined to believe these promises, and what became of the promises. A good illustration of the promises is found in the speech two days after the coup was carried out, Mohamed Siyaad Barre gave as the leader of the SRC and the "revolution" on 23 October 1969,. He said:

> We want to restore the honor of our people at home and abroad; we want to develop the resources of our land with our own efforts so that prosperity prevails in our land... We want to extend material support to those working for world peace; we want to fight the colonizer of the mind and soul, be they at home or abroad...we want to advance the economic development of our people and land...[1]

The idea that the Somali armed forces were free from political ambition and they existed only to serve and protect the nation was an opinion not only held by Mohamed Siyaad Barre. It was also assumed by most Somalis and accepted as a truth. After all, the armed forces took power following the crisis in the civilian administration and the assassination of the President. Most Somalis believed that the armed forces intervened to save the nation in time of crisis. Few question if the coup and the assassination were somehow linked, that some ambitious men planned the assassination as well as the coup. Almost none anticipated that the quickly forgotten murder of the President would open the way for the murder of countless others also quickly forgotten.

The coup leaders promised that they would clean up the government, restore the honor of Somalis, and bring economic prosperity to the country. This was believed by the people. The majority of Somalis believed the armed forces were above the dirty politics and the political ambition that led to the country's ruin. Mohamed Siyaad Barre and the coup leaders took advantage of the circumstances and told them what they wanted to hear. Mohamed Siyaad Barre and his "friends" won half the battle by winning public acquiescence while developing and perfecting the system of oppression. By the mid-nineteen-seventies, dictatorship and oppression were fully in place.

Table 1 listing the names, rank, and clan identity of SRC members shows the change that took place at the pinnacle of power.

Table 1
Members of the Supreme Revolutionary Council
1974

Name	Rank	Clan	Sub-Clan
General Mohamed Siyaad Barre	President	Daarood	Mareehaan
Hussein Kulmiye Afrah	Member	Hawiye	Abgaal
Mohamed Ali Samatar	Member	Tumaal	Iise-'Aade
Abdalla Mohamed Faadil	Member	'Arab	Yemeni
Mohamed Mire Musa	Member	Daarood	Ogaadeen
Mohamed Sheekh Osmaan	Member	Hawiye	Murasade
Ali Mataan Haashi	Member	Daarood	Mareehaan
Ahmed Sulieman Abdalla	Member	Daarood	Dhulbahante
Ismaiil Ali Abokor	Member	Isaaq	Habar Jélo
Muuse Rabiileh Good	Member	Gadaburs	Mahad-Case
Faarax Waays Dulleh	Member	Iise	Wadool
Mohamed Ali Shire	Member	Daarood	Dhulbanate
Ahmed Mohamed Faarax	Member	Isaaq	Habar Awal
Mohamuud Geelle Yuusuf	Member	Daarood	Mijeerteen
Abdirazaaq Mahamuud Abubakar	Member	Daarood	Mijeerteen
Abdilqaadir Haaji Mohamed	Member	Daarood	Mareehaan
Mohamed Umar Gees	Member	Daarood	Ogaadeen
Abdi Warsame Isaaq	Member	Dir	Gaadsan
Osmaan Mohamed Jeelle	Member	Hawiye	Hawaaadle
Ahmed Hassan Muuse	Member	Isaaq	Habar Jélo

The table shows that the SRC membership of 25 in 1968 reduced 20 members by 1974 after five members (three Hawiye, one Isaaq, and one Daarood) were removed from membership. Mohamed Siyaad Barre continued to serve as President while the others were listed as members of the SRC. This time, there were no Vice Presidents as in 1969. General Mohamed Áynaanshe Guuleed was executed and General Qorsheel imprisoned.

Having fully consolidated his power, Mohamed Siyaad Barre wanted to give none of his colleagues the illusion of being his deputy. There had to be no mistake about his newly found dictatorship. In addition, he wanted to place a clan stamp on his regime by increasing the dominance of the Daarood in the SRC in 1974.

Chart 1 shows the clan distribution of SRC members in 1974.

Chart 1
Clan Distribution of SRC Members, 1974

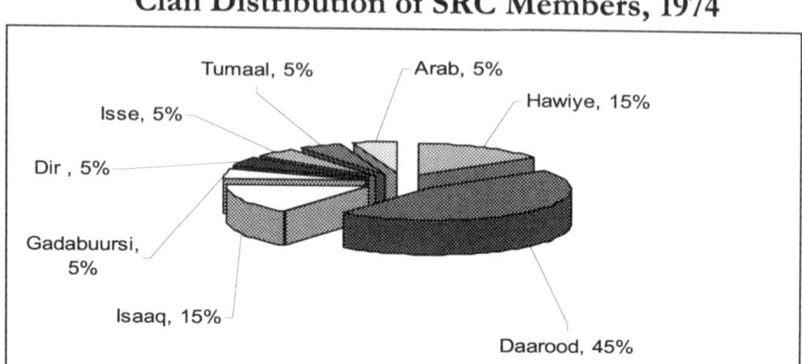

In comparison to the SRC announced in 1969, the percentage of Daarood members in the 1974 SRC rose from 40% to 45% while that of the Hawiye and Isaaq declined from 24% to 15% and from 16% to 15% respectively. Among the Daarood, a third (33%) were Mareehaan, the largest representation in the higher echelons of power this sub-clan ever received before 1974. Clearly, the clannism the coup leaders promised to root out was getting worse than the past. However, few paid attention; if they did, they kept tight lip for fearing charge of "anti-revolutionary."

In addition to the symbolism of power and clan predominance in the SRC, the machine of oppression was also perfected and grinding in full gear. At first, it began at the macro-level of experience and society. The coup leaders first took control of the state and its conduits of power. By bringing the armed forces and police under their control, they monopolized the organization and its deployment of violence. Anyone bearing arms was considered a threat and a criminal to be punished. While their use of violence was legitimate, the use of violence by others was illegitimate a fact was the foundation of their power and tyranny. They became the sole negotiator of Somali relations with the international community; they abolished all political parties, the parliament, and the constitution; and they usurped the power to make and enforce laws. Having affirmed that the SRC is the sole authority in the land, they issued laws that suited their vision and their interest. These laws legitimized and galvanized their power.

At the macroeconomic level, the SRC nationalized major businesses and banks. It became the sole authority to mint money, print notes, and set exchange rates in the country. It controlled the terms of import and export and determined flow of money both in and outside of the country. It took charge of bilateral and multilateral aid and decided with which institution or country it negotiated loans. At the cultural level, the military regime took control of the media, and all avenues of expression, converting the intelligentsia to its cause. By exploiting the gift of the spoken word, the regime controlled how the citizens saw their world and defined their experience in it. The SRC adopted socialist ideology that was considered "progressive" and even "revolutionary."

Cain's System or auto-colonialism also found application at the micro-level. It restricted accesses and use of basic dimensions such as space, time, matter, and energy. Thus, the Somali who historically had lived in a large expanse of land found that his space was controlled and restricted by the military regime. The land was no longer his. Since the SRC had appropriated it by force, he was a stranger to his land, a squatter that could be expelled. The plot of land he inherited from his ancestors became government property. Even his home was liable to searches that had become commonplace under the SRC. His time also was controlled and restricted. Curfews dictated when he could move and with whom he could associate. Orientation centers could call him any time for "community service." His material possessions were only his conditionally and temporarily as the regime could confiscate them. The search-and-seizure practice imparted the feeling that those who govern consider ownership to be illegitimate as if one were a criminal.

Government employees could not negotiate the terms of employment, strike, or resign. A businessman could not conduct his trade without paying bribe, nor could he set prices without permission from authorities. A farmer was required to turn over his produce to the states. Regardless of one's occupation, at least a portion of what was earned was appropriated through taxes imposed without representation. Even the self-help programs were ordered and managed from the top. The citizen did not participate in these programs in response to coercion. Armed checkpoints ensured that activities were monitored. Pass cards for free movement *(Warqadda Dhaqdhaqaaqa)* similar to the "passbooks" of apartheid South Africa controlled his movement. One's life was not his own; the regime could seize a person anytime and induct him into war. He could be arbitrarily detained or executed.

The regime strictly controlled all reading material. It "nationalized" the press, thereby controlling the content and form of information, and censored ideas and words. Spies were reminders to keep mouths and ears closed. The regime determined one's values and provided a code of contact whose violation brought harsh punishment. Prisons waited for those who did not follow the norms. The Orientation Centers created conflict in the family and a wedge between couples.

The *Tabeleh System* that the regime implemented in Somaliland during the nineteen-eighties listed the number of persons in each household. State agents monitored designated number of homes. They reported to authorities who visited the family, where each family member was, and what relations they had with others. Personal identity was tampered with. The law prohibiting the traditional role of clan elders was intended to isolate and control people. Ritual burial of 'tribalism" was designed to deny the majority emotional attachments to clan while it gave cover to its use by those in power. In fact, the regime wanted the citizen to forget not only his clan but also his own father and instead to praise the cruel Machiavellian man dubbed, "father of knowledge, father of the nation."

What is remarkable is that the majority of Somalis acquiesced to the Cainetic system or auto-colonialism for well over two decades. Could this system be maintained only by force if there were no aspects in the Somali culture, psyche, and social relations that contributed to the rise and continuation of auto-colonialism? We will examine these aspects after we describe how the use of brutal force played a central role in the system.

Cain's Prisons

There were three main prisons before the military coup and all were built during colonial rule. The Central Prison in Mogadishu was designed for a maximum of 5,000 prisoners. The other major prisons were in the former British Protectorate. The Mandheera Prison between Hargeysa and Berbera had a capacity of 3,000. The Central Prison in Hargeysa could accommodate a maximum of 1,000 prisoners.

After the military coup, hundreds of prisons sprouted up throughout the country. The most infamous were the Laanta Buur Prison, the Buurweyn Prison, and the Labaatan Jirow Prison. Laanta Buur Prison was located 40 km away from Mogadishu. It was designed to occupy prisoners in agricultural production but it became a place of incarceration. The Buurweyn Prison was located 20 km south of Buulaburde, a small town. It was intended for prisoners whose whereabouts and conditions the regime wanted to conceal. The Labaatan Jirow Prison was located 20 km northeast of Baydhabo and in thenineteen-nineties came to be known internationally as 'the place of death.'

Labaatan Jirow was developed with the financial and technical assistance of East Germany. It had specially designed underground cells. Prisoners were political detainees held incommunicado in solitary confinement for an undetermined length of time. Only Mohamed Siyaad Barre could decide the length of detention or time of release of prisoners at Labaatan Jirow Prison. If a prisoner was released, it occurred late at night and without warning. The prisoner was taken from his cell and by heavily armed soldiers. The practice was intended to make the prisoner believe that his execution was happening. To his relief, he was taken to the President's Palace in Mogadishu where, he received an offer of clemency from the President. He also heard excuses for why he had been detained and why he had been forgotten in prison. The unexpected way this ordeal concludes, just as one thought he was being executed, left most prisoners grateful to the President. By then, the prisoner was so traumatized that he would immensely be thankful to his torturers for a smile, a kind word, a cigarette.

The old and new prisons were filled to maximum capacity by the nineteen-eighties. Overcrowding and poor hygiene were common. Torture was also frequent, including pulling nails and teeth with pliers, administering electroshock on testicles, hanged for hours upside down, being downed in a tank, hands and feet tied, but taken out in time before dying. In fact, getting into prison was easy, but getting out was rare. Many were forgotten in prison because there was no record of charges against them and no one came back to release them. As a result, prisoners languished in prison for years with an open-ended commitment. The anxiety of not knowing if or when they would be released broke their defenses, making grim any thought of the future. It left one vulnerable to self-doubt eating away the inner core of one's personality, crushing the soul more than did the time-limited and localized physical tortures.

Tyranny of this type permeates the environment with apprehension and fear. It also turns anger of the victim onto himself because doing so is safer for the prisoner and the self is the most accessible object to him. It is not only the prisoner who turn anger inward; the relatives and friends feel self-blame because they know that they should something to help the victim but can not, they feel shame for reflexively choosing self-protection over rescue of the victim. Attempt to help attracts scrutiny and suspicion; therefore, the safest course was to take minimal action on behalf of victims and, when in doubt, to err in favor of oppression. If they do not physically end in prison in due course, they subjectively live in prisons without walls. Even the state agents feel apprehensive since most know that they are tomorrow's victims.

The number of prisons and prisoners increased rapidly and Somalia itself became a prison. The moral order collapsed and the value of life diminished. Tyranny was relayed from the top to the bottom, with civil servants, security agents, and teachers serving as the purveyors, each victimizing subordinates. The family also was divided and no longer offered a refuge from the tyrannical demands of the external world. Mothers left their peace and family chores to attend to the rituals of the neighborhood associations. Fathers accepted indignity to keep their jobs, and to avoid detention. The children sang praises of a 'Nation's Father' who was said to possess greater authority, knowledge, and wisdom than the one at home. Seeing the father at home harassed by a lowly state agent diminished not only his image but also the child's view of himself.

Filling these prisons were a swarm of law enforcement agents who persecuted citizens everywhere. They included the *Guulwadayaal* (Victory Pioneers), the National Security Services, the Presidential Guards also known as the *Koofiyad Cas* (the Red Caps), the armed forces Security Service known by their acronym HANGAASH (*Hay'adda Nabadgelyada Gaashandhiga*). Known also as the *Dhabar-Jabinta* (the Back-Breakers), HANGAASH was established following an attempted coup in 1978. Its members were exclusively of the Mareehaan clan.

It is said that the founder and mentor of HANGASH was the first and older wife of Mohamed Siyaad Barre who had felt a need to develop an intelligence and security agency in competition with the NSS. HANGASH became more feared than the NSS for its cruelty and speed of destruction. Added to these law enforcement agencies were the National Audit Office *(Hisaabi Xil Ma Leh),* the National Security Court, the Police, the Armed Forces, and the Custodian Forces, each of which had full authority to detain a person for any reason and any length of time. There was myriad of other state controls such as the *Halganka Hoose* (the Under-Cover Revolution) and *Guddiga Baadhista Xisbiga* (The Parliamentary Investigation Board) which was free to scrutinize and terrorize any branch of government.

As we saw in the preceding chapter, the *Gulwadayaal* and the "orientation centers" over which they presided enabled the state to infiltrate into the neighborhoods and families of the ordinary citizen. Brutal force was used against suspected *Kaán-diid* (anti-revolutionaries) and the ordinary citizen was terrorized by crude and subtle tactics. The pervasive insignia of the BIG EYE transmitted messages of being watched by the "Green Dogs" at every turn. The government-controlled airwaves were saturated with the following song:

Our red eye
Wherever you notice it
A tree can't hide you from it
Dodger, dodger, dodger,
Dodger, it sees you! [2]

The lyrics of the song had the power of evoking fear since the red eye implied conviction of crime violent retribution. The BIG EYE symbol was everywhere, with the intended effect that everyone was being watched. The song also betrayed one central orientation of the regime — everyone was guilty unless proven otherwise. Paranoia and persecution were the order of the day. The *Gulwadayaal,* pervasive and invasive, identified and eliminated opponents who exist anywhere. There was no hiding place from the authority and punishment of the state. The impact of the song was reinforced by the fact that the NSS and the *Gulwadayaal* had the power to search without warrant, and arbitrarily arrest anyone at any time.

The National Security Services (NSS) which was developed with technical assistance from the Soviet Union and East Germany was a more feared and efficient instrument of terror. Its officers consisted of an elite force drawn from the military and the police. It was headed by Ahmed Suleymaan Ábdulle, a son-in-law of Mohamed Siyaad Barre. The NSS learned methods of detecting and suppressing "anti-revolutionaries," techniques of inflicting torture to gain a confession, and controlling people through fear and terror from its Soviet block tutors. The job of the NSS was to silence the opponents of the regime or to intimidate others into surrender; it also took draconian measures to weaken social bonds among the people and to control unofficial contacts with the external world.

Dictators abhor social bonding and free flow of information; they seek to rule individuals stripped of human connections. They also limit knowledge of possibilities beyond the world of tyranny. Hence, the NSS restricted association among citizens. A gathering of more than several people constituted a threat to the state or even evidence of conspiracy. The government also kept close surveillance and control on unapproved communication with visiting foreigners and embassy officials. In 1974, all government employees were required to sign a statement of loyalty to the regime and to avoid unapproved contacts with foreigners.

The National Security Court, established in April 1970, worked closely with the NSS and the *Gulwadayaal*. Initially, it heard cases concerned with the assassination of President Ábdirashiid Ali Sharmaarke and charges of corruption imposed on members of the previous regime.[3] The court's function broadened to trying cases involving political crimes. The NSC consisted of three members—a member of the SRC serving as President of the court and two other military judges. A special military attorney general served as the prosecutor. None of these men had legal training; yet their verdicts were final and in some cases, a sentence of execution could be carried out within a few days. No other court could review sentences meted out by the NSC; appeals could be heard only by the SRC and only Siyaad Barre had the power of granting mercy to the accused—a power he rarely exercised.

On 20 April 1970, General Jaamá Áli Qorsheel was arrested. He was the First Vice-President and a key member of the SRC. He was also a Commandant of the Police, a post previously held by General Mohamed Abshir Muuse who was arrested soon after the coup. He was charged for plotting a coup in cooperation with a foreign power and was imprisoned and later released. On 6 March 1970, two members of the SRC, General Mohamed Áynaanshe Guuleed and Colonel Salaad Gabeere Kediye, were arrested. Áynaanshe was Vice-President and colonel Kediye was the Minister of Public Works. General Jaamá

Áli Qorsheel was more fortunate than Áynaanshe and Kediye executed by a firing squad.

The case of Ahmed Yuusuf Samatar (known as Bardaád) illustrates how long-term imprisonment could be unjust. He had not committed a crime except that he was a known Somali socialist long before Mohamed Siyaad Barre had become a turncoat socialist and an ally of the Soviet Union. After the coup, the presence of Bardaád as a free man stirred anxiety and insecurity in Mohamed Siyaad Barre who feared that this man, with stronger socialist credentials than he, might lure the Soviet Union to carry out his own "revolution." Mohamed Siyaad Barre alleviated his worries by keeping Bardaád in solitary confinement for eighteen years. After his release, Bardaád asked the President why he was imprisoned without cause and without a trial. The President answered: "We needed to put you in jail but not with the intention that you serve such a long time. It should have been only for a few years."[4]

The President's view of arrest for "a few years" sounds like a weekend inconvenience. His explanation that he was "forgotten" in prison for eighteen years was itself indicative of Cain's arrogance as manifested in Mohamed Siyaad Barre. Bardaád left his meeting with the President with no admission of guilt, no request for forgiveness, no offer of compensation. It seems that even such a politically conscious man, victim of a dictator and injustice, could not free himself from clannism and politics of the *Klan* long after he was released from prison. It is said that Bardaád was a chief supporter of Col. Ábdulaahi Yuusuf Ahmed during his 2004 presidential campaign at Mbagathi, Kenya. The two men are of the same clan. It is an irony pervading Somali politics and life.

Arbitrary arrests and long-term incarceration without cause, as Bardaád experienced, were common. Such practices were most prevalent in communities and clans that the regime identified as enemies of the state. During the nineteen-eighties when armed struggle against the regime gained momentum, the Mijeerteen and the Isaaq were frequent targets of indiscriminate arrest, torture, and executions. When the Mijeerteen achieved a truce with the regime, the weight of tyranny fell on the Isaaq who continued to fight the regime until its demise in January 1991. In fact, Africa Watch documented that Cain's 'System of Terror' evolved to frightening levels as applied to the extremes of cruelty on the Isaaq.[5]

Life in the prisons of Mohamed Siyaad Barre was always harsh and humiliating even if one escaped torture. For instance, the UFO imprisoned and tortured for rehabilitating hospitals described the pathos of these prisons. Ábdi Aadan Haad (Ábdi Qays), the talented poet and imprisoned several times for antirevolutionary ideas, told me the following story to underscore the absurdities of life in these prisons. There was one donkey detained in one of the large prisons where Ábdi Qays spent years without either a sentence by court or knowledge of how long he would be prisoner. Qays and the other prisoners inquired of the head warden why the donkey was kept in the prison. He explained that an agent of the state had brought the beast to the prison for unknown reasons and added that only the person who brought the donkey to prison can release it, the same way the warden can not release any prisoner until the person who brought him lets him go.

The prisoner left the head warden disappointed. They later came up with the solution. They collected money and approached the head warden again. They proposed to buy a young donkey to replace the aged one that had lost time in fathering young donkeys or enjoying his freedom. The head warden accepted their proposition assured that, if the jailer of the first donkey came, he would show him the younger donkey. Thus, they released the first donkey and his jailer never returned. Meanwhile, Ábdi Qays composed a play in which the old donkey, released from prison, recounts the injustice of his imprisonment. He also talks extensively about how the streets and life in Mogadishu had changed while he (the old donkey) languished in prison.

Two years ago, this play won an award for literary excellence in one of the Nordic countries. Unfortunately, the poets and singers that contributed to public awareness and resistance to oppression had lost their revered place in society after the state collapse, as did the value of ideas once warlords and wielders of AK-47 terrorized the public in decentralized dictatorship in which only the violent and cruel count.

Cain's Executions

The regime was not only using detention to punish its opponents. In September 1970, it issued a new law guaranteeing punishment (including the death sentence) to anyone compromising the unity, peace or sovereignty of the nation. Within the first year of the military takeover, the number of persons executed was greater than the number executed during nine years of civilian rule. This indicated that the coup leaders would not hesitate to kill anyone deemed a threat to their power. In addition, the executions were carried out in public, something the civilian regime had never done.

In subsequent years, their power and representation grew even more as Mohamed Siyaad Barre, the Grand Wizard, became the supreme dictator. In fact, they became the key power brokers. While the Isaaq and other clans were under-represented, the Hawiye lost their historic competition with the Daarood more under the reign of Mohamed Siyaad Barre than under the preceding civilian administrations.

The songs whose theme were about change, hope, and salvation gradually turned violent. When the National Security Court condemned its opponents to death, radio Mogadishu played a song that everyone associated with an impending execution:

Repudiator of goodwill
Awaiting you is a trap
By which you will be executed
You, opportunist, your fate
Is death by hanging
With no trial or appeal.[6]

The song was heard throughout the city; vans mounted with loudspeakers ensured that everyone was sufficiently informed and terrorized. The song and the executions evoked horror and terror that the public felt but each individual privatized. As natural emotions of fear were concealed, the healing power of language and discussing the terror was banished along with the impulse to resist the cruelties of the state. The only reaction permitted was obedience to the regime.

Executions and capital punishment did not cease and the guiding principle was this: *if you cannot control opponents, get rid of them, body, mind, and soul.* As the number of citizens falling victim to the executioners' cruel methods of elimination increased, the majority of citizens sought refuge in the silence and conformity that provided them a temporary reprieve but also encouraged the tyranny imposed on them.

Dictators are not content with obedience and submission alone; they want in addition to keep their people in constant terror. It is their way of satisfying pathological wishes beyond the exercise of power.

One of President Mohamed Siyaad Barre's early decisions was to dismiss three of the most senior members of the SRC. Mohamed Áynaanshe Guuleed (Isaaq, Habar Yoonis) and Jaamá Áli Qorsheell (Daarood, Warsangali) were both generals and held the post of Vice-President. The third was Col. Salaad Gabeere Kediye (Hawiye, Abgaal), a key figure in carrying out the coup of 1969. Mohamed Siyaad Barre viewed these three men as threats to his power.

Mohamed Áynaanshe and Salaad Gabeere had expressed differences with him on policies of abolishing clannism while, in fact, Barre pursued it in practice. First, the regime imprisoned the three men and executed two of them, Áynaanshe and Gabeere, for plotting a coup along with Major Ábdilqaadir Dheel Ábdulle (Daarood, Mijeerteen). The three men were arrested on 6 March 1971. Also later dismissed from the SRC were Mohamed Yuusuf Élmi (Hawiye, Habar Gidir) and Ahmed Mohamuud Ádde (Hawiye, Abgaal).

It is said that Mohamed Yuusuf Élmi to have gone, while inebriated, to the prison where Áynaanshe and Gabeere were imprisoned. Assuming the mantle of SRC member, he tried to release them. The man in charge of the prison was a Mareehaan officer. He called Mohamed Siyaad Barre who ordered the immediate imprisonment of Mohamed Yuusuf Élmi. He remained in prison for years. He died in the nineteen-nineties during the inter-clan fighting of the USC in Mogadishu.[7]

Áynaanshe, closer in age and experience to Barre, was an old colleague who knew much about Mohamed Siyaad Barre and his tactics. The two men were among the officers sent to Italy in 1956. Barre considered him a threat because Áynaanshe knew his colleague's questionable activities and his ambition for power. Gabeere was an energetic and ambitious man who played an important role during the coup of 1969. He was also the son-in-law of former President Aadan Ábdulle Ósmaan and therefore had a grudge against the regime of Sharmaarke and Égaal.

The three men were executed by a firing squad on 23 July 1972. Ironically, according to Colonel Ábdi Isxaaq Hiniin, a Mareehaan military officer who was close to Mohamed Siyaad Barre, Ábdilqaadir Dheel Ábdulle was the person who, in 1969, betrayed the coup plans of General Mohamed Áynaanshe and his colleagues. He explains that although Dheel was part of the plot, his loyalty to Ábdirashiid Áli

Sharmaarke was due to their shared kinship as Mijeerteen and this took precedence over his loyalty to Áynaanshe, an Isaaq.[8]

The executions of Gabeere, Áynaanshe, and Dheel had served two purposes. First, Barre eliminated potential competitors for power, in particular, Áynaanshe and Gabeere; Dheel was only a sacrificial lamb. Second, it tested and broke down the myth of invincibility associated with the three major clans in Somali society. Gabeere was a Hawiye, Áynaanshe, an Isaaq, and Dheel, a Mijeerteen. In fact, Barre's experiment succeeded perfectly, the three clans did not retaliate. On the contrary, they publicly acquiesced to it, as did the rest of the population. The execution of the three men delivered a chilling message not only to the major clans but also to all other clans. Barre and the SRC sent the message that any form of opposition to the "revolution" would bring swift and brutal retribution.

The identity of the soldiers who fired the bullets at close range to the three victims was hidden from the public by pieces of cloth covering their faces (except their eyes and mouth). Mohamed Aadan Ábdulle Ósmaan, the son of former President Aadan Ábdulle Ósmaan and brother-in-law of Gabeere, informed me years ago that Mohamed Siyaad Barre used Ábdalla Mohamed Faadil and Mohamed Áli Samatar to entrap their friend Salaad Gabeere by inviting him to lunch, capturing him disarmed and defenseless. According to his brother-in-law, Gabeere's wife had a premonition when Faadil and Samatar came to her house. She suspected that something terrible was afoot when the two men invited Salaad to lunch. Taking him aside, she advised her husband not to go with his so-called friends. Nevertheless, Salaad did not share his wife's intuition nor did he think that his friends would betray him. They did.

Mohamed Siyaad Barre orchestrated the public execution of Áynaanshe, Kediye, and Dheel for political gains. The men were executed in a key location in Mogadishu where large numbers of citizens could watch. The hail of bullets instantly killed Áynaanshe, Salaad, and Dheel. A doctor approached to examine if indeed the men were alive and they were not. The fact that the public accepted and watched these brutal murders sent a chill throughout Somali society. It also encouraged the emerging dictator to carry out any abuse of power with impunity. The abuse of power intensified once the dictator found public acceptance of his excesses, because the public feared for their lives.

Decades later, in 1991, Ábdalla Mohamed Faadil was killed in Mogadishu by Salaad Gabeere Kediye's clansmen. During the chaos that followed the collapse of the regime, Faadil's body remained for days on a street near Hotel Juba, rotting and disfigured. Mohamed Áli Samatar now lives in Virginia, in the United States of America.

Another symbolic act the regime instituted to divide society was the Family Law issued on 11 January 1975. The law provided greater rights to inherit property and to initiate divorce than the tradition or religion permitted. Some religious leaders viewed aspects of this law as violating the teachings of the Koran. On 15 January 1975, only five days after the law was issued, eleven religious leaders who voiced opposition were publicly executed. The pretext and speed in which the men were condemned and executed took everyone by surprise. The law was an outright provocation for potential opponents. Calls for tolerance, dialogue and clemency were rejected.

Wearing the mantle of social reform, Siyaad Barre recruited women to his cause. He presented himself as champion of women's rights to win the allegiance of women. In particular, he wanted exploit tension between men and women, particularly those marriages according to Somali tradition. In fact, Siyaad Barre intended no genuine reform; he himself was married to two women and would have been the first to object if either wife claimed greater rights of inheritance or initiated divorce. In addition to exploiting traditional conflicts between men and women, the law gave a needed pretext for a showdown with men of religion, the last bastion of potential opposition. The isolated resistance of the religious leaders could have been ignored or resolved through dialogue, but Siyaad Barre used their protest as justification for their physical elimination.[9]

The elimination of the military officers removed immediate competitors. The intelligentsia had surrendered following "orientation" in Halane Camp, stick-and-carrot tactics, cabinet reshuffles, unexpected demotions and promotions, and arbitrary dismissal and detention. Students were held in check by the programs of indoctrination and their parents' fears. The elimination of the religious leaders symbolically completed the elimination of all men from the political landscape. It also sent shock waves and terror greater than the previous executions. For if Siyaad Barre did not spare religious men who posed little threat to the state, if he did not fear the wrath of Allah, then no one was safe, despite the illusion of security from loyalty to Siyaad Barre.

In fact, as we have seen in the preceding chapter, Mohamed Siyaad Barre was conciliatory toward Islam before his regime gained strength. Nevertheless, by 1975, he was bristling for confrontation with religious leaders after issuing the Family Law that they opposed. His declaration that, had the Prophet lived, he would have endorsed the Family Law was unbelievably arrogant. He provoked outrage with his assertion that statements or articles contained in the Qur'an, specifically in Al-Nisa Sura, on inequality of women and men "have been rendered irrelevant."[10]

In any case, Mohamed Siyaad Barre expunged from the SRC those persons deemed a threat to his power. He promoted the remaining members of the SRC—those who were colonels became generals, majors became colonels, and captains became majors. In addition, members of the SRC were given greater symbolic authority in the armed forces. Even those with a higher rank than the SRC were to salute them and treat SRC members as if they were higher in rank than they were. Such symbolic gestures of power and the chilling execution of their eminent colleagues made them prone to cooperate with Mohamed Siyaad Barre.

As repression intensified, those who were able fled the country. Many found jobs in oil-rich Arab states like Saudi Arabia; others stayed in Somalia hoping that the regime would collapse from its internal rot. Meanwhile, they found no alternative but to live in a world strewn with prohibitions and to feign cooperation with the system of oppression. Every day in which they escaped dismissal from their job was a victory and every night without their doors being opened with a booted kick was a reason to thank Allah for protection. Many saw oppression as a new opportunity for ill-gotten wealth and power. However, they knew that the circle of Siyaad Barre loyalists was more exclusive and secretive and that danger lurked everywhere. Life was one of anxiety and nightmares. The hard-core loyalists diligently continued their intimidation and persecution of others; they improved their techniques and technology of torture; they reaffirmed their loyalty to the "father of the nation" and his system by inflicting greater cruelty on the *Kaán-diid.* This too was a form of personal survival – survival of the meanest.

The determination to fight and change the regime was not yet born; at least, it remained unexpressed and privatized, consciously concealed or enacted in dreams of rage. A few years later, after the dictator embarked on a war with Ethiopia and experienced defeat, the myth of his invincibility dissipated; his rhetoric of revolution lost credibility, and his world of make-believe lost its potency. Nevertheless, long before he lost grip on power, he prepared his loyal forces, arming them with lethal arms. Meanwhile, he invested inordinate privilege on his paternal and maternal clans—the ***M**areehaan*, the ***O**gaadeen* respectively—and on the ***D**hulbahante*, his son-in-law's clan. Together, members from the three clans formed the infamous clan coalition known by the acronym M.O.D., constituting the ruling *Klan*. Nevertheless, like any clan coalition in Somali society, this alliance also proved opportunistic and temporary.

War with Ethiopia

Before Siyaad Barre's dictatorship took root, it was generally believed that the *raison d'être* of the Somali Armed Forces was to protect the nation and to liberate other Somalis. What freedom meant or required was not fully understood, nor was the meaning and pain of oppression, but the passion for it was intense. Frustrated hopes for freedom were pinned on the Somali army, and sorely needed resources were invested in its development and expansion. Even before the 1969 coup, defense costs exceeded the combined budget for health, education, and labor. By 1973, the public expenditure was $5 per capita for the military but only $2 per capita for health and $1 per capita for education. By 1975, the size, budget and equipment of the armed forces increased substantially.

In 1960, the Somali armed forces totaled 5,000. In 1970, it reached 12,000 and by 1976, it exceeded 25,000. Its approximately 250 Soviet-made tanks gave Somalia the largest force in black Africa. Its Air Force, though small in comparison to that of Ethiopia, was made formidable by the squadrons of MIG-17s, MIG-19s, and MIG-21s provided by the Soviet Union. By 1987, the Somali armed forces were estimated to be 62,000 strong, divided between its armored and mechanized brigades—the 250 tanks were complemented by 500 armored personnel carriers. The Navy had 23 patrol craft. The air force had about 60 combat aircraft. Supplementing the armed forces were militia that numbered 20,000 and a paramilitary force of around 8,000 men.

These figures, found in the archives, actually underestimate the strength of the Somali armed forces. In an interview aired by the BBC Somali Section on 12 October 2002, General Mohamed Áli Samatar Commander of the Armed Forces, Minister of Defense, and Vice President, affirmed that the Somali armed forces were 50,000 in 1977 when the war with Ethiopia started, and quickly reached 100,000 by the early nineteen-eighties. He added that the armed forces totaled 120,000 "when he left" office, by which he probably meant 1991 when the dictatorship he loyally served collapsed. Mohamed Áli Samatar also added that in the midst of the war with Ethiopia, the regime organized fighters according to clan brigades because they recognized that was the only way they could continue fighting with high morale.

Ironically, the military regime resorted to the clan system after years of denouncing it, in order to attain Pan-Somali-Unity. The liberation movements also eventually resorted to the clan system in fighting against the regime. Hence, the question of whether the clan system is inescapable fact of life, or an artifact of the elite, remains to be resolved not only intellectually but also in practice.

In his quest for personal power, Siyaad Barre misdirected and confused the armed forces and the nation. Instead of protecting freedom, he made the armed forces the primary bulwark of his regime and the guardian of his power. He corrupted Pan-Somali nationalism into a coalition of the Daarood, the President's clan-family straddling the borders of Somalia, Ethiopia, and Kenya. Despite this self-serving distortion of unity, Mohamed Siyaad Barre knew that all Somalis would be easily swept by nationalist fervor if he invaded Ethiopia and provoked war. This would give his regime a reprieve and a new lease on life. In addition, more territory means more resources, more power, and more people to govern. Beyond these immediate gains, Mohamed Siyaad Barre thought he would be hailed as the greatest hero in the annals of Somali history if he wrested the territory of Somalia controlled by Ethiopia. War with Ethiopia thus offered multiple advantages and Mohamed Siyaad Barre could not pass up the opportunity.

Ethiopia had sunk into violence brought on by an internal feud over power. Like Somalia, Ethiopia had its own military dictator and junta pushed citizens beyond the limits of human tolerance. While the crisis in Ethiopia festered and the war in Eritrea depleted its resources, the might of the Somali armed forces reached its zenith. Lean and well equipped, it needed to pursue other ambitions than the conquest of Somali citizens whose surrender was in any case complete. Keeping the soldiers in barracks, armed with sophisticated weapons and provided daily training on how to kill, was itself dangerous to the regime unless their energy and violence were directed elsewhere.

Siyaad Barre possessed a keen sense of timing when an opponent was most vulnerable and he had the skill to deflect danger to others. He ordered the armed forces to invade Ethiopia on 23 July 1977. To cover up the invasion and avoid international condemnation, his regime insisted that the invaders were none other than the fighters of the Western Somali Liberation Front (WSLF), the guerrilla movement of Somalis under Ethiopian rule. In fact, the regime of Mohamed Siyaad Barre distorted the truth of how the war started and who was fighting inside Ethiopia.[11]

Nonetheless, the Somali public received the attacks with zeal and euphoria. For many Somalis, this was a dream come true and Siyaad Barre became an instant hero. With dazzling speed but massive human toll for both countries, the Somali armed forces subdued the larger and demoralized Ethiopian army. Between September and October 1977, a large portion of the Ogaadeen was quickly "liberated." The Somali who felt helpless and hopeless before the war suddenly experienced a jolt of pride in victory. The war offered a chance of self-rehabilitation from the cowardice that led to surrender into Siyaad Barre's tyranny; in some magical way, it lifted the feeling of defeat which daily was experienced under the petty and mean agents of his regime.

The war brought the intoxicating passion of nationalism. It pit the "good *us*" into a violent confrontation against "the bad *them*" using steel and explosive neither Somalis nor Ethiopians produced. The imported lethal arms became instruments to settle old scores and canalize destructive passions devastating both countries. In this moment of collective dissociation and of *folie en masse*, all Somalis suddenly became brothers, at least comrades in arms, despite the fact it had been only yesterday that some kicked others with boots, broke their bones with batons, tortured them in underground cells, or killed by a firing squad. The passion for Pan-Somali-Unity and the dissociation the war engendered are illustrated by the military officers who were in prison at the time of the invasion but who, given a chance to fight, proceeded straight to the front-lines of the war. Most of them did not see their families as they left the prisons in which they were incarcerated. Some of them died on the war-front before they saw their families; others were executed after they returned from the war, defeated and exhausted.[12]

Even before the war began, the Soviet bloc had established (primarily through East Germany) links with Mengistu Haile Mariam, the Ethiopian dictator, because the USSR valued Ethiopia's strategic position in Africa and because they had increasing doubts about Mohamed Siyaad Barre's commitment to socialism. The Soviet bloc tried to mediate the conflict between Somalia and Ethiopia but to no avail. When it came to a choice between the two countries, the Soviet bloc sided with Ethiopia. Therefore, between November 1977 and February 1978, the Soviets provided arms and Cuban soldiers to assist the Ethiopian forces. The counteroffensive forced Somalis to withdraw from the territory they occupied in their quick victory. The regime of Mohamed Siyaad Barre abrogated the 1974 Somali-Soviet Friendship Treaty, and established relations with the Carter Administration.

As the rhetoric of revolution wore out and the public became increasingly disillusioned, the military regime moved away from reliance on propaganda and intensified its use of brute violence and repression. However, as the regime's control by promises and propaganda weakened, the regime resorted to violence. By 1974, when public disillusionment with the regime set in, the prisons were filled to capacity. The armed forces continued to consume a substantial portion of the nation's revenues and external aid even after its defeat in the war with Ethiopia.

In any case, following the defeat in 1978 and after the coup attempt in the same year, the armed forces waged war on its own people. The regime therefore continued to expand its armed forces not with the goal of liberating Somalis across the border, or defend the country from external aggression, but to demoralize, dominate, and defeat the very citizens who had maintained the armed forces with their taxes.

The 1977-78 war with Ethiopia produced unexpected consequences for the regime of Mohamed Siyaad Barre and for the Somali people. According to Mohamed Áli Samatar, the general commanding the Somali armed forces on behalf of Mohamed Siyaad Barre, there were approximately 5,500 military casualties on the Somali side and about 15,000 military casualties on the Ethiopian side.[13] These figures do not include civilian deaths. In addition to deaths, untold numbers suffered physical disability and psychological trauma. The war casualties were forgotten after the guns ceased firing, but their suffering and rage continued to haunt Somalis for years.

The violence and anarchy that brought down the regime is to some extent a legacy of the Ethiopian war and associated tyranny. After the regime fell in 1991, the country was awash with the lethal arms it accumulated before and after that war. There are also less tangible but equally important consequences of that war. After the war, Somalis broke down into warring clans. Armed movements against the regime began and these movements spearheaded a succession of wars that began with a desire for liberty but degenerated into anarchy and chaos.

Although the SRC and its leader had promised to root out "tribalism," it did not deliver on that promise. On the contrary, it reproduced the most blatant form of clannism. The regime did not publicly renounced clan as an organizing force in society changed its public views on clan during the war with Ethiopia. Desperate for new recruits for the supposed "war of liberation" against Ethiopia, the regime exhumed the "tribalism" it buried in 1971. General Mohamed Áli Samatar affirms that the military regime resorted to clan mobilization because it was the only effective means left for the regime to recruit soldiers from a population exhausted by the war and tyranny at home. The regime sought the help of the clan elders it banned in 1970 in order to mobilize the forces. In the hour of need, it embraced clan as the most effective means of organizing Somalis for war.[14]

This was an admission that clan and clannism are inescapable in Somali society and that, in the final analysis, appealing to clan identity and clan organization (not nationalism, religion, or monetary incentive) can motivate Somalis to the battlefield. The admission is most remarkable when offered by a general who is a *Tumaal*—one of the unjustly despised and segregated clans in Somali society—and who, as a result, would have every reason to minimize the importance of clan and clannism in Somali politics and society.

The armed movements that started after the war with Ethiopia proved the same point because, regardless of their effort to organize on national platform, they fell back on clan mobilization and their movements all ended up as clan movements. The ensuing years ushered in clan movements (first of the Mijeerteen, then of the Isaaq, and then of the Hawiye) that took up arms to fight the Daarood dominated regime of Mohamed Siyaad Barre. As a result, trashed and forgotten were traditional themes of Somali politics—homogeneity of the people, sanctity of the state, and commitment to Pan-Somali nationalism.

Once the clan system found new life in clan movements fighting a clan dominated regime, Somali politics and society took a new trajectory few anticipated in 1960 on the eve of independence and in 1969 when the armed forces took power. Once the clan *jinni* was out of the jar, it exposed that the declared brotherhood of Somalis was insincere and hollow, that the dream of Pan-Somali-Unity was sham.

To this day, Somalis wallow in the clan neurosis fostered by the culture and pushed to absurd extremes by the regime of Mohamed Siyaad Barre. What was this neurosis and how did it manifest itself in Somali politics? In what ways did Mohamed Siyaad Barre express his clan neurosis? How did 'the rule of the family' come about?

The next chapter provides answers to these questions.

9
CLAN NEUROSIS AND NEPOTISM

Tuug baladille, yaa reerkisa mari.
Killing a thief restricts travel among his clan.
—Somali proverb

It is one of the ironies of life that experiences in the past haunt us. We never fully outgrow our insecurities and fears of childhood—even in old age, we may not outgrow childhood phobias, we may carry with us hurts we suffered, or we may try to make up for the love denied us in childhood. Some of these enduring consequences of childhood may be a private torment with limited social consequences, although the pathology of an individual is never a private matter when a spouse, a child, a friend, a neighbors, or society suffers for it.

When one assumes power, the private and the public merge with enormous consequences; they become social malaise affecting the lives of millions. Often, the pathology of the individual is a product of an eco-pathogenic environment or relationship. If victim of child abuse, the person carries within him the abuse suffered somewhere in his unconscious and my repeat the abuse as an adult. If he grew in midst of pervasive spouse violence, he may also carry within him the terror or rage or both to later life, perhaps avoiding intimate relationships or repeating the abusive relationship he had known.

Assuming political power, the person may reenact past abuses on him in ways that affect the lives of millions. In his pathological attachment to clannism, Mohamed Siyaad Barre was probably compensating for unsatisfied needs and inferiority complex rooted in his past. In his case, the struggle he waged with the demons of his past distorted the lives of millions. His tortured past wrote the script for the generation for whom it became destiny.

How did the clan neurosis of Mohamed Siyaad Barre manifest itself? How did his clan neurosis—in this case his fetish of clannism and anxiety—spill over into the world of politics? Why did the man who depended on his own perseverance and will for survival, and who rose to power without the support of his clan, turn out to be pathologically insecure and clannish at the apex of power? How did his family and clan exploit his clan neurosis and status as a leader? What was their contribution to the erosion of power and ultimate downfall of Mohamed Siyaad Barre?

Clan Neurosis and Revolution

I define clan neurosis as the rigid but superficial adoption of identity based on the clan system to such a degree that one judges others their personality, their intent, and their behavior—only in terms of clan affiliation. There are two aspects to this inflexible clan orientation. On the one hand, the person suffering from clan neurosis finds comfort, feels secure, and extends trust to whomever he identifies as member of his clan. On the other hand, he feels anxious, insecure, and alienated in the presence of others who do not share the same lineage.

In both cases, he disregards behavior of others, forcing them into a classification based on their ancestral past and group myths. The clan neurotic is thus a slave to irrational division of people into "us" and "them" on the basis of clan delusions and clan myths. At the bottom of clan neurosis and sustaining its irrationalities is personal neurosis with roots that go back to childhood socialization later emerging as an orientation of clan competition and conflict. Feeling deeply insecure, the person seeks forsakes personal responsibility in exchange for clan identity, support, and protection. In time of failure and frustration, he deflects onto others his inadequacies, blaming others for his limitations.

The clan neurotic leader surrounds himself with inept cronies from his clan who in turn exploit their newly found power and privilege without restraint. In time, the system turns into a junkyard of clan misfits and government degenerates into a rule by the inept until it narrows down a rule of the family. Yet the more neurotic the leader the more he stimulates clan neurosis in others by re-enacting the self-fulfilling prophesy—the enemy fabricated in the mind materializes in reality, lurking everywhere. In short, clan neurosis is self-defeating because it creates avoidable enemies, stress, and anxiety in politics and human relations. The neurosis that began with the leader expands to a neurosis of the family, of the clan, of the nation. In short, the concept of clan neurosis explains many of the irrationalities in Somali politics and particularly in the behavior of the Somali elite. A non-clinical or an exclusively rational explanation fails to account for Mohamed Siyaad Barre's oppressive rule, his behavior, or that of the men who defended his regime. The neurosis engendered by clan dynamics must be included in the analysis.

Equally, those who took up arms against Mohamed Siyaad Barre's oppressive rule were themselves hosts to clan neurosis but they understood neither the dictator's clan neuroses nor their own. Confronting his neurosis with theirs, they broke no new ground in changing the relations of Cain and Abel. Though they toppled his regime, they only aggravated the old patterns of clan fusion and fission with pathologic relations associated with them. No wonder the anarchy and violence rages on in most parts of Somali society 17 years after the collapse of the state.

Neurosis does not motivate all revolutions. Some of them began with human values and genuine compassion for the oppressed while many begin with unwholesome goals, psychologically unhealthy leaders, and power-hungry warlords. Prolonged oppression is by its nature neurotogenic, even schizophrenogenic, and it haunts its victims and reproduces itself in subsequent generations. Revolutions that start without a preceding trauma and neurotic leaders are therefore as few as those that succeed in their declared mission of liberation. Often, self-declared revolutionaries plagiarize goals and rhetoric but only *practice* and *outcome*, moving rhetoric and grand promises, distinguish the genuine from the false revolution.

The "revolution" led by Mohamed Siyaad Barre is a case in point. His clan neurosis, previously private and circumscribed, became a national malaise and a public hazard when he became the leader of a self-serving "revolution." Somalis were ready to embrace any "revolution" so long as it got rid of the civilian administration that had misgoverned them since independence. Mohamed Siyaad Barre and his rhetoric of "revolution" thus came at the right time when military coups were common in Africa and at the right place where people were desperate for change and naive about politics. Their neurosis found a match in the neurosis of the leader.

Mohamed Siyaad Barre took power in collaboration with other military officers. He wrested power from his collaborators by setting them against one another and by manipulating their personal insecurities. After executing some, he used their individual vulnerabilities and fears to accumulate more power for himself. He also understood the aspirations of the public and told them what they wanted to hear. A swarm of his cronies embellished his speeches, recited them in poems, and sang them in schools, orientation centers, and public ceremonies.

When he became the ruler of the country, he kept a retinue of high officials queuing up every evening at his palace for the chance to see him. He listened to them and manipulated them all night until 8:00 AM, releasing them just in time to go to work in their offices. This was a form of torture reserved for the fortunate few who had escaped the persecution of the swarm agents who crawled all over the streets and neighborhoods in search for the *Kaán-diid* (anti-revolutionary).

His personal neurosis also expressed itself through sexual exploits of women, particularly the wives of both his opponents and cronies. He was hungry for rumors of scandals, particularly concerning high officials and his opponents. He was interested in consulting soothsayers, in order to divine the future of his rule. When his neurosis focused on clan, it gained incendiary power and produced the most disastrous consequences for the Somali. Mohamed Siyaad Barre knew the humiliation a person from a powerless minority feels and, given opportunity, he made sure that everyone around him felt the same even if they came from a clan that boasted of numbers and power.

The 1969 coup began with great promise expressed in the speech of Mohamed Siyaad Barre on 23 October 1969, two days after the coup. However, the promise degenerated to fear and despair once Mohamed Siyaad Barre consolidated his power. In that long speech, Mohamed Siyaad Barre explained why the armed forces had carried out the coup and what policies the coup leaders wanted to implement as part of their revolutionary program.

The speech was impeccable in presentation and timing, striking the right tone for what people wanted to hear—reassurance, denunciations of anti-clannism, commitment to Somali unity, promises of economic advancement, and anti-colonialism. In particular, he stated:

> If we ask why the officers and soldiers of the Somali armed forces carried out the coup, the answer is clear: not in order to replace one group with another, not in pursuit of rank or power for their own sake, not to serve the interest of one person or of a specific group. The armed forces could not ignore the pain the public experiences on the many problems the country faces including bribery, clan dis-

> crimination, embezzlement, breach of honesty, lack of order and discipline, undermining the religion, and lack of faith...
>
> What we want is to root out clannism with which we were manipulated and oppressed. When foreigners wanted to mislead us, they used it [clannism] and they asked, "What is your clan?" "You are of this or that clan." "So-and-so is related to you." "So-and-so had given a report about you..." The colonial system today has its local representatives among us... We want to destroy them and all traces of them, including all loopholes through which they enter...

With the prevailing optimism, one did not ask if Mohamed Siyaad Barre was sincere about his denunciation of clannism and breach of honesty in government. People wanted to forget the painful past and to ignore the background of their leader. In retrospect, Barre's description of how "foreigners," referring specifically to colonialists, had exploited clannism suggests he is a man with intimate familiarity with the tactics of sowing suspicion and discord among the colonized.

Throughout his long reign, he presented himself as anti-clannist and as an "anti-colonialist." Again, with optimism gripping the nation, few asked the past of this self-anointed anti-clannist and anti-colonialist? Using his experience in intelligence during the colonial era and his talent for double-talk, Mohamed Siyaad Barre pulled the wool over people's eyes. Had Somalis closely examined Mohamed Siyaad Barre's record, they would find ample evidence of his disreputable past. Yet, disregarding his shady past activities, including arrests of nationalists and his alleged complicity in political assassinations, he was able to stand in front of Somalis and sanctimoniously present himself a revolutionary, a liberator, and the long-awaited savior.

Of course, the man had audacity in making these claims that was remarkably glib and bold. He was able to dissimulate the truth and mesmerize the population with his words. He took advantage of the *zeitgeist,* the spirit of the time and trend of thought characteristic of the nineteen-sixties. In that decade, with independence from colonial rule fresh in the public mind, everyone took the liberty to call himself nationalist as long as he had the right skin-color and seem to choke with emotion when the new national anthem was sung.

Even the well-known anti-nationalists of the colonial era, including the once hated spies joined the fold as long as they spoke the right words and aligned their past with the *zeitgeist.* Somalis were, at the time, in a state of nationalist mind trance, oblivious to the past, too optimistic about the future, and as naive about politics as they were quick to forgive past crimes. In retrospect, it is not surprising that Mohamed Siyaad Barre could stand lecturing about revolution and liberation with no questions asked.

Nonetheless, Mohamed Siyaad Barre proudly stood to declare that the awaited revolution had come when clannism would be rooted out and nirvana was imminent. People believed him. Meanwhile, as he covertly advanced clannism, the SRC tried to strip the majority of Somalis of their clan identity and support so they would become isolated and weak. On 10 November 1970 the SRC, under the Barre's leadership, issued the decree called *"Difaaca Bulshada"* (Protection of Public Order) which abolished traditional titles and ranks like *Boqor, garaad, Suldaan, and Ugaas* as well as certain laws and traditional social contracts.

In December 1970, Mohamed Siyaad Barre and the SRC carried out a vigorous campaign against clannism that started with a public burial of an effigy representing the clan system. The campaign proceeded with fanfare accompanied by the destruction of historical records. In March 1970, Mohamed Siyaad Barre announced that all government employees would be evaluated on merit (by *what* you know, not *who* you know)." At about the same time, the airwaves were filled with the song, "*Turun turootoo, Kuftay, kuftay,, Ayaa taqaan?... Taladii seegtoo luntay, ayaa taqaan?—Ee maxaad taqaan?*"[1]

In 1971, as rhetoric on the revolution and Pan-Somali nationalism continued, Mohamed Siyaad Barre and his "friends" again orchestrated a public ritual of "tribalism" in which an effigy of the clan system was buried.[2] The ritual was reenacted in every major city and people from all walks of life participated. Each participant partook partly out of fear that he might be labeled *Kaán-diid* (anti-revolutionary) and partly out of a secret concern that the clan being buried was not one's own, but that of someone else. In fact, Mohamed Siyaad Barre was using the ritual to "bury" other people's clan and clannism, never his own.

While the ritual continued, the dictator was busy recruiting his clansmen for key posts in the government, the armed forces, and the secret service. Ominously, the ritual foreshadowed the approach of a man and a regime that when confronted with difficult or stubborn problems, sought the solution in burying "the problem." In this case, the problem buried was symbolically the clan but this prepared the way for *en masse* killing and burying of specific clans presumed to be the enemy of the regime.

By 1972, people realized that the dictator was not an anti-clannist but rather a rabid pro-clannist. In fact, it was apparent that the public denunciation of "clannism" was a ruse to hide the clan affiliation of the leaders, that the ritualistic burials were part of a strategy to conceal plans to monopolize power, as well as that the revolution was a vehicle to confuse the people. We note that Mohamed Siyaad Barre lost choice posts in both the armed forces and the police force for reasons he attributed to clan discrimination. Two younger colleagues of his—General Mohamed Abshir Muuse and General Daauud Ábdulle Hirsi—superseded him because the former was a Mijeerteen and the latter a Hawiye. Such incidents throughout his career must have instilled, deeply within him, his clannist orientation and preference.

Soon after he became Commandant of the armed forces, Mohamed Siyaad Barre called in a young and energetic captain whose duties included managing the office where military personal records were kept.[3] As soon as Barre entered the office, the captain saluted and stood attentively, waiting for instructions. With an unusual warmth and informality, Barre ordered him to relax and sit down on a nearby chair. The officer did. The young captain wondered what he had done to merit this friendliness. With a straight face and a calm voice, the Commandant ordered the young captain to conduct research for him and to document the clan of every officer in the armed forces.

The captain, himself a Daarood, responded that such information does not exist in the files. The Commandant, speaking in a fatherly manner, told the captain that he was too young and inexperienced to understand the value of such information. The captain (who eventually became general) reports that he considered the request bizarre and demeaning. When he refused the order—so he claims decades later—the Commandant transferred him from this post. About this time, Ábdulaahi Yuusuf Ahmed, now the President of the so-called Transitional Federal Government, returned to Somalia during a break from his military course in the former Soviet Union. He took the assignment to document the clan identity of military officers. In return, he received an extra-stipend and a car to facilitate his research Ábdulaahi until he completed the assignment.

Three years before the coup, therefore, Mohamed Siyaad Barre had the clan particulars of every military officer in the country. This is the type of information interested the former CID and intelligence expert and he knew how to exploit it for his ends. Mohamed Siyaad Barre was not only a clan addict of the extreme; he was also an unforgiving and vindictive man who never passed up the opportunity to even the score for a wrong suffered in the past. For example, there was a debate prior to the coup when the Égaal Administration was considering retiring Mohamed Siyaad Barre from the Armed Forces. One minister—Aadan Isaaq Ahmed—argued that, because Mohamed Siyaad Barre was old and weak, it was pointless to worry about a coup led by him. Individuals in the meeting understood the minister's argument as a defense of the Commandant, although the characterization of him as weak and old was not flattering.[4]

After the coup, the same minister was among the politicians imprisoned by the Supreme Revolutionary Council. One night, Mohamed Siyaad Barre visited the prison where the politicians and walked into the cell where the former minister was asleep on the floor. Waking up the prisoner with booted kicks, Mohamed Siyaad Barre looked down at the minister and said, "Hey, what do you think of your fate today? Do you still believe I'm weak and old?" The prisoner, confused and frightened, was unable to answer.

A folklorist and poet, tells a story which is uncorroborated but of interest. He said that several generations ago, a Mijeerteen Sultan had among his confidants and advisors "a Midgaan" whose loyalty and wisdom was highly valued. One day, the Midgaan asked the Sultan to show his appreciation for loyal service by giving him the hand of a woman with noble birth. The Sultan was in a dilemma because he wanted to comply with the request, yet to do so would violate custom. One of his Mijeerteen advisors then found a compromise solution by arranging a marriage between the Midgaan and a Mareehaan woman. Generations later, Mohamed Siyaad Barre remembered the injustice committed against the Mareehaan woman and the blot left on the honor of his clan.[5]

According to the folklorist, Mohamed Siyaad Barre avenged the "injustice" and "dishonor" after he assumed power. First, he fired the

Minister of Education, Yaasiin Ósmaan Kenadiid, whose grandfather was the Sultan, and then he appointed Ashkir Botaan, a Midgaan, as the Minister of Education. He also arranged a marriage between a Mijeerteen male singer and a Midgaan female singer. According to the folklorist, the Mijeerteen male singer was the grandson of the man who long ago had arranged the marriage of the Midgaan advisor to the Sultan and the Mareehaan woman.

Is the story true? Who knows? Anything is possible in the convoluted psychology of Mohamed Siyaad Barre. The folklorist, a man with extensive knowledge of Somali history, might also have relayed a fictional story as history for, as we know, the quest for truth in Somali society is often an impossible mission. Even those who question the folklorist's story affirm that both the Mijeerteen community and the family of the singer felt distressed by the marriage and that Mohamed Siyaad Barre went to the extreme to protect the marriage. In fact, the marriage was a state affair, given official welcome and celebration. Was this an illustration of Mohamed Siyaad Barre's progressive outlook or an expression of his vindictive streak?

One can question the truth of this rumor, although myths and mythmaking among Somalis is a fascinating subject. If true, it shows Mohamed Siyaad Barre's capacity to remember a clan grudge and settle the score with vengeance. If untrue, we should consider it the in its cultural context where, as they say, *Xooluhu waa caws ku nool, dadkuna was xan ku nool*—livestock live on grass, people on rumor. In other words, life would be boring without rumor. What matters is not the veracity of the rumor but its socially binding and entertaining value. For the more wicked and juicy a rumor, the more it entertains. The more secretive, the more the teller and the listener huddle together, sharing a conspiratorial moment in the forbidden.

Masking Clan Neurosis

Seven years after the coup, Siyaad Barre's tyranny outpaced his capacity to justify socialist ideology. When the rhetoric of revolution lost steam, he needed a cover for his clan neurosis and tyranny. The regime needed to make adjustments to give the appearance of collective leadership. The 25-member Supreme Revolutionary Council with which the coup gave way to a one-man rule with Mohamed Siyaad Barre the uncontested winner of power.

In 1971, there were plans to form a political party to replace the SRC, with the Soviet government promising further military aid, but nothing materialized until July 1976 when Siyaad Barre convened the first meeting of a new party, the Somali Revolutionary Socialist Party (SRSP). The party disguised Mohamed Siyaad Barre's clan neurosis and gave semblance of broad participation regardless of clan affiliation.

General Ismaíil Áli Abokor who was a key member of the SRC and Vice President confirms that leaders of the Soviet Union repeatedly advised Mohamed Siyaad Barre to form a political party akin to theirs if he was sincere about his claim of adopting socialism.[6] They asserted that no socialist revolution reached its full potential under a military regime. The general added that more was actually involved than ideological purity. The foreign policy makers of the Soviet Union believed that an institution like a political party would protect their geopolitical investment in the Somali regime for a longer period than reliance on one man who would die or be overthrown.

When they saw his resistance, they advised that he form a party whose members comprise trusted loyalists that give the appearance of public participation. When the socialist masters upon whom her relied for military and financial assistance advised him to form a socialist political party, Mohamed Siyaad Barre had no choice but to comply in a manner suiting his own interest—getting rid of the SRC, a nuisance to his dictatorship, and forming a party predominated by trusted loyalists from his clan. In fact, before the SRC members realized it, he had mobilized for party members a swarm of supporters, mostly from the M.O.D Alliance with emphasis on his clan, the Mareehaan.

Using the party, he emasculated SRC members by diffusing their power and concentrating it to himself. Managing almost illiterate and inexperienced loyalists was indeed more congenial and safe than continue to rule with the support of the SRC with some members feeling cheated and angry while others still entertained ambition to replace him. Thus, whether driven by external pressures or by local considerations, Mohamed Siyaad Barre formed the party and soon used it to consolidate his power.

On the first day the party convened there were 3,000 participants called the "founders of the party." Mohamed Siyaad Barre and his cronies selected party members on proven loyalty to the "revolution," a euphemism for loyalty to Mohamed Siyaad Barre. The selection process began with a circular ordering the Political Office, headed by an Army officer, Ahmed Muumin Dolaal, an army officer, to direct regional and district units to identify potential party members from the armed forces, government agencies, and the civilian population. With Mohamed Siyaad Barre's supervision and approval, his cronies developed a final list of party members. The process of selection ensured that members of the party were "yes-men" who hailed the Chief without restraint and applauded whenever he spoke. In one of his speeches, Mohamed Siyaad Barre stated this criterion in no uncertain terms: *"Maxaad taqaan waan dhaafnay ee maxaad aaminsan tahay ayaan gaadhnay"*—we surpassed the stage of *what do you know*, we reached the stage of '*what do you believe*.'[7]

Predictably, the assembled party members consisted of Mohamed Siyaad Barre's relatives by clan or marriage, loyal army officers, select members of the cabinet ministers, and young ideologues trained abroad (primarily in the Soviet Union). Included in the party were also civil servants and security agents who knew how to keep their mouths closed and to look the other way when impropriety and abuse were present. In their first meeting, the party members nominated and selected Mohamed Siyaad Barre for the General Secretary of the Party, Chairman of the Central Committee, Chairman of the Council of Ministers, and President of the country. They nominated no one else.

In addition to these new titles and powers, Mohamed Siyaad Barre was the Commander-in-Chief of the Armed Forces. The Politburo replaced the SRC; the Council of Ministers succeeded the Council of Secretaries of State. The Politburo consisted of five military officers: President Mohamed Siyaad Barre, his three Vice-Presidents (Mohamed Áli Samatar, Hussein Kulmiye Afrah, and Ismaíil Áli Abokor), and his son-law, Ahmed Suleymaan Ábdulle. Other members of the SRC and loyal allies among the intelligentsia joined into the Council of Ministers.

General Mohamed Áli Samatar continued to serve as the Minister of Defense and Commandant of the Armed Forces. General Hussein Kulmiye Afrah and General Ismaíil Áli Abokor continued in symbolic positions. Ahmed Suleymaan Ábdulle, Barre's son-in-law, remained head of the National Security Services. The Party and the Council of Ministers took nominal roles and powers. However, in reality, the Politburo was the highest authority in the land. It alone decided domestic and foreign policy. Yet within the Politburo, power exclusively rested in Mohamed Siyaad Barre.

Mohamed Siyaad Barre not only exercised his authority at the level of the Politburo or Council of Ministers, he also exerted his power through party bureaus concerned with economic, security, ideology, social, finance, and party affairs. Clan relatives of Mohamed Siyaad Barre chaired the most important and influential of these committees. For instance, a Mareehaan, Mohamed Mohamuud Warsame (nick-named *Jaan Go'an*) chaired the Party Bureau on Security called the *Gudiga Baadhista ee Xizbiga*; Dr. Mohamed Aadan Sheekh, a Mareehaan physician-turned-politician headed the Ideology Bureau; Ábdilqaadir Haaji Masale, a Mareehaan military colonel, headed the Bureau of Mobilization known as *Gudiga Abaabulka.*

These bureaus had special functions and authority. The Bureau of Security harassed and persecuted citizens throughout the country; the Bureau of Ideology indoctrinated the populace and justified its tyranny; the Bureau of Mobilization recruited, trained, and organized defenders of the regime. Dr. Mohamed Aadan Sheekh, the physician turned the political ideologue of Mareehaan supremacy and a key advisor of the dicatator, is said to be the author of a long-term plan with which the Mareehaan were supposedly to rule Somali politics for at least ninety years.

The plan was that the Mareehaan would govern by exercise of violence for thirty years, use of money for the next thirty, and excel in educational credential for the next thirty years. The plan assumed that the first thirty years would enrich the Mareehan and the next thirty years would bring a significant number of their own who would benefit from the special opportunities opened for them by Mareehaan control of the state purse and scholarships. If it is true that the doctor or the regime had set up such a plan, fate too had its own plans concealed from mortals.

The Mareehaan indeed obtained immense political and military power, but their reign by use of violence could not exceed twenty-one years. Some of them, like Ábdi Ashkir Hoosh and Ábdirahmaan Jaamá Barre, also acquired immense wealth by illicit means, yet (as we shall see later) their money had little redeeming consequences for the Mareehaan. As for education, few of their young men and women wanted to give up life of plenty, social merriment, and pleasure of imported trinkets for the drudgery of study and grueling examinations. What is more, a monster assisted in pursuit of personal power or the limelight eventually turns on those who in the beginning had nurtured it on injustice and violence. Hence time did come when Dr. Mohamed Aadan Sheekh himself would become a victim of the regime and the dictator in whose service he had devoted his keen mind and warm personality. The danger and delusion of which all ideologues suffer are that their idealistic and partisan fixations ensnare them in a web of illusions and elusive goals they come to regret. At least, this doctor knew when he erred and, for this, he was imprisoned, though not with traumatic consequences meted out for his non-Mareehaan colleagues.

In short, the Somali Revolutionary Socialist Party (SRSP) gave the illusion of change and democratic participation in socialism as understood in those times. However, its structure and function revealed what people knew since the early nineteen-seventies—that Mohamed Siyaad Barre was the only man in charge, that he was the alpha and omega of power, the ultimate dictator. The appointment of three members of the Mareehaan to the three most important party bureaus emboldened him to reveal his clan neurosis without disguise. From here on, he recruited mostly from the Daarood and particularly from the Mareehaan clan to take charge of the party and its key political functions.

The composition of the Central Committee changed during its existence, often adding or removing members on whim of Mohamed Siyaad Barre. Despite its revolutionary rhetoric and claims of being the people's party, Mohamed Siyaad Barre remained stuck in old patterns that gave dominance to the Daarood in all respects. In fact, the role of the SRSP was to cover to the power of the core *Klan* and its Grand Wizard who selected members using clan criteria. And it did for a while. One would have expected that, at least in the start of the so-called revolutionary party, the dictator would disguise his clan obsessions. He did not.

Table 5 presents the composition of the Somali Revolutionary Socialist Party's Central Committee by clan. The first column presents the different clans, broken into sub-clans where possible. The last column presents the total number of persons appointed in the SRSP Central Committee.

Table 1
Composition of SRSP Central Committee
July 1, 1976

Clan \ Sub-Clan	Majerteen	Mareexaan	Ogaadeen	Dhulbahante	Habar Gidir	Abgaal	Xawaadle	Murasade	Habar Je'lo	Habar Awal	Habar Yonis	Arab	Xeebjiire	Gaadsan	Sheekhaal	Digle	Dishishe	Ortable	Waldool	'Iise-'Adde	Iidagale	Madhibaan	Durugbe	Lyeylakase	Yahar	**Grand Total**
Daarood	10	8	7	6													1	1						1		**34**
Hawiye					4	4	2	1							2											**13**
Isaaq									4	4	3										1					**12**
Raxanwein																1										**1**
Gadabursi													1													**1**
Dir														1												**1**
Iise																			1							**1**
Tumaal																				1						**1**
Madhibaan																						1				**1**
Reer Xamar																							1			**1**
Arab											4															**4**
Yahar																									1	**1**
Grand Total	**10**	**8**	**7**	**6**	**4**	**4**	**2**	**1**	**4**	**4**	**3**	**4**	**1**	**1**	**2**	**1**	**1**	**1**	**1**	**1**	**1**	**1**	**1**	**1**	**1**	**71**

Chart 1 presents the clan distribution of the party's Central Committee.

Chart 1
Clan Distribution of SRSP Central Committee, (July 1, 1976)

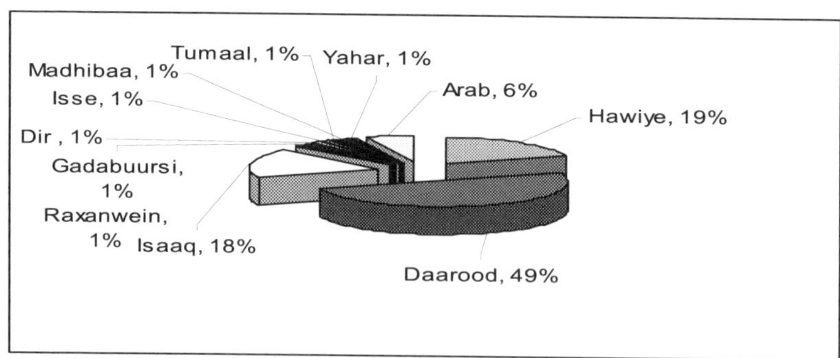

It is obvious from the table that the three major clans (Daarood, Hawiye, and Isaaq) dominated the SRSP Central Committee, as they dominated Somali politics since 1960, although the Daarood consistently obtained a lion's share of power in excess to their comparative population. Stacking the SRSP Central Committee with Daarood members may have reassured Mohamed Siyaad Barre, but this only intensified the simmering resentment of other clans. Several years later, some of these clans took up arms to fight the regime and, fifteen years later, clan massacres followed.

About half (49%) the members if the Central Committee were Daarood and the Hawiye, Isaaq, Rahanwein, Dir, and Gadabuursi combined had only 40%. The only modification from earlier patterns is that the Central Committee incorporated previously neglected groups, the Reer Hamar, Tumaals, Madhibaan, Yahar, and Arabs (mostly of Yemeni origin.) Even in these instances, the dictator chose 'representatives' of these groups—General Mohamed Áli Samatar (Tumaal), Ahmed Ashkir Botaan (Madhibaan), and Ábdalla Mohamed Faadil ('Arab)—for their personal loyalty and service.

Within the Daarood, the Mijeerteen (despite their opposition to the regime) maintained dominance in party representation and the Mareehaan who in earlier regimes were rarely found, became formidable leaders in the party, the cabinet, the armed forces, and the diplomatic corps. Members of the MOD Alliance comprised 68% of the Daarood representation in the party and 30% of the total membership in the Central Committee. Little changed in the Central Committee's clan composition the regime announced on 1 July 1982 and on 1 July 1986.

Yet, even minor changes reflect a change of tactics. For instance, the composition of the Committee in July 1982 was 42% Daarood, 20% Hawiye, and 13% Isaaq; the composition of the Committee in July 1986 rose to 46% Daarood, 21% Hawiye, and 13% Isaaq.[8] The representation of Arabs was always greater than that of the Rahanwein, the Dir, and the Gadabuursi. In short, the rhetoric of the new party and its democratic reforms were a sham through and through.

To fortify the illusion of change and democracy, Mohamed Siyaad Barre held a "general election" in 1979. The Somali Revolutionary Socialist Party (SRSP)—the only party allowed to register and campaign—won 99.91 per cent of the vote; three years later, it won 99.86 per cent of the vote. According to official records, 171 candidates ran for the National People's Assembly and 1,174 candidates competed for local government assemblies in the 84 districts. All the candidates were members of the SRSP. Of the 4,220 citizens who voted, only 470 voted against the official party candidates. All the 171 who campaigned were members of the SRSP. These included 46 new faces.

The six members of the National Assembly that the President nominated won without any pretense of election.

Everyone understood that the "general elections" were blatantly phony. Yet most people went along with it in order to save their job or their welfare. Despite the promise of reform with which the "new party" began, the ordinary citizen remained unmoved and unconvinced. His pessimism deepened. The only groups who took this game seriously were the loyal allies of Mohamed Siyaad Barre, including clan cronies, the *Gulwadayaal,* and opportunistic members of the intelligentsia, all seeking their personal gain.

Many of these groups sacrificed their self-respect for secure jobs or promotion years earlier. With the misuse of power all around them, their tolerance for injustice heightened. They cared least about the abuse of others as long as they felt secure and comfortable. Competing with one another on who was most loyalist of Mohamed Siyaad Barre, they gave up on truth or justice. They went along with the lies because they lacked the courage to stand up for the common good. They were prisoners of Mohamed Siyaad Barre's web of illusions and of their own private delusions. To please Barre, the party members offered him the title of Field Marshal in the founding congress. He refused the title with feigned humility.[9]

The majority of citizens remained unconvinced by the new rhetoric and unmoved by the new promises. Talk of revolution, a new party, or programs of reform turned trite and stale, no longer capable of stimulating hope or further sacrifice. Any mention of "revolution" or "comrade" discredited the speaker as either a spy or an opportunist. The people lost faith in politics and politicians –they lost trust in leadership of any type. The new party only deepened their cynicism, but, out of fear of reprisal, they kept their feelings bottled up. Their discontent simmered, their rage festered. The explosion was to come, but no one knew when or how.

Before the explosion came, people resorted to jokes, the one avenue of release available to the oppressed. Jokes provided a temporary relief to pent-up frustration and bind people by reaffirming trust and affiliation, two human attributes that oppression steals. Jokes are also a form of resistance, a rebellion with words and laughter. Laughing at the absurdity of those in power and at themselves, the oppressed temporarily eject the oppressor within and reaffirm their humanity. The celebrated master of these jokes is Faarah Golloolay.[10] One of his popular sayings was *"ama af-kaaga hayso, ama Af-gooye tag!"* – 'either shut your mouth, or go to Af-gooye!' Af-gooye is a town on the outskirts of Mogadishu where Mohamed Siyaad Barre's security agents imprisoned and tortured opponents.

Another is the story of Mohamed Siyaad Barre visiting Lazaretti Mental Hospital in Mogadishu. Before he arrived, his heavily armed bodyguards occupied the mental hospital and positioned themselves in strategic posts. Immediately after the dictator arrived with additional armed soldiers, one of the mental patients shouted: "Please take me out of this place!" The hospital attendants tried to calm him but to no avail.

The Minister of Health who accompanied Mohamed Siyaad Barre then asked calmly, "What's the matter, my comrade?" The patient answered, "Each of us was brought here by a relative or a policeman. It took a whole army to bring this man. He must be extremely violent. I don't want to stay for the massacre when the soldiers leave him with us!"

Mohamed Siyaad Barre invoked socialism and revolution as an ideological cover for tyranny. There was nothing sincere about his socialism or revolution. He hoped to exploit the magic of words, offered a convoluted s reasons for the virtue of a one-party system—the system of political sorcery rife throughout Africa since independence. One recalls Barre's contemporaries such as Idi Amin, Bokassa, and Kamuzu Banda, all of whom justified their tyranny in similar terms.

Chris Nteta, a medical doctor and advisor to Kamuzu Banda of Malaw, gave the most amusing justifications for imprisonment and torture. In a BBC interview, Nteta stated that God's kingdom is a one-party state excluding Satan. By simple extension, he argued that his government has every right to punish the opposition, the Satan of today, since what is good for God is also good for Malawi.[11] The tragedy was that a medical doctor with the training and skill to heal had become a tool of a dictator oppressing his people.

Siyaad Barre used socialist justification to the same end, perhaps believing that the kingdom of Lenin was a one-party state from which opponents of the regime were banished, and that what is good for the Soviet Union was good for the Somali Democratic Republic. Kamuzu Banda was forthright in that he openly called himself President-for-

Life. Mohamed Siyaad Barre maneuvered for the same goal more deviously and treacherously.

Like Kamuzu, Barre behaved like a demigod who alone knew what was best for the nation and had the right to expel anyone from his kingdom by use of imprisonment or execution. Those whom Mohamed Siyaad Barre expelled from his kingdom were from the clans he feared for his power. By so doing, Mohamed Siyaad Barre set the terms for his own expulsion from power. He also set the stage for the total ruin of Somalis.

From Rags to Riches

The most amazing example of Mohamed Siyaad Barre's Mareehaan cronies who became extremely wealthy from the regime's favors is Ábdi Ashkar Hoosh.[12] This man benefited from the injustice of clannism that all Somalis passionately detest but they acquiesce to it when one of their own clan benefits from it. Late in the nineteen-fifties or early nineteen-sixties, Aadan "Law"—a leading Mareehaan politician who was a Minister during the civilian regime of President Ábdirashiid Áli Sharmaarke and Prime Minister Égaal—brought Hoosh from the rural areas.

Hoosh became a driver of a water truck owned by the wife of Aadan "Law" who was also the sister of Mohamed Siyaad Barre's younger wife, Dallaayo Haaji Haashi. He lived in a shack rented from a Hawiye woman at the monthly rate of 15 Shillings, at that time, at that time a high sum that was bearable for a truck driver of Hoosh's standing. Because he had failed to pay his rent regularly, his lady forced him out of the shack when could pay 30 Shillings that he owed her for rent. However, his fortunes took a sudden turn for the better a few years later when Mohamed Siyaad Barre became the President in 1969.

By the early nineteen-seventies, Mohamed Siyaad Barre vigorously embarked on his program of lifting the Mareehaan from their poverty and lack of political influence. Hoosh was among the young men to whom the regime and Mohamed Siyaad Barre extended bank "loans" and other government assistance. Hoosh was an active and enterprising man who effectively took advantage of all opportunities offered him. One of the government contracts was to haul goods from the port on big trailers bought for him with public funds. With the support of the port authorities, he had the ability to move containers from the port to any location in the city. He also had the special privilege that port officials could not open, check, or delay containers under his company name. No one else had that kind of dispensation from the rigid controls of the regime.

Hoosh was upset when port workers complained about the efficiency of his service because the government favored him and gave him a special dispensation. The port workers feared that Hoosh's service would throw them into the ranks of the unemployed so someone opposed to Hoosh approached Mohamed Siyaad Barre. He presented the problem in a manner that would prompt the dictator to act quickly. He told him that the containers brought arms into the country and released by port authorities unopened and unchecked. Highly sensitive about public accessibility to arms, Mohamed Siyaad Barre readily believed the report and issued firm orders that port authorities open and check all containers, without exception. Naturally, this slowed Hoosh's operation. However, it did not stop his ability to amass wealth by other means.

A remarkable element to this story is that oppressed people are not always naïve or fools. Sometimes, they get crafty and cunning; the even fool the dictator, the master swindler and trickster of all. Another is that the most rustic and rough characters among them, like Hoosh, could find himself catapulted to amazing wealth and heights to power by sheer luck of sharing clan affiliation with a dictator while those more capable and deserving could rot in poverty or prison.

Another contract that added to Hoosh's growing wealth involved the armed forces where he was to bring caps and buttons to the armed forces. Many people saw this as a minor contract—caps and buttons are no big deal! On the contrary, it was a big deal because such contracts offered a cover for Mohamed Siyaad Barre's program of Mareehaanization. Hoosh provided caps and buttons for all the armed forces. He also received the contract to purchase all furniture and building material for Hotel Úruba, the largest and best hotel built in Mogadishu by the military regime. A bigger break came to Hoosh during the 1977-78 war with Ethiopia. He had a contract to bring all rations and supplies to the armed forces and soon became one of the arm-dealers of the regime. Military aid acquired from other countries, such as Iraq, was billed as arms purchased by Hoosh and the proceeds were transferred to a special account known as XX account. Even the Minister of Defense, General Mohamed Áli Samatar, had no access to the account.

By the nineteen-eighties, Hoosh was one of the wealthiest and most influential men in the country. He could arrest anyone for the slightest reason. Because they either feared him or got a nice tip from him, the police and the security forces did what he told them. Sometimes, relatives of the detained appealed to Hoosh who ordered their release with a bundle of cash as a gesture of forgiveness. A throng of young girls also lined up in front of his office to get cash by simply offering him greetings, smiles, or their bodies. Being a wealthy playboy, any skirt that caught his eye was fair game. Hoosh, the villager and truck driver who could not pay rent for a shack turned into a prince only because he belonged to the right clan.

The government contracts continued and Hoosh became a multimillionaire, owning some of the largest buildings in Mogadishu. He had a fleet of expensive cars and all the valuables that money could buy. He even got the contract to bring in and fix Mercedes cars in a country where such cars barely existed. His accounts abroad increased in number, location, and size. He also bought houses abroad—in Kenya, Europe, and North America. Hoosh no doubt had an insider in the dictator's nuclear family, probably one of the President's wives, who continuously endeared him to Mohamed Siyaad Barre and secretly shared with him the wealth he amassed.

By 1991, after the fall of the regime, Hoosh managed to escape to Nairobi with much of his wealth saved from the pillaging and plundering raging in Mogadishu. His trailers were in the care of one of the Hawiye warlords who himself rose from a humble beginning, subsequently entered the car-fixing and truck-driving business, and then leapt to the status of multimillionaire.

It is said that a number of Mijeerteen swindlers had for years drawn large sums of money from Hoosh by telling him false stories that the Daarood were about to retake Mogadishu by force and needed arms or supplies to flush out the Hawiye pockets of resistance. Hoosh believed these stories and thus paid generously for the 'cause'. Only much later did he find out that others exploited him the same way he exploited the country. It is also said that the United Nations paid Hoosh huge sums of money after he presented deeds in his name for the compound that UNOSOM used during its operation in Somalia.

Yet for all his wealth and charm, Hoosh remained a country boy who could not outgrow his rough edges. A Mareehaan diplomat told the following story: Hoosh visited the United States in 2000, landing at Kennedy International Airport. He called a Mareehaan diplomat in Washington to pick him up from the airport. The Mareehaan diplomat explained to him that Washington D.C. was far from Kennedy International and advised Hoosh to take the shuttle to Washington, DC.

Confused by the crowds and the many airlines at the airport, Hoosh called again for help. The diplomat again explained that Hoosh should take the shuttle to Washington, D.C. Asked if he understood the instructions given to him, Hoosh confidently stated that he did, promising to be with his friend in a short time. Hoosh boarded the plane, acting like a man who knew his destination.

The plane landed in Buffalo, New York. He waited for his friend to pick him up. When he could not find him, he called again. The diplomat sent a driver to Washington National Airport. There was no sign of Hoosh who called later to report that he was in a place called Buffalo that must be quite close to Washington, D.C. When he realized his mistake, Hoosh did not have the will to try again. He therefore pleaded with the diplomat to send someone to rescue him. A person flew to Buffalo to bring the princely Hoosh to Washington, DC.

Hoosh was an example of how wrested power and ill-gotten wealth worked together to make a travesty of the promise that Mohamed Siyaad Barre gave at the beginning of the coup that 'merit' (*maxaad taqaan* – what you know) would take precedence over 'cronyism' (*ayaad taqaan* – who you know). Of course, there also was a horde of other beneficiaries from Mohamed Siyaad Barre's dictatorship, including those who rose to heights of power because they were married to the President's daughters. Of these, the most notable are General Ahmed Suleymaan Ábdalla (Daffle), head of the NSS and later Minister of the Interior and Vice-President; and General Mohamed Saíid Hirsi (Morgan), the cleft-lipped sadist and one of the architects of the genocide perpetrated on the Isaaq.[13]

There are also many other less known beneficiaries whose only qualification for unimaginable power and wealth was the accident of being born Mareehaan. They included drivers turned tycoons, half-literate soldiers promoted to generals, and ill-prepared youngsters catapulted to diplomats. To underscore this sudden change of fortunes, I wrote in 1981 a long satirical poem called "The Confession of Siyaad" in which the dictator recounted how he rose to power and lifted his clan from poverty and powerlessness:

Mareexan boys and girls
I improved your lot
Exalted you to the skies.
I lifted you from penury
The poverty rut
Hurting every Somali gut.
Your mediocrities are today
Millionaires.
Your delinquents have turned
Diplomats.
Your sergeants I made them
Generals.
Disarming everyone else
I arm you to the hilt
In order that you shall rule
The walking dead of our land.[14]

An example of the arrogance and disregard for human life the Mareehaan coteries acquired is the cruel action of one of them, a military colonel reassigned from Presidential guard for insubordination (the *Red Caps*) to head the port authority in Mogadishu. Angered by the actions of port workers, he detained eleven porters in a container. They died of suffocation and heat exhaustion.[15]

Such cruel acts were common. The average citizen often heard or suffered such cruel acts with unspoken horror. In fact, as the beneficiaries of clan neurosis and nepotism increased, other clans in society were busy condemning, envying, and fighting the system of inequity over which Mohamed Siyaad Barre had presided. The conflict between the Mijeerteen and the Mareehaan is a case in point. This conflict is important because it was the first that adopted clan character following the coup and because it affected the course of the regime's political repression and the form of resistance it provoked.

Before the regime of Mohamed Siyaad Barre degenerated into the "rule of the family," its backbone was clannism and cronyism. Barre stacked the government with members of his clan, and appointed relatives by clan and marriage to posts where money and power were concentrated. These positions included ministries of interior and finance, foreign embassies, and the armed forces. Most of the appointees were not qualified for these posts. Recruited from the rural areas or from the urbanized sectors of society, they compensated for their ignorance and incompetence with defensive arrogance and cruelty.

Mohamed Siyaad Barre was once asked why he chose to fill critical posts with such simpletons and he answered, *"Midkaan anigu surwaalka u galiyaan ugu jeclahay"* (I prefer most the one on whom I put his first trousers.[16] After the attempted coup in 1978, he told members of the Mareehaan: *"Dawladda idinkaa iska leh ee ilaashada"* ("the government belongs to you alone; you defend it.")[17] The same leader often passionately preached others about nationalism and patriotism—hog wash!

It turned out that the ill-gotten money quickly vanished for most of the Mareehaan whom the dictator enriched. They lost the wealth for three reasons. First, a great deal of their wealth poured into wars aimed at regaining power in Somalia. Second, the bankruptcy of BCCI—the bank started by a Pakistani that went bust during the early nineteen-nineties due to charges of money laundering and fraud. It was one where the cronies of Mohamed Siyaad Barre stashed their money. Third, most Mareehaan could not enter into business ventures of their own without the invisible hand of the government. They were not entrepreneurs who made wealth by their intelligence and sweat, nor were they prudent with their savings, so many of the dictator's cronies lost their capital by entering into unproductive ventures or by living lavishly after the state collapsed. The exception is Ábdirahmaan Jaamá Barre who lives in the United States and remains a wealthy man.

Mohamed Siyaad Barre also promoted clansmen to the pinnacle of power by putting them on the fast track of the armed forces. Mareehaan generals numbered more than fifty, perhaps the largest number of generals of any clan. The author met one of these generals in Paris in 1981 at a dinner in a friend's home. A Mareehaan general, serving as military attaché in Somali Embassy in Paris, joined the group for dinner. The man introduced himself as General Bihi. Later, my cousin and friend, the late Saíid Ábdilahi Égaal, a former colonial in the Somali armed forces and one of the founders of the Somali National Movement, joined us. The colonel had taken asylum in Sweden after he joined the opposition to the regime.

Before Saíid arrived, the General told the host and me incredible stories of his military expertise and bravery intended to impress but only revealing his ignorance. In one of them, he related that he was among the officers assigned to work with the American Rapid Deployment Force in the Horn of Africa during the Cold War. He bragged about how good the Somali armed forces were in comparison to their American counterparts. He claimed that Somali soldiers excelled in military maneuvers and that he was among the officers asked to train the American soldiers.

To remind the fool that his stories were out of place, our host informed him that I was an American who came from the United States only a week earlier. However, the so-called General continued his boast and bluster. Unable to listen to the hokum, I finally said, "*Wax kale aan ka sheekaysano, riwaadanna duulal-jaan iyo dameero u sheeg!*"—Let's talk about something else; as for this drama, tell it to phantoms and donkeys!

The General was upset. Remembering that our host introduced me as a mental health specialist, the term *duulal-jaan* specially offended him because he explained that the remark accused him of madness. The host intervened and diverted the conversation to more mundane topics. Before the dust settled, Saíid entered the room. He and the phony general greeted each other like two long lost friends. The General showed Saíid intense respect and courtesy, standing up until Saíid told to sit down.

After leaving the friend's house, I asked Saíid when and where he knew the General.

"I knew him as a barely literate private, a foot soldier."

"But he is now a General, you only a Colonel," I commented.

"He is one of the Mareehaan catapulted to the rank of General after I left the armed forces."

"Why did he accord you such respect, as if you were his commander?"

"He may act like a General with you and others. With me, he knows that he was my driver. His salute and respect to me is part of a repertoire he had learned long ago and can't easily erase."

I learned years later that the so-called general died of bullet wounds after the regime collapsed and the Mareehaan were target of clan reprisal.

Rule of the Family

As we have seen, the military coup that began with great promise degenerated into a dictatorship with clan domination. The circle of the rulers and the privileged, the *Klan*, narrowed following the defeat of 1978. By the nineteen-eighties, the regime over which Mohamed Siyaad Barre had presided became rigidly clannish to the point that the

M.O.D. Alliance had started to weaken although it remained operative until the demise of the regime in 1991.

The jostling for replacement of Mohamed Siyaad Barre by his relatives and cronies started as early as May 1986 when the dictator suffered serious injury in a car accident. Thus, without the armed resistance, the tyranny would continue for a longer period under a successor, perhaps long after Mohamed Siyaad Barre left the political arena due to death, ill health, or old age. The relatives of Mohamed Siyaad Barre did not succeed in replacing him, but they exploited their status as the immediate kin of the dictator to the maximum extent possible.

By the late nineteen-eighties, the "rule of the family" was in high gear. The *Klan* narrowed to an even tighter circle of close relatives. For instance:

- The President was Mohamed Siyaad Barre.
- The Chief of Staff was Maslah Mohamed Siyaad Barre (his son, then in his 40s).
- The Minister of Foreign Affairs was Ábdirahmaan Jaamá Siyaad Barre (his cousin).
- The Head of Administration and the Presidency was Ayaanle Mohamed Siyaad Barre (his son, then in his early twenties).
- The Vice-Minister of Health (actually the sole authority on health matters) was Ábdulaahi Mohamed Siyaad Barre (his son).
- The Supervisor of the Mechanized Division of the Army in the Mogadishu Area was Hassan Mohamed Siyaad Barre (his son).
- The Director General of the National Budget Division (also the sole authority on all budget matters in the nation) was Ánab Mohamed Siyaad Barre (his daughter).
- The Director General & the Minister of External Tourism Development was Haawa Mohamed Siyaad Barre (his daughter).
- The President's Advisor in Financial Matters was Diiriye Mohamed Siyaad Barre (his son, then in his twenties).
- The Brigadier General, Minister of Interior, and Chairman of the Security Committee was Ahmed Suleymaan Ábdulle (his son-in-law).
- The Brigadier General and Commander of the Police Force was Ábdirahmaan Hassan (his son-in-law).
- The Deputy Minister of Defense was Mohamed Saíid Hirsi, nicknamed "Morgan" (also his son-in-law).

The story of Ábdirahmaan Jaamá Barre and Ayaanle Mohamed Siyaad illustrates the absurd extremes to which the regime pushed incompetence and corruption. Ábdirahmaan Jaamá Barre, a cousin of the President, had served as the Foreign Minister for 16 years. He began his career in the Foreign Ministry as a lackluster and dull employee who performed minor and nonessential duties. His nickname, *Buluq buluq*, aptly described his chubby, clumsy body and his poorly developed intelligence and personal character. After he became the Foreign Minister, he liked to dress in flashy clothes, and to engage in sexual escapades as if to make up for his poor intelligence and uninspired character.

His political and financial fortunes rose when the Foreign Minister, Úmar Árteh Qaalib, proposed to the President and the Council of Ministers that Ábdirahmaan Jaamá Barre be appointed as the Director General of the Ministry of Foreign Affairs. Although the proposal sounded preposterous to all who heard it, except for the President, many understood the Minister's proposal as unabashed opportunism. Someone in the Council of Ministers that day recalled how Mohamed Siyaad Barre managed to promote his cousin while not taking responsibility for it. After hearing the Foreign Minister's proposal, Mohamed Siyaad Barre ostensibly advised against the appointment of his cousin to the post when, in reality, he had endorsed it without delay.[18]

This was an example of Mohamed Siyaad Barre's double-talk developed to the level of art. It turned out that Ábdirahmaan Jaamá Barre elbowed out Omar Árteh Qaalib from the post of Foreign Minister had assumed the job for 16 years. It was also an example of how blind ambition to please the dictator becomes self-defeating.

During the tenure of Ábdirahmaan Jaamá Barre, the Foreign Ministry and the embassies of Somalia became institutions of embarrassing incompetence, cronyism, and corruption. Barre had amassed enormous wealth during his tenure as Foreign Minister and later as Minister of Finance. In the same way that his cousin ran the country as he wished, without limits to his power, Ábdirahmaan administered the Foreign Ministry as his fiefdom. He controlled its finances and siphoned its funds to private accounts abroad, making him one of the wealthiest persons in the country. He appointed his favorites to critical posts, giving preference to the Mareehaan who possessed similar attributes of incompetence and corruption as he did.

Under his leadership of the Ministry, embassies were no longer serving the Somali interests abroad. They too became extensions of him and of his family. In the Emirates, in Europe, and in the United States, embassy personnel kept busy purchasing, packaging, and sending for him and his family consumer goods, including the latest models of clothes, furniture, and other symbols of good living. When he traveled abroad, he took a large entourage of aides who stuck to him like leeches.[19]

If the story of Ábdirahmaan Jaamá Barre is an example of ineptitude raised to unbelievable heights of power and wealth, that of Ayaanle Mohamed Siyaad demonstrates how the regime had became a family-owned shop in which all members could meddle with it. Ayaanle, the youngest and favorite son of Mohamed Siyaad Barre, was born a few days after the coup of 1969. His name translates to "the fortunate one." He was 16 years old when Mohamed Siyaad Barre a car accident seriously injured him and left him incapacitated for months. A teenager with limited education and experience, Ayaanle assumed the awesome job of managing administrative affairs of the Presidency. He quickly assumed responsibilities of recruiting, firing, promoting, and demoting at his own discretion those officials in lucrative posts in government, in return for a kickback for himself.

One can imagine the humiliation felt by men who were old enough to be his father and yet placed in the position of giving bribes to a teenager in order to gain a living. One can also speculate on the lavish life-style and arrogance of a teenager naming his price for appointing or firing officials at will.

His brother, Maslah Mohamed Siyaad, the oldest son of the President, had gone for training in the Soviet Union where he attended few classes and failed the required exams. Sent back to Somalia by frustrated college administrators, he became an officer in the armed forces. Lacking the street smarts and ambition of his father, he exploited his status as the President's son and therefore won quick promotions in the armed forces. Supposedly trained as a military engineer, he built up a fortune from lucrative contracts awarded to him by the government. He spent much of the proceeds on lavish life-style and sexual escapades.

After the attempted coup of 1978, he headed the powerful military sector No. 77 based in Mogadishu. Armed with the best weapons and manned mostly by Mareehaan soldiers and officers, this sector of the armed forces had the responsibility of ensuring the security of Mogadishu and strategic facilities located around Mogadishu. On occasions when Maslah and his colleagues in Sector No. 77 needed quick cash, they sold arms to whoever would purchase them. An example was the conflict involving the Gaalgale and Abgaal when the latter purchased arms from Sector No. 77 and changed the balance of power against the Gaalgale who supported of the regime and persecuted the Abgaal.[20]

Ironically, these arms had contributed to the uprising against the regime that eventually brought its downfall. During the nineteen-eighties, Maslah became the de facto Minister of Defense. His status as the "crown prince" came under challenge when the car accident seriously injured his father, the President, in 1986. Along with General Mohamed Áli Samatar, the First Vice-President, General Ahmed Suleymaan Ábdulle, and even the teenaged Ayaanle, Maslah was one of the contenders for the post in case the President died or resigned. However, Mohamed Siyaad Barre did not let his cronies to push him out of power.

After the regime fell in 1991, Maslah lived in poverty. The last thing known about his is that he was languishing in Nairobi, unemployed and broke, begging for financial help from a Hawiye junior colleague of his who had become wealthy after absconding with the private accounts they both jointly owned in foreign banks during the heyday of Mohamed Siyaad Barre's rule.

Behind Maslah's candidacy as a "crown prince" was his mother, Khadiija Maálin, the first wife of the President, who wielded formidable power behind the scenes. She was of the Mareehaan sub-clan, and married Mohamed Siyaad Barre when he was young, poor, and inexperienced. She was at his side through the good times and the bad. She bore him many children and saw him through difficult years. She provided counsel and comfort to him as he faced difficult choices and challenges in his career. For these reasons, she had a great influence on the President. As the first wife, her children also enjoyed, according to Somali and Islamic tradition, preferential rights for inheritance.

Whatever was her personality before to the coup, Khadiija's formidable power and influence had come to public attention particularly during the nineteen-eighties when she earned the reputation for get-rich-quick schemes and for imposing her will on others. A Mareehaan banker said that she would send orders to bank officials who readily doled out to her or her dispatchers any amount of cash she requested or else face severe reprisals.[21]

By the late nineteen-seventies, Khadiija had formed her own intelligence agency called *Hangash*, or *dhabar-jabinta* (the backbreakers). Some claim that she developed *Hangash* with three goals in mind: to give employment to young Mareehaan males, to protect the interests of her husband, and to develop a parallel and competing organization to the feared National Security Service. It comes as no surprise that when Mohamed Siyaad Barre came was called the nation's "father", she too was dubbed 'Mama Khadiija.' Unlike the President's second wife, Khadiija was the Maria Theresa of Somalia.[22] She reached the height of greed and cruelty so that if some had informed her of the poverty and misery of the citizens, she might very well have answered, "Let them eat one another!"

Mama Khadiija died in Dubai in September 2005 in poverty and dejection. Somali residents in the UAE collected donations for a modest burial of her. Dallaayo Haaji Haashi, his second wife, died in Columbus Ohio in July 2004. Like their husband, Mohamed Siyaad Barre, both wives died while refugees and in despair. Such are the ironies of history and the bitter fruits of living on the suffering of others.

Aadan Ábdulle Ósmaan

Ábdirashiid Áli Sharmaarke

Ábdirazaaq Haaji Hussein

Mohamed Ibraahim Égaal

1956 Picture of Military Officers including Mohamed Siyaad Barre (standing back 3rd from left), Daauud A.Hirsi (standing back 5th from left), Mohamed Abshir Muuse (standing middle 5th from left), Mohamed Áynaanshe Guuleed (sitting, 3rd from left), and Hussein Kulmiye Afrah (sitting, 4th from right).

Daauud Ábdulle Hirsi

Mohamed Siyaad Barre

10

OLIGARCHY SOMALI STYLE

Fiqi Tolki kama jano tago.
Even the most religious man never abandons his clan for paradise.
—Somali proverb

In *A Pastoral Democracy*, I.M. Lewis stated that clan genealogy is the key to Somali politics. Genealogy is still a key to Somali politics but in ways different from how I.M. Lewis observed and explained it almost half a century ago. As a social anthropologist studying Somali culture and social organizations, Lewis focused his study on the clan system in its indigenous and pristine form. He explained that traditional politics was founded on egalitarian system of self-governance, confirming Richard Burton's description of Somalis a century earlier as a 'nation of republicans' consisting of scattered, independent, and proud clans.

Much indeed changed in Somali society and politics since I.M. Lewis wrote his pioneering work. Somali society is no longer egalitarian or a 'nation of republicans.' The growth of the state in post-independence—its monopoly of violence and resources, its pervasive presence and corruption, its intrusion into all aspects of life—has turned the former colonial state into an oligarchic polity first disguised as civilian-led democracy, then military dictatorship justified as socialist revolution, subsequently the cause of disastrous conflict and anarchy. This was far cry from the descriptions given of Somalis by I.M. Lewis and Richard Burton.

After examining the history of Somalis for about one hundred years and almost a half century after Lewis presented his classic, we ask: what changes have taken place in the use of clan in Somali politics since 1956 when I.M. Lewis carried out research for his work? If the Somali elite had institutionalized oligarchy after independence, as suggested by the previous chapters, did they do so as members of clan, class, or both?

Since also no system of injustice endures for long without serving the interest of some groups invested in its continuity, who primarily benefited from this oligarchic rule? Why do the Somali elite repeatedly choose oligarchy and hegemony as their standard model of governance? And why does the Somali public acquiesce to these forms of government even when they publicly declare abhorrence to its inequity and injustice?

Although I focus in this chapter on the relevant data from 1960-1991, I shall return to the question of oligarchy and hegemony in Chapter 13

Oligarchy and Hegemony

Oligarchy is government in which a small group exercises control while *hegemony* is dominant influence or authority one group, clan, or nation has over others. While oligarchy emphasizes concentration of power in a few persons, hegemony refers to monopoly of power and influence by a group but power distributed among a large number of its members.

Before colonial rule, Somalis governed themselves by egalitarian tradition—that is why Richard Burton called them "a race of republicans." Under colonial rule, however, they lived under one or another form of racial oligarchy with power concentrated in a few white men. After independence, the trio we discuss in this work—the flawed state, the distorted clan system, and the malfeasant elite—worked jointly to sustain class oligarchy often combined with either clan hegemony or sub-clan oligarchy.

Diagram 2 highlights forms of hegemony and oligarchy by class and clan.

Diagram 2
Hegemony and Oligarchy

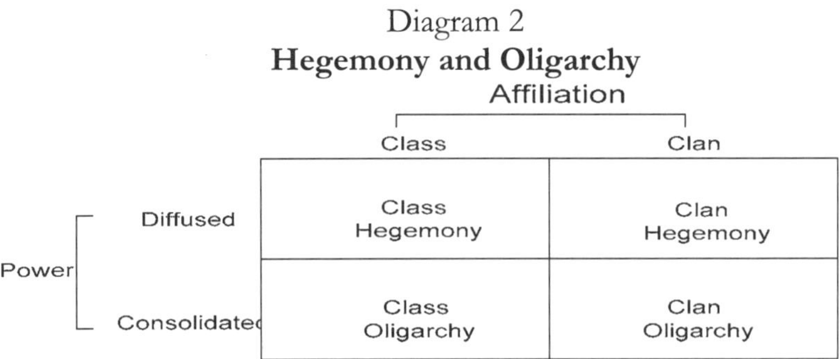

Class hegemony is exercise of power or influence by a group with common economic interest but their power and influence is more diffuse than in class oligarchy—the latter being consolidation of power in a few members sharing class (chiefly economic) interests. Clan hegemony refers to dominant power or influence exerted by a group sharing common genealogy at a higher level of segmentation such as for instance the Daarood, the Hawiye, or the Isaaq. In clan hegemony, power and influence are more diffuse whereas clan oligarchy arises when power in a few persons concentrates in a group sharing common genealogy at the level of sub-clan or extended family.

Although these four categories of hegemony and oligarchy characterize Somali politics, they seldom operate in pure or isolated forms. The four categories often interlace and overlap—such that class hegemony and clan hegemony occur in tandem, as do class oligarchy and clan oligarchy. Thus, wherever there is class hegemony, the symbols and substance of power do not distribute equally among clans. One clan inevitably enjoys greater power or influence over others. Where there is class oligarchy, power and influence also consolidate soon or later in the sub-clan or extended family of the leader. Complicating matters, there is always a veneer of democracy, socialism, or religious ideology that deceptively gives the impression of inclusion, equality, and justice. However, the veneer hides hegemony or oligarchy in the form of class, clan, or both.

The existing data shows that government in Somali society in the first thirty years of self-governance (1960-1990) was first and foremost class oligarchy in which power concentrated in hands of the elite, the *Klan*, who differentiate themselves from the rest of the population by level of education, economic advantage, and life style. In time, the Klan oligarchy enlarges into clan oligarchy at the level of the *primal clan* (what I.M. Lewis calls *clan-family*) by which Somalis differentiate themselves as Daarood, Hawiye, Isaaq, Rahanwein, etc.

By its nature, oligarchy is a gradation of inequity and exclusion which rewards a few and frustrates the majority. The gradation of inequity and exclusion take place not only between classes and primal clans but also within the ruling elite and ruling clan. Hence neither all members of the ruling elite nor all members of the ruling clan obtain equal share of power and state resources. The inequity reproduces itself at different levels of society such that there is often an oligarchy within oligarchy. For this reason, it generates resentment within and without the ruling group, making politics not the art of achieving the possible but the sorcery of realizing the impossible.

There are different ways by which oligarchy manifested itself in Somali society. One good indicator of it is who and how cabinet members enjoyed exercise of power during thirty years of self-governance from 1960 to 1990. Selection of cabinet members is indeed the most important political decisions a leader makes. These members play crucial roles in governing. They help formulate and implement policy of the regime, they serve as loyal confidants and agents of the leader, they influence his decisions; they influence who is promoted, demoted, or dismissed; they issue grants, contracts, and favors to their allies; by the information they provide, they also influence the leader's opinion of other individuals and clans. In addition, the leader's choice of cabinet members reveals his political views and practices, the persons he trusts, and the clan as well as class strategies he adopts to meet changing political demands.

I highlight below the ministerial appointments made in 1960-1969, the period of civilian rule, and 1969-1990, the era of military dictatorship. I later add other indicators of inequity in the armed forces, the police, and the diplomatic corps.

Klan Oligarchy

Somali politics from 1960-1990 was dominated by an oligarchy of the *Klan* and this oligarchy followed clan pattern in distribution of power. Individual members of the oligarchy distribute by name and clan. Yet, within the oligarchy, members possessed unequal power and privilege. Some members of the oligarchy were kinsmen of the leader and they enjoyed his trust; some belonged to other clans and held on substantial influence because they loyally executed his wishes; still others rose to power like a meteor and vanished in quick succession because they did not perform according to the standard set by the dictator.

Often, members of the oligarchy concentrated in the cabinet—the highest echelon of formal power under the President and the Prime Minister. The cabinet formally developed and approved government policies, budgetary decisions, and promotion of key personnel. At minimum, a person in the cabinet had access to vital information on affairs of the state, and access to vital information constituted power unto itself. Permanent or temporary members of the oligarchy occur in the pattern of cabinet changes that took place in the thirty years of independence. When cabinet changes took place, a few continued to hold on to key posts, playing musical chairs; others temporarily joined the oligarchy once or twice only to be dismissed, jailed, or forced to exile.

Although at the beginning the oligarchy came from the elite drawn from different clans, the Daarood members often dominated in number and power. For instance, if we examine the number of Presidents and Prime Ministers, we find that in the thirty years of independence (from 1960-1990) a Hawiye was President and an Isaaq Prime Minister only one time (disregarding the short-lived and superficial appointments of Mohamed Hawaadle Madar before the state collapsed.)

In contrast, there were two Daarood Presidents—one Mijeerteen, the other Mareehaan—the latter ruling society for twenty-one years. There were also two Daarood Prime Ministers in addition to two nominal Prime Ministers—one Tumaal, the other Isaaq. The Commanders of the Armed Forces and of the Police were Daarood for most of the thirty from independence to the collapse of the regime, except for a brief period (1961-65) when a Hawiye, General Daauud Ábdulle Hirsi, served as the army force's Commander.

The distribution of ministerial posts from 1960-1990 also affirms two recurrent pattern— firstly that a small number of individual constituted the ruling clan, secondly that Daarood members were most dominant in the ruling *Klan*. Table 1 shows the number and distribution of ministerial posts from 1960-1990.

Table 1

Clan and Sub-Clan Distribution of Ministerial Posts

1960-1990[2]

	Sub-Clan																														
Clan	Majerteen	Mareexaan	Habar Awal	Habar Gidir	Dhubahante	Ogaadeen	Abgaal	Habar Je'lo	Habar Yoonis	Xawaadle	Samaroon	Isse-'Adde	Gaadsan	Dabarre	Yemeni	Murasade	Warsangali	Iidagale	Durugbe	Eelaay	Giible	Sheekhaal	Ortable	Ujejen	Disow	Ajuraan	Makaahiil	Dishishe	Tuuni	Others	**Total**
Daarood	78	50			36	33											10						6					3			**216**
Hawiye				42			32			19						11						7		6		4				4	**125**
Isaaq			45					25	22									9												1	**102**
Raxanwein																				7	7				5					5	**24**
Gadabursi											19																4				**23**
Digile														13															3	1	**17**
Tumaal												17																			**17**
Arab															13															2	**15**
Dir													14																		14
Reer Xamar																			8											2	10
Issa																														2	2
Madhibaan																														2	2
Total	**78**	**50**	**45**	**42**	**36**	**33**	**32**	**25**	**22**	**19**	**19**	**17**	**14**	**13**	**13**	**11**	**10**	**9**	**8**	**7**	**7**	**7**	**6**	**6**	**5**	**4**	**4**	**3**	**3**	**19**	**567**

Chart 1 summarizes the percent distribution of ministerial posts by clan for the thirty years of self-governance.

Chart 1
Percent Clan Distribution of Ministerial Posts
1960-1990

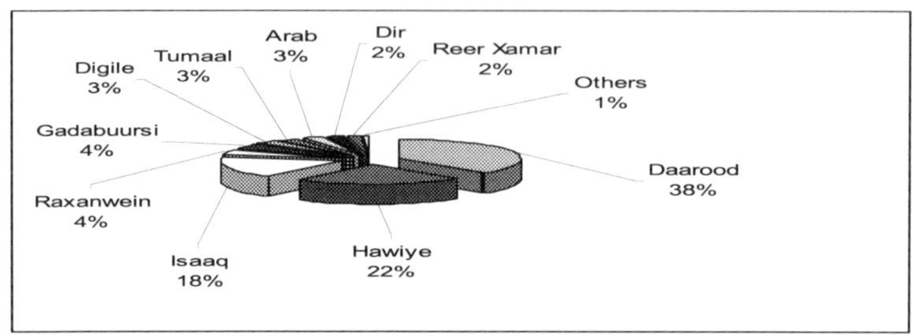

As shown in Table 1, the total number of ministerial appointments in the thirty years of Somali self-governance was only 567. This group of cabinet ministers, comprising a special club, occupied key cabinet posts in government and made critical decisions for a population of about 7 million. They enjoyed the highest political power and privilege in Somali society.

More remarkable than the limited number of cabinet appointments (i.e. 567) for a population of 7 million is that the 567 cabinet posts were occupied not by 567 individuals but only by 158 persons during the thirty years of self-governance from 1960-1990.

Further analysis shows that three clans—the Daarood, the Hawiye, and the Isaaq—dominated this ruling clique of 158 and obtained 84% representation in ministerial posts during the thirty years of self-governance (1960-1990). When we compare the size of representation among the three dominant clans, the Daarood alone had 41% percent of ministers, almost the combined representation of the Hawiye and the Isaaq. Other clans—including the Rahanwein, the Dir, the Gadabuursi, the Digil, and many minority groups—obtained only 16% representation in the cabinet. As we shall see later, this pattern of inequity also obtains in the distribution of all posts in government.

Since oligarchy and inequity reproduce themselves at all levels of government, we discover a predictably consistent pattern in the distribution of the 158 persons who held cabinet appointments in the thirty years of self-government from 1960-1990. There are two consistent patterns we note here particularly—firstly the unequal distribution of cabinet posts to clans, secondly the unequal distribution of posts among the 158 persons appointed to cabinet posts. From this, we discover that there is not only clan oligarchy but also oligarchy within oligarchy. That is, the oligarchy in society reproduced within the cabinet itself.

Table 2 presents the persons who occupied cabinet posts 10 or more times from 1960-1990.

Table 2

Clan Distribution of Persons Appointed 10 or More Times,

1960- 1990 [2]

Name	Clan	Sub-Clan	Times
Mohamed Ali Samatar	Tumaal	Iise-Adde	16
Abdiqaasim Salaad Hassan	Hawiye	Habar Gidir	13
Abdisalaam Sheekh Hussein	Digile	Dabarre	13
Abdirahmaan Jaamá Barre	Daarood	Mareehaan	11
Aadan Mohamed Ali	Daarood	Mijerteen	11
Muse Rabileh Good	Gadabursi	Mahad Asse	11
Abdi Warsame Isaaq	Dir	Gaadsan	10
Ahmed Mohamuud Faarah	Isaaq	Habar Awal	10
Hussein Kulmiye Afrah	Hawiye	Abgaal	10
Mohamed Buraaleh Ismaíil	Daarood	Dhulbahante	10
Mohamed Sheekh Osmaan	Hawiye	Murasade	10
Umar Arteh Qaalib	Isaaq	Habar Awal	10

Chart 2 presents the clan and sub-clan distributions of persons appointed to ministerial posts for at least 10 or more times.

Chart 2

Clan Distribution of Persons Appointed 10 Times or More, 1960-1990

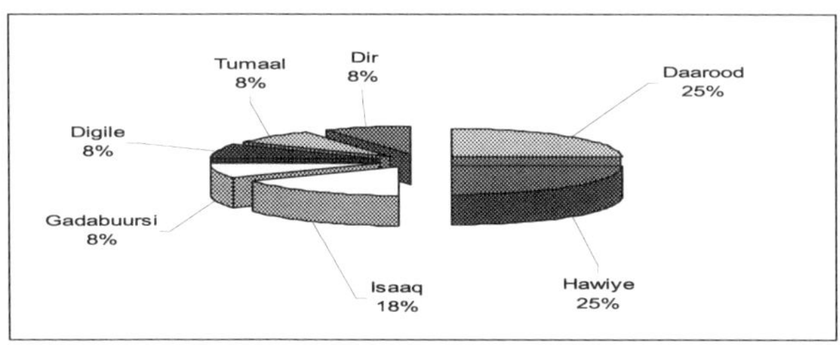

The trust of the dictator was most important in the frequent appointment of the other nine persons. Their presence also served another function: it gave symbolic clan representation in the highest echelon of power as if the dictator shared power with different clans. For instance, the dictator appointed General Mohamed Áli Samatar to ministerial posts more frequently (16 times) than any other individual in Somali history. That he is a member of the clans discriminated against—hence least likely to obtain ministerial post even once—is a historically significant t, but Mohamed Siyaad Barre had altogether a different motive than restoring justice or making history. He trusted Mohamed Áli Samatar for his compliant and loyal disposition above all.

Table 3 presents the list and clan distribution of the persons who became ministers more than five but less than ten times.

Table 3

Persons Appointed More than 5 but Less than 10 Times

1960-1990[3]

Name	Clan	Sub-Clan	Times
Ábdulaahi Óssoble Siyaad	Hawiye	Hawaadle	9
Ósmaan Jaamá Áli	Isaaq	Habar Yoonis	9
Ábdalla Mohamed Faadil	Arab	Yemeni	8
Ahmed Habiib Ahmed	Reer Hamar	Duruqbe	8
Ahmed M. Mohamuud (Siilaanyo)	Isaaq	Habar Jélo	8
Mohamed Hawaadle Madar	Isaaq	Habar Awal	8
Mohamed Geelle Yuusuf	Daarood	Mijeerteen	8
Ábdirazaaq Mohamed Abubaker	Daarood	Mijeerteen	7
Jaamá Mohamed Qaalib	Isaaq	'Iidagale	7
Mire 'Awaale Jaamá	Daarood	Majerteen	7
Mohamed Áli Xaamoud	Rahawein	Gillble	7
Yuusuf Áli Ósmaan	Daarood	Mijeerteen	7
Ábdulaahi Ílise Mohamuud	Hawiye	Habar Gidir	6
Ahmed Suleiman Ábdulle	Daarood	Dhulbahante	6
Bile Rafle Guleed	Daarood	Ogaadeen	6
Hussein Ábdilqaadir Qaasim	Daarood	Ogadeen	6
Mohamed Áli Nuur	Hawiye	Abgaal	6

Chart 3 shows the clan distributions of persons appointed to ministerial posts more than five times but less than ten times. Again, this chart gives proof that *Klan* oligarchy overlapped with clan oligarchy.

Chart 3

Persons Appointed to More than 5 but less than 10 Times

1960-1990

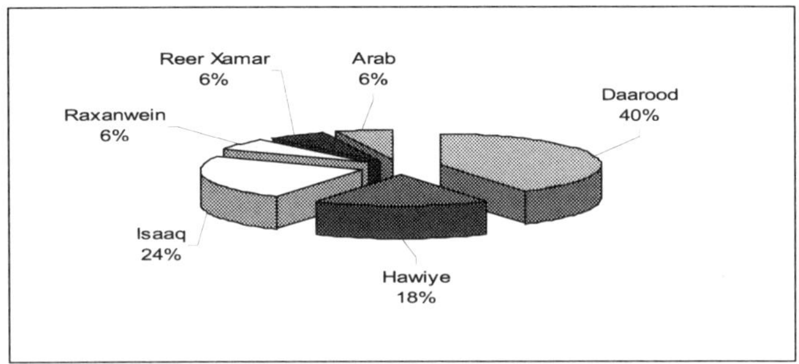

The Daarood had overwhelming dominance of representation (40%) in this group of 17. The Isaaq with 24% were second—a rare event since the union—while the Hawiye had 18%. The Rahanwein, the Reer Hamar, the Arabs of Yemini descent had one person each appointed to ministerial posts more than five times. While the Daarood maintained dominance at all times, the other clans kept more or less the same pattern with two exceptions in this instance: reversal of the Isaaq and the Hawiye was unusual because the Isaaq often were distant third in the hierarchy of clan advantage.

In its early years of revolutionary rhetoric, the military regime had drawn into its cabinet and administration the Isaaq members who had well-established credentials like Ahmed Mohamed Mohamuud (Silaanyo) who is an economist trained in Britain. By 1974, two developments became clear: the military regime turned into a dictatorship that would not leave power on its own and the clannism it had promised to root out had enlarged clan hegemony.

By 1975, the regime began to dismiss or demote many Isaaq civil servants and military officers, adding them to the category of clans opposed to the regime. By 1976, the demotion or dismissal intensified while many members of the Isaaq, seen the writing on the wall, left the country, most of them seeking jobs in oil-rich Arab countries like Saudi Arabia. By 1981, they took up arms against the regime under the Somali National Movement. Ahmed Mohamed Mohamuud (Silaanyo) became was the SNM Chairman after he too fled the country.

Table 4 presents the names and clan distribution of persons who held cabinet posts for exactly five times from 1960-1990.

Table 4
Persons Appointed for Five Times
1960-1990[4]

Name	Clan	Sub-Clan	Times
Ábdirazaaq Haaji Hussein	Daarood	Mijeerteen	5
Ábdilqaadir Mohamed Aadan "Zoppe"	Rahanwein	Habar Yoonis	5
Jaamá Rabiile Good	Gadabursi	Mahad Ásse	5
Mohamed Aadan Sheekh	Daarood	Mareehaan	5
Mohamed Áli Munasar	Arab	Yemeni	5
Mohamed Ibraahim "Liiq-Liiqato"	Hawiye	Sheekhaal	5
Mohamed Mohamuud Warsame	Daarood	Mareehaan	5
Mohamed Saíid Mohamed "Gacmay"	Daarood	Warsangali	5
Sheekh Hassan Ábdulaahi Faarah	Isaaq	Habar Yoonis	5
Yuusuf Hassan Élmi	Hawiye	Habar Gidir	5
Ábdulaahi Mohamed Mireh	Daarood	Ogaadeen	5
Jaamá Gaas Maáwiye	Isaaq	Habar Jélo	5

Chart 4 shows the clan distribution of persons appointed for five times.

Chart 4
Persons Appointed for Five Times
1960-1990

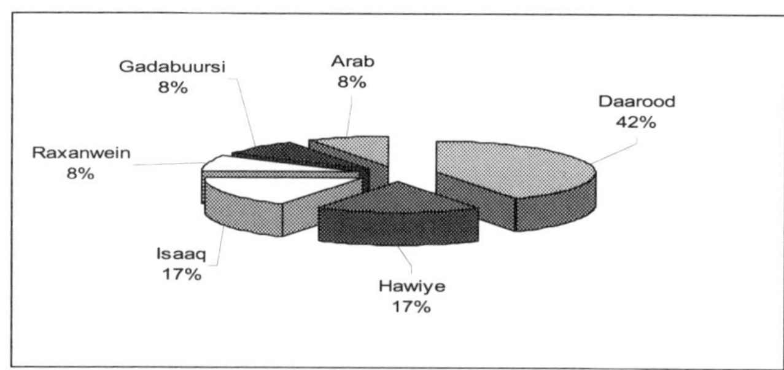

Table 4 and Chart 4 again affirm that power was held by an exclusive clique of the *Klan* and that some clans had more power in this special clique. The Daarood had 42% of the total cabinet appointments in this group. The Hawiye and the Isaaq had each 17%. The Rahanwein, the Gadabuursi, and Arabs of Yemeni descent had each 8%. Except for one person (Ábdulaahi Íise Mohamuud), the military regime appointed all others

There was not only a core group of 158 persons who decided the fate of over 7 million people for thirty years or unequal clan distribution of ministers during this period but also there was inequity within this oligarchy. For instance, the 10 individuals (6% of the 158) who were appointed to cabinet posts for ten or more times (see Table 2 above) occupied 115 (20%) of the 567 ministerial posts appointed in the thirty years. The 17 individuals (11% of the 158) who occupied ministerial posts for more than 5 but less than ten times (see Table 3 above) occupied 123 (22%) of the 567 ministerial posts. The 12 persons (8% of the 158) appointed to ministerial posts for five times (see Table 4 above) occupied (60 (11%) of the 567 ministerial posts.

When we combine the 10 persons who held ministerial posts for ten or more persons and the 17 persons who held ministerial posts for more than five times but less than ten times, these 27 persons (17%) held 238 (42%) of the 567 ministerial posts. The total 39 individuals (25%) appointed to ministerial posts for five or more times occupied 289 (51%) of the 567 the available cabinet posts in thirty years of self-governance. The remaining 119 persons (75% of the 158) appointed for less than 5 times occupied 278 (49%) of the available 567 ministerial posts.

In short, a core group who repeatedly played musical chairs to give the illusion of change dominated Somali politics during the thirty years of self-governance. In reality, however, there was an oligarchy of the *Klan* and this oligarchy was the dominated by the Daarood. In addition, inequity and oligarchy reproduced within the ruling elite. Although the pattern of clan inequity and class oligarchy existed since independence, the military regime aggravated both in its 21 years of tyrannical rule.

The ruling elite in the first nine-years of civilian rule was few in number and largely naive about world politics; they run a fledgling state and experimented with democracy with little understanding of what a modern state requires to advance national development or render justice to its population. The civilian rule was short-lived. It ended after the assassination of the President—a tragic event that involved a well planned and covered up conspiracy of the *Klan* and specifically of the Daarood members of it.

The twenty-one years that followed the civilian rule was the period of military dictatorship that began with the rhetoric of revolution only to rapidly degenerate into worse corruption than Somalis experienced under the civilian rule. The system came under absolute control of Mohamed Siyaad Barre and his clan neurosis provoked not only the clan neurosis of the elite but also national psychosis which brought the total collapse of the state and continued to cause havoc for more than fifteen years.

Existing data provides valuable information on how Klan oligarchy coexists and enlarges into clan oligarchy, leading on the one hand blatant abuse of power and on the other simmering anger which to this day makes Somali society an arena of violence for which neither Somalis nor the international community found solution. One reason solution eludes both is that the key causes of the conflict is often evaded. One of these causes is clan oligarchy that I illustrated above but needs to further analysis.

Clan Hegemony

When we examine the historical record with regard to primal clans competing for power and state resources, we discover that from 1960 to 1969 the Daarood were the primary beneficiaries in the hierarchy of power, followed by the Hawiye and the Isaaq respectively. The other clans (like the Rahanwein, Gadabuursi, and Digile) obtained minimal share of power and benefits.

As suggested earlier, clan oligarchy is by the few which takes on clan character when members of the ruling elite and their cronies come from one clan or sub-clan. Hegemony enlarging the number who wield and influence power also becomes clan hegemony when the majority of these come from one clan or sub-clan. Yet in neither clan oligarchy nor clan hegemony do members of the same clan have equal access to power. The select few or major wielders of of power in time distinguish from other members of their clan by social class since power produces wealth and wealth too brings power. Whereas the ruling elite of class oligarchy and class hegemony give their rule the appearance of multi-clan representation, clan oligarchy and clan hegemony takes clan configuration when the ruling elite abandon this semblance of clan representation for biased recruitment and promotion of their clan for key posts in government. Both remain essentially class oligarchy and hegemony even though they conceal themselves in their surface clan appearance. In addition, the system becomes clan oligarchic or hegemonic when the majority of the ruling elite's kinsmen attain subjective gains by viewing the government as their clan turf.

Table 5 presents the clan distribution of cabinet members for the civilian governments from 1960 to 1969.

Table 5

Clan and Sub-Clan Distribution of Ministerial Posts 1960-1969[5]

Clan \ Sub Clan	Majerteen	Abgaal	Habar Awal	Dhulbahante	Habar Gidir	Habar Je'lo	Ogaadeen	Disow	Habar Yoonis	Mareexaan	Ujejeen	Gaadsan	Xawaadle	Makaahiil	Tunni	Ajuraan	Eelaay	GaalJe'el	Geedowfade	Jajeele	Geledi	Murasade	Samaroon	Warsangeli	Yantar	**Grand Total**
Daarood	17			7			6			5														1		**36**
Hawiye		10			7						5		4			2		2		2		1				**33**
Isaaq			9			6			5																	**20**
Raxanwein								5									2		2						1	**10**
Gadabursi														4									1			**5**
Digile															3						1					**4**
Dir												4														**4**
Grand Total	**17**	**10**	**9**	**7**	**7**	**6**	**6**	**5**	**5**	**5**	**5**	**4**	**4**	**4**	**3**	**2**	**2**	**2**	**2**	**2**	**1**	**1**	**1**	**1**	**1**	**112**

Chart 5 presents the clan distribution of cabinet members for the civilian governments from 1960 to 1969.

Chart 5

Percent Clan Distribution of Ministerial Posts

1960-1969

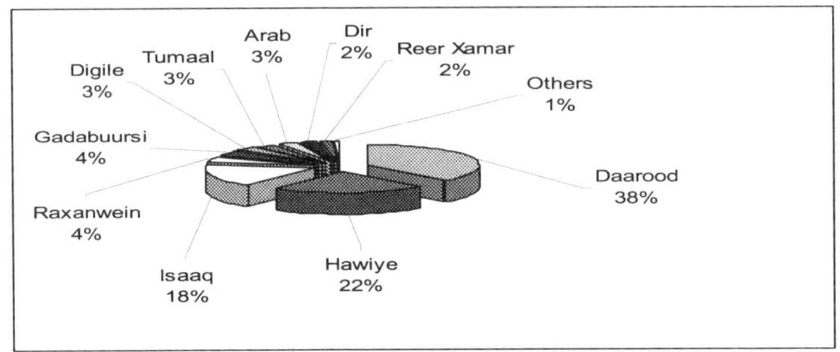

Of the 112 persons who held ministerial posts from 1960-1969, 36 (38%) were Daarood, 33 (22%) Hawiye, and 20 (18%) Isaaq, and 10 (4%) Rahanwein. When we examine the historical record from 1969-1990, we find that inequity in share of power is more pronounced under the military regime than under the civilian administration.

Table 6 presents the clan distribution of ministerial posts from 1969 to 1990.

Table 6

Composition of the Cabinet by Clan and Sub-clan 1969-1990[6]

Clan	Sub-clan: Mareexaan	Majeerteen	Ogaadeen	Dhulbahante	Warsangali	Ortable	Dishiishe	Habar Gidir	Abgaal	Xawaadle	Murasade	Shiikhaal	Ujejen	Ajuuraan	Habar Awal	Habar Je'lo	Habar Yoonis	'Iidagale	Arap	Mahad 'Asse	Reer Nuur	Dabarre	Eelaay	Ashraaf	Gibile	'Isse 'Adde	Madhibaan	Gaadsan	Durugbe	Reer Xamar	Waldool	Yemeni	Grand Total
Daarood	45	61	27	29	9	6	3																										180
Hawiye								35	23	14	10	7	1	2																			92
Isaaq															36	20	16	9	1														82
Gadbuursi																				17	1												18
Digile																						13											13
Raxanwein																							5	2	7								14
Tumaal																										17							17
Madhibaan																											2						2
Dir																												10					10
Reer Xamar																													8	2			10
'Iise																															2		2
'Arab																																15	15
Total	45	61	27	29	9	6	3	35	23	14	10	7	1	2	36	20	16	9	1	17	1	13	5	2	7	17	2	10	8	2	13	2	455

Chart 6 presents in percent the clan distribution of ministerial posts from 1969-1990.

Chart 6

Percent Clan Distribution of Ministerial Posts

1969-1990

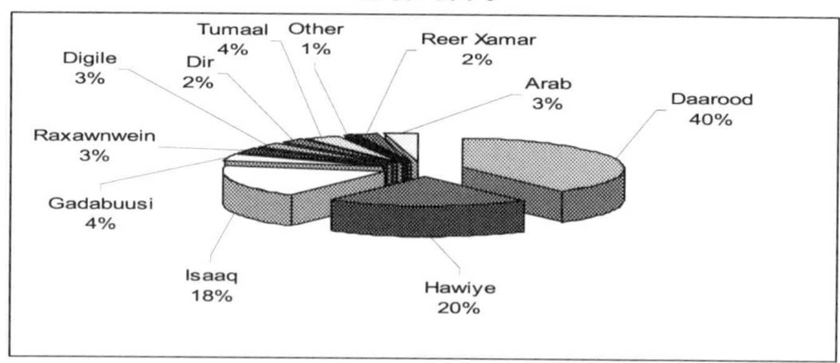

Of the 455 cabinet posts from 1969-1990, the Daarood occupied 180 (40%) of the cabinet post, the Hawiye 92 (20%) posts, and the Isaaq 82 (18%) posts; the Gadabuursi and the Rahanwein held 18 (4%) posts respectively; the remaining clans occupied 61 (13%) posts. Ironically, the Rahanwein, by no means a minority clan, obtained the same number of ministerial appointments as the Arabs of Yemen origin who constitute a very small minority. The Digile and the Dir whose number far exceeds that of the Arab minority also obtained less cabinet appointments (only 1 minister) during the military regime.

That the military regime appointed ministers from the Tumaal and Madhibaan—both socially despised and excluded clans—was a bold step affirming the progressive ideology that the military regime had espoused. However, these appointments involved mainly General Mohamed Áli Samatar who, though respected for hi military credentials, remained trusted crony of the dictator until his regime fell.

Thus, both under the civilian and military regime, the order of clan beneficiaries stayed remarkably consistent for the thirty years of independence from 1960 to 1990, although the armed forces justified their coup of 1969 with the goal of ending clan inequity, corruption and nepotism that characterized the civilian governments that preceded their regime. Instead, the military regime enlarged and deepened clan inequity, corruption, and nepotism.

Daarood representation in key posts was highest immediately after the armed forces took power when talk of change and revolution was most intense. Later, the representation of the Mareehaan, the President's sub-clan, increased by leaps and bound. Diagram 1 sums up the clan hierarchy of power as reflected in the distribution of cabinet posts from 1960-1991.

Diagram 1

Clan Hierarchy of Power in Cabinet Posts 1960-1991

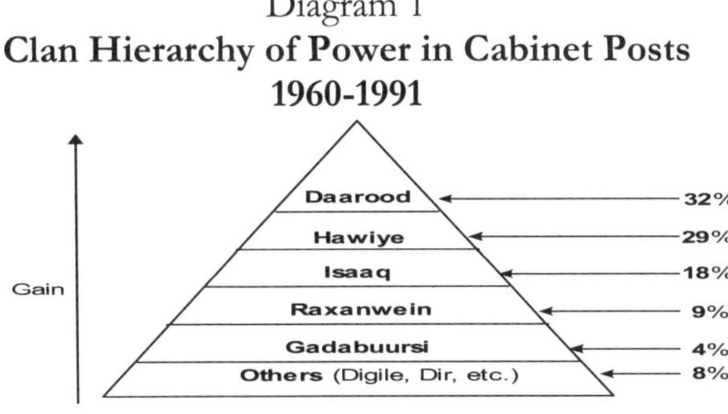

This distribution of power was based neither on population census nor popular consensus. In some respects, the roots of unequal clan distribution go back to the colonial past when some clans were assimilated into colonial service (as cook, guides, guards, soldiers, policemen and interpreters) faster or in greater numbers than other clans.

Other Indicators of Clan Oligarchy

It was not only at the level of cabinet ministers that clan nepotism operated. Like the selection of cabinet minister, whom the President promotes to the rank of general in the armed forces and the police is a critical decision. The generals are the highest commissioned officers in the armed forces and the police. They make critical decision on the officers they promoted, demoted, or dismissed. They also make vital decisions on budget, arms, and guiding strategy of these two critical forces.

Table 7 presents the number of military generals by clan and sub-clan.

Table 7
Clan Distribution of Military Generals
1960-1991[7]

	Sub-clan																					
Clan	Mareexaan	Majeerteen	Ogaadeen	Dhulbahante	Warsangali	Awrtable	Laylikas	Habar Gidir	Abgaal	Xawaadle	Shiikhaal	Iidagale	Habar Je'lo	Habar Yoonis	Habar Awal	Gaadsan	Mahad 'Ase	Geledi	Begedi	Barawaani	Yemeni	Grand Total
Daarood	16	11	10*	6	3	1	1*															48
Hawiye								7	8*	3	2											20
Isaaq												1*	2	1	1							5
D/Midhfle																		1*	1			2
Dir																1						1
Gadbuursi																	1					1
Gibil'ad																				1		1
'Arab																					3	3
Total	16	11	10*	6	3	1	1	7	8*	3	2	1	2	1	1	1	1	1*	1	1	3	81

** One of them was NSS officers who originally was in the police or armed forces.*

Chart 7 presents the clan distribution of the military generals.

Chart 7
Clan Distribution of Military Generals
1960-1991

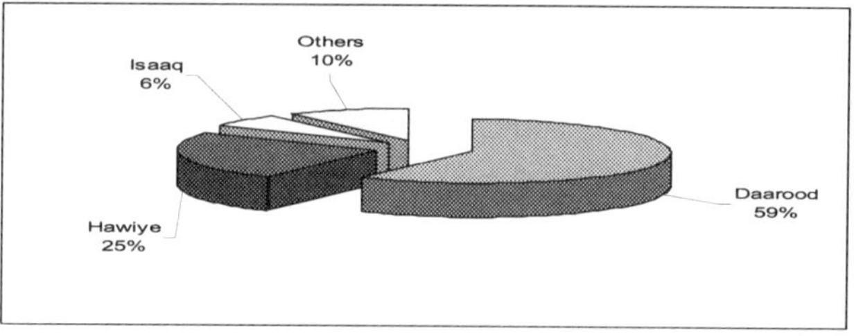

Well over a half (59%) of the officers promoted to the rank of general were Daarood. Clearly, clan inequality and Daarood hegemony was greater in the armed forces than in the cabinet. The Daarood had disproportionate number of the generals not because they had the largest number of officers in the armed forces, or they possessed greater ability than officers from other clans, but because the President and previously the Commander of the Armed Forces who made decision on promotion consistently favored them for reasons of clan affiliation.

Table 8 and Chart 8 show the clan distribution of generals in the police force from 1960-1991.

Table 8
Clan Distribution of Generals in the Police Force
1960-1990[8]

	Sub-clan														
Clan	Majerteen	Ogaadeen	Dhulbahante	Warsangali	Habar Gidir	Abgaal	Xawaadle	Sheekhaal	Karanle	Habar Je'lo	Habar Yoonis	'Iidagale	Luwaay	Yemeni	Grand Total
Daarood	10	3	1	1											15
Hawiye					2	2	1	1	1						7
Isaaq										1	1	1			3
D/Midhifle													1		1
'Arab														1	1
Total	10	3	1	1	2	2	1	1	1	1	1	1	1	1	27

Chart 8 presents the clan distribution of general in the police force.

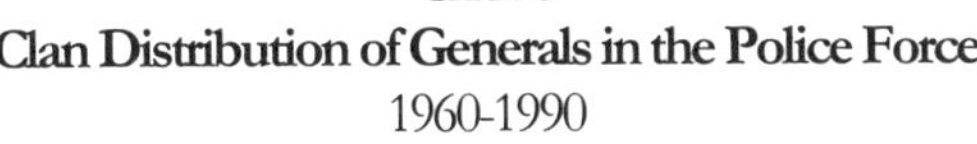
Chart 8
Clan Distribution of Generals in the Police Force
1960-1990

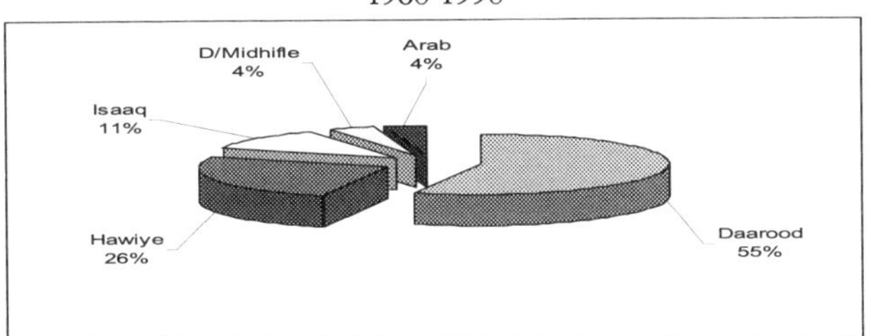

From independence in 1960 to the collapse of the regime in 1991, the Daarood had well over half (55%) of all the generals in the police force of whom 67% were Mijeerteen generals. The Hawiye and the Isaaq had respectively 26% and 11% of the generals in the country. Clearly, the clan factor remained the most robust and consistent determinant of power and promotion in Somali society.

Note, as in the cabinet, the small community of Arabs from Yemen had equal number as the generals of Digile & Midhifle and more appointments than other clans like the Dir and the Gadabuursi. Similarly, the clan distribution of governors for the 18 regions illustrates how the five Daarood clans—the Mareehaan, the Mijeerteen, the Dhulbahante, the Ogaadeen, and the Warsangali—enjoyed disproportional power while certain clans whom the regime considered a threat were given less share of power altogether excluded.

Though governors were less powerful than cabinet members, they carried out the policies of the regime, affecting the daily lives of ordinary citizens in the regions they control. Often, they reproduced the dictator in the way they administered the regions. In addition, the governors interpreted and used gray areas of the law and policy as they saw fit. Hence the identity (personal and clan) of whoever became governor was important indicators of the dictator's views and wishes. From the clan distribution and post assignment of governors, we can surmise which clan the dictator favored and trusted.

Table 9 presents the clan distribution of governors for the 18 regimes of the country in early 1990.

Table 9

Number of Governors by Clan and Region

Early 1990[10]

Clan	Gedo	J/Hoose	Bay	Sh/Hoose	W/Galbeed	Togdheer	Sanaag	Sool	Mudug	G/Guduud	Hiraan	Sh/Dhexe	Banaadir	Nugaal	Bari	J/Dhexe	Awdal	Bakool	Total
Daarood																			**12**
Mareexaan	1	1			1					1	1	1							6
Majeerteen			1																1
Dhulbahante						1		1											2
Ogadeen									1										1
Warsangeli				1			1												2
Hawiye																			**4**
Abgaal													1	1					2
Xaw aadle															1				1
Gaalje'el																1			1
D/Midhifle																		1	**1**
Gadabuursi																	1		**1**
Total																			**18**

Chart 9 presents the clan distribution of governors.

Chart 9

Clan Distribution of Governors

Early 1990

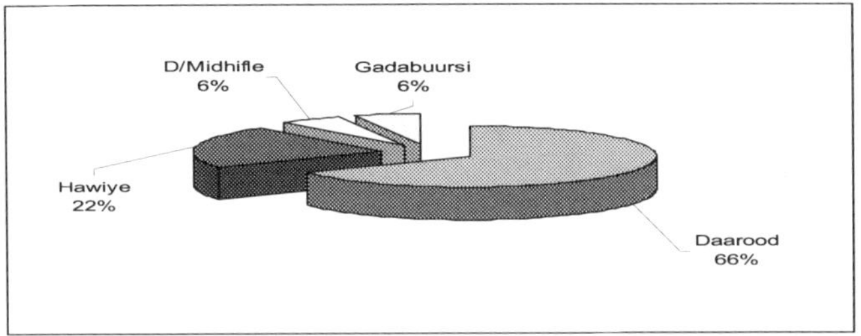

The above table and chart, like the others preceding them, present an illustrative snapshot of the prevailing clan pattern in the political administration of the country.

The majority (66%) of the governors were Daarood. The Hawiye kept more or less the same percent (25%) representation in governors as they did in the cabinet and generals in the armed forces. The Isaaq who had a minority representation in all respects in the past did not figure at all in the late nineteen-nineties in administering even their regions.

Further analysis shows that a third (33%) of the governors for the 18 regions was Mareehaan. They were also a half (50%) of the Daarood governors and close to a half (46%) of the non-Daarood. In addition, the Daarood governors and particularly the Mareehaan governors governed strategic regions. Mohamed Siyaad Barre appointed the Daarood and particularly the Mareehaan in key posts of government not only in the cabinet or the armed forces did. He did the same in the diplomatic corps.

Before we review the record of appointments, one important fact needs emphasis: No government, certainly none in Africa, takes lightly whom it appoints to serve as ambassador in North America, the United Nations, the European Union, and European countries. Whom Mohamed Siyaad Barre trusted the most with regard to the financial and military aid he desperately needed was reflected by the ambassadors he appointed to the United States, the United Nations, Belgium where the European Union is based, the U.S.S.R., United Kingdom,

Italy, West Germany, East Germany, and France. They were all Daarood.

Table 10 and Chart 10 present the clan distribution of ambassadors in North American and European countries.

Table 6

Ambassadors to North American & European Countries, Early 1990[11]

Name	Post	Clan	Sub-Clan
Ábdikariim Áli Úmar	U.S.A. (Washington, D.C.)	Daarood	Ogaadeen
Ábdilaahi Saíid Ósmaan	United Nations (New York)	Daarood	Ogaadeen
Ábdirazaaq Ártan Aadan	Canada (Ottowa)	Daarood	Mareehaan
Yuusuf Áli Ósmaan	Italy (Rome)	Daarood	Mareehaan
Ahmed Jaamá Ábdulle	U.K. (London)	Daarood	Dhulbahante
Saíid X. Mohamuud (Dheere)	France (Paris)	Daarood	Dhulbahante
Áli Hassan Áli	Belgium & E.U. (Brussels)	Daarood	Warsangeli
Hassan Abshir Faarah	W. Germany (Bonn)	Daarood	Mijeerteen
Ahmed Shire Mohamuud	E. Germany (Berlin)	Daarood	Mijeerteen
Yuusuf X. Saíid Mohamed	Sweden (Stockholm)	Daarood	Warsangeli
Ábdulaahi Égaal Nuur	U.S.S.R. (Moscow)	Daarood	Mareehaan
Faadumo Isaaq Biihi	Switzerland (Geneva)	Daarood	Mareehaan
Mohamed Aadan Tafadal	Romania (Bucharest)	Daarood	Wasangeli
Faadumo Mohamed Enow	Yugoslavia (Belgrade)	Dig/Midhifle	Rahawein
Hussein Hassan Bullaale	Turkey (Ankara)	Isaaq	Habar Awal

Chart 10 presents the clan distribution of ambassadors to North America and Europe.

Chart 10

Ambassadors to North American & European Countries

Early 1990

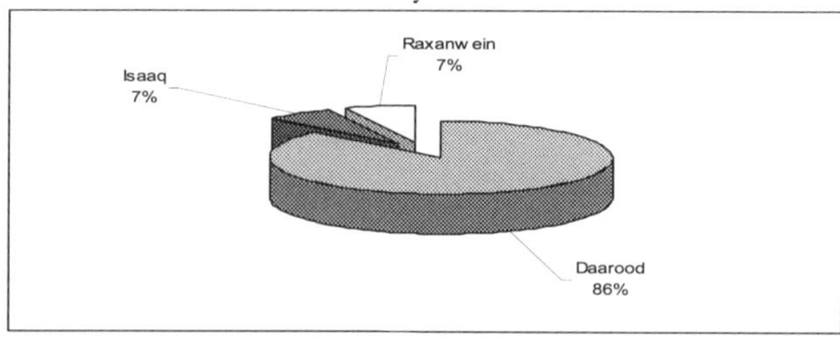

Of the 15 ambassadors appointed to this category, 13 (86%) were Daarood. The two non-Daarood ambassadors in the list (a Digil/Midhifle and an Isaaq) were in the least priority countries in this category, namely Yugoslavia and Turkey. Romania provided little material aid to him, but Mohamed Siyaad Barre was a close friend of Nicolae Ceausescu, the Romania dictator he admired. He relied on a Daarood to convey advice and gifts to Ceausescu whom he liked and admired.

The Daarood ambassadors came from clans in the MOD. Alliance complemented by the Mijeerteen who by the mid-nineteen-eighties joined in the defense of the regime after the SSDF disintegrated.

Representation in Asia countries was not as important as in North America and Europe but they held second priority in economic, military, and diplomatic influence. Hence, Mohamed Siyaad Barre made sure that he appointed Daarood Ambassadors (all in the M.O.D. Alliance) to represent him in the most vital countries, particularly Japan, China, Iran, the United Arab Emirates, and Yemen.

The importance of Japan and China are obvious—both held priority over other countries in the Far East because of their financial and diplomatic power. Mohamed Siyaad Barre made sure that only trusted ambassadors represented him in these countries. The United Arab Emirates were also important because they provided a steady and generous aid to the regime. Iran and Yemen too could not be ignored—the first for its role among Islamic countries, the second for its geographic proximity and reciprocal influence.

Table 11 presents the list of ambassadors to Asian countries.

Table 11

Ambassadors to Asian Countries

Early 1990 [12]

Name	Post	Clan	Sub-Clan
Daahir Faarah Afey	Japan (Tokyo)	Daarood	Ogaadeen
Mohamed Hassan Saíid	China (Peking)	Daarood	Dhulbahante
Ábdi Shire Égaal	Iran (Tehran)	Daarood	Mareehaan
Aadan Hirsi Ílise	U.A.E. (Abu Dhabi)	Daarood	Mareehaan
Ábdisalaan Maálin Diini	Yemen (Saná)	Daarood	Mareehaan
Ábdisalaan X. Ahmed Liibaan	Pakistan (Karachi)	Hawiye	Habar Gidir
Ílise Áli Mohamed (Dheere)	Iraq (Baghdad)	Hawiye	Abgaal
Mohamed Ósmaan Úmar	India (New Delhi)	Others	Gibilád
Shariif Mohamed Úmar	Qatar (Doha)	Others	Gibilád
Ábdilqaadir Amiin Sheekh	Kuwait (Kuwait)	Others	Gibilád
Ahmed Ábdalle Mohamed	Saudi Arabia (Riyadh)	Others	Gibilád
Mohamed Saban Nuur	Oman (Muscat)	Gadabuursi	?

Chart 11 shows the clan distribution of ambassadors in Asian countries. Here too, the majority of the ambassadors were Daarood

Chart 11
Ambassadors to Asian Countries
Early 1990

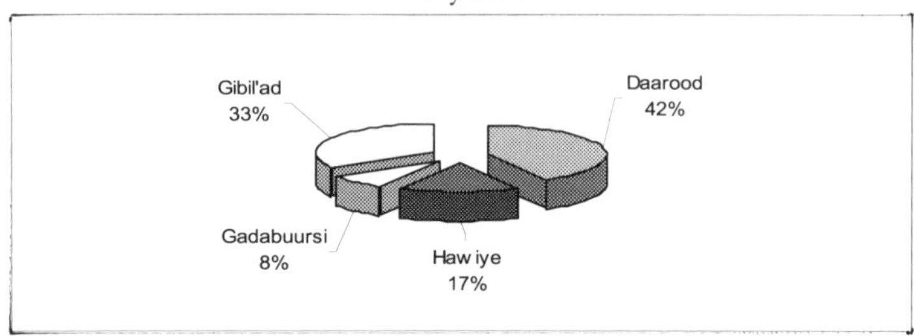

An interesting question is this: Why did the Gibilád, a very small minority clan based mainly in the ancient port city of Barawa, get 4 ambassadors (33% of the total appointed to Asia) when for instance neither the Hawiye nor the Isaaq were included in the list? Ábdilqaadir Ósmaan Mohamed suggests that Ábdirahmaan Jaamá Barre, half-brother and cousin of the dictator, favored the Gibilád because his second wife was a Gibilád.

Table 12 presents the clan distribution of ambassadors in African countries in early 1990.

Table 12
Ambassadors to African Countries
Early 1990[10]

Name	Post	Clan	Sub-Clan
Ahmed Sheek Mohamuud	Kenya (Nairobi)	Daarood	Mareehaan
Ibraahim Haaji Muuse	Ethiopia (A. Ababa)	Daarood	Mijeerteen
Mohamed Ábdilqaadir Warsame**	Uganda (Kampala)	Daarood	Mareehaan
Ahmed Jaamá Saíid Handulle	Djibouti (Djibouti)	Daarood	Mijeerteen
Mohamed Sheek Ahmed Timaádde	Sudan (Khartoum)	Daarood	Ogaadeen
Áli Ábdi Gurxan	Senegal (Dakar)	Daarood	Ogaadeen
Ábdulaahi Mohamed Hassan	Algeria (Algiers)	Daarood	Ogaadeen
Úmar Mohamed Ummal	Zambia (Lusaka)	Daarood	Dhulbahante
Mohamed Sheekh Hassan	Nigeria (Lagos)	Gadabuursi	Reer Ogaas
Ábdulaahi Sheek Ismaíil	Tunisia (Tunis)	Dir	Biyomaal
Ábdirahmaan Ósmaan Saíid (Geelle)	Libya (Tripoli)	Dir	Gaadsan
Ábdirahmaan Áabi Hussein	Egypt (Cairo)	Hawiye	Sheekhaal

Chart 12 shows the clan distribution of ambassadors to African countries in early 1990.

Chart 12
Clan Distribution of Ambassadors to African Countries, Early 1990

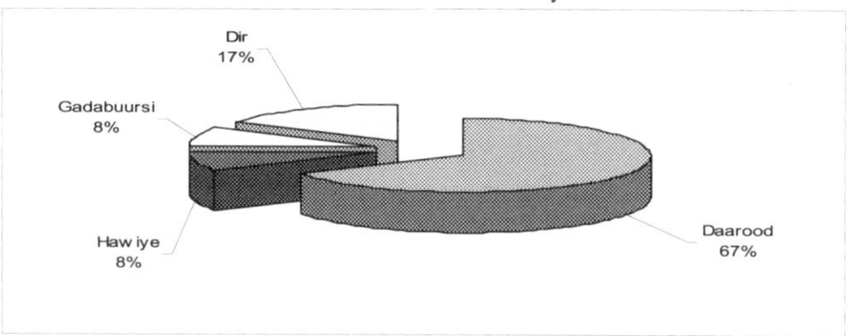

The majority (67%) of ambassadors in African countries was Daarood—all of them appointed to the countries the dictator considered most important. The exceptions were Nigeria, Libya, and Egypt. In these three countries, and in all cases where the ambassador was a non-Daarood, his deputy was invariably Daarood and probably a Mareehaan who monitored the activities of the ambassador and directly reported either to Minister of Foreign Affairs or to the President. For this reason, the appointment of a non-Daarood to ambassadorial post was mainly symbolic.

In fact, most embassies teamed with young, poorly educated, and inexperienced Mareehaan who occupied posts like Charge d'affaire, military attaché, or financial director. Often, they substituted for an absent ambassador and to whom all ambassadors deferred to them on most issues. In turn, the Mareehaan personnel flexed their power and acted as if the embassies were their clan turf, and it indeed was.

I met on several occasions the first crop of Mareehaan youth sent by the regime of Mohamed Siyaad Barre to the Somali embassy in Washington and to the Somali Mission for the United Nations. Barely educated and unable to speak English, they had the responsibility of occupying key diplomatic posts. Timid and uncomfortable in the jobs for which they were unqualified by education, age, and experience, they remained prisoners of their offices and their ignorance. On the few occasions they came out to talk to visitors, they wore Wall Street pinstriped suits as alien and uncomfortable to them as if they wore heavy armor. Defensive and shy, they could barely articulate their thoughts or feelings, let alone fulfill the diplomatic mission they were to accomplish.

These Mareehaan neophytes in time became fat and feisty, even arrogant and conceited. A few of them enrolled in school while the regime pampered them. Others stayed in their posts, counting on their powerful "uncle" who reigned supreme in Somalia. By 1980, the situation worsened and illiterate members of the Mareehaan from the countryside took the Somali embassies by storm. In his book, Failed States, Ábdulaahi Dool,' himself a member of the Somali diplomatic corps, documented his observations and anguish over the miserable state to which Somali missions abroad and Somali diplomacy had sunk.

Writing of Somali in Latin script in the early nineteen-seventies had undeniable social benefits but it also had its drawbacks. For one thing, writing in Latin script contributed to decline of standards in the civil service. For another, it served the goal of Mohamed Siyaad Barre and his incompetent cousin, the Foreign Minister, Ábdirahmaan Jaamá Barre, to fill key government posts with unschooled and barely literate kinsmen.

> When Somali was written in Latin script, the government immediately introduced legislation that the national language [Somali] was its official means of communication... In no time, the leadership sought to kill two birds with one stone: it took advantage of this achievement to introduce "affirmative action" based on clan and revolutionary loyalty. For instance, an illiterate person, even an ambitious nomad fresh from the countryside, needed only six months, to learn to read and write his language, and to qualify for any government post.
>
> In the embassies, illiterate soldiers who had been sent to guard them suddenly found their way into offices with decision-making and other administrative responsibilities. This new-found elite did not think they required anything other than their own imagination to write and submit political and economic reports and analyses for the Foreign Ministry. They became so sure of themselves, they avoided having properly educated and trained senior colleagues check their work. . . Thus, the quality of information available to government on which decisions were made, plummeted.[13]

Ábdulaahi Dool knew that neither the Foreign Minister nor the President had respect for the education or information needed for making sound decisions. More important to them was to fill posts with loyal kinsmen and to help the Mareehaan catch up with other clans. If there ever was a "revolution," its beneficiaries were the Mareehaan and their clan allies. The rest of the population and the resources of the country became fodder for Mohamed Siyaad Barre's private ambition—to lift up his clan and to remain hoisted in the pinnacle of power forever.

Mohamed Siyaad Barre achieved the first goal remarkably well. During his reign, the Mareehaan acquired power and wealth. They also learned to feel comfortable in pin-striped suits, to act pompous and polished, even to excessively imbibe liquor as if it were camel's milk. As for Mohamed Siyaad Barre's second goal—to keep himself and his clan hoisted in the pinnacle of power forever—he succeeded to rule for twenty-one years, indeed a very period by any human standard, but his regime ended in disgrace as did the oligarchy of his clan along with the power and wealth they enjoyed during his reign.

Sub-clan Oligarchy

Oligarchy, as pointed out earlier, reproduces itself at different levels of society. Oligarchy is a graduated system of inequity and exclusion—a hierarchy of injustice and misery that affects all people to varying degrees. It is not therefore surprising that inequity of power and material benefits existed even among the Daarood sub-clans who dominated the civilian and military regimes.

Chart 13 shows the sub-clan distribution of ministerial appointments different sub-clans of the Daarood obtained in the civilian governments from 1960-1969.

Chart 13
Ministerial Appointments of Daarood Sub-Clans
1960-1969

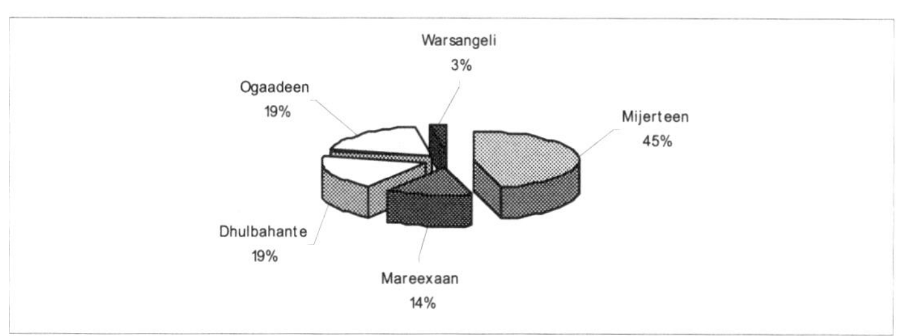

Of the 37 Daarood ministerial appointments made from 1960-1969, 17 (45%) were Mijeerteen, 5 (14%) Mareehaan, 7 (19%) Dhulbahante and Ogaadeen respectively, and 1 (3%) Warsangeli. The Mijeerteen kept under the military regime the superior advantage they had under the civilian rule, although they were the first sub-clan to oppose the military regime.

Chart 14 presents a similar pattern in the 21-years of military rule.

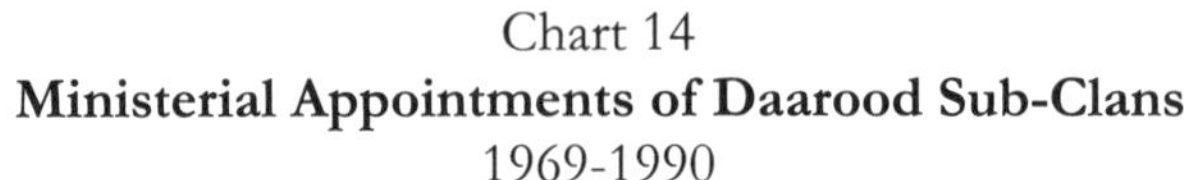

Chart 14
Ministerial Appointments of Daarood Sub-Clans
1969-1990

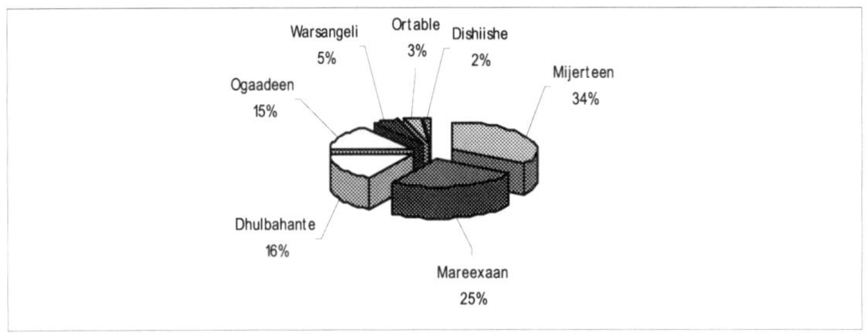

As noted earlier, the military regime came to power with promise of rooting out clannism, nepotism, and corruption. In reality, it proved to be worse than the civilian administration in these regards, giving caution toward all claims of "revolution" and change in Somali society. Of the 180 Daarood ministerial appointments made from 1969-1990, 61(34%) went to the Mijeerteen, 45 (25%) to the Mareehaan, 29 (16%) to the Dhulbahante, 27 (15%) to the Ogaadeen, 9 (5%) to the Warsangeli, 6 (3%) to the Ortable, and 3 (2%) to the Dishiishe.

Chart 15 shows the pattern when ministerial appointments for the thirty years of independence are combined.

Chart 15
Ministerial Appointments of Daarood Sub-Clans
1960-1990

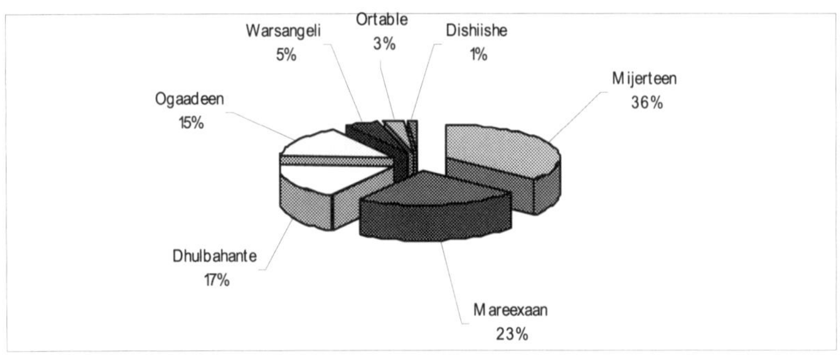

In fact, unequal sub-clan distribution of benefits existed at all levels of government for the Daarood sub-clans as it did for other primal clans. For instance, Chart 16 shows the sub-clan distribution of generals in the armed forces.

Chart 16
Sub-clan Distribution of Military Generals
1960-1991

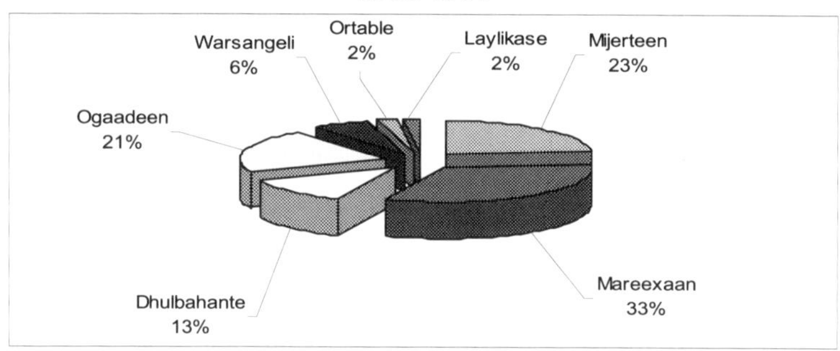

Of the 48 generals promoted in the armed forces from 1960-1991, 16 (33%) were Mareehaan, 11 (23%) Mijeerteen, 10 (21%) Ogaadeen, 6 (13%) Dhulbahante, 3 (6%) Warsangeli, and 1(2%) each from the Ortable and Lilikase.

Of the Daarood, the Mareehaan were the greatest beneficiaries during the military regime. Prior to 1969, they had no more than two generals but they obtained under the military regime the largest number of generals (33%). Most of them rose rapidly from the lower ranks with comparatively little training and experience.

Stories are replete of Mareehaan officers returned from training abroad because they could not meet the academic and practical requirements of their training. This is illustrated by two cases— the son of the dictator, Maslah Mohamed Siyaad, and his distant nephew, Mohamed Haashi (Gaani). Both men returned several times from military colleges in the U.S.S.R. and Italy, but both had meteoric rise to the rank of generals.

Next to the Mareehaan in number of generals were the Mijeerteen who, in spite of their opposition to the regime of Mohamed Siyaad Barre, enjoyed a substantial number of generals (23%) among the Daarood. In the hierarchy of power and resources, the Ogaadeen and the Dhulbahante stood third and fourth, respectively. Together, the four sub-clans of the Daarood had 43 generals, accounting for 90 %of Daarood generals and 53% of all generals in the armed forces.

Among the other Daarood sub-clans, the Mijeerteen always occupied a leading role in Somali politics, often taking a lion's share of power as well as state resources. The Mareehaan, the Ogaadeen, and the Dhulbahante were late comers to the political limelight, increasing their share of power and resources mainly during the reign of Mohamed Siyaad Barre. The Warsangeli, the Ortable, and the Dishiishe—minority sub-clans of the Daarood never challenged the regime; they worked closely with the M.O.D. Troika to defend the regime, taking their share of power and resources wherever they could.

It is not therefore surprising that the first clan that opposed the dictator as early as 1969 were the Mijeerteen who resented that the power they enjoyed under successive civilian governments but diminished by the military regime. They also resented that the Mareehaan, previously a minority and powerless sub-clan of the Daarood, poised to replace them in the apex of clan hierarchy of power long established in Somali politics.

In fact, Mohamed Siyaad Barre could not dislodge the Mijeerteen from his government even if he wanted to. Successive civilian administrations before the coup placed the Mijeerteen in key posts of the civil service, the police, and the armed forces. To dismiss all of them was well-nigh impossible. Not only were entrenched in the government before the 1969 coup that brought him to power but also the dictator needed the Mijeerteen to defend his regime and therefore Daarood interest when the need arose.

As we have seen, Mohamed Siyaad Barre tried to appease the Mijeerteen while he kept a vigilant guard on Mijeerteen threat to his power. He also purged some of the leading politicians and military officers, although others continued to hold key posts in government and the armed forces. The coup some Mijeerteen officers attempted in 1978 confirmed his worst fears. In reaction, the Mareehaan mobilized in defense of the regime and pushed the dictator to rely almost exclusively on the Mareehaan backed up by the Ogaadeen and the Dhulbahante.

After the coup attempt, the regime executed some of the Mijeerteen coup plotters and their supporters. Others fled to Kenya and Ethiopia and formed political opposition to the regime as early as

1979, culminating in the establishment of the Somali Salvation Democratic Front (SSDF) in October 1981. However, even in the midst of Mareehaan-Mijeerteen conflict over political supremacy, the Daarood coalition for hegemony continued and many of the Mijeerteen in the country served in key posts of the regime, exerting significant influence on Somali politics and institutions. Not surprisingly then, most Mijeerteen opponents to Mohamed Siyaad Barre quickly joined forces with the M.O.D. Alliance to defend the regime after the SSDF disintegrated and many of its officers and fighters accepted an amnesty Mohamed Siyaad Siyaad Barre extended to them. The coalition of the Daarood, despite serious political differences, driven home for other clans that Somali nationalism was farce—a ridiculous mockery and empty show

The Ogaadeen always occupied a contradictory place in Somali politics and the armed forces. Straddling the Ethiopian and Kenyan border, they organized themselves as one sub-clan due to genealogy. Because of belief in Pan-Somali-Unity, despite internationally sanctioned borders, they enjoyed equal rights of citizenship as other clans within the borders of independent Somali state. Under the military regime, they obtained greater share of power and material benefits than did other clans like the Hawiye, the Isaaq, the Rahanwein, and the Gadabuursi. Their Daarood identity of course helped, as did the fact that the dictator's mother was Ogaadeen. For these reasons, Mohamed Siyaad Barre trusted and rewarded them; in return, they defended him and his regime to the end, although, as we shall see later, they were partially alienated when the regime gave up on the pursuit of liberating Somalis in Ethiopia.

Officers from the Ogaadeen clan comprised one-third of the Somali armed forces. Most of them joined the armed forces for a nobler cause—to liberate their kinsfolk across the border, not to oppress Somalis in the new republic. However, after liberation failed in 1978, the Ogaadeen serving in the armed forces and in the Western Somali Liberation Front (WSLF) turned their attention to resettling the refugees who fled Ethiopia within the territory of the Somali Democratic Republic. Gradually, the idea of permanently settling these refugees among their hosts became a goal of the regime and the WSLF.

Resentment eventually built up among Somalis who originally lived in the areas where the refugees were resettled.6 The resentments changed to anger and hostility when the original settlers of the land discovered that the refugees not only got better government aid in food and health services but also received greater arms and political privileges from the regime. Indeed, the original settlers of the land concluded that the regime had plans to dispossess them of their land, property, and citizenship.

From the start, the Somali interpretation of "liberation" rested on achieving the explicit goal of Pan-Somali-Unity that rallied all Somalis to a common cause. However, there was also the implicit and narrow goal of achieving Daarood dominance in a large and independent Somali territory since the Ogaadeen and other sub-clans would enlarge the size of the Daarood sub-clans (e.g. Mareehaan and Mijeerteen) residing in the Somali Democratic Republic. Nevertheless, this misuse of Pan-Somali-Unity to Daarood ascendancy backfired.

Untutored in the true meaning of liberation or of human rights, the proponents of this misuse of Pan-Somali-Unity threw themselves into the role of oppressor of the very citizens who were their hosts and benefactors. They turned their guns on the very people who shared with them the dream of liberating Somalis, fought for their liberation, supported the war through tax revenues, paid for their education, and contributed to salaries in the armed forces.

Because the defeat in 1978 ended both goals, attention of the regime and its Daarood ideologues sought to permanently settle the Somali refugees in the Somali Democratic Republic, particularly in the Northwest (Somaliland). The emergence of the Somali National Movement in 1981 and the guerrilla war it waged for nearly ten years frustrated that goal. Ogaadeen soldiers were also alienated from the regime when Mohamed Siyaad Barre, sought rapprochement with the Mengistu regime of Ethiopia. The alienation of the Ogaadeen weakened the M.O.D. Alliance.

The Dhulbahante fared third in the alliance of the three clans and in the hierarchy of influence. They controlled the NSS headed by Ahmed Suleymaan Ábdulle a Dhulbahante, known as Dafle, the son-in-law of the President and a member of the SRC. In addition, they enjoyed the privilege of recruitment and promotion in the diplomatic service but also in the armed forces. Disproportionately represented in both services, their qualification for these privileges was simply membership in one of the three clans constituting the M.O.D. Coalition.

Any member of the three clans who had an ally (like Ahmed Suleymaan Ábdulle) achieved choice assignments in the armed forces or in the diplomatic service. If assigned to the diplomatic service, he and his family enjoyed the comforts and glamour of life abroad, distanced from Somalia's poverty and, disease.

Relations between the Ogaadeen and the Mareehaan soured during the mid nineteen-eighties partly because Mohamed Siyaad Barre retreated from his commitment to liberate Western Somalis under Ethiopian rule. By 1987, Hussein Ábdilqaadir Qaassim, a former member of the Somali Revolutionary Socialist Party's central committee and a rising star in the regime's elite, had defected and taken refuge in the United States.

With resentments simmering between Mareehaan and Ogaadeen members in the armed forces, occasional skirmishes took place between the two clans. The Mareehaan and Dhulbahante alliance also broke down due to resentment over the inequality of power and privileges that the Mareehaan received but also to hostility over encroachment into what the Dhulbahante saw as their share in the intelligence and diplomatic services.

The creation of the Mareehaan-dominated HAANGASH weakened the monopoly on terror and persecution in the Dhulbahante-dominated NSS. The appointment of many members of the Mareehaan clan to embassies abroad alienated the Dhulbahante and other clans who previously enjoyed preference for posts in the diplomatic corps. Resentment and hostility toward the Mareehaan weakened the M.O.D. Alliance but it did not lead to its breakdown. In fact, if the alliance could no longer be justified, the anger and hostility provoked in other clans bound them as a minority with a destiny irrevocably linked for better or for worse.

After 1985, the Mijeerteen joined the M.O.D. alliance in defense of the regime; subsequently, the competition for power, resources, and prestige escalated into Daarood verses non-Daarood conflict in the mid-nineteen-eighties when the SSDF disintegrated. As we have seen, the escalation of conflict into war of primal clans pitting the Daarood against the non-Daarood had thrown Somali society into a cataclysm of violence and disaster from which it never recover to this day. But before this plunge to total calamity took place, Mohamed Siyaad Barre attempted shifts of tactics that show firstly the importance he attached to clan distribution of ministerial posts, secondly his attempts to woo clans he defined as his "enemies" as the political fortunes of his regime changed.

Shift in Clan Tactics

Because the military regime reigned for twenty-one years, it offers a unique window to explore how Somali leaders use clan tactics to acquire and maintain power but also change clan tactics to reward or punish clans. Ministerial appointments are one barometer of how a leader tries to cope with challenges he faces and his ideas of what he wants to accomplish.

Hence, as shown in Chart 17 below, Mohamed Siyaad Barre changed the size of his cabinet in the twenty years of his reign. We note from the chart that, like Somali leaders before him, he tended to increase the size of the cabinet, thinking that more ministers would be a better solution that less. The period from 1989-90 is an exception. This is when he most of his tactics of ruling failed, his trust and confidence declined significantly, and he surrounded himself with the most trusted cronies.

Chart 17
Increase in Composition of Government by Clan
1969-1990

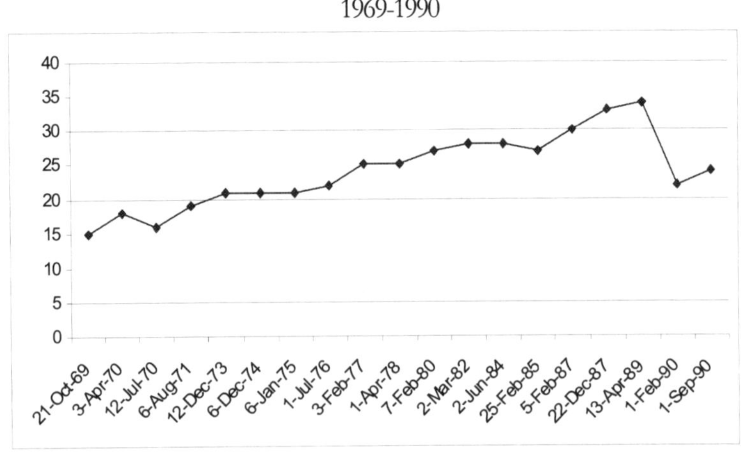

One approach is to examine ministerial appointments by dividing the regime into periods of change and conflict. In this respect, we can divide the 21 years of military rule into three periods, each lasting for about 7 years, each period providing a bird's eye-view of the regime's tactics.

The First Period (1969-1975) was a period of euphoria about "revolution" and hope for political change. The period began with collective leadership by the Supreme Revolution Council that declared "scientific revolution" as its guiding ideology and political practice. It is also in this period that self-help schemes proliferated, the writing of Somali script became institutionalized, students mobilized for literacy campaign, land was reclaimed from encroaching sand dunes, schools grew in number and size, and the armed forces acquired the best of training, equipment, and public support. Only in this period could some in the public give a shred of credence to the state ritual of burying "tribalism."

By 1974, the so-called "revolution" lost steam as Mohamed Siyaad Barre usurped power and he surrounded himself with "yes-men." In the Second Period (1976-1983), the dictator was in full control. A sham revolutionary party emerged as a new tactic to hold on to power in 1976. The country waged a disastrous war with Ethiopia, the former Soviet Union and its allies propping the regime withdrew their financial and military assistance. An aborted coup took place in 1978 making the dictator nervous and insecure, forcing him to fall back on his clan for protection. In this period, the regime's propaganda ceased to inspire or confuse the public; the songs praising the dictator turned stale, even ludicrous in light of the growing tyranny and deepening misery.

As state repression intensified, more individuals and clans were alienated. In 1981, the Somali Salvation Democratic Front and the Somali National Movement declared armed resistance against the regime. As war clouds hang in the air, the regime resorted to what it knew best—brute violence to punish opponents and hold the lid on pent up anger. The prisons filled to capacity, the underground torture cells worked around the clock, the economy was in shambles, state corruption increased, foreign debt and debt service ballooned, and the IMF's structural adjustment cornered and confused the regime, with no relief or improvement in sight.

In the Third Period (1984-1991), the armed opposition grew in size and effectiveness, gradually winning support within the country and abroad, mostly from members of their clan. Their periodic attacks on the armed forces inside the country heightened the regime's anxiety and their prestige. The myth of invincibility the regime enjoyed since 1969 cracked as the armed opposition refined their guerrilla tactics, forcing the regime to abandon parts of the countryside and the armed forces to travel only in heavily armed convoys. If previously the dictator adhered to clannism largely due to neurosis, he now threw himself to it with abandon to defend his waning power.

The M.O.D. Alliance proving inadequate to the challenge in the Third Period, Mohamed Siyaad Barre rallied others who shared Daarood lineage. By 1985, the SSDF weakened due to its internal feuds prompted by the dictatorial leadership of its Chairman, Ábdulaahi Yuusuf Ahmed. As a result, some of the SSDF founders left the organization altogether, a few joining the Somali National Movement. Many of its members accepted the amnesty the dictator extended to them. With their help, Mohamed Siyaad Barre intensified repression and carried out clan cleansing, first in the former British Protectorate, later in Somalia.

By 1988, the regime raised Hargeysa to the ground, its atrocious human rights record isolated it, the foreign aid it desperately needed began to dry up, and the state inexorably headed toward collapse as majority of the Hawiye joined the armed opposition. When the Mijeerteen joined the M.O.D. alliance in defense of the regime, the war that started primarily with political motives changed into an outright and expanded clan war. But neither the Daarood nor the non-Daarood expected that the clan war would rage on for well over a decade and cause cataclysmic disaster for all. The war of clans have taken different turns and twists for the worse. Almost eighteen years later, none can predict how long the death, destruction, and mass trauma sired in the heart and mind of Somalis will be forgotten or forgiven.

In retrospect, then, it is interesting to see how Mohamed Siyaad Barre used ministerial appointments to manage the growing political crisis in the three periods. The ministerial changes he made did not save his regime but they reveal his tactics of playing one clan against another. The three clans that most preoccupied his mind were the Daarood, the Hawiye, and the Isaaq.

Chart 18 plots pattern of change in the composition of the government focusing on the three major clans in the 1st Period (1969-75), 2nd Period (1976-1983), and 3rd Period (1984-1990).

Chart 18

Change in Composition of Government by Clan

1969-1990

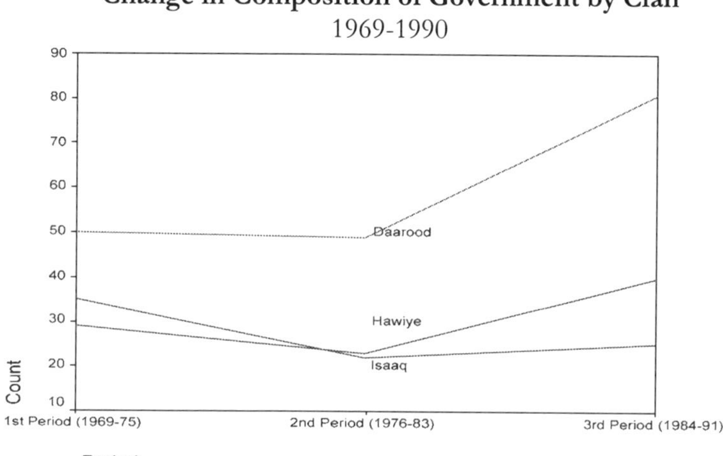

In the First Period (1969-1975), the Daarood were most dominant in the cabinet and key leadership posts. In this period, the Isaaq held a more favorable position in comparison to the Hawiye, but both clans lagged far behind the Daarood.

In the Second and Third Periods, the Daarood gained substantially, Isaaq declined, and the Hawiye gained moderately. The decline of the Isaaq in the Second and Third Periods had to do with their alienation that began in 1975 when many of Isaaq civil servants, military officers, and members of the diplomatic corps were dismissed, precipitating the launching of the Somali National Movement six years later.

The increase for the Daarood and Hawiye in the cabinets of the Second and Third Periods suggests Mohamed Siyaad Barre's wish to shore up support from these two clans in his war against the Isaaq. Still, on closer examination of the appointments made during the 21 years of military dictatorship, we find that, from the perspective of the dictator, the Daarood were not created equal or deserved equal benefits. The M.O.D. alliance—comprising the Mareehaan, the Ogaadeen, and the Dhulbahante—had decisive advantage over all other Daarood supporters of the regime.

As we have seen earlier, he believed that the Mareehaan (his clan), the Ogaadeen (his mother's clan), and the Dhulbahante (his trusted son-in-laws clan) deserved the choice assignments and ranks in the regime. The other Daarood sub-clans—like the Warsangeli, the Dishiishe, Ortable, and Lilakasse—found better benefits than non-Daarood clans, but they belonged low in the hierarchy of Daarood beneficiaries.

Ironically, the Mijeerteen who opposed the regime were the second beneficiaries in appointment of cabinet ministers to clans in the M.O.D. alliance, suggesting that the dictator had an ambivalent relationship with the Mijeerteen, although he often tried to woo significant number of them to neutralize his Mijeerteen opponents. However, his attempt to neutralize the Mijeerteen did not work mainly because they understood, with justification, that Mohamed Siyaad Barre's military coup had undermined Mijeerteen political supremacy in Somali politics from 1960-1969. They also viewed that the rise of new regime beneficiaries (like Daarood sub-clans in the M.O.D. alliance, particularly the Mareehaan) had gained state power and largesse at their expense.

When we consider changes in the number of Daarood ministers from 1960-1990, we see the ambivalent relationship Mohamed Siyaad Barre had with the Mijeerteen.

Chart 19 shows changes in the number of Daarood ministers.

Chart 19

Changes in Number of Daarood Ministers

1969-1990

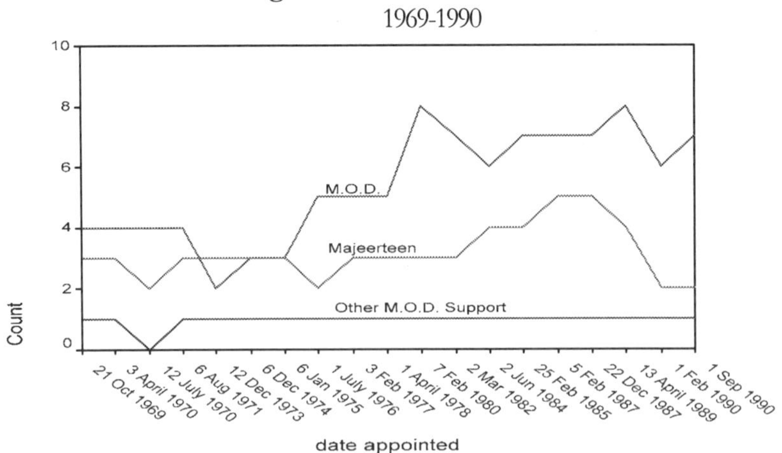

Mohamed Siyaad Barre started with a significant number of M.O.D. ministers from 21 October 1969 to 12 December 1973 when he reduced their number in the cabinet but increased their number by

8 January 1975. After the attempted coup of 1978, Mohamed Siyaad Bare increased substantially the number of ministers from the M.O.D. Alliance but temporarily reduced their number in June 1985 to accommodate the Mijeerteen who came to his fold in large numbers after he extended amnesty to them as SSDF disintegrated due to internal feud. The other Daarood sub-clans (the Warsangali, the Ortable, and the Dishiishe) were third in the hierarchy of Daarood beneficiaries but the number of ministers from this group did not increase after August 1971.

After 1985, the Daarood (including the Mijeerteen) joined forces against the Isaaq led by the Somali National Movement. Their alliance against the Isaaq continued after Hargeysa was raised to the ground. The clan war took a cataclysmic turn for the Daarood when the Hawiye joined the Isaaq in the war against the regime and brought its total collapse in 26 January 1991.

Chart 20 suggests Mohamed Siyaad Barre's thought about the Isaaq and the Hawiye during his long reign.

Chart 20
Changes in Number of Isaaq and Hawiye Ministers
1969-1990

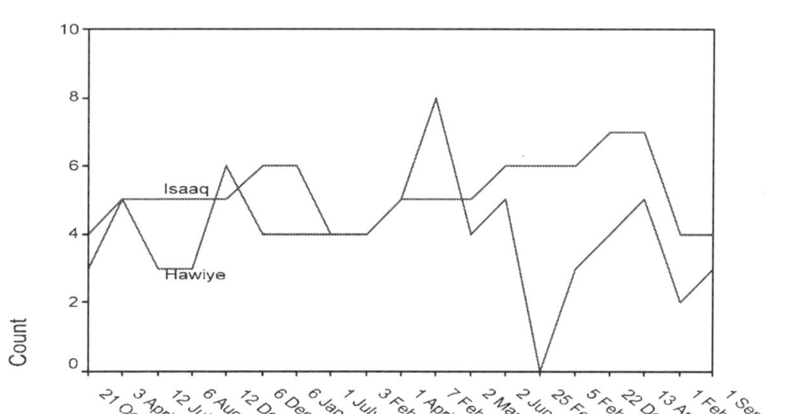

The relationship of the Hawiye with the regime was more or less stable except between July 1970 and August 1971 and particularly after August 1989 when the Hawiye joined in growing numbers the opposition to the regime under the leadership of General Mohamed Faarah Áydiid. The dictator's relationship of the Isaaq with the regime waxed and waned. It peaked after the attempted coup of 1978 when the dictator wooed the Isaaq, but dropped precipitously after June 1987 when growing numbers of the Isaaq the Somali National Movement.

After raising Hargeysa to the ground in 1988, the dictator again tried to woo the Isaaq by increasing their number in the cabinet and even by offering the post of Prime Minister to them. However, the ploy did not work for two reasons—firstly the Isaaq individuals he promoted were not credible, secondly the dictator's symbolic overtures were too feeble to erase the crimes of genocide and property destruction the Isaaq had suffered.

From the above, it is clear that Mohamed Siyaad Barre had an abiding conviction in Daarood hegemony with him as primal clan's unquestioned leader; for this reason, he relied primarily on the M.O.D. Alliance to achieve that mission, that he continuously wooed the Mijeerteen to join the fold, and that he succeeded in doing so after 1985. Further, we notice that he often rewarded the Mijeerteen each time they caused him trouble while he severely punished the Isaaq and the Hawiye when he found them resistant.

Rebellion of Primal Clans

In brief, three parallel and complementary developments escalated conflict within the elite for power and resources to conflict of primal clans. The first development was the failure of the elite to deliver on the promises of liberation and prosperity they promised when they agitated for independence prior to the nineteen-sixties and mobilized Somalis for Pan-Somali-Unity.

The second development was the failure of the military regime to bring about the radical changes it promised, instead putting in place a tyrannical rule that concentrated power in a dictator and his cronies.

The third development was installation of a clan oligarchy that enlarged into Daarood hegemony when the Mijeerteen, the first opponents of the regime, joined forces with the M.O.D. alliance in defense of the regime.

The agitation independence in nineteen-fifties proceeded with the expectation that all Somalis would enjoy equally the freedom and Pan-Somali-Unity for which the public mobilized. As shown earlier, the civilian administrations that governed from 1960-69 failed to deliver on these expectations. Simmering resentment against growing clannism, nepotism, and corruption grew to boiling anger during the nine years of civilian rule.

As noted earlier, the coup of 1969 was widely welcomed because the public thought that the coup leaders would save the nation from the misrule of the civilian rulers. In addition, the coup leaders started with a political program that promised to root out clannism, making merit and qualification—"what you know," not "who you know"—the and criterion of employment and promotion. They also promised justice, prosperity, and unity of all Somalis.

The public took to heart these promises at face value. They clung to hope of change four years; they also willingly participating in different self-help schemes presented as part of the military's "revolutionary" agenda. Meanwhile, they ignored abuses of power by agents of the state in the hope that the anti-clannism, freedom, and unity the military promised would come due course if only they remained patient and endured these temporary abuses. This was not to be. Once again, Somalis fell back to familiar despair.

By 1974, the "revolution" the military launched five years earlier lost steam. The rhetoric of revolution and socialism turned stale and no longer credible in light of deepening poverty and intensifying persecution. The "Old Man" (Mohamed Siyaad Barre) thought to be only a symbolic figurehead of a collectively led Supreme Revolutionary Council usurped absolute power; in time, absolute power deformed him absolutely.

Clannism and nepotism grew in every branch of government; prisons filled up with "anti-revolutionaries" persecuted on the slightest pretext of opposing the regime; individuals whom the dictator found a threat to his power and therefore executed; terror and self-censorship therefore gripped the nation, replacing the frustration openly aired under the civilian governments.

The regime needed a new smokescreen to confuse and mislead the public. To obscure the tyranny and nepotism that became as blatant as it was crude, the dictator established in 1976 the Somali Revolutionary Socialist Party (SRSP) that gave the impression of collective leadership and mass participation in decision-making at the highest pinnacle of power. The dictator called 3,000 participants as the "Founders of the

Party" but all knew the dictator was the only founder, arbiter, and beneficiary of the new party. In addition, a ritual called "general election" followed in subsequent years to give democratic guise to the dictatorship. The results of these elections only gave proof to what a thinly veiled secret.

For instance, in the "general election" of party members, the ruling SRSP won 99.91 per cent of the vote. The "general election" on 31 December 1984 won 99.86 per cent of the vote. Again, only one party (SRSP) represented 171 candidates for the National People's Assembly and the 1,174 candidates for local government assemblies in the 84 districts.

The results of the so-called "election" were as preposterous as were its intent and design. Officials claimed that 4,220,466 citizens cast their vote in support of the party candidates, with only 4,700 voted against them. In these and subsequent "general elections," one candidate—Mohamed Siyaad Barre—stood for General Secretary of the Party, Chairman of the Central Committee, Chairman of the Council of Ministers, and President of the country. Since the party members nominated no one else was, the dictator won with total unanimity. In short, the dictator's urge to flaunt absolute power contradicted and undermined his deliberate effort to disguise tyranny.

By then, opposition by the SSDF and the SNM took root and presented major challenges to the autocratic rule of Mohamed Siyaad Barre and the oligarchy of the M.O.D. Alliance. As we have seen earlier, the SSDF formed in October 1981 was unification of several smaller political parties, some of which began in 1979 or earlier. Six months after the declaration of the SSDF, in April 1981, the Isaaq formally launched their opposition movement called the Somali National Movement in London, establishing bases in Ethiopia a year later. The SSDF and the SNM did not coalesce into one organization, as their Ethiopian hosts wanted without understanding the clan distrust and contrasting propensities of leaders that kept insoluble wedge between the two organizations.

After the SSDF disintegrated due to internal conflict among its leaders, many of its members who accepted the amnesty joined the M.O.D. alliance to defend the regime. When the Mijeerteen joined the Mareehaan, the Ogaadeen, and the Dhulbahante in defense of the regime, all of the defenders being sub-clans of the Daarood, the war drastically shifted in meaning and organization. No longer a war against a dictatorial regime, it turned into an open war of Daarood versus non-Daarood and more specifically Daarood versus *Irir* (the latter including the Isaaq and the Hawiye).

For the first time, then, political contest shifted wars of primal clans. It appeared that the Daarood coalition was determined to save the regime, despite its tyranny and nepotism, and to keep clan oligarchy intact using all violent means, including targeted clan cleansing and indiscriminate bombardment of population centers. For the Isaaq, the Hawiye, and parts of the Dir, the war was not merely dislodging a dictator but of Daarood hegemony that began after 1960, grew rapidly under the nine-years of civilian rule, and enlarged into a formidable machine of oppression.

The elite and clan neurosis grew into a national psychosis. Hence, the cycle of violence between primal clans escalated to unprecedented levels in Somali history. Waged with massive weapons imported from abroad, it led to genocide and destruction of cities, in the end to total collapse of the state. The Isaaq and the Hawiye took control of their traditional areas of settlements, pushing the Daarood defenders of the regime and clan hegemony to their traditional areas of settlement.

For sixteen years, the international community spent massive resources on fifteen so-called Somali reconciliation conferences with little understanding of the fundamental causes of the conflict that began with the establishment of a flawed state in 1960 and continued to enlarge in flaws, size, and clan hegemony. These reconciliation conferences simply recreated the flawed state, paying attention to the surface appearances of the conflicts, not to their fundamental causes and deed structures.

Attempts to solve Somali problems would bring better results if the following central facts are taken to heart: Firstly, recreating the flawed state reproduces only the flawed politics of the last forty years. Secondly, the Somali elite, the *Klan*, are incapable to govern democratically or justly because they learned no alternative to oligarchy. Thirdly, the class oligarchy they understand as the best model of governance quickly degenerates to clan oligarchy. Fourthly, the shift to clan oligarchy brings to full enactment of the pastoral ethos and delusion of clan superiority contradicting the goals of an inclusive and just state. Fifthly, only a fundamental change in thought and action are necessary if Somalis are to find solution to their problems, or else they will experience re-colonization or even extinction, culturally if not physically.

I shall return to these issues in Chapter 13, but how did the regime fall and what were the causes of the collapse? Chapters 10 answers the first question and Chapter 11 the second.

11

FALL OF CAIN IN UNIFORM

Maanigii roonaabay i rogatey?
Was I, the victor, defeated?
—Somali proverb

The fall of a regime following a period of violent armed struggles is supposed to mark the end of an era, ushering a new system of government, new leaders, and new ways of dispensing justice. Sometimes it does, but frequently it does not. Often, the leaders and the led forget after victory the rhetoric of revolution and promises of change with which the armed struggle for liberty started. Unanticipated problems emerge and draw attention away from realizing the promised change. Gradually, the old habits of misrule, corruption, and tyranny return in imperceptible ways until they become as blatant as practices of the earlier regime, giving rise for another call for regime change. Hence, the cycle continues of hope and disappointment continues like a seesaw that goes up and down, but at uneven pace—the downs being longer than the occasional and fleeting ups.

In reality, regimes do not fall easily or frequently. On the rare occasions they do, the state continues to function under new management. The Somali state and the military regime presiding over it followed a different course. For two decades, people considered the state and the military regime invincible. Their sudden crash revealed that those who organized and led the armed resistance had no viable organization of power to holds society together, let alone effect the change promised. Chaos, anarchy, and mayhem therefore followed. The Somali case underscores the pitfalls of relying on emotion and waging resistance to oppression without theory.

What actually brought about the fall of the military regime? Who were the key players that brought about its collapse? What motivated and guided their resistance? How did the dictator and his supporters respond before the state collapse? What happened to them after their fall from power?

Answers to these questions provide a glance to one of the most dramatic and most tragic moments in Somali history.

Prelude to the Explosion

While the regime waged war against the Isaaq, Somalis in the former Italian colony enjoyed a period of relative peace.[1] The residents of Mogadishu carried out the usual routines of their daily life. Children went to schools, mothers shopped for food in the bustling marketplace. Businesses continued their pursuit of profit. Government employees carried out their administrative chores. Cabinet ministers pursued their get-rich-quick schemes. Construction workers enjoyed a building boom from a steady flow of foreign aid diverted to private accounts.

After work, the *nouveau riches* drove home in expensive cars to new neighborhoods such as *Booli Qaran*—Plunder of the Nation—which was built with funds embezzled from taxes and foreign aid. The poor wearily trudged home to hovels in shantytowns euphemistically called "Argentina" and "Tokyo." After dusk, a swarm of young women of the night strolled to nightclubs and bars, dressed in their best, stalking men with their eyes in bars that mushroomed throughout the city, either selling their bodies for cash or hunting for husbands that would make up for the education, career, and financial independence society denied them.

In other parts of the city, however, security agents kept surveillance and vigil in the streets. The President held his usual evening sessions with a throng of supporters until early morning when he went to bed and the citizens awoke. He was a nocturnal man who developed this habit when he was a security agent conducting his business mostly at night when ordinary citizens slept. Each night, high officials went through the humiliating ritual of waiting in long queues to talk to the President about matters of urgent national concern only to suffer the indignity similar to plantation workers whose master had little time or patience to hear their report. Waiting for him for hours was part of a ritual of humiliation that tested their patience and loyalty. It was common for them to spend the night at the palace, drinking coffee and rehearsing what they would say to him, only to return home without seeing him at all.

For the Southerners and the residents of Mogadishu in particular, the carpet-bombing of Hargeysa and the massacres perpetrated on the Isaaq during the nineteen-eighties occurred in a land 1,500 km away. These distant events had no direct bearing on their lives. The people battled in daily struggles for survival in a nation racked by corruption and tyranny. They had no interest in learning about the troubles of people far removed from them in distance and clan identity. If news of the war reached them at all, it was a censored and distorted account of it. They accepted the government's claim that the Isaaq, like the Mijeerteen before them, were traitors who conspired with Ethiopia and willfully committed treason against the Somali nation.

Mogadishu residents and Somalis elsewhere never imagined that the carpet-bombing of Hargeysa was the death throes of a regime that was losing grip on power as it unleashed total violence on its people. Nor did they ever imagine that the ragtag fighters of the Somali National Movement would prove the myth of its invincibility as they relentlessly fought not only the dictator but also the clan hegemony represented by the M.O.D. Alliance that had eroded the patriotism and feeling of shared destiny that in the past mobilized Somalis for defense of the regime. That is why the regime resorted to forced recruitment of young men into the war front, many of them quickly deserting as soon as the opportunity availed itself. Few of them wanted to die for a cause that no longer made sense.

Still, the government's propaganda intensified the southern clans' biases against Northerners. The government also exploited the view, deeply ingrained in Somali psychology, that responsibility for crime, including treason, rested not on individuals committing it but to the clan as a whole, that therefore the entire clan deserved indiscriminate and collective punishment. Even the intellectuals from whom could expect more open mind or support for freedom fighters followed the same logic—"If the Isaaq challenged the state, let them perish and die like vermin!"

The Mijeerteen encountered the same cruel response from other clans. The few who knew better or sympathized with the rebels understood the cruelty and military might of the regime. However, they did not want to risk suspicion that somehow they understood the plight of the Isaaq. They also believed that the Isaaq's armed confrontation against the regime was tantamount to suicide. Yet, from the perspective of the SNM fighters, there were only two options producing the same result—either *do-and-die*, or *do-nothing-and-die*. They chose the former option: to fight the regime and die for a cause.

What the majority of Southerners (people of Somalia) did not realize in 1988 was that the culture of silence and acquiescence to tyranny offered only a temporary sanctuary. Security obtained in this manner was illusory. Soon or later, the war would be at their doorsteps and the regime itself would treat them like the enemy. By the late nineteen-eighties, there were disturbing war clouds gathering all over the country. The armed forces could not win the war against the SNM, and the government brought a steady stream of wounded soldiers to Mogadishu. As the number of families in the south who lost loved ones in the war increased, so too did questions and doubts about the real purpose for the war. General Mohamed Faarah Áydiid left his post as Ambassador to India in 1989. Soon after he defected to Ethiopia, Áydiid set out to reorganize the United Somali Congress. In his war against the regime, he also formed an alliance with the Somali National Movement.

Meanwhile the regime continued to intensify its tyranny against opponents in Mogadishu. It acted on the presumption that enemies lurked everywhere, thereby harassing innocent citizens and pushing them into the camp of the opposition. After raising Hargeysa to the ground, the regime used the capital city was used as killing-ground of the Isaaq, exemplified by the Jazira Beach Massacre. As a result, public anxiety particularly of the Non-Daarood grew and underscored the fragility of peace even in Mogadishu. By then, residents of Mogadishu understood that the worst was yet to come. They felt that they, too, would become victims of the regime's violence. However, few of them anticipated that the violence would be as cataclysmic and total as it turned out to be in the nineteen-nineties.

Delivering the Coup de Grâce

The Isaaq fought the regime for about ten years in the North and the Hawiye initially either stood on the sidelines or defended the regime during the nineteen-eighties. In the months following the Jazira Beach Massacre, the clan wars gathered momentum and intensity. Developments after the massacre began to draw the battle-lines emotionally and militarily. Either one belonged to the camp of government supporters who mostly were of the Daarood clan-family, or one sympathized with the opposition consisting mainly of the Isaaq and the Hawiye clan-families.

To ensure that the Hawiye did not join the opposition, the regime mollified them with government posts, land grants, and business opportunities. The United Somali Congress was too weak to mount an armed struggle until General Mohamed Faarah Áydiid came to Ethiopia to organize and strengthen its members. As long as the USC was floundering, the Hawiye were unable to unify them.

In January 1989, the United Somali Congress formed in Rome under the leadership of Áli Mohamed Óssoble. Until the USC formed, the regime of Mohamed Siyaad Barre had little reason to consider the Hawiye a threat. On the contrary, he used as foot soldiers in the war against the Mijeerteen and the Isaaq. With a few exceptions such as the Hawiye pilot who fled with his MIG-17 plane to Djibouti when Hargeysa was being carpet-bombed, most of Hawiye officers had actively participated in the defense of the regime.[3]

In the South, the Saád sub-clan was the first Hawiye sub-clan to challenge the regime of Mohamed Siyaad Barre. They did so by agitating in the southern part of the Mudug region and by assuming the leadership of the Ethiopian-based USC with General Mohamed Faarah Áydiid. The extent to which these two wings of Hawiye opposition – the one operating in Somalia, the other based in Ethiopia, had cooperated and coordinated activity is unclear. What is clear is that the regime of Mohamed Siyaad Barre tried to solve the emerging political differences with the Hawiye with violence, another instance of the fool who, with a hammer in hand, treated everything as if it were a nail. A case in point is the response of the regime toward the Hawiye in eastern and southern Mudug.[4]

When the Habar Gidir and the Saád organized a rebellion of nomadic communities in this region, including the Hawaadle and the Hiraan, 'armed forces' 21st Division and its commander, Colonel Ábdi Ósmaan *(Ábdi Áluuq)*, reacted brutally. This commander appointed three Mareehaan captains to take charge of a unit he named *Horinta Daroogo*—the Drugged Brigade—consisting of 120 soldiers headed by a Mareehaan sergeant. They won that name because they looked and acted brutally as if drugged, even though they did not take drugs.

Arming the brigade and providing it rapid mobility, Colonel Ósmaan ordered it to eliminate opponents of the regime, using the same techniques of mass persecution that had used in the North against the Isaaq. The unit subsequently killed all Hawiye and 'Hawaadle sympathizers and supporters of the USC by executing them in mass, looting their property, and burning their villages.

The first group to react against this brutal repression was of Hawiye officers and soldiers who were members of the 21st Division, in particular the brigade based in Gaalkaáyo. These officers and soldiers deserted the armed forces and joined the USC fighters led by General Mohamed Faarah Áydiid. Unlike Mohamed Ibraahim Égaal who returned when called from his post as Ambassador to India, only to suffer several years of harsh prison life, the General saw the writing on the wall, quit the same post proactively, and moved to Ethiopia to organize the USC.

Following the death of Áli Mohamed Óssoble, known also as Áli Wardhiigle, Mohamed Faarah Áydiid named himself the Chairman of the USC on 6 December 1990 and established his base near the town of Mustahiil on the Ethiopian-Somali border, in an area north of Baladweyne. The desertion of the Hawiye officers and soldiers strengthened his hand, as did subsequent desertions prompted by the heavy-handed response of the regime to opposition.

News of the regime's scorched-earth tactics in eastern and southern Mudug, and the desertion of the Hawiye from the armed forces, reached Hawiye residents of Mogadishu who were already alarmed by the regime's indiscriminate repression in and around the capital city. News that the USC began to fight the regime brought to the surface the repressed anger and grievance of Hawiye. The news of killings by the regime, burning of villages, and military desertions provoked the Habar Gidir Hawiye to support, materially and morally, the armed struggle against the regime. In particular, many traders of the Saád sub-clans, sharing genealogy with Mohamed Faarah Áydiid, gave large sums of money to enable their kinsmen to purchase arms.

Ironically, the vendors were mostly Daarood officers who had become addicted to the pursuit of wealth.[5] Deserting Hawiye officers and soldiers took arms with them while Hawiye fighters across the border were given weapons given by Ethiopia. There were instances in which Hawiye and Isaaq officers moved arms and ammunition from government depots, claiming that they were transferring them to forces in other regions when in fact they were clandestinely armed Hawiye opponents of the regime.

In addition to mounting grievances against a tyrannical regime, the Hawiye struggle against the regime became a cause for restoring clan pride and integrity, which stimulated Hawiye clan focus. In the process, current problems mixed with old clan animosities existing between the Habar Gidir and the Mareehaan, or between the Hawiye and the Daarood. The USC fighters under the leadership of General Mohamed Faarah Áydiid were infiltrating into territories inhabited by the

Hawiye and engaging the armed forces that, as in their fight with the SNM, did not possess the same passionate commitment as the opponents of the regime.

As the USC fighters pressed on, the armed forces consisting of different clans broke up. As Hawiye officers and soldiers deserted and joined their kinsmen against the regime, the chain of command broke down. Daarood members of the armed forces fought with weak resolve or fled. Further weakening their social and military standing, they took to looting and terrorizing the population. The brutal violence the regime used to intimidate and force submission fast reached diminishing return. The more unleashed, the more it provoked rage and risk-taking in rebellion.

Once the Habar-Gidir and the Hawaadle found a core of supporters and sufficient arms, they challenged the regime in the rural areas. Two key questions were of paramount importance – how could they take the war to Mogadishu and how could they induct the Abgaal into the armed struggle. With regard to the first question, the USC and its supporters sent political agitators and disguised military officers into Mogadishu. Hawiye opposition within the capital city burgeoned and many Hawiye residents kept abreast of the armed engagements of the USC in the countryside. Some knew that their clan relatives fell victim to the regime's brutal violence or had joined the armed struggle. Hawiye passion ran high and, many who identified themselves as Hawiye, including *lumpen* elements within the city, were already agitated due to the regime's intensifying harassment and terror.

By early 1990, gunshots rocked n some neighborhoods of the capital city that had previously been safe and serene. The crime rate and political violence increased. News of a murder became frequent, with confusion about who committed the crime and why. Crime and political violence became fused and confused. Everyone knew that, sooner than later, an earth-shaking explosion would occur.

For the explosion to ignite in Mogadishu, mobilizing to action the large Abgaal population inhabiting strategic locations was an essential but difficult challenge. Generally known to be a tolerant and largely apolitical, the Abgaal were in addition loyal and friendly to the regime. When nothing could mobilize them against the regime, a conflict between them and the Gaalgale pushed them into the fray. The Gaalgale is a minority group whose members had lived within the Abgaal for generations, perhaps for centuries. Although traditionally despised by the Abgaal, the Gaalgale traditional maintained identity and livelihood within the Abgaal.[6]

A conflict emerged between the Abgaal and the Gaalgale at the very time the regime was trying to stifle Hawiye opposition within Mogadishu. There are at least two versions of the conflict between the Abgaal and the Gaalgale that emerged at this critical juncture, and both versions affirm that the conflict was instigated from outside. One version names the government as the instigator; the other points a finger at the USC. According to the first version, the Gaalgale, claiming to be of Daarood origin, sided with the regime and it in return heavily armed them. Motivated both by clan alliance with the Mareehaan and an age-old resentment toward the Abgaal who despised them, the Gaalgale served as a fifth column for the regime and even partook in terrorizing the population in general and the Abgaal in particular.[7]

In support of this version, some cite an incident of terror organized by the regime in 1990 that focused on a shantytown called "Argentine" whose residents were predominantly Abgaal. Prompted by news of hidden armed caches in this shantytown, the regime laid siege on this community and, using terror tactics, conducted house-to-house searches. This offended and provoked the Abgaal who turned their rage against the Gaalgale whom they believed had betrayed them. Revenge killings erupted between the two clans. The government sided with the Gaalgale and Hawiye opposition came to the defense of the Abgaal. The revenge killing between the two clans continued to parallel the wider war between the regime and the USC.

The second version of why the two clans fought claims that the Hawiye organizers of the opposition sent *agent provocateurs* to Mogadishu whose mission was to instigate war between the Abgaal and the Gaalgale.[8] According to this version, the ultimate goal was to alienate the Abgaal from the regime and to bring them into the Hawiye fold. Once in Mogadishu, the *agent provocateurs* dressed in the military uniform of the *Coffiyad Ás,* the Red Berets, who served as the president's bodyguard and were known for violent repression. Claiming to follow orders and implicating the Gaalgale as the fifth column, they embarked on acts of terror, including murder and pillage, against Abgaal neighborhoods.

To forestall the crisis, Mohamed Siyaad Barre assembled Abgaal elders and explained to them that the Habar Gidir were behind the acts of violence, intending to foment trouble between the government and the regime. The dictator said, *"Nin gurigiisii soo gubay yuu gurigiina gubin!"* – "*He who burned his own house should not burn yours.*" In this remark, he was referring to the Habar Gidir and the Isaaq whom he considered troublemakers who destroyed their homes. The Abgaal elders believed him; they also accepted his reassurance and warning.

However, Abgaal activists saw it differently. They retorted: *"Ubba abeeso ku jirtaa Abgaal ku istijoon rabaa!"* – "*the Abgaal want to wash their private parts by using a gourd containing a snake.*" They thought of Mohamed Siyaad Barre as the snake that will inevitably kill whoever trusts him. In the end, the activists won over the Abgaal in favor of the USC and in opposition to the regime. According to the second version then, the mission of the USC *agent provocateurs* to induct the Abgaal into the Hawiye cause had succeeded, in the same way their mobilization of the Hawiye in the countryside had succeeded when they told them that Mogadishu and its riches was theirs by birth.

The truth in these two versions is hard to determine. I am inclined to believe that the opposition of the Abgaal developed in stages as it did in other clans. They supported the government, then a small minority joined the opposition, and finally the majority joined the ranks of the opposition. Probably, the truth lies in synergic actions of the protagonists. That is, both the regime and the opposition contributed to the escalation of violence in Mogadishu. Regardless of the acts of the two parties locked in conflict, I believe the overall determination to find a solution to the political crisis rested primarily on the regime that created the tyranny against which citizens had taken up arms.

Since every *action* has a *reaction*, the regime *acted* unjustly and violently while the citizens *reacted* with peaceful and rational resolutions of conflict. The regime reacted in greater violence to the reaction of the rebels, hence a spiral of violence developed. Whenever the opportunity for dialogue arose, the regime refused to take advantage of it because it preferred to impose its will on the people by use of violence. The inability of the regime to be flexible and open to dialogue had forced many to take to the streets if they did not join the armed opposition. Demonstrations became a means to vent grievances. Demonstrations often led to mob action, heavy-handed tactics of repression by the regime, and civilian casualties that put the regime in bad light, unified public sentiment, and emboldened citizens.

As early as 27 March 1989, students took to the streets of Mogadishu for the first time since 1969. The security forces fired on them killing one student and wounding eight others. On 13 July 1989, Sheekh Ábdirahmaan Áli Suffi preached antigovernment sermons at the feast of Íid at the Mosque of Sheekh Áli Suffi at the junction of Casa Popular and Africa Village. He called for "holy war" against the regime and, soon after, he and at least three imams landed in prison. The public reaction was intense. Three days later, preachers in mosques throughout the city condemned the arrest. Public demonstrations followed. According to government reports, at least 24 died and 60 wounded when security forces fired on the demonstrators. Africa Watch put the number of casualties at over 400. The incident so angered the Italian government that it evacuated its personnel from Somalia.

Many Somalis believed that the regime orchestrated the murder of the Catholic Bishop in order to end his advocacy for human rights. They were offended that the regime offered such a high amount for the murder of a foreigner when it killed citizens at will, without compensation or due process of law. The assassination recalled that of Kamel Eldin Salah in 1957, the Egyptian diplomat and member of the Internal Control Commission that monitored the U.N. Trusteeship of Somalia. The pattern of the assassination pointed toward Mohamed Siyaad Barre. Ábdirashiid Áli Sharmaarke was probably another victim of the same perpetrator who skillfully worked behind the scene, hoping to gain from his assassination.

Throughout 1989, the demonstrations continued. The regime responded in its usual violent ways, aggravating its image and escalating grievances against it. However, such violent tactics only added fuel to the fire. An important event that showed the regime's disregard for its war heroes took place on November 2, 1989. When Ethiopian authorities released Somali war prisoners two months earlier, Mohamed Siyaad Barre greeted them as heroes and promised them quick restitution and reintegration into society. Because the dictator failed to keep his promise, the war prisoners took to the street in protest on that day.

Joined by 2,000 sympathizers, they marched in front of the president's residence. Fighting broke out when police tried to disperse the crowds and, in the violence that ensued, at least two police officers were serious injury. Three days later, the wounded veterans forgotten in run down hospitals in Mogadishu held a demonstration of their own. The sight of the veterans, many of them disabled, graphically displayed the callousness of the regime to those who had risked their lives for its defense. Those who fought in its defense, risking limb and life, understood that similar neglect awaited them.

That the regime raised Hargeysa to the ground did not incite rebellion or sympathy among residents of the capital city or other parts of the country. However, it communicated that the regime would unleash total violence to keep the dictator in power and clan hegemony in place. By carrying out massacres like the one at the stadium that killed 150 citizens also demonstrated to the public the regime's cruelty and disregard for basic human rights. The regime was on a skid and each action it took only increased the downward momentum. The dictator and his crony run out of ideas and behaved like the fool carrying a hammer and for whom everything turned into a nail in need of pounding.

By 1990, the peaceful demonstrations to which the regime responded with brutal force gave way to subversive acts including selective assassinations and car jacking of government vehicles. In view of the growing lawlessness and the tyranny that provoked it, the historic document of 15 March 1990 called *Bayaanka Muqdisho ee Koowaad*—The First Manifesto of Mogadishu—presented to Mohamed Siyaad Barre. This document was signed by 114 people including prominent politicians, elders, businessmen, and intellectuals. They represented all clans, regions, and professions, and they lamented the violence rapidly engulfing the nations. They cited the escalating civil war, destruction of major cities, the thousand of innocent civilians killed en masse, the economic and social crisis, the corruption and mismanagement of public funds, the escalating lawlessness and crime, and the consistent disregard for human rights. They proposed a peaceful and democratic transition of power in 1990 in response. The manifesto was a bold initiative intended to forestall the violence rapidly escalating in Mogadishu and already raging in parts of the country.

Mohamed Siyaad Barre, alarmed by this manifesto denied that he had ever received it. However, as the manifesto circulated throughout the city and country, the regime accused the signatories as being remnants of the reactionaries who sought to install themselves in power by illegal means, thus committing treason against the nation.

The regime arrested most of the signatories and charged them with 18th article of Law No. 54 issued 10 September 1970 that prohibited all acts of planning, preparation, and dissemination of propaganda threatening the existence of the Somali nation. Mass demonstrations within the country and abroad followed their arrest. Western countries like the United States, Italy, Germany, and others on whose aid the regime depended also protested the arrest. Even though he had implored his National Security Court to impose the severest punishment on the signatories, Mohamed Siyaad Barre caved to the pressures put on him from both within and without of Somalia.

Following the release of the Manifesto Group, the public in Mogadishu found new courage and began to view the Dictator, not long ago appearing larger than life, as a simple paper tiger. The regime too, considered invincible, revealed its impotence. Writing protest letters, and antigovernment pamphlets, and participation in public demonstrations against the regime became common. The Hawiye who previously were intimidated by the might of the regime and had acquiesced to its tyranny became firebrand agitators in every neighborhood, shouting, *"Down with Mohamed Siyaad Barre!"*

If passengers in cars responded likewise, they pass through without violence. If they suspected them to be supporters of the regime, they threw stones and insults at them. Even the *lumpen* elements within the city rallied behind the cause of the USC and found a chance to integrate into a community that previously had rejected and despised them. These are bold and destructive acts because, fighting demons of their own, these elements unleash their rage on whoever possesses the authority, wealth, and advantage they had been denied.

A political struggle such as emerged in Mogadishu in 1990, did more than rehabilitate the *lumpen* and antisocial elements to a social cause. Even the most stable and morally grounded person found within him the darker side of human nature–violence, revenge, and treachery. The meeting of these two polar opposites in the continuum of morality and decency had the effect of suspending reason and ethics in the conduct of human affairs. All that counted was killing the enemy within and without, in quick succession, by all means available.

The absence of organized political principles and the lack of a politically developed liberation movement produced a moral and political wasteland in which the boundary between good and evil had blurred. None anticipated the consequences of this vacuum in leadership and ideas. Left to chance or to fate by those focused exclusively on getting rid of the dictator without any thought of future implications, or consequences of rebellion led to tragedy.

The agents of the regime had also long ago abandoned conscience, morality, nationalism, and basic human decency. They learned that only the use of violence would make a difference in keeping power and controlling people. The agents of the regime embraced the ideology of *Cainism* which presumes that two brothers cannot live together in peace and therefore, that one of them must perish for other to survive and thrive. The clan system defined the path that *Cainism* took in Somali society, and its ruling elite identified itself as Daarood and acted through the MOD Alliance. Reaction to it evoked *Irirism* of the nineteen-sixties when the Hawiye, Isaaq, and the Dir clans formed a coalition to counter *Daaroodism*. The difference is that the two camps competed through use of the ballot box during the nineteen-sixties while confronting each other by means of deadly violence in the nineteen-nineties.

Ironically, the national military service that the regime imposed on students and government employees, contributed to the effectiveness with which the Hawiye and the Isaaq rebels fought. The national service requirement provided military training to all recruits, both male and female. In the first decade of revolutionary activity, the idea behind national service was to prepare citizens for self-defense against external invasion. It was recruits initiated into the rigors of military discipline and how to handle light arms, particularly the AK-47, that in subsequent years became all pervasive and readily accessible. The second initiation concerned the reduction of fear in the face of authority. Imprisonment, torture, and executions raised fear and anxiety but the indiscriminate use of these terror tactics also had the effect of *criminalizing* and then *desensitizing* the population.

The cumulative effect of the regime's injustice and clannism had alienated the public to such an extent that fewer counted on its survival. When a clan like the Isaaq and Hawiye finally took up arms against the regime, even the coward displayed surprising bravery. This is explained by Somali proverb *"Xininyo ma aha kuwa kugu jira ee waa kuwa lagula bar-bar joogo"* which literally translates to: 'balls are not what you carry with you but the sum of balls with which others back you up." A coward with the supported by his community is a dangerous missile. The 'balls' of those who defended the regime were based on the regime's political legitimacy that had long eroded.

By October 1990, violence in Mogadishu intensified as robbery, car-jacking, demonstrations, and mob actions increased. The regime prepared for the October 21 celebration marking the anniversary of the coup. The Hawiye opposition mobilized its forces in the region of Hiraan and Galgaduud in order to attack the refugee camps inhabited mostly by the Ogaadeen who fled Ethiopia. They also assaulted government garrisons in the border areas. The roads linking Mogadishu to Hiraan and Galgaduud were impassable and telecommunication services destroyed. The news reaching Mogadishu was of the opposition's success in battle and its brutality on captured government troops and refugees. Adding to the panic, rumors circulated that the USC forces were only 50 km away from Mogadishu. The regime could not celebrate with the fanfare and pride as it had in the past due to mass panic.

Flight *en masse* of those residents who could afford a ticket and a visa ensued as those who had money and connections sent their wives and children abroad—their money and gold followed. Even government loyalists, including Mareehaan officials and soldiers, who could not send their families abroad rushed to their distant clan settlement, far away form the violence brewing in Mogadishu. Meanwhile, thousands of the Daarood and the Hawiye who fled the violence in the rural areas flooded the capital city in search for security and food.

The government armed the refugees if they were Daarood and sent them to defend the government that was theirs by clan and destiny. The opposition also recruited the Hawiye to push out the Daarood and to reclaim the government and the capital city that were theirs by lineage. The refugees escaped the misery they had known and hoped to make a new life in Mogadishu, even though it had become a city divided by the elite of both camps. Thus each camp was in grip of clan-mind-trance that intensified the violence in Mogadishu and the rest of the country. As he lost control, Mohamed Siyaad Barre contributed to further escalation of violence. When he heard that even his palace guard were about to mutiny because of dissatisfaction with their salaries and rate of inflation, Mohamed Siyaad Barre paraded the soldiers in front him, took a rifle from one of the men and said, *"He who has this will never go hungry."* He then walked briskly away, leaving the soldiers to figure out the message on their own. To loot was not only a necessity but also a virtue.

The tinderbox of deepening poverty and festering clan antagonisms, finally exploded in Mogadishu. Although the violence built since the early nineteen-eighties and had escalated after 1988, the critical date for the purpose of history was 30 December 1990. From that day on, Mogadishu was never the same bustling and peaceful city where the elite rode in fancy cars, lived comfortably in plush neighborhoods, or the ladies of the night danced until dawn. The new masters of Mogadishu were a breed of men whose language was violence and terror as their only means of human relations.

In peacetime, before Mogadishu became a war zone, the winners of regional football competitions met in the capital city for the finals.

On 30 December 1990, the finals for the "game of violence," fought viciously first in the countryside and then in small towns, began in Mogadishu. Giuglo Marchesi, the cultural attaché of the Italian Embassy, summed up the fear and frustration of the diplomatic community in Mogadishu when he said, as he was preparing for his flight to Italy: "Given the choice, I'd be home watching all this on TV."[9]

The Italian diplomat was lucky to have the choice. Having exercised that choice, he probably watched the finals on TV at home in Italy. Unfortunately, many residents in Mogadishu had no choice—they died because of it, or they were traumatized by it. Those who fled on time were lucky if they reached their destination safely. On the surface, there were winners and losers – the rebels won in the countryside, and the armed forces withdrew to the capital city. However, the rebels did not know how to constructively use and hold on to their victory, and they too became losers.

Regime Final Collapse

There is a fascinating story that captures the heightening anxiety of the public and how the regime played down the escalating turmoil. The story revolves around a conversation between Mohamed Siyaad Barre and his tailor, Muudey, who had served the President and his family for years. Muudey came from an oppressed and despised group, originally of Bantu stock, and deridingly called *"Jareer,"* meaning people with kinky hair. Long ago, Muudey and his people were enslaved or sold as slaves by their more "fair featured" compatriots. In other words, they were the "Niggers" of Somalia, a population who would be referred to as such in Europe and North America.

Every society has its "Niggers" who constitute the oppressed socially, politically, and economically. They also serve as the repository of the negative attributes that their oppressors project on them. These attributes include genetic or character defects, cowardice, and inarticulate speech. As the story goes, Muudey had such attributes. However, what the Somalis often forget, as racists elsewhere forget, is that oppressed peoples have a reservoir of unacknowledged intelligence, sense of humor and sarcasm concealed in their simple words and obsequious behavior.

In any case, Muudey came to Mohamed Siyaad Barre in the days when Mogadishu was embroiled in an escalating civil war. He knew that the President liked praises. Muudey spoke in the simple style befitting his group stereotype in the following conversation.[10]

Muudey:	Papa Siyaad, you're my father. You've always treated me well. You did all you could for me.
Siyaad:	I'm glad I could help.
Muudey:	Today, I've two wives and I own four sewing machines in a well-stocked shop. Thanks to Allah and to you.
Siyaad:	It is pleasure to help you.
Muudey:	You gave me all that wealth. Without you, it would be a life of misery. But I'm puzzled by one thing. These days, I hear that a war is raging in the country. I hear about people killed, about Beledweyne turned into a war zone. Is this true?
Siyaad (laughs):	Aah, aah, aah! It's a joke; they are fooling you; *it's a game, only a game.* Don't worry about what they say. Go and mind your own business.
Muudey:	Oh! *It is only a game.* Papa Siyaad, I was truly afraid. Thank you for telling me the truth. I feel reassured.

Two weeks later, Muudey again heard disturbing rumors—people killed in Beledweyne; vehicles on the road looted; Buula Burde pillaged; Jawhar occupied; Áliyow Aweyski Shiidle (one of the persons whom Muudey admired intensely) also killed, his property plundered; many people fled their homes. Indeed, conditions had turned very grave. Yet, Muudey could not reconcile these rumors with what the President had told him. He decides to accept the President's version of the rumors. After all, Papa Siyaad said that *it is a game, only a game.* Papa Siyaad would never tell a lie.

Next evening, Muudey heard a radio broadcast informing the public that the rebels attacked Beledweyne and residents of Buula Burde fled. The rebels reached Jalalaqsi and Jowhar. A policeman was murdered, two were wounded; the shops were looted. Residents of these towns fled. Conditions were very grave indeed.

Again, Muudey could not reconcile the disturbing news with what the President had told him. Either the radio reporters or the President is lying. It is extremely difficult for Muudey to decide which. The *government radio* would not report a lie since the President dictates everything to it – including the news and commentaries. The President would not lie to him directly, in person, because Papa Siyaad would never tell a lie.

Muudey is on the horns of a dilemma. Again, between the two versions, Muudey places his confidence in the President. After all, Papa Siyaad said *it's a game, only a game.* He never tells a lie.

Still, wanting to be reassured, Muudey decides to visit the President again. He walks toward the President's palace. The security guards know Muudey and they let him enter the palace. The President's secretary says that the President is in a meeting. Yet, knowing that Muudey is never turned away, the secretary motions to him toward the President's conference room. Muudey walks quietly as if he wants no one else but the President to notice him. Seeing Muudey, the President turns toward him and asks Muudey what he wants.

Muudey:	Papa Siyaad, greetings to you. I've come only to offer my greetings. Are you in good health? You know, I pray for you everyday. I've the feeling that my prayers are answered. You look good.
Siyaad (smiling):	I accept your greetings with pleasure. But what can I do for you?
Muudey:	Papa Siyaad, you know that I am quite satisfied with you and that I love you. You've treated me very well. I'm in full prosperity, for I'm married to two wives and I have a big shop with four sewing machines.
Siyaad:	As I said before, it's pleasure to help you.
Muudey:	But I'm worried again. I hear that war has broken out, getting closer to the capital. I hear that there was fighting in Mahadaay and Jowhar, that one Policeman was killed. The shops looted and many people fled. Now, sir, I'm really scared.

Siyaad:	Muudey, there's no reason for you to fear.
Muudey:	You know all that takes place in this country. I care less about the news and rumors I hear from other people. Tell me, Papa Siyaad, what is going on,?
Siyaad (laughing)	Aah, aah, aah! Do not take all you hear seriously. Just go home and mind your business *All of it is a game.*
Muudey:	Papa Siyaad, you keep telling me the same thing—that *it's a game, only a game.* Your words are always true. *If all I hear is a game, then, as usual, the final games will be played in Mogadishu! [This time, Muudey leaves, laughing aah, aah, aah!]*

Indeed, the *final games,* the *deadly games of war*, the *mother of all war games in Somali history*—soon came to Mogadishu and played intensely. Muudey, the man considered a fool and a coward, understood something fundamental and true which Mohamed Siyaad Barre, the President, had not understood. The anecdote subtly shows the real fool. The President misses the point altogether.

Muudey's sarcasm and laughter at the end of the conversation are a testimony to his intelligence, conveniently concealed in his simple and obsequious words. His laughter at the end also shows his defiance and courage. Having discovered that a violent upheaval was fast approaching, Muudey whom others (including Mohamed Siyaad Barre) considered the coward laughs at them to his heart's content. In fact, he is a rebel of sorts, an unconventional guerilla whose weapon is wit and intelligence hidden in a veneer of profuse subservience, a disarming expression of gratitude, and feigned simplicity.

Days after this conversation, as Muudey predicted, Mogadishu became the venue for the final games, after all other cities plunged into lawlessness and some, like Hargeysa, reduced to total rubble. On Sunday, 29 December 29 1990 the armed forces cordoned off the neighborhood of War-Dhiigleh as a reprisal for Mareehaan officers who were killed as they tried to loot a store. By Monday morning, 30 December, heavy guns roared in the northern part of the city. The USC fighters had already infiltrated the city and the government soldiers began looting and hoarding. Thus, the "finals of the game" effectively started on 30 December 1990. Those who were witnesses reported that the government forces provoked the showdown.[11] Adding insult to injury, the government forces wrote on their guns *"Hawiye dhabe"*—the Hawiye fucker.[12]

During the days immediately prior to 30 December, the Hawiye rebels regrouped in Ceel Cirfid, in the outskirts north of Mogadishu. The fighters prepared to make an assault on Mogadishu by dividing themselves according to sub-clans and the neighborhood in which each sub-clan predominated. Meanwhile, the regime embarked on massive house-to-house searches in select neighborhoods and detained suspected opponents. The regime also distributed arms to the Daarood civilians, particularly arming the Mareehaan, the Ogaadeen, the Dhulbahante, and the Mijeerteen. The rebels also armed themselves, mostly by purchasing weapons from the Daarood who sought fast and easy cash. In fact, the price of weapons suddenly grew and, depending on one's point of view, the finals were on the offing. The two protagonists were ready for the final showdown before 1990 ended and 1991 began.

On 30 December 1990, fighting broke out early in the morning in some sections of the city. It began north of the city. By the afternoon of 30 December, gunfire rocked the city. There was pandemonium set in and everyone not engaged in the fighting ran for cover in any shelter possible. A few neighborhoods, like Casa Populare, were calm and some continued to chew *qat* that afternoon, adding to the eerie contrasts of the city. However, the residents of these neighborhoods knew that the growing tumult and violence would soon engulf them.

General Mohamed Saíid Hirsi (Morgan), the President's son-in-law who played a key role in the carpet-bombing of Hargeysa, convinced Mohamed Siyaad Barre that only the roar and destruction of heavy bombs fired from Katyusha rocket launchers, APCs, and T55 tanks would subdue the rebels. The President accepted the advice of the mass-murderer, showing that both shared in cruelty and disregard for human life.

From 30 December 1990 until the end of January 1991, the violence and pandemonium spread to other neighborhoods. Every night, the city was lit by a multi-color the flare emitted by bullets and bombs fired in all directions. By 2 July 1991, the chain of command broke down, increasing the desertion and demoralization within the armed forces. Increasingly, the war was one between the Daarood and the rest of the population. Supporting the MOD alliance and defending the regime were the Mijeerteen who, like their comrades in the losing war against the Hawiye, set up their clan-based command-and-control post within the city.

The choice had come down to get rich personally or retain clan power and the overwhelming inclination was toward individual wealth. That is why the same soldiers whose job it was to restore law and order had taken to looting of foreign embassies, businesses, and homes. They brought their booty to their command-and-control posts, wetting the appetite of their protagonists who wanted to push them out of the capital city; to appropriate their loot. The regime's defenders began random killing of whomever they suspected to be Hawiye or Isaaq. This angered the rebels and their supporters who in retaliation threw themselves into revenge killing, raping, and looting of anyone identified as Daarood.

By mid-January 1991, civilian members of the Mareehaan fled Mogadishu in droves leaving behind their newly found riches. This time, the choice came down to either remaining rich and risking death, or remaining alive and returning to poverty. The gravitation was toward remaining alive. The Mareehaan members of the armed forces who were supposed to defend the regime with the greatest determination, showed their lack of resolve and fright. Most of them had sent their families to the countryside if unable to send them abroad.

Even their two commanders of the tank divisions (one of them, Colonel Ibraahim Hassan (Ánjeeh), who commanded the unit that carried out the gruesome Jazira Beach Massacre) had fled the city by mid-January 1991. Those who remained used Villa Somalia as their post while the palace turned into the prison of Mohamed Siyaad Barre. They positioned themselves and their lethal weapons on the strategic hill on which Villa Somalia was located and on key streets leading to it. By then, the war engulfed the city, the outskirts, and the countryside.

On 20 January 1990, the residence of the Khadiija, the President's first wife, the headquarters of the NSS and the Immigration Department, the old port in Mogadishu, the telecommunication headquarters, and other key departments fell into rebel hands. Strewn in the streets were the bodies of top Mareehaan officials, like the powerful Nuur Bidaar, head of the Immigration Department. General Mohamed Ábdalla Faadil's corpse remained in the street for days, as were those of hundreds of others strewn in the city center. Included among the victims were countless individuals whom one camp or another had killed in reprisal for mistaken identity. Decomposed bodies filled the air with an overwhelming stench of death and, some of the bodies run over by rushing traffic.

A survivor in a neighborhood during those days described the sound of bodies, bones, and skulls crushed by rebel vehicles in hot pursuit of fleeing civilians. The survivor lacked the basic human emotions as he described this gruesome scene, emphasizing how quickly people descend into inhumanity and depravity under conditions of war and disaster.

Panic seized the Mareehaan defenders of Villa Somalia and the President when they learned that the Somali People's Movement (SPM) led by Ahmed Úmar Jees had captured the military base of Bali Doogle which is 90 Km out of Mogadishu,. The SPM that consisted of Ogaadeen fighters had broken away from the Government after they fought against the Isaaq in the North. The SPM had become an ally of General Mohamed Faarah Áydiid who led the USC fighters. The news that the SPM had captured of Bali Doogle military base had alarmed the Mareehaan defenders of President because, by closing the only road linking Mogadishu and the Lower Juba, the SPM would deny any chance of safe exit for the President and his supporters if the defenders of the regime were routed in Mogadishu.

It was obvious that these defenders of the regime were losing the war in Mogadishu, the roads leading to Villa Somalia were becoming difficult to defend, and chance of exit out of Mogadishu was getting slimmer by the day and by the hour. Even then, Mohamed Siyaad Bare had acted as if the violent tumult going on in Mogadishu and in the country would quickly pass. Mohamed Siyaad Barre surprised people who visited during this period by his composure and calm appearance while fire and fury engulfed the city. On the contrary, they report, he seemed to enjoy the panic and despair of those who were with him at Villa Somalia. Supporting his covert pleasure at what was going on was a report by two people who visited him on 25 January at about 5:00 PM at Villa Somalia. [13]

According to their report, they saw him dressed up immaculately in his best uniform, holding a book in hand and a shining scepter under his arm, as if he was ready to chair a grand meeting in a state of total peace. Talking with remarkable composure, he recounted an event that took place fifty years earlier. Two Habar Gidir sub-clans – the Saád and the Suleymaan—had fought a bitter war. In the din of battle, a Suleyman pursued a fleeing Saád fighter. To dissuade the

Suleyman fighter from the pursuit, the Saád fighter dropped his gun. The Suleyman fighter responded: *"Iima dhigtid, kaagamana haro, mana bujin aqaano"* – don't drop it, for I will not cease to pursue you, and in any case I don't know to squeeze it [the trigger]."

By that story, Mohamed Siyaad Barre was perhaps telling his visitors, most of them his cronies and collaborators, that the Hawiye will continue to mercilessly pursue them to the end, until death, regardless of what concessions they give them. As Mohamed Siyaad Barre retold the story, the visitors noticed that a heavily armed unit and vehicles were ready for him whenever he decided to flee from Villa Somalia and the capital city.

In fact, on the evening of 26 January 1991, Mohamed Siyaad Barre and his heavily armed guards have left Villa Somalia and the capital city without warning or fanfare. A few minutes earlier, the rebels consisting of trained guerilla fighters, the lumpen elements of the city, and ordinary citizens in frenzy and clan-mind trance, had stormed Villa Somalia, climbing the walls of its well-fortified compound and coming from all directions. The dictator and his defenders fled in the last moment. Had they caught him, they would have unceremoniously executed him like Ceausescu of Romania. The dictator knew this peril well and with sound mind, but he had decided to die in Villa Somalia.

Earlier, when his fall from power was certain, Shiekh Zayid Bin Sultan Al-Nahian, the leader of the United Arab Emirates, offered him comfortable refuge in his land. But Mohamed Siyaad Barre refused the offer. Perhaps, he saw no point in living as a fallen dictator. Perhaps, something within him held him back to face the execution he was sure to face. Perhaps too, he might have believed unconsciously that he deserved execution for the crimes he had committed. In any case, Mohamed Siyaad Barre wanted to stay in Villa Somalia, whatever the consequences. It was not to be.

In an interview by the author, Colonel Ábdi Isaaq Hiniin, a Mareehaan officer in the armed forces and once the head of the feared *Kofiyad Ás* (Red Berets) had described to me what had happened during the last days before the collapse of the regime and the ensuing months. The Colonel was with the dictator back in 1986 when the dictator the car accident seriously injured him and six years later when he fled to the countryside.[14]

The colonel describes the scene at Villa Somalia in vivid details when the rebels storm it in endless wave of men falling of its walled compound. When finally the defenders of the dictator, fighting with immense firepower, could not stem the mass of rebels besieging the palace, the Mareehaan soldiers, reduced to 130, decided to force the president out of Villa Somalia on January 26, 1991, exactly at 6:30 PM.

The Mareehaan defenders finally decided that it was suicidal to continue listening to the confusing orders of the dictator who, on the one hand, wanted them to fight, and on the other, did not want them to kill the civilian youngsters attacking them. Adding to their befuddlement, the dictator gave a speech in a radio broadcast on January 25 admonished the rebels to lay down their arms and go back to farming. It was clear to them that he did not understand the deadly peril of the situation. If he did, he no doubt wanted to die in Villa Somalia in the hands of the rebels. He preferred death than life as an ousted dictator.

However, the Mareehaan fighters did not want to die, with or without Mohamed Siyaad Barre. They decided to leave Villa Somalia and physically force Mohamed Siyaad Barre into an armored carrier ("pepe") waiting in the compound. Riding in the 25 vehicles and armored carriers, they drove away from Villa Somalia through the southern gate – the only gate open to them. The residents of Mogadishu heard next morning that the dictator had left Mogadishu. By then, Mohamed Siyaad Barre and his military escort had reached Kismaayo where many Daarood officials, including cabinet ministers and military officers, had taken refuge when Mogadishu had turned into a battle zone and a veritable inferno.

According to Colonel Ábdi Isaaq Hiniin, Mohamed Siyaad Barre and his Mareehaan escorts stayed in Kismaayo for a few days and they moved on to Baardheere, then to Buur Dhuubo. There, short of money, the dictator looked into a briefcase that he had used in his last travel abroad. In his worst hour of need for cash, the man who ruled Somalia for twenty-two years and created instant millionaires was able to find only about $900 in his briefcase. Worse, he soon discovered that one of his Mareehaan escorts stole $500 of it. After a few days, Mohamed Siyaad Barre and his armed defenders reached Garbo Haaray where his immediate clansmen whom he had enriched and empowered beyond their imaginations did not allow him to enter.

Once the dictator had fallen from power, they rejected him and pushed him out of Garbo Haaray. Mohamed Siyaad Barre rediscovered a lesson he had known years ago but he forgotten while in the pinnacle of power. Somalis rarely like a person for what or who is;

they only like him for his capacity to dole out money or to hoist them to power. Once he loses that capacity, the man has no value or consequence to anyone but to his immediate family. Given the prevailing culture and the exigencies of life, even his family may quickly forget his value as a person.

A telling but cruel proverb is, *"Nin dhintay kabahiisa dhaama"*—a dead man's shoes supersede him [in value]. For in the crassly utilitarian and heartless psychology of the Somali, a dead man's inheritance—e.g. his shoes) —are utilized by the living as soon as he is buried away. Having fallen from power, Mohamed Siyaad Barre was in effect a dead man even to those whom he had enriched and who in the past reated him like a demigod. In pushing out of Garbo Haaray, they might very well argue that they did him a favor since they did not kill him physically and then wear his shoes.

Attempts to Regain Power

Forced out of Garbo Haaray, Mohamed Siyaad Barre and his defenders returned to Buur Dhuubo where they stayed for months because they found a better reception. There, the former dictator was offered marriage to a beautiful and young lady who bore him a son. After a period of stay, his daughter in Nairobi had sent a huge sum of money withdrawn from one of the family's fat bank accounts abroad replenished with funds siphoned from the country's treasury and funds for development assistance. In addition, she had sent 10 trailers of patrol and a large shipment of arms.[15]

In any case, using these resources, Mohamed Siyaad and his Mareehaan loyalists regrouped and prepared for another military assault on Mogadishu, driven by dreams of a comeback to power. They raised a large force consisting of former members of the armed forces and new recruits from their clan. Well-armed and wearing new fatigues of the same color, they drove their 128 "technicals" toward Mogadishu in late March and early April 1992. While in Baydhabo, Mohamed Siyaad Barre consulted a soothsayer who predicted that he was destined to win and return to power if only his fighting force was exclusively Mareehaan, except for General Mohamed Saíid Hirsi (Morgan) who had joined them on their way to the finals in Mogadishu.

According to Colonel Ábdi Isaaq Hiniin, it was not only the soothsayers advice alone that led to the decision of the Mareehaan to launch an attack on the capital city on their own, without the support of other Daarood clans. An earlier attack jointly taken in March and April 1991 by a coalition of Daarood clans had failed miserably and they wanted to avoid the same mistakes again. The coalition consisted of the Ogaadeen and the Mareehaan who came under the SPM and the Harti with overwhelming representation from the Mijeerteen. In that joint operation, called *Dagaalki 'Armiska*, the Daarood forces fought their way back to Afgooye and to the outskirts of the capital city.[16]

It is then that a self-defeating conflict had emerged over which person and which clan would assume power *after* the Daarood confederation retakes Mogadishu. A dispute over who would take power had surfaced on the battlefield in Afgooye, only 25 km away from Mogadishu. According to one view, the Mareehaan were determined to restore Mohamed Siyaad Barre to power after they retake Mogadishu. They even placed pictures of him on the side of their vehicles.[17] Supporters of this view blame the ensuing defeat of the Daarood forces on the Mareehaan who refused to provide the resources the controlled if their man—Mohamed Siyaad Barre—was not accepted as the leader.

According to the Colonel, however, the Mijeerteen had their own hidden agenda that became obvious when one of their generals broke off with over 400 fighters exclusively from his clan. He hastily moved toward Mogadishu in order to install his clan in power *after* he takes Mogadishu whose defense seemed to him definitely too weak and quite inviting. In fact, he had miscalculated. The Hawiye had tactically retreated from the outskirts of the city but they set a clever trap for the advancing Mijeerteen invaders. As the latter entered the zone of peril, the Hawiye fiercely and suddenly attacked them, wiping the Mijeerteen invaders completely. None of the Mijeerteen fighters had returned alive. When the other Daarood fighters heard the terrible news, they did not want to make the same mistake of rushing into their death.

Thus, Colonel Ábdi Isaaq Hiniin presented a different view of why the Daarood forces were defeated. In addition, he states that General Mohamed Abshir Muuse was mishandling their supply of fuel and provision, forcing the Daarood forces to withdraw back to their traditional areas of settlement and to existential despair. From the colonel's account, some unanswered and intriguing questions remain. Was Mohamed Abshir Muuse sacrificing the other Daarood fighters because the Mijeerteen goal to power was unattainable? Was this a case of a policeman's ineptitude in military logistics for which he had no training or experience? The Colonel answered both questions in the affirmative. More interesting, whoever ever imagined that the day would come when Mohamed Siyaad Barre and Mohamed Abshir Muuse would ever fight for the same cause, huddled together in the same camp?

Such indeed is the vicissitudes, conundrums, and paradoxes of clan dynamics and of Somali leaders when it comes to the pursuit of power. The human and cost of this failed operation was enormous for the Daarood. For instance, there were alleged brutal retributions of the Hawiye for the death of Colonel Ibraahim Rooble Warfaa "Doonyaale". According to Aw Jaamá Úmar Íise, Áli Mahdi, had declared that the death of Colonel Doonyaale should be avenged by the murder of 150 Daarood members in Mogadishu and wherever they could be found. Aw Jaamá adds that instead 300 members of the Daarood had been killed in cold blood to avenge the death of the Hawiye colonel.[18]

In the second attempt to retake the capital and power, the exclusively Mareehaan operation had started in the first week of April 1992 with determination and ample resources withdrawn from millions of dollars stashed away by the family of the former dictator. There was however one crucial hitch: the conflict between Mohamed Siyaad Barre and Mohamed Haashi Gaani had presented an insurmountable hurdle to the Mareehaan. The conflict had been brewing ever since Mohamed Siyaad Barre had removed General Mohamed Haashi Gaani from the North when ruled the Isaaq like a pampered, arrogant, and cruel prince.

Following his removal, Mohamed Siyaad Barre appointed him as a Deputy Minister when the General expected a higher post in government. Adding insult to injury, he appointed him to this post at the same time that he had appointed a lady of questionable repute to the same rank in another ministry. Gaani was extremely offended by this unflattering appointment and by the concurrent appointment of the lady to a similar post. For this, he bore a grudge he never forgave. In addition, with his own ambition for power, he wanted get rid of the former dictator who frustrated his ambition.

There are other grounds for the conflict between the dictator and General Gaani not mentioned by Colonel Hiniin. For instance, it said that General Gaani, disappointed with his removal from the North, had complained to the dictator that he was not given the reward he deserved when in fact had committed many atrocities on the Isaaq in loyalty to Mohamed Siyaad Barre and in defense of Mareehaan ascendancy. In a vein similar to Siyaad Mohamed Ábdulle Hassan's response to the man who killed his son, Mohamed Siyaad Barre responded to Gaani's complaint: "Who told you to commit these atrocities against the people?" By this question, the dictator was accusing Gaani alone for the atrocities, with himself taking direct or indirect responsibilities for it.

Gaani was not only dumbfound by the accusation but also angered by the implicit message that he might face punishment for his actions by the regime, turning him into the sole victim of Isaaq reprisal. It is for this reason that, when brought to court to bear witness in the National Security Court against some Isaaq members accused for treason and for planning political assassination, Gaani had shocked everyone by his statement that he knew nothing of the alleged charges. In issuing that statement, Gaani was trying to mend fences with the Isaaq whom he had mistreated when he was the prince of terror. In any case, the conflict between the two men came to the open before the Mareehaan had mounted their operation to retake Mogadishu and power. However, the Mareehaan needed both men to lead them back into power and the two men needed each other in pursuit of their separate aims.

On the way to battle, the conflict between the two men first emerged in Baydhabo with regard to who deserved to sleep in the largest and best residence reserved for government officials. Mohamed Siyaad Barre stayed in the residence—an honorific treatment the general intensely resented. In addition, he was upset by the name the Mareehaan had given to the operation to retake Mogadishu and power. The name *"Rug Cadaagi Soo Rogaal Ceeli"*—The Come Back of Seasoned—communicated to the general that the dictator was still in charge. Further, when he asked what message they should transmit when they capture Mogadishu, Mohamed Siyaad Barre answered, "Just say the former government has returned to power."

This last order was the straw that broke the camel's back. In retaliation, according to Colonel Ábdi Isaaq Hiniin, the General Mohamed Haashi Gaani had made a secret deal with General Mohamed Faarah Áydiid. Gaani accepted Áydiid's offer of $4 million dollars in return for sabotaging the operation. When Gaani assured himself that the money was in possession of his cousin, Saíid Faarah Garaad, in Nairobi, he fulfilled his promise. While the Mareehaan invaders were in Afgooye, he gave each driver of the 128 'technicals' about $10,000 to disable their vehicles. They did.

Meanwhile, according to Colonel Ábdi Isaaq Hiniin, the Hawiye, led by Colonel Shabeel, attacked the Mareehaan fighters. To their dismay, mobility denied to them because of their disabled "technicals". In addition, the conflict between the two leading generals of the lot had surfaced among the Mareehaan fighters. Demoralization and fear set in. Meanwhile, the Hawiye attack became relentless and fierce. The Mareehaan voted by their feet. Killing or capturing many of the Mareehaan fighters, Shabeel's forces pursued the Mareehaan survivors were all the way Garbo Haaray. Mohamed Siyaad Barre and a contingent broke away earlier, fleeing in another direction. General Áydiid had nearly captured the Mohamed Siyaad Barre who, in the last minute, had escaped. Pursued all the way to the Kenyan border, Mohamed Siyaad Barre boarded on April 27, 1992 a plane offered by Kenyan authorities in Habaaswayne.

Safe under Kenyan protection, he ordered his Mareehaan escorts to hand over their weapons. As he left of Nairobi, they had found themselves disarmed and abandoned. This was the dictator's reward for risking their lives on his behalf. However, he never looked back. Failing to find permanent refuge in Kenya, he proceeded to Nigeria where he found asylum on humanitarian grounds. It was in that country that he lived in desolation and despair until he died. All those who once claimed to respect and love him, including many his immediate relatives, had abandoned him to life in an alien culture, isolation and gloom. Perhaps, the only good news the former dictator had received during his exile in Nigeria concern two items—one political, the other personal. With regards to politics, he heard that the people he had ruled for 21 years had turned ungovernable – that indeed some look back to his reign with nostalgia because men more brutal than him and conditions worse than people had known during his reign have surfaced in Somalia. On the personal side, the young girl he had married in Buur Dhuubo had given birth to twin boys.

Perhaps, these two events were consolation enough for a fallen dictator who at least was in his mid nineteen-eighties and who, if he knew how to put a pen on a paper, could have written the classic on how to destroy a country. He could also have written on how to have a surfeit of children with an age range of nearly sixty years between the oldest and the youngest. Perhaps too, there was a third piece of good news for Mohamed Siyaad Barre while he remained in exile. Rumor has it that President Bill Clinton, embarrassed by General Mohamed Faarah Áydiid's insolence and tired of the Somali crisis, had called Mohamed Siyaad Barre the night preceding the dictator's death. According to this rumor, President asked Mohamed Siyaad Barre by what means he managed to rule Somalis for twenty-two years when the international community could not do so for even one year. In addition, deeply frustrated and angered by Somalis, so goes the rumor, President Clinton promised to assist Mohamed Siyaad Barre to wrest power again if he wished. However, fate put to rest whatever plans the two leaders hatched up.

Even if the rumor is wholly untrue, I know the international community is anxious to cobble up state for Somalis, however flawed and by whatever means possible. The latest proof of this has been progress since the beginning of 2007 when Ethiopian forces invaded and occupied Somalia with United States military and financial assistance in the name of helping restore peace and state for Somalis. Both powers want to nib in the bud the rise of a state led by Muslim fundamentalists. The United States played the role of the Portuguese in the sixteenth century and the British did so at the turn of twentieth century when they fought the Dervishes led by Mohamed Ábdulle Hassan.

We leave discussion of this remarkable replay of history and associated geo-politics for discussion elsewhere. Suffice to mention here that the invasion by Ethiopian forces left Mogadishu in ruin and Somalis in worse state of disaster than they had known in the absence of the state for sixteen years or even under the tyrannical reign of Mohamed Siyaad Barre.

Hence, the more things change, the more they remain the same for Somalis. Like other people in the world, they have the right and responsibility to fight oppression, but they cause themselves greater disaster if their struggle lacks theory—a developed consciousness of the past with an envisioned future and calculated means to attain it.

12

CAUSES OF THE COLLAPSE

Kudna waa diley, waana loo weheliyaa.
Anthrax killed it, aggravated by other causes.
—Somali proverb

The causes of state collapse in the Somali Democratic Republic are many and complex. However, we can point to several key causes of which the armed resistance to the regime is the most important since a tyrannical regime rules by violence, ignoring all reasonable appeals for reform and therefore forcing its opponents to mount counter-violence to the only means of resistance it understands.

However, violence alone did not bring about the collapse of the regime. There were other causes as well. For instance, the degeneration of the economy played a key role; so did the growing conflict within the clan loyalists of Mohamed Siyaad Barre and his regime. Publicizing the human rights violation of the regime also helped raise the concern of the international community. The role of poets and musicians who risked their lives by speaking out was equally vital since they articulated the hopes, fears, and frustrations of the public, while raising public awareness on the cruelties and corruption of the regime.

Each of these factors, whether a cause or contributor, deserves at least a brief discussion. The belief that only armed resistance brought down the regime is understandable because oppressed people need to exaggerate their potency in light of their past impotence and powerlessness. Yet to attribute the collapse of the state to violence alone is shortsighted since, even if violence eventually brought down the regime, combination of the factors mentioned above had weakened the strength, resources, and will of the regime.

We therefore ask, how did the armed opposition to the regime start? How did the economy weaken the regime of Mohamed Siyaad Barre? What brought about conflicts within the loyal forces of the regime? What role did Somalis living abroad, human rights organizations, poets, and singers play in bringing down the regime?

Clan Wars of Liberation

The Mijeerteen were the first clan to experience repression by the regime of Mohamed Siyaad Barre. They were also the first take up arms against the regime in 1978. The Isaaq were the second clan to suffer the regime's persecution; they were also the second to fight the regime in 1981, debilitating the seemingly invincible regime. The Hawiye followed suit in 1989 and delivered the coup de grace in 1991.

One after another, these three major clans became targets of discrimination and repression and, one after another, they fought the regime until it lost authority and legitimacy, inexorably headed toward collapse. The regime could have saved itself and the country if it listened to the grievances of these clans and carried out the necessary reforms. But dictators are impermeable to reason; they suffer illusions of invincibility and permanence. Coming also to power by violence, they rely on violence alone to sustain their tyranny. The regime of Mohamed Siyaad Barre was not different.

Mohamed Siyaad Barre and his cronies relied only on violence. Similar to the proverbial fool who, handed a hammer, treated everything as if it were a nail, Mohamed Siyaad Barre and his cronies used violence to quell all opponents to their rule. They did not realize that prolonged and unjust violence hardens oppressed people, that it trains them to use counter-violence, and that their counter-violence in time would bring down the regime. Armed opposition to the regime started slowly and with limited capacity but, as the regime alienated one clan after another, it grew in frequency and effectiveness until the regime collapsed in 1991.

The clan neurosis and malevolence Mohamed Siyaad Barre harbored toward these exacerbated the objective inequities of power and the repression they experienced. It is no secret that Mohamed Siyaad Barre had a deep aversion to the Mijeerteen and the Isaaq. He disliked, envied, and feared the Mijeerteen. Given their history of dominating Somali politics, he knew that if ever any clan could undermine his regime, it would be the Mijeerteen.

The coup attempt organized by the Mijeerteen in 1978 confirmed Barre's worst fears. He also disliked and distrusted the Isaaq whom he derided as *"imaan la'aweyaal"*—the greedy people, the people without scruples—deriding their business acumen and independent enterprise. The dictator also harbored similar misgivings about and scorn on the

Hawiye. Although he thought them more manageable than the other two clans, he feared their pervasive presence and strength in the capital city and in south-central Somalia.

His open attack on the three clans reached its peak in the nineteen-eighties, although it began early in July 1971 when he executed Salaad Gabeere, Mohamed Áynaanshe, and Ábdilqaadir Dheel for allegedly conspiring to carry out a coup. The clan identities of the three men were respectively Hawiye, Isaaq, and Mijeerteen. Their execution therefore served him two goals: to get the three men out of the way, removing threat within the armed forces, and implicitly communicate to their three clans that challenge to the dictator's power would face severely punishment.

Indeed, the three clans and the rest of society inferred the implicit message and did not challenge the regime's autocratic rule for ten years. But the regime took the silence for license to intensify its tyranny. The open resistance the dictator feared surfaced in 1978 when a group of mainly Mijeerteen officers and soldiers attempted a coup under the leadership of Colonel Mohamed Sheekh Ósmaan *(Iron)*. The coup was planned during the 1977-78 war with Ethiopia or perhaps earlier and, as we have seen, officers of other clans who refused to join the plot suffered execution on the trumped-up charge of disobedience or desertion during the war.

The coup that did not materialize during the war; the plotters attempted it at the end of the war. Organized and led by Mijeerteen officers, Colonel Mohamed Sheekh Ósmaan was to capture Mogadishu. Colonel Ábdulaahi Yuusuf Ahmed, now the President of Somalia, was to occupy the south-central regions. Ábdirahmaan Warsame Élmi *('Alas Áare)* was to capture Hargeysa and the north. Doonyaale was to organize the opposition to the regime in Mogadishu.

When the coup failed, the regime executed in Mogadishu twenty-two men, including Colonel Mohamed Sheek Ósmaan *(Írrö)*. Many more Mijeerteen officers were arrested including Ábdulaahi Aw Mohamed Hassan (Matukade), Colonel Ahmed Sugulle Mohamed, and Ahmed Grasse Hassan. Colonel Ábdulaahi Yuusuf fled to Kenya, subsequently to Ethiopia to lead an armed opposition to the regime.

Mohamed Siyaad Barre's aversion to the Mijeerteen has a long history. General Mohamed Abshir Muuse personified, for him, the envy and fear he found in the Mijeerteen— that is why he quickly sent him to prison after the coup of 1969. Perhaps, too, that is why in 1971 he dismissed twenty-two Mijeerteen army officers and filled their posts with Mareehaan clansmen. In reaction to the dictator's aversion and systematic persecution, the Mijeerteen reciprocated Mohamed Siyaad Barre's aversion. This set in motion a complex process of mutual paranoia and delusion of clan superiority leading to the 1978 coup attempt and subsequently the emergence of the SSDF.

The SSDF was the first armed movement that challenged the regime of Mohamed Siyaad Barre. It was also the first armed opposition to cross the Ethiopian border and ally itself with the Ethiopian regime in order to fight the regime of Mohamed Siyaad Barre. Going against the sacred cow of Somali unity and becoming an ally of "the enemy" across the border was indeed a bold decision that first isolated the Mijeerteen from other opponents of the regime but, in time, they followed the example of the SSDF.

Like the SSDF, these movements used Ethiopia for base, they discarded the sacred cow of pan-Somali nationalism, and they became political movements whose leaders as well as members came mostly from one clan. The example of the SSDF and duplication of it by the other armed movements had a lasting and detrimental effect on how Somalis fought the regime of Mohamed Siyaad Barre—relying on futile strategy of clan division, each disconnected from and hostile to other clans before as well as after the collapse of the regime.

The SSDF was actually a union of several organizations. When in 1978 the coup attempt failed, many Mijeerteen officers fled to Ethiopia and joined intellectuals of their clan who earlier formed the Somali Democratic Action Front (SODAF). These two groups formed the Somali Salvation Front, renamed the Somali Salvation Front (SSF). In October 1981, SSF amalgamated with two small left-learning political organizations—the Somali Democratic Liberation Front (SDLF) and the Somali Workers Peoples' Party (SWPP), both based in Aden. The combined organization called itself the Somali Salvation Democratic Front (SSDF).

The SSDF, led by Colonel Ábdulaahi Yuusuf Ahmed, received generous military and financial support from Libya, given on condition of adopting Muamar Al-Qaddafi's "Green Book." Subsequently, it carried out a number of military attacks against the regime of Mohamed Siyaad Barre. For instance, the SSDF in collaboration with the Ethiopian armed forces attacked and seized Balambale and Geldegob in June 1982. The regime of Mohamed Siyaad Barre admitted the attack and seizure but claimed that the invaders were primarily the Ethiopian armed forces. However, the SSDF claim of victory turned force when by Ethiopian government insistence that the areas seized were part of Ethiopian territory it reclaimed. The combined SSDF and Ethiopian forces pulled out of these areas when the USA brought emergency military aid to the regime of Mohamed Siyaad Barre.

Such attacks caused political damage not only to the regime but also to the SSDF. On the one hand, they emboldened other opponents to mount similar attacks; on the other, they demonstrated that the SSDF leadership, driven by ambition for power and hatred of the regime, was willing to advance Ethiopian penchant for expansion. The other movements lacked the generous aid in money and military hardware the SSDF received from Libya. They therefore had no option but to rely on their own resources and employ guerrilla warfare. In contrast, the SSDF became dependent on Libyan and Ethiopian aid to wage conventional warfare using heavy guns, tanks, and armored personnel carriers.

The autocratic control of Colonel Ábdulaahi Yuusuf Ahmed and the pervasive disputes on clan or sub-clan dominance in the organization hastened the demise of the SSDF. The colonel and his supporters wanted to keep the SSDF a Mijeerteen dominated organization. The left-learning members wanted to free the organization from the colonel's despotic control, diversify its clan membership, and adopt a progressive agenda. The dispute spawned a revolt by some members against whom the colonel used the money and arms he received from Libya. He also made deals with Ethiopian authorities to purge the leftists. The conflict culminated in political assassinations allegedly linked to the colonel. Among the assassination victims were Ábdirahmaan Áydiid and Iiker Mohamed Hussein.

By 1984, the SSDF disintegrated as the Ethiopian officials purged some members and the Barre regime gave others monetary inducements or high posts if they deserted the organization. By 1985, the SSDF ended military skirmishes against the regime and subsequently all operations when Ethiopian authorities imprisoned Ábdulaahi Yuusuf. In the early years, the Mengistu regime found in Ábdulaahi an ally carrying out its bidding; Mengistu turned against him when it became clear that Ábdulaahi adversely influenced key military officials by dolling out the generous funds he received from Libya. After the imprisonment of the colonel, many of the remaining SSDF members accepted an amnesty extended to them by Mohamed Siyaad Barre. The returning SSDF members joined the Mareehaan-Ogaadeen-Dhulbahante (M.O.D.) alliance in defending the regime, turning the conflict between the regime its opponents into an all-out clan war—the Daarood on one side, the Non-Daarood on the other.

The first non-Daarood armed opposition, the Somali National Movement, launched in London on 6 April 1981. The SNM was in gestation at least since the mid-nineteen-seventies when the regime summarily and without stated cause dismissed many Isaaq civil servants, military officers, teachers, and members of the diplomatic corps. There was no hint of challenge the Isaaq issued toward the regime to explain the mass dismissal. Thus, from the perspective of the Isaaq, was sudden and unprovoked. One thing is however sure: the mass dismissal coincided with a time when the regime started its policy of clan domination and paranoia that prompted it to sack non-Daarood officials in the system. In addition, the dictator's reflexive distrust of the Isaaq came to the surface when he attained full powers of a tyrant and wanted to secure his autocracy from the threats of a clan he believed was responsible for the defeat of Mohamed Ábdulle Hassan.

Many of dismissed Isaaq sought work in oil-rich Arab countries in need of skilled and unskilled labor. The generous remittances they sent to relatives in Somaliland enticed others to resign their government employment or simply flee the country to find their fortunes abroad. Bringing with them their anger against the regime, these expatriates formed discussion groups that in time evolved to the decision of launching an opposition political movement against the regime. Three groups in particular had contributed most in the birth of SNM: the expatriates in Saudi Arabia, those remaining in the home front, and the intelligentsia (mostly students) in London.

Each group had its distinct contribution and limitation. The Saudi group had money and (in the absence of their families) the raw energy of celibates, but they lacked freedom to politically organize in the highly conservative and controlled environment of Saudi Arabia. Those in the home front—led by Ábdi Ismaíil Yoonis (Duse), Saleebaan Nuuh Jaamá, Ismaíil Áli Abokor, and others—possessed up-to-date knowledge of facts on the ground and close contact with the populace, but they lacked freedom of speech and association under the tyranny of Mohamed Siyaad Barre. The London group enjoyed these very freedoms and used them maximally, but they were mostly young, politically naïve, and short of money to organize a vibrant and sustainable organization. Only when the three groups coordinated ideas and action was the SNM declared in London on 6 April 1981.[1]

The launching of the SNM was a momentous event for the Isaaq who for two decades simmered in frustration and despair as the union they hastily threw themselves brought neglect and subsequently escalated to clan persecution. The SNM revived the old dreams of freedom and provided an outlet to anger repressed for years. At the same time, the launch not only confirmed the dictator's fears and distrust of the clan but also justified full and indiscriminate persecution of its members. From there on, the SNM and the regime headed toward a violent collision which escalated into a disastrous clan war of Daarood versus Isaaq, particularly so when the Mijeerteen deserting the SSDF joined in droves the M.O.D. alliance in defense of the regime.

The arrival of the SNM in Ethiopia brought the conflict to a head. When early Ethiopian efforts to unify the SSDF and the SNM failed, each movement assumed responsibility to wage war against the regime of Mohamed Siyaad Barre in its way and clan territory. The SNM was at comparative disadvantage because it lacked the generous support of Libya or the full trust of the Ethiopian authorities that the SSDF enjoyed. However, these limitations were a blessing in disguise. It forced the SNM to rely on its resources and creativity to wage a guerrilla war against a formidable regime. It also secured the organization from interference by a "big brother" like Qaddafi or Mengistu, and to forge a democratic system by which it selected leaders and ran its affairs.[2]

The Ethiopian authorities expected less of the SNM than of the SSDF enjoying massive military and financial support from Gaddafi of Libya. However, their cynicism turned to disbelief in 2 January 1983 when the SNM, though ill-equipped and unfunded except by its supporters abroad, took the war deep inside the territory the regime of Mohamed Siyaad Barre and released over 700 detainees (most of them political prisoners) in the Mandheera Prison, the most secure and the largest prison in Somaliland. Another bold operation followed in April 1983 when several SNM fighters released their colleague, Col.

Ábdilaahi Askar Barkhad, from detention in the Bir-Jeeh military headquarters in Hargeysa.

SNM carried out in 1984 the invasion known as the War of the Mountains in the West and East involving attack of military garrisons inside the border, followed by assassination of the regime's top security officer on broad daylight in Hargeysa in December 1986. The Invasion on the Cities in 1988 came right after the Mengistu regime had signed a peace accord with the Barre regime on 2 April 1988. To protect their accord, the Ethiopian officials had asked the SNM to remove their fighters away from the border to limit their struggle to occasional, clandestine skirmishes with light arms.

Not surprisingly, the Ethiopian officials wanted to simultaneously eat and have their cake—to keep the SNM alive in needed in the future but keep on short leash to implement the accord. The SNM officers decided to disregard this order and take a full assault on the cities without the knowledge of Ethiopian officials. The invasion was indeed a perilous political and military gamble, but the SNM officers and fighters felt that they had no choice. The accord the Ethiopian demand for restraint suggested that their movement was to end in the same way as did the SSDF.

At first, the SNM political leaders did not approve the plan. They hesitated and sought an easy way out. However, when the officers insisted on carrying out the invasion, the politicians fled to the safety and comforts of Europe, never to look back until much of Somaliland became free from occupation of the Daarood-dominated armed forces and Ethiopian refugees who supported them. The invasion of the cities was catastrophic for the population because the regime's armed forces indiscriminately fired heavy artillery and strafed the survivors all the way to the Ethiopian border.

The debate on whether the invasion of cities was necessary or wise is now simply academic and speculative. The officers who led the invasion claim this loss of life and destruction of cities was inevitable, given the regime's boundless cruelty and design for genocide. They also argue that their movement would silently perish, as did the SSDF, if they accepted the Ethiopian ruse; besides, the regime would avoid the blow the SNM inflicted on it, hastening its collapse.

Before they carried out the invasion of cities, the SNM fighters mounted offensive attacks against the armed forces of the regime.

They started operation from the bases they had established in Togwajaale, Godka, and Ged-Balaad. On 27 May 1988, the SNM forces took off from the Raqmaale Base and attacked Buró early in the morning. Other fighters took off from Kabo-Qorray Base in the afternoon of 31 May and attacked Hargeysa. By early June, the SNM launched an all-out attack on the three major cities of Hargeysa, Buró, and Berbera.

In retaliation for these attacks, the armed forces killed anyone suspected to be an SNM fighter and indiscriminately massacre civilians. The genocide would seem exaggerated or fabricated if there did not exist a documentary filmed by the regime's agents for Mohamed Siyaad Barre and found in his palace in Mogadishu after he fled in January 1991. The documentary shows the commanding officers conferring at the military headquarters of Hageysa and carrying out in chilling details heavy artillery bombardment on Hargeysa, the second largest city in the country. Justifying the indiscriminate artillery with claims of defending the city from SNM invasion, they decimate the civilian population.[3]

After the men gave their orders, a colonel on a nearby hill faced the camera and explained the type of guns that would soon appear in every neighborhood. The soldiers then drove around the city to photograph the ruin and devastation inflicted on the city. After carpet-bombing, leaders of the armed forces assembled in the Military Headquarters to hear reports on the fate of civilians who had escaped. The military had orders to kill anyone fleeing to the Ethiopian border.

There exists no accurate count civilians killed or wounded in this campaign of Isaaq genocide; a conservative estimate is 50,000 persons (although it is probably double that number). The number of wounded is more, at least 200,000 persons, and the number of persons suffering from posttraumatic stress disorder is mind-boggling. Twenty years later, the victims of this disorder abound in Somaliland. Some are victims of more recent armed conflicts, but the majority of them are victims of the carpet-bombing in Hargeysa in the summer of 1988.[4]

The SNM fighters retreated to the countryside due to coordination issues and a shortage of ammunition. Refugee camps formed on the Ethiopian borders. The two protagonists in this war were unequal in the size of their forces, the power of their arms, and their financial resources. Mohamed Siyaad Barre's regime had armed forces considered among the best in black Africa, with stockpile of military hardware and ammunition acquired from its socialist allies like the Soviet Union. From the nineteen-eighties to its collapse in late 1990, the Somali armed forces also received aid from the west, in particular the United States.

On the other hand, the SNM relied on limited military assistance, mostly from Ethiopia. Ethiopian support was minimal and unreliable since it pursued its national interest to gain as much as it could from the Somali regime. Mohamed Siyaad Barre's regime not only received financial aid from the Arabic Emirates and Saudi Arabia, Italy, and the United States but also from the World Bank and the International Monetary Fund. The SNM relied on minimal financial support from Isaaq communities in the Diaspora and on the meager resources of nomadic communities whose herds diminished due to both the war and drought.

The regime replenished its forces from a large population; the SNM relied on a core of military officers and a small pool of civilian volunteers who were hastily trained and ill equipped. The SNM failed to form an alliance with other clans due to its ideology and organization; the regime used its nationalist rhetoric to rally the support of many clans who lived in settlements contiguous to the Isaaq. These clans intermingled with the Isaaq through intermarriage; they knew the Isaaq community well; they harbored resentment from past relations with the Isaaq. Therefore, they provided the regime a strategic alliance.

The contrast between the two protagonists could not have been more striking. The SNM and its Isaaq supporters continued their guerilla war, carrying out surprise attacks on military bases, ambushing convoys, and keeping the enemy constantly on the defensive. Because they fought for a cause they believed in, they had a firm resolve to fight and die, many of the SNM attacks were called suicidal by the regime, and, in fact, they were. Like the Tamil Tigers who carry poison pills with them in case of impending capture, each SNM fighter carried his *kaffan* (the white piece of cloth with which a dead Muslim is properly buried) with him. Each fighter considered himself *Mujaahid*—a man driven by the passion for a higher goal than himself as in a holy war. His colleagues and loved ones also considered him a *Mujaahid*, thereby giving him respect for his sacrifice for a shared commitment. Armed with community and family blessings, the SNM fighter was determined to die as long as he could cause maximum harm to the enemy. He also had the advantage of fighting in a terrain he knew well amidst a population that identified with him.

Even when the SNM fighter lacked sufficient arms, organization, or discipline, he had a clear mission. He was in the fold of clan and family, enjoying the advantages of the terrain. In contrast, the armed forces of Mohamed Siyaad Barre were *an occupying force.* The majority of the soldiers were not of the land and soil; they came from other regions, some were forcibly conscripted. Others were recruits driven by incentives like money and rank. Many disliked the prospect of dying in a war they barely understood and they would have preferred to stay with their families in Mogadishu. In the final analysis, they were engaged in war to pursue more income and a comfortable retirement *after returning home alive.*

It is not surprising that the armed forces mostly remained in well-fortified bases and, for security, moved in large convoys. Often they unleashed their anger on the civilian population, unarmed men, women, and children. Such soft targets allowed the reluctant fighter to show off false bravery and cruelty on defenseless civilians. It also gave their bosses the false impression of a job done well. This type of warrior fights on two battlefronts, one within and the other without. In the battlefront within, his actions contradicted his conscience. Each time he killed innocent citizens, his shame undermined his self-respect. If his conscience was undeveloped before the war, his cruel actions--murder of unarmed citizens, rape of women, pillaging the innocent—inspired in him the gnawing fear that he too might face the same fate in the hands of his enemies.

Therefore, the battlefront within is the most difficult one. With or without a developed conscience, the warrior who lacks a goal, other than material gain or rank, faced two enemies—himself as his own victim and the SNM fighter as his protagonist. As he victimized others, he was also his own victim. A fighter, torn by guilt, shame, or fear, cannot give his best on the battlefront. He cannot bring out his best when faced with an enemy supported by his community and with a willingness to sacrifice his life. The American soldier learned this in the Vietnamese war. More than thirty years after its conclusion, the American veterans of that war are still suffering from its psychological effects.

Seventeen years after the collapse of the dictatorial regime, one still finds former Somali soldiers roaming the streets of major towns in Somaliland still reeling from the trauma of wars concluded ten years ago. These veterans probably presumed dead by their relatives but still fight lonely apparitions a disturbed psyche. They are poorly clothed, sometimes carrying sticks in the shape of a gun, and mumble insults such as they did on SNM fighters.

The SNM victors laid down their arms after taking control of their land. They understand the tragedy of these tormented souls and let them live amidst them unharmed. Of course, psychological trauma is not limited to these former soldiers; psychological trauma is also rampant among former SNM fighters and civilians who during Mohamed Siyaad Barre's tyranny, happened to be of the *wrong clan* (Isaaq), in the *wrong place* (Hargeysa), at the *wrong time* (the summer of 1988 when the city was carpet-bombed).

While the Isaaq armed struggle against the regime continued, the Hawiye also took up arms in 1989. Their conflict with the regime quickly enlarged into Hawiye-Daarood conflict because they fought not only the Daarood as a whole, including the Mareehaan, the Ogaadeen, the Dhulbahante, the Mijeerteen, and smaller Daarood sub-clans. Hawiye-Daarood competition for power dates back to the formation of the SYL after World War II. Spearheading this clan competition were Saád of the Habar Gidir sub-clan on the side of the Hawiye and the Mijeerteen sub-clan of the Daarood. The competition peaked during the last years of the U.N. Trusteeship when Ábdulaahi Íise was the Prime Minister and the Hawiye was in control. Prior to independence, the selection of Aadan Ábdulle Ósmaan, a Hawiye but politically moderate and married to a Mijeerteen, pacified the two clans and negotiated a truce between them.

The primary focus of competition between the two clans centered on the political arena, in particular the choice positions in government each obtained. After independence, political leaders paid special attention to distribution of power and representation in government between the Hawiye and the Daarood. Thus, from 1960-1967, a Hawiye President (Aadan Ábdulle Ósmaan) always had a Daarood Prime Minister (first Ábdirashiid Áli Sharmaarke, followed by Ábdirazaaq Haaji Hussein, both of the Mijeerteen sub-clan). Similarly, the Commander of the armed forces (General Daauud of the Hawiye clan) provided clan balance with the Commander of the police (General Mohamed Abshir Muuse of the Daarood clan).

The death of General Daauud in 1965 and his replacement by General Mohamed Siyaad Barre, his deputy, tilted the balance toward the Daarood. The election of Ábdirashiid Áli Sharmaarke (Daarood) as President, followed by his selection of Mohamed Ibraahim Égaal (an Isaaq) as Prime Minister, eliminated the Hawiye from the upper echelons of power. Balance in cabinet representation also shifted in favor of the Daarood under Sharmaarke's leadership.

By the late nineteen-seventies, usurpation of power by the Mareehaan followed the concentration of power in the hands of the Daarood and the M.O.D. Alliance particularly. This disempowered the Hawiye who in pre-independence had the upper hand. Yet the Hawiye enjoyed symbolic concessions, such as the appointment of Hussein Kulmiye Afrah as Vice-President, and they did not suffer the indiscriminate persecution reserved for the Isaaq. The Hawiye cooperated with the ruling Daarood in making the Isaaq and other clans scapegoats for collaborating with the state. The periodic rise of *Irirism*, particularly in the mid nineteen-sixties, often created anxiety among the Daarood who ensured that the Hawiye-Isaaq alliance never materialized.

The emergence of the SSDF and the SNM changed the landscape of Somali politics. Some Hawiye intellectuals and activists became members of the SSDF but, like other members of the Mijeerteen, they could not continue to support it because of the dictatorial streak of the SSDF, Colonel Ábdulaahi Yuusuf Ahmed. Most of them joined the SNM to the chagrin of Mohamed Siyaad Barre. When the SNM conferred the position of Vice-Chairman, (the highest position a non-Isaaq had ever held) to Áli Mohamed Óssoble (Wardhiigle), a Hawiye, the regime dreaded the prospect of another *Iririst* alliance. To avert this prospect, it placed pressure on Wardhiigle and other Hawiye members of the SNM. The subsequent resignation of Wardhiigle did not diminish Hawiye opposition to the regime, in fact, anti-regime and anti-Daarood sentiment grew among the Hawiye in the mid nineteen-eighties.

The decision for an independent armed movement by the Hawiye emerged in 1989, two years before the collapse of the regime. Violence escalated and no clan could remain on the sideline. After 1989, the Hawiye threw themselves into the fray with abandon. Although a group of Hawiye intellectuals registered with the USC in Rome in February 1989, held a number of Hawiye meetings in the country (such as that at Balli Dhuumoodle in 1988), the USC did not become a genuine armed movement until General Mohamed Faarah Hassan (Áydiid) came to Ethiopia. He found support for the SNM, and boldly challenged the regime on its home turf.

In fact, the arrival of General Mohamed Faarah Áydiid in SNM camps was an historical landmark in Isaaq-Hawiye collaboration and in the fight against the regime. As the Hawiye resistance gained momentum, the Daarood confederacy carried out violence against the Hawiye, including mass-murders as it had done with the Isaaq. The Hawiye reaction, like the Isaaq reaction, was not abstract as merely a fight for democracy, but it was concrete and clan oriented consistent with Somali tradition and thought. The Hawiye understood aggression perpetrated on them as targeting them as a clan and carried out by the Daarood. By then, clan neurosis within both clans had come out in the open with fury.

The war raging in the countryside reached Mogadishu in 1990. By December of that year, the city became a veritable war zone. The regime and its allies (specifically the M.O.D. confederacy) responded with cruelty against the Hawiye and against whomever else it deemed enemy. The Hawiye, in turn, extracted retribution against the Daarood. By January of 1991, mayhem became so pervasive that rape and pillage diminished to minor acts of violence. Strewn in the streets were the abandoned corpses of the regime's loyalists, and the stench of death enveloped the city for weeks.

Aftermath of the War

The collapse of the regime did not occur only because its opponents excelled in the practice of violence. In reality, before Somalis took up arms against the regime violence, the economic, political, and moral arrangements with which it controlled people eroded in the late nineteen-seventies. Of its growing woes, the fiasco of the 1977-78 war with Ethiopia emboldened opponents of the regime and hastened its demise. In particular, the regime's rapid decline began after the war when the USSR switched sides from Somalia to Ethiopia and brought over 17,000 Cubans and Southern Yemenis to help defend Ethiopia, the joint forces outgunning and outmaneuvering the Somali fighters.

The shift of the USSR support to Ethiopia isolated and weakened the regime. In retaliation, it sought help elsewhere. Using its strategic location as bait, the regime wooed the West, particularly the United States, in order to obtain the economic and military assistance it desperately needed. The West welcomed Somalia's shift away from its cold war opponents, but it did not provide the extensive help the dictator sought and needed. Worse, the shift of alliance made his regime less insular and more vulnerable to external pressure for economic and political reforms. Demand for reform came even from the conservative Reagan administration. In addition, as we shall see later, the International Monetary Fund pressed for privatization and economic reforms while other organizations mounted charges of human rights violations.

Further, the shift to the West required changes in the regime's ideology and the manner in which it conducted foreign relations. To please the West, the regime abandoned its socialist pretensions and tried to give civilian face to its dictatorship. But these maneuvers convinced none; besides, the help the regime obtained from the West was too little-too-late as its internal rot and its opponents enlarged.

Long before the war, the pool of competent civil servants and technicians also dwindled. Many of the Western-educated elite fled the country fearing arbitrary dismissal and imprisonment. Disillusioned by the clannism of the regime, they either sought employment in the oil-rich countries or asylum in the West. As a result, the regime had to rely on inept loyalists like Ábdirahmaan Jaamá Barre, the Foreign Minister who ran the country's foreign policy into the ground.

From 1969-77, the regime depended on massive assistance—militarily, economically, and technically—from the USSR and it socialist allies. The loss of that assistance spelled doom to the regime and nothing the West provided could safe it from its growing woes. After the 1977-78 war, the country's economy was in shambles. The war was followed by a serious drought in 1979-80. Unlike the devastating drought of 1974, the regime could not mobilize resources to undertake bold initiatives or fight wars without USSR assistance.[2]

As its reliance on external military and economic aid reduced, the regime could no longer monopolize the use of violence. The counter-violence of the SSDF and later the SNM gradually demonstrated their capacity to hurt the regime and frustrate its defenders. Addicted to use of violence, the regime could and did not change tactics. Even when the dictator sought political reconciliation with his opponents—such as when he sent ministerial delegations to Isaaq elders and businessmen in Hargeysa to isolate the SNM—he dismissed the recommendations of the delegations he had sent when they failed to follow his script and wishes. In reality, reconciliation was not what Mohamed Siyaad Barre wanted; he thought that these gestures of negotiations would divide and isolate his opponents, or else buy him time to mobilize his forces to vanquish them. Nevertheless, his opponents saw through these maneuvers and rarely believed his reconciliatory gestures which they saw as sign of weakness.

In addition to its reliance on violence, the regime identified with a clan or a coalition of clans while unleashing indiscriminate violence on other clans. The exclusive reliance on violence and clan partisanship only strengthened the armed opponents who found larger and more committed members joining their ranks, providing a fresh pool of recruits. They knew that the more the regime used indiscriminate violence, more people became alienated from it and helped their cause.

Deepening Economic Crisis

The economic crisis that helped bring down the regime began in 1960 when expectations of freedom and prosperity took root in Somali consciousness. Each time a new group came to power, they made unrealistic promises and inflated public expectation for short-term political gains. Meanwhile a vulnerable public listened to only what they wanted to hear.

A population of paupers, crushed by poverty and despair, needed inflated hopes and dreams to endure pain of living and look forward to better days in the future. The politicians not only catered to these needs of the public but also gave the illusion of change as new personalities replaced the too familiar, or the latter abandoned stale rhetoric with fresh and even 'revolutionary' bombast. It was a game everyone played all along with knowledge that little would objectively change. Thus, long periods of despondence followed the fleeting moments of optimism and this fluctuation from hope to disappointment infected the economy as well as politics.

Successive civilian governments failed to improve the economy and the government increasingly became not only the primary employer but also repository of public taxes and foreign aid wetting the appetite of the elite for the get-rich-quick schemes. From the start, the civilian governments depended on foreign aid to forestall economic crises and to give the illusion of progress while fostering dependency and corruption. While mismanaging scarce resources of the country, the elite siphoned the aid it received, giving Somalia the reputation of being *the grave of foreign aid.* In fact, Somalia was also the grave of promises and dreams. Later it became the grave of people killed en masse by starvation or Somali soldiers.

This addiction to charity under the SYL and siphoning off the aid to private accounts prompted Ábdilaahi Suldaan (Timaádde) to affirm after the election of 1964:

> *The SYL has no fear of Allah or blazing fire of hell*
> *We set out to unite the original Somalis*
> *Those entrusted to that job have betrayed it*
> *The predatory ministers seek European charity*
> *They're branded [like slaves] in hidden spots.*[5]

The first few years of the "revolution" declared by the military junta after the coup of 1969 disposed the public to expect better life. Early initiatives (like nationalizing private concerns, starting self-help schemes, distributing land and assisting farmers, establishment of cooperatives, the writing of Somali script, and regaining lands from creeping sand dunes – gave cause for hope. In time, however, the military junta turned its attention away from these initiatives as nepotism, mismanagement, offset the early gains. The junta chose to rely on persecution to keep the people controlled until tyranny forced them to take up arms against the regime.

Even with the stern controls of the military junta, the gloomy economy of the country did not substantially change. From independence to 1989, almost a year before the regime collapsed, it suffered from a deficit in foreign trade that had deteriorated over the years. For instance, trade deficits grew substantially from 43 per cent of total export proceeds in 1970 to over 200 per cent by 1981, a deficit that grew larger in subsequent years.

The Somali state was literally insolvent from beginning to end and would have gone out of business if it were a private establishment or it did not find foreign donors bailing it out and debtors willing to modify the terms of payment. It was state top heavy but weak legs to keep it standing up without external buttress and prop. Though the state collapse would surely come, the false generosity of foreign aid and mounting debt postponed the crush to take place after three decades of mass heartache, inter-clan acrimony, and social burden.

Table 1 shows the trade deficits from 1984 to 1989.

Table 1
Trend of Foreign Trade
($ mn)

	1984	1985	1986	1987	1988	1989
Exports fob	62	91	90	91	58	78
Imports cif	-406	-380	-447	-488	-458	-389
Balance	-344	-289	-357	-397	-400	-311

Source: Government of Somalia, presentation to UN Conference on Least Developed Countries, April 1990

Exports traditionally were mainly livestock and bananas. There was export of hides, skin, and frankincense but they played a minor role. Periodic droughts and a livestock ban by Saudi Arabia seriously affected the size and value of exports. The figures for imports presented in the table include government and private sector imports (a broad definition including capital goods for development programs).

The consistent deficit shows that in terms of trade, Somalia's *needs* and *wants* are greater than its capacity to pay for them. The country would have gone bankrupt if foreign aid had not kept it afloat. The regime's economic crisis began in the early nineteen-seventies and was aggravated after the 1977-78 war with Ethiopia. After this war ended, the government severed its relations with the former Soviet Union and its allies because they sided with Ethiopia during the war. The regime retaliated by establishing relations with the United States.

The regime obtained substantial aid from 1971-90, especially from Italy which provided economic assistance exceeding $1 billion, making Italy the largest donor to Somalia. For access to the ports and airports of Berbera and Mogadishu, the United States provided the regime with more than $800 million in economic and military assistance between 1979 and 1991. It provided about $600 million in economic aid, amounting to 16.8 percent of the total aid extended to the regime during this period. From 1982 to 1990, the United States also provided over $200 million in foreign military aid used against Somali citizens opposed to the regime.[6]

Without foreign aid to keep it afloat, the regime would have collapsed on its own for economic reasons. From 1970 to 1980, Somalia depended heavily on financial and military aid from the former Soviet Union and its allies. The Cold War enabled Mohamed Siyaad Barre to exploit the strategic location of Somalia. Following the break with his socialist patrons, Mohamed Siyaad Barre turned to the West and to Arab countries.

Table 2 presents the aid the regime received from the West and Arab countries. The table indicates only development assistance. If military assistance is included, the monetary value of the aid extended to Somalia would be much larger.

Table 2

Gross Official Development Assistance

($ mn)

	1983	1984	1985	1986	1987	1988
Bilateral	193.8	217.7	213.2	358.4	416.9	326.0
Italy	51.8	107.5	60.6	159.3	232.5	197.2
West Germany	25.1	17.7	20.7	43.6	50.9	31.6
USA	48.0	52.0	56.0	82.0	52.0	24.0
OPEC Countries	40.0	20.7	43.3	4.5	1.1	11.4
Multilateral	159.2	150.5	154.8	169.7	181.6	119.1
UNCHR	5.2	42.4	40.9	52.1	48.1	34.3
WFP	24.6	34.8	38.1	26.4	48.8	23.4
IDA	21.4	20.5	39.1	47.8	39.6	23.0
EC	19.6	19.3	10.5	10.7	9.4	15.2
Arab/OPEC Agencies	22.6	9.4	1.9	3.0	1.6	0.8
Total	353.0	368.2	368.0	528.0	598.5	445.1
Of which are grants	218.1	217.7	244.7	415.7	440.2	395.2

Without including military assistance, it is clear that Somalia received substantial aid. The table does not exhaust all the aid Somalia received from 1983-88, but it provides an overall estimate of the aid that period. Aid from the three western countries (Italy, West Germany, and the United States) and from OPEC members averaged $ 443 million per year from 1983-88, with Italy providing the greatest amount every year. Aid from OPEC countries tapered off from 1986-88 perhaps because of the problem of arrears on Somalia's debt accumulated over the years. A very high proportion (89%) of the total disbursement came as grants. These grants averaged $ 322 million annually. Still, this level of assistance still could not keep the regime afloat due to internal corruption and mismanagement. When the 50 parastatals created in 1969 closed down and external pressure mounted, the military regime made feeble efforts to encourage the private sector. The privatization programs did not bring the expected results due to clannism, cronyism, and corruption. The GDP fell by an average of 3 percent annually between 1978 and 1980.

External debt soared as deficits grew. The small surplus the central government registered for the period between 1971 and 1978 could offset the deficit exceeding 32 percent of expenditures during the nineteen-eighties. The trade deficit of 43 percent of total exports in 1970 reached 200 percent by 1981. This forced the government to negotiate a series of stabilization programs with the IMF in 1980.

One result of these negotiations was a continued devaluation of the Somali shilling. Another was the abolition of price controls imposed during the socialist period. Somalia's balance of payments and foreign exchange position continued to aggravate during the nineteen-eighties. Debt servicing arrears reached $214 million at the end of 1984. Under pressure from the IMF, the devaluation of the Somali shilling continued. In 1984 it was devaluated 32 percent, followed a year later by an additional 29 percent devaluation.

The rate of exchange of 36.6 shillings to the dollar set by the government in 1985 rose in the market from 300 Somali Shillings per dollar in early March 1988 to 400 Somali Shilling per dollar in mid-April of the same year. Curbs on imports and incentives for exports were attempted but the curbs did not produce the intended effect because the regime did not implement proper economic. The regime tampered with market forces that would determine the rate of hard currency exchange in order to accommodate Mohamed Siyaad Barre's relatives who feverishly pursued get-rich-quick schemes.

A highly publicized scandal regarding foreign aid occurred when Somali authorities launched a liable case in 1988 against the Italian Magazine *Europea* after it reported irregularities in the aid given to Somalia. Áli Khaliif Galaydh provided testimony in the trial and he accused the government of embezzling millions of dollars on wasteful projects. The scandal involved the Italian aid fund, FAI, headed by an associate of Bettina Craxi, a former Prime Minister. The scandal made headlines in Italian papers and provoked debate on the misuse of Italian aid.[7]

In July 1988, the London-based *Africa Analysis* leaked another example of the misused aid. The report presented minutes of a meeting between Somali officials and a West German delegation in November 1987. It documented that funds worth $5.7 million set aside for foreign exchange auction only augmented the wealth of Ábdi Haashi who illegally became the sole recipient in breach of the agreed upon terms for the auction and signed by the World Bank in 1987. As we have seen in Chapter 9, this man was an illiterate truck driver who turned into one of the wealthiest persons in the country only because of his clan and family links to President Mohamed Siyaad Barre. There were indications that the regime used the funds to purchase arms on the black market in order to subdue its opponents, mainly the SNM in Somaliland. A substantial amount of it also found its way to private accounts.

The economic liberalization begun in 1983 also failed to produce the expected results. Inflation and debt soared. Table 3 shows the external debt of the country from 1983-1988.

Table 3

Somalia's External Debt ($ mn)

	1983	1984	1985	1986	1987	1988
Total external debt	1,400	1,487	1,632	1,803	2,006	2,035
Public disbursed	1,217	1,283	1,419	1,559	1,739	1,754
Debt service	24	20	34	77	55	5
Total external debt/GNP (%)	187.5	194.3	189.3	206.4	207.4	214.8
Debt service ratio	12.2	18.5	26.7	66.7	38.7	6.8
Interest arrears on long term debt	19	43	25	68	89	113

Source: World Bank, World Debt Tables 1990 (summarized)

The total external debt rose from $1,400 million in 1983 to $2,035 million in 1988. By the nineteen-eighties, Somalia's long-term debt burden increased steadily. By the end of 1984, the debt servicing arrears reached $214 million, leaving the country's balance of payments and foreign exchange position in serious trouble. Somalia had a theoretical debt service ratio of over 120 per cent in 1986.

Indebtedness continued to increase, particularly to multilateral creditors who provided two-thirds of the disbursed loans. In 1986, the debt exceeded the country's GNP for the first time in Somali history. However, the government was unable to pay those debts in full as scheduled. Most of the creditors either stopped disbursement or rescheduled payment. As the table below shows, total external debt grew from $1,400 million in 1983 to $2,035 million in 1988.

Much of the debt was long-term. Somalia's poor credit rating had reduced its short-term debt to $166 million in 1988, and even publicly guaranteed private creditors refused to take new risks with the Somali government. As a result, the IMF froze its standby credit and Structural Adjustment Facility in September 1987 and made Somalia ineligible for further borrowing in May 1988.

The poor credit rating of the regime reduced its capacity to borrow money to offset its worsening economic performance or to initiate new development programs to stimulate the economy. The war in the north with the SNM and the Isaaq had increased the regime's requirements for foreign capital, producing a foreign exchange crisis in 1989. In 1987, when the regime failed to implement reforms required by the IMF, only two countries (Italy and Saudi Arabia) provided support for balance of payment. The USA, West Germany, Japan, the World Bank, and the African Development Bank froze their funds unless the regime met its obligations for arrears to the IMF. The regime could not meet its obligations.

The deteriorating trade deficit forced the military government to negotiate a series of stabilization programs with the IMF. The first began in 1980 and other agreements followed in subsequent years. Once in need of assistance from the IMF, the regime had on relent to its demands, including the devaluation of the currency, abolition of price controls, the restriction of credit, reduction in the civil service, improvement of debt management, increased interest rates, and reform in the public sector.

The military regime that once applauded socialist rhetoric, succumbed to IMF in return for economic assistance. Accepting the IMF demands had their consequences that aggravated certain aspects of the economy (e.g., the cost of living index) and social services, particularly for the poor. Even without the IMF intervention, the average exchange rate of the Somali shilling has been weakening for decades. It stood at 6.30 per dollar in 1973-81, but dropped to 10.75 in 1982, 15.79 in 1983, 20.02 in 1984, 39.49 in 1985, 72.00 in 1986, 105.2 in 1987, 170.5 in 1988, and 490.7 in 1989.

The exchange rate in the parallel (black) market was worse. As part of the IMF program, the regime introduced a dual exchange rate in July 1981. In September 1986, it also introduced foreign currency auctions on a fortnightly basis. However, these measures did not diminish the country's economic woes. The value of the Somali shilling declined even more after the collapse of the state. In 2001, for instance, it exceeded 20,000 shillings to the dollar!

A Nation of Paupers

It was not only the government that had confused basic *need* with boundless *want*, directing sorely needed resources to private accounts and consumptive habits of the ruling elite. Somali citizens too lost their capacity to feed themselves as their taste and habits changed to what they wanted but could not afford. For instance, a World Bank study in 1988 reported that Somalia which had previously produced all the food it needed, had become "alarmingly" dependent on food imports since 1975. According to the report, dependence on external assistance for food became a permanent characteristic of the Somali economy. Flooding the market with food aid, particularly rice and wheat, at below market prices, had discouraged farmers who traditionally produced basic staples like maize and sorghum. In reaction to the over-dependence on food imports, the farmers moved to non-consumable crops or left farming altogether.

The World Bank study recommended lifting controls on grain prices, eliminating the subsidies given to urban consumers, and providing credit facilities to enable small farmers to increase productivity. The government did not act on these recommendations, therefore food aid intended to be a temporary fix to help the poor until locally grown food could meet the demand became a permanent curse on society. Meanwhile, the appetite for imported food, particularly rice and spaghetti, had become a daily necessity for a population that in all respects lived beyond its means.

The capacity of Somalis to produce the food they needed had diminished; and industry did not grow substantially from independence in 1960 to 1991 when the Somali state collapsed. From 1969 to 1984, the 50 parastatals created by the military regime dominated the industry sector. The most important manufacturing activities in this sector concerned food processing, fishing, and the curing of skins and hides. The largest facilities were the sugar factory at Jawhar, two meat canneries, three fish canneries, a diary plant, four tanneries, a textile factory, and a cigarette factory.

A report by the IMF showed that since 1974, growth of domestic manufacturing was minimal. With encouragement from the IMF, the regime promised to change unprofitable parastatals into private enterprises. However, the government dragged its feet and those by West Germany and diverted to Sudan through a shipment of arms sealed in crates which were marked as agricultural produce) had made foreign donors weary of a regime that engaged in self-defeat.

The livestock ban imposed by Saudi Arabia in 1983 also had a devastating impact. Earnings from livestock exports fell from $72 million in 1983 to $26 million in 1984. Total export fell by 26 and 39 percent respectively in 1983 and 1984. In 1988, fighting between the armed forces and the Somali National Movement led to a 36 percent drop in total export earnings and a 54 percent drop in livestock export.

The influx of refugees from Ethiopia following the 1977-78 war and the ensuing drought also placed an enormous burden on the economy and the land. A conservative estimate of the number of refugees reached one million, although the regime claimed it was 1.6 million. Refugees fleeing the 1984-5 Villagization Program in Ethiopia added to the economic and social problems of the country.

In short, the economy was in serious trouble and life for the majority was extremely difficult. War, drought, and mismanagement were responsible. Life became even more difficult for the majority as the government became the primary source of income and the privileged turf of certain clans who were primary beneficiaries.

Even basic commodities that grew in the country became scarce. Imported goods became even more expensive and, due to lack of foreign exchange, a fuel shortage was frequent which, on occasions in May 1988, prompted demonstrations in Mogadishu. Despite wage increases in 1987 and again in 1990 for civil servants and the armed forces, devaluation of the currency and a rise in the price of imported commodities forced workers to seek other sources of income. Often, they turned to corruption, bribes, and outright looting.

When the government imposed price controls despite the requirement of the IMF, produce was withdrawn from sale and the parallel (i.e., black) market flourished. When it followed IMF requirements, the economy showed little improvement. In part, this was because of structural adjustment programs that did not suit the needs of the country and because the regime declared that such measures favored of clannism, nepotism, and cronyism.

This regime established rigid controls inhibiting initiatives during its socialist pretensions and later adopted capitalist pretensions and produced the worst of two approaches toward economic and social development. It produced a cutthroat world in which a few could feast in the midst of poverty because they were the relatives or cronies of the dictator. The majority lived in misery.

Meanwhile, unemployment in the urban labor market rose and the creation of new jobs could not keep up with 80,000 new entrants in the labor force each year. Unemployment worsened since 1983 when the government withdrew its practice of offering government jobs to secondary school graduates. The number of unemployed rose in subsequent years, adding to discontentment of the masses ready to join rebellion against the regime.

The regime with its inept planners and administrators could not envision how its policies were breeding conditions for social discontent and conflict. It was more concerned with winning wars with its political opponents than in preventing them. It did not endeavor to address the deepening misery of its people.

UNICEF reported a steep decline in social services in 1989. For instance, 73 percent of the population had no access to health services and over half of the administrative districts outside the capital had no midwife, no public dispensary, and no functioning hospital. At the same, the government cut from 9 percent of total budget expenditure for education to 2 percent in 1986. In the same period, it also cut the budget for health from 4 percent to 1.3 percent. Thus, while the regime fought its opponents on different fronts, it also cut essential services and mismanaged on the economic front, led by inept and corrupt officials.

In short, the Somali state began with insolvency and sank deeper into bankruptcy. The ruling elite, greedy and inept, deepened the poverty and despair. Following their example, the population too changed from a *homo-sapient* (*thinking* beings) and *homo-fabre* (*working* beings) to a voracious but unproductive *homo consumen* (*consuming* beings) living on international charity. In fact, the ruling elite dispensed with thought and work as unnecessary toil to become rapacious machines that loot the state and consume everything within reach—the imported and expensive being the most popular. In time, predatory behavior and looting the public treasury and cannibalizing one another developed into a sub-culture.

It is against this deteriorating economic and social background that Somalis played out the political conflicts of clans and clan neuroses that escalated into violent conflagrations and collective psychosis. Taking up arms against the regime was reaction to the regime's violence which increasing alienated the population.

Conflict within the Loyalists

Another key contributor to the weakening and eventual collapse of the military regime was dissention within the loyalist camps. The M.O.D. Alliance looked away as Mohamed Siyaad Barre concentrated power in his own hands, compromised on long-standing policies toward Ethiopia, and then gave preferential treatment to members of his clan.

Mohamed Siyaad Barre lavished the Mareehaan with power and wealth, particularly the aborted coup of 1978 when, as a clan, they defended the regime. The aborted coup also made Mohamed Siyaad Barre increasingly wary about other clans and more dependent on the Mareehaan to protect his dictatorship. As the power he denied other clans transferred to his own clan, the Mareehaan saw their future in strengthening and prolonging the regime that in effect became their dominion and turf.

By early 1982, Ábdirahmaan Jaamá Barre led an effort to expand the membership of the Politburo from 5 to 18 in order to accommodate more members of their clan in this critical body. Mohamed Siyaad Barre said that he would do so if the other four Politburo members agreed with this proposal. He knew, however, that the other four members (Mohamed Áli Samatar, Hussein Kulmiye Afrah, Ismaíil Áli Abokor, and Ahmed Suleymaan Ábdulle) would reject the proposal. This was his way of turning the anger of his clan against the four members of the Politburo and disempowering them. Disempowering his closet colleagues and concentrating power on himself, made him even more dependent on his clan for support and loyalty. His dependence on them only intensified their ambition for power and their ownership of the regime.

After the May 1986 accident, Mohamed Siyaad Barre lost his alertness and vigor. This made him dependent on family members to care for him and the affairs of the regime. Family rule intensified both competition and alienation within the Mareehaan clan. Near the end of the decade, challenge to the regime came from different clans and the Mareehaan demanded more power in deciding the policies of the regime. As the end of the regime seemed in sight, many of wavered and began to have cold feet or simply fled as the going became rougher. These actions seemed to hasten the collapse of the regime.

The Ogaadeen provided the largest number of officers and soldiers for the regime. Dependence on them for defense of the regime also stimulated their ambition for power. They resented the excessive power the Mareehaan enjoyed. Their alienation from the regime increased when Mohamed Siyaad Barre sought to integrate the armed Ogaadeen militia (including the Western Somali Liberation Front) into the armed forces. Their alienation increased even more when the dictator signed a peace accord with Ethiopia on 2 April 1988 to isolate and defeat the SNM.

In addition, the accord included demilitarization of a 15 km wide zone on both sides of the Somali-Ethiopian border. Both governments implemented the accord in 25 May 1988. In return for ceasing Ethiopian support to the SNM, the Somali regime renounced its claims to the Ogaadeen and recognized the territorial integrity of Ethiopia. Integrating the Ogaadeen militia into the armed forces would deny this significant clan the independent force to threaten the regime. It would also end independent armed engagement in Ethiopia.

The signed accord was humiliating to the Ogaadeen who not only comprised about a third of the armed forces, but also had been strong supporters of the regime of Mohamed Siyaad Barre. Dissatisfaction among the Ogaadeen surfaced earlier, as shown by the 1987 defection to the United States by former minister, Hussein Ábdilqaadir Qassim, who also was a member of the party's central committee as well as a leading politician of the Ogaadeen clan. The regime demoted, retired, or sent abroad a number of Ogaadeen officers. In May of that year, there were also clashes between the Ogaadeen and the Mareehaan.

There were also instances of open revolt by Ogaadeen soldiers who protested Mareehaan dominance, fueled by the regime's renouncement of its claims to the Ogaadeen. One instance occurred in March 1989 when 600 Ogaadeen officers and troops stationed in Kismaayo Military Academy revolted. Another revolt occurred in mid-April 1989 when 400 Ogaadeen officers and troops mutinied. Almost 3,000 armed militia, formed from unemployed youth and deserters, had joined the mutineers and terrorized the Mareehaan in central Somalia. They joined the *Abris* militia and captured the town of Bu'aale. Such incidents are examples of recurring conflicts within the M.O.D. Alliance that existed from the start.

To a lesser extent, the concentration of power in Mohamed Siyaad Barre and his Mareehaan cronies alienated the Dhulbahante. The internal clan competition—for instance the competition of the Faarah Garaad and Mohamuud Garaad that started as early as 1835—continued to the nineteen-eighties and aggravated tension within the M.O.D. alliance. Despite these internal conflicts, the M.O.D. Alliance held firm to the end because all three clans comprising it knew that fate bound them by lineage as well as the violence they perpetrated against other clans.

Since each clan within the coalition crossed the threshold of abuse and violence against other clans, it could not suddenly abandon loyalty to the regime. In fact, fear of reprisal for the shared crimes they jointly committed against others clans as well as the temporary rewards of power bound them in complicity more than lineage. Had it not been for their shared enmity toward the other clans, the recurring fissures within the M.O.D. Alliance would have escalated into violent and lasting conflict among its clan members. Nonetheless, periodic conflict and chronic resentment within it weakened and demoralized alliance, particularly so as opposition to the regime gained momentum and strength.

Even the Mareehaan loyalists and members of the president's immediate family had problems with their amassed power and wealth. For instance, rumors circulated that the aging president, then 70, was positioning loyal members of his immediate family, particularly his son, General Maslah, to critical posts to prepare for his succession. His serious injury in a d in May 1986 raised doubts about the president's health and longevity.

The rumor stimulated infighting within the family while increasing the ambitions of loyal generals like Mohamed Áli Samatar, Ahmed Suleymaan Ábdulle, and Hussein Kulmiye Afrah. Joining the fray was Ábdirahmaan Jaamá Barre, the president's cousin who moved from the Ministry of Foreign Affairs to head the Ministry of Finance and State Revenue. Even though his incompetence was widely known, the fact that he controlled the country's economy increased his ambition.

Even Ayaanle, the president's youngest son, presented himself as a candidate for succession. His mother and her supporters lobbied for him as the rightful successor to his father's dictatorial throne. General Mohamed Haashi Gaani who had considerable support among Mareehaan members of the armed forces, and General Mohamed Saíid Hirsi (Morgan), the president's son-in-law were also minor—though active contenders—also contributed to the growing power struggle among the loyalists.

The tyranny and unpopularity of Mohamed Siyaad Barre as well as the conflict within the loyalists reached such extremes that in 26 May 1989, a Mareehaan delegation of senior officers, members of parliament, and businessmen presented an ultimatum to the president. They demanded that he introduce sweeping political reforms or else they would withdraw support to him and his regime.

Their ultimatum included that Mohamed Siyaad Barre must declare on television and radio that his policies had failed; that he must form a provisional government within six months; that he must revise the constitution; and that he must permit the three parties to compete in free and democratic elections. Also included in their ultimatum was that he must allow multiple candidates to run for president. They also included that he must form a commission to reconcile with 'the North' and that reconstruction of ruined state and private properties would begin.

This was indeed a tall order. No doubt, the Mareehaan delegation knew as much. It was clear that Mohamed Siyaad Barre would not accept the ultimatum as it was also equally clear that he could not afford to lose the support of his clan. Many interpreted the ultimatum as an indication that the Mareehaan read the reading on the wall – that the regime of Mohamed Siyaad Barre from which they had gained special power and wealth was in grave danger of collapse—and that they ought to distance themselves from it.

Not wanting to accept their ultimatum but seeking a face-saving exit, Mohamed Siyaad Barre stalled by announcing on 29 May that he needed suggestions from all Somalis both at home and abroad on how to solve the political crisis. It was obvious that Mohamed Siyaad Barre who would not heed the advice of those within his trusted circle also would not accept suggestions from a mass of faceless and nameless people.

Subsequently, he organized a meeting of the Somali Revolutionary Socialist Party to pass a resolution that supposedly would give the impression of a collective decision, a strategy he crafted to hold on power. In addition, to dismiss the call for a multiparty system, he orchestrated a demonstration in favor of a one-party state. In the end, all of this led to one conclusion that "a fox cannot protect the chicken coop, nor can a leopard can not change its spots." The ultimatum was simply lip service since no Mareehaan would bite the hand of Mohamed Siyaad Barre that fed him in the feast of clannism and cronyism.

Meanwhile, as these conflicts within the rank of the regime's loyalists emerged, Mohamed Siyaad Barre reshuffled his cabinet, as if changing names and personalities offered a special magic. Even though Mohamed Siyaad Barre pursued his own machinations behind the ritual of a cabinet reshuffle, frequent changes in government gave an aura of political instability, keeping aspirants for office in a constant state of anxiety. In reality, such reshuffles were one of the means by which he rewarded, demoted, and controlled loyalists.

He began this practice in the nineteen-seventies, increased its frequency during the nineteen-eighties continued the reshuffling until his fall from power. On the eve of cabinet changes, he would call the ministers he planned to dismiss and commend them for the great job they rendered him and the nation. On rare occasions when he offered such praises, it was never clear what he really meant – a genuine commendation or censure followed by dismissal.

This ambiguous language kept his ministers in a state of constant insecurity. Even though some of them remained in the cabinet following each reshuffle. An interesting example is Ábdiqaasim Salaad Hassan who became the President of the Transitional Government formed in Árta, Republic of Djibouti. Mohamed Siyaad Barre appointed him Minister of Public Works in 1985, one the Ministers of State in 1987, as Minister of the Interior in 1988, as Minister of Commerce in 1989, and so on. He was not a member of the Mareehaan clan, or the son-in-law of Mohamed Siyaad Barre, but had become a fixture in the inner circle, and this raised serious questions of opportunism, ethical impropriety, and corruption. A more serious charge was that he was Minister of the Interior when Hargeysa was carpet-bombed and therefore belonged to the camp that had committed crimes against humanity.[8]

Despite the dissension within the loyalist camps, Mohamed Siyaad Barre intensified his tyranny. The prisons filled to capacity as the regime deployed its myriad of security agencies—including the NSS, the HANGASH, the Guulwadayaal, the National Audit Office, the Somali Revolutionary Socialist Party, the National Army, the Red Beret, and the Police. When the regime itself brought the war against the Isaaq into Mogadishu, the political temperature rose and terror gripped the residents of this once calm city. The Jazira Beech Massacre, in particular, did much to yank the residents out of their indifference forcing them to realize the gravity of the dangers threatening them.

Human Rights Activists

Complaints about human rights abuses by the regime of Mohamed Siyaad Barre went unheard in the early nineteen-eighties, particularly in the United States who pandered to this brutal dictator in order to gain geopolitical advantage over the former Soviet Union. During the Cold War, the Reagan-Bush administrations ignored and dismissed charges of human rights violations by the Somali regime. The dictator became a United States ally after the USSR and Cuba sided with Ethiopia during the 1977-78 war. Throwing out his socialist allies who provided him military hardware and training for years, the dictator turned to the U.S.A. for financial and military support. They obliged while other western governments (like Italy and West Germany) also provided assistance.

A proverb he liked to quote summarized the dictator's tactic: *Ama buur ahaw, ama buur ku tiirsanaw*—either be a mountain, or lean on a mountain. The tactic worked well for him. Those of us who publicized in the Unites States the regime's atrocious human rights record in the nineteen-eighties met a deaf ear. Except for a few like the lawyer Ismaíil Jumáalle in Mogadishu, the human rights activists at that time lived abroad and were almost exclusively Isaaq. This was in part because the regime specially targeted the Isaaq for its most intense and sustained violence, in part too because some were human rights activists by personal inclinations before the Isaaq became target of clan cleansing.

Isaaq students and intellectuals in North America and Europe spearheaded the revelation of human rights violations by the military regime through a series of demonstrations and public speeches. These demonstrations rallied many members of the Isaaq all over the United States and often held in Washington, D.C. and New York City. In those years when the Isaaq were the primary victims of the regime, other Somalis assumed that the condemnations of the regime's policies served only Isaaq agenda to destroy Somalia. Since the abuses of the regime did not yet hit their clan as fully as they victimized the Isaaq, they were content to watch from the sidelines or even denounce the demonstrations.

They dictatorial regime was not pleased with these demonstrations, but it was outraged by series of writings and TV debates in subsequent years. One of them was an article I and my friend, Ahmed Saíid Faarah, wrote in 1980. This was one of the first articles on the regime's human rights abuses including my satirical poem, "Confession of Siyaad", which formed the bulk of the article. At the time, Ahmed and I were editors of the *Horn of Africa Journal* in which the human rights article and poem appeared. That we published the article and poem under pseudonym of Mohamuud Hassan shows our desire to keep the image of political neutrality for the journal.

My *OpEd Page* article in the New York Times, March 5, 1982, published in my name only a few days before the dictator's visit to the United States, had foiled the dictators aims of getting more support from the United States. In his first public speech in New York City, the dictator revealed his anger and distress at the article by accusing me to be an ally and spy of Ethiopia who wants to deny financial and military assistance Somalia needs desperately. In those years, it was enough to call an enemy of Somali nationalism or, worse, an Ethiopian spy to assassinate his character and person.

Another human rights activist who contributed much to the cutting of US aid to the Somali regime was Ahmed Hussein Íise. He was the primary contact for a group of us in early nineteen-eighties to the prestigious Academy for Sciences in Washington, D.C. The Academy held a series of conferences on human rights violation of the regime and in the end sent a team of highly respected scientists to visit Mogadishu, resulting in a most damaging report on the regime's human rights violations. Publicity like this and others—in writings, speeches, and demonstrations—brought about the ending of the US financial and military aid the regime desperately needed, as shown by its collapse soon after support of its most important ally ended.

The work of human rights activists did not end with the collapse of the regime. After the fall of the regime, the United States Congress held a series of hearings. With invitation, I presented testimony on the regime's brutality in a hearing held by the Africa Subcommittee of the House and later by the highly influential Foreign Relations Committee of the Senate. The former committee was chaired by Congressman Wolpe of Rhode Island, a steady supporter of Africa; the latter by Senator Simon of Illinois, a powerful and highly respected voice in the Senate.

I was also one of two Somalis whom Senator Simon called to his office for more in-depth discussion of what the United State should do on the Somali problem. This was a few months before the United States launched Operation Restore Hope. The Senator wanted to learn of our thoughts on US military intervention in Somalia. I the more than an hour of exchange, I argued that Somalis firstly need food assistance to stem the raging mass starvation and death, secondly financial and technical assistance on reconciliation and conflict resolution. The other Somali, one called General Hoolif, insisted that nothing would work except overwhelming military force on Mogadishu and rest of Somalia. I learned later that the General was a Mijeerteen who wanted to subdue the Hawiye with US military force. I left the meeting saddened by how the two of us took diametrically opposed views, thereby wasting a rare opportunity to help save lives instead confusing the Senator.

After founding *Africa Watch*, Raaqiya Ábdilaahi Omaar had done superb job near the end of the decade in advocating on behalf of the victims, as shown in the Africa Watch reports she spearheaded like *A Government at War with Its Own People,* an Africa Watch Report in January 1991. In addition, Raaqiya took the baton of human rights activists soon after the fall of the regime when the UN under the leadership of Boutros Ghali was determined to recreate the flawed state first by diplomatic means and later by use of force. None who watched her articulate and strident TV debates can forget the anger they provoked in UN and US diplomatic circles. Other human rights activists, including Mohamed Saíid Urdooh, also exposed the plight of Isaaq survivors of the regimes systemic violence and in particular the war criminals seeking asylum in North America. As a result, some of them were forced to leave Canada.

At the time, most non-Isaaq intellectuals abroad either stood on the sideline or defended the regime. Coupled with the Cold War and the regime's alliance of convenience with the West had made the task of human right activists difficult. However, two developments—the indiscriminate bombardment of Hargeysa in 1988 and the Jazira Beach Massacre—had exposed without doubt the brutality of the regime we had strenuously tried for years to explain to American politicians who often heard criticism of African regimes but mostly turned a deaf ear.

After 1988, following the carpet-bombing of Hargeysa, the regime could no longer conceal its brutalities. A report by the U.S. Government Accounting Service, accompanied by a documentary on the destruction of Hargeysa, confirmed what human rights activists had been claiming along while the Reagan and the Bush, Administrations ignored. Reports on the bombardment and accounts of survivors in refugee camps across the Ethiopian border helped immensely to show the regime's brutality that in turn motivated some relief organizations and the media to give proof of e the regime's human rights abuses.

By 1989, the regime could no longer hide its cruelties. In that year, the Jazira Beach Massacre took place. While of short duration compared to the carpet-bombing of Hargeysa, it occupies an important place in history because it not only exposed the regime's brutalities against the Isaaq but also raised public consciousness in Mogadishu.

Most residents in the capital city knew that war raged on in "the North," but, since the scene of armed conflict was far away the public was removed from it. The Jazira Beach Massacre changed all that.

The Jazira Beach Massacre began as a reprisal to an antigovernment speech followed by a mob scene resulting in wounding or death of a Mareehaan officer. The massacre took place on 14 July 1989. On that night, Mareehaan members of the armed forces cordoned off Bulo-Hubey, a section of the Medina District of Mogadishu whose predominant inhabitants were "Northerners". About midnight, after the soldiers assured themselves that all residents of the neighborhood had returned to their homes, the soldiers closed off all roads to and from the neighborhood. In the middle of a strategic intersection, sealed off from pedestrians and motor vehicles, their commanding officer (Col. Ibraahim Hassan, nicknamed *Ánjeeh*) and his lieutenants sat comfortably on couches looted from nearby homes.

In that tightly controlled street, the Commander and his lieutenants established themselves as inquisitors. They interrogated terrified residents and queried them about their name, occupation, and clan identity. The singled out anyone suspected to be Isaaq and ordered to squat in a military formation under the glare of a blinding light. Many of the captured thought this roundup was for recruiting military conscripts. Far from it – unknown to them a worse indeed fate awaited them. Those who were not Isaaq claimed to be so because they believed that this clan identity would disqualify them from military conscription to the war against the Isaaq. Sadly, they were wrong.

When the soldiers filled three military trucks with their human cargo, they sped away to Jazira Beach. There, the captives were summarily executed and buried. The massacre at the beach would have remained a secret if one of the victims had not survived and managed to walk away wounded after the soldiers left the scene of these gruesome killings. He was composed enough to go directly to the home of Hussein Áraj, a Dhulbahante military general. Accompanied by a clansman serving as Director General in one of the government ministries, Hassan took the young man to General Ahmed Suleymaan Ábdulle who at the time was Minister of the Interior. The next morning, these men and General Ahmed Jaamá Muuse, an Isaaq, visited the scene of the massacre and discovered the bodies. Soon, story of the massacre became public.

The Jazira Beach Massacre had both international and local repercussions for the regime. Internationally, it provided uncontestable evidence of the regime's blatant violations of human rights. Until then, the regime seemed impervious to the mounting charges of human rights violations presented by Amnesty International, Africa Watch, and Somalis in the Diaspora.

The Reagan and Bush administrations were unsympathetic and resistant to human rights concerns in developing countries. Obsessed with superpower geopolitical competition, without any qualms, they supported dictators as long as they cooperated with the U.S.'s Cold War strategy. Neither administration wanted to see Mohamed Siyaad Barre removed from power since he had permitted the United States to use the strategically located Port of Berbera. Somali troops in 1983 and 1984 had participated in joint maneuvers of the U.S.'s Rapid Deployment Force.

The Jazira Beach Massacre brought the brutal practices of Mohamed Siyaad Barre's regime to the attention of wider and influential circles such as the U.S. Congress and the international media. The Bush Administration habitually had looked the other way, but could no longer ignore pressures from the Congress and the media. Following the Jazira Beach Massacre, the U.S. Department of State issued a press release announcing a drastic cut of development assistance (PL-480) for fiscal year 1990. In addition, on 4 January 1990, the Congress imposed the Brooks Amendment that precludes non-humanitarian assistance on Mohamed Siyaad Barre's regime.

A more detailed report by the U.S. Department of State specifically mentioned the reprisal killings of Isaaq civilians by the government following a landmine explosion on the Berbera-Buró road and the Jazira Beach Massacre. Major newspapers like the New York Times and The Guardian also reported on this massacre. With dwindling foreign aid, the regime could not keep itself afloat for long, especially since its handlers were increasingly avaricious and its opponents were on the rise.

The Jazira Beach Massacre also had repercussions in Mogadishu itself. The failure of the government to bring the criminals to justice showed residents of the capital city that the security they had enjoyed was a mirage, a false security. They realized, with mounting evidence providing proof, that government soldiers could snatch anyone they wished, any time, and from any place. They understood that one was punished or rewarded because clan identity, not because of his character or actions. Regardless of his other attributes, the decisive factor for life and death was clan identity.

Thus, one was forced to embrace his clan identity and seek security in one's clan, to associate with its members, to share news, to live and die in its midst. Under these conditions, even the most *de-clannized* Somali, long ago alienated from his clan, found no option but return to the clan fold, become an advocate of its cause focused on its survival in the midst of cataclysmic and senseless violence. In the context of primordial clan wars, no Somali, even the most cosmopolitan and open-minded, could escape this leap backwards to the fold of clan.

Onslaught of Poets and Singers

After the fiasco of the 1977-78 war with Ethiopia, the power and prestige of regime steadily declined. Its decline began in the hearts and minds of the people, chipping away at the regime's claim to legitimacy. The poets who often gave voice to the hopes and frustrations of the public started to challenge the regime in subtle ways that eventually became incendiary and explosive.

For instance, a 1978 poem by Mohamed Haashi Dhamá (Gaariye) affirms the responsibility of the poet in society as he rejects the poet's past role in pandering to the dictator and the corrupt regime. In fact, despite the risks of living in Mogadishu like his friend Mohamed Ibraahim Warsame (Hadraawi), the poet refuses to shower the dictator with praises but instead rebels with a frontal attack on him.

The man who deceives the community
If buried in a crumbling mountain heap
By Allah, I do not unearth (rescue) him
By Allah, the swindler with a pen
Crimes committed against the nation
I never hide from the masses
By Allah, the festering wound
I never treat its surface alone.
If frustrated public rises in revolt
Ceasing fear and self-censorship
By Allah, I do not fetter it in shackles…[9]

Long before the war with Ethiopia and the aborted coup of Colonel Mohamed Sheekh Ósmaan (Írro), the regime had lost the hearts and minds of the citizenry that it had won by promises of revolution. After the war and the coup attempt, the nation turned inward, focused on the rot and the misery of the regime. The poets Mohamed Haashi Dhamá (Gaariye) and Mohamed Ibraahim Warsame (Hadraawi) who started the series of poems called *Silsilaaddii Deeley* were among the first to give voice to Abel (Qaabiil), the oppressed.

As Gaariye himself recounts in an unpublished collection of his poetry, *Deeley* followed another series by Khaliif, a Mijeerteen and member of the newly formed Somali Salvation Front (SSF). He composed a widely publicized poem in which he blamed most Somali clans for their unwillingness to take on the regime and join the SSF movement. At the time, even the ardent opponents of the regime rejected the SSF because its leadership and most of its members belonged to one alone—the Mijeerteen. This armed political movement was also based in Ethiopia, a country which at the time most Somalis viewed as an enemy.

An Isaaq poet, nicknamed *Dhirbaaxo-Jin*, the Slap of Jinn, replied in defense of the Isaaq, attacking the Mijeerteen and Khaliif. A series of poems, *Silsiladdii Miinleey*, followed. The regime encouraged these poems because they deflected public attention from itself and, because some of the poems stimulated sympathy and support for the Daarood. These poems dredged up the worst of clan abuse and prejudice, threatening to unleash clan conflict.

Gaariye started *Silsiladdii Deeley* with a poem called *"Dugsi mal leh qabyaaladi'* – 'Clannism has no shelter.' In essence, Gaariye refocused public attention away from clan disputes to the political actions resulting in mass suffering.

He who fosters clannism [is a fool]
And foolishness is a disease
If you had substance
Just look around you
How many are the widowed wives!
How much blood was shed!
How many men were eaten alive!
How many people suffered national defeat![10]

Gaariye emphasized the unity of Somalis in order to avert clan feuds that clan poetry of the day supposed to instigate.

Somalis are an integral whole

With the exception of the guilty
They're[united like] one stick and its sheath
They're neighbors and kin
Divided by the pursuer of selfish ends.[11]

Having underscored the ruin brought by clannism, he castigated the elite and the political leaders the "fat-asses" who use clannism as "concealed trap" to deceive and plunder the nation. Some of them with empty [false] degrees and big drums, the use clannism for their own private ends and for exploiting the labor of Abel [Haabiil}:

Summing up altogether
It's a class greedy for assets
The stamped is for one reason alone:
For my sweat (labor) of gold
To be hurriedly swallowed.[12]

Mohamed Ibraahim Warsame (Hadraawi), Gaariye's friend, responded with a poem called *Daalaán*, the second in the series that came to be known as *Silsiladdii Deeley*. He began with an affirmation of his readiness to join his friend with a "speedy horse, reddish in brown" in the war for unveiling the truth and changing the system.

Hadraawi affirms that successful oppression depends on two qualities of the protagonists: on the one hand the oppressor's determination and vigilance, on the other the lack of consciousness and resolve of the oppressed. He places the cause for oppression and liberation not on clan dominance but on the citizen's (Abel's) failure to assume their historic responsibility for self-liberation.

He who in faltering moments and
inner weakness exploits me
it's due to his vigilance
and my defenselessness
for throughout history
and in the national archives
whatever clear debt (responsibility) I have
depends on my will to attack and counterattack.[13]

Hadraawi contrasts the greed and corruption of the ruling elite (*Cain*) with the patience and tolerance of the citizens (*Abel*) who:

Our community is of people
sincere and with great modesty

made of silken thread
they mistreat none
they live in Allah's grace
they're vulnerable to feelings
But, mind you, fools they are not. [14]

Hadraawi adds that, although the citizens are tolerant to even the tyrant, giving him time to mend his ways, they do not forget his crimes which they preserve in stories [social memory]. He further affirms that clannism will not end as long as mass poverty and class exploitation are rife; that clannism will never end because *"Cilmi diiddan baa jira"*—'there is a system resisting change.' He concludes by urging the people (Abel) to unite, seek honest leadership, and work hard to find their own redemption.

For your well-being, you people,
in being united
and with honest leadership
and your hard work
therein lies your medicine
if any aspect (of these) falter
your fate is doomed.
Is there last warning left [to utter]? [15]

Under the prevailing tyranny and paranoia of the regime, Gaariye's and Hadraawi put themselves in evident danger. To articulate this veiled and not so veiled criticism of the regime in Mogadishu, right in the belly of the beast, required immense courage. Fortunately, though, a flood of poems in the same genre and passion followed, some poets attacking the regime, others defending it. The poetic exchange caught fire throughout the nation because nothing catches the mind and heart of Somalis as does as poetry—it puts them in trance.

The regime at first thought this series of poems would deflect public attention from its internal rot but the criticism dominated the poetic exchange and, in turn, it emboldened its critics. The dictator considered several options—imprisonment or execution of his critics in the poetic series. In the end, he decided to prohibit the series and declared them seditious.

Poetry such as the *Deelleey* series conditioned people to focus attention on the regime, it raised public consciousness, undermined the potency of the terror it inspired, and chipped away at its legitimacy. The lyrics of Ábdi Muhumad Amiin, sung by Saado Áli in late 1989, are examples of open challenge to the ruling oligarchy. The song derided those who were proud to own and drive Land Cruisers that had become the rage among government officials and the elite in the midst of national misery and suffering, yet pleading for foreign aid. Mohamed Siyaad Barre was in the audience the night Saado first sang the song. Everyone understood to whom the song referred.

It's a confused mind
and wicked conscience
to buy a Land Cruiser
yet beg for maize [aid].
My beloved and kinsmen
did you decide [with lucid mind]
while pervasive deprivation
prevails in our homes
to remain undisturbed
in a comfortable car
the Land Cruiser you bought
So that it confers nobility to you
Horn of Africa.[16]

The song began with veiled innuendo, as shown in the first stanza when the Horn of Africa is mentioned, seemingly harmless criticism of a whole region. But it ends with direct criticism of the ruling Somali elite and the regime, the song simulates in a few minutes the path which the armed revolt had taken in years—from indirect criticism, to peaceful demonstration, and finally to violence. The target of the attack—the ruling elite who waste resources including aid—contrasts to the object poverty crushing the rest of the population. Why so?—simply in order attain the delusion of nobility!

Buy a Land Cruiser
While the home is dark
Water is lacking
The children are dying
It is the peculiarity of Somalis
And their distinction
By which they are recognized
Let its sound delude you
That you attained nobility by it.[17]

The song was a political landmark of sorts for several reasons. First, Saado sang in front of Mohamed Siyaad Barre, demonstrating the momentum that the public rebellion against his regime had gained. Right to his face, the song declared that the king is naked,. Second, the singer was a clan member of the M.O.D. coalition that served as the primary bulwark of the regime. Action against her would further weaken the alliance that Barre desperately needed. Proving his political impotence, the despot let the singer go unscathed, as well as the composer, and others associated with the song,.[18] Third, the song suggested a budding solidarity between those who opposed the regime and those who supported it. Hence, the isolation and weakness of the dictator was becoming evident. Last, the song appeared at a critical juncture in history when the air was explosive and the regime was on the brink of collapse.

It is clear from the above that poetry and songs are potent tools of war and peace, as they are the medium of expressing love, hurt, and hope. In traditional society, a clan without a poet was as vulnerable and defenseless, the same way it would be if it lacked fighting force. Of course lacking both, it suffered humiliation, domination, and enforced silence.

Armed men defend life and property in the immediate term; they may even bring a fleeting victory. Without a poet, however, the grievances and valor of the group quickly vanish; even victory of military heroes fade from memory. However, the words of the poet keep alive in the minds and hearts of generations to come. Poetry preserves only the group's grievances but also its valor and claim to clan superiority.

Moreover, the poet can invent nobility in peace and inspire courage in war. Although the words he mints and his message exist only in the mind, people readily accept them as facts that took place in real life and in the din of battle. Further, the poet's message has magical power of dispersing quickly and widely by word of mouth, without the use of modern press or telecommunication services.

No wonder then the poet occupies a critical role in Somali life and politics. No wonder too that the poets and singers who popularized the military regime in its early years had struck a fatal blow on it with their words when they joined the opposition, contributing to its collapse as did the men who fought with the gun in the field, the pen in the media, and speeches in influential circles abroad.

Unfortunately, poets and singers experience financial strains in a society respecting neither copyright nor intellectual property. In addition, there are no institutions offering them grants, no nurturing institutes giving them intellectual shelter, and no conscious public protecting their independence, politically and financially. Since they often depend on government for disseminating their entertaining and educating messages, they remain vulnerable to official manipulation and misuse. They are not only the first to be censored but also the first to be persecuted since their words can be as lethal as arms. Thus in the oppressive system that often prevails in Somali society, they are under constant pressure— intellectually, they already live in a prison, though physically they may live outside its walls.

When the poets and singers find society in the throes of crisis, they are among the first to risk life for freedom, the first to articulate the suffering of the people, the first to be censored and persecuted. Though financially and politically vulnerable, they ignite the minds and hearts dampened by fear; as they incite rebellion of people cowered into self-censorship and submission. And when they join the armed opposition, they are warriors whose fiery words echo in the minds and mouths of generations to come, long after people forget the men who courageously fire bullets and hurl bombs.

The population counts on them because they are society's *organic intellectuals*. Of course, a few of them sell their words and souls to the highest bidder, and the public readily forgives these betrayers, as they should, because their dire financial conditions push them to desperate solutions in a society that loves their poems and songs, yet neglects even the bread and bed they need to sustain life.

Despite their continued neglect, the poets and singers seldom complain, for they know firstly that bread and bed are scarce necessities for the majority of the population whose suffering they unveil, secondly that the ruling elite, engrossed with their selfish interests, are the last to extend generosity or solution to anyone unless it benefits their quest for power, wealth, or prestige.

In short, it is in this world inhabited by contrasting realities and incompatible interests that the poets and singers bridge, bind, and illuminate by self-sacrifice and with the magic power of the word. It is also the torment and trauma of this world that is the source of their creativity and commitment. That is why I call them the true *organic in-*

tellectuals of Somali society while the ruling elite represent Cain dis-simulating as liberators of Abel.

13

CONCLUSION

Ceelna uma qodna, cidina uma maqna
No wells dug for them, no rescuers on the way
—Somali proverb

As shown in the preceding g chapters, Somalis have had a very difficult one hundred years, beginning with colonial occupation and partition, followed by imposition of an alien state without their consent. Later, the local elite inherited the colonial state and ran it aground after three decades of misrule and corruption, resulting in succession of wars, material ruin, ruptured human connections, and pervasive trauma.

Bearing testimony to the tragedy are the ruined and bullet-ridden buildings, the painful memory and bitter words of survivors, the vacuous and distant eyes of trauma victims. Most of all, it is the children's eyes and faces that haunt one the longest. Seeing them, one wants to do something instantly to bring them back to the vocation and avocation of children everywhere—play and laughter. Yet the obduracy of an unjust world and inept leaders reminds us that we must first break through the stubborn barriers to feeding, housing, covering, and healing their naked, emaciated bodies. Sadly, the project of educating them and building playgrounds for them cannot start in earnest until solution is found for the flawed state and the malfeasant elite.

The point in retelling this story of disaster and malfeasance was not to lament the past, nor heap accusations on others, nor plead for sympathy from outsiders. It is to impart understanding on why the past one hundred years have been a century of torment and tribulation for Somalis, what forces brought about this predicament, and how Somalis themselves, in particular the ruling elite, contributed to the tragedy still raging in parts of Somali society.

Since my goal was not to only record that history but also interpret it, I identify in this concluding chapter the root causes of why Somalis, traditionally egalitarian and self-sufficient, have become freaks and charity cases of the international community, and why they continue to inflict on themselves injuries deepening their torment and trauma.

Several key causes of and contributors to the Somali disaster are outlined below, although I present detailed discussion on each of them in *Pathology of History*. I review these key causes and contributors because only when people identify and understand the core problems can they realistically find solution.

As I explained in Chapter 1, the following remarks refer to all territories where Somalis govern themselves as sovereign states or proxies of neighboring governments that benefited from colonial partition of Somalis.

Muddled Environment

Muddle is the confused mix of things—a turbid and muddy state producing jumbled thought and aimless action. When social and political structures that shape and influence human thought and behavior are flawed, people become troubled and troubling to others. When also their beliefs and values are in muddle, confusion and disorientation become the norm. None escapes the insidious but cumulative effects of muddled structures, beliefs, or values. One way or another, even the healthiest members succumb to their corrosive influences. In time, muddled and confused existence becomes the order of the day.

Contemporary Somalis have inherited a muddled mix of structures, beliefs, and values, and they carry on life as if the jumble were the natural order of the world. Because they do little to analyze and change their predicament and jumbled legacies, the muddle of incompatible structures, beliefs, and values produces muddled thought, policies, and behavior. In fact, the muddle continues like untreated and growing cancer.

Three factors—the flawed state, the distorted clan system, and the malfeasant elite—are the most important causes of the muddle in Somali thought and action. We must understand the muddled mix of clan and state in order to identify the root causes of muddled existence in Somali society.

One basic principle of change is this: *change the social structure, and human behavior changes.* Here is another: *Change the core beliefs of people, then their thoughts, emotions, and subsequently their behavior change.* Thus change of the social structure or of core beliefs has more or less the same in effect, although by different means, each producing repercussion on the other. But before setting out to change the social structure or core beliefs, it is necessary to understand how they became *eco-pathogenic*—an environment that frustrates human needs, producing pathologies of history and existence.

Following colonial occupation of Somali territories, Europeans imposed the state—a political organization that monopolized the use of violence in society. At the same time, the previously stateless Somalis held on to the clan system with which they organized, governed, and sustained themselves. The colonizers enlarged and empowered the state while marginalizing the clan system. Unable to destroy the clan system altogether, they left intact aspects of it that served their goals, undermining features impeding their divide-and-rule policy.

In time, the two systems—clan and the state—intermingled and clashed, producing on the one hand coerced order and fragile peace, on the other simmering confusion and conflict that mostly remained dormant until post-independence when Somalis discovered that the coerced order, the fragile peace, and the simmering conflict were integral component of the state they inherited from colonial rulers. In addition, the interaction of the two systems gradually altered the state and the clan system from their original forms. The result of their combination was a jumbled mix of incompatible authority structures and power relations that gained life of their own, contributing to a succession of disasters. This becomes clear when we understand each in its original form and distinct history.

The State and Clan System

The state and the clan system have a long history and they moved in two different trajectories. After a long period of gestation and development, the state emerged in Europe. Its beginning goes back to ancient Greece and the Roman Empire when agriculture was the predominant sources of livelihood. In this agrarian system, over 80 percent of the population consisted of slaves and a small minority owned not only the land but also the slaves. On each plantation, the owner of land and slaves was king; he also took the entire surplus and lived in luxury.

The decline of the Roman Empire was followed by the Middle Ages (roughly from 500 to about 1350.) Technological improvement in agriculture and transportation brought in the thirteenth century the dissolution of feudalism and the beginning of modern capitalism. Increase in production and population stimulated growth of towns, in turn encouraging on the one hand urban migration of the nobility to seek more wealth, on the other swarms of peasants to look for work after they were dislocated by the enclosure movement and poverty.

Migration to the cities increased capital investment and pool of cheap labor for industries. Improvement in shipbuilding lowered cost of transportation. Inventions like the telescope and the compass enabled long-distant navigation that advanced growth of trade and commerce. Monetization of economic tasks brought new class of people selling their labor; this in turn enlarged the profits of capitalists who, by investing more capital, earned more profit.

By the fifteenth century, the new capitalist class (known also as the middle class or the bourgeoisie) began to replace the nobility in dominating the economic and social system. In fact, the emergence of the nation-state marked the growing economic and political dominance of the new class who allied themselves with monarchs seeking to defeat feudal rivals. At the same time, growth of industries, long-distance commerce, and the African slave trade increased the wealth and population of Europe.

Eric Williams and Walter Rodney explained in their seminal works the devastating consequences of the Triangular Trade and colonization on Africa. These works show that the rapid growth of capitalism in Europe and North America would not be possible without the exploitation of African human and material resources, that therefore the *underdevelopment* of Africa is directly related to the *development* of Europe and North America.[1]

As the middle-class gained greater political power, a shift in values and outlook took place in the old feudal. The associated paternalistic ethic that condemned greed, selfishness, and acquisitive behavior lost ground. Individualistic ethic that removed the moral restrictions against profit, selfishness, egoism, and acquisitive motives replaced the paternalistic ethic. In particular, the Protestant movement that rebelled against some doctrines of the Roman Catholic Church gave moral and religious justification for this new ethic that provided further impetus and justification for capitalism.

The feudal system, having proven obsolete to political and commercial needs, gave way to a new order better suited to the demands of the market. The rise of capitalism subsequently brought more reforms in not only to the old political, social, and religious outlook but also the institutions and practices of Europe. In addition, capital and skilled labor flowed where greater profits could be earned. To ensure that feudal princes do not hamper free flow of commerce and capital, the power and sovereignty of the state was increased, giving almost exclusive power to monarchs.

Many treaties, notably the Treaty of Westphalia in 1648 vested sovereignty in a central authority (the monarchy) to make and enforce laws. This treaty and others that followed gave special powers to this central authority. Firstly, the sovereign (the monarch) became be above the law. This meant that he made and enforced laws, limited only by self-imposed constraint. Secondly, the treaty made inviolable the territorial integrity of each state and promoted noninterference in its internal affairs. Enormous power thus centralized in the state and the king, both protected from external interference. As a result, Europeans were able to develop stable societies enabling peaceful exchange of goods and therefore growth of capitalism.

By the seventeenth and eighteenth centuries, European societies gradually changed the political order dominated by the monarchy and the church, making it more compatible to the newly emerging economic and social orders. The old social and psychic structures (resting on unquestioned obedience to and dependence on feudal authority) also changed to meet the requirements of the emerging market-driven society where division of labor engaged individuals in different means of earning livelihood while social classes differentiated on income and access to power. Moreover, expression of individuality grew in the marketplace, politics, and the family. Public participation in political decision also enlarged, permitting individuals more political and social rights in society.

The late eighteenth and early nineteenth centuries brought the Industrial Revolution—a period of unprecedented technological innovation resulting in increase of human productivity, wealth, and improved standard of living, albeit in uneven pace for the different classes. The same period also brought demand for social justice and organized revolts against exploitation of the industrial workers and farmers. In response to these demand and revolts, the state incorporated reforms that included more checks and balance of power, protecting citizens from the obvious abuses that earlier generations of Europeans had known. In time, state *sovereignty* translated into state *responsibility*. Although the state continued its original function of maintaining law and order, managing and preventing conflict, it gave in to demands for representation which in turn made the state legally and fiscally more accountable to citizens than it had known in the past.[2]

By the eighteenth century, the state acceded to *civil rights* of individuals, including equality before the law, the right to own property, and freedom of speech, press and assembly. By the nineteenth century, citizens attained increased *political rights,* including participation in political decision making in the form of universal suffrage. By the twentieth century, citizens demanded and obtained greater *social rights* including rights to welfare, education, health, and retirement.

Thus the state that began in feudalism with crude violence and exploitation, bolstered by old religious doctrine and justifications, increasingly became inclusive and responsive to citizens as it modified to accommodate new economic and political requirements. In fact, the concept of *citizenship* increasingly took on real meaning and substance when the state, under sustained pressure, granted civil, political, and social rights to citizens. In consequence, food production and populations grew, as did technology and commerce. At the same time, the demand for inclusion and equality of citizens found legal concessions that, though partially realized in practice, encouraged citizens to identify with and defend the nation-state.

In contrast to this evolution and trajectory of the state in Europe, a nomadic, pastoral people who moved from one location to another in search of grazing and water with the least material encumbrance developed the clan system. A family could load all its household possessions in a camel or two. The society had no centralized authority, not fixed in one geographic location, not coordinated by one administrative headquarters, nor founded on elaborate division of labor. Loosely organized, it had no monarchs, no salaried administrative personnel, no standing army, no fixed system of taxation, not even a written script. It functioned with a degree of disorganization, even managed chaos, permitting improvisation of rules as needed and promoting selective memory of the past in a population dependent on the spoken word.

This social structure moved Somalis on a path drastically different from that which Europeans treaded to become firstly masters of *things*, then of *people* whom they treated like *things*—no different from the fauna and flora of the lands they had occupied. Developed in conditions of material scarcity and competition for scant resources, the clan system evolved economic and political relations drastically different from the economic and political relations that gave rise to feudalism and capitalism in Europe. The segregation and humiliation meted out for the Gabooye and the Tumaals, the repositories of traditional technology and medicine, show the low priority traditional culture gave to the world of things whose mining and molding, planting and harvesting, manufacturing and distributing not only satisfy human needs and wants but also advance intellectual, commercial, and technological development.

The primary goal of the clan system is not wealth accumulation or development of central authority or promotion of technology but ensuring basic survival of members. To achieve this goal, the traditional system socializes members to identify exclusively in terms of lineage, differentiating layers of kinship extending from the nuclear family to an ever-widening circle of people. Rote learning of genealogy provided illiterate population a simple cognitive map guiding them on who they are, where they belong in their world divided into clans, and what rights and responsibilities they can expect as members of a clan. Encoded in genealogy is thus the identity and history of groups.

Because the division of society based on genealogy promotes group identity and cohesion learned in the nuclear family, the clan simulates the *family writ large*, building on the emotional and social bonding learned in childhood. Accident of birth, not individual merit or achievement, determines clan membership—hence once a member of a clan, always a member, the same way a member of the nuclear family remains such forever, even if the person were retarded or insane. The clan thus comprises members of different abilities and personalities, including the competent and the incompetent, the genius and the idiot, the kind and the cruel, the courageous and the coward, the generous and the miserly. Its goal of clan survival forces it to tolerate within-group differences, serve the majority, and abhor change.

To accommodate this diversity within the group and remain comprehensible to all, the clan system functions at or below average talent and contribution of its members. For the same reason, it also forsakes the gains accruing from rewarding individual talent and merit that would advance technological and social development. Though the egalitarian tradition and the unpredictable exigencies of the semi-desert permitted individuals a significant degree of freely expressing opinion and personal initiative, the stability and cohesion of the clan system needs to fulfill its function also impose clan tyranny and partisan morality at the expense of individuality and universal morality.[3]

While the clan system aims to save and serve the majority of its members, the individual too, always embedded and submerged in the clan, defends his clan, right or wrong, and dispenses justice and generosity only to clan members. The clan also controls mistreatment of clan members, but not abuse of people outside the clan unless they fit especial categories (like women, children, elderly, religious leaders, etc.) who are protected by the ethic of *bir-magaydo.* It also condones looting property (camels), causing injury, or even committing homicide outside the clan. Only fear of clan revenge, not internalized universal moral standards, modulate and control social behavior. Similarly, shame and guilt have meaning and restraining power only within the clan, but revenge and fear of it control behavior toward others outside the clan.

The tradition of violence outside the clan reached such extremes that some clans required young men to use the murder of an "enemy" or even a stranger as rite of passage to manhood, the head or testicles of the victim as trophy, the proof of valor. Probably other Somali clans had similar tradition but they abandoned the gruesome ritual because heads and testicles, including their own, would be in short supply. On the other hand, the tradition of camel looting and clan revenge persisted in all clans; the elite re-directed the tradition to looting the state treasury and employing state violence, as we shall see later.

Thus, whereas the plantation served as the nucleus of economic and social relations for feudal society, the factory and the market the hub of capitalist production and exchange, the pastoral society made the nuclear family and genealogy the crucible of identity, kinship, and social as well as political relations. Traditional Somalis developed the ascetic self-denial and stoic indifference with which they met scarcity and hardship. Hence they did not expend energy to produce goods beyond what is necessary for basic survival; they did not accumulate wealth for its sake, and they did not develop markets for exchange of goods and labor—behavior and relations essential to the development of capitalism, differentiation of social classes, and evolution of the state.

On the contrary, the traditional Somalis gave primacy to subjective gains (like clan and personal honor or prestige) when survival of the individual and group was assured. Even the herds of camels that pastoralists consider the most valuable material possession and the enticing allure of looting provided mostly for honor and prestige, not for consumption or profit. Preferring also stability, they avoided change. Being highly conservative, they sought to preserve the old beliefs, values, and norms handed down by past generations. The majority living at subsistence level, with little investment in production and accumulation of material resources, social classes also did not differentiate and evolve.

Although frequent wars erupted in pastoral communities over pasture, water, and clan honor, no revolutions in thought, politics, technology, and society resulted. The victors were satisfied with enlarging grazing land, their herd, and clan honor. They imposed no system of governance, no taxation, not even their genealogy. The vanquished kept their clan system, their clan identity, and most of their land if they did not migrate to another territory. In the meantime, they garnered men and arms to even the score whenever possible. Thus, as the tit-for-tat of attack and revenge continued, little changed in the structure, beliefs and values of society. The most visible spoils of war were mostly camels, grazing land, and clan honor—not changed systems, practices, or state of mind.

Consolidating the essential conservatism of the culture, Somalis embraced the rituals of Islam prescribed for worship, without benefiting from Islam's long and rich contributions to science, mathematics, medicine, philosophy, and jurisprudence. Somalis did not benefit from this Islamic revolution because their link to the Islamic world were two essentially conservative societies—Yemen and Saudi Arabia—neither of them significantly affected by this revolution.[4] Relying also on rote learning of religious texts in a foreign language (Arabic), they held on to the basic liturgy and interpretation of the faith that illiterate and non-Arabic-speaking population easily comprehend and practice.

Little wonder then that to this day Somalis conveniently invoke fatalism—that all is predestined—to excuse lack of personal drive and discipline. Fatalism also provides ready-made defense for individual irresponsibility and lethargy, a quick rejection of all critical thought and analysis. an abiding desire to follow the herd for fear of straying into the precipice of hellfire which, according to the sermons of half-literate preachers teeming society, is only a step away in any direction one moves, if it is not blazing right under one's feet. Thus, instead of seeking causes for problems or working for change, one avoids to question authority or outcome of action and to endure suffering with one crisp remark, "All was meant to happen in this way!"—hence, it is futile to worry, question, or plan in a world where everything is predestined.

Yet, in essence, the clan system achieved the goal of promoting survival of members in the semi-desert where human and animal predators abound. However, since every solution has its own hidden limitations, the drawbacks of the clan system surfaced in due course. For instance, success of traditional society in its goal of achieving survival was adequate so long as Somalis remained isolated from political and economic currents elsewhere in the world. Its fundamental limitations surfaced when Somalis encountered in the late nineteenth century Europeans armed with superior technology and using better organization for war.

As we have seen in Chapters 2 and 3, Somalis were politically, socially, and psychologically unprepared to protect themselves and their freedom from colonial occupation, partition, and rule. Even when they put up formidable resistance lasting for twenty years, as did the Dervishes, the first aerial bombardment in Africa quickly ended their resistance. The British who could not quell this resistance by conventional war for twenty years did so by unleashing aerial bombardment for about a month in 1920.

In one of his last poems, Mohamed Ábdulle Hassan explained his utter befuddlement and despair when the aerial bombardments left him and his forces no option but to flee. To one of his detractors who jeered his flight, he responded thus with his usually candid words:

Their echoing boom filled the sky and earth
Flying vultures they brought from Aden [in Yemen)
Well, tell me Smart Alec, what else can one do but flee? [6]

A year after the aerial bombardment crushed his movement, Mohamed Ábdulle Hassan died of influenza in the area of Iimay. Following the defeat of his forces, the state in its distorted form was imposed on Somalis without the economic and social foundation that brought about and supported its development in Europe.

It was not only Mohamed Ábdulle Hassan and his dervish forces who, befuddled and demoralized, found flight the most sensible option when "vultures" rained down devastating bombs on them. Somalis have since been befuddled and demoralized by a succession of predators using lethal weapons, including airplanes, to subjugate and rule them. As I explained in Chapters 10, even the Somali government unleashed its own set of "vultures" that rained deadly bombs on the Isaaq in 1988, forcing the survivors to flee to refugee camps in Ethiopia.

Exactly eighty-seven years after the defeat of Mohamed Ábdulle Hassan, the 'vultures" also came back in 2007 to defeat the Union of Islamic Courts, leaving some of its leaders no sensible option but to flee to Eritrea. This time, Ethiopia and the United States brought and piloted the 'vultures" that rained down deadly bombs claiming more lives than those which forced Mohamed Ábdulle Hassan and his forces to flee. I discuss the irony and consequences of the latest comeback of the "vultures" in *Return of Cain—Why Freedom Eludes Somalis.*

Not only did the state and the clan system emerge in drastically different social and political conditions but also they moved their respective societies in contrasting trajectories. Whereas one engaged in the world of things for use and surplus value, the other gave priority to group survival and clan honor in a harsh environment. Whereas one welcomed change and modified its moral and religious precepts accordingly, the other clung to stability and conservative orientation to life. Whereas one encouraged individual talent and technological advancement, the other gave primacy to group uniformity and cohesion, even at the cost of clan tyranny and poverty. Whereas one developed a concept of citizenship, theoretically associated with inalienable rights for all, the other conferred 'citizenship' only to members of the clan.

Muddle of Structures

The Europeans who colonized and partitioned Somalis in the late nineteenth century were products of the European history and culture sketched above. Energized by ambition for power, driven by pursuit of profit, and armed with sophisticated technology, they colonized a people stuck in insular mode of adaptation that changed little for centuries. That is, the material production and cultural adaptation of traditional Somalis were not only different from frozen in historical, economic, and political conditions giving rise to the state and capitalism in Europe but also they were 'frozen' in time, space, and mind.

A clash of cultures and systems was therefore inevitable when Europeans imposed the state on hitherto stateless and classless but clan-based Somalis. In addition, the state Europeans imposed was substantially different from its European prototype in at least three respects. Firstly, the state imposed on Somalis by violence was an alien system that had not organic link to the culture and history of the colonized. Secondly, it lacked the political and legal controls that checked abuse of power in Europe. For instance, it did not safeguard rights of political representation, rights to integrity of body and property, freedom of speech and assembly, writ of *habeas corpus* against illegal imprisonment. Thirdly, the *raison d'etre* of the state imposed on Somalis was not to serve society or even a specific class within it but to uniformly oppress and exploit the conquered population.

The state alone did not change from its prototype when transplanted in Somali society. The clan system too modified and distorted from its original form during colonial rule. Colonial rulers were not social engineers who had the best interest of the ruled in mind. Unable to do away with the clan system, they suppressed aspects of it—for instance *clan fusion* (unity) and joint defense—that opposed their colonial aims and they retained other aspects—for instance *clan fission* (disunity) and inter-clan conflict—that promoted divide-and-rule. The selective suppression and retention of traditional society resulted in uneven and incoherent changes in the indigenous structures and values of traditional society.

Though the state in Europe of the late nineteenth and twentieth centuries improved significantly the political and social rights of the ruled, the version of it transplanted in Africa degenerated to almost its sixteenth century or even feudal version. Its degeneration was not only a product of the crude despotism colonial administrators; most Europeans, including even their intellectual luminaries also approved its crass and callous application of it in Africa. For instance, John Stuart Mill, the English philosopher and economist, had stated, "Despotism is a legitimate mode of government in dealing with barbarians, provided the end be their improvement."[5] In other words, European abuse of power and economic exploitation were justified so long as white men concocted claims that such practices benefited Africans who supposedly did not know what is good for them or act on their behalf.

Worse, as we have seen in Chapters 2 and 5, the most brutal version of Benito Mussolini's fascism became the foundation of the state in the Italian colony. The fascist state influenced the worldview and practices of the local elite while it crushed the rest of the population with its draconian measures. Except for a short period during the British Military Administration, which itself was highly violent and oppressive, the fascist state—with its Mafiosi-type tactics of cruelty, corruption, nepotism—continued to shape the form of political system and ethos that were to emerge in Somalia after independence. The ten-years of UN Trusteeship that might have reversed the legacy of fascism and Mafiosi tactics kept it in place when Italy took responsibility to "prepare" Somalia for independence.

The union of the former Italian colony with the former British Protectorate, far from changing or diluting these legacies and tactics, only disseminated wide and institutionalized the buccaneer-type of looting the state treasury and abuse of power the elite had learned under the fascist state. Because also Somalia's local elite had obtained greatest leadership role in post-independence—while Mogadishu became the hub of Somali politics, business, and education—the legacies of fascism and its crude tactics infected other Somalis, deepening among Somalis everywhere the misinterpretation of politics as *Polly tricks* in pursuit of individual or clan superiority in power, wealth, and prestige.

Not that the elite of Somaliland were any more ethical than those of Somalia or that they grew up in a more democratic state, but they lived under a form of colonial rule whose administrators were very few, detached, and minimally interested in developing the authority. The British invested little on Somaliland and their tight control on expenditure gave little room for corruption. The schools were comparatively fewer, entrance requirements more competitive, fees required too high except for wealthy families or those willing to sell their livestock. Hence, the number of local elite emerging in Somaliland was small; even then, cheap Indian expatriates filled most positions below British administrators. Applying also indirect rule in the Protectorate, the British type of colonial rule was less intrusive to the traditional culture and clan system than its Italian counterpart. The latter, as we have seen in Chapter 5, used massive violence and dislocation of the indigenous culture in its program of rigid control and establishing white settlers with large plantations.

After the union of the two former colonies, the Somaliland elite—more naïve and fewer than their southern partners—quickly caved in and emulated their southern partners. Equally influenced by a culture that encouraged looting outside the clan and by colonial education that predisposed them to class entitlement, the Somaliland elite responded in the manner of the opportunist suggested by one proverb: *Meel aan doonaayey baa roob ma igu heelay!*—to the very place I wanted, didn't [auspicious] rain force my drift to it! Thus, without questions or qualms, the Somaliland elite too, misinterpreting independence as license for get-rich-quick schemes and wresting personal power using any means, happily joined the stampede for plunder of the state.

Further, the union of the two former colonies, prompted more by emotion than reason and plan, only augmented the muddle of structures and colonial legacies. The Somalis elite under Italian British rule had cut their teeth in different systems of administration, laws and law enforcement, and judicial procedures. To carry out official business, they even spoke different lingua franca—Italian for Somalia, English for Somaliland. It took years to reduce the muddle and the mutual incomprehension, but not enough thought and energy went into building a coherent and sustainable system of governance.

The elite were preoccupied with internal competition for power-grab and wealth. Hence, the mix of the two colonial systems aggravated the muddle that each territory inherited. When the jumble formed into a system, the result was neither fish nor fowl, muddle of systems and practices that not only confused the public but also allowed the *Klan* of the two former colonies to carry on their class mischief. In fact, the muddle did not stay at the level of political and social structures. It also permeated beliefs and values that further amplified the befuddled existence of Somalis had known before the former colonies united.

Muddle of Beliefs and Values

In his pioneering works, *The Protestant Ethic and the Spirit of Capitalism,* Max Weber detailed how psychological traits—like hard and methodic work, diligence and self-discipline, active mastery and pursuit of material gain, self-denial of immediate gratification, both materially and emotionally—had played critical role in the rise and growth of capitalism in Western Europe. Even the most radical anti-capitalists (like Lenin and the Bolsheviks) conceded the vital significance of these traits for economic and social development. In addition, the remarkable advances of Japan and other Asian countries confirm the vital role of these traits to economic and technological development.

When we examine Somali culture and psychology, we discover that the traits Max Weber called the *Protestant Ethic*—including hard work and active mastery for personal gain, self-discipline and controlled emotion, frugality and calculated accumulation based on self-denial—are incompatible with what I call the *Pastoral Ethos* that Somalis internalize in childhood and reenact in society. By Pastoral Ethos, I mean the core beliefs and values that distinguish and guide Somali pastoralists. Core beliefs and values—usually global, inflexible, and resistant to change—influence the thought and behavior of people socialized into them in childhood and later sustained by habit and social relations.

I detail the Pastoral Ethos in. Suffice it to mention here that the Pastoral Ethos encourages members to:

- Consider genealogy as key to human relations; that therefore one should never disregard it in dealing with others;
- Be proud of your clan because it is superior to other clans;
- Help and defend the clan, right or wrong;
- Always remain vigilant of clan enemies lurking to take vengeance,
- Most of all, beware of authority outside the clan for it only seeks to deceive and oppress your clan;
- Accept looting other clans is not only acceptable but also a display of bravery;
- Realize that what is owned collectively is owned by none; therefore appropriate it if you can take and defend it;
- Immediately gratify needs for you may die sooner than you think;

- Recognize that only misers accumulate wealth while the noble share; and
- Work hard of necessity, but enjoy leisure every chance you get.

It is obvious from the above that the Pastoral Ethos Somalis internalize early in life and reinforced by society in the life cycle of the individual is in profound contradiction with the ethics of inclusion, equality, nationalism, hard work, and even law and order as defined and expected in contemporary society. Faced with these contradictory values, Somalis prefer to follow the Pastoral Ethos deeply ingrained in their psyche and reinforced by their society.

Is it any wonder then that the ruling elite compulsively act nepotistic, loot the public treasury, surround themselves with clan loyalists, and treat other clans as their sworn enemies when they show the slightest sign of opposition? Is it any wonder too that the majority of Somalis are devoid of nationalism but steeped in clannism, that they envy and admire those who behave according to the Pastoral Ethos even when all—the elite and the public alike—recited the sermon of nationalism, equality, and justice?

A most virulent aspect of the Pastoral Ethos, inciting hatred and conflict among Somalis, is what I call *Delusion of Clan Superiority* that all Somalis harbor due to childhood socialization and subsequently reinforced by society. Because Somalis internalize in childhood the delusion—by definition is a false belief—it nests in the unconscious of even the most enlightened Somalis. The delusion is a culturally induced neurosis all Somali suffer in one way or another. The crass and violent features of the delusion lie dormant or superficially controlled in time of social peace and interpersonal harmony, but they surge among the elite and the public with irresistible force in time of clan conflict and political campaigns of the *Klan*.

The delusion has several key aspects. First, the clan divides the world as "us" versus "them." Second, it compares itself to other clans using the mythic mode where sensory and rational data have no persuasive or restraining force. Third, the clan chooses for comparison only criteria favorable to it, often distorting facts to its advantage. It associates "our clan" with "the good" and "their clan" with "the bad"—treating these conclusions as incontestable truths.

Delusion of clan superiority runs the gamut from speculation on population size, land quality, ancestral nobility, and/or other fictional criterion.

Table 1 illustrates how Somalis express the delusion of clan superiority by contrasting "our clan" with "their clan."

Table 1
Delusion of Clan Superiority

OUR CLAN	THEIR CLAN
1. We are the majority – the largest in size.	1. They are a minority – fewer than us.
2. We possess the largest/richest land.	2. They inhabit smaller/poorer land.
3. We have a glorious past.	3. They have an infamous past.
4. Nobility runs in our blood.	4. They are ignoble by birth.
5. We are related to the Prophet .	5. Nobody knows their origin.
6. We are blessed.	6. They are cursed.
7. We possess culture and honor.	7. They have no culture or honor.
8. We confer honor to in-laws.	8. They bring disgrace to in-laws.
9. We are generous and kind.	9. They are miserly and mean.
10. We are courageous.	10. They are cowards.
11. We are rational and flexible.	11. They are irrational and rigid.
12. We are honest and hard-working people.	12. They are thieves and thugs.
13. We are fair and just.	13. They are unfair and unjust.
14. We are open to dialogue and negotiation.	14. They respect only violence.
15. We deserve to rule.	15. They deserve to be ruled.
16. We do not get our fair share of power.	16. They have the lion's share of power.

Distorting sensory data which can be objectively verified, the delusion contradicts even objectively verified or verifiable findings like census and geologic studies. For instance, members claim that "our clan" is larger than "their clan". Although we can empirically test this claim, there is no census on clans or generally on the population. Even if there were census, each clan would inflate its number by moving to the next level of segmentation, or it would claim the census biased.

Similarly, we can objectively test the claim that "our clan" possesses the largest or richest land, but there is no documentation on clan territories. If the available facts contradict the claim, one still asserts that "our clan" has richer land than "their clan." Alternatively, one changes tactics by simply asserting that the land has more unexplored minerals or untapped agricultural possibilities. In fact, there will never be a census or geologic findings that Somalis will universally accept as fair and accurate so long as the delusion of clan superiority dominates thought and social relations. As with other forms of neuroses, like the phobic and conversion disorders, the delusion of clan superiority is not persuaded by logic and empirical truth. Rooted in subjective fixation, the delusion is its own truth, impervious to proof.

Since the delusion rests on a Manichean division of the world—"us" versus "them"—even outsiders who come up with estimates or conclusions contradicting a clan's delusion will be condemned to have their hidden agenda or siding with the opposing clan.

Illustrating the dissatisfaction of Somalis steeped in the delusion of clan superiority is the distribution and land settlements of major Somali clans presented by the *CIA World Factbook* in Figure 3 below. Almost all Somalis will take offense in one way or another to distribution of "Somali Ethnic Groups" presented in the Sourcebook.

Figure 3

Somali 'Ethnic Groups'

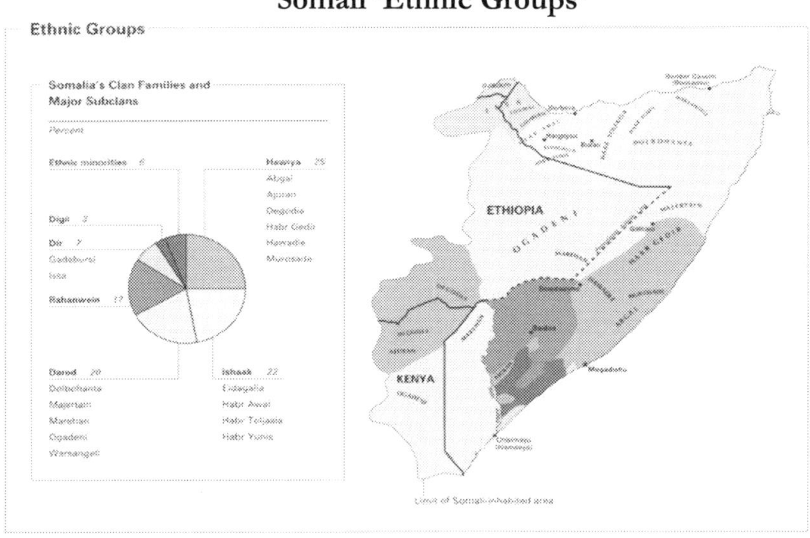

From Wikipedia, the free encyclopedia

Scanning the above map and clan distribution, some Somalis will find fault with the percent estimation of their number, others with the land size allocated to them, still others with their inclusion in one group, their exclusion altogether, or how their name is changed. Typically, every clan has its own fixed notion of their number, land size, and clan composition or purity. Anything contradicting their fixed notion, they condemn as inaccurate or infer hidden agenda of the estimator. Hence, the delusion of clan superiority is not only a self-fulfilling prophesy but also a belief impervious to both the sensory data and the judgment of outsiders. To be sure, cite the above figure not to affirm or disconfirm its information but only to illustrate that it serves like a Rorschach test for delusion of clan superiority among Somalis.

Often, the delusion is most intense among clans/sub-clans living in close proximity to each other. It also intensifies when clans are embroiled in conflict. For these clans, contest on delusion of clan superiority precedes and motivates armed conflict. Taking up arms is only an escalation of a war that began with words long ago. In addition, the delusion dehumanizes the other as categorical inconvertible "enemy"—a conclusion that removes guilt and shame not only the kill the specific opponent but also to slaughter his kin. If the tradition of clan revenge also kicks in its indiscriminate murder and mayhem, the conflict that started at the level of subjectivity enlarges into a group disaster. God forbid that poems of valor and defeat are not recited to remind generations of their obligation to avenge aggrieved ancestors!

Because training in delusion of clan superiority starts in childhood, it endures for a long time, often outliving the individual as he or she passed it on to younger generations. That parents, sibling, and extended family instill the delusion, associating it love and loyalty for one another with hate and aggression on others, intensifies the delusion and nest in the psyche. Take for instance how traditional mothers encourage their children to drink milk: *Haddii aanad dhaqo caanaha dhamin, Wallee waxa kaa booby qowlaysatadii reer hebel!*—'If you don't quickly drink your milk, by God, the bandits of clan so-and-so's will loot and gobble it up!' In response, the child gobbles down the milk before the enemy lurking nearby loots the cup of milk.

From a loving and nurturing source, the child learns that he and his clan alone have something valuable others clans lack and want to plunder, that therefore he must at all times keep vigilant. Often the clan portrayed to be so cruel as to plunder a child's milk is not distant, geographically and perhaps genealogically. The image of that clan or generally "the enemy" remains etched in the psyche of the child, lying dormant until some conflict later in life exhumes it violent defense or at least guarded apprehension toward that clan or generally toward people. The delusion therefore instills not only pride but also paranoia.

Just as clans competed for material necessities in the harsh ecology of the semi-desert, they also competed for nobility, honor, and prestige in a society where everyone lived at subsistence level. Often, loss in competition for material resources (usually water and grazing land) also entailed loss of nobility, honor, or prestige. In fact, pursuit of honor and prestige as well as material gain motivated the tradition of camel looting. The clan that looted with impunity proved its superiority in power and bravery.

Force was therefore the final arbiter of who gained materially and subjectively. Size of the clan and its ability to mobilize violence also correlated with how much of the tangible resources (e.g. pasture and livestock) and intangible rewards (e.g. honor and prestige) the clan obtained. Following victory, the clan always exaggerated its achievement and its offspring took this victory as proof of their clan's permanent superiority. Thus, the delusion quickly transmuted to the *mythic mode* that rests on irrational and subjective processes, in contrast to the *sensory mode* based on rational and verifiable observation.[7]

The clan unable to defend itself and its members from external contest over material and subjective rewards suffered abuse, exploitation, and possibly obliteration of its lineage, thereby losing it clan identity and becoming an ancillary unit of a more powerful clan. Thus if the clan survived physical annihilation, it suffered psychological and social death, as illustrated by the history and predicament of the Gabooye, the segregated and despised clan in Somali society, almost equivalent to the Untouchables of India. At bottom, the fear of being reduced to the status of the Gabooye, hence oppressed and segregated, is the source of the culturally induced neurosis.

The segregation and disparagement of the Gabooye remain largely in enforce to this day and therefore the delusion of clan superiority controls the psyche of other Somalis. Deep down, then, every Somali clan dreads the prospect of slipping down into the derogated status and fate of the Gabooye. To avoid this prospect, every clan puts strenuous effort to defend its material possession and honor. Yet doubt and insecurity assails every clan at the level of the unconscious; hence, each clan consciously exaggerated its virility and greatness.

That is why Somalis cling, as if by instinct, to clan loyalty and pride even when they reside abroad and objectively have little to fear of skidding down to the status and fate of the Gabooye. That is also why in contemporary politics every clan wants one or more of its members to assume power—as president, cabinet member, or legislator—to reassure itself that its secret dread of clan inferiority is baseless and that, on the contrary, it has reason to feel noble and honorable.

The Delusion in Politics

Following migration to the cities, the elite have exploited the delusion of clan superiority to rally kinsmen in competition for personal power and wealth. With little or no hope of economic improvement, the ordinary people on their part found in the delusion of clan superiority a bubble of security in the herd and promise of vicariously obtaining subjective satisfaction from the misrule by their kinsmen in power. Falling back on the mythic mode, they use the formal position of kinsmen in government as *proof* of clan honor and superiority.

For instance, the clan that finds one or more of its members in key posts—like president, cabinet minister, or commander of the armed—feels victorious, vindicated, and secure even if majority of its members are objectively in worse economic conditions in comparison to clan members. They are convinced that critics of the regime are also opponents of the clan, as if their clan alone has eternal contract of political hegemony and monopoly of state resources. If the regime caves in to the opposition, bringing new leaders to power, they self-righteously declare, "Our regime and rights have been wrested by clan so-and-so." Hence, they wait for their day when they can take revenge and even the score.

On the other hand, the clans that have no members in key posts of government feel vulnerable, offended, and insecure. They look at the state as an alien force of occupation and misrule. They distrust it because the pastoral ethic affirms: "beware of authority outside the clan, for it only seeks to deceive and oppress your clan." Besides, their delusion of clan superiority is disproved and frustrated. The delusion rests on comparative advantage or misery, not objective criteria. While one clan enjoys the symbols of power and therefore is prepared to risk life for defense of the regime, the other is poised to wrest the symbols of power denied to them and equally ready to risk life for these symbols when their threshold of insecurity, inferiority, or frustration intensifies.

Thus because the state has become not only a means by which the elite attain power and wealth but also a screen on which ordinary Somalis project their delusion of clan superiority and securing vicarious satisfaction, it is caught in perpetual conflict and instability. Many armed conflicts in Somali society derive from such ill-defined and subjective causes often missed by outsiders, as demonstrated by the fourteen failed reconciliation conferences sponsored by the international community for Somalia.

Traditional theories of the West, be they Marxist or liberal, often ignore the important role played by contest over subjective rewards in pastoral societies. Emphasizing material motives, they miss a good deal of what preoccupies and torments people who exist at subsistence level, with little interest in accumulating wealth. Little wonder Somali conflicts baffle the outsider who takes standard approaches. Because they ignore the underlying subjective causes, Somali armed conflicts seem to them convoluted, incomprehensible and elusive. The conferences of reconciliation they sponsor and the agreements signed with fanfare and in plush hotels abroad repeatedly fail because the essential motives provoking and sustaining conflict are misunderstood.

Worse, as I demonstrate in *Return of Cain*, these conferences not only recreated the flawed state which repeatedly failed Somalis but also they installed the same inept elite exploiting the muddle of structures and values including the delusion of clan superiority. That recreating the flawed state and installing the inept to power the same inept elite were doomed to failure would be obvious if the sponsors took into account the muddle of structures, beliefs, and values that give Somali politics their peculiar turns and dizzying twists.

The system of governance that best allows the elite to grab personal power and wealth, at the same affords their kinsmen a bone to gnaw on in order to satisfy their passion for clan honor is either clan hegemony or clan oligarchy which characterizes the auto-colonial rule recreated in Somali society since independence. We therefore must understand how oligarchy and hegemony emerge in Somalis society, subsequently explaining the inner contours and dynamics of the auto-colonial state.

From Hegemony to Oligarchy

In chapter 10, I outlined four forms of hegemony and oligarchy that emerge in Somali society and I presented historical data to demonstrate their operation from 1960-1991. To comprehend why the Somali state fails so often and bogs down in incessant conflict, we must understand not only the structural flaws and muddled values but also the following essential principles or use of power in Somali society:

1. Given history and socialization, *the so-called Somali elite operative in either of two forms of rule—oligarchy or hegemony*—their preference being oligarchy even at the risk of incurring the wrath and envy of their peers within the elite who on their part try to bring down the sky until they turn over the table and concentrate power in their hands;
2. *Hegemony sooner or later degenerates into oligarchy and oligarchy to dictatorship*—a degeneration that pushes society into succession of conflicts making the state dysfunctional or causing its total collapse; and
3. Since there are no clear and robust institutions for checking abuse of state power and resources in Somali society, *misrule by means of hegemony, oligarchy, or dictatorship reinvent themselves* causing conflict, state collapse, material ruin, and trauma.

The discussion below highlights how Somalis reenacted ad nauseam these three principles of power since independence from 1960-1991. The diagram below sketches the transition from oligarchy of one type to hegemony and back to oligarchy of another type in Somali society since colonial rule to the collapse of the state in 1991.

Note that the transition simultaneously takes place at the level of clan and social class which constantly interact because the ruling elite are members of both social classes and clans, readily exploiting the identity that best serves their interest at a given point.

Diagram 3

Hegemony and Oligarchy by Clan and Class

1880 -1991

CLAN	Race Oligarchy 1880 - 1960	Clan Hegemony 1960 – 1975	Clan Oligarchy 1976 - 1980	Sub-clan Oligarchy 1981 - 1991
CLASS	Race/Class Oligarchy 1880 - 1960	Class Hegemony 1960 - 1969	Dictatorship & Class Oligarchy 1970 - 1991	

In brief, the former Somali Republic, later named the Somali Democratic Republic, began with *race oligarchy* during the colonial era. After independence, *class hegemony* of the elite replaced the rule of a few Europeans supported by their powerful governments and local minions. After independence, Somali politics shifted to hegemony, oligarchy, or a combination of the two using class or clan configuration.

Colonial rule (1880-1960) was by its nature oligarchic—a few white men, supported by powerful European governments ruled with iron fist without the consent of the governed. This period was characterized by both race and class oligarchy, although the race factor was most fundamental. Colonial rule ended in 1960 and the class oligarchic system it put in place remained intact with some window-dressing by the Somali elite.

The civilian elite who inherited the state grew under this oligarchic system of colonial rule. They understood change mainly as replacing white oligarchs with black oligarchs with façade of being democratic and inclusive. Though the ruling wanted to reproduce the oligarchy they knew in the past, they sought to accommodate public demand for freedom and desire for broad inclusion in governance. Hence they established a parliament in which many members of the elite could feel included; they also set up the ritual of periodic elections by which clans could elect their most vociferous and tenacious politicians to represent their interest in the National Assembly.

The National Assembly, comprised of 135 members, was at first a powerful institution in comparison to the oligarchic system of colonial rule. For instance, the members elected the President, they approved his nominee for Prime Minister and other cabinet ministers, they proposed and ratified legislation, and they influenced the national budget. Theoretically, then, a democratic system of government was in place which included a relatively large number of the elite in governance and enabled most clans participation through their elected representatives.

In reality, however, the actual arrangement of power was hegemonic—power distributed among a select group of the elite and certain clans enjoying dominant influence. In time, this hegemonic arrangement skewed toward oligarchy since only key members of the Somali Youth League obtained appointment to high office. Hence, the President, the Prime Minister, and most of the cabinet posts were members of the SYL, the largest political party in the land. In addition, the Mijeerteen had dominant representation not only in the high posts of government—two successive Prime Ministers and one President in the first nine years—but also they occupied key and dominant positions in the executive branch including the police force from Commander to the Regional chiefs of Police, as we have seen in the preceding chapters.

Yet so long as the elite accommodated one another in sharing power through different institutions—e.g. the legislature, the executive, and legislative branches—Somalis, the elite and the public alike, maintained fragile peace and tolerated frustration. But this status quo did not last long. The parliament, supposedly the institution where elected representatives spoke on behalf of constituencies and the nation, proved to be a den of self-styled looters of state power and resources. There they exchanged acrimony, favors, votes and government contracts. When they gave voice to the public, they also bought and sold votes, rigged elections, changed the outcome in their favor. In time, the veneer of class and clan hegemony gave way to class and clan oligarchy.

Thus, by the time Ábdirazaaq Haaji Hussein succeeded Ábdirashiid Áli Sharmaarke as Prime Minister, both of them leading members of the SYL and belonging to the Mijeerteen sub-clan of the Daarood, resentment began to build up against not only the fake parliament and elections but also the emerging class and clan oligarchy, as illustrated by a chant of the Hawiye:

Once Rashiid, then Rizaaq,
Are other people merely bread [for the feast]!

The election of Sharmaarke as President further intensified simmering resentment of other clans who felt excluded from share of power. It also alienated key members of the Mijeerteen who in the past partook in the class as well as the clan hegemony of the status quo ante. In fact, anger at Sharmaarke's accession to the Presidency was so intense that, as we have seen in Chapter 5, some of his former allies in the Daarood hegemony planned a failed plot to blow up the parliament building in the morning of his swearing-in ceremony.

Among the most ardent critic of the Sharmaarke-Égaal Government was Ábdirazaaq Haaji Hussein, a former ally of Sharmaarke when the two politicians along Mohamed Abshir Muuse—known as the "Croce del Sud Group" of the Mijeerteen—opposed Prime Minister Ábdulaahi Íise Mohamuud during the late nineteen-fifties. By 1967, the two former allies turned into sworn enemies The conflict between emerged after independence when Prime Minister Sharmaarke and President Aadan Ábdulle Ósmaan had serious political differences and the latter replaced Ábdirashiid with Ábdirazaaq for the post of Prime Minister. The Commander of the Police, General Mohamed Abshir Muuse allied himself with President Ósmaan, married to his aunt.

The break up of the former allies into feuding cliques within the Mijeerteen had other fallouts. General Mohamed Siyaad Barre, whom Ábdirazaaq supported to become the Commander of the Armed Forces after the death of General Daauud, also allied himself with Ábdirazaaq. In addition, while the feud of the two camps intensified after the election, the Sharmaarke-Égaal Government dismissed General Mohamed Abshir, the Commander of the Police. Rumors also circulated that Prime Minister Égaal was about 'promote' General Mohamed Siyaad Barre out of his job by sending him for training to the former USSR.

At least Mohamed Siyaad Barre did not wait quietly wait for his planned demotion or dismissal. In addition to rallying the intervention of key persons on his behalf, we know from General Ismaíil Áli Abokor's account, that he had planned a military coup early as 1967 when Sharmaarke became President. But he bid his time and made his move two years later when military coups were the fashion in Africa and public frustration with the civilian regime had intensified. Following assassination of Sharmaarke on October 15, 1969—an assassination in which Mohamed Siyaad Barre and other yet unconfirmed accomplices had a hand—the military coup took place on October 21, 1969. After herding the civilian politicians into prison, the coup leaders promised fundamental change.[10]

Since people believed and wanted to believe their promise, there were no obvious harbingers of the dictatorship or sub-clan oligarchy that would emerged in time, nor of the horrendous crimes the military regime would committed in its long reign. At first, the transition from class oligarchy to dictatorship, then from clan hegemony to sub-clan oligarchy, took place in gradual steps. Unlike the civilian ruling elite, the coup leaders did not disguise their class oligarchy with parliamentary façade or election rituals. They offered the nation no choice but the Supreme Revolutionary Council consisting of 25 members and their shadow civilian administration, the Council of Ministers. Moreover, socialist revolution was a convenient cover for outright oligarchy and use of violence against "anti-revolutionaries".

As the SRC members acceded to the wishes and decision of the "Old Man" partly as show of respect and partly due to underestimation of his skills, Mohamed Siyaad Barre increasingly concentrated power unto himself. The execution of General Mohamed Áynaanshe Guuleed and Colonel Salaad Gabeere Kediye gave him free hand to intimidate the other SRC members and rule society with iron fist. After he became the dictator, he weeded out potential opponents and surrounded himself with loyal cronies—first from different clans, later from his sub-clan, then from members of his family.

After the oligarchy of the armed forces changed to dictatorship, the class hegemony (involving different clans in the SRC and Council of Ministers) with which military regime began shifted to clan hegemony involving selected sub-clans of the Daarood, as illustrated by the M.O.D. alliance. Actually, Daarood hegemony began soon after the coup—as we saw in Chapter 6, eleven (40%) of 25 SRC members were Daarood, maintaining the old distribution of power that had favored the Daarood since independence. The Daarood also predominated the Council of Ministers since, of the 15 members in the Council, eight (53%) were Daarood.

Still, the revolutionary rhetoric and the public trance of the day predisposed the majority of Somalis to overlook this clan preponderance in both the SRC and the Council of Ministers. Typical to Somali lack of foresight and prevention, the non-Daarood (particularly the Isaaq and the Hawiye) ignored the growing Daarood hegemony evolving to oligarchy until it grew into a well-tuned and repressive machine. Somali history might have been different if they resisted it at the early stages when it was nascent, weak, and amenable to change. But this inattention and lack of foresight is characteristic of Somalis who tolerate dictatorship and oligarchy so long some of their kinsmen are included in the cabal to loot state resources and bask in power. They criticize or even take up arms against the regime only when systematically excluded from a share of the loot or they enjoy symbolic power and prestige.

By 1976, when the dictator caved in to Kremlin demand a political party, Mohamed Siyaad Barre put sub-clan oligarchy in full gear as he filled membership of the party with handpicked members of the Mareehaan and placed his most loyal kinsmen in key posts of the government. As mentioned in previous chapters, the troika of the M.O.D. alliance consisted of the Mareehaan (his clan), the Ogaadeen (his mother's clan) and the Dhulbahante (his son-in-law's clan)—all three of the Daarood clan. However, all began to unravel after 1977 when Mohamed Siyaad Barre invaded Ethiopia, confident that he would "liberate" the Somali territory Ethiopia occupied with European assistance under Emperor Menelik II.

Victory in "freeing" Somalis from Ethiopian rule would not only put Mohamed Siyaad Barre in the annals of Somali history but also turn public attention away from his failed revolution. But the dictator miscalculated, as did Benito Mussolini's entry into World War II only when he believed that Germany would come out the victor. Mohamed Siyaad Barre invaded Ethiopia when he realized that his revolution lost steam and thought internal conflicts weakened Ethiopia. However, the opportunism backfired when the former USSR on which he relied for arms and advisors changed sides and supported Ethiopia.

The fiasco of the war with Ethiopia brought two unanticipated consequences—on the one hand the weakening and demoralization of the armed forces the dictator depended upon to sustain his tyranny, on the other the emergence of armed clan opposition against his regime. In particular, the 1978 coup attempt confirmed the dictator's worst fears. Since 1969, Mohamed Siyaad Barre knew that the Mijeerteen who primarily controlled and benefited from the clan hegemony of the civilian administrations would challenge him. For nearly ten years, he managed them by carrot-and-stick policy, but their coup attempt forced him to rally the Mareehaan who by then they believed to the state to be their clan dominion.

Reliance on the Mareehaan had other consequences. The Daarood hegemony began to fizzle gradually, giving way to sub-clan oligarchy of the Mareehaan, though the unraveling of this clan hegemony took about a decade when clan cleansing brought the most sordid chapters in Somali history, erasing Somali belief in common destiny into a dark abyss with no sign of its retrieval or resurrection in the foreseeable future. And while Mohamed Siyaad Barre dictatorship found complementarily in sub-clan oligarchy in the early nineteen-eighties, the enemies of the regime grew slowly but steadily, like the creeping underground tremors of a volcano building up steam and lava to cataclysmic explosion. Yet the dictator and his cronies believed that all they would managed all by using brutal terror on the population and bulldozing its opponents, real or imagined.

After his injury in the 1986 car incident, the sub-clan oligarchy degenerated into "rule of the family" whose members competed for supremacy with the mean subterfuges and acrimony characteristic of a polygamous family fighting over inheritance. Joining the scramble for power with a hefty war chest garnered as Minister of Foreign Affairs and Minister of Finance, even Ábdirahmaan Jaamá Barre—the half-brother of the dictator—joined the fray. In time, the underground tremors of the volcano, no longer inaudible or confined to the rural areas, reached the capital city. By 1989, the war clouds the intensified after the armed forces raised Hargeysa to the ground and airplanes strafed the survivors also gathered momentum and moved toward Mogadishu to rain blood.

And yet this was only the "semi-final of the game" of which dictator's tailor, Muudey, had spoken with his wise yet euphemistic wit. The "finals" indeed came when the eye of the storm moved toward the capital city where the dictator and his sub-clan oligarchy enjoyed the loot, like gang of camel-looters confident that the victims of their plunder possessed neither the means nor the will to put up the ante to far greater and disastrous conclusion than they had ever imagined. That is when the Hawiye, under the leadership of General Mohamed Faarah Áydiid and an ally of the SNM, took the war to Somalia, then to Mogadishu, subsequently to the palace of the dictator. After his clan defenders abandoned him in droves, the dictator fled to Kenya and later to Nigeria where he died in despair and isolation. However, unlike Mussolini whom the partisans kills and left hanging by his feet for days, the Somali dictator died of natural causes, or so we learn. If he did not commit suicide, an unlikely event for a man who killed others by devious means, the angel of death probably came to him while he suffered a bout of deep depression.

This terrible way of dying, at least in despair and isolation, was not limited to Benito Mussolini or Mohamed Siyaad Barre alone. The Shah of Iran, Marcos of the Philippines, Somoza of Nicaragua, Haile Selassie of Ethiopia, Ceausescu of Romania, Mobutu of Zaire, Sgt. Doe of Liberia, and Saddam Hussein of Iraq—to just name a few—

had met with the same fate, leaving behind traumatized populations, tattered nations, warped legacies. For all their skills in attaining and retaining power, dictators lack foresight and sense of history in the height of their power. They ignore that history's recursive movement will some day play a cruel joke on them. The so-called Somali elite too have similar lack of foresight and reflection even when they do no enjoy power, real or symbolic.

In short, then, the first thirty years of independence demonstrate that the ruling Somali elite rule only by hegemony and oligarchy, the latter being their preferred system of rule. And by whatever name—democratic or socialist—they call their system of rule, they govern by a mixture of hegemony and oligarchy, based firstly on class, then on clan. Even when the Somali state begins with hegemonic rule with either class or clan character, it inevitably degenerates into oligarchy and dictatorship. Class oligarchy turns into despotism of one man., clan hegemony into sub-clan oligarchy, and sub-clan oligarchy into "rule of the family."

Obviously, then, the ruling Somali elite are incapable of thinking and acting except in hegemonic and oligarchic terms. The state they fashion, even the political party they establish, begins in hegemony of one kind or another, degenerating into oligarchy and despotism. Thus their proclamations of lofty ideals—whether political or religious—should never be taken at face value because such pronouncements are anesthetic device or dose of sorcery administered to lull the public and induce relaxation of vigilance toward the auto-colonial state with which they govern.

The Auto-Colonial State

Colonial rule gave Africans ample excuse to deny and evade responsibility for their contributions to the oppression they had experienced. So long as colonial rule persisted, they convenient blamed outsiders for all the ills of society. Independence did not force them to own their responsibility since for a while formulating problems in terms of *neo-colonialism*—meaning in effect the return of colonial rulers by the back door—provided them a ruse by which they could blame outsiders and evade responsibility.

However, the reality and experience of *auto-colonialism*—oppression sustained by groups within the formerly colonized communities—could no longer be denied a decade or so after independence, although consciousness and articulation of this new from of oppression did not dawned for a while since denial and displacement are common defenses of the misruling elite of Africa.

The Somali history we reviewed shows the transition from colonial rule to auto-colonialism, no doubt with aspects of neo-colonialism mixed with the latter. We have seen that Somalis failed to transform the flawed state that entered their political and social life in the nineteenth century and took root after World War II. Responsibility for the failure rests mainly on the local elite who proved to be a case of the fox tending the chicken coop, or a case of the half-blind leading the blind. Yet the majority of Somalis were neither innocent nor passive victims. They too contributed their part by keeping the *Klan* in power by pursuing vicarious gains like clan honor, thereby giving up responsibility for their destiny and allowing the elite to retain essentially the colonial institutions, laws, and policies with only symbolic changes—like colorful flags and black leaders—under an *auto-colonial state.*

Concentration camp reports demonstrate that the most brutal tyrants were often Jews the German Gestapo chose to administer horrendous cruelties on their people before they too ended in the gas chamber. Black Americans prisoners also report that black prison employees inflict the greatest brutality on those who share skin-color with them. In both concentration camps and American prisons, the Jewish and Black from whom one would expect greater empathy and mercy are on the contrary the cruelest because they want to prove that are different from the condemned and oppressed, as if their actions would override or annul their ethnic and race attributes. In trying to prove loyalty to the oppressor, they also demonstrate betrayal of their people and in the end their own self-betrayal.

Likewise, the auto-colonial situation brings to power members of the oppressed who reproduce the abuses they had experienced in the past and give free reign to their pervert wish to be like the master they overtly hated yet covertly admired. However, never secure in their tenuous and ambiguous status, the inheritors of the colonial state and promoters of the auto-colonial rule pursue two irreconcilable wishes—one the one hand to be the European colonial masters, on the other the liberators of their people. The love-hate relationship they had with the former also permeates their relationship with the latter. Hence, we should never be surprised to find in the auto-colonial situation brutal and indiscriminate use of violence that even colonial masters would consider unnecessary unless required by special exigencies like outright rebellion and revolt.

When the local elite assumed control of muddled structures, beliefs, and values profoundly incompatible with one another, they took 'under new management' the job of stewing toxic potpourri of contradictions in the cauldron of auto-colonial rule. By its nature, the auto-colonial situation agitates the mind and soul. A breeding ground for trauma, it deems certain fundamentals thoughts, behavior, and personalities superfluous if not inimical to the status quo. For instance, it does not comport with logic and rationality, integrity and transparency, merit and competence, public service and social harmony. The naïve idealists who uphold these principles or seek to reform the auto-colonial state are readily condemned subversive and somehow silenced. They do not understand that the opposite of these values—illogic and irrationality, corruption and deception, nepotism and ineptitude, divide-and-rule and individual aggrandizement—are not superficial blemishes changed by tinkering with the system or exhortation to lofty ideals or religious sermons on human virtue. They are inherent to the auto-colonial situation.

Further, the local elite have free hand for deception and looting under the auto-colonial state since they make the laws, interpret them, and enforce them. Their rhetoric of change and occasional burst of conflict do not usher change of the system, but only change of new managers later kicked out by the same tactics of subterfuge and deception they had pushed out those who preceded them. Hence errors of the past repeat and, if they do not, worse blunders emerge to set a new benchmark others repeat or exceed. How often have we seen so-called revolutions become smokescreen for despotism, nationalism for clan hegemony, sub-clan oligarchy to rule of the family, and claims of religious salvation for the rise of another elite to power?

Like its colonial predecessor, the auto-colonial state monopolizes violence without checks and balance of power. Hence, it is patently oppressive, intrusive, and exploitative. Not acknowledging the civic, political, and social rights of citizenship, it continues to treat the ruled as the vanquished and occupied. Fiscal accountability and transparency are not its creed, nor are competence and merit its governing norm or goal. Often the inept and the subservient gravitate to it, like scavengers to a carcass. Resting also on divide-and-rule, it foments clan division and conflict to govern and sustain itself.

The auto-colonial state is therefore a system in continual stagnation or else incessant conflicts and crises. Because competition within the elite follows winner-takes-all, minor differences quickly escalate to violent conflicts that in turn cause maximum torment and tragedy for the ruled. In addition, the auto-colonial state was first introduced as redeemer and guarantor of freedom but soon proved to be its primary extinguisher and barrier, particularly so when the ruling elite, brought up in muddle of structures and thought, misinterpret freedom as license to advance personal, class, and clan interest, real or symbolic.

Profile of the Auto-Colonialist

A cardinal mistake incurable optimists and idealists commit is their belief that the auto-colonial state is open to new ideas or blood. It is not and never will be of its own accord. On the contrary, it is a closed system in which only a select few of the elite qualify to partake in its cupidity and cruelty. Among the first group the system ejects like an organ transplant or avoid like the plague on first sight are well-trained and competent person who by their very presence point an accusing finger at the ignorance and ineptitude of the ruling elite who occupy highest posts of the government. The next trashed are those prone to guilt over the blatant and pervasive injustice or feel empathy for the victims of the system. The third in line are those who, whatever their levels of competence, take their job description literally—therefore work hard and honestly.

The members of the *Klan* most qualified for auto-colonial service are individuals who possess the following characteristics: intense passion for power, thrill in flaunting personal superiority, absence or guilt or shame, extreme sensitivity to criticism, and vindictive streak toward opponents, real or imagined. Of course, the configuration and intensity these characteristics exist among managers of the auto-colonial state vary, as do the combination and preponderance of signs and symptoms for any clinical syndrome. However, all or most of these characteristic exist in persons occupying high posts of the auto-colonial state.[8]

Without intense passion for power, a person has little motivation to enter service in the auto-colonial situation strewn with peril and pain. If the person enters service without such passion, it is so because he did not find alternative avenues of work (as in business, religion, or health) which some of his type had chosen to channel their energy, leaving politics to seasoned predators pursuing abundant prey euphemistically called citizens. The businessman, the religious man, and the healer too may exploit another set of victims in the auto-colonial situation, but the latter often come to them out of their own will and need. At least, some of these 'victims' have some choice with regard to whom they go for services, while the state predators exploit a captive population who must pay taxes and submit to power on pain of imprisonment, torture, or death.

Yet power by itself is nothing in the auto-colonial situation unless flaunted as proof of one's superiority to others. One way of flaunting power is to affirm superiority by exercising it with despotism, to make others cower and cringe in the presence of the power wielder, or to inflict searing pain on the disobedient by torture. Another way is to show off material rewards of power—like a big car, big house, clothe of the latest design, golden rings, expensive electronic gadgets, strong-smelling perfumes. Often, despotism and material greed go together, but different persons have their predominant bent.

As I suggested earlier, Mohamed Siyaad Barre was an exception in this regard. He preferred exercise of crude despotism to material accumulation. Mohamed Ibraahim Égaal too did not accumulate wealth for its sake but he used money to win friends and defeat foes while Mohamed Siyaad Barre used brute force. In fact, Égaal entered bouts of depression if he lacked ample reserve of money to purchase alliance and loyalty; Mohamed Siyaad Barre experienced panic if someone seemed to carry or prepared a bigger club in the politics of the jungle he excelled. Other Somali leaders before 1969 and after 1991 cut a different profile. The most mediocre see power as the royal road to personal wealth.

To attain power and accumulate wealth in the auto-colonial situation, with its distinctly jarring mass poverty and economic underdevelopment, does not come without breaching ethical standards and casting morality to the wind. In fact, politics in the auto-colonial situation is not a means to serve the good of society or to pursue lofty ideological goals. Power is a reward unto itself—in having it, one feels more secure and better than others. Permits one to loot state resources, obtain bribes, and even expropriate the property of others, power is the royal road to wealth, the quickest means to become rich.

But to get rich by these unethical means and in the midst of misery requires absence of guilt or shame—at least hard entrails for ignoring the suffering of others and committing injustice. In the Somali context, the delusion of clan superiority, bolstered by public admiration of those who boldly loot state resources or prey on the defenseless, is often a convenient antidote to guilt and shame.

Moreover, the auto-colonial situation and the many injustices it breeds cannot sustain where state records and individual actions are transparent, public debate and the media uncover unseemly behavior of officials, or the competitors over power present alternative programs and leaders. That is why in the auto-colonial situation the media is gagged; the budget for law enforcement and prisons outstrips those for education and health combined; swarm of undercover agents serve as 'ears' and 'eyes' of the state.

Even the constitution affirms a legislative branch and an independent judiciary, these institutions quickly prove to be window-dressing intended to hide the essential despotism and corruption of leaders. Often too, the persons shunted to these institutions are mostly clueless, toothless, or both—they neither understand the constitution, nor dare to monitor and punish official wrongdoing. Faced with the dilemma of living with unemployment or working for the system, the best among them try to do the least harm.

In short, the auto-colonial state and its managers have a lure for people that can neither think nor talk—a population that sleepwalks through daily life and history. If some among them talk and question, it expends sorely needed resources force their submission to silence them for good. What makes the auto-colonial state most treacherous is that those who manage it—from top to bottom—are often unforgiving and vindictive to those whom they identify as opponents, real or imagined. In fact, one marvels at the ingenuity, energy, and money the auto-colonial state expends on developing tactics of eavesdropping on citizens, torturing persons accused of subversion, and execution of the condemned, thereby sending people to caves of pain and death while other nations channel resources toward national development including sending astronauts beyond the earth's atmosphere.

Feast on Phantoms

The local elite do not sustain the auto-colonial state. The public too, confused by the muddled structures and incessant feuds of the elite, gave up hope of attaining freedom and development, turning attention and energy on surviving poverty and predators, the same way their ancestors did for centuries. Only this time, they endure crushing misery in the anonymity crush of enlarging urban wasteland and the isolation of hovels called home. In traditional and pastoral communities, the clan system did not enrich them, but it made suffering a shared experience and insulated them from despair. In the auto-colonial situation, the distorted clan system entraps them, making ready tool and cheap fodder for elite competition on who rules and exploits them.

Long ago when colonialism was taking root, it weeded out the elders with integrity by dismissal, imprisonment, and exile. They were replaced by more malleable and amenable coterie who willingly served colonialists by collecting taxes, capturing rebels, gathering intelligence, and encouraging obedience to the colonizer's laws. After independence, the local elite took charge of the seasoned betrayers or cultivated their ilk to serve and sustain the auto-colonial state. Even if some of the elders enter the auto-colonial system with sincerity and integrity, the ruling elite quickly corrupted them by doling out money to buy their loyalty and souls, perhaps purchasing for them a Land Cruiser for bonus. It is then that these new recruits and seasoned traditional elders—wearing colorful turbans, caressing rosaries, poised as impeccable devotees to the faith—sell their people to the highest bidder as if they were cattle in the marketplace.

As a result, the victims of the auto-colonial situation are subjectively and objective hemmed by pressure from all directions. Their political elite promise change that they never deliver. Their traditional elders preach restrain and collaboration with the oppressive state. They consciously want to become full citizens of the nation, to enjoy equal rights under the law, to channel their energy in productive work, simultaneously feeding loved ones and contributing to the development of their society. Unconsciously, however, they know that the clan system does not acknowledge citizenship of members outside the clan. On the contrary, it encourages clan hegemony if not oligarchy over other clans. The pastoral ethos nested in their psyche is also fundamentally incompatible with contemporary requirements for economic development and social justice.

Face with these contradictory demands of the state and the clan system, driven by the revolution of expectations inflamed by the elite's exaggerated promises of freedom, yet frustrated by lack of objective improvement, ordinary Somalis fall back to comparison of vicarious the subjective gains (like clan honor and prestige) they can snatch from the success of kinsmen in power. Having lost the struggle on the objective (economic) domain, lacking material resources to meet basic needs, they throw themselves with abandon on contest on the subjective realm—comparing whose misery is worse, whose defeat more humiliating, or whose boast of clan honor more credible.

Thus the struggle on the sensory and reality mode—objective and verifiable—gives way to one on the mythic mode—subjective and modified according one's fantasy. Since basic needs as food and shelter are frustrated, Somalis resort to feasting on phantoms in the form of Clan X, Y, and Z pitted against another on contest of valor, honor and prestige. These clan phantoms created to satisfy socially constructed delusion of clan superiority for defense against dreaded individual and group inferiority therefore provide temporary refuge for majority of Somalis who lost on the objective, material domain of life.

So long as Somalis are preoccupied in the world of phantoms, including delusion of clan superiority and subjective clan wars, they will find neither time nor energy to canalize thought and action toward objective change of the auto-colonial state. This feast on phantoms not only perpetuates the auto-colonial state and even encourages mutual-cannibalization on the abstract but also constitute a national addiction. The feast on clan phantoms provides Somalis a jolt of adrenalin and gives them fleeting satisfaction. Of late, however, the feast on clan phantoms is inadequate to give them the transient satisfaction and bubble of security they seek even when they take the feast to brutal pitch, acting out their fantasies in violent altercations.

Thus to calm their nerves from their mounting stress and side-effects of qat, they also use to frightening scale psychopharmacological agents imported from abroad by unscrupulous businessmen and sold at pharmacies without control or prescription, is fast catching up with the cultural addiction for delusion of clan superiority which the ruling elite exploit and sustain the auto-colonial situation. Most popular drugs these days are Diazepam, an addictive drug with anxiolytic properties, and Amitriptyline, one of older antidepressant. Add to these the ever-pervasive addiction to *qat* (an amphetamine-like substance) and you have a nation addicted to multiple substances, each intensifying the need for the other and whose interactions complicating resulting side-effects.[9]

The ruling elite show neither thought nor alarm on this aggravating state of their people. On the contrary, they encourage the multiple addictions since an anesthetized or spaced-out population does not question or threaten their auto-colonial rule. In addition, the imported drugs and qat bring substantial taxes to the state treasury, replenishing the amounts withdrawn to private bank accounts and stashed away in private chests at home. And when they want fighters and fodder for their internal squabble, they find armies of kinsmen stupefied enough by drugs and delusion of clan superiority to kill without distinction and mercy any group identified as the "enemy."

In reality, the elite have their own dilemmas. They want a 'modern state' and 'contemporary life' as they understand these goals, yet they want to grab personal power and amass wealth. They want to develop a nation, yet they do not discard the traditional values they internalized in childhood. They never tire of promising economic development and social justice while competition for power and wealth among their peers repeatedly contradict and undermine their promises.

Caught in this impossible world of contradictions, they too fall back on cannibalizing their people, selfishly pursuing power and wealth while pushing them into greater misery and mayhem. This deadly game shall continue so long as the majority of Somalis obtain vicarious satisfaction from the actions of kinfolk in high places bent on usurping power and looting state resources.

Thrill and Theft of Maandeeq

The struggle for control over the state boils down to who owns and controls *Maandeeq*, the milk-fecund and cherished camel used as symbol of freedom and prosperity in the heyday of anti-colonial struggle and thereafter. Maandeeq is actually more than a metaphor of the state; on the contrary, the state itself is metaphor of Maandeeq. Somalis who knew little about the alien state except its tyranny and torment—a monster that only oppressed and killed people during the colonial era —had to find a way of making the state benevolent, nurturing, and alluring.

The most apt and evocative name Somalis gave to the state—a name which a population of camel-herding pastoralists could readily understand and appreciate—is Maandeeq, the name of a she-camel, which literally means *satisfier of the soul.* It is not only that Maandeeq provides milk nourishing the body, a service a cow or another camel can render, but also the name conjures up images of nurtured mind and soul. In addition, Maandeeq represents the ultimate the symbol of power and prestige for anyone who owns it. Maandeeq also confers honor not only to the owner but his clan. Thus the name *Maandeeq* became a powerful means of rehabilitating the bad name and memory of state associated with alien domination and violence.

Similarly, traditional Somalis who for centuries inhabited in scattered and insular clan settlements without a central state could not readily comprehend the concepts of nation and nationalism. The poet and composer, Ábdi Iidaan, reported that he moved from the rural areas to the city in the early nineteen-fifties when nationalist fervor was at its peak. Discovering his poetic talent, inhabitants of the city asked him to compose nationalist poems. He said that he did not know what nation and nationalism really meant, but he interpreted them according to what he knew best—the clan system as the medium of social relations and politics. He therefore conceived nation as the unity of many clans into one large clan and nationalism as fraternity and common destiny. Framing it in these terms, he then utilized the repository of poetic knowledge he had in which, true to the delusion of clan superiority, one glorified his clan and vilified the clans of others. Thus, the Somali nation became "our clan" and the enemies—for instance Ethiopian and European colonizers—became "their clan."

Ábdi Iidaan was not alone in this reinterpretation of nation and nationalism. Most Somalis understood the concept of nation in terms of *clan writ large* with ambiguous genealogy but conceived as shared culture, language, religion, and territoriality. However, the reinterpretation of the nation as the clan writ large would have little appeal without the concept of *Maandeeq* that lent it emotional content and magical attraction. Without Maandeeq, it would be an empty scaffold, a home without love, even the Élmi Boodhery's tree of poverty in a barren land. However, once the state and nation paired with *Maandeeq,* the two alien concepts gained meaning and appeal for Somalis in both urban and rural communities.

The culturally rooted emotional allure for *Maandeeq* the she-camel also coincided with the adoration the public had for a popular singer in the late nineteen-fifties and early nineteen-sixties *Maandeeq*. Her melodic and pleasant songs of the Qaraami genre enchanted Somali audiences everywhere. Akin to Robert Flack's songs—exemplified by "Killing me softly"—*Maandeeq's* smooth, sweat, and rhythmic tunes on the one hand lamented jilted love, on the other expressed the experience of nirvana realized in union with the other near.

Maandeeq the she-camel, the singer, and the state therefore fused in the public mind, making the amalgam a household object of endearment, nights of wet dreams, and daily public obsession on freedom. The blend of the three—the allure of the she-camel, the evocative tunes of the singer, and the new meaning of the state—mesmerized and possessed Somalis of that era. To this day, the she-camel and the singer remain fused in the Somali psyche but the state shriveled in the heart and mind when it turned into a deadly monster. It also died in a whimper in the heart and mind before its explosive collapse as an institution in 1991.

In reality, the reinterpretation of nation and nationalism as Maandeeq was from the start forced for convenience in the heyday of anticolonial struggle. By culture and history, Somalis had not known consolidated and massive *clan writ large* including all of them one tent. Traditional socialization and genealogy, the Pastoral Ethos and the delusion of clan superiority, clan fusion and fission—in short Somali psychology and social relations—contradicted this newly formed social construction. Perhaps this social fiction would endure longer and even take root if it found new material and social conditions to affirm and sustain it. Such material and social conditions did not develop. The ruling elite left it for singers, the poets, and the public to celebrate Maandeeq the state while they looted and bled it dry, later turning it into a hairy, ugly, and brutal ogre devouring adults and children alike.

The new socials fiction called nation soon after independence faced a new contradiction nested in Somali tradition and psyche: Would *Maandeeq* the state exist for the benefit of all, an inheritance and dominion of all Somalis, or only for those who could loot it according to the camel looting tradition? For *Maandeeq* the state to exist as the common inheritance and right of all Somalis, as the paper and imported constitution declared, it would have laws and institution neutral to all clans, ensuring that none is above the law and that all have equal opportunity to enjoy the legal, social, and individual rights of citizens.

This could not be in a society and culture where each individual and clan, steeped in the Pastoral Ethos, nursed the private ambition of looting Maandeeq the she-camel, the beautiful singer, and of course the state that represents the dialectic synthesis of material gain and honor. In fact, the tradition of camel looting co-existed with the tradition of men looting or eloping beautiful women in the next hamlet or clan. A fascinating genre of folklore and poetry exists on how traditional Somalis looted young women or even a married wives, as shown by Aw Jaamá Úmar Íise who presents in *Damac Rag iyo Qurux Dumar* five riveting examples of clan wars precipitated by contest of leaders over women.

However, whoever looted and defended *Maandeeq* the state by force obtained far greater material gain and the highest of honor those who traditionally looted *Maandeeq* the she-camel and the beautiful lady since the plunder of the state also brought ownership of all three. Besides, to loot the state proves personal and clan superiority over those who forced to submit to its rule. Yet the tantalizing question was this: Who really has the will and means to loot, defend, and own *Maandeeq*?

After few years of independence, it became evident that only a minority of the elite could loot, defend, own, and exploit *Maandeeq*—and they did. The prize they sought and found in looting *Maandeeq* was not only the life-giving 'milk' of the state, or the feminine soul and persona the beautiful singer represented, but also the personal and clan honor affirming superiority of character and genealogy. Hence wresting *Maandeeq* involved dual victory—firstly enjoying benefits of the loot, secondly proving one's superiority over others. Worse, the ruling elite who looted commonly owned resources of the state arrogantly and shamelessly flaunted their loot in the form of imported clothes of the latest design; large, plush homes cordoned off by high walls; wives behaving like Imelda Marcos; children and expensive cars—like the Land Cruisers about which Saado Áli sang with contempt in late 1989.

Illustrating the fate of the Somali state is Somali Airline, another symbol of *Maandeeq*. Started in July 1964 in partnership with Al-Italia, the airline was the first and only national airlines that provided domestic and international airlines. Although its beginning was modest, Somalis were proud of it as symbol independence and an efficient means of transport between major cities linked in the past by rough and hazardous roads.

The Example of Somali Airlines

Lufthansa provided training and technical assistance to Somali Airlines after Mohamed Siyaad Barre collaborated with West Germany in a terrorist incident involving the hijacking of a Lufthansa plane and landed in Mogadishu in the late 1979. West German forces stormed the plane, killed some of the terrorists and captured others, releasing the passengers safely. The success of the project brought steady financial and technical support to the Somali government. One of the beneficiaries of West German assistance and largesse was Somali Airlines.

In 1987, Somali Airlines acquired an Airbus A310-300 in a complicated arrangement to finance the acquisition with France's Banque Indosuez Industries at the estimated cost of $55-60 million. The poor credit of the Somali regime would have prevented the acquisition of the plane without support from Germany. In addition, the plane would regularly land in Rome and Frankfurt—a flight schedule that assured the financiers that they could repossess the plane in case of default on payment.

It is said that Ábdirahmaan Jaamá Barre, the half-brother of the dictator and minister of finance, arranged for the purchase and obtained for commission no less than $5 million. According to employees of Somali Airlines, the Airbus plane was busy and profitable before the state collapsed. The Airbus was flying from Mogadishu to Dubai when the regime collapsed on January 26, 1991. After the passengers disembarked at their destination, the crew grounded the plane in Rome. Later, the plane flew to Frankfurt where it remained for months until repossessed for default of payment to the bank that financed it and for accumulating airport charges while grounded.

The fate of other planes of Somali Airlines—specifically two Boeing 707s, and several smaller planes, including at least Fokker planes—

did not fare better. A Boeing 707 plane was stranded in Mogadishu after it sustained some damage from the shooting and pillaging that followed the collapse of the regime. The other Boeing 707 was stuck in Nairobi until repossessed by the American who financed it.

Only one Fokker plane escaped the rampage in Mogadishu. That plane landed in one of the traditional settlements of the Mareehaan, the dictator's clan. Looters and nomads subsequently dismantled it to pieces. Only the shell cabinet and seats remained intact and used as teashop by Mareehaan woman who entertained customers with stories of her prized inheritance from the collapsed regime. All the remaining assets of the airlines—spare parts, large cash, tickets, technical and office equipment—were looted in Mogadishu, Hargeysa, and other Somali locations where Somali Airlines had offices and stores.

In addition to the sordid way a profitable service and symbol of national pride had ended, there is also another sordid part to the story of Somali Airlines. When Áli Mahdi Mohamed declared himself Interim President in 1991, he dismissed the manager and key officials of Somali Airlines fled to Rome. The manager was a Mijeerteen and the key officials belonged to other sub-clans of the Daarood. Playing tit-for-tat through clan politics, Áli Mahdi replaced these men with members from the Hawiye, his clan.

No doubt, Áli Mahdi's motivation was more than clan gesture since the replacement would bring him steady cash that he would use for personal and political goals. He knew that Somali Airlines was a source of steady revenues the collapsed regime and its clan beneficiaries handsomely exploited. Taking control of it promised a handsome inheritance from the fallen regime. However, the exiled manager and his associates refused to resign and the dispute foiled plans to rent the Airbus to other airlines to cover at least financial obligations to creditors until an internationally recognized and stable government took responsibility for it. The Somali disputants—Áli Mahdi on one side, the officials of the Airlines on the other—did not accept this arrangement. Their dispute continued while the financial obligation excessively mounted forcing the creditors to sell the plane to the highest bidder. Yemen bought the plane.

This ending of Somali Airlines illustrates not only the consequences of state collapse but also the personal greed and the absurd tactics of the Somali ruling elite, new and old. The other assets of the regime—including cash, bank account, tickets, spare parts, and furniture—fell to whoever had the means to pillage and pulverize Somali Airlines, the same as other assets of the state vanished soon after the collapse of the state.

Years later, when I served as the Director of the Academy for Peace and Development, a Somali from Mogadishu approached me in 2002 to inquire if the Academy was interested in purchasing over fifty volumes of testimony, witness reports, and legal briefs of the National Security Court—that deadliest instrument of the regime's repression and summary executions.

The offer was attractive for its historical value, but we had to decline purchase of the volumes because the price demanded was too exorbitant even if we took the risks it entailed since the documents would reveal the names and damaging testimony of many Somalis who today masquerade as patriotic citizens and paragons of virtue.

The Last Straw...

Somalis have been in the forefront of things—both good and bad—in Africa during the past one hundred years. After their land was occupied and partitioned without their consent, they survived four types of colonial rule—British, Italian, French, and Ethiopian. Not only did they survive the onslaught of formidable foes, but they also achieved what no other African countries did on their own. As soon as two of these former colonies gained independence in 1960, they spontaneously united while leaders of other African countries preached the virtues of African unity. This day, their sermons remain rhetorical and hollow.

In fact, these leaders barely sustain the unity of peoples in the territories they inherited from colonial rulers. When Somalis sought greater unity with their people across the arbitrary borders drawn by colonial powers, most African leaders insisted on "the sanctity of colonial borders." By this insistence, they kept intact the Ethiopian Empire that worked hand in glove with European colonialists and profited from the partition of Somalis; they also thwarted the principle of self-determination that would give Africans the right to choose their system of governance and destiny without use of violence. As a result, African leaders kept in place the flawed states and unjust borders that colonial rulers had left in much of Africa, damping hopes of freedom and right of self-determination.

Even then, the new Somali Republic, formed from the union of British Protectorate and the Italian colony, became a save haven for other Africans—including South Africans, Mozambiqueans, Eritreans, even Ethiopians—who fought apartheid, colonial rule, or African governments oppressing their own people. After the military coup of 1969, the Somali regime also provided training and arms to African freedom fighters, passports to exiled African politicians, and scholarships to students, convinced that their cause was just and sacrifice of scant resources the least Somalis can do for fellow Africans.

The Ethiopian leaders who in 2007 and 2008 ordered the heavy artillery on population centers with the excuse of defending a fictional Transitional Federal Government of Somalia were beneficiaries of Somali assistance when they were in exile. Perhaps, they rationalize their intervention as show of gratitude and neighborly sacrifice, although most Somali view the intervention in light of historic territorial expansion poisoning relations between peoples who together would prosper in just peace and cooperation than war that always impoverishes both, at the same time causing death, trauma, and prolonged misrule.

Somali achievements were not limited to moral and material support to fellow Africans in their hour of need. There were other accomplishments at home. They include: the writing a script for a society that in the past relied on the spoken word; literacy campaigns in rural areas that made over 70% of the population; innovative programs of reclaiming the desert from encroaching sand dunes; developing numerous schools and key institutions of higher learning. Equally remarkable is the project of saving drought-stricken nomads by moving them in airplanes and trucks to fishing and farming communities thousands of miles away in order to give them sustainable means of earning living.

These were no small achievements for an African country strapped for resources, reeling for generations from colonial fragmentation, neglect, and contradictory legacies of two colonial administrations—British and Italian. These achievements would have stood as stellar examples of what Africans can do for themselves instead of waiting for charity or wallowing in despair. However, all these achievements, except the writing of script, vanished due to the corrosive effects of the flawed state, the malfeasant elite, and the distorted clan system.

Somalis learned from this experience that the climb upwards towards self-help and innovation was steep and elusive, but the slide downwards to conflict and despair was easy, rapid and precipitous. Whereas the climb upwards required the unity and energy of all citizens, the slide downwards occurred in division, discord, and malice.

Most of all, it is the elite entrusted with power who are responsible for the failure of politics as means to advance the welfare of society or as the art of achieving the possible good for the benefit of all. Instead, they made politics as the *poly-tricks* to hoodwinking their people and enrich themselves. From the beginning, they failed to critically examine and change the muddled structures and values they had inherited from the colonial era. This failure kept in place institutions, ethos, and practices that kept in place colonial oppression in auto-colonial form managed by black leaders, enforced by black agents of repressions, and disguised with false symbols of freedom.

Promising more than they could deliver, the elite raised expectations far beyond what could realistically achieve under the prevailing muddle of systems and practices. Forgetting their promises and the responsibilities entailed, they gave highest priority to acquiring personal power and wealth by pitting one clan against another, in consequence tearing asunder a society that needed mending from decades of colonial divide-and-rule and despair. Equally critical, they relied on first on deceit, then on raw violence, to achieve their private ambition for power and wealth, not realizing that deception and violence produce many unintended consequences including their boomerang in self-victimization.

After nine years of civilian rule marked by raging corruption and rigged ballots, the armed forces intervened and took control of the state with their new rhetoric of socialist revolution. People believed these new leaders as they did those who had preceded them in the heyday of anti-colonial struggle. Yet the military junta, instead of solving the prevailing muddle of structures and values, added another layer of incongruous ideology and organization. The new idols they introduced and glorified were Karl Marx and Lenin, though these proselytizers of the new religion were almost as ignorant of its fundamental tenets as were the public they preached.

Turning away from the West for what Somalis found as negligent and unjust as it was in the days of the colonial scramble, the military junta threw itself into the lap and tutelage of Soviet masters seasoned in the practice of bulldozing revolution from the top, without regard to human values and the number of people sacrificed in the process. Oblivious to the damaging consequences of colonial past, they imported Stalinist approach of terror as anvil with which to crush and defeat their people.

The approach fit the mind-set of the military leaders and the political climate of the time when socialism of Soviet-type promised the fastest means to nirvana. Besides, the Cold War was boon for leaders like Mohamed Siyaad Barre who, playing one superpower against another, found the former Soviet Union and East Germany most accommodating to requests for arms, military training, and methods of controlling people by means of propaganda and calibrated force. When his socialist allies disappointed him during the Somali-Ethiopian War of 1977, he humbly turned to the West with begging bowl in hand.

The junta's rhetoric of change and isolated reforms during the first few years of the so-called revolution lulled the majority of Somalis into believing that the swarms of security agents and the pervasive repression were temporary nuisance or isolated mistakes that would diminish as the revolution took root and the regime settled into its declared goals of liberation. However, this was not to be. After Mohamed Siyaad Barre singled himself out of the pack, emerging as the most supreme of the Supreme Revolution Council, he acquired absolute power and focused his energy on remaining hoisted on the throne. Not content with absolute power, he also surrounded himself with loyal cronies, mostly from his clan, and set out to take pre-emptive strike at "anti-revolutionaries" before they spawned and propagate in society.

Saddam Hussein once declared that he intuitively knew his future opponents before they had become conscious of their incipient rebellion. Driven by paranoia, his mere suspicion affirming as proof of treason, he eliminated his suspected opponents before they knew of their "crime." Mohamed Siyaad Barre was no different. He too was host to similar paranoia, although his method of eliminating opponents was not as swift as that of the Iraqi dictator. He often used mind-game on his allies and his opponents by keeping them guessing their fate, killing their dignity and self by promotion or demotion, dismissal or imprisonment, resorting to execution in cases where he felt opponents were stubborn and unredeemable. For those who retained personal integrity and dignity but presented no immediate threat, he enjoyed prolonging their suffering until they either submitted or, after long-term imprisonment, sought refuge in frank madness.

Thus after 1974, the machine of tyranny that started with military coup was in full gear in the new name of Somali Democratic Republic—a name given to the state to affirm its socialist credentials. Subsequently, the swarm of state agents—from the National Security Service, the *Guulwadayaal*, and the National Security Court—rounded up and brutalized opponents, real or imagined. Somalis who prided themselves in their capacity to meet hardship with stoicism and courage found themselves cowering to submission, enduring the abuses of someone who, after for decades of experience as a security agent, knew too well their vulnerable spots and tactics of denuding individuals from their clan armor.

Yet so long as the regime retained oligarchy of the elite drawn from different clans, the dictator literally got away with murder. Somalis tolerate corruption and misrule as long as members of different clans share the symbols of power and get a share of the loot. The excluded majority may circulate rumors of scandal, criticize, and let off steam, but they endure corrupt leaders and political abuse so long as a few of their members of their clan show visible symbol of power and flaunt personal wealth derived from official malfeasance, although such gains of their kinsmen do not objectively benefit them. That they obtain vicarious subjective gains—honor, pride, and vindication—are enough for them to feel contented but also to risk life in defense of the status quo.

By 1977, convinced that he fully conquered his people, Mohamed Siyaad Barre embarked on the biggest gamble of his life—he waged war with Ethiopia. The crushing defeat that followed had major consequences for Somalis. Firstly, it struck the last nail on the coffin of pan-Somali nationalism. Secondly, it depleted the steam of the so-called revolution whose rhetoric no longer inspired hope or commitment. Thirdly, it cracked the myth of the regime's invincibility. Once the regime's vulnerabilities surfaced, opponents came out of the woodworks and openly challenged the dictatorship until the regime collapsed.

If it true that those who live by the sword also die by the sword, it is also true that those who seek to free themselves only by the sword, with no guiding moral compass or rational end, turn into worse predators than those who preceded them. The collapse of the state brought Somalis a succession of disasters. Seventeen years later, the guns fired in opposition to the military dictatorship have yet to cease. If they do not snuff out life of civilians caught in crossfire as in Somalia, their roar reverberates in the dreams of survivors in Somaliland, showing their residues in the muddled language, the broken syntax, and the articulate silences of the mad who today roam the cities.

Lessons Not Learned

To summarize, Somali society entered a stage of unprecedented social and cultural crisis beginning in the late nineteenth century when Europeans imposed colonial rule and partition on Somalis. In time, the crisis seeped into almost every domain of life and turned chronic to the point that today Somalis accept all crises as the natural order of life or as divine damnation insoluble by human intervention.

Under this condition, each individual and group seeks temporary reprieve from poverty, powerlessness, and exploitation at the expense of others forced to suffer these triple and crushing scourges. For this reason, living is no longer a right or blessing but a penalty and punishment paid by the majority who die due to preventable hunger, disease, and war. Somali politics is therefore not a means to seek or find solution for the benefit of the collective but the art of disempowering and dispossessing the majority kept in perpetual misery to the benefit of the elite.

The political and social crises that began over a hundred years ago continue to this day because three factors instigate and maintain them. The first factor is the flawed state that took root under colonial rule; the second is the local elite that transformed the colonial into autocolonial order; the third is the distorted clan system and associated pastoral ethos that serve as the social and political bulwark for elite misrule and mystification. If Somalis are to live in peace under a political system in which all clans enjoy rights of inclusion and equality before the law, they must give serious thought to rectifying these three causes of oppression and underdevelopment.

To wait for new ideas or solution from the ruling Somali elite is a pipe dream because the flawed and corrupt system of governance often winnows out the competent and honest, selecting the technically inept and the financially unscrupulous to assume leadership at most levels of government. Thus, contrary to elite theories like Vilfredo Pareto and Gaetano Mosca, the best or most competent in society do not lead or govern everywhere, certainly not in Somali society. Slavishly carrying the script of the flawed state and its colonial architects, the Somali elite constitute society's crudest, cruelest, and greediest lot, bearing testimony to the saying that "filth floats to the top."[5]

The word 'elite' in its best meaning is therefore an inappropriate name for this group, for they are not 'the cream' of society but its organized and heartless thugs. Despite this, I refer to them generally as the 'elite' for wont of a better term and their ruling members as the *Klan* since, like the KKK, they constitute a mean and deluded minority who pursue private and sordid interests by exploiting the name of a collective—a sub-clan, a clan, or a nation.

Complicating matters, the distorted clan system and traditional culture encourage and justify nepotism, corruption, and clan hegemony—all harking back to the pastoral ethos of helping and defending the clan, right or wrong. Integral to this ethos are the tradition of camel looting for fast material gain in an environment of poverty and the *delusion of clan superiority* to compensate for the unconscious insecurity and anxiety assailing Somalis accustomed to life in the perilous semi-desert. I described in the preceding pages how the clan and age-old cultural legacies combine with the flawed state and the tactics of the power elite to give Somali politics its peculiar twists and torment.

The goal of inclusion, equality, and justice which Somalis consciously and passionately seek will continue to evade them so long as the incongruent mix of the flawed state and the distorted clan system prevail, the Somali elite persist on their habitual power-grab and qet-rich-quick schemes, and the majority of Somalis, steeped in self-defeating ethos, fall victim to the elite's clan manipulation. Denied basic rights and accustomed to hand-outs, the majority also acquiesce to oppression for ephemeral subjective gains, though these gains involve nothing more than the *delusion* of faring better in comparative distribution of misery.

Instead of visionaries leaders—like Gandhi, Nehru, Mandela, Cabral—Somalis have had the misfortune of misguided, corrupt, and inept leaders who, given time, degenerated into tyrants. The public, misinformed about their rights and responsibilities, accept incompetent and corrupt leaders. Focusing on the biography of Mohamed Siyaad Barre who ruled Somalis for twenty-one years, I demonstrated that leaders are as much makers of society as they are products of it. Thus if Mohamed Siyaad Barre did not come to power, Somalis would create his ilk—and they did, as shown by the rich harvest of inept and tyrannical leaders who have come to assume power since the collapse of the regime in 1991. In fact, the leaders who emerged since then are far less talented and charismatic than Mohamed Siyaad Barre, though on the whole they are as mean and cruel as he was.

Because Somalis and their ostensible international benefactors ignore these three factors, they compulsively recreate the flawed state, despite its patent and repeated failure, restore the malfeasant elite to power, ignoring their proven ineptitude and corruption, and maintain the distorted clan system as if it were the natural and sole destiny of Somalis. In fact, the state and the clan system are social constructions developed to meet human needs. These social constructions in time developed into institutions and social structures with life of their own, appearing to be impervious to human intervention. In reality, we can *de-construct* all social constructions if we have the will for change and know how to develop alternative social constructions meeting human needs. Somalis have not given sufficient thought to this fact. That is why the proverb introducing this chapter—*no wells dug for them, no rescuers on the way*—gains especial meaning and relevance.

The Somali example also shows the absurdities to which the so-called elite push socially constructed differences to secure for themselves power and material gains. If nothing else, it underscores that we must become vigilant whenever someone or a group points to differences of people using socially constructed terms like clan, nation, and race; we must also examine what interest lies behind the exaggeration, aggravation, or invention of differences before we act on them. Too often and tragically, we commit injustice and atrocities on others distinguished from us on fictitious differences.

Thus the barriers to change are not only the flawed state and the malfeasant elite—the first controlling the institutions and political behavior of the ruled, the second resisting all change threatening their unearned power and privilege. The covert yet most unyielding roadblock to change is the distorted clan system that dominates the Somali psyche, permeates their social relations, and sustains the Hobbesian status quo of each person or clan against all. The pastoral ethos, the delusion of clan superiority, the treacherous processes of clan fusion and fission—these throwbacks to the primordial past—keep Somalis confused and busy in outmaneuvering, undercutting, or killing one another, in the end destroying any residue of collective will and talent that would canalized to promote life and development. These political, social, and psychological barricades—more than external forces—today keep Somalis stuck in stupefying anarchy or stagnation.

It is obvious from the preceding chapters that clan is simultaneously myth and reality, social metaphor and social organization, crucible of identity and social differentiation, means of group cohesion and paranoia, a tool for collective self-defense and divide-and-rule. It is also a form of sport providing fleeting entertainment and instigator of wars whose contestants are quickly swept away by intense passion to win. In its crass and cruelest forms, clan is a convenient justification to loot the property of others and take cover in the defense of the clan. One even commits murder, letting the clan to assume collective culpability and pay blood-compensation.

Nothing therefore whips Somali passion to hysteria, even collective madness, as does the clarion call to defend clan survival and honor. Even in peacetime, Somalis interpret interpersonal conflicts as clan contest, ignoring altogether the class and personal interests of those who instigate and promote conflicts. Members of the *Klan* know this well and rally their clan by crying *"tollaayey!"* in their pursuit of personal power and wealth. It is then that their kinfolk, without question or thought, rush to their defense, impelled by the irresistible trance of primordial clan identity and loyalty.

Jumping into the fray in response to calls of *"tollaayey!"* provides new and fleeting jolt of adrenaline to the masses caught in permanent state of misery, ennui, and despondency. It binds the group into a cohesive gang against others, providing defense against the horror of clan inferiority assailing all Somalis deep in their psychic. Let us not also forget—clan brings vicarious and subjective gains (like group honor and prestige) if the clan member wins the contest. That is why

Somalis mobilize with remarkable zeal behind kinsmen in time of political campaigns and armed conflict. That also is why regimes, political movements, social clubs, and religious movements turn clannish. Even while living abroad, Somalis carry with them the clan outlook and biases they had internalized in childhood. At minimum, they sympathize and side with their clan—their most favored 'sports team'—when it is engaged in political campaign or armed conflict. More often, they raise funds for purchase of votes and arms.

Often forgotten is that each conflict of the elite into which kinsmen throw themselves deepens their festering physical and mental wounds long after the politicians for whom they fought disappears into the world of power and wealth, cordoning themselves with high walls and armed guards. Ironically, as if possessed by evil forces they failed to exorcise, Somalis again throw themselves into the next fictional 'clan contest' before the wounds of past conflicts have healed and the grieving of the dead has ended.

Hence beware of any group of the Somali elite—whether they wear pinstriped suit, army uniform, or religious apparel—who blurt out mesmerizing rhetoric and offer ready solutions to Somali problems. They promise justice and egalitarian rule, but quickly impose *class* hegemony and oligarchy, followed by *clan* hegemony and oligarchy, degenerating at last to rule of the family. Regardless of their garb or rhetoric, the so-called elite continue the cycle of promises they make but break, the seesaw from hope to disillusionment their people repeatedly experience, and the recurring fluctuation for short-lived euphoria to chronic despair we have seen in the past one hundred years.

The choice is clear: Somalis will transform themselves, their worldview, and their behavior in ways affording them a chance of survival in this ever-competitive and globalizing world; or they shall perish in their current predicament of *in-betweenity*, neither here nor there, caught in succession of conflicts within the clan and against others, including their colleagues, compatriots, and neighbors. Somalis led by the Klan have proven their exceptional talent and efficiency for self-destruction. If they show the same talent and efficiency in saving lives and make traumatized children to smile again as they have in killing one another and destroying their property, their society will be among the most vibrant and enterprising in the region, free from the charity of their former rulers who never tire of blurting out complaints of "compassion fatigue."

If Somalis are to survive, they must therefore end the flawed state, the rule of malfeasant Klan, and the distorted clan system. The nineteenth century state and associated nationalism are today in their death throes. After two devastating world wars and countless smaller wars, even Europeans are fast replacing their insular states and fetish of nationalism by larger social constructions pooling their human and material resources. In consequence, they are poised to become another superpower while China and India are steadily approaching their nadir. Africans have yet to go beyond the flawed state that so often failed them or the fetish of dissimulated nationalism contradicting their history or cultural heritage.

As we have seen in the Somali example, the flawed state and the dissimulated nationalism serve the interests of the ruling elite but bury the misinformed citizen in heaps of accumulated external debt siphoned off to private accounts, a system of tyranny killing the will for freedom or creativity, and a succession of wars leaving death, destruction, and trauma. Even democracy has turned into a cruel joke, as demonstrated recently in Kenya and Zimbabwe where the leaders seem to declare, "I'm a democrat only if I win the election, but not so if I lose it." After loss of elections, their cronies justify tyranny by asserting that the exercise of democracy expected of them is un-African in history and culture. The implication is that tyranny and torture are African!

The absurd twists of African politics reached extremes when President Mbeki of South Africa, one of the most promising African leaders to emerge in recent years, shocked the world by declaring that Zimbabwe was in no crisis at all, in absolute contradiction to the obvious falsification of the election results and the blatant refusal for peaceful transition of power. On that day, the dream of African Union (like its predecessor, the Organization of African Unity) proved another contrived ploy of the African ruling elite to hold on to power and defend the malfeasance of a ruthless dictator who ran his society aground and pushed his people into crushing misery.

Somalis too will sooner or later tread the path spearheaded by Presidents Kibaki and Mugabe. They will find leaders who under internal or external pressure agree to hold elections whose outcome they want to control by using bribes, voting rigging, and intimidation. But when the results do not please them, they will declare that democracy is not un-Somali and therefore unnecessary. Crying "*tollaayey,*" their kinsmen then rush to their defense to return Somali politics to the cycle of degeneration and destruction to which has been doomed under the flawed state, the malfeasant Klan, and the distorted clan system. Change will not therefore take place as long as these three problems of Somali politics persist.

Those who argue for the unity of Somalis before solving these three problems have not understood why Somali history since independence in 1960 was a history of degeneration and destruction, not of development or democratic evolution. Nor have they grasped that the breakaway Somaliland is a safe haven from the political tyranny and clan cleansing Somalis had inflicted upon one another for decades. In reality, false unity under the flawed state which the Klan readily exploits has proven irredeemable bankrupt and disaster-prone; hence, there is no point in repeating the old mistakes, rebuilding the failed structures we have seen in the preceding chapters. Genuine unity—the only means of surviving in an ever competitive and confederating world—requires conditions which to this elude Somalis.

Yet there is another tragedy: into every island of peace Somalis rebuild on the ruins of war and misery, the same Klan infects its characteristic ineptitude, nepotism, and corruption. Somaliland is not an exception, although the evident inferno and vortex of mayhem Somalia had become since the collapse of the military regime had made Somaliland a place of refuge for all Somalis. In the final analysis, however, the Somali predicament under those three factors at work is a case of jumping from the frying pan into the fire, then leaping up from the fire into the frying pan! Clearly, then, the old and tired politics of the flawed state, the malfeasant Klan, and the distorted clan system must end and Somalis must invent new solutions if they are to successfully meet the challenges and imperatives of the 21st century.

Little in people's history happens by accident. History is the story of those who, with knowledge of their past and of who they are, envision a destination and know how to get there. Confused and divided selves relive pathology of history, repeating errors of the past, where today is only a repeat of yesterday and tomorrow is no different. Befuddled suckers and easy victims, they find predators at home and abroad who happily exploit them. Somalis found both in abundance. They shall continue to be suckers sleepwalking through history until they come to terms with their past, apprehending who they are, where they want to go, and how they shall get there.

Developments during the seventeen years after collapse of the state in 1991 show what Somalis did *to* themselves or *for* themselves. However, that is another story for which I devote a separate volume.

REFERENCE

Afrah, Mohamed Daahir (1987) *Fan-Masraxeedka Soomaalida*, Kenya.

Africa Watch (1990) *Somalia: A Government at War with its Own People.* Published by the Africa Watch Committee, New York: January 199.

Albertoni, Ettore. 1987. *Mosca and the Theory of Elitism.* Oxford: Basil Blackwell.

Andrzejewski, B.W. and Lewis, I.M. (1964) *Somali Poetry, An Introduction*, Oxford University Press.

Bottomore, T. (1993) *Elites and Society* (2nd Edition), London: Routeledge.

Brons, Maria H. (2001) *Society, Security, and the State in Somalia,* Utrecht, the Netherlands: International Books.

Bulhan, H. A. (1979) *Black Psyches in Captivity and Crisis*, Race & Class, 20(3), 243-261,

___________ (1980) *Psychological Research in Africa: Genesis and Function,* Presence Africaine, 116, 20,

___________ (1980) *Dynamics of Cultural In-Betweenity*, International Journal of Psychology, 15, 105-121,

___________ (1985) *Frantz Fanon and the Psychology of Oppression* New York: Plenum Publishing Corporation,

___________ (2004) *Ruin and Rebuilding – the Story of Somaliland*, World Bank,.

Burton, Richard F. (1894) *First Footsteps in East Africa.* London: Tylston and Edwards.

Ciise, Aw Jaamác Cumar. (1994) *Qaranjabkii Soomaliya.*, Mombasa, Kenya.

Davidson, Basil, Let Freedom Come, Africa in Modern History, Boston: Little, Brown.

Deng, F.M. et al (1996) *Sovereignty as Responbility—Conflict Management in Africa*, Washington, D.C. Brookings Institution.

Dool, Ábdulaahi (1998) *Failed States –When Governance Goes Wrong*, London: Horn Heritage Publications.

Drysdale, John (1964) *The Somali Dispute*, London: Pall Mall Press.

Drysdale, John (1994) *Whatever Happened to Somalia? A Tale of Tragic Blunders.* London: Haan.

Farah M. Mohamed (2004) *Timelines of Somali History*, Columbus, Ohio: Somali Media Network.

Ghalib, Jaamác Mohamed (1995) *The Cost of Dictatorship.* New York: Lilian Barber.

Hunt, E.K. (1981) *Property and Prophets— the Evolution of Economic Institutions and Ideologies*, New York:: Harper & Row Publishers.

Hobsbawm, Eric. 1991. *The Age of Empire,* London: Abacus.

Holcomb, Bonnie and Ibssa, Sisai. 1990. *The Invention of Ethiopia—the Making of a Dependent Colonial State in Northeast Africa.* New Jersey: The Red Sea Press.

Ibister, John (1995) *Promises Not Kept—the Betrayal of Social Change in the Third World*, Hartford, Connecticut: Kamarian Press,.

International Crisis Group (July 28, 2003) Report No. 66: *"Somaliland: Democratisation and Its Discontents."* Nairobi/Brussels.

Kapchits, G.L. (1998) *Gaamuuska Maahmaahyada Soomaaliyeed* (The Dictionary of Somali Proverbs). Moscow: Vostochnaya Literatura.

Lewis, I.M. (1994). *Blood and Bone, The Call for Kinship in Somali Society*, Lawrenceville, New Jersey: Red Sea Press.

LeShan, Lawrence (1992). *The Psychology of War—Comprehending its Mystique and its Madness,* Chicago: Noble Press.

Lewis, I.M. (1965) *The Modern History of Somaliland: From Nation to State*. London: Weidenfeld and Nicolson.

_________. (1961) *A Pastoral Democracy*. London: Oxford University Press.

_________ (1994). *Blood and Bone: The Call of Kinship in Somali Society*, New Jersy: Red Sea Press.

Mohamed, Ábdilqaadir Ósmaan(Oroomo), *Jamhuuriya*, June 29 and July 2, 2006

Hagi, Aves Osman Hagi and Hagi, Ábdiwahid Osman, (1998) *Clan, Sub-Clan and Regional Representation in the Somali Government Organization, 1960-1990: Statistical Data and Findings.*

Marcus, Harold. (1995). *The Life and Times of Menelik II – Ethiopia 1844-1913*, Lawrenceville, N.J.: Red Sea Press

Menkhaus, Ken, and J. Prendergast (1995) "Governance and Economic Survival in Post-Conflict Somalia." CSIS African Notes, Center for Strategic and International Studies, Washington, D.C.

Muxamed, Ibraahim Muxamed (Liiq Lliqate), *Taariikhda Soomaaliya,* Mogdishu. (No date of publication or publisher cited.)

Omar, Jaamá Mohamuud, 1992. *Maa-maaho iyo Maanso Soomaaliyeed*, Stockholm: Skolverket.

Omar, Mohamed Osman, 1992. The Road to Zero, Somalia's Self-Destrution. London: Haan Associates.

Rieber, R. W. and Green, M. 1995, "The Psychopathy of Everyday Life: Antisoical Behavior and Social Distrss," in R.W. Rieber (Ed.), *The Individual, Communication, and Society,* New York: Cambridge University Press, 1989.

Rieber, R.W.1997. *Manufacturing Social Distress—Psychopathy in Everyday Life*, New York: Plenum Press.

Rodney, Walter. 1974. *How Europe Underdeveloped Africa*, Washington, D.C: Howard University Press

Williams, Eric. 1966. *Slavery and Capitalism*, New York: Capricorn Books.

Walsh, L.P. 1890. *Under the Flag and the Somali Coast Stories*. London: Andrew Melrose.

Weber, Max. 1958. *the Protestant Ethic and the Rise of Capitalism*, New York.

Zartman, William, *Collapsed States—The Disintegration and Restoration of Legitimate Authority*, Boulder, Colorado: Lynne Rienner Publishers, 1993

NOTES

Preface

1. Quoted by William Zartman, Collapsed States, *The Disintegration and Restoration of Legitimate Authority*, Boulder, Colorado: Lynne Rienner Publishers, 1993, p. 3.
2. To be sure, his neurosis is neither unique nor isolated. It is a manifestation of an affliction rampant among the Somali elite, as I show in my work, *No Longer Myself.* For a detailed discussion of neurosis and generally alienation in situations of oppression, see my book, *Frantz Fanon and the Psychology of Oppression,* New York: Plenum Publishing Corporation, 1985. For discussion on alienation among Somalis, see my work on *No Longer Myself.*

Chapter 1

1. For detailed analysis of Somaliland history and politics, see my *Cinderella in the Horn—Conflict and Chang in Somaliland.*
2. For a review of the Ethiopian intervention and the Union of Islamic Courts, see, *Return of Cain,* a follow-up volume for this work.
3. The fact that today Somalis live under different political entities—including the Republic of Djibouti, Ethiopia, Kenya, Somalia, Puntland, and Somaliland—is not really as fundamental as often suggested. I shall return to this point in Chapter 13.
4. Many commentators, including Somalis, make the mistake of confusing tribe and clan. They use the two terms interchangeably. Members of a tribe may share a distant common descent but often they share common custom, language, and territory. Clans on the hand are *groups of families* whose members share a common ancestor. In this sense, Somalis belong to one tribe in the same way as do for instance the Yoruba of Nigeria and the Kikuyu of Kenya.
5. Quoted by Eric Hobsbawm in *The Age of Empire,* 1991, p. 1.
6. Somalis had no script until 1974 when a Latin-based orthography was developed and officially enforced by the military regime.

Chapter 2

1. There is disagreement as to the identity of the leader Somalis know as Ahmed Guray and described in Amharic literature as Ahmed Gragn. According to Somali accounts, Ahmed Garaad Ibraahim (Ahmed Guray) was born in Hobat, near Jileysa, halfway between Harar and Zayla. According to this, there is no doubt that Ahmed Guray was a Somali, although he drew his forces from different groups including the Afar and the Oromo who professed Islam.
2. The proxy wars continued to recent decades. Thus, from the nineteen-sixties to the early nineteen-eighties, the region was a venue for

superpower geo-political contest between the United States and the former USSR. Somalis and Ethiopians were once again pawns in this superpower contest, though each of them pursued local interests and pushed by demons of the past conflicts.

3. Richard F. Burton, *The First Footsteps in East Africa*, New York: Dover Publication, Pp. 77-78.
4. Ibid, 5 p. 79.
5. Quoted by Basil Davidson, *Let Freedom Come, Africa in Modern History*, p. 78.
6. Ibid., p. 79.
7. Quoted in Holcomb and Ibssa (1990), *The Invention of Ethiopia*, p. 93.
8. Ibid. p. 105. For a detailed discussion of Tewodros, Yohannes, and Menelik II, see Harold Marcus, *The Life and Times of Menelik Iil – Ethiopia 1844-1913*, Lawrenceville, N.J.: Red Sea Press, 1995.
9. See H.G.C. Swayne, Early Days in Somaliland and Other Tales, Durham: Pentland Press Ltd, 1996, p. 227.

Chapter 3

1. For the original poem in Somali (quoted by B.W. Andrzejewski and I.M Lewis, *Somali Poetry, An Introduction*, 1964, Oxford University Press, P. 57) is the following:

   Ingriis, Amxaar iyo Talyaan way akeekami ye,
   Arlada waa la kala boobayaa ka u itaal roon ee,
   Waa duni la kala iibsaday aan nala ogaysiin ee,
   Anse la ah, Aakhiru Sabaan iligyadiisii ye.

2 For detailed discussion on these meanings of possession, see *No Longer Myself.*

3 For the original poem in Somali is the following:

   Waa cadow Axmaarka galbeed, ka cartamaayaaye
   Waxa badaha ceegaaga waa, ciidan Fransiise
   Ingriisna Cadan buu ka iman, waana cudud weyne
   Gildhigaan caliqan sow Talyaan, soo camiri mayo?

4 For a detailed discussion, see Muxamed Ibraahim Muxamed (Liiq Lliqate), *Taariikhda Soomaaliya,* Mogdishu.

5 See I.M. Lewis, *Blood and Bone: The Call of Kinship in Somali Society*, Lawerenceville, N.J. 1994, p. 5.

6 Lij Iyasu was the heir apparent of the empire that Menelik II had developed from the small kingdom of Shawa. Soon after Lij Iyasu succeeded Menelik, the Highland Chrisitans accused him of being Muslim. Before he formed alliance with Mohamed Ábdulle Hassan, Lij Iyasu was dethroned and imprisoned until his death.

7 The original poem in Somali is the following:

   Dawa lagama helo gaal haddaad, daawo dhigataane
   Waa idin dagaayaa kufriga, aad u dabcaysaane

Dirhankuu idiin qubahayaad, dib u go'aysaane
Marka hore dabkuu idinka dhigi, dumar sidiisiiye
Marka xiggana daabaqadda yuu, inin dareensiine
Marka xiga dalkuu idinku odhan, duunyo dhaafsada ee
Marka xigta dushuu idinka rari, sida dameerahae...

8 The original poem in Somali is the following:

Irdihi biyaha waxa la dhigay, aarmi iyo xoog e…
Waa duni Adari iyo laysku xidhay, koonfur iyo Ayl e
Waa duni lakala iibsadoo, nala ogaysiin ee
Bahal samada eeraabayoo, aad u kala jeexay
Addimmadda ku soconeynin, oo la ambaqaadaayoo
Waa duni waxaa lagu arkiyo, Aakhir Sabankaase…

9 The original excerpt in Somali (taken from a recording by Jaamá Faarah Mohamed (Únaaye), assisted by Haaji Áli, and colleced by Hurre Walanwal) is the following:

Mar haddii gar-sare laga baqiyo, baadiyihi dibadda…
Banderkiina iimoobay, badow ka so maagay
Oo la buriyey diintiiyo xaqqaa, lagu badbaadaaye…
Oo ay bulshadu kadan tihiyo, baadi walligeedba…
Oo boogta kii dhayi lahaa, boqonta sii gooyey
Billaahaan ku dhaartee ma jiro, baarax nabadeede…

10 See L. P. Walsh, *Under the Flag and the Somali Coast stories*, London: Andrew Melrose, 1890.

11 Ibid, p. 215.

12 His father was also a colonial soldier before him until he was killed.

13 For detailed discussion on the BMD and history of the Somali police, see Jaamá Mohamed Ghalib, *The Cost Dictatorship—the Somali Experience.*

14 Personal communication from the late Robleh Michael Mariano, September, 28, 2000.

15 Only France continued to rule its colony based in Djibouti.

16 The original poem in Somali (quoted from Farah M. Mohamed, *Timelines of Somali History*, Columbus, Ohio: Somali Media Network, 2004) is the following:

Dorraad baa Bashiir lagu shanaqay daar agtiina ahe
Dahriga iyo laabtay rasaas kaga daloolsheene
Digashiyo dihaaniyo cag baa loogu sii daraye
Meydkiisa daahira markii dibada loo saarey
Ee aaska loo diidey waad wada dul joogteene
Ma damqane jidhkiinuye markaa waad ku digateene
Nasab hadaad durrayadii tihiin kama dareerteene
Waa dabac idiin gooniyaan duulna waafiqine.

17 I credit the list and clan description of ministers and others to Aves Osman Hagi and Ábdiwahid Osman Hagi, *Clan, Sub-Clan and Regional Representation in the Somali Government Organization, 1960-1990: Statistical Data and Findings, 1998.*

18 See Muxamed Ibraahim Muxamed (Liiq –Liiqato), *Taariikhda Soomaaliya,* p. 110

19 John Drysdale, *Stoics without Pillows*, Haan Associates Publishing, 2000, p.68.

20 Alex Qolqolle served as interpreter for the colonial administration.

21 The original song in Somali is the following:

Soomaaliyeey tooso
Tooso isku tiirsada ee
Kulba kina taag daran
Taageera waligiine..

22 The song in Somali (quoted in *Fan-Masraxeedka Soomaalida*, by Mohamed Daahir Afrax, 1987, Kenya) is the following:

Ka kacaay! Ka kacaay!
Laysku soo korodhyee, ka kacaay
Kaftankii ma jiree ka ka kacaay
Kooraleey la gubyee ka kacaay....

23 The song in Somali is the following:

Dhallintii waddankiyo dhulkaynu nahoo
Labood iyo dhaddig, wax meel dhiganno
Inaanu dhimanniyo, inaanu dhallanno
Maantaan waxba nooga dhexaynayn!

24 The original poem in Somali (quoted from *Maa-maaho iyo Maanso Soomaaliyeed*, by Jaamá Mohamuud Úmar, 1992) is the following:

Awowgey ninki indhaha tiray
Ninkii aabbahay addoonsaday
Ninkii anigana i iibsaday
Ninkii ifka igu adduun tiray
Itaal li'ibaa ishaa i bide
Haddaan ogohoonan ka aarsan karayn
Haddaanan Aadanow unuuka jarayn
Ninkaa aragiisa urkaan ka necbee
Aan ooye albaabka ii xidha.

25 Ceding the Haud and the Reserved Area to Ethiopia was included in the 1897 Anglo-Ethiopian Treaty. Somalis became aware of the treaty and its full import only in 1934 when a joint commission, representing Britain and Ethiopia, had started to demarcate the boundary as agreed in the 1897 Anglo-Ethiopian Treaty.

26 For a detailed discussion on the betrayal of the NFD, see John Drysdale, *The Somali Dispute*, London: Pall Mall Press, 1964.

27 The original song in Somali is the following:
Meykal waa Kristaan
Ahmed baa Muslinee
Raaca yaa waddani…

28 The original song in Somali is the following:
Maqalay war la'ay
Meykal iska eeq
Maska daba socdiyo
Meykal iska eeg
Midiibu sita
Meykal iska eeg
Yaanu ku makalin ee
Meykal iska eeg...

29 The original poem in Somali is the following:
Halkii aan dad ii soo kordhiyo, darar ka eegaayey
Iyaba waa darxumo ii maqan ee, dacar miyaan leefay,
Ma dorraato raadkaan dhigaan, dib ugu soo laabtay
Sidiiyoon dayays nahay miyaan, dawgii ka habaabay
Isma doorin Gaalkaan diriyo, daarta kii galaye
Dusha midabka Soomaalidaad, dugul ka mooddaaye
Misna laguma diirsado qalbiga, waa dirkii Karale.

30 The original song is the following:
Hir bay laacayoo hinqaday
Hillaac bay baxoo handaday
Haddana waayayoo hakaday…

31 The original song in Somali is the following:
Adduunyo hal baan laha
Hashii horror baa la tagay
Hadhuub madhan baan sita.

Another verse affirms:
Hadhuub nin sitoo, hashiisso irmaan
"Ha maalin" la leeyahaan ahay..
(A man with a container, [his] camel fucund wih milk
Yet I am told "don't milk it")

32 The poem in Somali (quoted from from *Collection of Ábdillaahi Suldaan's (Timaádde) Poems* written by Ábdi Yuusuf Duáale) is the following:
Qasaaraa dhexdeena ah haddaan, laysku qabanaynin
Qabaa'il iyo jeeroo la naco, qaadkan lagu waashay
Qasdi jeeroy wada yeelatoo, qawlka ku heeshiiso
Qabyo weeye Soomaalidaay, qiiradaadaniye.

33 In fact, Shuriye was favored over Ábdilaahi (Mohamed?) Sheekh Muuse, a Sacaad Muuse candidate, and Úmar was favored over another member of the Isaaq majority.

34 The original song in Somali is the following:

Qolaba Calenkeedu, waa Caynoo
Innaga keenu, wa cirkoo kale e
Aan caadna lahayn, ee caashaq ee.

35 The original poem in Somali (included in *Collection of Ábdillaahi Suldaan's Poems,* compiled by Ábdi Yuusuf Duáale, Boobe) is the following:

Soomaalidoo calan taagta
Saakay noogu horreysoo
In sidayda tihiin iyo
In kalaanan saxaynine
Saddex 'wiig' iyo maalmo
Haddaan soor cuni waayo
Safrad layga ma yaaboo
Sari na meyso naftayda e
Saaxirkii ka la guuraye'
Sarreeyow ma-nusqaamow
Aan siduu yahay eego e'
Kaa na sib kan na saar.

36 John Drysdale, *Stoics Without Pillows,* p. 71.

37 List of names for the table and data for chart were drawn from the work of Aves Osman Hagi and Ábdiwahid Osman Hagi, ibid. To avoid repitition of the same statement, similar information and data presented in subsequent pages are drawn from the same source.

38 John Drysdale, Stoics *Stoics Without Pillows*, Haan Associates Publishing, 2000.

39 In fact, Aadan Ábdulle Ósmaan had continued his moderating influence in subsequent years after clan politics became most deadly and destructive. Unfortunately, the events unfolding after the nineteen-seventies had overwhelmed the goodwill and conciliatory power he could muster. He also has the credit of being the only politician who peacefully left office by vote and turned to admirable private life, mostly on his farm.

40 From personal conversation with Ábdirahmaan Shuke.

Chapter 4

1 The Somali elite's use of the terms "tribe" and "tribalism" reflected the language of the colonialists whom they emulated. For the colonialists, Africa was the Dark Continent where social differences did not matter and subtlties did not exist. One never hears Europeans defined in terms of tribe; they are discussed in term of nations.

Only with respect to non-European populations, particularly Africans, is the concept of tribe invoked, to implicitly suggest low evolution in their sociology, culture, and politics.

2 For discussion on delusion of clan superiority and Horror of clan inferiority, see Chapter 13.

3 The original poem in Somali is the following:

Aan dallaco aan daar dheer u baxo oo daaqadda ha taaban
Aan dibbiro dulbaaxdana aan cuno iina dudi maysid
Deynkiina ii keen waxaan qabayna waa duudsi
Waa xaal Diktaatooriyaan dad isku raacayne
Doqon baa sidaa laga helaa diidney oo keliya

4 The allegation that the two men were dismissed because of alleged mental illness may very well be an exaggeration, although both might have been dismissed for old age.

5 These characterizations of Ábdirashiid Áli Sharmaarke were provided by persons who knew him, including Ábdi Hassan Buuni, who worked as his deputy from July 22, 1960 to July 27, 1961. Buuni shared with me his assessment of the man in evening discussions at Xaraf Restaurant in 2006.

6 The 13 members expelled included ministers (Ósmaan Mohamuud Ádde and Ismaíil Duáale Warsame) whom Ábdirazaaq had earlier dismissed from his cabinet. Also included in the group was "Awil Haaji Ábdulaahi who had resigned from Ábdirazaaq's cabinet.

7 See Hagi, Aves Osman Hagi and Hagi, Ábdiwahid Osman, (1998) *Clan, Sub-Clan and Regional Representation in the Somali Government Organization, 1960-1990: Statistical Data and Findings.* P. 18

8 In a speech he delivered to a Somali audience in Virginia in September 2002, he explained that he spent much of his inheritance on pursuit of politics and women.

9 The original poem in Somali is the following;

Danlaydaan arrad-beeline…
Ku dul qaadayo roobku
Neefkay daajinayaan iyo…
Cashuurtaa wanka daylan
Shilinkaan ka dayayno
Nin intuu dem ka siiyay
Daaro dheer ka samaystay
Intaa aan la dabraynineen
Degdeg loo xukumaynin…
Cigaalow degi meyso.17

10 For detailed discussion on manipulation of votes in this election, see Jaamá Mohamed Gaalib's *The Cost of Dictatorship—The Somali Experience,* New York, L. Barber, 1995.

11 The original poem in Somali is the following:

Sidi baan Makale lagu gubtiyo
milic u joogaaye
Sidi baan madaal dheri karshiyo
rodol u miistaaye
Sidi baan tacliin uga madnahay
machadkii diineed...
Isagaa maqsuudee wax kale
nooma maamuline
Bal muxu, macneeyoo, i taray
ministarkaan doortay?

Quoted by Mohamed Daahir Afrax, *Fan-Masraxeedka Soomaalida*—a valuable work on the history and analysis of Somali theatre and drama. Pp. 64-65.

Chapter 5

1 For detailed discussion on the psychosocial functions the dream of Pan-Somali Unity had served, see H.A. Bulhan, *Pathology of History.*

2 The original poem in Somali is the following:

Dugsigii Barlamaankiyo
Dekeddii Hamar baa leh
Berbera daadku ha qaado
Doonniyi yaanay ku weecan
Duqeydii Barlamaankaay
Labadaa ka la daaya oo
Yaan loo deymo la'aan.

3 Jaamá Mohamed Galib, *The Cost of Dictatorship—The Somali Experience,* New York, L. Barber, 1995, p. 123

4 The original Somali song is the following:

Tan iyo qaylo doonkii
Gumaystihii qudhmuunaa
Aan ku qaadno lagu yidhi
In yar oo qaloocdo
Qaadhaab doona mooye
Qiiradu makalahadhin
Lagu Qaaday calankii
Qoob kalese lama rogin.
Bal wax qabasho daayo
Qima dawladnimo iyo
Qaranimo la duuduub
Qoloqolo dib loo raac.

5 Personal communication, General Mohamed Hussein Hiirane, Silver Spring, Maryland, summer 2001.

6 Personal communication from Ábdiraxman Shuke in June 2003 while we flew in ECHO plane, a UN-chartered plane, from Hargeysa to Nairobi.

7 Personal communication in January 2004 from Mohamed Haaji Aadan, at one time a key member of the SSDF and subsequently of the SNM. Mohamed is belonged to the wing of the SSDF opposed to Colonel Ábdulaahi Yuusuf Ahmed, the President of Puntland.

8 To set the record straight, neither General Mohamed Hussein Hirane nor Ábdiraxman Shuke directly or indirectly connected Ábdirazaaq Haaji Hussein in the assassination of President Ábdirashiid Áli Sharmaarke. Moreover, this author who had known Ábdirazaaq Haaji Hussein when he served as the Somali Representative in the United Nations believes that the man possesses neither the personal inclination nor mean streak to join an ssassination plot for the sake of power.

9 The suggestion of KGB involvement in the assassination of President Sharmaarke came up in a wide-ranging afternoon conversation I had with Mohamed Saíid Gees, Saíid Ahmed, 'Abdirahmaan Waabare, and others on April 26, 2008 at the Academy for Peace and Development, Hargeysa, Somaliland.

10 The original song in Somali is the following:

Qiiqbaa saro u kacay
Qayadiisa roobkana
Dhibico gururux ah keeneen
Qawlaysta timid
Isticmaar qabbaan u ah
Wax qaboojiyaa jirin.

Chapter 6

1. For detailed discussion on the history and development of the Somali police force, see the website allrefer.com and H.A. Bulhan, Ruin and Rebuilding – the Story of Somaliland, World Bank, 2004.
2. There is a question of whether Mohamed Siyaad Barre had first joined the Mussolini's colonial system or if he was recruited into the police during the British Military Administration. A Mareehaan military officer, Colonel Ábdi Isxaaq Xiniin, who personally knew the dictator for decades and fought on his behalf to the end of his reign claims that it was his father, nicknamed Siyaad Garabwayne, who had served as a sargeant in the Italian fascist forces.
3. According to Colonel Ábdi Isxaaq Xiniin, Mohamed Siyaad Barre was indeed an only son but that he had numerous sisters. This account contradicts the claim of Siyaad Barre's sterility.
4. Fasci or fascio, the root term for fascism, was the symbol of bound sticks used as totem of power in ancient Rome.

5. For details on the cruelties of Italian colonial rule in Somalia, see Sylvia Pankhurst, *Ex-Italian Somaliland*, London: Watts & Co., 1951.
6. Richard Greenfield confirms the admiration Mohamed Siyaad Barre had for these leaders. See "Obiturary: Siyaad Barre" in www.netnomad.com, January 3, 1995.
7. As mentioned earlier, rumors of illigetimacy are common tools of character assassination particularly in Somali society. Not surprisingly, one also hears today in Somaliland similarly hushed rumors about the illegitimacy of the late President of Mohamed Ibraahim 'Égaal—again a rumor intended to undermine him with words when political or military action failed.
8. The eight men sent to Italy for training were: Saddex Xarigle Mohamed Siyaad Barre, Saddex Xarigle Hussein Kulmiye Afrah, laba Xarigle Mohamed Ibraahim Mohamed (Liiq liiqato), Laba Xarigle Mohmaed Abshir Muuse, Laba Xarigle Ábdalla CÁli Mohamed, Xarigle Daud Ábdulle Hirsi, Xarigle Mohamed Aynanshe Guled, and Xarigle Mohamed Bin Khamis. For details of the political context in which these men were sent for training, see Taarikhda Soomaaliya by Muxamed Ibraahim Muxamed (Liiq Liiqato).
9. Jaamá Mohamed Ghalib, *The Cost of Dictatorship—the Somali Experience*, New York: Lillian Barber Press, 1995, p. 41.
10. General Mohamed Hussein shared with me this view of Mohamed Abshir Muuse in a conversation I had with him in 2000 in the United States. In this and other conversations, it was clear to me how profoundly General Mohamed Hussien (Xiirane) respects Mohamed Abshir Muuse and in equal measure hated Mohamed Siyaad Barre. He added that Mohamed Abshir shied from making his belief known to others.
11. Mohamed Gees, former Minister of Finance for the break-away Republic of Somaliland and now Director of the Academy for Peace and Development, reports that General Mohamed Qoorsheel who succeeded Mohamed Abshir Muuse as Commander the Police affirmed the same before his death.
12. Jaamá Mohamed Ghalib, *The Cost of Dictatorship---the Somali Experience*, NewYork: Lilian Barber Press, 1995, p.67.
13. Personal communication, 2006, Hargeysa, Somaliland.
14. In the BBC series on Somali history, Colonel Ábdulaahi Yuusuf Ahmed told his version of how the coup of 1969 had been planned and carried out.
15. Ábdulaahi openly admitted to that effect in the BBC series on Somali history.

16. Mohamed Sheekh Aadan, a leading activist in the SSDF and Mijeerteen politics, shared this behind-the-scene account with me in 2005.
17. The account presented here was told to the author by Hussein Áli Duáalle in September 2001 in Hargeysa.
18. Ábdilaahi Adan Rayiid was not a graduate of Sandhurst. He was trained in Egypt. Áwil claims that he was a graduate of the Royal Military Academy at Sandhurst. But this is contradicted by former graduates of the Academy like General Ismaíil Áli Abokor who affirmed that Áwil belonged to a group provided a short course of six months training in Britain.
19. Personal communication in Hargeysa, August 2004.
20. Some people state that their problem began before the union took place when Mohamed Ibraahim Égaal failed to upgrade their ranks to give them the edge they over their southern counterparts who were policemen transferred to the armed forces with minimal military training. If Egaal had devalued them, the Southerners followed suit. And if this claim is true, one would not be surprised that they held no loyalty to Egaal in subsequent years, especially so when Mohamed Siyaad Barre was planning a military coup in 1968 and 1969.
21. Some people describe this event as a "coup attempt." I prefer to call it a revolt because, having taken place in Hargeysa, it was too remote to effect change in structure of the state, neither in Mogadishu nor in Hargeysa, and too short-lived to have significant effect in the balance of power.
22. Among the men appointed to diplomatic posts were Hassan Ábdulle Walanwal (known as Hassan Kayd), the leader of the revolt, and the two men who had visited General Daud Ábdulle Hirsi and General Mohamed Siyaad Barre in 1961.
23. BBC series on Somali history.
24. The original poem in Somali (in Aw-Jaamác Cumar Ciise's *Qaranjabkii Soomaaliya,* 1995, p. 20) s the following:

    Run Illaah Rashiidow ma tihid kii Illaah rabaye
    Soomaali baad kala rartay oo reerba meel degaye
    Rafaad noqotay dunidii markii rays lagaa dhigaye
    Kol haddaan Ra'iis sida Jaamáal laguugu raacaynin
    Rucbi kugu dhaca iyo cudur xunoo raarta kula jiifa
    Ruush iyo midaan laga daaweyn Rooma iyo Kiinya
    Kursigoo kula Ruxda iyo Ciidankoo talada kaa riixda
25. Personal communication from Mohamed Saqadhy Dubad at the Hargeysa Club, January 2005.
26. Pesonal communication with Ja'far Gaadaweyne.

27. The original song in Somali is the following:

Same diidow
Dabin baa kuu dhigan
Lagugu dili doono
Daneystow duugtaadu
Waa daldalaad
Aan dacwo laheyn.

Chapter 7

1. Personal communication, August, 2004, Hargeysa.
2. Personal communication by Mohamuud Saalah Nuur (Fagadhe), January 2004, Hargeysa
3. For detailed discussion of secrets and rumor in Somali society, see *Archeology of Experience.*
4. The original song in Somali is the following:

Qaaradda madow een
Qaynuunka guud iyo
Qaabkaba wadaangnaa
Quluba-gediga iyo
Midka goriga haystaa
Qabsadaa ku badan yahay
Waase loo qormeeyo
Qiil bay u haystaan
La yidhaa wax lama qaban.

5. See Aw-Jaamác Cumar Ciise, *Qaranjabkii Soomaliya*, page 27.
6. Jaamá Mohamed Ghalib, *The Cost of Dictatorship,*p. 67
7. Ibid, p. 68.
8. Hussein Áli Duáale (Áwil) shared the story with me in December 2000 in Hargeysa.
9. John Drysdale, *Stoics without Pillows*, Haan Associate Publishing, 2000, p. 71
10. Personal communication with Mohamed Saqadhe Dubad in January, 2005 at the Hargeysa Club, Hargeysa, Somaliland.
11. By Somali reckoning of time, "last night by nine" translates into "last night by 3:00 A.M". The song refers to the very hour when the coup was carried out.
12. The original song in Somali is the following:

Haddii xalay sagaalkii
Xilqaadkii noo hagaagay
Oo maanta xooggii haystoo
Xamddi Ilaahay weeye
Magacii waa xoroobee
Magacii waa xoroobee.

Xalaal dhammaan u ciidaa.
Xukuumaddi qabiil iyo
Xumaaha noo horseeday
Haddii dhammaan la xooray
Oo maanta xooggii haystoo
Magacii waa xoroobee
Magacii waa xoroobee

13. The original song in Somali is the following:
    Run haddan ku hadlaynoo
    Rabbigeen ka baqaynno
    Raggiinan aarmiga haystaa
    Mar inaad rogataan
    Annagu waan rabnayoo
    Raali baan ka ahayne
    Idin kaa naga raagay…

14. For further details on the subject, note Ábdi Daahir Afay's discussion in the BBC series on Somali history and Mohamed Siyaad Barre's explanation on October 21, 1972 duplicated in Yaasin Kenadiid's *Qaamuuska Af-Soomaaliga*, Mogadishu, 1976.
15. The BBC series on Somali history, 2000
16. Personal communication with General Ismaíil Áli Abokor in Ming Sing Restaurant, Hargeysa, August, 2004.
17. Ibid
18. Ibid
19. See A Government at War with Its Own People, An Africa Watch Report, January 1991.
20. Since 1971, the Special Prosecutor was Mohamed Ghelle Yuusuf – a man known for callousness and cruelty.
21. The song in its original Somali is the following:
    Turun turootoo
    Kuftay, kuftay
    Ayaad taqaan?
    Talaabsan weydoo
    Dhacday, dhacday
    Ayaad taqaan?
    Taladii seegtoo luntay
    Ayaad taqaan?
    Ee maxaad taqaan?

22. *"Qof kasta oo mas'uul meel ka ah oo aan lo socon ujeedada Kaánka waxaa waajib ku ah in uu shaqada iskaga tago",* quoted by Aw Jaamác Cumar Ciise, *ibid*, p. 37.
23. These two statements are quoted by Aw Jaamác Nuur, p.48.
24. The song in Somali was the following:

Waddadii caddayd
Cagta saartayee
Ku carraabiyo
Cimrigii jiryoow
Jiryoow, jiryoow
Caynaanka hay
Hay, hay,
Waligaa hay...
Caqi toosanoo
Caafmaad qabaad
Nagu caymisee
Cimrigii jiryoow
Jiryoow, jiryoow
Caynaanka hay
Hay, hay,

25. General Ismaíil Áli Abokor assisted FRELIMO in Mozambique. Included in this elite corps was also Colonel Ábdilqaadir Kosaar who had spent years in training fighter sin Equatorial Guinea. During the nineteen-eighties, he joined the Somali National Movement in order to fight against the very regime that had sent him to train other Africans to win their liberty. After a short service to the SNM as its chairman, Kosaar died before his movement reached its goal of liberating Somaliland
26. The song in Somali is the following:

Guul wade Siad
Abihii Garashada
Gayigaayagow
Hantiwadaagga waa habkaa
Barwaaqo noo horseedayee
Bullaankan baxaaya
Nuurkan bidhaamaya
Dhawaaqa oo isu baqaya
Waa barbaartiyo shaqaalaha
Oo is biirsaday
Bar-bar taagan towradooda
Ra'yigii ka so baxa
Oo ballan qaaday
Ha... Ha...

Hantiwadaag inay badbaadiyaan

27. See Mohamed Osman Omar, author of The Road to Zero, Somalia's Self-Destrution.
28. The Somali name for this daily was Xiddigta Oktoobar -- commemorating the month when the 1969 coup was carried out. A periodical called Halgan (The Struggle) was also among the most known medium in this genre supporting the regime and its dissimulated socialist ideology. Its founder and director was Dr. Mohamed Adan Sheekh, a Mareehaan and medical doctor, who served as close advisor of Mohamed Siyaad d Barre until he opposed the regime's policies in its last years and was imprisoned.
29. Personal communication by Ibraahim Meygaag Samatar, 1997.
30. For a detailed discussion of these and other aspects of the regime's instruments of control, see Ábdulaahi Dool, *Failed States – When Governance Goes Wrong*, London: Horn Heritage Publications, 1998.
31. The song in its Somali original was the following:

    Ma ogtahay Hindiya Ooshin baan ku ag wareegaye
    Ma ogtahay askari jaahilaan amar ka qaataye
    Ma ogtahay anfacaan cunaa ma laha iidane
    Ma ogtahay waxaan eersadaa Odayga weeyaane.

    See Aw Jaamác Cumar Ciise, *Qaranjabkii Soomaliya,* 1995, p. 38. I later learned that the composers of this song included Faisal Ali Mushtake and other teachers from the former British Protectorate now called Somaliland.

32. Mohamed Hassan Gani informed me that Ceel Jaalle existed in Amoud and perhaps Qalax Gabiley.
33. List cited by Aw Jaamác Cumar Ciise, *Qaranjabkii Soomaliya*, 1995, p. 74
34. The song in its Somali original was the following:

    Guul wade Siad
    Abihii Garashada
    Gayigaayagow
    Hantiwadaagga waa habkaa
    Barwaaqo noo horseedayee…

Chapter 8

1. See the Somali version of the speech in Aw-Jaamác Cumar Ciise, *Qaranjabkii Soomaliya*, 1995, Pp. 28-32. It is from this source that selected the above excerpt and translated it into English.
2. The original song in Somali is the following:

    Ishayada guduudan

Goobta aad ku aragtaan
Geed kaama qariyee
Gabade, gabade, gabade
Gabade, way ku aragtaa…

3 Many Somalis believe that there was conspiracy to assassinate President Sharmaarke, that Mohamed Siyaad Barree was involved in this conspiracy, and that the man excuted for the murder was merely an underling of Mohamed Siyaad Barre. The investigantion of the assassination was perfunctory and secretive, as was the court hearing. Instead of properly investigating and trying the assassination, the NSC focused greater attention and effort on silencing "anti-revolutionaies" by sentences of long-term imprisonment or execution.

4 Quoted in Ábdulaahi *Dool's* *Failed States*, London, Horn Heritage, 1998, p. 24.

5 I highlight how the system of terror threw its full weight on the Isaaq in next chapter. For detailed discussion on this topic, however, see A Government At War with Its Own People, An Africa Watch Report, January 1990 and my book *Injuries of A Generation.*

6 The original song in Somali is the following:

Same diidoow
Dabin baa kuu dhigan
Lagugu dili doono
Daneystow duugtaadu
Waa daldalaad
Aan dacwo laheyn

7 This inter-clan fighting, among the worst experienced in the early nineteen-nineties, was mainly between the Habar Gidir and the Abgaal, both of the Hawiye clan-family.

8 There is a troubling inconsistency here. If Colonel Xiniin's story is true, either Dheel was part of the coup planned by Áynaanshe in 1969 but, having betrayed it, he would not be trusted by the latter in another coup attempt, or the colonel's story on Áynaanshe's coup plans and Dheel's betrayal is not true.

9 As mentioned earlier, manipulating women's sympathy and support had been a favored tactic of Siyaad Barre. Whenever he found the opportunity, Siyaad Barre used women to entrap, humiliate, or break his male opponents, real or potential.

10 These two statements are quoted by Aw Jaamác Cumar Ciise, p.48.

11 Some members of the Somali Revolutionary Socialist Party (SRSP) report that General Mohamed Áli Samatar, briefing party members at the Peoples' Hall, officially stated that the war started on 7 July 1977. They add that Ahmed Suleymaan Dafle, briefing mem-

bers of the party on the same topic, stated that the WSLF infiltrated into Ethiopia and started attacks earlier in 1976.

12 In the BBC interview aired on 12 October, General Mohamed Áli Samatar declared that causalties of the Somali armed forces totalled 5,500. He estimated casualties of the Ethiopian forces totalled between 15,000 and 17,000.

13 BBC series on Somali history, 2000.

14 Ibid.

Chapter 9

1. For details on the song, see the preceding chapter.
2. As I mentioned earlier, the term "tribalism" is inappropriate in the Somali context. Technically, Somalis are differentiated on the basis of clans – not tribes. They all belong to one "tribe".
3. Personal communication, General Mohamed Hussein Hiirane, Silver Spring, Maryland, summer 2001.
4. The minister was Aadan Isaaq Ahmed, a Gadabursi and the former Minister of Education.; Ábdirahmaan Ábdilaahi Jumáalle reported this account in 2002.
5. Personal communication by Ahmed Sheik Jaamá, Hargaysa, May 2004.
6. Personal communication, July 2007.
7. Statements like these did not only guide the selection of party members; it also gave the dictator license to the myriad of security agencies to intensify their persecution of people on the basis of their *belief*, or even *presumed belief*. It was no longer necessary to judge someone on his words or deeds – inference of his belief on any basis had constituted sufficient proof for promoting, demoting, imprisoning, torturing, or executing him. From there on, judgement of one's guilt or innocence became exclusively a prerogative of the state.
8. Note the size of the Committee changed from a total of 71 in 1976, to 56 in 1982, to 47 in 1986.
9. Ábdi Yuusuf Duáale (Boobe), personal communication.
10. For examples of these jokes, see my manuscript, *Demons in Somali Politics*.
11. I heard this statement reinvoked in a BBC interview with Dr. Chris Nteta – a medical doctor turned politician who was a key advisor to Kamuza Banda.
12. This story is told to me by my Somali friends whom we exchange news and stories at Starbuck in Silver Spring, Maryland. They include professionals of different fields, a former military general and a cornel, a prominent businessman and politician – all from Mogadishu or Puntland.
13. For further details on the genocide, see *Injuries of a Generation*. Incidentally, Mohamed Saíid Hirsi wears a big moustache and a beard to hide his cleft-lip. But will he find a cover for his crimes against humanity? Will the day of reckoning come for him in a court of justice like that at Hague? Or, will he continue to find refuge in the fold of his clan?

14. I published the poem n the *Horn of Africa Journal* in 1981 under the pen name of Mohamoud Hassan because, as one of the editors of the journal, a pen name retained the image of neutrality to the journal.
15. See Ábdulaahi Dool, Failed States, p. 146.
16. Ábdulaahi Dool, Failed States, p. 135.
17. Ibid, p. 87
18. Personal communication by Ahmed Mohamed Mohamuud (Siilaanyo), 2001, Hargyesa.
19. For the detailed discussion on intrigues and incompetence of the Foreign Ministry and the embassies, see Ábdulaahi Dool, *Failed States – When Governance Goes Wrong!*, London: Horn Heritage Publications, 1998.
20. See Aw Jaamá *Qaranjabkii Soomaliya*, Mombasa, Kenya, 1994.
21. Personal communication, Ahmed Aadan Sheekh (Jangali), Washington, D.C., 1995.
22. The President's second wife, Dalaya Haaji Hashi, was reputedly a a modest and cordial women who kept herself out of the public arena and the rough politics as well as get-rich-quick schemes for which Khadiija was known.

Chapter 10

1. The military regime and generally the elite chose aspects of tradition that suited them, dismissing those that did not. For instance, they embraced the clannism and tradition of looting, but they ignored prohibition of the indigenous culture placed against certain abuse and cruelty even in time of war. These injunctions evolved from the social values and code of conduct (*dhaqan*) that was no less binding than customary law (*xeer*). An example of these was the custom of *bir-magaydo* that specified the ethics of war. It prohibited abuse of certain groups like children, women, disabled persons, religious leaders, and poets. Members internalized rules guiding their behavior toward others, as illustrated by the proverb: *Wallaalka maragga ku fur, magtana la Bihi*—'Bear witness against your brother [for a crime you know he committed], but share with him payment of compensation.'
2. The list and clan description are from the collection by Aves Osman Hagi and Ábdiwahid Osman Hagi on *Clan, Sub-Clan and Regional Representation in the Somali Government Organization, 1960-1990: Statistical Data and Findings, 1998.*
3. Ibid
4. Ibid
5. Ibid
6. Ibid
7. The table distilled from names and clan identity of police generals provided by Ábdilqaadir Ósmaan Mohamed (Oroomo), *Jamhuuriya*, June 29 and July 2, 2006.

8. Ibid
9. Ibid
10. Ibid
11. Ibid
12. Ibid
13. Ábdulaahi Dool, *Failed States – Why Governance Goes Wrong*, London: Horn Heritage Publications, 1998, pp. 56-57.

Chapter 11

1. In this chapter, I will use the terms "South" and the "North" to refer respectively to the territory formerly ruled by Italy and the former British Protectorate. These terms were used since the union of the two former colonies in 1960. Today, following the unilateral declaration of independence in May 1991, the "North" prefers to be called and is called Somaliland.
2. The regime's responses to the drought of 1974, called *Daba Dheere*, was historic and momentous. It moved thousands of drought-stricken nomads to farming and fishing communities not only to save them but also to transform their way of life. Unfortunately, the bold initiative and experiment had failed later because the regime's bureaucratic rigidity and Mohamed Siyaad Barre's stultifying personality cult had undermined it.
3. This pilot made history by showing his humanity and genuine commitment to Somali people. It is unfortunate that he is neither recognized for his courage and commitment nor enticed back from life abroad to help in the reconstruction of the country. The moral, ethical, and national example he set is to this day sorely needed.
4. See Aw Jaamác Cumar Ciise, *Qaranjabkii Soomaliya.,* 1994, Mombasa, Kenya.
5. In his *Qaranjabkii Soomaliya*, Aw Jaamá argues that it was the Mareehaan who sold the arms to the Hawiye. In contrast, a former Mareehaan colonel, Ábdi Isaaq Xiniin, argues that the Mijeerteen sold the arms to the Hawiye.
6. According to some, the Gaalgale belong to the Daarood Clan-family and to the Mijeerteen sub-clan. Called Nuux Mohamuud, their lineage joins the Mohamuud Saleebaan. See Aw Jaamá Íîise, *Qaranjabkii Soomaliya*, p. 134.
7. One leader of the Gaalgale—nicknamed *Geeda Qore*—had even made a sculptor of Mohamed Siyaad Barre to show his admiration and love of the dictator. It is said that, in return, Mohamed Siyaad Barre lavished him with gifts and gave his clan extensive arms in order to defend the regime.
8. See Aw Jaamác Ciise, *Qaranjabkii Soomaliya,* p. 134.
9. Quoted by Mohamed M. Afrah, *The Somali Tragedy,* 1994, p. 42.

10. For a detailed version of this story in the "Jareer" vernacular, see Aw Jaamá Cumar Ciise, *Qaranjabkii Soomaliya,* pp. 130-133. I translated Aw Jaamá's version and modified it to make more readable.
11. Personal communication from Ábdiraxman Ábdilaahi Jumáalle and Ábdiraxman Yuusuf 'Artan.
12. The late Bashiir Buux affirmed that he saw these words written on the weapons the regime's soldiers carried with them.
13. See Aw Jaamác cumar Ciise, *Qaranjabkii Soomaliya,* p. 139.
14. According to the colonel, Mohamed Siyaad Barre was never the same after the car accident. He adds that the death of his regime began after the car accident.
15. This daughter of Mohamed Siyaad Barre is also the wife of General Mohamed Saíid Hirsi (Morgan)—the last Minister of Defense under whose call Mogadishu went up in smoke and, three years earlier, Hargiesa was raised to the ground.
16. *Dagalkii Carmiska* could be the translated as the War of 'Armiska – 'Armiska being a place near Afgooye. If the word is literally translated, it could also mean the War of Teaching Lessons.
17. For this perspective on why the Daarood forces were defeated, see Aw Jaamác Úmar Ciise's *Qaranjabkii Soomaliya,* pp. 152-153.
18. See Aw Jaamá Úmar Íise, *Qaranjabkii Soomaaliya,* p. 153.

Chapter 12

1. For a detailed discussion of SNM history, see my work on Cinderella in the *Horn: Conflict and Change in Somaliland.*
2. Ibid.
3. I found a copy of the film accidentally in one of my visits of Hargeysa in 1997. The person who had possession of it entrusted it with me to take it to the United States to make copies of it and to disseminate it. What I found interesting is that it became news in Hargeysa when a Minister of the Somlailand Government brought a copy of the film from the United States. This event underscored for me how often officials and others ignore historical, cultural or social facts available in their own land only to hail it as worthwhile news when brought from Europe and the United States.
4. See *Injuries of A Generation* for further details on the effects of such violence on civilians, men and women, adults and children.

The original song in Somali is the following:

SYL Illaah ka ma baqdiyo, ololii naareede….
Asalkeeda Soomaali baan, ururinaynaaye
Kuwii loo igimaday waa kuwaa, aakhiro u ridaye
Wasiirradan ugaadhsiga bartee, Orobo ka dhowrtaysta
Astaan bay ku wada leeyihiin, meel aan la arkayn.

(This abbreviated stanza was taken from Ábdi Yuusuf Duáale's book on Ábdillaahi Suldaan (Timaádde). The English translation is mine.)

5. See *Humanitarian Aid in Somalia*, report of the Refugee Policy Group, Washington, D.C., 1994, pp. 6-7.
6. Áli Khalif Galaydh who became the Prime Minister of the so-called National Transitional Government formed in 'Arta, Republic of Djibouti, in the summer of 2000 had lost parliamentary vote of confidence following charges of fiscal irregularities and inability to restore peace in Mogadishu, let alone the rest of the country. No evidence was presented to support the first charge while the second was based on unrealistic expectations since even President Ábdulaahi Yuusuf and two successive of Prime Ministers during his tenure could not restore peace in Mogadishu even with massive and brutal Ethiopian military support.
7. Ahmed Muuse Geedi, a former official of the anti-corruption organization called *Xisaabi Xil Maleh* says that Ábdiqaasim Salaad Hassan personally was charged for corruption prior to the coup of 1969 before Mohamed Siyaad Barre appointed him to a high post. The relationship between the two men remained very close until the collapse of the regime.
8. The original poem in Somali is the following:

Ninkii beesha qaayimaQ
ar hadduu ku soo dumo,
Wallee ciiidda kama qodo.
Wallee qalin-daraalaha
Dambi qaranka laga galay
Kama qariyo wadhatadaW
allee qoonta mililka leh
Qaarka sare ma dhaydhayo…
Shacbi qawdhamoo kacay
Qarqarsiga hadduu jaro
Wallee qoofal kuma xidho…

9. The original poem in Somali is the following:

Nin qabyaalad doojaw
Doqoniimo waa cudur

Haddii aad dux leedahay
Bal docdaada uun eeg
Inta dumar agoomo ah!
Inta dhiig dad lagu qubay!
Inta darib nin lagu cunay!
Inta duul ku qaran-jabay.

10. The original poem in Somali is the following:
Soomali waa duud
Dakan-qabe ha joogee
Waa ul iyo diirkeed
Deris iyo tol wada yaal
Nin dan laan kala gura.
11. The original poem in Somali is the following:
Isku soo dabbaaloo
Waa dabaqad maal jecel;
Waxa loo dig leeyey
Dhididkayga dahabka ah
Sidii loo dudubin laa.
12. The original poem in Somali is the following:
Ninka xagal ka daac iyo
gol daloolo iga hela
isagiyo digtoonkii
anigiyo dagnaantay
taariikhdu duuggeed
diiwaanka qarankiyo
wixii deyn cad ii qoran
dirirtioy rogaalkay.
13. The original poem in Somali is the following:
Bulshadeenu waa duul

daacad iyo xishood badan
dun xariira weeyaan
qofna uma darraadaan
dar Allay ku dhaqantaa
dareen waw dhegweyn tahay
ogow doqonse maahee.

14. The original poem in Somali is the following:
Ummadyahay daryeelkaa
isku duubnidaadiyo
madax daacad noqotiyo
adigioy dedaalkaa
dÁwadaadu waa taas
dhan hadday ka debecdana
gabbalkaa dam weeyaan.
Ma dardaaran baa hadhay?
15. The original song in Somali is the following:
Waa maan gura'an
Iyo garasha jaan
Landcruiser gado
Soo bari galleey
Gacal iyo tollow
Ma gudoonsateen
Bahida gudban ee
Gurigeena taal
Innagoon ka guban
Gaadhi raaxo leh iyo
Landcruiser gado.
Guuxiisa mood,
Gob inaad ku tahay
Geeska Africaw!
16. The original song in Somali is the following:
Landcruiser gado
Gurigoo mugdi ah
Biyuuhu go'een
Gabanadu jesheen
Soomaalay u gaar
Iyo gooni u tahay
Oo lagu dartaa
Guuxiisa mood, mood
Gob inaad ku tahay.
17. It is said that Saado Áli was imprisoned but only briefly and then released.

Chapter 13

1. See Eric Williams, *Slavery and Capitalism*, New York: Capricorn Books, 1966, and Water Rodney, *How Europe Underdeveloped Africa*, Washington, D.C: Howard University Press, 1974.
2. For an informative discussion of the evolution and role of the state in Europe, see F.M. Deng et al *Sovereignty as Responbility – Conflict Management in Africa*, Washington, D.C. Brookings Institution. 1996. In more truncated form, Maria H. Brons discusses the same in her *Society, Security, Sovereignty and State in Somalia,* Utrecht, Netherlands: International Books, 2001.
3. For detailed discussion on the clan system and associated culture, see my *Kinship and Conflict—Cultural Roots of Somali Resilience and Violence.*
4. Quoted by Eric Hobbsbawm in *The Agee of the Empire*, London: Abacus, 1995 p. 33
5. For more detailed exposition on the Islamic revolution Somalis had mÍised, see my *Archeology of Forgotten Experience—Reconstructing the Distant Past of Somalis.*
6. The original poem in Somali is the following:

   Cirkii iyo dulkii baa isqabsaday carrarraqdoodii e
   Coomaadi duullaaya bay Cadan ka keeneen e
   War adiguba caqlaad leedahe carar maxaa dhaama?
7. LeShan, L. (1992). The Psychology of War—Comprehending its Mystique and its Madness, Chicago: Noble Press.
8. R. W. Rieber and M. Green (1995) described passion for power, thrill-seeking behavior, and absence of guilt as psychopathic characteristics of person in 'high places' of government and business. These three characteristics are relevant in the auto-colonial situation. I believe that finding thrill in flaunting superiority, extreme sensitivity to criticism, and unrelenting vindictive streak are implied in the formulation of Rieber and Green but need to be made explicit here because they gain especial significance in the auto-colonial situation.
9. I discuss details on qat use and addiction, see my *Miqaan and Madness—Qat Use and Addcition in Somaliland,* an unpublished manuscript.
10. After releasing the civilian politician herded into prison after the coup, President Mohamed Siyaad Barre appointed Ábdirazaaq Haaji Hussein to the choice post of UN Representative. As a person and politician, Ábdirazaaq deserved the appointment, but the question had been raised as whether this was an expression of gratitude for Ábdirazaaq's political support when Mohamed Siyaad Barre needed support as he struggled to become

the Commander of the Armed Forces. Some go so far as to suggest a more sinister connection—a suggestion that is both incredible and unlike the integrity of Abdurizaaq.

11. For the theories of Vilfrado Pareto and Gaetano Mosca, see for instance T. Bottomore (1993), *Elites and Society* (2nd Edition), London: Routeledge and E. Albertoni (1987), *Mosca and the Theory of Elitism*, Oxford: Basil Blackwell.

INDEX

Welcome to
Tayosan International Publishing!

Publisher and Distributor of African Books,
Magazines and Audio-visual Products

Other Tayosan's publications by Dr. Hussein A. Bulhan include:

Archeology of Experience–Reconstructing the Somali Past
Kinship and Conflict–What Keeps Somalis Wretched Yet Resilient?
Mirqaan and Madness–Qaat Addiction in Somaliland
Pathology of History–Why Peace and Freedom Elude Somalis
Cinderella of the Horn–Conflict and Change in Somaliland
Injuries of A Generation–the Cost of Auto-Colonialism
Return of Cain–Conflict and Chaos after State Collapse
No Longer Myself–Alienation and Torment of Modernity
Camels in the Sky–Somali Myths and False Consciousness

How to Contact the Author

Dr. Bulhan provides consulting service on psychiatric problems, cross-cultural psychology, qaat addiction treatment and prevention, conflict resolution, and generally on Somali history, culture, and politics. Requests for information about these services, as well as his availability for speeches and seminars, should be directed to the author at *drbulhan@yahoo.com*

The author invites readers of this book to contact him at *drbulhan@yahoo.com* with comments and ideas for future editions.

ATTENTION: Quantity discount for this book or others listed above are available for universities, colleges, corporations, and professional organizations. For information, please contact Dr. Bulhan in Africa at drbulhan@yahoo.com or Ms. Oumie Joof in the United States at oumskie@yahoo.com

INFORMATION FOR AUTHORS

Tayosan International Publishing has the mission of documenting and disseminating the voice of the voiceless and publishing the contributions of new and established authors.

To that end, Tayosan takes special care to:

- Attract new authors whom standard publishers seldom consider;
- Produce and sell high quality publications at cost; and
- Distribute valuable works to audience whom standard publishers do not reach.
-

If you want Tayosan International Publishing to consider your work for publication, please follow Tayosan's submission policy and send:

1. A book proposal outlining the purpose, organization, anticipated length, and target audience;
2. A brief autobiography and your previously published works (if any); and
3. Your address, telephone number, and email.

If the Manuscript Committee approves your project, the Committee will request from you:

1. A brief explanation of the published works on the same topic or area as your project;
2. How your manuscript is different from existing works on the same topic or area;
3. One or two chapters of your manuscript for review;
4. Your suggestions for distribution of your work; and
5. What role (if any) you intend to play in the distribution of your book.

If you want us to explore with you publication of a project in progress or you have completed, please contact Ms. Oumie Joof at:

1. oumskie@yahoo.com, or
2. Tayosan international publishing, P.O.Box 30602, Bethesda, Maryland, 20824

GIFTS OF THIS BOOK

If you want to give gift of *Politics of Cain—One Hundred Years of Crises in Somali Politics and Society*, check your local bookstore or order here:

☐ Yes, I want ____ copies of the Politics of Cain at a discount of $25.00 (25% less than listed price for 3 books or more) excluding shipping cost.

Name____
Organization______________________________________
Address____
Phone___________________E-mail__________________
Card#____
Exp. Date_______________Signature_________________

INVITATION TO SPEAK OR OFFER SEMINAR

☐**Yes,** I am interested in having Dr. Hussein A. Bulhan speak or give a seminar to my school, company, association, or organization. Please send me information to the following:

Name____
Organization______________________________________
Address____
Phone___________________E-mail__________________

TAYOSAN INTERNATIONAL PUBLISHING
Publisher and Distributor of African Books,
Magazines and Audio-visual Products
P.O.Box 30602
Bethesda, Maryland, 20824